PSYCHO
AND CATHOLICISM

In this historical study of psychology and Catholicism, Kugelmann aims to provide clarity in an area filled with emotion and opinion. From the beginnings of modern psychology to the mid-1960s, this complicated relationship between science and religion is methodically investigated. Conflicts such as the boundary of "person" versus "soul," contested between psychology and the church, are debated thoroughly. Kugelmann goes on to examine topics such as the role of the subconscious in explaining spiritualism and miracles; psychoanalysis and the sacrament of confession; myth and symbol in psychology and religious experience; cognition and will in psychology and in religious life; humanistic psychology as a spiritual movement. This fascinating study will be of great interest to scholars and students of both psychology and religious studies but will also appeal to all of those who have an interest in the way modern science and traditional religion coexist in our ever-changing society.

ROBERT KUGELMANN is a professor of psychology at the University of Dallas. He has written two previous books: *The Windows of Soul* (1983), and *Stress: The Nature and History of Engineered Grief* (1992).

PSYCHOLOGY AND CATHOLICISM

Contested Boundaries

ROBERT KUGELMANN

CAMBRIDGE
UNIVERSITY PRESS

CAMBRIDGE UNIVERSITY PRESS
Cambridge, New York, Melbourne, Madrid, Cape Town,
Singapore, São Paulo, Delhi, Mexico City

Cambridge University Press
The Edinburgh Building, Cambridge CB2 8RU, UK

Published in the United States of America by Cambridge University Press, New York

www.cambridge.org
Information on this title: www.cambridge.org/9781107412736

First published 2011
First paperback edition 2012

A catalogue record for this publication is available from the British Library

Library of Congress Cataloguing in Publication Data
Kugelmann, Robert, 1948–
Psychology and Catholicism : contested boundaries / Robert Kugelmann.
p.   cm.
ISBN 978-1-107-00608-9 (hardback)
1. Psychology and religion.   2. Catholic Church – History – 20th century.   I. Title.
BF51.K84   2011
261.5´15088282–dc22
2011005955

ISBN 978-1-107-00608-9 Hardback
ISBN 978-1-107-41273-6 Paperback

CONTENTS

ACKNOWLEDGMENTS

"In the middle of the journey of our life," I found myself beginning to study the relationships between psychology and Catholicism. There have been many twists and turns along the way, and I had many guides. While I cannot say that I always went in the direction that they indicated, I am thankful for their help. This aid came in conversation, in emails, in letters, in phone calls. Some of my guides read various versions of my efforts and provided important insights and corrections.

When I was just beginning this work, Dr. Philipp Rosemann of the University of Dallas philosophy department directed me to the contributions of Cardinal Mercier and the Louvain school. Dr. Charles Fischer of Franciscan University, Steubenville, told me to talk with Dr. LeRoy Wauck, which I did. Dr. Wauck was most generous, loaning me some of his books and newsletters published by the American Catholic Psychological Association, and reading an early version of a paper I wrote on that organization. Phyllis Wentworth generously shared important primary material with me, such that this work became, early on, a historical investigation. Closer to home, Dr. Leo McCandlish of Dallas, who had studied at Fordham and Loyola of Chicago in the 1950s, was an important source of information about Catholics in psychology in mid-century and beyond. His gift to me of books by such notables as Magda Arnold, his dissertation adviser, from his personal library, I will treasure always.

Along the way, the insights by many other scholars, some of whom were participants in this history, have proven invaluable: the Rev. Daniel C. O'Connell, SJ, and the Rev. Adrian van Kaam, CSSp, offered corrections and directions that I still follow, as did the Rev. Gerald A. McCool, SJ, and W. Norris Clarke, SJ (whom I never met, but who were generous with their time and knowledge). Dr. Amedeo Giorgi, who has been in important ways a teacher of mine for many years, shared his experiences of his graduate study at Fordham, and he shared some of his vision for psychology. Dr. William Coulson was generous with his time and insights.

At various stages, I consulted with some fine writers, who gave me critical comments and correctives. Dr. John Sommerfeldt, my colleague at the University of Dallas, read much of the manuscript and helped me make it more readable. Dr. Jacob A. Belzen, Professor of the Psychology of Religion at the University of

Amsterdam, has been a delightful collaborator, and has spent hours reading portions of this book, helping me with his excellent editorial eye. Lindsey Schutze read the final version and with good sense, good grammar, and a sense of style, improved the writing a great deal.

Others have read sections, chapters, articles that have been reworked for this book, and to whom I owe a debt of gratitude: Dr. Hendrika vande Kemp, Dr. Frederick Wertz, Dr. Kathryn Benes, Dr. Gladys Sweeney, and the Rev. Vincent W. Hevern, SJ (who also provided many significant comments at meetings of Cheiron – thanks, Vinny!). The Rev. Kevin Gillespie, SJ, has likewise provided important direction, and his book pioneered this field after it lay fallow for decades. Dr. Mark Mattson's investigations into the history of psychology at Fordham filled in important missing pieces.

Much of the material in this book was presented at meetings of Cheiron: The International Society for the History of the Behavioral and Social Sciences over the past decade. Some was presented at meetings of the European Society for the History of the Human Sciences (ESHHS), and once, at a joint meeting of the two organizations. It is an understatement to say that I have benefited from the collective wisdom of the members of these groups. The first presentation I did on this topic, however, was at a meeting of the Society of Catholic Social Scientists, thanks to the encouragement of Charles Fischer. One ESHHS presentation became a chapter, "Importing phenomenology into North American psychology," in *Recent Contributions to the History of the Human Sciences*, edited by Annette Mülberger and Beni Gómez-Zúñiga (München: Profil, 2005). I have used portions in Chapter 8.

Thirteen graduate students read the penultimate draft of this manuscript and gave me comments, criticisms, and editorial recommendations. They were superb readers and critics, and I thank: Mark Alonzo, Christian Angle, Elizabeth Bergstrom, Idalie Beyer, Rustic Bowen, Gary Hominick, Angela Howey, Elizabeth McShurley, Christina Rodriguez, Amanda Runyan, Ingeborg Saenz, Lindsey Schutze, and Rebecca Zufelt. I think we had a good semester!

I received valuable help from archives. John Waide at the St. Louis University Archives was most helpful, as I would stop in from time to time during trips to St. Louis to see my daughter, Verity, who was studying at SLU. Steven Szegedi at the Dominican University Library Archives uncovered material about the Chicago Society of Catholic Psychologists that was a real find. I thank also the archivists at the Loyola University of Chicago Library and at the Midwest Jesuit Archives. Finally, I am most grateful to Dr. David Baker and the staff at the Archives of the History of American Psychology (AHAP) in Akron, Ohio, for their guidance when I was a novice in archival research, and they helped me with the holdings of the American Catholic Psychological Association.

The writing of this book has been supported in part by release time from the University of Dallas, and I thank colleagues in the faculty and the administration for continued support. I obtained a sabbatical in the fall of 2003, when

I completed drafts of Chapters 4 and 6. King-Haggar Faculty Development funds provided me with opportunities to visit the AHAP and the St. Louis University archives.

My wife, Laurie, has been most generous in her support, encouragement, and understanding. During the time it took to write this book, the children (Verity, Colin, Kateri, and Andrew) have gone from grade school children to adulthood. Their flourishing brings us joy.

For "From substance to phenomenon: A concept of the 'soul' for phenomenological psychology," *Journal of Phenomenological Psychology, 19* (1988). © 1988 by Koninklijke Brill NV. Adapted with permission. The use of this information does not imply endorsement by the publisher. Portions of this article were adapted for Chapter 10.

For "Neoscholastic psychology revisited." *History of Psychology, 8* (2005). © 2005 by the American Psychological Association. Adapted with permission. The use of this information does not imply endorsement by the publisher. Portions of this article were adapted for Chapters 2 and 3.

For "Out of the ghetto: Integrating Catholics into mainstream psychology in the United States after World War II," *History of Psychology, 12* (2009). © 2009 by the American Psychological Association. Adapted with permission. The use of this information does not imply endorsement by the publisher. Portions of this article were adapted for Chapter 7.

For "An encounter between psychology and religion: Humanistic psychology and the Immaculate Heart of Mary nuns," *Journal of the History of the Behavioral Sciences, 41* (2005). © 2005 by John Wiley and Sons. A portion of this article was adapted for Chapter 8.

1

An introduction

The science and profession of psychology emerged in the mid- to late nine-teenth century. In all its varieties, including "pop psychology," psychology is one of the ways that we in the contemporary world ask the questions: "Who am I?" "What sort of things are we?" "How shall I live my life?" "What makes me happy, sad, confused, anxious?" These questions arise not only in the abstract, they occur also in activities of healing, correcting, adjusting, guiding, treating, managing, counseling. Even though in many quarters, psychologists have distanced themselves from such questions – call them philosophical – the inescapable truth is that they surface in all psychologies, pure and applied. Psychology asks these questions and psychology answers them. Questing for the nature of human nature, of mental illness, of cognition, of personal growth, for the tasks and challenges of childhood and old age, and in countless other ways, psychology addresses the vexations of living and dying.

And so psychology is an ethical science, ethics being the discipline that seeks to know how we should live our lives. Textbooks and clinicians and researchers, in one way or another, advise us how to conduct our lives. At the very least, they provide information, but all such information implicitly offers guidelines for conduct: description is prescription. This is not an indictment of psychology, for there is great effort to be fair and neutral within the field; it is simply stating the obvious case that no science that describes and explains human behavior and mental life can avoid indicating better and worse ways to act, think, and feel.

For these reasons, psychology makes claims in areas already occupied by the religious traditions – traditions that not only have positions on our nature and our place in the cosmos, but also on how we should act, think, and feel. Religions offer care for the soul in sickness, depravity, and loss. The Catholic Church is no exception in this regard, having a long history of reckoning with the nature and rectification of human life. So when psychology emerged in the nineteenth century, and as it continued to grow, bubbling forth from the ground of twentieth-century life, there were bound to be points of difference and convergence between psychology and Catholic thought and traditions. The philosophical presuppositions of some prominent psychologists, for example, were precisely the kinds of doctrines identified in the 1918 *Code of Canon Law*

(*Codex iuris canonici*, 1918) as being antithetical to the Catholic faith. Some psychotherapeutic practices, in how they encouraged patients to think and act, were called immoral by some Church officials and by some Catholic psychologists. The fact is that psychologists take positions on ground deemed sacred and protected by the Church. Psychological expertise proclaimed on this sacred ground cannot be sheltered from religious counterclaims when the Church has provided other knowledge and guidance for centuries.

This book explores some of these conflicts and convergences. The primary focus is on what those psychologists who were also Catholic said and did about the relationships between modern psychology and Catholicism. The book further has an emphasis on the American scene. Without a doubt, modern psychology and, of course, Catholicism, are international in scope, but there were some particulars of the American social landscape that individuate that history. Distinctive features of the American context, such as its traditions regarding the separation of church and state, were not shared everywhere, and in some countries at some times, political regimes imposed religious orthodoxies, and some of them were Catholic. Until the 1960s, because they came primarily from immigrant groups, American Catholics often felt a need to justify their being both Catholic and American. There was in the Catholic subculture a lively sense of being a minority group. There was both a sense of superiority of the traditions and teachings of the Church and a sense of inferiority, especially regarding participation in the intellectual life of the nation. Nevertheless, the narrative cannot be confined exclusively to these shores, as many ideas and people came or visited here and contributed mightily to what happened. In several chapters, the focus will indeed be in other places, including Belgium (for the beginnings of experimental psychology within a Catholic setting), France (in dealing with some of the spiritualist and miraculous phenomena), Ireland (in dealing with an early Catholic response to psychoanalysis), and Switzerland and England (especially for consideration of Catholic Jungians). The Vatican, the home of the Pope and seat of the Church, naturally plays an important role in this history, from beginning to end. In fact, a papal document serves as one bookend for the story: *Aeterni Patris* (1879/ 1954) was a call by Pope Leo XIII for a renewal of Thomistic thought and its positive engagement with the modern world, especially the modern sciences. This document sounded a receptive tone and thus helped to justify the cultivation of modern psychology in Catholic circles. The Second Vatican Council of the 1960s marked the end of an epoch in the questioning of boundaries between psychology and Catholicism, and there our study – although not the story – will end. After that time, things changed, and even if the components remained, their relationships did not. Finally, *Ex corde ecclesiae* (Pope John Paul II, 1990/2000) raised the question of the meaning of institutions that are both Catholic and universities, there being presumably no contradiction between the two. This document suggests a reconsideration of some of the solutions to the sometimes difficult relationships between psychology and Catholic thought.

Non-Catholic readers, especially non-Christian readers, may wonder at this point about the relevance of what follows for a more general understanding of relationships between psychology and religion. Those relationships are very important and will remain so. Understanding one history of the conflicts and cooperation between science, however conceived, and religion, also however conceived, can provide some clarity in an area fraught with vague generalities. Hence the plan of this book is to study a specific religion and to differentiate the psychologies that it encountered. I do not assume that the relationships between psychology and Catholicism can be automatically generalized to those between other religions and other sciences. It may well be that they cannot. However, if we can talk about specific relationships and what actually happened within them, perhaps we can discern a wider range of possibilities. With that aspiration, I would say that one need be neither Catholic nor a psychologist to follow the thread of meaning through this book. The issues addressed are important for us all.

The question of boundaries

How can there be contested boundaries between psychology and the Catholic Church, since psychology is an empirical science whose sole duty is to discover the facts and then propose the theories that explain them? The Church has to do with beliefs and values. This division of labor between facts and values, between objective data and subjective beliefs, is still our taken-for-granted way of ensuring peace within ourselves and in our society. If this position, called naturalism, were the correct way to frame the relationship between psychology and religion, there could be contests of will and power, but not of knowledge. The reason for this is that, according to naturalism, the only way to gain certainty in knowledge is by natural scientific means. What we *ought* to do – ah! This the scientist cannot answer, because it is not a factual concern. At best, the psychologist could predict what consequences follow any course of action. A naturalistic philosophical presupposition, one that underlies much thinking in psychology, would ignore claims of psychological knowledge coming from a religion, because religion does not discover scientifically whatever it uncovers.

But since the beginnings of natural scientific psychology, and since the beginning of the profession of psychology in psychoanalysis and the like, church leaders, philosophers, theologians, and yes, church psychologists, have questioned psychology's knowledge claims and scientific authority. These figures have contested the boundaries between the knowledge domain of psychology and that of the church in various ways. Some have disputed the claim that psychology can be a natural science. For others, even if psychology were what some psychologists say it is, namely, an empirical science just like biology and physics, even then, as repeated incidents over the past century show, Catholic thinkers inside and outside psychology have disputed the limits of the competence of the psychologists. (The boundaries are contested in biology and physics, too, as debates over evolution and creation illustrate.) The reasons for these disputes are many, but central to them are the objects of investigation of the various sciences. For the sciences do not have the only access to these objects – such as living things, the object of biology, and material things, the object of physics. This is all the more the case when one turns to psychology, for here is a science – of disputed character – that deals with what? It deals with behavior, with experience, with the mind, with personality, with human beings and what they think, feel, and do. What are closer to the heart of the Church, of any church, than those things? It does no good to set up in the abstract a division of labor between psychology and the Church. That has been tried repeatedly, only to founder on the rocks in the tumultuous straits of human existence. Psychologists deal with flesh and blood human beings, often with their most intimate concerns. So does the Church, which has also as its concern the eternal destiny of these human beings. So how and where can we set up a clear and distinct partition? Where shall we find one when human thought, feeling, and action are involved?

The boundaries of science

Thomas Gieryn (1983) provides a solid sociological analysis of ways that scientists engage in "boundary-work," that is, make "attributions of selected characteristics to the institution of science for purposes of constructing a social boundary that distinguishes 'non-scientific' intellectual or professional activities" (p. 791). His examples include the efforts of John Tyndall in the nineteenth century to claim for scientists some of the academic authority that religion had had in Great Britain: "The Church . . . held power over educational institutions and used it to stall introduction of science into the curriculum" (p. 784), a situation that was repeated later to counter psychology's efforts to find a place in the curriculum. According to Tyndall, science differs from religion in four ways:

(1) Science improves our material lot; religion provides emotional comfort and consolation.
(2) Science uses experimentation to discover the attributes of nature; religion describes spiritual entities that cannot be empirically verified.
(3) Science does not follow any authority except the answers Nature gives to experimental questions; religion "continues to respect the authority of worn-out ideas and their creators" (p. 785).
(4) Science is objective; religion is subjective.

These four arguments elaborate one central point, namely, that science yields knowledge whereas religion produces feelings. In claiming this distinction between objective knowledge and subjective feeling, Tyndall sought to claim for science some of the authority that the Church had in his day. His boundary-work, demarcating the difference between the outer world and the inner world, served to determine a domain over which religious claims were invalid. Today, when scientific authority is common sense, some religious positions seek the status of scientific authority, as in the case of arguments for Intelligent Design.

Central to Gieryn's study is the conditions under which boundary-work is likely to occur. He identifies three situations: "(a) when the goal is *expansion* of authority or expertise into domains claimed by other professions or occupations . . .; (b) when the goal is *monopolization*[1] of professional authority and resources . . .; (c) when the goal is *protection of autonomy* over professional activities" (pp. 791–2). Gieryn concludes that "the boundaries of science are ambiguous, flexible, historically changing, contextually variable, internally inconsistent, and sometimes disputed" (p. 792). This analysis helps discern how boundaries are drawn without deciding in advance what significance to give to the truth claims of the participants.

Tyndall's demarcations serve to point to a larger issue, namely the question of what distinguishes something called "science" from other types of activities that also make knowledge claims. Gieryn's (1999) sociological studies of disputes over the nature of science illustrate the difficulties. Science as it exists in the "wild" is a complex thing:

> [It] is not embodied only in these first-time-through practices, instruments, research material, facts, and journals; it has several other realities too. Science [is] . . . a bit of the cognitive schema we use everyday to navigate material and symbolic lands. Science also exists in codified bureaucratic procedures, as when university catalogs divvy up the universe of learning into natural science, social science, and humanities.
>
> (pp. 19–20)

It is this cultural complex called "science" that is at issue in this book, not some supposed ideal essence of science. In the chapters that follow, we will attempt to find out what the science of psychology has meant by examining what the participants in the various struggles have claimed it was. This view of the authority of science based on its knowledge claims is critical for the analyses in this book. In psychology, the basic questions about human beings are far from settled. As a consequence, what type of knowledge counts in psychology? Who can legitimately speak of human psychology, to put the matter bluntly, if to be human means to have an eternal destiny? Does not any science which

---

[1] Gieryn (1999, p. 16) calls this "expulsion," that is, the effort to deny the epistemic authority of science to contenders whom the other players deem non-scientific.

ignores that destiny ignore the most important point? Or is that destiny a matter of faith alone, and has the science of psychology plenty to do without tackling the questions of the soul? Questions such as these have been behind the boundary-work between psychology and the Catholic Church.

For Gieryn, the difficulty is not simply that boundary-work has occurred, because it might be the case that some contestants are simply wrong if, for example, we take the view of science developed by the philosopher, Karl Popper. Then we might say that psychoanalysis and Neoscholastic psychology (a type developed in the Catholic world) mistakenly called themselves sciences, but in fact they were not, because their key proposition could not be falsified, meaning that no scientific test could dispute their knowledge claims. One such claim would be the Neoscholastic conclusion that the evidence of psychology points to the reality of the rational soul as a spiritual, not a material, substance. From a Popperian point of view, how could such a conclusion be tested empirically? Therefore, so the argument would run, Neoscholasticism is not science. If Neoscholastic psychologists engaged in boundary-work, claiming scientific status for their psychology, that would not legitimate it as science, because it did not conform to the canons of science. But efforts to define in advance what science is by asserting a criterion such as falsifiability play only one part in determining what science is and what is the authority of science. Other considerations and other participants, sometimes remote from the laboratory or the university, decide what counts as science. At the same time, this does not mean that "anything goes" with science, because the cultural institutions that have stakes in science will object and will exclude or protect its autonomy and thus their epistemic authority. In this book, we will not define in advance what science is and is not. We will look at the disputes over its limits in order to see what science has become for us.

Such a strategy is vitally important for psychology, in which disputes over the nature of the discipline, its status as a science and, indeed, the meaning of "science," have been and remain integral to the kind of thing that psychology is. That is, boundary-work is not something psychologists do only when pressed by contenders; boundary-work is a distinguishing characteristic of psychology. Using Thomas Kuhn's terminology, we can say that boundary-work is part of "normal science" psychology and not only a part of "revolutionary science."

For psychology, there is the ever-recurring boundary dispute between the natural science and the human science approaches, with some attempting to define psychology as a natural science to the exclusion of a human science approach, and others seeking to enlarge the meaning of "science" to include the human sciences. Rather than rehash these arguments, this book takes the position that all science is interpretative or hermeneutical activity. Don Ihde (1997), approaching the natural sciences from a philosophical angle, argues that the tried and true differentiation between the natural sciences and the human sciences in terms of the former explaining nature and the latter interpreting human realities has been challenged on the ground that the natural sciences too are interpretative. Ihde develops a theme from Bruno Latour, who presents the case that science works by producing a series of representations, each one of which becomes data for further interpretation, and that the very instruments used in the laboratory (the epitome of "real" science) are devices that inscribe – and Ihde adds, depict – something. Scientific activity entails, among other things, reading these inscriptions and depictions. Thus all science is an interpretative activity, and not only the human or social sciences. Heelan (1998) furthers this conception by using the metaphor of the library: when nature and Scripture are read, in terms of which library are they read? The modern sciences, starting with Galileo, read natural phenomena in terms of a mathematical library, in contrast with ancient science, which turned to other sources. This view of science differs from Gieryn's sociological analysis, but it is a reminder that whatever else science is, it is an activity performed by members of a larger cultural community. It also serves as a reminder that science has a history, and that it has had other libraries to draw upon.

Science and religion: the larger picture

What holds true for science in this study also holds true for religion. Both have histories, and the question "Whose Science? Whose Religion?" (Brooke and Cantor, 1998, p. 43) is relevant. Religion, whatever it is, does not claim to be – with some exceptions, such as Christian Science and Scientology – science. In this book, the parallels between science and religion are fairly precise, because here we are not dealing with religion in general but with a specific religion, Roman Catholicism.[2] With this religion, the questions of authority and of who speaks for the Church seem much clearer than with science, and especially with psychology. The Church has a hierarchical structure, and the Pope has, in a very real sense, the last word. Psychology has no pope. Even acknowledging the more or less fixed structure of the Church, in this study we are not dealing with an abstract entity, but with a living community composed of individuals responding to unique cultural and historical events. In addition, the Church is no monolithic structure, so that the questions of what the Church is and how it responded to developments in the sciences do not have univocal answers. As we shall see, there have been boundary disputes between the Church and psychology, and

---

[2] Because of this limitation, the whole question of what is and what is not a religion can be avoided, although others have not avoided it. Pargament (1999) has made one attempt to define religion, especially in relation to spirituality. As he points out, authors going back to William James (1903) in *The varieties of religious experience* have had to make decisions about what to include and what to exclude. The present effort has the same limitations. So nothing in this book should be assumed to apply *a priori* to other religions or forms of religion. I do not think that there is an essence of religion that would permit us to draw the lines of demarcation between religion and psychology deductively.

moreover, boundary disputes within the Church between Catholic psychologists and other Catholics, some of whom were also psychologists.

The larger vicissitudes of science and religion I shall not discuss (see Asad, 1993; Pickstock, 1998). Assuming that they are not fixed entities, their relationship cannot be defined categorically. Brooke (1991) has described three standard concepts of the relationship: conflict, complementarity, and mutual advantage. The conflict model is familiar these days in the political wrangling over creationism, but Brooke has shown with specific historical examples that conflict is not a necessary relationship between religion and science, and creationism is as much a conflict between theologies as it is a conflict with science. Complementarity can take many forms, including the one Tyndall described. Typically, perhaps, it takes the form of a division of labor, especially where a natural scientific psychology prevails. Mutual advantage can occur at the practical as well as at the theoretical level. When a church hires a psychotherapist, or a religiously affiliated institution establishes a psychology department, we have examples of mutual advantage. When Victor White sought to collaborate with Carl Jung, he intended mutual advantage for both Thomistic theology and for analytical psychology. Brooke (1991) has concluded that no simple answer to the relationships between science and religion exists and that they are better addressed with examinations of specific instances.

Boundaries between psychology and religion

One of the significant ongoing boundary-making efforts that define psychology as a science has been its relationship with spiritualism. Coon (1992) observes that, over the past century, "psychology has been a magnet for cultural anxieties about the hazy borderline between science and pseudoscience, between the natural and the supernatural" (p. 143). Coon's study of how early experimental psychologists came to grips with the claims of the spiritualists, including mediums, "mind-readers," and mental healers, is a good case in point for the difficulties in drawing the lines between what is science and what is not (and what is religion and what is not). Coon concludes in part by saying:

> In an era of increasing skepticism about God, scientific naturalism offered the latest and best substitute providing order and reason in the universe. In this worldview, espoused by the majority of experimental psychologists, psychophysical parallelism held sway. Physical phenomena could only occur as the result of physical causes. Psychological phenomena might bear a one-to-one correspondence to physical phenomena but could not cause or be caused by them.
>
> (p. 149)

Psychophysiological parallelism was a position close to that of the spiritualists, who asserted the effectiveness of the parallel world of the spirit in the material world. Efforts by some early psychologists to distinguish themselves from the spiritualists were complicated by the fact that William James, the premier psychologist at the turn of the twentieth century, took the spiritualists' claims seriously. In reaction to what were seen as the spiritualists' excessive claims, many in psychology found the embrace of a materialistic conception of science enticing. Where did this outcome leave the psychologist who was also a religious person, for whom the physical world could feel the effects of the action of the spiritual? Where did it leave the psychologist who at the same time rejected spiritualism and its promise of "a new secular faith" (p. 144)? This was the position of the psychologist who was also Catholic, who held that the immaterial soul acted on the body, and that miracles, such as those reported at Lourdes, happened. This is an example of the problem that faces us.

Many have been the boundaries drawn between psychology and religion, and between psychology and theology. Bear in mind that these lines often serve practical purposes, such as securing the independence of a psychology department in a college, or persuading a congregation that its members suffering from addictions or abuse need counseling in addition to prayer. Others erase or redraw the lines in order to deal with the less than sage advice, in the name of some enlightened theory or other, that therapists may give to their Christian clients. But these practical matters often arise from or lead back into more speculative ones. The fact is that, before the nineteenth century, the boundary between psychology and the care of the soul did not exist. Even when physicians, lawyers, and bankers offered clients advice on living the good life, in much of the western world prior to the nineteenth century, there was more of a common ground for ethical decision-making than now exists (MacIntyre, 1984). I am not prejudging the issue here, and throughout this text I will avoid slipping into either a "grand narrative" of progress or of regress. Moral pluralism is our condition, and in light of the extant alternatives, we may hope it remains our condition. The point is that given our contemporary situation, the question of boundaries between psychology and religion promise to remain viable and contested.

So how have the boundaries been drawn? Without pretense of being complete,[3] here are the main ways.

---

[3] This way of describing interactions between psychology and religion is not the only one. Kevin Gillespie, SJ, offers another one, drawing on the work of John Haught. In this view, there are five types of relationship between psychology and religion: conflict, contrast, contact, confirmation, and – to be avoided – conflation. Conflict occurs when "science invalidates religion" (Gillespie, 2007a, p. 176); contrast means that science and religion have nothing in common (for example, there is no theology of reaction time or color vision); contact means that the two differ but can interact (Gillespie uses the setting up of the American Catholic Psychological Association as an example); and confirmation signifies how the two work toward a common end. Conflation is psychology-as-religion. These categories overlap the ones I am using: Haught and Gillespie's conflict is "psychology as religion"; contrast is the "divorce" of psychology and religion; contact is similar to the

(1) *Psychology divorced from philosophy and theology.* First, and most common, is that which derives from the stance that psychology is a natural science. As such, it derives its data from empirical investigation, and on that basis it forms theories to explain the relationships between the facts. Psychology so conceived makes no philosophical, theological, ethical, or political statements. Indeed, if it is indeed a natural science, it cannot make them. In this view, the boundary seems clear.

(2) *Psychology bound to philosophy and theology.* A second position is that since all psychology has underlying presuppositions, philosophical, cultural, and historical, the lines between psychology and religion are not easy to draw. This position may push the question about boundaries to philosophy, where a boundary question also arises: "Can there be a Christian philosophy?" This position also makes it imperative to probe the presuppositions of psychological theory, and to ask of them their compatibility with views of human nature stemming from religious tradition. In principle, the autonomy of psychology is recognized, but it is not absolute, since competing and even superior claims must be acknowledged.

(3) *A Christian psychology.* Third is the view that scientific psychology has largely been a secular affair and that what is needed today is a Christian or even, more specifically, a Catholic psychology. This position sees secular psychology as hostile to the claims of religion and as competing with them.

(4) *Psychology instead of religion.* A fourth position asserts that psychology is a more rational approach to living than is religion and should replace it. A variant on this theme is more irenic, and it significantly alters the nature of the boundary. In this view, psychology does not replace religion; it rather participates in one of the traditions of "unchurched spirituality." This route appeals to those for whom religions, with their teachings and competing claims to ultimate truth, seem irrelevant, but for whom matters of the spirit are vitally important. The "spiritual but not religious" portion of the contemporary population often turns to psychology of one sort or another instead of to religious faith. This group probably makes up the majority of those who pursue this fourth path. "Where religion was, let psychology be," seems to be the heart of this approach.

If the first two alternative ways of drawing a boundary are guided by the principle that "good fences make good neighbors," the second two challenge

---

second alternative presented here, except that "contact" has to do with ways that psychology and religion interact positively, and this, in my view, can be seen in a variety of ways under my second category, although my way stresses more the theoretical. Virtually all the topics covered in this book could fit under "contact." "Confirmation" is also largely handled in my second category. "Conflation," "psychology as religion," I would see in terms of unchurched spirituality and contend that it is not conflation but a unique formulation of a psychologized spirituality. A purely Christian psychology could be a better example of conflation.

the disciplinary autonomy of any scientific psychology. Let us look at each of these ways of drawing the lines more closely.

Psychology divorced from philosophy and theology

This first position has much to do with the history of psychology defining itself by its adherence to the so-called scientific method. Wisdom about human nature abounds, so this view goes; however, only with the rise of a scientific psychology do we have the foundations for an empirical science of human nature. The Bible and Shakespeare may exceed psychology in penetrating insights, but psychology like the other sciences only makes a genuine contribution when it renounces the wider view and humbly pursues the data in methodical ways. Howard H. Kendler (2005) recently reaffirmed the first position by defining the boundary between psychology and (in this instance) ethics by means of "the fact/value dichotomy that denies the possibility of logically deriving value judgments from empirical evidence" (p. 321). Kendler wants to safeguard psychology from self-destruction: "An educated democracy will not buy the idea that psychology is capable of identifying the right political policy or the correct way to live" (p. 323). This position is probably the most widely accepted one in psychology. It rests, however, on a contentious principle, namely, the fact/value dichotomy. The principle underlying this dichotomy (with the "/" as the boundary we are discussing) is that the methodologically purified evidence of our senses cannot determine values. Ethical judgments, in this view, are subjective – that is, based on feelings. Feelings have no epistemological status in science. It follows that religion is a private matter, and it ought not to interfere with or be adversely affected by science. In other words, Kendler shares Tyndall's view of the matter.

An important variant of this first position affirms the autonomy of psychology even as it acknowledges the necessity of its integration with theology. In reviewing the state of things in the limited area of the psychology of religion – where the question of boundaries is ever-pressing – Vassilis Saroglou (2003) has asserted that psychology, in order to make any contribution to the topic of religion, must "be based on the methods of observation and of explanation used in the different psychological fields . . . The utilization of these methods guarantees a capacity to reduce, insofar as possible, the influence of the subjectivity of the researcher" (pp. 474–5). One reason for this insistence on psychology's autonomy is that for, and especially for, a psychology of religion, "the legitimacy of its approach depends on the recognition by one's peers [in psychology], a recognition based on its ability to refer to theories and methods in general psychology" (Saroglou, 2000, p. 752). Psychology can make no contribution if it is absorbed into philosophy or theology, and it does have an independent standpoint.

The levels-of-explanation approach, which David C. Myers has done much to champion, adheres to this position. It holds that "all levels of reality are important (the physical, chemical, biological, psychological, social, and theological), that each dimension or level of reality is uniquely accessible to study by the unique methods used in each discipline, and that the boundaries of each should not be blurred" (Johnson and Jones, 2000a, p. 38). According to Johnson and Jones, those who take this approach are Christians and academics who hold that "true science will be impeded by the intrusion of faith beliefs from *any* quarter that cannot be empirically documented" (ibid.). In this concern, Christian psychologists such as C. S. Evans (1982) resemble the Neoscholastics, those philosophically-based psychologists who sought to carve out a space for scientific psychology in Catholic higher education in the first half of the twentieth century. Scientific methodology, in this way of marking the boundary, does not carry with it its own presuppositions.

Boundary maintenance from this point of view means justifying "methodological atheism" (Teo, 2009, p. 61) or "methodological naturalism" (Bishop, 2009, p. 109). Bishop states that this position claims to make no judgment concerning the reality of God; it simply seeks "natural causes as explanations of events in nature and see how far such explanations will go for particular limited purposes" (ibid.). We shall attend to a surprising example of methodological naturalism in the debates over the reality of miraculous cures at the French shrine of the Virgin at Lourdes (in Chapter 4). There, the Catholic position was to consider only those cures as miraculous that could not be explained through natural causes, thus excluding the cures of all functional or psychosomatic diseases. As we shall see, methodological naturalism in this case intended to strengthen the claims for those cases deemed miraculous, in the face of "metaphysical naturalists"[4] who *a priori* dismissed the possibility of miracles.

So we need not assume that this way of drawing the lines makes for conflict. Indeed, complementarity and mutual advantage could be the outcome of defining psychology narrowly as a natural science. Then, psychology like medicine becomes something useful, especially when it shows respect for the ethical boundaries set for it by the churches.

Psychology bound to philosophy and theology

The second way of drawing the lines has many variants. William James sketched out one possibility for the subordination of psychology when he argued in *The Principles of Psychology* that psychology as a natural science

---

[4] Bishop (2009), among others, distinguishes methodological and metaphysical naturalism. The latter dismisses the idea of God categorically. Even methodological naturalism is problematic from some theological points of view, particularly those that stress the freedom of Divine Will. The Neoscholastic point of view, however, was compatible with methodological naturalism.

assumes that states of consciousness follow one another in a deterministic manner, but that ethics assumes freedom of the will, and that, in the order of things, ethics has the higher claim. The Neoscholastic psychologists argued in a similar vein for the proper autonomy of psychology, while owning that psychology's basic categories derived from philosophical inquiry into first causes, and that philosophy was ancillary to theology. So psychology's autonomy was relative, and it had a subordinate place in the unity of knowledge.

This way has long been the stock-in-trade of the human science approach in psychology, which argues that there are no facts without theories and no theories without philosophical presuppositions. This position, which owes much to the phenomenological and Kantian traditions, has support from those in the history of science, such as Thomas Kuhn (1970) and Peter Galison (1999), who describe the theory-laden character of facts in the physical sciences. Stenner's (2009) elaboration of this approach is apropos here, as he shows that the very concept of "nature" assumed by methodological and metaphysical naturalists, as well as by some of the theistic opponents of one or both (see Slife and Reber, 2009a), was itself a theological concept forged by, among others, Isaac Newton, for whom "science (or rather natural philosophy) was the ideal territory on which to clarify theological matters" (Stenner, 2009, p. 104). So however we understand the *natural* sciences, we are at the same time affirming philosophical and theological conceptions of the real. *A fortiori*, the same applies to psychology.

In a related approach, *Psychology and Christianity* (Johnson and Jones, 2000b) presents four ways of conceiving the relationship between psychology and religion, including the "integration" model, which binds psychology to theology. Widely pursued in contemporary evangelical circles in psychology, the integration model in some ways resembles the Neoscholastic approach in the Catholic world, but with a characteristic theological difference that pertains to evangelical Christianity. While the Neoscholastics affirmed the unity of all truth, they typically stopped at the level of philosophical discourse, unlike the integrationists, who have sought to develop "a biblically-based" psychology. In the words of Bruce Narramore (1973), a leading integrationist, "we are in a position to gather relevant objective data, seek well constructed theoretical views and find improved techniques for applying our biblical and psychological data" (p. 17).[5]

---

[5] Note the use of the term "data" in this quotation from Narramore. Rhetorically, it serves to legitimate bringing biblical considerations into psychology without abandoning the claim that psychology is a science. However, as with Neoscholastic theology, which held that divine revelation could be expressed in propositional form, Narramore risks a kind of theological positivism. In what sense except the metaphorical can Scripture provide "data," as that term is employed in scientific discourse? Data are sense data, whereas Scripture claims a higher authority than that of the senses. Myers (2000) uses a similar phrase: "Knowing that no one is immune to error and bias, we can be wary of absolutizing human interpretations of either natural or biblical data" (p. 58). In this context, the use of "data" supports Myers' "levels-of-interpretation" approach, meaning that empirical data in

So, whereas the Neoscholastics sought a pre-theological philosophical integration of psychology with the Catholic faith, Evangelicals do not, insisting that psychology acknowledge explicitly the truth claims of Scripture.

Integrationists, Catholic and Evangelical alike, affirm that there is only one ultimate Truth, namely God's Truth, which is in fact a person: "I am the Way, the Truth, and the Life." Carter and Narramore (1979) sketch the ground for integration in these terms: "Our position is that there is a unity of truth and such conflicts do not in fact exist. We hold that all such conflicts between theology and psychology are conflicts between theory and interpretation of the facts rather than between the facts themselves" (p. 27). Here the trouble begins, for facts do not exist in themselves, independently of theory and interpretation. This is complicated further when they assert: "a fully integrated model ... requires a full commitment to both the learned facts of psychology and the revealed truths of Scripture" (p. 104). If this be the basis of integration, then the result would be diversity bordering on chaos: surely it makes a difference which conception of the truth of Scripture is affirmed, as surely as it makes a difference which are the facts of psychology. Hence, in this position regarding psychology and religion, underlying assumptions become key considerations.

Central to the concerns of both the Neoscholastics and the Evangelicals – taking these psychologists as representative of this second type of boundary-work – is the pluralism of contemporary society. Catholic psychologists in the mid-twentieth century felt the sting of dwelling in an intellectual ghetto – the term has often been used – and part of the Neoscholastic strategy was to carry forward a Catholic position without being dismissed by non-Catholic psychologists as dogmatists. Hence their emphases that psychology is a natural science and that psychology has philosophical presuppositions that cannot be determined empirically. The Evangelicals, too, worry about isolation, as Narramore (1973) observes: "As Christians we will lose our effectiveness if we develop a superior or paranoid attitude toward the world ... An isolationistic attitude may maintain our doctrinal purity but it will cause us to fail to grab hold of a large portion of God's general revelation" (pp. 16–17). These issues of marginalization and purity loom large in discussions of the relations between psychology and religion, and these Neoscholastic and Evangelical views are representative of one of the central ways of doing this boundary-work.

A Christian psychology

The third approach divides the psychological world into secular and non-secular psychologies. This approach also takes many forms. In recent years,

psychology do not necessarily support what Christian psychologists think that Scripture says. While Narramore means to include biblical "data," Myers argues for the independence of empirical data vis-à-vis theology. This use of "data" is a good example of what Gillespie (2007a) means by conflation.

especially as psychology-as-science has come under scrutiny from a variety of sources – the critical, postmodern, and hermeneutical among others – proposals for Christian psychologies have become more common, and they have come to hold a more mainstream position within psychology. Christian psychologists have American Psychological Association (APA) approved graduate programs, they have journals, and they have organizations.[6] Robert C. Roberts (2000) spells out the goals of a Christian psychology in these terms:

> A primary aim of Christian psychology is to make available the distinctive psychology of the Christian tradition to the intellect and practice of persons in our times. It is a different enterprise from integration [of psychology and theology], whose aim is to produce a happy blend of one or another of the twentieth-century psychologies with the thought and practice of the church. The goal of Christian psychology, then, is two-dimensional: to read the tradition *pure* and yet to read it for what we and our contemporaries can recognize as *psychology*.
>
> (p. 155)

While his conception of integration (what I am calling the second approach) may be debatable, what is noteworthy in Roberts' approach is his claim that what we call psychology today is that of the "psychological 'establishment' – represented by psychology departments in major universities and the American Psychological Association" (p. 149). For Roberts, a main limitation of establishment psychology is its historical amnesia rooted in its Enlightenment and Romantic past, from which it derives its bias against Christianity. Roberts would define psychology more broadly, and so include the psychologies of Aristotle, the Desert Fathers, Augustine, Aquinas, Jonathan Edwards and others – and above all others, the Bible. Roberts challenges the positivistic narrative that has defined mainstream psychology for much of the past century.

Roberts' approach does not seek to subsume the psychology of the APA to Christian psychology. Indeed, from his point of view, that cannot be done, because "the psychologies of the twentieth century are all, in one way or another, rivals and alternatives to the Christian psychology" (p. 155). Hence his concern with purity and the dangers of secular psychology. Brent Slife and Jeffrey Reber (2009a) make a similar but more nuanced case for institutionalized biases – against not Christianity alone but theism in general – in mainstream psychology. They conclude that "theists require God as a

---

[6] Graduate programs in the United States include the Fuller Theological Seminary, Regent University, and the Rosemead School of Psychology. The Institute for the Psychological Sciences is a Catholic graduate program aiming at integration of psychology and theology. Journals: *Edification: The Interdisciplinary Journal of the Society for Christian Psychology* and the *Journal of Psychology and Christianity*. Organizations include the Christian Association for Psychological Sciences, the Society for Christian Psychology, and the Society of Catholic Social Scientists.

primordial premise . . . and naturalists deny this requirement" (Slife and Reber, 2009b, p. 130). While they seek dialogue with naturalistic (meaning metaphysically naturalistic) psychologists, still, they see no way to merge a theistic with such a psychology. So like others who take this third position, there is no unifying set of assumptions to bridge a psychology-with-God and one without God.

Catholic examples of this approach exist. A century ago, there were Catholic criticisms of the new psychology because it was a "psychology without a soul." But even when this new psychology was disparaged for its neglect of the soul and for being materialistic, the Catholic psychology proposed in reply was not meant simply to exist alongside the materialistic one: it was meant to replace it. This could be proposed because these psychologists, Neoscholastic or not, did not intend to bring theological concepts or principles directly into psychology. Rather, the philosophical psychology that they articulated was sufficient to their purposes, especially as it provided proofs for the existence and immortality of the soul and its special creation by a Creator. Paul Vitz's criticisms of secular psychology fall into this third type, because he seeks to base psychology on Christian principles.

Psychology instead of religion

The fourth alternative is the secular counterpart to the third. Freud's *The Future of an Illusion* was a clear statement of it, an enlightenment essay that argued that, as religion no longer keeps human passion in check, there is the necessity – if we value civilization – to provide a more rational means for dealing with our desires. That alternative was, of course, psychoanalysis. Freud was not alone in seeing psychology as superseding religion. Freud's was one way to read the positivist's dream of the triumph of reason and science. John B. Watson's radical behaviorism was another variant, as is Martin Seligman's positive psychology.

Perhaps the most common form of this approach is that of positivism. Positivism derives from the nineteenth-century French thinker and founder of sociology, Auguste Comte. Comte proposed a history of human thought that progressed from religion and myth, in which natural events had divine causes – the gods cause lightning – to philosophical systems that purport to explain nature – the final cause of rain is to make the flowers grow – to the period of positive science, which is empirical and experimental. Positive science rejects religious and philosophical explanations, and the natural sciences have progressed by liberating themselves from religion and philosophy. A theme of the "new psychology" at the end of the nineteenth century was that psychology had indeed freed itself from philosophy, building on the other natural sciences: physics, chemistry, and physiology. Not all the significant psychologists a century ago accepted this positivist reading, including Wundt, but in the North American scene it was and remains the dominant view. Not all theologians of the time were hostile to this reading of intellectual history, and many, especially liberal Protestant thinkers, agreed to the superiority of a purely naturalistic interpretation of natural events.

This fourth approach need not be as strident as the positivism of Freud or Watson. Taylor (1999) describes a spiritual tradition in American society, stretching back to colonial times, of people finding spiritual sustenance outside the established churches, largely through the cultivation of religious experiences. Much of this tradition entailed psychological theorizing and therapies, visible in the ways that phrenology and hypnotism were assimilated into nineteenth-century American culture, and also in what was called "New Thought" a century ago and called "New Age" today. For Taylor, in the rise of transpersonal psychology, this tradition of dissent, this tradition of the personal pursuit of spiritual growth, has found an institutional home within psychology. William James' (1903) century-old set of lectures, *The varieties of religious experience*, is the key document of this attempt to transcend the boundaries between psychology and religion. Vitz (1994) and Myers (2000) take a less benign view of psychology-as-religion approach, seeing in it an idolization of the self. However, this spiritual-but-not-religious mindset has deep roots, going back, in other forms to be sure, to the fourteenth century. Hanegraaff (1996) sees it as a counter-movement to the rise of the natural sciences, flourishing first in Renaissance hermeticism and natural magic, and changing over time. Characteristic of the contemporary epoch is what he calls the "psychologization of religion and the sacralization of psychology" (p. 224), which may be a good definition of much of contemporary interest in New Age spirituality and in personal growth. Over the past forty years or so, this psychologized spirituality has earned institutional respectability and even legitimation, generating graduate programs and empirical research.[7]

Perhaps the most common form of this approach is less theoretical than practical: many people turn to one psychology or another in addition to the churches for spiritual sustenance. Some psychologies – Jungian, for example – often seem to promote this kind of psychology-as-religion (or unchurched spirituality), with their psychologized and symbolic readings of the Bible and of myths. Carter and Narramore (1979) depict this position in terms of two "models," both of which tend to strip Scripture or theological formulations of any transcendent reference and make them "symbolic" of psychological categories. Thus, sin becomes a violation of the moral code (according to their reading of Orval Hobart Mowrer and Karl Menninger), rather than "an offense against God" (p. 84), and God "is certainly in some way a projection of our inner self" in the psychology of John Sanford, again according to Carter and Narramore. For Erich Fromm, "religion is constructive (and congruent with

---

[7] For example, the Institute for Transpersonal Psychology and Naropa University. There is a *Journal of Transpersonal Psychology*.

psychoanalysis) to the degree that it promotes freedom, love, truth, and independence" (Carter and Narramore, 1979, p. 83). If this variant substitutes psychology for religion, it provides a bridge to the religious realm for those who find themselves at odds with it. Psychology as a kind of secular spirituality de-emphasizes transcendent notions of the divine, seeking the holy within. At the same time, by drawing on contemporary physics, it articulates a spiritualized picture of the cosmos, so becoming a type of scientific spirituality.

All four approaches engage in boundary-work of one form or another. A common factor is that they identify psychology with mainstream scientific psychology, the "psychology of the American Psychological Association," as one Neoscholastic (pejoratively) put it. This is because natural scientific psychology, for all its own diversity, is the dominant social, political, and economic force in psychology.

The boundaries today?

We live in a time of porous boundaries, insecure boundaries, invisible boundaries on every level. Political, economic, geographical, informational, social, and interpersonal boundaries are not what they used to be. Boundaries of the beginnings and ends of life lack clarity in the public sphere, and the margin of uncertainty grows in what Ivan Illich called our "amortal" society. Psychology, ever a twig in the cultural stream, follows suit. Some thirty-five years ago, the Dutch phenomenological psychologist, J. H. van den Berg (1971) wrote that, whereas in Freud's day sexual matters lay in the unconscious, in the present moment, there is a "spiritual unconscious." Well then, from a van den Bergian perspective, existence has mutated once again. Listen to the psychologists: it is now possible to speak of spirituality, "psychology's clearest taboo" (Miller, 2005, p. 14). The taboo gone, we see that "disciplinary allegiance to secularism has long blinded psychology to phenomena that are of natural interest in understanding human behavior and has encouraged psychologists to divorce their science from the insights and priorities of a theistic perspective" (p. 15). Delaney and DiClemente (2005) reiterate this point: "Throughout most of the 20th century, the idea of taking Judeo-Christian teaching seriously within psychology was generally considered taboo" (p. 31). Transpersonalists and others, such as the Jungians, may object that they had not encountered the spiritual as a taboo, but truth be told, those groups continue to dance at the margins of the "psychology of the American Psychological Association." What is different now is that in terms of working assumptions (such as the existence of choice in human action), topics (correlation of spiritual well-being and mental health), and methods (qualitative research primarily), religion and spirituality do not threaten mainstream psychology. Of course, this means a change in the mainstream, with developments such as positive psychology and its studies of character and virtue. So the taboo against religion has crumbled.

Other conflicts will arise. It is not difficult to imagine that this new interest in religion and spirituality will produce a secularist countermove across the boundary. Will psychologists in general think it is an advance that some psychologists can now speak of sin, to pick a prime example? What else comes through the embrace of a postulate for psychology of "an unseen spiritual dimension of reality to which humans are meaningfully related" (Miller, 2005, p. 16)?

A critical perspective

Religion and spirituality are surely basic foci of human action and thought, so it is important that psychology reckon with them. Nevertheless, there is reason to express concern over the violation of the old taboo against psychology making inroads into religion and spirituality. I will express this concern by taking a critical perspective in the course of relating the history of psychology and Catholicism. Let me explain the critical psychological approach I will take, since there are various things that fall under this name.

A clear account of a critical approach is Kurt Danziger's (1994) discussion of how the history of psychology is written. He distinguishes two: internal and external histories. Internal histories are those written by psychologists for psychologists and, Danziger asserts, they tend to be celebratory. Like Little Jack Horner, the celebratory historian shows how psychology has overcome past obstacles and come to a clear road to the truth. This is the kind of history one sees in textbooks, and Boring's *History of experimental psychology* (1950) is the classic example of celebratory insider history. Hans Van Rappard (1997), in partial rebuttal to Danziger, notes that some insider history is more lamentation than celebration, and he has a point. The history of psychology from Christian perspectives concentrates more on the secularism of psychology than on its glorious rise as a science. For example, Johnson and Jones (2000a) write that "the 'new' or *modern* psychology, then, was birthed through the union of a legitimate quest for empirically validated truth with a modernist worldview that separated psychology from theology and philosophy" (p. 31). This way of construing the history both celebrates and laments, for in invoking "modern-ism," Johnson and Jones mean a "tendency to empty culture of its religious significance, discourse, and symbols" (p. 14). Nevertheless, in recent years the laments have turned to cautious alleluias as psychology has shown interest in religion and spirituality again, this time casting them in a favorable light: "For the first time in its history, the American Psychological Association has published a series of books on the interface of psychology with religion and spirituality" (Miller, 2005, p. 14). Whether they praise or blame, however, these histories of psychology and religion are insider histories.

Danziger calls for insider histories that take an external or critical stance, and in light of the importance of the topic of psychology and religion, I find that this area is in need of such an approach. What characterizes it? A critical approach looks for the conditions of possibility for the manifestation of a phenomenon but, following Danziger, I take these conditions of possibility to be historical conditions. That is, I will not be seeking the ontological possibilities for the appearance of contested boundaries between psychology and Catholicism, as if there were some rift in the nature of the cosmos demanding them. The critical approach here means an examination of the historical conditions of possibility for boundary-work. Psychology's categories and methods are historical phenomena. What this means is that concepts such as personality, memory, perception, intelligence, need, neurosis, drive, etc., can be shown to have had historical contingencies at the basis of their formulation. Because of the human tendency to appropriate what is said about human nature, not only the categories of psychology have historical contingency: "human subjectivity, the reality behind the objects of psychological investigation, is itself strongly implicated in the historical process, both as agent and as product" (Danziger, 1994, p. 475). One of the chief ways that human subjectivity has been agent and product over the past century has been through the emergence of psychology in its various forms. We come to know ourselves and others, seek to change ourselves and others, through psychology. Other ages had other means at their disposal, as Foucault (1978) illustrated: stoic maxims, monastic ascetic practices, disciplines of the school, the prison, and the factory, were all means of coming to know and work with our very selves. So a critical approach seeks the historical conditions that made possible the emergence of particular forms of "psychology," "subjectivity," "religion," etc.

The study of the historicity of subjectivity and of psychology brings an "outsider" perspective to psychology. Nevertheless, it is a perspective that has a place and a hearing within psychology these days (Blackman, 1994; Danziger, 2003; Greer, 1997; Rose, 1996; Staeuble, 2006; Van Hoorn, 1972). This critical approach has a complex lineage itself, with the influences coming from phenomenology (van den Berg, 1972), Foucault (1972), social constructionism (Gergen, 1997), and other studies that take the historicity of the mind seriously (Duden, 1991; Vernant, 1991).

What this critical approach means for this book is that we shall look at the various conflicts as arising in specific cultural and historical moments. The conflict indicates what counted as "psychology" and what counted as "religion" at that moment. Moreover, within the conflict, we shall examine the particulars of the conflict. For example, one conflict was over confession and sexuality, and another over that of the will and obedience. What were these objects at the heart of each contested boundary between psychology and Catholicism? Most important, we shall ask about the configuration of human subjectivity in the conflicts. In each conflict, the character of subjectivity was at stake. Often enough, that this was at stake received recognition by at least some members of the conflict. For example, in early Catholic criticisms of a "psychology without a soul," there was a clear understanding that what was at issue was not simply a philosophical concept, but that there were clear implications for the conception of the subject as an individual and as member of larger social bodies, implications for education, and most important of all, implications for human self-understanding as having an eternal destiny or not.

Part of the methodology that I will employ draws on what Foucault (1972) called "contradictions," here, the contradictions between psychology and the Church during the past century: "contradictions are neither appearances to be overcome, nor secret principles to be uncovered. They are objects to be described for themselves, without any attempt being made to discover from what point of view they can be dissipated, or at what level they can be radicalized" (p. 151). I take this as a heuristic, intended to offset the "passion for unity" that fires many in the study of the relations between psychology and religion. Foucault continues: "By taking contradictions as objects to be described, archaeological analysis does not try to discover in their place a common form or theme, it tries to determine the extent and form of the gap that separates them ... [It] describes the different *spaces of dissention*" (p. 152). If we look at "spaces of dissention," this does not mean ignoring or denying spaces of consensus or convergence. It means, in my reading of it, suspending all assumptions of unity and harmony between psychology and religion. This kind of intellectual discipline is appropriate for the current moment, when mainstream psychology now studies religious topics and even, in some quarters, adopts religious presuppositions. Beliefs in pre-established harmony in this area are as commonplace as assertions of the fact/value dichotomy.

Foucault described types of contradictions, two of which are especially relevant: extrinsic and intrinsic. Extrinsic contradictions "reflect the opposition between distinct discursive formulations" (p. 153). Relevant to our study are those contradictions arising from differences between psychological discourses and the religious and theological discourses that were mingled with those of psychology. An example of that would be efforts to integrate natural scientific facts with biblical teachings. Intrinsic contradictions, writes Foucault, unlike extrinsic contradictions, "derive from a single positivity" (ibid.). These intrinsic contradictions are "two ways of forming statements, both characterized by certain objects, certain positions of subjectivity, certain concepts, and certain strategic choices" (ibid.). The single positivity at the heart of our analysis is that of "psychology/Catholicism." Examples of intrinsic contradictions include the place of the soul in psychology, the meaning of symbols in our psychological lives, and the meaning of obedience to authority.

The political battles between evolutionary theory and creationism, for example, indicate extrinsic contradictions, since each side disputes the legitimacy of the ground from which the other speaks, biology and biblical fundamentalism not participating in the same knowledge system. In the intrinsic contradiction between the Church and psychology, however, both the subject[8] and the objects belong to a single and common ground and area of concern: "modern man in search of a soul," to borrow Jung's (1933) phrase. Of course, both psychology and the Church are not simply bodies of thought; they are complex institutions with considerable overlap, making for possible conflict. The "single positivity" within which intrinsic contradictions between psychology and the Church arise is the teaching authority and the pastoral activities of the Church, which correspond to the expertise of psychologists, particularly in applied areas such as education and psychotherapy. I call them intrinsic rather than extrinsic contradictions in order to stress, at least as a hypothesis, that those who have claimed that in some way psychology substitutes for religion (I include Sigmund Freud, Carl Jung, and John B. Watson here, as well as their critics in psychology, such as Rudolf Allers and David Powlison) notice *something* that those who see the two as capable of being integrated or otherwise harmoniously related miss. Not that the claims for hegemony are simply correct on their own terms, but that there is a region that psychology and religion co-occupy.

An overview of psychology and Catholicism: contested boundaries

The critical approach brings a number of questions to each topic. In addition to the obvious ones, such as attending to the specifics of person, place, and time for each of the contests that we will review, there are others. These questions include:

(1) In each instance, what is meant by "psychology"? What kinds of claims are made about this object of the discourses under question? What is the perceived history and organization of this object? These questions are necessary because "psychology" means a number of things: the new experimental psychology, psychoanalysis, humanistic psychology, psychotherapy, etc.

(2) From where in the Catholic Church does the opposition to psychology arise? Into which context do we need to situate the conflict from the point of view of the Church? Does the source of the opposition lie at a local level, national level, or at the level of the Vatican? What is at stake?

(3) For both psychology and the Church: who has the authority to take up the "subject position" in the dispute? Who, that is, is in a position to speak the truth? How is authority understood, and what are its bases?

(4) Which types of discourses and practices frame the contest? Is it a discourse on modernism, on progress, on democracy? Are the practices those of teaching, counseling, administering the sacraments, etc.?

---

[8] "Subject" refers to who or what can make authoritative statements: who speaks for psychology? Who speaks for the Church? By the term "objects" is meant the categories of things that "subjects" can speak about: What is psychology? Is psychoanalysis a substitute for Confession? What is intelligence? Motivation? Will?

(5) Not to invent a contest where none exists: if there is agreement or harmony, in what terms is it meant and carried out? Does the harmony take place within a larger contest?

With these questions in mind, let me turn to the specific issues that will occupy the body of this book, chapter by chapter.

Chapter 2. The major fault line: modernism and psychology

No discussion of psychology and Catholicism can ignore the trauma of the modernist crisis of a century ago. Modernism was a name given to many things, but for many in the Catholic Church it signified a profound threat to the integrity of Christian teachings. Modernism chiefly meant attempts to update church teachings and organization with the findings of the modern sciences. Modernism, it was claimed, was the desire to substitute "science" for "religion," using quotation marks to indicate that we will need to specify exactly what was supposed to replace what. The shadows of this crisis fall on boundaries between psychology and the Church to this day in a variety of ways. Psychology was implicated in the modernist crisis, at least indirectly, since many of the modernists, real and alleged, made appeal to experience and to the subjective a part of their theology. The name of William James appeared in modernist literature. The 1918 *Code of Canon Law*, which solidified the Church's position against modernism, named many of the philosophical bases of psychology as antithetical to Christianity. But the modernist crisis is not only of historical significance: it plays through much of the discourse over the place of psychology in the Church to the present day. One of the earliest and most important Catholic psychologists, Cardinal Mercier, articulated a clearly anti-modernist foundation for psychology at the turn of the twentieth century. However, the intertwining of his story with that of one of the leading modernist, George Tyrrell, who adumbrated a psychology of the subconscious, shows how deeply the emergence of scientific psychology was tied to this major and divisive issue in the Catholic world.

Chapter 3. Neoscholastic psychology

Neoscholastic psychology was the major Catholic response to modernism and to the rise of the new psychology in the first half of the twentieth century. The Neoscholastic empirical psychologists walked a fine line between charges from some Catholics of abandoning authoritative Church teaching on the one hand, and accusations by some psychologists of being unscientific on the other. Neoscholastic psychology became the Catholic response to the new psychology because in 1879, Pope Leo XIII institutionalized a return to the thought of St. Thomas Aquinas as the foundation for Catholic thinking in philosophy and theology. Any psychology that developed after that time was supposed to conform to the categories of Thomistic thought. At the same time, this Thomistic view recognized that psychology, like all the sciences, had its proper autonomy. Neoscholastic psychology developed two paths: the first a philosophical psychology that articulated a theory of the soul, and the second a scientific psychology, employing experimental and statistical methods to compete with positivistic conceptions of psychology. Neoscholastic psychology flourished in both academic and applied settings until the Thomistic "synthesis" broke up in the wake of the Second Vatican Council (1962–5).

Neoscholastic psychology led to the first contest we shall examine: debates over the rise of the "new" psychology at the end of the nineteenth century. This new psychology was an experimental psychology and it was a physiological psychology. For some Catholics, these characteristics were sufficient to call it into question as a "psychology without a soul," since characteristic of much of the new psychology, although not of all, was its abandonment of metaphysical questions, including those about the soul. Nevertheless, it was more the practical applications promised by the new psychology that made it suspect in Catholic circles. At the same time, the practical implications of psychology proved to be the royal road to the acceptance of psychology in Catholic communities.

Abandoning the soul meant a number of things beyond the loss of a metaphysical center for the human person. It also meant the reduction of thinking to the level of sensation, and the human ability to conceive universals was important in Catholic thought in the early twentieth century, because our ability to do so was said to rest on the immateriality of the rational part of the soul. Also threatening Thomistic teachings on the intellect was the elevation of the importance of the instincts and feelings, which seemed to pervert the Church's image of human nature. So we shall investigate what the Neoscholastics had to say about human cognition.

In so doing, especially looking at the work of Thomas Verner Moore and his students, we see that they developed a psychology that, while Neoscholastic, drew on other streams of thought too. Moore was not a purist in his psychology, and he received some criticism for it. What happened was that a modern Neoscholastic psychology developed, with the ability to engage the Catholic and the larger psychological communities at the same time. We shall also look briefly at other contributions to Neoscholastic psychology, in particular developmental psychology and clinical assessment, there focusing on work of Magda Arnold and her students.

Chapter 4. *Psychology as the boundary: Catholicism, spiritualism, and science*

Whatever their limitations, the Neoscholastics had an expansive vision of human life. Death was not its end, and they argued that the facts of human life led to the conclusion that we are ensouled, that the soul is immaterial, and that we have an immortal destiny. They rejected materialism and phenomenalism. The spiritual world was real, we have access to it, and it had its powers, promises, and dangers. Mainstream psychology, with some exceptions, such as the all-encompassing William James, held the spiritual world at arm's length after a brief love affair with the psychic researchers. That being said, the squeamishness of the experimentalists was not shared by all who had psychological interests and – given that psychology was not defined solely by the academics – we see that psychology in other contexts was very much a spiritual psychology. I refer here to that broad sea of interest in the influence of the mind over the body and, with it, of the transcendental view of mind that has characterized much of American popular religion and psychology from colonial times onward. Called the "shadow culture" by Taylor and the "unchurched" by Fuller, this tradition has taken various forms over the past three hundred years. In most cases, it involved the incorporation of non-Christian, pantheistic or quasi-pantheistic views of the universe with some form of Christianity. In more recent years, under the umbrella name of "New Age" thought, the Christian component may be muted. It definitely relativized Christian teaching, typically asserting that Christ was one of those enlightened beings who appear from time to time – and who foreshadow the inevitable evolution of human consciousness to a higher state. This chapter looks at the ways that in the arguments over spiritualism, hypnosis, and various forms of mental healing, including Christian Science and Mind Cure, psychology played a boundary role between the Spiritualists and modern science. It is a complex story, because there was a Catholic version of spiritualism and mental healing, associated with shrines, in particular with that at Lourdes in France. Here the Church defended the miraculous nature of some of the cures, using psychological categories to discriminate between real and merely psychological healing. The chapter closes with attention to James Joseph Walsh, a New York physician and author of *Psychotherapy*, an early twentieth-century attempt to integrate the results of the study of hypnosis, spiritualistic phenomena, psychological medicine, and Catholic teaching.

Chapter 5.   Psychoanalysis versus the power of will

As a means for treating mental disorders and as a compelling theory of the soul and, indeed, of religion, psychoanalysis threw down the gauntlet to people of faith throughout the twentieth century. The story of Catholic responses to psychoanalysis is a complex one, ranging from outright rejection to measured embrace. Early Catholic responses focused on the relationship between psychoanalysis and the sacrament of confession. Not doubting psychoanalysis' effectiveness (unless to denounce it as pseudo-science), views ranged from analysis as a complement to the confessional to it being an inferior replacement of it, thus affirming the power of confession not only to forgive sins but also to heal the sufferings of the soul. And if confession does the latter, what is the purpose of psychoanalysis?

Neoscholastic interpretations of Freud's work varied, with Thomas Verner Moore giving measured acceptance to some of the techniques, if not to the theory behind them. Then there is the story of Edward Boyd Barrett, the Irish Jesuit who came to the United States in the 1920s. His work is often referred to in histories of the Catholic critiques of Freud, but less well known is how he developed his own version of psychoanalysis, how he left the Jesuits, hung out his shingle in Greenwich Village, and then, late in life, how he reconciled with the Church. His writings, especially on sexuality, before and after his break with Rome, show two strikingly different interpretations of Freud and of Catholic thought and life at the time.

Psychoanalysis did have an impact on one area of traditional Catholic practice – the training of the will. Will-training was no doubt less a Thomistic than a Cartesian practice, but it was widespread throughout the period covered in this book. Psychoanalysis cast doubts on it, and Moore, with his dynamic psychology, agreed with the critiques. Nevertheless, Catholic psychological thinkers kept a place for the will in their psychologies, from Moore and Boyd Barrett to van Kaam, despite the eclipse of the will as a category in mainstream psychology.

In 1940, the Viennese psychiatrist Rudolf Allers attacked Freud's theory and therapy as incompatible with Catholic principles and anthropology. His colleague at the Catholic University of America, Monsignor Fulton J. Sheen, took up Allers' position and reopened the conflict. In 1947, Sheen denounced Freudianism from the pulpit of St. Patrick's Cathedral in New York City, raising a storm of protest from Catholic psychiatrists in the area. Among the marvels of that furor was that no one questioned the effectiveness of psychoanalysis. Its allegedly destructive effects on the soul, making peace of soul impossible, were the object of Sheen's criticism.

In the 1950s, more nuanced interpretations of Freud appeared, often published in the Catholic periodical, *Cross Currents*. In addition, new versions of psychoanalysis served to dispel some of the antagonism with religion. With the decline of psychoanalysis as the dominant form of psychiatry, much of the conflict abated.

Chapter 6.   From out of the depths: Carl Jung's challenges and Catholic replies

Forty years ago, one could speak confidently about ours being a secularizing age: the more science and technology progressed, the more religion receded. Carl G. Jung could write about "modern man in search of a soul" as a consequence of secularization, with religious symbols, rituals, and beliefs losing their force in increasing numbers of lives. There were for the first time in history entire nations, especially the Soviet Union, dedicated to atheism. The positivist dream was being fulfilled.

But secularization has not simply progressed. The public sphere is in many ways increasingly areligious, but this is highly contested ground. If much of Western Europe and Canada seem contentedly secular, in the United States, as in many nations in the east and the south, intense religious ferment has exploded on the cultural and political stages. Religious and spiritual issues, once on the fringe of mainstream psychology, as represented by the APA, have come front and center. Even biomedicine, that bulwark of secularized views of the body and illness, acknowledges more readily the spiritual and religious dimensions of life and their usefulness in preserving health and fighting illness. One cannot speak of desecularization, however, for secularization proceeds apace. The situation is more complex and fragmented, and within and without the dominant secularized and tolerant culture, there are pockets of resacralization and large areas where religious views, often hostile to the natural sciences, hold sway. Most telling of all is the increasing presence among us of those who are "spiritual but not religious," those simultaneously secularized and engaged with the sacred.

If we turn to the question of spirituality in psychology, in relation to the Catholic Church, the work of Carl Jung is most prominent. Jung is an important thinker in this area, and his work itself occupies a boundary condition. One of the most important psychologists of the twentieth century, his work rarely finds a place in academic psychology, although it has influenced literary, religious, and cultural studies in the universities. Jungian psychology verges on "pop" psychology, despite Jung's enormous erudition and despite his lack of the easy optimism and the positive thinking that characterizes popular spiritualized psychology. Jungian psychology thrives at independent institutes and through the practice of analytical psychology. Catholic takes on Jung and the Jungians are various as well, and this chapter begins with the Catholic (mis)appropriation of Jung. While a number of psychologists and theologians will occupy attention, at the center is Victor White, the English Dominican theologian who had a complicated relationship with Jung and Jungian thought. The deaths of White in 1960 and Jung in 1961 mark the end of the pre-Vatican II era, when anxieties over modernism were foremost.

The starting point for the significance of Jung's thought is the "wasteland" motif of the post-World War I period. There was a widespread sense that modern men and women were cut off from the myths and traditions that rooted and nourished human living. The "hollow men" who could no longer believe in Christian teachings turned to Jung for help. Jung's claim to be a natural scientist was granted him by many a Catholic thinker, although others, such as Agostino Gemelli and Magda Arnold, questioned the basis of his psychology.

Jung, unlike many of his contemporaries in psychology, actively sought out theologians, philosophers, classicists, and others for purposes of understanding the nature of the soul. In this way, Jung provided a model for how a psychology interested in its relationships with Catholicism (and religion generally) might move forward today in recovering from its amnesia and connecting with the long traditions of thought and action about the human soul and its well-being. In this chapter on Jung, we thus look at the Catholic thinkers who participated in the Eranos conferences from the 1930s to the 1950s. We then turn to how Catholic psychologists replied to Jung's work on the cure of the soul, especially the work of Raymond Hostie, Josef Goldbrunner, and centrally, Victor White. White's Thomistic interpretation of archetypes and symbols was an important contribution to the development of a Catholic perspective in psychology.

Chapter 7.   Institutionalizing the relationship

The boundaries that psychology staked out in Catholic contexts were not only theoretical and practical, they were also institutional. Psychology confronted and contacted (Gillespie, 2007a) Catholicism in the establishments of psychology departments in American colleges and universities, a process that was still contested as late as the 1950s in most Catholic colleges, even later in a few others. In this chapter, we look at the Catholic universities that had the first graduate programs in psychology. The incorporation of psychology into what had previously been a domain of philosophy and theology, shows a surprising development. In all four of these universities, psychology established itself in part by showing its applicability to pressing social problems that were the pastoral concern of the Church. While often beginning as experimental programs, their genius lay in applied psychology.

Then we turn to Catholic psychological organizations, starting with a brief look at the Chicago Society of Catholic Psychologists, begun by Charles I. Doyle, SJ,[9] in the 1930s. Doyle was present when, after War World II, the American Catholic Psychological Association (ACPA) was formed. Then, we turn to the 1952 founding of the Guild of Catholic Psychiatrists (later, the National Guild of Catholic Psychiatrists). These professional organizations provided a ground, within an identifiably Catholic context, for the cultivation of psychology and psychiatry. The differences between the ACPA and the Guild shed much light on the differences between psychology and psychiatry as they do on two ways of rapprochement between psychology and Catholicism.

Chapter 8.   Humanistic psychology and Catholicism: dialogue and confrontation

The "third force" in American psychology promised a new conception of the boundary between psychology and Catholic thought in the 1950s and 1960s.

[9] SJ, the Society to Jesus, i.e. the Jesuits.

Here was a psychology that was not reductionistic and that did think that questions of value and meaning were important in human life. But the humanists and the phenomenologists also questioned the boundaries between religion and science by first challenging the conception of science that the Neoscholastics had accepted. The old division of labor between the philosophical and the empirical psychologies broke down in this challenge. In addition, humanists and existentialists alike challenged religion by delving into spiritual issues. The picture is complicated by the fact that these trends in psychology coincided with the "cultural revolutions" of the 1960s, which cast all authority into question. As an example, in 1968, a group of psychologists active in the ACPA raised a series of questions in response to the encyclical, *Humanae vitae*, asking if the understandings of human relationships in the encyclical were based on sound knowledge of human nature.

We examine humanistic challenges both to natural science psychology and to the Neoscholastic formulation of a basis for natural science psychology. Psychologists did not initiate the latter – the break with Neoscholasticism originated with theologians and philosophers. Later, in the 1950s, a number of Neoscholastically trained psychologists turned to the humanistic psychology of Carl Rogers and to phenomenological thought (which had many ties to Neoscholasticism). The work of Charles A. Curran and Adrian van Kaam features large in this transition, although so does the work of Magda Arnold, Raymond McCall, and Alden Fisher.

The chief significance of humanistic and phenomenological psychologies for our story, however, is its relationship to Catholic spiritual psychology. So this older psychology is presented – an ascetical psychology with deep roots – and its continuation and transformation in the work of van Kaam and others. Themes of the will and of the spirit emerge, as well as how these themes played themselves out in the distinct historical movement of the 1960s. The meanings of "authority" and "obedience" were irretrievably altered as a result.

Chapter 9.   Trading zones between psychology and Catholicism

At boundaries, other things than conflicts occur. One of the most important is trade or commerce – a hermeneutic enterprise par excellence – and in this chapter we will draw on the notion of "trading zones" developed by the historian of science, Peter Galison. We will look at two different trading zones, one in education, the other in counseling. To establish a presence in Catholic universities, psychologists such as Moore developed a "pidgin," a way of speaking that both the psychological and the Catholic communities could understand, even if they understood the key terms in strikingly different ways. A key word of this pidgin was "personality," which evoked the soul and the unity of human nature for the Catholic community, and empirical studies of traits for the psychologists. At the level of praxis, the development of pastoral psychology in the 1950s was a prime example of a trading zone, as a full-fledged "creole" formed to create a new discipline in the Catholic psychological world. What we see, however, is that after Vatican II, the older pre-established harmony between psychology and moral theology broke down, within both sciences and between them, as psychology removed homosexuality from its roster of psychopathologies, and some moral theologians rejected earlier objectivistic views of human action. This topic points to conflicting boundaries that developed after the period addressed in this book.

Chapter 10.   Crossings

At this point in our history, it is time to look ahead and see what the prospects are for future contested boundaries. The nature of the person is the most central, and in terms that psychology used to understand, the nature of the soul is perhaps the most pressing. A term that itself sits on the boundaries that are at question in this book, a notion of the soul is the most easy to reject as being unscientific and as importing into psychology something that is best left out. In reply, I contest that boundary. Without committing to a particular conception of the soul, the question arises, as it did for Franz Brentano more than a century ago, whether psychology loses something central in losing the soul. Drawing on the previous chapters, this final chapter asks if there is a conception of the soul or the psyche that has a place in psychology, however defined. It asks further: can there be a conception of the soul rooted in empirical evidence, in experience? Can such a concept lend itself to philosophical and theological discourse? To anticipate: there is such a conception, and it has roots in Neoscholastic, psychoanalytical, Jungian, and phenomenological approaches in psychology. Formulation of this concept of the soul marks the boundary of the present study.

To proceed with the new crossings of the boundaries between psychology and Catholicism, crossings that do not follow the worn paths of modernism and Neoscholasticism and Jungian psychology and humanistic psychology, to turn toward the future, that is, we must Janus-like turn to the past. In conclusion, I propose a *ressourcement*, a turn to the sources of our collective discourses on all things psychological, pure and applied, to find the refreshment needed to forge ahead into uncharted regions of the borderland.

Is there a Catholic psychology?

Henryk Misiak and Virginia Staudt asked this question in their landmark work, *Catholics in psychology* (1954). Their answer? It is a complex answer, an unreconciled answer. First of all, they assert:

> There is no Catholic psychology any more than there is a Catholic biology, Catholic physics, or Catholic medicine ... The fact that in scientific

psychology there is no discussion or mention of the soul need neither surprise us nor create any hostility toward psychology, or suspicion or condemnation of it, such as was found among so many Catholic scholars in the early history of psychology.

(p. 13)

Misiak and Staudt drew the boundaries by asserting that psychology is a natural science and so makes no philosophical or theological claims. In this, their position is that of Kendall's, described above. In fact, they state that "Catholic psychologists can still retain their philosophical and religious beliefs, while collaborating with materialists or physicalists in the discovery of the facts" (p. 14). They go further:

> Since Catholic psychologists are not only psychologists but also Catholics, they will always endeavor to integrate psychology, philosophy, and theology . . .; but this endeavor does not preclude their participation in science even if this science assumes physicalistic methodology or is culti- vated by people who do not share or care about Catholic philosophy or theology.
>
> (ibid.)

The integration will be in the person of the psychologist and not in psychology. But this division of labor, which allows the Catholic psychologist to function in what sounds like a hostile environment within psychology, is complicated by the fact that "all three – psychology, philosophy, and theology – besides having a common object of study, namely, man, also have a common goal, the pursuit of truth" (p. 15). In their schema in which these three studies exist within a hierarchical relationship, there can be only apparent conflict and not real conflict, since truth is one.

But what if the hierarchy breaks down? What if how the "common object of study" construed philosophically within psychology conflicts with how the object is conceived within the regnant theology? What if presuppositions in psychology really matter, as many have argued over the years? Then what? It seems that if any of these questions are pursued, then the question of a Catholic psychology surfaces, as has the possibility of an evangelical Christian psychol- ogy. In other words, the question is not so easily settled. So the question will haunt the entire book. Only at the end can we return to it.

The major fault line: modernism and psychology

The two deepest characteristics of the new order are the scientific spirit and the democratic movement – a new conception of truth and a new conception of authority and government.

George Tyrrell (1908), *Medievalism*, p. 120

This chapter explores the narrative of modernism that has pervaded the debates between psychology and religion, particularly Christian religion, over the past century. For Freud, psychoanalysis was the logical successor of religion, because it provided a rational grounding for mental health and moral action. For some Christians, psychology (and of course psychoanalysis) is an ersatz religion, founded by people disenchanted with religion and hostile to the notion of divine revelation. Many of the founders of experimental psychology, of psychoanalysis, and of humanistic psychology, were modernists. In Catholic circles, modernism is now an old charge, stemming from controversies internal to the Church in the early twentieth century. These controversies culminated during the reign of Pope Pius X, who sought to defend the faith from subversion by the modernists within the Church. Given the Church's embrace of the modern world during the Second Vatican Council, especially its openness to the human sciences, it might seem a dead issue, but in recent decades charges of modernism have persisted. Indeed, some non-Catholic Christian psychologists have even joined the chorus and accused psychology of modernism. To address this perceived flaw, we see Christian counseling and Christian psychology programs, accompanied by criticisms of the secularist assumptions of mainstream psychology. Christian psychology, which was once an eccentric backwater of the discipline, has increased visibility these days. Modernism is such a vague term, and how the Church used it resembles the way American politicians spoke of Communism (modernism having obtained political power) as lurking everywhere. Modernism is a difficult topic to address, for even today, as Cadegan (2002) notes, how one narrates the events surrounding it reflects contemporary divisions within the Church, so that "a neutral assessment of theological modernism and its condemnation is impossible in the current context" (p. 100). We will explore the history of the modernist crisis with an eye to how it affected the position of psychology within the Church. We conclude this chapter by asking if the modernist crisis is over.

For many non-Catholics and non-Christians, this controversy may seem like a tempest in a teapot, especially if they are inclined to view modernism favorably. Is not the correction of primitive and medieval beliefs by the clear light of scientific research a rational move to make? I urge such readers to suspend judgment for the time being for several reasons. First, the nature of what counts as knowledge is precisely one of the issues at these contested boundaries, and the example of those between psychology and Catholicism may have value for other disputes. Second, these boundary disputes exist today in worldwide confrontations and commerce among cultural traditions, and it has become clear, as in the indigenous psychology movement, that western scientific psychology cannot claim with good conscience to be a universally valid psychology. Third, as the epistemic authority of science has become more widely challenged in recent years, it is useful to examine an earlier well-reasoned challenge to claims made in the name of science, even if one thinks the challenge wrong-headed. Thinking is, after all, argumentation, and this challenge was significant, although it was not only a rational one, but also a political one. Finally, in more general terms, the modernist crisis in the Catholic Church was an important episode in a broader debate in western societies over secularization. Secularization is not the monolithic movement that some accounts make it, but the delineation of an autonomous secular public sphere, secured from intrusions of the sacred and the religious, is one of the notable features of modern life. These separations of church and state, of science and religion, of the sacred and the profane, it must be remembered, were not only accomplishments of thought, in movements such as the Enlightenment of the eighteenth century, they were also a reply to bloodshed, achieved through bloodshed. Catholics were at both ends of the gun and the knife in these conflicts, as were Protestants and others. To grasp the shock of this violence is to see into the modernist crisis. If secularization was, to use the title of Marjorie Hope Nicolson's book, *The breaking of the circle* (1960), the Catholic world was in important ways the circle that was broken. Violence and the effects of violence echoed across the generations. Until today. So onward to the dispute.

The persistence of modernism

Benedict J. Groeschel, CFR,[1] is a renowned writer, spiritual director, and pastoral psychologist. Among his many books is *Spiritual passages* (1983), which examines both psychological and spiritual development, drawing on

---

[1] CFR, the Community of the Franciscans of the Renewal, an order of Catholic priests and brothers.

modern psychologists such as Erik Erikson, and on the analysis of three stages of the spiritual life in the Catholic tradition: the purgative, the illuminative, and the unitive ways. Groeschel's book is an effort to pour the best of psychology into the larger vessel of traditional Catholic understandings of the spiritual life. In discussing the "Religion of Maturity," he compares two prominent English Catholics, John Henry Newman and George Tyrrell. The former, says Groeschel, achieved spiritual maturity, and the latter, given the testimony of his friend, Baron Friedrich von Hügel, "died a bitter man, a tragic example of the perennial conflict of the adult adolescent who cannot make the leap to believe and love; thus he lived a life of unresolved conflict and rage" (p. 69).[2] Tyrrell, according to Groeschel, was a rationalist, and he explains what this meant for spiritual maturity:

> The difference between Newman and Tyrrell is presumably the giant step to mature religion, the transcendence of self or, if one prefers, the death of self ... The childish impulse to control God by prayer and works and the attempt of the adolescent mind to control Him by speculation and understanding must come to an end.
>
> (p. 70)

The casual reader will no doubt affirm Groeschel's distinction between adolescent and adult spirituality and acknowledge that many adults do not die to themselves so that they may live. But who was George Tyrrell? Why this example?

George Tyrrell (1861–1909) was born into a poor Protestant family in Dublin, Ireland. Attracted first by the liturgy of the Catholic Mass, he converted to Catholicism as a young man (in 1879) and became a priest, joining the Jesuits in 1891. Tyrrell was a graceful writer and, by all accounts, a difficult man. In his collective biography of the Catholic modernists, Marvin R. O'Connell (1994) writes of Tyrrell:

> Increasingly he saw his role as a ministry to Christian men and women who found the traditional modes of religious expression incompatible with modern culture. What science had wrought for such people was a crisis of faith to which, Tyrrell was coming to believe, the institutional church responded too often with barren abstractions or even out-and-out humbug.
>
> (p. 189)

Tyrrell came to be at odds with the Vatican and, after the condemnation of modernism, he was excommunicated in 1907 (he had already left, or been

---

[2] The position of von Hügel in the modernist controversy seems to rage on. See McKeown (2002, pp. 120–3).

expelled from the Jesuits in 1906) for his opposition to the papal encyclical[3] of that same year, *Pascendi Dominici Gregis* (Pope Pius X, 1907). When he died in 1909, he was denied burial in a Catholic cemetery, although he did receive the last rites. However, there must be something more at work in Groeschel's depiction of Tyrrell as a chronically spiritual adolescent, since the passage from von Hügel that he cites is a sentence wherein von Hügel, fourteen years after Tyrrell's death, acknowledged his contributions to *The mystical element of religion* (1923), von Hügel's most important work: "Father Tyrrell has gone, who had been so generously helpful, especially as to the mystical states, as to Aquinas, long before the storms beat upon him and his own vehemence overclouded, in part, the force and completeness of that born mystic" (p. vii).[4] To understand what happened to him, we need to look at the modernist crisis.

Prelude to the modernist crisis

The modernist crisis in the Catholic Church was, strictly speaking, an occurrence of the last years of the nineteenth century and the first years of the twentieth. It more or less coincided with the pontificate of Giuseppe Sarto, Pope Pius X (1903–14). Its roots go much deeper, to the loss of the Vatican's political power in the mid-nineteenth century and the subsequent necessity to rethink the place of the Church in the modern world. There was much political turmoil in the mid-nineteenth century, with the Papal States finally being seized by the newly formed Italian state in 1870. This event solidified papal opposition to the new government, and Pope Pius IX forbade Catholics from voting in elections in Italy. At the time of this invasion, the First Vatican Council was being held. The major results of this Council were declarations on papal infallibility in certain specific circumstances[5] and on the primacy of the pope as the successor of St. Peter. Just at the moment when the pope lost temporal power, his ecclesiastical authority was strengthened, making the pope nearly an absolute monarch. With modern transportation and communications

---

[3] An encyclical is an official letter written by the pope to bishops. Such a letter deals with matters of faith and morals and is considered authoritative in the church.

[4] According to O'Connell (1994), Tyrrell edited von Hügel's *The mystical element of religion* extensively: "He worked at it diligently for as much as six hours a day, trying to make it readable. And trying too to respect von Hügel's stated conviction that the institutional church, for all its faults, had to be maintained – convictions Tyrrell had long since given up" (p. 331). Because of his situation (he was no longer a Jesuit and had not found a bishop who would accept him as a priest in his diocese), he wrote to von Hügel: "Indeed I am going to ask you to erase my name when it occurs in two or three places of [your] . . . MS" (quoted in ibid., p. 332). Is not this erasure of self a sign of spiritual maturity?

[5] They include the pope speaking in an official capacity on matters of dogma. There have been two such occasions since this teaching was ratified at the First Vatican Council.

(the railroad, the telegraph, etc.), the reach of the Vatican and its bureaucracy, the Curia, was reinforced.

Coupled with the troubled nature of authority in the Church in a modernizing Europe was a response to philosophical trends of the day. In 1864, a few years before the First Vatican Council, Pius IX had issued a "Syllabus of Errors" (Pope Pius IX, 1999), listing eighty propositions that the Church declared false. Among them, and relevant to present purposes, were the following:

> 9. All the dogmas of the Christian religion are indiscriminately the object of natural science or philosophy, and human reason, enlightened solely in an historical way, is able, by its own natural strength and principles, to attain to the true science of even the most abstruse dogmas; provided only that such dogmas be proposed to reason itself as its object.
>
> ...
>
> 13. The method and principles by which the old scholastic doctors cultivated theology are no longer suitable to the demands of our times and to the progress of the sciences.
>
> (pp. 28–9)

The Syllabus opposed the rationalization of religion, the denial of its supernatural origin, and the claim that the human intellect solely "by its own natural strength" can grasp dogmatic statements about God. It criticized investigation using natural scientific methods into matters beyond the proper domain of science, and it defended the ways of philosophizing of "the old scholastic doctors." In expressing its concerns in the way it did, the Syllabus called into question the autonomy of scientific (including historical) inquiry. The new psychology would fall under the cloud of this suspicion because it extended the methods of the natural sciences to the region of the soul, and it investigated religious belief scientifically.

The Thomistic revival: Response to the political and intellectual developments of the modern world

When Gioacchino Pecci became Pope Leo XIII in 1878, one of the first things he did was call for Catholic theology and philosophy to return to the teachings of Thomas Aquinas, the thirteenth-century thinker who was credited with synthesizing Aristotelian with Christian thought. His encyclical, *Aeterni Patris*, officially inaugurated Neoscholasticism. He instituted Neoscholasticism not only as a return to the so-called medieval synthesis (which made his move "Scholastic"), but also as a dialogue with – and an absorption of – "what is best in modern thought" (McCool, 1989, p. 9) in general, and in the sciences in particular (which accounts for the "Neo"). The Neoscholastic revival of the late nineteenth century was a conscious effort to address the modern world. Catholic philosophical thought earlier in the century had been primarily

Cartesian,[6] not Scholastic, and there had been other trends, such as Fideism,[7] which severely constrained the scope of human reason. Leo XIII understood that the stakes in the philosophical questions extended beyond the classroom. The fate of the modern world hung in the balance:

> Whosoever turns his attention to the bitter strifes of these days and seeks a reason for the troubles that vex public and private life must come to the conclusion that a fruitful cause of the evils which now afflict, as well as those which threaten, us lies in this: that false conclusions concerning divine and human things, which originated in the schools of philosophy, have now crept into all the orders of the State, and have been accepted by the common consent of the masses. For, since it is in the very nature of man to follow the guide of reason in his actions, if his intellect sins at all his will soon follows; and thus it happens that false opinions, whose seat is in the understanding, influence human actions and pervert them.
>
> (Pope Leo XIII, 1879/1954, pp. 32–3)

From the beginning of the Scholastic revival, matters of politics, science, and faith were central to its philosophical teachings, thus establishing horizons of significance that would affect psychology as well.

That is one face of the Neoscholastic revival. The other was a defensive effort to deal with the modern world in its political as well as intellectual forms. There were reasons to be defensive, as anti-religious sentiment was often couched in a scientific, really a scientistic, discourse. Science, moreover, was often aligned ideologically with efforts to replace monarchs and aristocrats with more democratic and representative forms of government. Neoscholasticism presented a bulwark against these legacies of the French Enlightenment. From the Vatican viewpoint, attacks on the pope as a secular ruler and as a spiritual monarch were two forms of the same thing. As Lester Kurtz (1986) explains:

> Nineteenth-century political battle lines were frequently drawn so that affinities were defined between particular approaches to scientific and religious thought on the one hand, and various political and social alliances on the other. If one supported the replacement of the monarchy with a republic, especially in France, one was expected to oppose Catholicism and to favor the expansion of scientific research, while most who elected to be defenders of the Catholic faith also tended to oppose republicanism and science and to defend the monarchy. Monarchical models of authority

[6] Cartesian, that is, rooted in the philosophical tradition stemming from Descartes. A main difference between the Cartesian and the Thomistic is the radical separation of soul from body in the former, along with its emphasis on epistemological questions.

[7] Fideism is "a philosophical term meaning a system of philosophy or an attitude of mind, which, denying the power of unaided human reason to reach certitude, affirms that the fundamental act of human knowledge consists in an act of faith, and the supreme criterion of certitude is authority" (Sauvage, 1909, p. 68).

were used by clericals to defend Catholic orthodoxy, just as scientific
models of inquiry were used by anticlericals to attack that orthodoxy and
the monarchy which it legitimated.

(pp. 13–14)

Neoscholasticism, by returning to "the *philosophia perennis* which, elaborated
by the Greeks and brought to perfection by the great medieval teachers"
(de Wulf, 1911, p. 746), sought to heal the wounds of the Enlightenment and
the French Revolution by connecting modern with a largely misunderstood
medieval thought (McCool, 1994, p. 2). So if on the one hand, Neoscholasticism
was an effort to integrate the new sciences with the perennial philosophy, on
the other hand it attempted to protect the teachings of the Church, formulated
in Thomistic terms, from the corrosive effects of science, especially as it was
being applied to things theological.

   This twofold mission of Neoscholasticism gave it the possibility of very
different applications. In the hands of Monsignor Désiré Mercier, whom Leo
XIII had appointed in 1882 to head the *Institut supérior de philosophie* at the
University of Louvain, Neoscholasticism engaged in an effort to integrate the
findings of the natural sciences with Thomistic thought. Nowhere was this truer
than with psychology. Mercier himself, returning from Rome after meeting
with the pope and prominent Neoscholastics, spent some time in Paris studying
in 1882 with Jean-Martin Charcot. A renowned neurologist, Charcot's work on
hysteria and hypnosis was controversial at the time. He helped to make
hypnosis a respectable medical procedure in 1882, after it had been condemned
and ridiculed for much of the nineteenth century in academic medical circles
(Ellenberger, 1970, p. 90). While Mercier's choice to study briefly with Charcot
was understandable, given Charcot's reputation, it was not unproblematic. As
Ellenberger has pointed out, Charcot "was stamped as an atheist by the clergy
and the Catholics ... but some atheists found him too spiritual" (p. 96).
Whether or not Charcot was an atheist was beside the point, as the mere
suspicion could have been reason for Mercier to forgo the opportunity to
study with him, given the delicacy of Mercier's new position. In other respects
as well, Mercier showed himself open to modern psychological thought, even
when it strongly deviated from Neoscholastic philosophy, as in his enthusiastic
reading of William James' (1903) *Varieties of religious experience* (Misiak and
Staudt, 1954, p. 41). For Mercier, Neoscholasticism was an opening to modern
science, and not a bar against it.

   The details of the story of Mercier's study with Charcot after being charged
by Leo XIII to set up the Thomistic program at Louvain are instructive.

> At the moment Charcot's observations and theories on nervous cases
> treated in the hospital of La Salpétrière in Paris were everywhere exciting
> the world of science. How could Mercier investigate the experiments of the
> famous physician? How, especially, could he profit by them? Having the

will, it was easy to find the way. The young teacher let his beard grow, donned civilian clothes, and set out for Paris. A few days later there could be seen at Charcot's lectures a young man of distinguished bearing but of severely plain attire (plain, in spite of a pin with a double eagle that he was using for his cravat). He went by the name of Doctor Mercier. He was in reality the canon of Louvain.

(Laveille, 1928, p. 58)

Jan Goldstein (1982) provides the political and medical background necessary to see why Mercier's doffing of clerical garb was a necessary move at the time. Charcot had been named to the first chair in the diseases of the nervous system in 1882 by the anticlerical government of the Third Republic. Paul Bert, Minister of Public Instruction and Religion, "was a thoroughgoing positivist in his own physiological researches" (p. 233), a philosophical conviction Charcot shared. At the same time, Désiré-Magloire Bourneville, "the consummate hybrid psychiatrist-politician" (p. 223), led the charge to laicize French hospitals, a program carried out in Paris in 1883. Finally, there was professional rivalry between psychiatrists and clerics at the time: "The clergy, after all, were the traditional healers of the maladies of the soul and hence significant rivals of the professional newcomers, the psychiatrists" (p. 230). Thus, Mercier's decision to study with Charcot at this time was in effect a statement of his confidence in the Thomistic system to incorporate modern science while stripping it of its misguided philosophical presuppositions.

One could not say that all Neoscholastics held a benign view of modern science. To understand this other, more protective, use of Neoscholasticism, it is important to recognize its relationship to the dogmatic teachings of the Church. According to the Neoscholastics, philosophy had reached a high water mark in the Middle Ages, and afterward had been in decline. The Thomistic revival was the Church's answer to the spread of other philosophical systems, including those of Kant, that called into question the ability of human reason to come to know God. Neoscholasticism asserts the existence of truth and of the ability of the human mind to know it. This assertion applies to dogma as well: "The dogmas of the Church, such as the existence of God, the Trinity, the Incarnation, the Resurrection of Christ, the sacraments, a future judgment, etc. have an objective reality and are facts as really and truly as it is a fact that Augustus was Emperor of the Romans, and that George Washington was first President of the United States" (Coghlan, 1909, p. 90).

Given this conception, the way was cleared for the Neoscholastics to define the relationship between theology and philosophy. In the wake of the modernist crisis, Pohle (1912) wrote:

> The [First] Vatican Council ... solemnly declared that the two sciences [theology and philosophy] differ essentially not only in their cognitive principle (faith, reason) and their object (dogma, rational truth), but also

in their motive (Divine authority, evidence) and their ultimate end (beatific vision, natural knowledge of God). But what is the precise relation between these sciences? The origin and dignity of revealed theology forbid us to assign to philosophy a superior or even a co-ordinate rank ... When philosophy came into contact with revelation, this subordination was still more emphasized and was finally crystallized in the principle: *Philosophia est ancilla theologioe.*

(p. 583)

But which philosophy will most truly serve as the "handmaid of theology"?

Theology may be conceived as a queen, philosophy as a noble lady of the court who performs for her mistress the most worthy and valuable services, and without whose assistance the queen would be left in a very helpless and embarrassing position. That the Church, in examining the various systems, should select the philosophy which harmonized with her own revealed doctrine and proved itself to be the only true philosophy by acknowledging a personal God, the immortality of the soul, and the moral law, was so natural and obvious that it required no apology. Such a philosophy, however, existed among the pagans of old, and was carried to an eminent degree of perfection by Aristotle.

(ibid.)

The Scholastic method in theology seeks to make dogma available to human reason without forgetting the necessity of grounding interpretation of dogma within the tradition of the Church:

In attempting this task, the theologian cannot look for aid to modern philosophy with its endless confusion, but to the glorious past of his own science. What else are the modern systems of philosophy, skeptical criticism, Positivism, Pantheism, Monism, etc., than ancient errors cast into new moulds? Rightly does Catholic theology cling to the only true and eternal philosophy of common sense, which was established by Divine Providence in the Socratic School, carried to its highest perfection by Plato and Aristotle, purified from the minutest traces of error by the Scholastics of the thirteenth century.

(ibid.)

This position was directed not only against skeptical modern philosophers, including the modernists, who espoused the notion that the truths of the faith must be understood in the light of modern, especially scientific, thought, but also against the political implications of those views. Attacks on the Church's position in society were at one with attacks on her dogmas. According to McCool (1994), Neoscholasticism, "when employed by the theologian, ... could organize the various parts of Catholic theology into an integrated, coherent whole; and it could provide the effective arguments needed for controversy with the Church's enemies" (p. 34).

Modernism

There are a number of good accounts of the modernist crisis of the early twentieth century, and it is not my intention to rehash that history, except insofar as it implicated how the Church responded to modern psychology, which was developing at the very moment that modernism was the word of the hour. The term "modernism" has been subject to much controversy, and it was not one used by any of those later accused of being modernist until after the 1907 papal encyclical, *Pascendi Dominici Gregis* (Pope Pius X, 1907), brought the conflict to a head. Modernism challenged both Catholic dogma as Neoscholastically defined and a monarchical conception of the Church. It was an affair primarily of France, Italy, and England. In France and Italy, the theological and philosophical issues were inseparable, in the eyes of the Vatican, from ongoing political struggles with the governments of those two nations. The most prominent of the modernists was Alfred Loisy, a French priest and Scripture scholar, who used the relatively new method of historical criticism to understand the nature of the Bible. His historical investigations led him to the conclusion that Scripture was not the inerrant word of God, but the product of the human response to God. Church doctrines were symbolic representations of "the eternal truths" (Aubert, 1981, p. 434). Loisy defended this position, which was contrary to contemporary Church teaching, on the grounds that he was writing as a historian, and that historical science can know nothing of transcendent realities. For Loisy, the subject of history is "not the existence of the resurrected Christ, but solely the disciples' belief therein, a belief undergoing progressively precise definition" (quoted in ibid., p. 435). So, for Loisy, human understanding of Church doctrines evolves. He was excommunicated for holding to these positions after the condemnation of modernism in the 1907 encyclical, which had his writings in mind. Loisy's position is important for our study because of his insistence on the autonomy of history as a science from theology, for history's "methodological independence" (O'Connell, 1994, p. 215). Not that there is any direct connection, to my knowledge, between Loisy and the new psychology, but the existence of his contentious thesis helped set the tone for early Catholic responses to psychology, especially in light of some prominent Catholic psychologists who left the Church. But more on that later.

Tyrrell's psychological modernism

George Tyrrell was a leading light of modernism, according to both contemporary (Mercier, 1910) and recent (Maggiolini, 1996, p. 229) accounts. His mission as he saw it was to try to reconcile the Christian faith with the scientific mind. Like Loisy, he sought to distance himself from liberal Protestantism on the one hand, which capitulated to modernity, and Neoscholastic theology on the other hand, which resisted historical criticism of Scripture and Tradition, by formulating the teachings of the Church in ahistorical terms. Tyrrell wrote in his last book, *Christianity at the cross-roads* (1910): "By a Modernist, I mean a churchman, of any sort, who believes in the possibility of a synthesis between the essential truths of his religion and the essential truth of modernity" (p. 5). That sounds reasonable enough to our eyes and ears, but in the context of the time, they were fighting words. Tyrrell wrote them on his deathbed, excommunicated but not returning to the Anglican Church of his childhood. His synthesis included the historical evolution of Christian doctrine and a reversal of the centralization of power in the Vatican. At a time when the Church was being attacked politically as well as intellectually, Tyrrell's challenges were inopportune.

Both the notion that doctrine evolves and his criticism of the static, ahistorical nature of Neoscholastic theology roused a definitive reply from the Vatican. Tyrrell drew on non-Thomistic philosophical approaches to epistemological questions, including those of Maurice Blondel, a French philosopher and layman who, although accused of being a modernist, did not suffer the ecclesiastical fate of Loisy and Tyrrell; of Henri Bergson for his criticism that conceptual formulations distort reality, which is ever in flux; and of Hugo Münsterberg, the experimental psychologist, for his views on history. That is, Tyrrell drew upon a dynamic, developmental, and evolutionary view of history and the human mind. O'Connell (1994) summarizes Tyrrell's views in these words:

> "We are nothing else but will," said Tyrrell, quoting Saint Augustine . . . "Affection" and "sentiment" therefore precede thought, not the other way around. To seek identity with the divine will "is the foundation of the religious sentiment or affection, which is inclusive and regulative of the sentiments of particular and collective love founded on the other relationships" . . . The instruction offered by religion "is not in the interest of intellectualism, but of life and action . . . Its chief aim is the shaping of the affections and sentiments."
>
> (pp. 277–8)

The consequences of this view for the doctrines of the Church? According to O'Connell, "Creeds and dogmas, therefore, as well as institutional forms, must be judged by their utility, and their usefulness in promoting proper affections and sentiments for one generation does not guarantee a usefulness for the next" (p. 278). Unlike liberal Protestants, however, Tyrrell did not throw out the doctrines as simply outmoded, and his complaint against liberal Protestants was that they reduced religion to ethics (Tyrrell, 1910, p. 66). According to Tyrrell (1908):

> He [the Modernist] does not view the essence of Christianity as consisting of one or two simple principles given from the first and abiding unchanged beneath a bewildering mass of meaningless and mischievous encrustations.

Its essence is continually being built up by the expansion and application of these normative principles; by their combination with all that is good and true in the process of human development. It consists not merely in the leaven but in the whole mass that is leavened and christianized, and that grows in bulk from age to age. So far as he agrees with the [Neoscholastic] Medievalist against the Protestant. But he does not believe that the process stopped with the thirteenth century.

(pp. 148–9)

So doctrines are not discarded, for that would not be "development." Instead, given what we can call his "dynamic psychology," they are preserved even as they change. As Schultenover (1981) states Tyrrell's position:

With regard to creedal statements, we know their truth only by appeal to faith. Appeal to the intellect and reason is irrelevant. If it were not, unbelievers and evil persons, for whom reason works equally well as for good persons, could be brought to faith simply on the strength of logical argument. Rather the critical element in knowing the truth of creedal statements is faith, and so we are thrown back again on revelation as an inward experience. Creedal statements are "not divine statements but human statements inspired by divine experience." For these inspired human statements to come alive with religious meaning, faith experience is a prerequisite.

(p. 352, quoting Tyrrell, "Revelation as experience")

Significantly, even as Tyrrell emphasized the importance of religious experience, he also held to the transcendence of the Divine. Von Hügel (1909–10) wrote of Tyrrell after the latter's death: "Thus ... we find him, at times ... so insistent upon the utter Transcendence of God, as apparently to reduce all our concepts of, and approaches to, Him to an equal worthlessness. And, in another mood, God's Immanence becomes so over-emphasised ... Yet both these excesses sprang doubtless, primarily, from the keenness with which he realised God's immense otherness, and yet His unspeakable closeness to us" (p. 250). Tyrrell's position drew on some of the psychological thinking that was current at the time, but he was not limited by it.

Tyrrell's contributions to a psychology of religion

Important trends in early modern psychology influenced Tyrrell's approach to religion. For example, in contrast to the Neoscholastics, for whom faith was grounded in the objective truth of the Gospels, Tyrrell stressed the importance of personal experience of the divine. Tyrrell did not reduce God to something like a Jungian archetype, but he did affirm that our access to Him is through experience. As Daly (1980) states Tyrrell's position: "religious man must recognize that he meets God in his 'own dim spiritual experience and its imaginative symbols' and must school himself 'to submit to the limitation *consciously*; to realize that our best God is but an idol . . .'. The ontological reality of God's transcendence is never questioned in Tyrrell's last book [*Christianity at the Cross-Roads*], as von Hügel, for all his hypersensitivity on this issue, recognized" (p. 144). But it was this psychological aspect of Tyrrell's writings (and of some other modernists) that was one of the main difficulties with the Vatican, for his appeal to psychological explanations was seen as supporting agnosticism.

Tyrrell drew, perhaps loosely, on Cardinal John Henry Newman's notion of "Christianity as the development of an 'idea'" (Tyrrell, 1910, p. 29). An "idea" is not an "intellectual concept . . . from which a doctrinal system could be deduced syllogistically" (p. 29), as the Neoscholastics claimed. For Tyrrell:

> Theology and Revelation must be distinguished. The content of Revelation is not a statement, but an "idea" – embodied, perhaps, in certain statements and institutions, but not exhausted by them. This embodiment is susceptible of development; but the animating "idea" is the same under all the variety and progress of its manifestations and embodiments. There is a development of institutions and formulas but not of the revealed "idea," not of the Faith.

> (p. 32)

For Tyrrell, we do meet God through the symbol, and included in the category of the symbol, which is always inadequate in representing God, would be the teachings and sacraments of the Church.

The future development of human religion will be along the Catholic model, which for him was "more nearly a microcosm of the world of religion than any other known form" (pp. 254–5). The development of religion will be the development of its "idea," as found in the Christ's revelations. As religion, "the adjustment of our conduct to a transcendent world" (p. 256) evolves, it moves from external forms, expressed in myth and in tribal gods, to an internal form. Religion moves from being primarily an external force, as it had been in earlier ages, to an inner force in the modern world, when

> it is no longer from without, but from within, that God reveals Himself as a mysterious, transcendent force, counteracting and interfering with the natural order of events, overcoming the forces of egoism and individualism, and through the action of spiritual personalities, interfering with the course of history as shaped by natural, self-centered man.

> (pp. 259–60)

Tyrrell gives this development a psychological form: "At the end of the religious process he explicitly recognizes this inward principle as the Divine Spirit, the condition and foundation of his personality. For what is personality if not that which is divine in man, that which makes him master of the determinism of nature of which he is at first the slave? . . . And to the fulness of this personality he can only attain by identifying himself with that indwelling Spirit which is transcendent over nature" (p. 260). This notion of religiosity moving from outer to inner forms was a common understanding of many in psychology in the twentieth century, including notably James and Jung. It has roots in the Reformation, and it was a staple of nineteenth- and twentieth-century notions of individuality and of the spiritualizing of religion, with the concomitant shedding of the husk of external forms.

So Tyrrell had intellectual connections with the new psychology. And this was essential to the difficulties that the Vatican had with his teachings. O'Connell (1994) suggests that "in clashing theories of knowledge, lay the central quarrel of the Modernist crisis" (p. 344). In contrast to the Neoscholastics, Tyrrell mistrusted the intellect. Tyrrell emphasized the priority of lived experience for the religious life. Intellectual formulations come after the lived experience and, in trying to formulate what has happened, concepts render the dynamic experience static, giving it a permanence that it really does not have. Hence the appeal of Münsterberg, although not of the latter's conception of psychology but of history, to which Münsterberg contrasted psychology. For Münsterberg, history deals with the "will acts" of subjects, and psychology deals with mental events taken as objects. Tyrrell read widely, regularly supplied with "assignments" especially of German authors by Baron von Hügel, and he found appealing those views of the mind that supported his arguments against the overly intellectualized views of the Neoscholastics. In addition to Bergson and Münsterberg, he read Pierre Janet and William James, as well as Lotze, Fechner (on belief), Dilthey and Wundt, all important thinkers for the emerging psychology.

If Tyrrell's conflict with Rome was epistemological, it was also psychological, for there were contrasting conceptions of the person. Tyrrell formulated a dynamic psychology, one that stressed the priority of the non-rational aspects of mental life over the rational and, indeed, of the "subconscious" over the conscious.[8] In an essay devoted to the mystic, Juliana of Norwich, Tyrrell (1902) commented on her visions, in part, by stating:

> St. Ignatius almost invariably speaks, not, as we should, of thoughts that give rise to will-states of "consolation" or "desolation," but conversely, of these will-states giving rise to congruous thoughts. Indeed, nothing is more familiar to us than the way in which the mind is magnetized by even our physical states of elation or depression, to select the more cheerful or the

---

[8] Tyrrell studied scholastic psychology, to be sure. "The whole doctrine of *species sensibiles et intelligibiles*; the magic-lantern or photographic-camera categories by which intellect was explained; the question-begging *vis æstimativa* or *cogitativa*; the scale and weights view of the will and its motives" (Tyrrell and Petre, 1912, vol. 1, p. 275) left him cold, because of the mingling of an out-dated science with philosophy.

gloomier aspects of life, according as we are under one influence or the other; and in practice, we recognize the effect of people's humours on their opinions and decisions, and would neither sue mercy nor ask a favour of a man in a temper. In short, it is hardly too much to say, that our thoughts are more dependent on our feelings than our feelings on our thoughts. This, then, is one possible method of supernatural guidance which we shall call "blind inspiration" – for though the feeling or impulse is from God, the interpretation is from the subject's own mind.

(p. 29)

One's "true self," which Tyrrell "wanted to call the 'subconscious self'" (Schultenover, 1981, p. 212), was "the 'not-present,' and therefore the past and the future, both of which characterise our present choice; the one by way of obscure memories, the other by way of obscure anticipations" (Tyrrell, quoted in ibid., p. 213). Another term for this "true self" was for Tyrrell, "personality," taken, as Schultenover notes, from Bergson. For Tyrrell, personality "means our freedom, in greater or less degree – our self-possession and deliverance from the determinism of nature" (p. 409, n. 155, quoting Tyrrell, *Religion as a factor in life*, p. 51, n. 11).[9] Not only deliverance from nature, for as Tyrrell argued, but also deliverance from passive obedience to political and Church authority: "If we have no responsibility; if our sole duty is to obey passively and blindly in the service of ends that are unknown to us . . .; if we are little better than witless forces to be disposed of by our rulers, we cease to be persons, and the boundaries of our own separate individuality become those of our interests" (Tyrrell, 1908, p. 135). For Tyrrell, in the final analysis, the person, history, and doctrine were all in flux. There was an end or goal, however, and that was the development of the idea that constitutes the heart of the Christian message.

Tyrrell translated Henri Joly's (1898) *The psychology of the saints* and wrote a review of the book, "What is Mysticism?" (in Tyrrell, 1904, pp. 253–72). In this essay and elsewhere, Tyrrell contributed to the psychology of religion,

---

[9] In *Medievalism*, Tyrrell (1908) said of the Gospel message: "It was not the light of a new theology, but that of a new revelation, a new experience, a new life, a new ideal of human personality" (p. 64). Maude Petre expanded on this theme: "This distinction between the psychic, i.e. the narrow, individualistic, life and the spiritual, i.e. the broad, personal life, is one of the leading categories of Tyrrell's thought as in conduct, so also in faith. For the single soul, as for the collective Church, this striving from the self-centred to the universally centred life from the Ptolemaic to the Copernican conception, was the one thing really needed. Hereby personality was not destroyed, for personality was best manifested by self-determination in view to that universal end in which all find the true scope and reason of their being: 'Since the true spiritual self, potential in all of us, is the image and likeness of God, to find God, to be united with God, is morally the same thing as to find and be united with our true self'" (Tyrrell and Petre, 1912, vol. 2, p. 205, quoting Tyrrell, *Lex Credendi*, p. 183).

which was in its first flourishing during the last years of his life. Joly and Tyrrell drew on the work of Pierre Janet to understand the ways in which saints are more like the rest of us than they are marvels – and so unlike us that mere mortals cannot really hope to emulate them. Tyrrell stressed the ways that will and feeling can exceed reason's grasp, and how as a result, religious awareness has a history, both developmentally and culturally. In his psychological reflections, Tyrrell was critical of the "scholastic psychology," even citing Dante against it.[10] Tyrrell's contributions were not lost altogether for psychology. James Bissett Pratt[11] included discussion of Tyrrell's views in his *The religious consciousness: A psychological study* (1920). Tyrrell's type of dynamic psychology had much in common with later trends, especially along Jungian and humanistic psychological lines, with his emphasis on will and feeling. Where he differed from much of these psychological developments, however, was in his decidedly theological basis. He is certainly worth remembering in any future syntheses of psychology and religion, as well as in the psychology of religion.[12]

Such were the views of one of the chief modernists, Tyrrell. I have presented him in some depth in part because his views were cited, as we shall see below, by Cardinal Mercier in his condemnation of modernism. Moreover, Tyrrell inclined toward some of the theories of the new psychology, those that would prove most problematic in the eyes of the Vatican. Let us now turn to the Church's response to modernism.

---

[10] "Here the mystics seem to come into conflict, not so much with theology, which denies to the Saints on earth all direct intuition of the Divine substance in the sense of mental penetration or grasp, as with the scholastic psychology, which leaves no room for what we have endeavoured to describe as 'tactual intuition' – something less than face-to-face vision; something more than the quickest inference, a sort of coming behind and touching the hem of God's garment. But it must be confessed that the mystics have in many respects a psychology of their own" ("What is Mysticism?" in Tyrrell, 1904, p. 268).

[11] Pratt (1875–1944) completed a doctoral dissertation in philosophy under William James in 1905. He taught philosophy and psychology at Williams College, and he published widely on religion. Pratt (1920) referred to Tyrrell's theories of religious development and used Tyrrell's autobiography as data for understanding religion in developmental terms.

[12] As a further example of Tyrrell's use of psychology, he wrote a Preface (Tyrrell, 1905) to Francis Thompson's *Health and holiness*, in which he stated: "To adhere rigidly and blindly not merely to the ascetical principles of the Past, but to their old-world applications, were to ignore the bewildering changes that have since swept over the face of society, and to deny all value to the light which has been given us from the Giver of all light through the progress of Physiology and Psychology" (p. ix). In this, Tyrrell challenged Church traditions in the name of psychology. When members of the ACPA questioned the 1968 encyclical on birth control, and when van Kaam and others offered reforms for an understanding of the meaning of obedience in religious orders, they made arguments similar to Tyrrell's. These criticisms put the body at the core of the disputes between psychology and elements of the Church.

Modernism, "the Synthesis of all Heresies"

Official response to the modernists had been gathering for some years and on many fronts. Although the conflict was in some respects over epistemology (that way of stating it does not grasp the enormous anxiety that seeped through the documents, and it must be stressed that philosophical questions are not only philosophical), it had political ramifications as well. Historical criticism of Scripture often went hand-in-hand with anti-authoritarian views. In 1905, the republican French government passed a bill that separated church and state, a shocking incident when viewed from the Vatican and from the point of view of many French Catholics, who held to an older conception of church–state relations. O'Connell (1994) sums up the significance of this event: "institutional Christianity could no longer claim to be an integral part of the *res publica* of Western nations. What had begun with Constantine had finally passed away, and religion, if it were to survive at all, would have to survive as a private concern" (pp. 310–11). As Leo XIII had warned in 1879, intellectual errors led to others, including those in the political sphere. The response of the pope to modernism must be understood in this light: the teachings declared erroneous were dangerous because they threatened the foundation of the Church.

The year 1907 proved decisive. The papal decree, *Lamentabili Sane Exitu* (Pope Pius X, 1999b) appeared in July, a new "syllabus of errors" listing sixty-five condemned propositions, derived mainly from Loisy (O'Connell, 1994, pp. 338–9), but without naming him or anyone else. Among the propositions condemned was number 64: "Scientific progress demands that the concepts of Christian doctrine concerning God, creation, revelation, the Person of the Incarnate Word, and Redemption be re-adjusted." But *Lamentabili* was just the first salvo, and in September, the encyclical *Pascendi Dominici Gregis* appeared, which condemned modernism as the "synthesis of all heresies" (Pope Pius X, 1907, § 39, p. 221). The encyclical did attempt a synthesis of modernist writings (see O'Connell, 1994, pp. 342–3 for Loisy's assessment), tying together various strands among a diverse group of thinkers. The basic charge in *Pascendi* was agnosticism:

> According to this teaching human reason is confined entirely within the field of phenomena, that is to say, to things that appear, and in the manner in which they appear: it has neither the right nor the power to overstep these limits. Hence it is incapable of lifting itself up to God, and of recognizing His existence, even by means of visible things. From this it is inferred that God can never be the direct object of science, and that, as regards history, He must not be considered as an historical subject.
>
> (Pope Pius X, 1907, § 6, p. 183)

The encyclical charged that modernists held the position that we cannot know God by the use of reason, a position attributed to a variety of philosophers, but especially, in the eyes of the Neoscholastics, to Kant. The force of the argument against the way the modernists appropriated Kant is clearly seen in the third and final official salvo, the *motu proprio*,[13] *Sacrorum Antistitum*, of September 1910 (Pope Pius X, 1999a), containing an oath against modernism, which the clergy and seminary professors had to sign. The oath declared that the signatory affirmed that God "can be known with certainty by the natural light of reason from the created world." Faith, that is, is rational; human beings can attain knowledge of God even without Revelation (in the Scriptures and Tradition). It also affirmed the Church's historical continuity with Christ and the apostles as well as the principle that dogma does not evolve: "I sincerely hold that the doctrine of faith was handed down to us from the apostles through the orthodox Fathers in exactly the same meaning and always in the same purport. Therefore, I entirely reject the heretical misrepresentation that dogmas evolve and change from one meaning to another." The oath included a psychological thesis, namely, "that faith is not a blind sentiment of religion welling up from the depths of the subconscious under the impulse of the heart and the motion of the will trained to morality; but faith is a genuine assent of the intellect to truth received by hearing from an external source."

Together these documents show that in responding to threats to the integrity of the Catholic faith, the Pope and his allies drew on Neoscholastic philosophy. In the end, Rome won (see O'Connell, 1994, p. 355). The modernists, real and perceived, retreated in disarray. Those that objected, such as Loisy and Tyrrell, were excommunicated, and others fell silent or in line.[14] As Gabriel Daly (1980) states the case: "Authority, not reasoned argument, extinguished the crisis" (p. 215). And since *Pascendi* ordered the bishops to be vigilant in watching for signs of "whatever savors of Modernism" (Pope Pius X, 1907, § 50, p. 232), preventing their publication and, failing that, preventing their distribution, for a generation or more, there was no ground for dissent. The encyclical listed signs of the slightest hints of modernism, including one with profound implications for the establishment of psychology in Catholic higher education: "there is no surer sign that a man is tending to Modernism than when he begins to show his dislike for the scholastic method" (§ 42). Indeed, *Pascendi* called for the creation of Councils of Vigilance (§ 55) in every diocese to make sure that

---

[13] *Motu proprio* means "by his own impulse" and it "is a letter written at the personal initiative of the pope and signed by him" (O'Connell, 1994, p. 351, n. 84). It is a type of decree, that is, a legislative act of the pope.

[14] Von Hügel (1909–10) wrote a memorial of Tyrrell shortly after the latter's death, in which he stated: "as to *Pascendi* his anger arose from its apparent contempt for mysticism and all the dim, inchoate gropings after God; its wholesale imputation of bad motives to hard-working scholars and thinkers; and its disciplinary enactments" (pp. 245–6).

no modernist or modernist sympathizer would infect anyone with his disease, a metaphor used in the encyclical.[15]

Among the many replies to *Pascendi*, Tyrrell's stood out: "whereas it [the encyclical] 'tries to show the Modernist that he is no Catholic, it mostly succeeds only in showing him that he is no scholastic'" (Tyrrell and Petre, 1912, vol. 2, p. 337, quoting a letter of Tyrrell to the *Times*). Suspicion toward non-Scholastic philosophizing would prove to be a major source of difficulty for psychology within the Church for the next fifty years.

Was psychology directly implicated in the condemnation of modernism? There were two references to psychology in *Pascendi*, both negative. The first dealt with how the modernists deal with Christ as a historical figure: given (for the modernists) that history must be agnostic (an early statement of methodo-logical naturalism), "when treating of Christ, the historian must set aside all that surpasses man in his natural condition, according to what psychology tells us of him, or according to what we gather from the place and period of his existence" (Pope Pius X, 1907, § 30, p. 211). That is, psychology can serve the reduction-istic efforts of modernist biblical criticism. The second was that for the mod-ernists, "controversies in religion must be determined by psychological and historical research" (§ 35, p. 216), and not by appeals to the truths of Scripture and Tradition. These passages do not condemn psychology, and if there were a negative halo circling about, it would all the more apply to history, which was a primary object of the encyclical, insofar as it studied both the Bible and the Church. In itself, then, *Pascendi* did not address the discipline of psychology, especially the new experimental psychology. But since the modernists appealed to experience and to the subjective, psychology in some of its manifestations would be likely to fall under suspicion. And indeed, that was the case.

The agnosticism of the modernists, in the view of *Pascendi*, was in part rooted in their faulty (non-Scholastic) view of the mind, in the way that the two sides, the modernists and the pope, understood "experience," and in the modernists' assertion that there is a "subconscious" aspect of the mind, wherein one finds the human "need" for God. The Neoscholastics had an overly intellectualized view of the human mind, and the modernist position opposed experience and cognition, to the detriment of the latter. For the Neoscholastics, as presented in the papal documents condemning modernism, faith is intellectual assent to revelation as presented in Scripture and the Tradition. For someone like Tyrrell, faith arises first of all in a religious experience, which is completed by the teachings of the Church. Those teachings, as we have seen, are subject to revision as they reflect or fail to reflect experience (see Maggiolini, 1996, p. 235).

---

[15] "With regard to priests who are correspondents or collaborators of periodicals, as it happens not infrequently that they contribute matter infected with Modernism to their papers or periodicals, let the Bishops see to it that they do not offend in this manner" (Pope Pius X, 1907, § 53).

The term "subconscious" occurred also in two sections of the encyclical, each time in a negative light. The modernists drew on this notion to explain the immanence of God in the mind: "This need of the divine, which is experienced only in special and favorable circumstances cannot of itself appertain to the domain of consciousness, but is first latent beneath consciousness, or, to borrow a term from modern philosophy, in the subconsciousness, where also its root lies hidden and undetected" (Pope Pius X, 1907, § 7, p. 185). The subconscious is a non-rational part of the mind and, by making it and the "inspiration" that emerges from it the ground of religious experience, the modernists undermined the objective truth of Catholic teachings. In contrast, the Neoscholastic approach to knowledge asserted two things. First, as a form of realism, it held that we can know objectively the existence of God. Second, according to Arthur Vermeersch, SJ,[16] (1911) who contributed the article, "Modernism," to the 1911 *Catholic Encyclopedia*, the limitations of the human mind necessitate external supports for access to reality:

> Catholic philosophy does not deny the soul's spontaneous life, the sublimity of its suprasensible and supernatural operations, and the inadequacy of words to translate its yearnings. Scholastic doctors give expression to mystical transports far superior to those of the modernists. But in their philosophy they never forget the lowliness of human nature, which is not purely spiritual. The modernist remembers only the internal element of our higher activity ... When deprived of the external support which is indispensable to them, the acts of the higher intellectual faculties can only consist in vague sentiments which are as indetermined as are those faculties themselves.
>
> (p. 419)

Any psychology that denied the intellect pride of place in the human mind or asserted immanence as the basis for our conception of God was thus suspect in the wake of the modernist crisis.

Finally, any psychology that drew upon evolutionary thought was suspect. In the minds of the anti-modernists, "Liberal Protestantism, Kantian and Spencerian philosophy, Jamesian psychology, and Darwinian evolutionism" (Daly, 1980, pp. 215–16) were all condemned as modernist. It would seem that psychology was under a cloud, and that it would have a difficult time within Catholic circles. For the boundary line had been drawn and it was watched with vigilance.

---

[16] According to Daly (1980), Vermeersch, who was teaching at Louvain when he wrote this article, soon thereafter was transferred to Rome, "and there to become the foremost moral theologian in the freshly centralized Catholic Church. He have it as his view that Pius X's *Motu proprio, Sacrorum antistitium* (September, 1910) had the effect of constituting the conclusions of *Lamentabili* and *Pascendi* as infallible utterances. Vermeersch, however, conceded that this view, extreme even for the age, was not universally accepted" (p. 216, n. 114).

Implications of the Modernist Crisis for Psychology

In this section, we look at the consequences of the modernist crisis. Psychology as a modern science, however defined, aroused suspicions in the wake of *Pascendi*, insofar as this document implied "outright rejection of key elements of the Enlightenment project" (Cadegan, 2002, p. 103). The necessity of Catholics interested in psychology to avoid modernism was all the more acute in the first half of the century because many of them were priests.

The caution of Misiak and Staudt

Henryk Misiak and Virginia Staudt addressed *Catholics in psychology* (1954) primarily to students in Catholic colleges and universities, in order to provide them with their own history. It was a time when the United States was more divided between Catholic and non-Catholic than it is now, when among Catholics there was a strong sense of religious identity, often accompanied with ethnic identity, such as Irish, German, or Italian. Misiak and Staudt hoped to inspire students to pursue psychology as a career, and even several years later, Misiak lamented the fact that Catholics were underrepresented in psychology. They also addressed the book to "non-Catholic psychologists who sometimes wonder if the Catholic faith is not a hindrance or a source of prejudice in scientific pursuits" (ibid., p. xiii). They did not think that it was; indeed, they saw their faith as opening "new vistas" in psychology. The potential biases of some of their non-Catholic fellows were no doubt rooted in American anti-Catholicism, which was stronger then than now, and they may have been thinking of Paul Blanshard's (1949) book, which had recently questioned the open-mindedness of Catholics. They may have also been thinking of some of the restrictions on inquiry at Catholic colleges, universities, and seminaries in the wake of the modernist crisis (see Gannon, 1971).

In any event, Misiak and Staudt did show some caution in the opening pages of their text. They go to considerable lengths to fend off the charge that the pursuit of scientific psychology is detrimental to the faith. The primary example of that possibility was the case of Franz Brentano, which they addressed directly: "Brentano is an interesting figure because of the controversy which developed around him, a controversy that seemed to suggest the impossibility of a scientist's reconciliation of science with his faith. Brentano's apostasy, unfortunately, led some people to think that faith and science were incompatible. Moreover, others very scrupulous in religious matters came to fear that the study of science, and of psychology in particular, might jeopardize an individual's faith" (Misiak and Staudt, 1954, p. 23). Without minimizing Brentano's break with the Church – it was over the First Vatican Council's affirmation of papal infallibility – they pointed out that Brentano, unlike Döllinger, did not join the Old Catholic Church, founded by some Catholics opposed to the teaching on infallibility. The name, Döllinger, is significant, and his rejection of the Council's proclamation on infallibility featured prominently in the modernist crisis, with Tyrrell, for example, being compared to Döllinger by Cardinal Mercier. Nor did Brentano become Protestant. They concluded their discussion of Brentano with "a feeling of regret that a scholar of such high intellectual integrity, and a man imbued with a sincere belief in God and in a life hereafter, could not reconcile his Catholic faith with science" (p. 29).

This sense of regret continued in the chapter, and Misiak and Staudt discussed three other early psychologists who abandoned the faith: Carl Stumpf, August Messer, and Karl Marbe. Stumpf, they wrote, left the Church for personal reasons, and Messer and Marbe because they "felt that their religion interfered with their freedom of thought" (p. 31). They concluded: "there are grounds that lead one to believe that the early Catholic antagonism to the new science was due in part to the unfortunate association between the pursuit of psychology and apostasy" (ibid.). They indirectly referred to modernism by stating that in the late nineteenth century, science appeared "dynamic," whereas the Church seemed "unduly static with its changeless teachings" (p. 32). But for Misiak and Staudt, there was nothing inevitable about the connection between science and apostasy, and the book sought to demonstrate that by recounting the lives and works of the many Catholics who were also notable psychologists. This caution illustrates how, nearly fifty years after *Pascendi*, modernism was still a thorny issue in psychology.

The frontispiece of *Catholics in psychology* showed the eminent Catholic pioneer in psychology, Cardinal Mercier. Mercier was the role model for the reconciliation of psychology and Catholicism.

Mercier's progressive Neoscholasticism

Just as the modernist crisis was reaching its climax, Désiré Mercier received two promotions in quick succession. In 1906, he was named as archbishop of Malines in Belgium, and in 1907, just before the publication of *Lamentabili*, his status was elevated to that of cardinal. This meant, it would seem, that Pius X had great confidence in his support in the battle against what the Vatican saw as a veritable fifth column, the Catholic modernists. Mercier was no lackey, as his stout and courageous confrontation with the occupying German army would show not too many years later. But in some ways, Mercier's position was precarious. He was a Thomist, of that there is no doubt. In the face of a polarized situation between science and religion, with the associated political implications of that divide, Mercier argued for the autonomy of philosophy and of the sciences from theology, and for the necessity of dialogue between the Thomistic tradition and modern philosophy. So the addresses that Mercier gave in the wake of *Pascendi* are interesting for the position that they attempted to take.

Shortly after *Pascendi* appeared, Cardinal Mercier addressed professors and students at Louvain. Mercier made a careful distinction, one that enabled him to affirm both *Pascendi* and the autonomy of science. Science – he named as examples, "physics, chemistry, biology, history, or social economy" (Mercier, 1907/2002, pp. 545–6; cf. Mercier, 1910, p. 9) – proceeds by isolating the "object" of that science without "searching for a confirmation of our religious beliefs" (Mercier, 1907/2002, p. 546). Is this not what Loisy claimed for his historical criticism? Yes, but for Mercier (1910), the modernists have "too blindly obeyed" (p. 10) philosophical presuppositions that have influenced their scientific research.[17] Every thinking person, Mercier stated, has a "system of philosophy" (p. 15), and the modernists have an inadequate one, based on the skepticism of modern philosophers. Better the realism of Aristotle and Thomas. Finally, in what may have been more to the point, Mercier gave another reason to heed the message of *Pascendi*: "To acquire science is not an end in itself. Duty ever comes before speculative reasoning; and the more a man increases his knowledge, the more is he responsible for his moral and social obligations, and for perceiving with pre-eminent clearness the true ideal of life" (p. 18).[18] The autonomy of science was, for one's life, relative, and beyond it existed more important relationships and allegiances. As a scientist, a philosopher, and a cardinal, these words spoke to Mercier's own commitments.

Mercier's modernist shadow

If this were a novel, I would here introduce in some subtle way the motif of the double. A double is the shadow of the main character, one who typically realizes the dark and evil possibilities that the protagonist struggles with. Doubles include Dr. Jekyll's Mr. Hyde, Raskolnikov's Svidrigaïlov in *Crime and punishment*, Humbert Humbert's Clare Quilty in *Lolita*, to name but a few. Here, Mercier's double is George Tyrrell. Since this is not fiction, I would not cast one as simply good or purely evil, and the fantasy, I must confess, is not mine. Rather, it belonged to the members of the *Sodalitium Pianum* or the *La*

---

[17] As in *Pascendi*, in this essay there was liberal usage of metaphors of sickness and health: modernism is an infection, the encyclical is the remedy, Thomism offers a "healthy, sound realism" (Mercier, 1910, p. 13). These metaphors underscored the emotional charge of the crisis and also that for the pope, modernism was a grave danger to the Church as an "organism."

[18] Kurtz (1986), taking a sociological approach to the modernist crisis, uses the concept of "sociological ambivalence" to understand the dynamics of both the modernists and Vatican officials. In the early twentieth century, "secular intellectual culture" clashed with "ecclesiastical culture" in such a way as to make belonging to both at the same time difficult. "The modernists responded with a neo-Catholicism that rejected the extremes of both scientism and scholasticism" (p. 55).

Sapinière,[19] founded in 1909 by Monsignor Umberto Benigni (1862–1934) to fight modernism. This secret society, dedicated to "integral Catholicism" or "integralism," acted as a kind of secret police, ferreting out modernists, real and imagined (Daly, 1980, p. 218; Kurtz, 1986, p. 160; O'Connell, 1994, p. 361), during the remaining years of the pontificate of Pius X. Aubert (1981), in summarizing the scholarship on Benigni, concludes that *La Sapinière*, while influential enough, was no more part of a monolithic conspiracy than were the modernists it fought. Nevertheless, it did have Pius's support and, given the anxiety in Rome about what was perceived to be the greatest threat to the Church since Martin Luther (p. 471, n. 55), the opinions of *La Sapinière* carried weight. Among the documents published in Émile Poulat's (1969) major study of integralism, were comments questioning Mercier's loyalty.

When the Jesuits expelled Tyrrell, he had to find a bishop who would agree to incardinate him, that is, accept him as a priest in good standing into his diocese. Offers, needless to say, did not come flooding in. But Mercier was willing to invite him. As Schultenover (1981, pp. 328–9) recounts the story, in 1906, the Vatican gave Mercier permission to receive Tyrrell (the inquiries between the two were made indirectly), on the condition that Tyrrell not publish anything on "religious questions" or even write letters dealing with them. Tyrrell found the conditions unacceptable, even after the offer was repeated, slightly modified. There the matter rested, until after the papal documents condemning modernism. Mercier (1908), now a cardinal, addressed a "Lenten Pastoral" on modernism to the bishops and clergy of Belgium. In it, Mercier named only one name, that of Tyrrell, "the most penetrating observer of the present Modernist movement . . . perhaps more deeply imbued with it than any other" (p. 26). Mercier accused Tyrrell of being imbued with the idea behind modernism, that is, Protestantism: "Little wonder, for Tyrrell is a convert whose early education was Protestant" (ibid.). Historians (Boudens, 1970; Schultenover, 1981) have wondered why Mercier singled out Tyrrell in this letter to his clergy, especially because Tyrrell's name was likely less known than that of Loisy or other French modernists.[20] Tyrrell replied, receiving permission from Mercier to publish a translation of the pastoral letter. It appeared at the beginning of *Medievalism: A reply to Cardinal Mercier* (Tyrrell, 1908). Tyrrell countered the assertions

---

[19] *Sodalitium Pianum* means "the Sodality [or Fellowship] of Pius"; *Sapinière* means "the piney woods" (O'Connell, 1994, p. 363).

[20] Schultenover (1981) writes: "it is ironic that Mercier, a scientist-philosopher who studied under Jean Martin Charcot in Paris and founded the Institut Supérieur de Philosophie at Louvain to promote the study of neo-Thomism after the mind of Leo XIII, should now turn against one who was so close to him in spirit" (p. 340). This and other ironies that Schultenover mentions have an explanation, he says, in a hypothesis that "No other prelate had identified himself as closely as Mercier did with one who was now ecclesiastically unclean. To prove himself clean, he had to perform the ritual sacrifice and bind himself by *Bluttkitt* to the antimodernist regime"(ibid.).

that Mercier directed against him, in part questioning Mercier's motives. Tyrrell expressed a sense of betrayal. In an unpublished reply to *Medievalism*, Mercier (in Boudens, 1970, pp. 340–51) in turn expressed his own sense of having been betrayed by Tyrrell. The incident terminated with Tyrrell's death in 1909.

Perhaps because of Mercier's attempts to help Tyrrell in 1906, or perhaps because of his efforts to synthesize the modern sciences into a Thomistic frame-work, an effort that resembled Tyrrell's to reconcile modernity and Catholicism, the files of Benigni's group show that Mercier was under suspicion as "known with ties to all the traitors of the Church" (Poulat, 1969, p. 330). Mercier thus in some respects walked a fine line, critical of both modernists and integralists (p. 559). In the eyes of some, then, the shadow of modernism fell across Mercier and, I would contend, with all of psychology, for some time to come.

Mercier's critique of psychology

As part of Mercier's project renewing Thomistic thought by integrating modern science, he published in 1897 *The origins of contemporary psychology* (Mercier, 1918). The work is an appreciative critique of modern psychology, with an emphasis on its grounding in modernity: for Mercier, Descartes' thought was indeed the origin of contemporary psychology. I say an apprecia-tive critique because in Mercier's analysis one does not find a combative rejection of all things modern. He discovered much to like in contemporary psychology and he agreed in one major way with the modern philosophical approach – namely, the centrality of epistemological (or as he named it, criteriological) problems. The book is "especially addressed to those who are no longer satisfied with the standard spiritualism [i.e. Descartes' philosophy], and if amidst the swarm of systems and growing crowd of facts that are around them they are in search of some guiding principle of thought" (p. vi), they might appreciate what Mercier presented, "the anthropology of Aristotle and the Middle Ages" (p. vii). In a word, and properly speaking, before the word became current, he objected to Descartes' modernism.

For Mercier, modernism in its philosophical form arose from Descartes' philosophy. The foundation of modernism was Descartes' "conception of a science of pure mathematics which would apply to every kind of research" (p. 3). This "geometrical spirit" led to disastrous consequences for his anthro-pology, that is, for his understanding of the nature of the human. But what led to these consequences – the dualism of a mind that is a thinking thing and a body that is a mechanical thing – was Descartes' starting point, methodical doubt: "To curtail the errors of the human mind, to uproot misleading illusions . . .; then, to set upon a solid and henceforth immovable foundation philosophy reconstructed on a new plan, such is the root-idea of the Cartesian system" (p. 4). Reviewing Descartes' *Meditations*, Mercier showed that Descartes reached his conclusion that the soul is an immaterial thinking substance whose attribute is thought by means of introspection, or of "all the facts perceived by the inner sense or consciousness" (p. 19). That is why, Mercier observed, modern psychology sees introspection of consciousness as its essential method. This psychology, he wrote, "is spiritualistic in excess" (p. 20).

Given this conception of the soul, what about the body? Descartes' well-known conclusion was that the body was an extended thing, operating as do all extended things, by means of motion transmitted mechanically. As to the union of soul and body, which Descartes understood that we sensed, as in pain and hunger, there was no way to think it clearly and distinctly. The upshot, Mercier concluded, was that Descartes left modern psychology a double legacy: idealism, which knows only the contents of consciousness, and mechanism, which knows only matter in motion.

The origins of contemporary psychology *compared with* Pascendi's Critique of modernism

After surveying the history of philosophy from Descartes' to his own time, Mercier presented three key figures of contemporary psychology: Herbert Spencer (1820–1903), Alfred Fouillée (1838–1912), and Wilhelm Wundt (1832–1920). Following that, Mercier spelled out what he considered the characteristics of modern psychology:

(1) "The *subject-matter* of psychology is confined to the *facts of consciousness*" (p. 160);
(2) "*Metaphysics* in general, and consequently what was formerly called *rational* psychology, are almost *universally given up*" (ibid.), replaced by a Kantian version of metaphysics, "the sole object of which is to determine the limits of thought" (ibid.). This trend has led to phenomenalism.
(3) "Empiricism and mechanical theory have helped to fasten the attention of psychologists to the *quantitative* aspects of psychic phenomena. The inquiries of *experimental psychology* have taken a great leap forward, and open up a future full of promise" (ibid.).

It is expanding upon the second of these three features that we discover that much of what Mercier found problematic in psychology reflected nearly point for point the objections made in *Pascendi* against the modernists. Mercier's text was written before the encyclical, so this was not a case of Mercier looking over his shoulders to see if the integralists were watching.

Agnosticism and positivism

When psychology abandoned metaphysics, by which Mercier meant Aristotelian metaphysics, psychology adopted a position of "metaphysical agnosticism," which because of Kant's influence, became phenomenalism and ultimately, "*idealist* and *subjectivist* monism" (Mercier, 1918, p. 164). As Mercier stated his objection, "The triumph of agnosticism in the sphere of metaphysics involves the negation of the *faculties*, of the *substantial Ego*, and finally, of any possibility, beyond phenomena, of a *thing-in-itself*" (pp. 164–5). Note that in this context "agnosticism" does not refer only to an inability to know if God exists, but if states of consciousness refer to anything outside of consciousness. In *Pascendi*, the first major objection to modernism is: "*Agnosticism*. According to this teaching human reason is confined entirely within the field of phenomena, that is to say, to things that appear, and in the manner in which they appear: it has neither the right nor the power to overstep these limits" (Pope Pius X, 1907, § 6, p. 183).[21]

Both *Origins of contemporary psychology* and *Pascendi* drew the same conclusion from this agnosticism: it laid waste to the scholastic teaching about the soul. Mercier drew this connection: because the soul was not itself a phenomenon, it had no place in science according to the agnosticism that reigned in psychology. *Pascendi* drew a related conclusion, although in applied terms: if the intellect cannot reach truth, then the only path left is that of sense: "Take away the intelligence [i.e. the intellect], and man, already inclined to follow the senses, becomes their slave ... Common sense tells us that emotion and everything that leads the heart captive proves a hindrance instead of a help to the discovery of truth" (§ 39, p. 222). *Pascendi* concluded that the abandonment of metaphysics and its teaching on the soul led to a degraded image of the human. For Mercier as well, the category of the soul was not simply a theoretical matter.

Tied to agnosticism was a second consequence of the abandoning of metaphysics, namely positivism. It too had its roots in Descartes because, according to Mercier, Descartes saw the mind as a purely spiritual entity. Therefore, it existed outside of time and space, so that scientific observation, which always has a spatio-temporal form, was impossible for mental activity. The conclusion followed that a scientific psychology was impossible, a view found in Auguste Comte, the founder of positivism. For Comte and the positivists, the only possibility of knowledge is that grounded in "the co-ordination of observed facts" (Comte, quoted in Mercier, 1918, p. 169), meaning spatio-temporal occurrences. As Mercier pointed out, Comte's positive philosophy excluded

---

[21] Tyrrell's views on positivism were expressed in a 1907 letter: "Then I ask whether recent epistemology or science-theories; whether the work of some of the pragmatists, and that of philosophers like Volkelt, James Ward, Poincaré, Adhemar, above all of Bergson, has not ruined the very foundation of Comte's trust in science; whether that trust itself has not been a passing stage and not the final stage of man's growth; whether finality is possible? What, I imagine, is the permanent value of Positivism is its spirit of fearless criticism, its refusal of any arbitrary dogmatism in things of the spirit. If Bergson is as right as I imagine, the scientific construction of the world possesses a purely practical value, but is the very furthest possible remove from theoretical truth" (Tyrrell and Petre, 1912, vol. 2, pp. 411–12).

psychology since the latter had introspection as its only method, and there is no science of what occurs outside time and space. The Neoscholastics, to the contrary, affirmed psychology as a science of the soul, with rational and empirical divisions.

Pascendi did not name positivism explicitly, but it did accuse the modernists of attempting to smuggle it into the seminaries:

> They wish the scholastic philosophy to be relegated to the history of philosophy and to be classed among absolute systems, and the young men to be taught modern philosophy which alone is true and suited to the times in which we live. They desire the reform of theology: rational theology is to have modern philosophy for its foundation, and positive theology is to be founded on the history of dogma. As for history, it must be written and taught only according to their methods and modern principles.
>
> (Pope Pius X, 1907, § 38, p. 220)

The document did not condemn "positive theology" as such, just that it needed to be balanced with scholastic theology and it must be practiced in "the light of true history" (§ 46, p. 230), that is, sacred history which is not simply empirical history, but also history in the light of God's revelation and human faith. Otherwise, a split between history and dogma, such as that advocated by Loisy, would result.

Idealism and the philosophy of immanence

A further consequence of Descartes' ontology, opposing positivism but unshakable from it, was the idealism of much modern philosophical and psychological thought, including that of the three main representatives of contemporary psychology, Spencer in England, Fouillée in France, and Wundt in Germany (Mercier, 1918, p. 174): in the final analysis, all we can know are the laws of consciousness. One outcome of this trend, in the late nineteenth century, was "the philosophy of immanence" (p. 179), which carries this trend further, asserting that "conscious being and real being are identical" (p. 180).[22] *Pascendi* had harsh words for the philosophy of immanence:

> when natural theology has been destroyed, and the road to revelation closed by the rejection of the arguments of credibility, and all external revelation absolutely denied, it is clear that this explanation will be sought in vain outside of man himself. It must, therefore, be looked for in man; and since religion is a form of life, the explanation must certainly be found

---

[22] Mercier did not lump all these trends together without distinctions. While he asserted that Wundt, for example, was "enveloped in *idealism*" (p. 155), still Wundt "believes in the *reality* of the facts of experience" (ibid.), and while under the sway of subjectivism, "he carefully and constantly tries to link up his highest metaphysical speculations with the surest facts of experience" (p. 156). In this section, we are highlighting only the major trends in order to compare them with *Pascendi*'s critiques of modernism.

in the life of man. In this way is formulated the principle of religious immanence. Moreover, the first actuation, so to speak, of every vital phenomenon – and religion, as noted above, belongs to this category – is due to a certain need or impulsion; but speaking more particularly of life, it has its origin in a movement of the heart, which movement is called a sense . . . This need of the divine, which is experienced only in special and favorable circumstances cannot of itself appertain to the domain of consciousness, but is first latent beneath consciousness, or, to borrow a term from modern philosophy, in the subconsciousness, where also its root lies hidden and undetected.

(Pope Pius X, 1907, § 7, pp. 184–5)

As with positivism, here the encyclical saw an implication in modern thought, one that was antithetical to Catholic thought, particularly in its Neoscholastic formulation. Mercier, in a later essay on modernism (1910), reiterated this charge found in *Pascendi*, that modernism denigrates the external voice of revelation, making of religion solely something that wells up from within, thereby making the Church superfluous.

Evolutionary theory

This may seem an odd transition, because what could be further from the subjectivism of Cartesian and Kantian thought than the theory of evolution as Darwin hammered it out in the nineteenth century? As Mercier (1918) argued, however, the main thrust of evolutionary thought in nineteenth-century philosophy and psychology was Spencerian rather than Darwinian. Spencer's theory of evolution[23] reconciled "subjectivist idealism and sensationalist empiricism" (p. 84). The "mechanical character of evolution" (p. 86), more commonly known as Spencer's law of "the survival of the fittest" (p. 85), governs all change in the cosmos, from the formation of solar systems to that of political systems. Spencer's law operates by chance, without any finality. So Spencer could reconcile subjectivism with empiricism by claiming to show that the forms of subjective experience have their origins in our evolutionary past: "man's mind was not at the outset a *tabula rasa*, for every *individual* inherits the accumulated experiences of his ancestors, and therefore there is some truth in the doctrine of Kantian idealism as to the *a priori* forms, but the cerebral structure of the individual at birth is the heritage of the experience of the past. Hence there is nothing in the mind of the *race* that is not the result of experience, and in this sense the *a priori* position of the German philosopher is counterfeited" (p. 87). Other combinations existed also, especially syntheses of evolutionary notions with Hegelianism, which Mercier found in many nations, including the United States.

---

[23] Evolution: Mercier (1918) wrote that "the word is Herbert Spencer's. From the year 1852" (p. 84).

Mercier pointed to Henri Bergson as a variant of this thought. He discussed how Bergson sought to overcome the opposition between matter and mind, but how, in the final analysis, Bergson's philosophy was a form of idealism (p. 189). Bergson, it will be recalled, was important to the thinking of Tyrrell, because for Bergson, fixities are the freezing, in spatial form, of the incessant flow of time, which is the essence of our existence. Bergson as a philosopher of life found resonance with many of the critics of Neoscholasticism, such as Tyrrell. *Pascendi* had indirect reference to this approach to the teachings of the Church:

> Dogma is not only able, but ought to evolve and to be changed. This is strongly affirmed by the Modernists, and clearly flows from their princi-ples. For among the chief points of their teaching is the following, which they deduce from the principle of vital immanence, namely, that religious formulas if they are to be really religious and not merely intellectual speculations, ought to be living and to live the life of the religious sense.
>
> (Pope Pius X, 1907, § 13, p. 190)

Again, what in Mercier's text was a philosophical foundation gone astray, the encyclical saw as having practical implications for the life of the faith. Here, it was a question of subsuming the teachings of the Church to evolutionary principles: because dogmas are fixities of expression and thought, they are subject to change over the course of time.

Conclusions

Mercier found the third characteristic of modern psychology, its experimental turn, to be a hopeful sign. Especially heartening, as he saw it, was that it had its justification in an Aristotelian, rather than in modern philosophy. What becomes clear from Mercier's exposition of the origins of contemporary psy-chology is that for all the strides of modern thought, it was founded on a philosophical error, the abandonment of Aristotelian and Scholastic thought: "the *abandonment of metaphysics* in the traditional sense of the word" (Mercier, 1918, p. 206). This was the very error of thought at the roots of modernism, according to *Pascendi*. The comparison of these two documents, then, leads to the conclusion that late nineteenth-century psychology, root and branch, was modernist. This criticism that psychology had erroneously jettisoned the only metaphysical foundation that provided a complete conception of the psycho-logical continued to be made throughout the twentieth century (for example, Brennan, 1945; Gruender, 1911). From this point of view, the only truly non-modernist empirical psychology would be one with a Neoscholastic foundation. Such a psychology did develop in the twentieth century, and in the following chapter, we survey its course.

These criticisms of psychology's foundations came from one of the defenders of the new experimental psychology. Mercier did not simply oppose the new psychology with the Thomistic, he sought to ground the new psychology securely in Thomism by providing it with a metaphysical basis and a sound philosophical anthropology. However, others in the Church were not as sympathetic to psychology or, indeed, to any alleged contribution of modernity. If even its sympathetic supporter cast it under a cloud, what can we have expected from those who concentrated more scrupulously on the theological and political implications of psychology's philosophical basis? After all, even Mercier was "suspicious, known to have ties to all the enemies of the Church."

A suspect science

A reading of *Catholics in psychology* (Misiak and Staudt, 1954) confirms that in the mid-1950s, a cloud still stood over psychology, a result of the modernist crisis. This was true both theoretically and institutionally, with Neoscholastic philosophical psychology still the dominant feature of the North American Catholic scene. Even though psychology of all sorts – including psychoanalysis – had made inroads and gained acceptance in Catholic circles, it still had a suspect aura about it. Limiting discussion to the time of Pope Pius XII (1939–58), we find that Pius (1952, 1953, 1958) was the first pope to address the question of psychology – in particular, the question of psychiatric treatment, especially along psychoanalytic lines (which at the time was the dominant theory in psychiatry). Additionally, while asserting the benefits of psychological treatment, he warned against a certain fragmentation of the human person that runs counter to the Church's teaching about the unity, rationality, and freedom of the human soul. Reviewing Pius's statements on psychology, Saroglou (2000) concludes that Pius's reception was "lukewarm" and that it was received in Catholic intellectual circles as condemning psychoanalysis (p. 722). With some exceptions: the American Catholic Psychological Association (ACPA) made lemonade out of what may have been a lemon in the pope's various statements, but then again, as we shall see, the ACPA did not envision psychoanalysis as central to its identity. Some ACPA members thought that psychoanalysis was not really scientific. Nevertheless, Pius saw some good in psychology, as long as it reckoned with the unity and the ultimate meaning and destiny of the human person, the person's capacity for moral judgment, and the necessity of self-mastery (p. 724). To the extent that psychology did not attend to these things, it remained a suspect science.

Is the crisis over?

Scitum enim est in sciente secundum modum scientis.

Thomas Aquinas[24]

---

[24] "Knowledge is according to the mode of the one who knows," Aquinas (1948, p. 73), *Summa Theologiae*, Prima pars, q. 14, art. 1, reply to objection 3.

The modernist controversy shows some of the complexity of boundary-work between psychology and religion. However one assesses *Pascendi* and Mercier, or Tyrrell and other modernists, it is clear that both sides had cases to be made. One of the particulars of the boundary disputes between psychology and Catholicism is that the official Church responses appealed to the philosophical tradition, from which psychology had emerged. Despite the differences, there was that common ground, or in Foucault's sense, an internal contradiction. This need not be the case for all encounters between psychologies and religions.

At the 1966 meeting of the American Catholic Philosophical Association, Mother Margaret Gorman, a leading member of the American Catholic Psychological Association, announced the end of the modernist crisis. I say this as a hyperbole, to be sure, but Gorman's (1966) words sounded a striking note. She said that Neoscholasticism as a system of knowledge was a historical construction, and that it was not the only one available:

> Regarding the body of philosophical thought of which we are heirs: I hold with many others that such thought is evolutionary. Man builds up on the insights of the past. Being evolutionary, such a development of thought is irreversible. Our way of looking at things must necessarily be different from the scholastic view, since in the interval, we have had the thoughts, questions and insights of Descartes, Kant, Hegel, Darwin, Freud, to mention a few.
>
> (p. 17)

Mercier's vision for scholasticism as a synthesis of religion and philosophy misunderstood Thomas's aim (p. 21). While we can remain true to scholasticism as a paradigm for philosophizing, Gorman asserted that it as important to "philosophize the more in terms of a pluralistic philosophy that speaks to modern man" (p. 29). These words had a modernist note, but what they signified was that Catholic thought had entered a post-modernist and post-Neoscholastic period.

While the Second Vatican Council did mark a decisive change from the integralist position of the early twentieth century, the ground had long been prepared. Without reviewing the changes in theological thinking over the past hundred years, suffice it to say that after World War I there were many innovations in theology, some drawing on the phenomenologies of Husserl, Heidegger, and Scheler, but also the philosophies of life, such as Dilthey's. Neoscholastic manuals did not disappear, and they continued to proliferate during this period, but the new currents continued to swell. In France, starting in the 1930s, there was renewed attention to the pre-Scholastic traditions of the Church, an "attempt to orient theology again more definitely to the biblical-patristic tradition, but in the horizon of modern thought and its *desiderata*" (Scheffczyk, 1981, p. 268). Many of these theologians, such as Henri de Lubac (to whom we will return in later chapters), suffered under suspicion around mid-century, but found themselves elevated during the

Vatican Council. The new approach had a "personalist concept of the truth of faith and its 'historicist' interpretation, and an option for a certain diversity in theology must have seemed dangerous to the representatives of a strictly oriented Thomistic theology of essence" (p. 269). These changes, focusing on the personalist and the phenomenological, in addition to the diverse historical strands in Catholic tradition, made for an opening to psychology and the other human sciences. Emblematic of this was renewed interest in the humanity of Christ (see p. 270) and of the importance of religious experience. Moral theology gave more attention to the psychological bases of moral teaching (p. 275), and in the 1930s, there was attention given to the contributions of psychoanalysis to a conception of morality (T. Müncker's work, cited ibid., p. 275). These various strands came together in some of the documents of the Second Vatican Council.

So is the modernist crisis over? In one sense, of course, because *Pascendi* dealt it a death blow. For another, modernism was not the cabal that the integralists claimed that it was. In yet another sense, though, modernism still haunts the discussion over the meaning of Christianity in the world today. Portier (2001) describes evangelical and fundamentalist Christianity as "a modern anti-modernism," in that it resists "secular pluralism" (p. 595) relativizing Christian claims. Some contemporary Catholics find common cause with these evangelicals. In addition, traditionalist Catholics, some of whom reject the authority of the Second Vatican Council, see the post-conciliar Church as having caved in to modernism (Appleby, 1995, p. 55). So the question remains, and it does inform to some degree the boundary work between the Church and psychology.

For psychology, the documents of the Vatican Council cast it and the other human sciences in a more favorable light. For mainstream conservative and liberal Catholics in the United States, the political battle is over as the separation of church and state, and the principle of tolerance of religious plurality, are generally accepted as good (Appleby, 1995), and not as disastrous consequences of the French Revolution. Theological pluralism is an acknowledged even if not always accepted fact in Catholicism today, and the Scholastic tradition is understood to have been more pluralistic than the Neoscholastics of the early twentieth century understood (Ashley, 1995). Given this profound change in the public character of the Church, the question of boundaries with psychology becomes much more fluid and easy to miss. Saroglou (2000) speaks of "psychology as a privileged partner in the dialogue of theology with the human sciences" (p. 733). Dialogue implies a common ground but also a dialectic, and so Saroglou notes that even in recent years, the Vatican has raised questions about the scientific status of psychology. With good reason. The boundary between psychology and the Catholic Church has as one of its premises that psychology is in one way or another a science. And, to be sure, the questionability of the scientific status of psychology is part of the very identity of this most characteristic modern discipline.

But the larger question, is the crisis over?, must be answered with some ambiguity. For the tension remains between a centralized ecclesiastical structure and the free speculations of theologians, philosophers, and psychologists.

3

Neoscholastic psychology

Vetera novis augere et perficere[1]

Leo XIII, *Aeterni Patris*, 1879

By the early twentieth century, psychology was securely a secular enterprise (Maier, 2004), even though this assessment was not universally affirmed, and even if this assessment did not necessarily carry modernist implications. As Wade E. Pickren (2000) observes, many early scientific psychologists sought to "make their case that they had something new to offer their audiences without its appearing to be a materialistic science, a psychology without a soul" (p. 1022). He writes that they did so often by portraying the new psychology as valid because it was scientific, and hence better than the old abstract theories (citing Edward A. Pace as an example) and useful in building character. Catholic psychologists, however, could not easily distance themselves from the old, philosophical psychology. They adopted a different strategy. In the Catholic world, moreover, psychology was a problematic development, because by its very name psychology was the science of the soul. How could Catholics participate in a secular science of the soul without crashing onto the rocks of materialism and modernism? Neoscholastic psychology was an answer.

When A. A. Roback (1952) included a chapter on "Neo-Scholastic psychology," he was giving attention to something the larger psychological community had ignored. When he revised his book, he added "A puzzling attitude" to this chapter (Roback, 1964). The puzzling attitude belonged to Misiak and Staudt, who in *Catholics in psychology* (1954) objected to Catholic psychologists being considered a separate school. For Roback, since they turned to Thomas Aquinas for a philosophical foundation and had established their own organization, the American Catholic Psychological Association, they indeed constituted a school. However, he sympathized with their objection, saying "the complaint of being treated separately savors of a minority's protest against segregation" (Roback, 1964, p. 445). Compulsory "schooling" may be inappropriate in historical work, but Roback had a point. Proposing a school of Neoscholastic psychology has

[1] "Strengthen and complete the old by aid of the new."

the merit of bringing together aspects of philosophical, experimental, and applied psychology that otherwise seem disparate. What these psychologists did have in common, in addition to their faith, was an eye for the philosophical presuppositions of psychology, especially as they relate to the nature of the "psychological," that vague and perplexing object of the discipline. Roback's comment about minority status hit the mark, too, for the Neoscholastics in psychology sought, in addition to the truth, a place in the mainstream of psychology: hence the protest by Misiak and Staudt.

This chapter looks at those psychologists who defined themselves in relation both to scientific psychology and to the Catholic Church, from the time of the "origins" of the new psychology and of Neoscholasticism in 1879 until the 1960s when, in the wake of the Second Vatican Council, Neoscholasticism lost its official standing. We shall see that the contests at the boundaries of scientific psychology and Catholic thought were complex, and that they occurred at both the theoretical and at the practical level. Indeed, part of what we shall see is that the theoretical and practical disputes were bound together. The particular ways in which the existence of empirical psychology contested boundaries with the Church make it relevant for both the history of psychology and of the history of the relationships among the sciences and religions, for two reasons. First, the chief issues in contest were philosophical, so that they were open to dispute. Pronouncements by authority played a role, to be sure, but they were couched philosophically. Second, with the complex allegiances of many of the psychologists involved, who were often Church officials, we see the interweaving of social institutions in psychology's investigative practices (Danziger, 1990). We thus see theory and research embodied in specific situations.

Philosophical Neoscholastic psychology

The fate of the soul in empirical psychology

Reflecting on her own experience with disputes over psychology in the Catholic world, Virginia Staudt Sexton (1986) later recalled:

> the negative attitudes toward psychology held by some of my fellow Catholics and especially by some of the Church leaders in the 1940s. At that time Catholic psychologists were engaged in a major struggle to extricate and emancipate themselves from the domination of Catholic philosophy and theology. Some Church leaders had a strong bias against psychology; others lacked the psychological sophistication to appreciate the way in which psychology could assist them.
>
> (p. 79)

Catholics in psychology (Misiak and Staudt, 1954) was one of the outcomes of this dissatisfaction. Staudt Sexton was an interested party, of course, as a

Catholic and as a psychologist. Misiak and Staudt wrote their text at an important moment in the history of the relationship between psychology and the Catholic church. Since the 1907 modernist crisis, a Neoscholastic orthodoxy had reigned in Catholic circles and, for two generations, Catholics had cultivated a Neoscholastic psychology. As Staudt Sexton's reminiscence indicates, tensions in the 1940s still were high. Many Catholic psychologists felt misunderstood by Church leaders, mistrusted for allegedly bringing the soul into the laboratory and for substituting secular treatment of mental maladjustment for traditional care of the soul.

Faith and Reason

Neoscholastics did not in principle assume the inevitability of conflict between psychology and Catholic thought. They did not generally pose the relationship as that between science and religion, but instead as between reason and faith. Reason is the natural, and faith is the revealed way to seek the same Truth, namely God. (Not all Christian theologies, including some Catholic, take such a benign position on the autonomy of human reason.) Neoscholasticism was a realist philosophy, which meant it held that by means of perception and cognition we can attain knowledge of the objective world. For the Neoscholastics, reason and faith follow different but complementary paths. They did not divide the world into that of fact (reason, science) and value (faith, religion). Such a position denied religion intellection and rational content, making it a soft cushion for hard science. Recall that essential to the condemnation of modernism was the charge that the modernists reduced faith to the outcome of certain affective experiences. In making the distinction between faith and reason, the Neoscholastics were not ceding reason to science: religious faith, too, is rational. From the Neoscholastic standpoint, the sciences complemented faith by learning of the proximate causes of things. Based on sense experience, the sciences cannot go beyond proximate causes to first causes, inquiry into which is the task of philosophical, metaphysical science. Yes, philosophical inquiry is, Neoscholastically considered, scientific, insofar as "science" designates systematic knowledge of the real. Philosophical knowledge is of universals, not of particulars. In this way, Neoscholastics, such as Mercier, divided the labor of human knowledge into the search for proximate and first causes. Psychology could be a natural science, because it studies a natural entity, the human being as an object of sense perception.[2] As long as the Big Philosophical Picture stays in view, this new empirical science can only contribute to our knowledge of reality.

As a result, "mutual advantage" (Brooke, 1991) between scientific and religious inquiries was the goal, because as science uncovers the laws of

---

[2] This included both inner sense (introspection) as well as outer sense (observation, etc.).

creation, we learn about the Creator using human reason. Since truth is one, greater empirical knowledge will make the rationality of Christian beliefs more evident. For the Neoscholastics, moreover, there was another advantage to be had in fostering modern scientific work: engagement with the modern world. It was necessary for Catholics to be scientists, so that science does not adopt an ill-conceived materialism for its philosophical foundation. In other words, Catholic fostering of science had an evangelical purpose.

The Soul

Within Neoscholasticism, however, a science/religion tension did arise, because psychology deals with the human soul. Chemistry and geology can be neutral on Catholic teachings on creation, but psychology has to take positions on the question of the soul, because the soul had been a fundamental category of philosophical inquiry into "the psychological" and of western conceptions of human nature. As the new psychology at the turn of the twentieth century sought to distance itself from notions of the soul, it ran head-on into Neoscholastic conclusions about the soul as a first cause of human life. For the Neoscholastics, psychology's abandonment of the soul was a failure of intellectual nerve at best or misguided materialism at worst.[3]

The soul really was the sticking point of this particular science/religion interface. For the Neoscholastics, the human – as opposed to the animal – soul is rational and is created uniquely by God for every human person. In Thomistic language, the rational soul is "infused" into the human embryo at conception or sometime thereafter (opinions differed). In the *Catholic Encyclopedia*, edited by many hands, including the psychologist and philosopher, Edward Aloysius Pace, we read in the article, "Soul," written by the renowned Neoscholastic psychologist, Michael Maher (1912):

> The rational soul is produced by special creation at the moment when the organism is sufficiently developed to receive it. In the first stage of embryonic development, the vital principle has merely vegetative powers; then a sensitive soul comes into being, educed from the evolving potencies of the organism – later yet, this is replaced by the perfect rational soul, which is essentially immaterial and so postulates a special creative act. Many modern theologians have abandoned this last point of St. Thomas' teaching, and maintain that a fully rational soul is infused into the embryo at the first moment of its existence.
>
> (p. 156)

---

[3] For empirical psychology's abandonment of the soul as a category of understanding, see important arguments by Franz Brentano (1874/1973) and William James (1890). In other quarters, soul (or its linguistic equivalents) was not dropped. We return to this topic in the final chapter.

While the origins of the human body can be explained in terms of natural causes, the specifically human aspects of our psychological lives – that is, the substantive form of the individual composed of intellect and will – cannot be so explained. Each soul exists, each person exists, because of a divine act. The soul is immortal, moreover, another conclusion of Neoscholastic philosophy. In other words, they held that this conclusion is pre-theological, based on reasoning alone and independent of Revelation by God. Intellect and will, the rational powers of the human soul in Neoscholastic terms, cannot be accounted for fully by reference to sensation, perception, instinct, and drives. So right in the very center of Neoscholastic psychology was the soul, which defied the division of labor between psychologists and philosophers. For the Neoscholastics, these teachings on the soul were not matters of faith, but of reason. They were the findings of rational psychology, which sets the ground for empirical psychological investigations. From a Neoscholastic point of view, empirical investigations, dealing with matters of sense experience, cannot refute or prove the metaphysical foundations established by rational psychology. Misiak and Staudt (1954) stressed the importance of the teachings on the soul (p. 10) and, at the same time, distanced themselves from them (p. 11). While the soul was fundamental to the Neoscholastic philosophical anthropology, there were various ways for Catholic psychologists, who sought to avoid being quarantined in the scientific world, to deal with this stumbling block.

Boundaries

If, as Cavanaugh (1995) asserts, in the modern division of labor between Church and State (and Science), the Church took care of the soul, here in modern scientific psychology was a science claiming expertise in the area assigned to the Church. Neoscholastic psychologists, even those who asserted the separation of scientific psychology from philosophy, could not develop "a psychology without a soul" and successfully claim disciplinary immunity in the eyes of the Church. The existence of the soul became the locus of "boundary-work" (Gieryn, 1983) between scientific psychology and philosophical psychology in Neoscholasticism. It would also figure into the negative evaluations by non-Catholic psychologists of Catholics in psychology: the Catholics had *a priori* dogmatic answers to what other psychologists saw as empirical questions, and the Catholics smuggled religious convictions into psychology. The notion of boundary-work helps to clarify some of the dynamics of Neoscholastic psychology, suggesting that its science/religion relationship was actively constructed by conflicts within the Neoscholastic movement, and by conflicts and accommodations between Neoscholastic psychologists and various outsiders, including ecclesiastical authorities and non-Neoscholastic psychologists. The boundary-work was complex, depending on who was drawing the line in the sand. The work sought to decide what counted as psychology and what as philosophy, as well as what counted as applied psychological activity and what as pastoral care of the soul. For many Neoscholastic psychologists, boundary-work centered on expansion of the emerging discipline of psychology and the concomitant protection of its autonomy; they feared that the philosophers or Church officials wanted a monopoly. For others, the emphasis on the scientific nature of empirical psychology was seen as an illegitimate expansion or as an attempt to exclude the Church's voice on matters of the human soul. The Neoscholastic solution to the problematic of science and religion in psychology was a careful distinction between two levels of analysis: that between the empirical and the philosophical, and that between the natural and the supernatural. We might say that the fate of psychology's soul was at stake.

In order to begin the historical analysis, we must first turn to the ecclesiastical background of the Neoscholastic movement, as well as its relationship to psychology. Following that, I will present the constituents of and contributors to Neoscholastic psychology. Finally, I will indicate the factors that led to the decline and transformation of this tradition.

Neoscholasticism and the new psychology

Two – not one – symbolic events occurred in 1879. In that year, Wilhelm Wundt opened his Psychological Institute in Leipzig and "inaugurated" experimental psychology. In the same year, Pope Leo XIII, as we have seen, officially inaugurated Neoscholasticism. Just as Wundt institutionalized a trend already occurring, so Leo did for Neoscholasticism, which was already in ascendance before Leo's papacy. Moreover, Leo put papal authority behind the movement.

Mercier's Neoscholasticism

We have already seen in Chapter 2 that Mercier's psychology was a response to modernism, even as it sought to be a modern, that is, a natural scientific, psychology. Now we shall emphasize the Neoscholastic grounding of his psychology.

Scholasticism developed in the Middle Ages as a type of philosophical investigation emphasizing logical disputation. Modern philosophical approaches, from Descartes and Locke, superseded it in most quarters since the seventeenth century. For Mercier, Scholasticism had never really died, although he thought it had retreated "into the cloisters" (Mercier, 1918, p. 323) in the eighteenth century. The institute that Mercier established at Louvain had a distinctive ambition to revive it:

1. Philosophy was not to be regarded as a mere *ancilla theologiae*, but to be studied for philosophy's sake. Catholic philosophers would thus frankly enter into the spirit of our time, and cease to be looked upon as mere apologists of their Creed.

2. Just as philosophy was to be studied for its own sake, so also was science. Neo-Thomists had to become true scientists, to construct laboratories, to make experiments, and ... to find in St. Thomas himself the reconciliation of science and philosophy.

(Perrier, 1909, p. 219)

Characteristic of the Neoscholasticism of his day, Mercier's position was that there is one Thomism, and that it is a complete philosophical system. He acknowledged that since the fifteenth century there had been degenerate forms of Scholasticism, but these did not represent the original impulse of Aquinas and the other greats of the thirteenth and fourteenth centuries. Mercier's Neoscholastic system had two aspects: "First is the union of reason and Christian faith; second is the union of observation and rational speculation, the combination of analysis and synthesis" (Mercier, 1882/1996, p. 297). To comprehend what was at stake in the relationships between Neoscholasticism and the New Psychology, these two points need clarification.

Reason and faith

Philosophy is "a 'natural' science, in this sense that it deals with an order of knowledge to which man can attain by the light of unaided reason and is opposed to that order of knowledge which, because it surpasses the power and needs of created nature, is called 'supernatural'" (Mercier, 1916a, p. 21). Philosophy, like other sciences, has its own principles and methods, and is autonomous in its own proper domain. That autonomy does not mean that the philosopher "may show a complete disregard of the teachings of revelation" (p. 22), however; the autonomy of science does not extend beyond the bounds of its competence. The Church has a mission to teach revealed truths, and it does not interfere with philosophy and science except to inhibit theories that contradict revealed truths. When such theories are proposed, "the Church cautions those who trust to her for guidance, and denounces the error the acceptance of which would run counter to belief in divine revelation. Her guardianship is thus negative and she herself does not positively teach either science or philosophy" (ibid.). (This position provided a justification for criticisms of the modernists, such as Loisy, who claimed that his work was historical, not theological.) What if reason would lead to conclusions contrary to faith? Mercier's Neoscholastic answer is that that is not possible, because God is the author of all truth, and truth cannot contradict truth. From this position, then, while science has an autonomous sphere of inquiry, this sphere is not absolutely independent of the Church and its teaching authority.

Analysis and synthesis

The union of these two intellectual processes overcomes the bifurcation in philosophy between empiricism and rationalism – two philosophical schools that arose beginning with Descartes, when the Scholastic method was discarded. For Mercier, "analysis consists in observing the exterior facts of nature and the interior workings of our life; in guessing by means of prudent hypotheses the intimate causes that explain nature, laws, origin and finality; and in rising ... to the certain affirmation and precise determination of these causes, principally of the first cause, that is to say of the absolute Being" (Mercier, 1882/ 1996, p. 301). The categories for the synthesis were those of Aristotle and Aquinas: the intelligibility of being, essence and existence, substance and accident, material and immaterial substances, act and potency, and the objective basis for law and ethics in a divinely created cosmos (Kelly, 1965). Mercier opposed the positivist and phenomenalist trends of the nineteenth century, trends that had enormous influence on the way that scientific psychology theorized about its data. Neoscholasticism countered what it saw as the illegitimate philosophical and theological claims of scientists when they stepped from their own turf on to that of the philosopher and theologian.

Mercier's Neoscholastic psychology

Mercier described a pattern that Neoscholastic psychologists would repeat over the years. His psychology proceeded from several assumptions:

(1) Catholics are isolated within scientific circles;
(2) scientific psychology has autonomy within a Neoscholastic framework;
(3) the Neoscholastic framework provides the ultimate interpretation for psychological findings;
(4) Neoscholasticism is superior to Cartesian and positivist philosophies for the development of a scientific psychology;
(5) psychology is the science of the soul, but as human beings are composites of matter, the body, and form, an immaterial soul, all psychological activity involves the body as well as the soul (with the exception of purely spiritual acts). Therefore, Neoscholasticism encourages experimental psychology as the study of embodied psychological activity, such as perception, emotion, imagination, and memory.

This framework supported an integrative strategy, which sought to contribute to the development of scientific psychology while maintaining a philosophical position that was compatible with Church teaching.

Catholic isolation within science

Leo XIII held that Catholics were decidedly isolated in the scientific world, and that they had been so since the Enlightenment (Boileau, 1996, p. 42). In his "Report on the higher studies of philosophy," Mercier (1891/1996) affirmed this position: "Catholics live *isolated* in the scientific world; they are marked by suspicion and treated with indifference; their publications have great difficulty crossing the fortifications of the believing world, and, if they do cross it, they are usually received without effect" (p. 344). The causes for this isolation need not detain us. Mercier's solution, however, is germane to the question of psychology. In this same essay he concluded: "We should be forming a large number of *men* who are devoted to *science for itself*, without professional benefit or direct apologetic goals, who *work first hand* to fashion the materials of the scientific edifice and thus contribute to its progressive elevation" (p. 349). Such were the goals of his Higher Institute of Philosophy at Louvain. In his 1891 Report, for example, he proposed: "This year, for example, in addition to the teaching of properly called psychology, it will be necessary to establish courses in general biology ... Finally, certain courses on experimental psychology or psycho-physiology, destined to examine closely the relations between the soul and the body" (p. 353).

Mercier detected a danger in Catholic neglect of the new scientific psychology, and of Catholic dismissals of it as a materialistic attempt to measure the soul: "Psychology today is undergoing a transformation from which we would be guilty to remain aloof. In Germany, Leipzig, Berlin, Paris, England, and the United States, laboratories have been constructed in which hundreds of young workers are dedicated to analyzing the contents of consciousness with a patience that one cannot fail to admire" (ibid.). If Catholics were to disdain this young science because some of its proponents espouse a materialist philosophy, the future looks bleak: "Here is a young, contemporary science that is in itself neither spiritualist nor materialist. If we do not take part in this, the psychology of the future will come to be without us and, as we have reason enough to fear, against us" (pp. 353–4).

Mercier's Neoscholastic project, then, was to develop scientific psychology on its own terms, without apologetic intentions. To achieve this aim, courses, laboratories, libraries, and publications would all be necessary. Neoscholastic thought had nothing to fear from experimental psychology, much to learn from it of the details of psychological operations and, finally, much to contribute to its metaphysical foundation. In his own life, Mercier implemented this strategy. From Louvain, he sent Armand Thiéry (1868–1955) to Leipzig to study under Wundt and when Thiéry returned to Louvain in 1894 he began a course in experimental psychology (Misiak and Staudt, 1954, p. 55). Albert Michotte (1881–1935), who developed a creative and fruitful experimental program, succeeded him after 1905.

The autonomy of experimental psychology

Mercier criticized Cartesian philosophy for its radical separation of soul and body. A Cartesian philosophy holds that only introspection gives us knowledge of the soul, and Mercier agreed with Comte's position that if self-contemplation were the only means to know the soul, then there would be no psychology, for introspection is notoriously unreliable (Mercier, 1902, p. 13). Since the

Neoscholastic position is that of hylomorphism (the unity of matter, *hylê*, with a formative principle, *morphê*, the soul), mental activity, with the exception of purely spiritual acts such as ideation, always has a material and hence measurable component. Even concept formation, which is a spiritual act, involves the nervous system, since thinking requires the prior operation of perception and imagination. Mercier's program of synthesizing modern thought with Thomism thus promoted the experimental method in psychology:

> This [development of experimental methods with Weber and Fechner] was a critical moment for psychology. If it remained refractory to the general conditions of progress, would it not virtually abdicate its claims of being a science? On the other hand, could it in any way attach itself to physics and mechanics and submit, by any title whatever or in any degree, to the experimental method without becoming materialistic? ... We believe that this is not the case. Neither the work nor the method of Experimental Psychology is opposed to the principles of spiritualistic philosophy.
>
> (pp. 18–19)

Mercier defined experimental psychology as the study of "mental states, their relation to one another, and the laws of their development" (p. 21). In the field of psychophysics, he noted, "materialistic prejudices" (p. 22) stake their claim but, he continued, the results of Weber's researches are more compatible with the Neoscholastic conception of the soul: "Sensation is an act of the nervous organ; it is therefore bound in its functions to the chemical and physical conditions of nervous activity. 'The acts of sensitive life,' says St. Thomas ... 'do not belong to the soul alone nor to the body alone but their subject is the combination of both'" (p. 28). In the study of reaction times and of the motor effects of mental activity, Mercier also found results conforming to Neoscholastic principles.

Mercier's position granted experimental psychology its autonomy as a natural science. This new science "helps to give a scientific basis to the philosophy of man" (p. 38). He saw this new psychology as a valuable aid in defeating the extreme dualism of Descartes on the one hand, and Comte and the associationists, with their "psychology without a soul" (p. 52), on the other. Mercier wrote that experimental psychology leads to metaphysical questions, especially to the question of "the nature of the conscious Ego" (p. 59).

The hierarchical relationship between philosophical and scientific psychology

Mercier's conception of philosophy was "encyclopedic" (MacIntyre, 1990), for ultimately it would be a complete system of all possible knowledge that the human mind is naturally capable of grasping. Hence, Mercier presented his philosophical system in manuals, typical of the time and certainly typical of the

Neoscholastic movement in general. The manual was a pedagogic tool that presented a totality of knowledge in systematic form. Mercier defined philosophy as "the science of things *through their simplest and most general reasons*, or again, *through their most far-reaching causes*" (Mercier, 1916a, p. 9). A cause is "a principle in virtue of which a being is what it is or becomes this thing" (p. 11), and for Mercier, there were four kinds of causes: the Aristotelian formal, material, efficient, and final causes. Philosophy has two divisions, speculative and practical. Among the speculative sciences, he included rational psychology along with ontology, cosmology, and natural theology. Using Aristotelian language, he defined rational or philosophical psychology as "the physics of the organic world" (p. 17); in particular, psychology "is that department of philosophy which contemplates the human soul" (Mercier, 1916b, p. 161). Unlike the Cartesian conception of psychology, for Mercier psychology is not limited to the immediate givens of consciousness, for "it is the *man* who feels and thinks, not his soul only" (p. 162), and therefore Mercier encompassed "*organic life, sentient life*, and *rational life*" (ibid.) in his philosophical psychology. In presenting the last part, rational life, Mercier divided his topic into the nature, origin, and destiny of the human soul and of the human being. Concerning both the origin of the soul and its immortal destiny, Mercier's position was that these are philosophical and not theological truths, matters of reason and not of faith. For Mercier, as others in the Neoscholastic tradition (e.g. Gannon, 1954), these propositions belong to science writ large, even if not to the experimental branch of science.

The changing and the unchanging in philosophical thought

One criticism of Neoscholastic philosophizing was that it was a fixed doctrine, unfazed by empirical findings. Mercier (1918) addressed this directly in citing criticism from Alfred Binet, the great French psychologist of the early twentieth century, in the context of an effort for Catholic and non-Catholic psychological thinkers to work together:

> M. Binet welcomed an invitation by M. Picavet to "a mutual tolerance between Catholics and their opponents for the greater advantage of science, and even of religion, of philosophy and civilization." Why, then, does he so far yield to prejudice as to continue: "To these sensible remarks let us add that when we take up our own special and limited standpoint of experimental psychology for forming an opinion of the new movement, we are unable to sanction a state of mind that uses observation and experiment to fortify a preconceived idea, especially when that idea is already many centuries old. On the contrary, we are accustomed to take observation as our starting-point, as the beginning of our investigations, and as the source of truth and the supreme mistress of science."
>
> (p. 337)

For Mercier, this was a misunderstanding of the Neoscholastic project in psychology. He saw the philosophical basis of psychology as necessarily unfinished, and he pointed particularly to the need for Neoscholasticism to take into consideration epistemological questions that modern philosophy raised and that the ancients and medievals did not see. Acknowledging the critical questions raised by Descartes and Kant, Mercier asked: "For whom are we philosophizing, unless it be for the men of our own times? And what is our object, unless it be to attempt a solution of the doubts which are an obsession in our contemporaries?" (p. 344). Nevertheless, the Aristotelian–Scholastic tradition provided a better ground for psychology than any other, and Mercier (1918) envisioned renewal of the tradition by means of experimental psychology:

> If neo-Thomism keeps faithful to this programme, it will be able to rejuvenate the philosophy of the School with fortunate discoveries, to renew its apparatus in part, and to wear in the eyes of posterity a very different aspect from that which it presents to-day. Nevertheless, those who would fathom its deepest possibilities will again find in the substructure of the building the soundness and completeness of the principles which governed the uprise of Western civilization. They will joyfully acknowledge that there has been progress without revolution, acquisition without loss, and the growth of a living unity which has been constantly enriched by the variety of the contributions made to it by all the branches of human knowledge.
>
> (pp. 350–1)

Being part of a tradition of thinking meant both continuity and change.

It is important to notice that this theme Mercier articulated here was subject to other readings and that criticism such as Binet's was shared not only by critics of Neoscholasticism but by some Neoscholastics. As an example, consider two reviews by Francis Patrick Siegfried, a professor of mental and moral philosophy at St. Charles Seminary in Pennsylvania, from the 1890s. In the initial review, he discussed the first edition of Michael Maher's *Psychology* favorably, and he looked forward to the time "when the old philosophy will combine with the new science, to grow, not each for itself, but as trunk and branch and flower and fruit of one grand organism of human thought" (Siegfried, 1891, p. 43). Yet in the second review, he claimed only limited results from this graft:

> there is no real discord, but, on the contrary, ... the recently ascertained results of experimental investigation on the organic side of psychology admirably confirm, complete and perfect the empirical content of the neoscholastic psychology. As to the rational or metaphysical side of the latter science, the wealth of doctrine handed on from St. Thomas, Suarez, and their commentators calls for no further development, and is unlikely ever to receive such.
>
> (Siegfried, 1897, p. 98)

So for Siegfried, the new psychology could only contribute empirical details that the medievals could not have obtained, because they were not experimentalists. The difference between Mercier and Siegfried may be one of emphasis, for neither would have concluded, on the basis of empirical investigation, for example, that the Scholastics were wrong, and that the soul was not immortal. That kind of conclusion could not come from empirical research, because the issue was not empirical in that sense. But between the Merciers and the Siegfrieds, we can say, there was considerable difference in terms of their assessments of the potential contributions of the new psychology. For the former, it had much to offer, even to philosophy; for the latter, it was mainly something to view warily, for the basic doctrine was set. What more, really, was there to learn?

Mercier as the guiding light

Mercier's framework held, in some circles, for the next 50 years, although Neoscholasticism developed in the twentieth century in many directions, eclipsing the contributions of Mercier (McCool, 1989). In many ways, Mercier's framework was robust enough to provide the means whereby both scientific and philosophical psychologies, conceived Neoscholastically, ultimately surpassed the framework itself. For within Mercier's vision for Neoscholasticism hid the possibility of its undoing. Mercier and others in his tradition, such as Michael Maher, Robert Edward Brennan, Thomas Verner Moore, William C. Bier, and Magda Arnold, did not question the scientific nature of the science of psychology. Because they could situate scientific psychology within a comprehensive metaphysical context, they took the scientific character of experimental psychology for granted, much as did their positivistic contemporaries. Steel notes that, "the modern sciences were integrated into a traditional metaphysical synthesis that, at the end, proved to be not much more than a theoretical superstructure" (1992, p. 199). We shall see how this limitation contributed, in the period after the 1950s, to new developments: first, to the assimilation of Catholic psychologists into mainstream psychology without visible remainder of anything distinctively Catholic or Neoscholastic; and second, to critiques of some crucial Neoscholastic presuppositions and a renewal of the questions raised by the Neoscholastics about the nature of psychology. In both cases, the "post-Neoscholastics" avoided framing their situations in terms of science and religion or faith and reason. In particular, they ceased speaking about the soul.[4]

---

[4] One of Mercier's contemporaries was Franz Brentano (1838–1917). While Brentano was an authority on Aristotle, and his *Psychology from an empirical standpoint* (Brentano, 1874/ 1973) shows a strong influence of the Scholastic tradition (in his re-introduction of intentionality, for example), Brentano was not a Neoscholastic. He was influenced by the British empiricist tradition and his work emphasized psychological acts and first-person

The American context for Neoscholastic psychology

Neoscholastic psychology was by definition catholic in scope, yet I restrict my discussion primarily to the North American context, because local conditions affected the ways that Neoscholastic psychology developed. For example, after the Civil War in Spain, the Franco regime imposed a Neoscholastic framework on psychology (Carpintero, 1984). However, the North American context was only relatively independent of European contributions throughout the period.[5] One local factor in the United States was that at the beginning of the twentieth century, Catholics were a minority group and they developed an independent system of education, which provided a fertile ground for Neoscholasticism. As a second local factor, the papal condemnation of modernism set the stage, to state it in positive terms, for the cultivation of a distinctive culture with a Neoscholastic intellectual foundation. After presenting these two broader cultural trends, I turn to Neoscholastic psychology itself. My argument will be that Neoscholastic psychology developed a solution to the problem of the philosophical basis of psychology. To demonstrate this point, after looking at the terms of the debate over psychology, I will focus on textbooks, as they were addressed to students and psychologists alike, and had wide circulation. Then I will turn to Neoscholastic psychologists who pursued scientific research. Following this, I will consider applied Neoscholastic psychology (counseling, psychotherapy, testing, etc.), which also emerged. Finally, I will indicate how Neoscholastic psychology surpassed itself and fell into decline.

Edward Aloysius Pace (1861–1938), a priest and protégé of Mercier, studied with Wundt and then established an experimental psychology program at the Catholic University of America in 1891. The university had been founded in 1887 in the midst of internal debates within the American Catholic community, with the intention of establishing a leading university that was also Catholic. Pace had been selected for the faculty in order to ensure that the Thomism at the university would be progressive, that is, engaged with the modern sciences. Pace sought to carry out the Neoscholastic program in both his writings and his administrative work. He conducted experimental studies early in his career, and he was elected to membership of the American Psychological Association (APA) at its first meeting. He wrote extensively on Neoscholastic philosophy, and he was one of the founders of the American Catholic Philosophical Association and its journal, *The New Scholasticism*. Pace devoted much effort

---

experience in a way that led to the phenomenological approach in psychology. As we have seen, Misiak and Staudt (1954) had to deal explicitly with Brentano's apostasy and defensively say that it was not inevitable for Catholics in psychology to break with the Church.

[5] A number of the thinkers discussed below, such as Michael Maher, SJ and Johannes Lindworsky, SJ, were not American and did not migrate here. However, their texts were widely used and thus I include them.

to overcome Catholic inferiority in the sciences. He echoed Mercier's warning about the dangers of Catholics not getting involved in psychology: "Either get hold of this instrument and use it for proper purposes, or leave it to materialists, and after they have heaped up facts, established laws, and forced their conclusions upon psychology, go about tardily to unravel with clumsy fingers, this tangle of error" (Pace, 1895, p. 160). This apologetical argument took aim at Catholic resistance to psychology.

Early on, Pace (1894) debated Thomas Hughes, SJ (1894), of St. Louis University, on the nature and usefulness of experimental psychology. Hughes decried the materialism of the new psychology, which Pace countered *à la* Mercier. Hughes also defended the traditional Jesuit form of education, which was under assault as secondary and higher education modernized. Pace, and his colleague, Thomas Edward Shields (1862–1921), who also taught psychology at the Catholic University, saw the need to adapt education to modern conditions. As such, they drew out implications for education from experimental psychological studies, while preserving the hierarchy of truths expressed in Neoscholasticism. Pace and Shields set the pace (we might say) for American Neoscholastic psychology, and Pace's student and successor as a psychology professor at the Catholic University, Thomas Verner Moore (1877–1969), also sought to involve Catholics in psychology in applied settings.[6]

Hughes' criticisms of psychology did not occur in a vacuum, and we must understand them within the larger Catholic context of the critiques of modernism and Americanism.[7] In the context of fears of modernism, psychology's focus on first person experience seemed in some Catholic eyes to have potentially dangerous implications for the objectivity of truth. Americanism – an

---

[6] The dispute between Pace and Hughes was not an isolated incident. Some years later, John A. O'Brien (1921) argued that the findings on modern psychology "have given us a wealth of psychological data concerning the various phases of the educative process which enables us to base our educational procedure not on the old *a priori* speculative hypotheses, but on definite, empirical, factual evidence, experimentally tested and verified" (p. 135). O'Brien (see Chapter 5 for further information) was writing, it should be noted, in the *Ecclesiastical Review*, a journal for the clergy. He was especially scornful of religious education, noting that the Baltimore Catechism (the primary text for religious instruction of the young, in various editions, used until at least the 1960s in the United States) "is almost barbarous" in its abstract approach and disregard for the mental development of children. He noted further that "the realization of the gross ineptitude of the present form of the Baltimore Catechism has induced the faculty of pedagogy of the Catholic University of America, as well as many other priests and nuns, to prepare other manuals wherein some recognition is given to these basic principles of pedagogy" (p. 134). Shields was instrumental in this reform.

[7] In a letter, *Testem Benevolentiae*, to Archbishop Gibbons in 1899, Pope Leo XIII warned against several deviations that some were calling Americanism, especially modifying traditional beliefs or downplaying some of them to appeal to modern people. Americanism, a variant of modernism, became something to tar one's opponents with for a while.

accusation waved at many American Catholic thinkers, including Pace – like modernism, referred to efforts to accommodate Church teaching and practices to modern life, with an emphasis on what the so-called Americanists deemed the goods of American life: the emphasis on liberty and on the progress of society and nature, "less tainted than European countries by [modernity's] irreligious features" (Gleason, 1995, p. 8). Opposition to Americanism and modernism had an ideological function of staking out the boundaries of what was possible in Catholic thought. Assessments of this period, from 1907 to 1962, vary, but some Thomistic philosophers later described restraints on the ability of Catholic philosophers to criticize Neoscholastic philosophy. James Weisheipl, OP.[8] (1968), for example, claimed that the modernist crisis produced "a literal reign of terror . . . in Catholic circles," with informers "encouraged to report suspicious Modernist tendencies among the clergy" (pp. 178–9). Ernan McMullin (1967), as president of the American Catholic Philosophical Association in 1966, seconded Weisheipl's view, as did another leading Thomistic philosopher, Norris Clarke, SJ (1968), who described "the somewhat totalitarian spirit of the high-riding Thomism of those days" (p. 191). While the United States had no Franco to enforce Neoscholasticism politically, to some extent it was "philosophy by decree" (McMullin, 1967, p. 9; Steel, 1992, p. 183). It is important to note that many of the Neoscholastic psychologists were members of the clergy, and as a result, in their education and in professional activities, had to respond to Church dictates in a way that the laity did not.[9]

---

[8] OP, Order of Preachers, the Dominican order. Thomas Aquinas was a member of this order.

[9] There are two related topics to mention in connection with this point that members of the clergy worked within ecclesiastical boundaries. The first deals with the obligation required of all Catholics, lay and clergy alike, to seek authorization to publish certain material. The Code of Canon Law (Codex iuris canonici, 1918), in a section devoted to the Teaching Office of the Church, indicated which books required prior censure before they could be published. According to an authoritative commentary, "all writings which contain anything of special importance to religion and good morals" (Bouscaren and Ellis, 1946, p. 713) needed permission. The local Ordinary (typically the bishop) oversaw this approval process, which included an examination of the text by the diocesan censor: "The indication of ecclesiastical approbation is customarily placed at the opening of the book. It contains the Nihil obstat (i.e. the decision of the censor) and the Imprimatur (i.e. the permission granted by the Ordinary) together with the time, date, and place where the authorization was granted" (Burke, 1952, p. 17). (Nihil obstat means "there is nothing objectionable"; imprimatur means "let it be printed.") The vast majority of Neoscholastic texts, because they treat of the human soul and human nature, included these authorizations. I was surprised to see that Catholics in Psychology did not contain them, and I presume that that was because it was a historical study. In addition to this ecclesiastic "peer review process," clerics had to receive permission to publish books and articles "even treating of profane subjects" (Bouscaren and Ellis, 1946, p. 714) from the Ordinary or the superior of their order. This permission did not require approval of a censor.

The second topic concerns the Index of Forbidden Books (Index librorum prohibitorum, 1948), the list of texts deemed antithetical to the Church and its teachings. No psychological

It would be a mistake, however, to see only repression in this period. Within the boundaries delimited by the perceived threat of modernism there developed a so-called Renaissance of Catholic culture, one that had a Neoscholastic base. The leaders of the Neoscholastic movement, including Leo XIII, saw the crisis of modernity as a failure of rationality and thus sought to provide a reasoned response to the rise of modern science and modern nation states deformed by faulty materialist and positivist conceptions of reality. Moreover, in the United States there was a cultural incentive to form a counterculture: Catholics still suffered the treatment afforded to many largely immigrant groups, and this sense of being under siege provided a justification for the development of a separate culture, with its own institutions and philosophy. This culture endured until the 1960s, when it broke down under the weight of external events and from internal structural weaknesses. I say it broke down, although the extent of continuity and discontinuity is hard to determine in this area, one so fraught with ideological conflict. For present purposes, however, it is important to note that it was within the Catholic counterculture of the first half of the twentieth century that Neoscholastic psychology took root in psychology and higher education.

Neoscholastic psychology: philosophical and scientific

Neoscholastic psychologists argued for the necessity of an explicit relationship between philosophical and scientific aspects of psychology. This argument began with criticism of the implicit or explicit foundations of much of the existing experimental psychology. Philosophical criticism was boundary-work, serving to justify scientific psychology for Catholics, and serving to steer psychology away from what were seen as inadequate philosophical foundations. Beyond this, it sought to establish a positive and mutually beneficial rapport between philosophical and scientific levels of inquiry.

Criticisms of the philosophical foundations of scientific psychology

Pace (1896) captured an essential aspect of Neoscholastic thought when he spoke of the desire "to pierce through the manifold of appearance to the

text of the twentieth century ever made the list before it was abandoned in 1966. The 1918 *Code of Canon Law* declared that among the books forbidden to Catholics *ipso jure* (by the law itself) were those "which in any way attempt to subvert the very foundations of religion (c. 1399, 2°)" (Bouscaren and Ellis, 1946, p. 727). Bouscaren and Ellis explain that this provision meant to include "most philosophical works of the Materialist, Positivist, Rationalist schools, books of Theosophy, and all forms of Pantheism" (p. 728). Given the materialist and positivist presuppositions of many works in natural scientific psychology, the Catholic psychologist in the first half of the twentieth century faced difficulties indeed.

The Code of Canon Law was revised in 1983, with the *imprimatur* and diocesan censors intact, although the provisions for them were considerably relaxed.

ultimate reality beneath" as "this passion for unity" (p. 192). The Neoscholastic philosopher sought to achieve a synthesis in a metaphysical system of the truths discovered by the positive sciences. What this meant in practice was chiefly a repeated critique of the inadequate philosophical bases of psychology and re-interpretations of research along Neoscholastic lines. Synthesis existed as an ideal, one that proved elusive to actualize.

Examples of the dual effort of criticism and reformulation come from the work of Hubert Gruender, SJ (1870–1940), at St. Louis University. Gruender, in addition to a background in Neoscholastic thought, had studied experimental psychology at the University of Bonn in 1912, when Oswald Külpe was there. Gruender's *Psychology without a soul* (1911) had two principal arguments. First, one cannot study human beings without studying the soul, since it is with the soul that we act, not only in distinctively human ways, but as living and sentient beings as well. Gruender defended this tradition against modernist deviations in philosophy. For Gruender, if thinking and sensing occur, they must be the acts of a subject. He and other Neoscholastics most strongly objected to the argument that a concept of soul was unnecessary for psychology (as Brentano, 1874/1973, argued), and certainly to the reduction of the soul or mind to the brain. Second, Gruender (1932) wrote: "All problems concerning the ultimate nature and origin of things are philosophical problems and must be solved by the methods of philosophy" (p. 439), thus attempting to refute the "behavioristic psychologist" who would interpret the predictability of much human action as evidence against freedom of the will. When faced with such ultimate questions, the scientific psychologist should *"leave them entirely to philosophy"* (p. 440, emphasis in original). In this insistence, Gruender engaged in boundary-work, with the distinction between scientific and philosophical levels of analysis keeping psychology in harmony with the Catholic faith. The philosophical teachings on the soul (here, the emphasis on the active subject and on the will) served as the boundary stone.

Gruender (1920) did conduct and teach empirical research, writing a text-book in experimental psychology.[10] Nevertheless, the resistance of Catholic thinkers to scientific psychology rested on a critique of the applicability of the natural scientific method to the life of the mind. While the majority position, following the lead of Mercier and Pace, was that scientific psychology, so long as it had a solid philosophical foundation, was acceptable as a way to advance knowledge in psychology, some contested scientific psychological methodology because it made studying distinctively human traits impossible. Ruth Katherine Byrns (1931), an educational psychologist, objected to the "almost unchal-lenged attempt to carry over into these [psychological and educational] studies the methods and techniques used in the purely physical sciences" (p. 184). She especially found fault with behaviorism for its "rejection of introspection,

---

[10] Gruender's work will be discussed further in Chapter 7.

experience, and opinion" (ibid.) in its desire "to be objective and scientific at any price" (p. 185). The scientific method in itself was not the problem, and Byrns conducted quantitative studies dealing with topics that included intelligence testing and academic achievement. The scientific method, however, "is not adequate as a means of studying human life, habits, and thoughts" (ibid.). The general position was that experimentation had its place, but that place had strict limits, and problems with experimentation arose when psychologists bent the human subject to fit into methodological Procrustean beds. Such criticism was not made only by Catholics; Gordon Allport (1940) stressed a similar point in his APA presidential address.

As an indication of the importance of psychology in Catholic circles, as well as the dangers of a misguided psychology, consider the "Preface" to *Introductory child psychology* (Kelly and Kelly, 1938) by Joseph Husslein, SJ[11] Husslein (1938) wrote that there was need of a child psychology text that "should take full cognizance of what is nominally at least the object of this study, the soul of the child" (p. ix). Husslein continued, seemingly condemning the book with faint praise: "For nineteen hundred years, now, the Church has been wisely familiar with every practical phase of psychology, without the label. Little has she to learn . . . from modern findings in this field, which in great part are rediscoveries of what she has benignly applied through the ages" (p. x). The child is no "mechanical automaton . . . no inert lump of matter quickened into motion by chemical and physical action and reaction only" (p. xi), reductionistic depictions repeated in modern textbooks "in the name of science" (ibid.). With such an attitude, not only critical of psychology but almost dismissive of it – ambivalently so, given that Husslein did publish it – it is hardly surprising that Catholic scientific psychologists would stress the autonomy of their research.[12]

The relationship between philosophical and scientific psychology

At the twelfth meeting of the American Catholic Philosophical Association in 1936, Neoscholastics debated the relationships between scientific and philosophical psychology. The variety of opinions illustrates the extent to which the autonomy of psychology was in question. In reiterating Cardinal Mercier's support for a physiological psychology, Joseph A. Schabert (1936) – of the College of St. Thomas in St. Paul, Minnesota – warned against apologetics in psychological texts (p. 105). All too often, Neoscholastic manuals "give the

[11] Husslein was the editor of *Science and culture texts*, a series of books for a broad Catholic audience.

[12] Husslein edited 213 books in his *A university in print*, including twelve by psychologists, including Gruender (1932), Francis Harmon (1951), Cavanagh and McGoldrick (1953), and others. See Werner (2001) for details on Husslein's work.

impression that they are trying to get the reader to believe something rather than help him to understand how man acts" (ibid.). For Schabert, psychology "does not belong to [n]or is it within philosophy. He advised projecting it against a background of Scholastic philosophy" (Weir, 1936, p. 109), because scholastically oriented psychology texts were academically isolated. Other participants claimed that psychology was leaving philosophy, while Louis J. A. Mercier[13] "was shocked at trying to separate psychology from philosophy" (p. 110). Harry McNeill,[14] who had a Louvain Ph.D. in psychology, "advised a separate department of psychology from the philosophy in the schools, or, if such is not possible, at least to put it in the hands of one individual. He advocated the establishment of laboratories" (p. 111). In contrast, "Father Barnhart, of St. Bonaventure ... approved an introductory course in experimental psychology which would lead up to the theory of the soul" (p. 110). This exchange illustrates the range of positions within the Neoscholastic community before World War II, and it indicates the active character of the boundary-work, both intellectual and institutional, in Catholic higher education. The debaters shared a common ground in their faith and on the philosophical foundations for psychology. The field of possibilities for scientific psychology was restricted to detailed empirical studies, but if psychology had to reiterate Neoscholastic formulations, Catholic psychologists would not get a hearing from their non-Neoscholastic peers. Hence the stress by McNeill and others on separate academic departments. Psychologists could also rally around methodological issues, as they helped mark the boundary between psychology and philosophy.

A leading Neoscholastic psychologist in North America was Robert Edward Brennan, OP (1897–1975). Brennan insisted on the link between the philosophical and the empirical sides of the discipline. According to Brennan (1940a), "Science progresses by a transition to new and better knowledge, often discarding the old as false or unsatisfactory. Philosophy, on the other hand, progresses by a richer and deeper understanding of principles that are already known" (p. 163). Scientific psychology contributes primarily details to the philosophical structure that gives psychology its moorings (a position we have already seen with Mercier and Siegfried): "Since psychology is simultaneously a branch of science and a branch of philosophy, there is the immediate possibility of uniting both its scientific and its philosophic analyses in one continuous doctrine in which philosophy will answer the fundamental

---

[13] Louis Joseph Alexandre Mercier (1880–1953) taught comparative philosophy and literature. In 1936, he was on the faculty of Harvard University. He was a member of the American Catholic Philosophical Association executive council in 1935–6. He was not related to Cardinal Mercier, to my knowledge.

[14] Harry V. McNeill had an undergraduate degree from St. Joseph's Seminary, Dunwoodie, where, after the modernist controversy, Neoscholastic philosophy reigned supreme. In 1936, he was teaching psychology at Fordham University.

questions . . . and science will resolve in detail the phenomenal character" of human activity (ibid.).

Brennan's remarks might vindicate the assumption that the Neoscholastics really were dogmatists. It is important, then, given that psychology is no stranger to dogmatism, to consider the justification for the Neoscholastics' position regarding the philosophical foundations of scientific psychology. For them, both philosophical and scientific psychologies are grounded in experience; that is, they are, in distinct ways, empirical. The difference is that scientific psychology develops from a special type of experience – the experiment – which enables more precision and control than is possible in ordinary experience. The basis of philosophy is also experience, more specifically "public experience," as Brennan described it in *Thomistic psychology* (1941), which all people share "by virtue of their senses" (p. 51), echoing Michael Maher (1918/1933), the author of the first Neoscholastic textbook in English, *Psychology: Empirical and rational*. Maher consistently appealed "to each man's inner experience" (p. 21) to support claims such as the human ability to introspect or to form abstract concepts. That the basis of philosophical psychology is public experience meant that anyone could potentially verify the findings of philosophical inquiry by testing them against personal experience. Three consequences followed from this: (1) No special scientific or philosophical training is needed to verify philosophical findings – this in contrast to the distinction between experts and laity that came to dominate scientific psychology (see Morawski, 1996). (2) Scientific psychologists carry with them into the laboratory the common experience which provides the raw material for their investigations. How could psychologists study learning or thinking, if they did not already have some pre-scientific acquaintance with them? Experimental investigations thus draw on the same source as do philosophical inquiries, and it is important that the scientist have clear concepts of their topics. Hence, scientists depend upon prior philosophical investigation. (3) While experimentation clarifies and specifies psychological phenomena, it does not change the basic philosophical findings. As James E. Royce (1961) argued, philosophical conclusions are independent of scientific inquiry. A set of data could prove neither a materialist nor an idealist position; in order for either position to oust a Neoscholastic one, they would have to be argued in philosophical terms. Not all Neoscholastic psychologists shared the easy confidence of Maher, Brennan, and Royce on this point. Johannes Lindworsky (1875–1939), for example, sought to develop a theoretical psychology independent of metaphysical considerations (Misiak and Staudt, 1954, p. 115). Lindworsky (1931) emphasized that the ancients and medievals wove but a few common experiences into metaphysical systems, so that we cannot assume that even the basic common experiences have been gathered. While Lindworsky sought to establish a theoretical psychology on its own terms, he did not attempt integration of scientific and philosophical psychology, as did many Neoscholastics. However, as Misiak and Staudt indicated, Lindworsky "assumed that such integration was beyond dispute" (1954, p. 124). That the ground of philosophical and scientific psychology was not fixed in stone became a point of departure in the subsequent development of this tradition, as we shall see below, when we turn to the breakup of the Neoscholastic tradition in psychology.

If one assumes, with the Neoscholastics, the autonomy of scientific psychology and its subordination to philosophical psychology, the way is clear for the development of a scientific tradition in psychology, both academic and applied. To that tradition we now turn.

Empirical Neoscholastic psychology

Academic Neoscholastic psychology

Neoscholastic psychology grew in the soil of American Catholic higher education, a system that was modernized in the early twentieth century along with the rest of higher education (Gleason, 1995). As older curricula, such as the Jesuits' century's old system of humanistic education – the *ratio studiorum* – gave way to one divided into departments and majors, with elective courses, psychology gradually gained a place.[15] As in non-Catholic higher education, at first psychology courses belonged in philosophy departments, but by the end of the 1960s independent psychology programs were the norm.[16] The writings of many Neoscholastic psychologists reflected and often promoted the administrative division of labor. In this section, we look at the branches of Neoscholastic psychology, beginning with academic writings, particularly textbooks, which show the most evident traces of the philosophical tradition. In addition to the textbooks, there appeared a body of scientific investigations that had a Neoscholastic philosophical background. Beyond this scientific basis, moreover, were Neoscholastic contributions to applied psychology, in such areas as psychotherapy and school counseling.

The textbook tradition

Textbooks are indicators of the received judgment of an intellectual community. They are the doors through which new members enter and, by defining the

---

[15] The history of the *ratio studiorum* (method of study) of the Jesuits has a much more complex history than can be addressed here. It dates from 1599 and had been changed many times, including in the nineteenth century. It was based on Greek and Latin classics and on a unity of education, defended by many American Jesuits well into the twentieth century. That it is still a topic in Jesuit education the book *The Jesuit Ratio Studiorum* (Duminuco, 2000) makes clear.

[16] Some of this history is treated in greater detail in Chapter 7.

discipline, mark what belongs and what does not. Textbooks tell students who they are and who they aspire to be (Morawski, 1996; Weiten and Wight, 1992). For the Neoscholastics, textbooks laid the foundations for all thinking in psychology. Differences among the texts show the tensions within Neoscholastic thought between those which emphasized the subordination of scientific psychology to philosophy (integrationalist texts), and those which emphasized the autonomy of scientific investigation, still within Neoscholastic lines, leaving it for others to complete an integration (autonomist texts).

Because of Neoscholastic psychology's position of hylomorphism, experimentation and quantification were valuable means for making psychology scientific. All the same, four Neoscholastic concepts differentiated this psychology from the mainstream of empiricist American psychology: (1) the existence of distinct psychological abilities, factors, capacities or, to use the older terms, faculties; (2) the originality of thought in relation to sensation; (3) freedom of will, however hemmed in by temperament and environment; and (4) the centrality of the study of the person or, in scientific psychological terms, personality and character. All four characteristics were implications of the Neoscholastic conception of the soul. The textbooks oriented the student by presenting these foundational concepts, and then by interpreting scientific findings by showing them to be instances of the concepts already presented.

Perhaps the most influential of integrationist textbooks used in the United States appeared in 1890 in the first of nine editions: Michael Maher's *Psychology*. Maher (1860–1918), a Jesuit who taught at Stonyhurst, an English Catholic public school, divided his text into two basic sections, Empirical and Rational Psychology. This division derived, of course, from rationalist thought, not the Scholastic tradition. Empirical psychology examined the powers of the soul, starting with sensation and the inner senses (imagination, memory, etc.), and proceeding to conception, attention, and volition. Rational psychology addressed the substantiality and immortality of the soul, and evaluated non-scholastic rational psychologies, such as Cartesian dualism and materialism. From edition to edition, Maher updated the suggested readings, citing, for example, Ebbinghaus on memory and Michotte and Prüm on will, without substantially altering his presentation.[17]

Other examples of this integrationist approach were Robert Edward Brennan (1937; 1941) and Francis J. Donceel (1955). Brennan covered essentially the same material as Maher, with chapters dealing with the powers of the soul,

---

[17] The fourth edition of Maher's book was reviewed in the American magazine, *Catholic World*, in 1901. The reviewer praises "the extensive consideration given to the modern or experimental school, something too often neglected by Catholics. Some have thought the school at least materialistic in tendency, if not essentially irreligious . . .. but we must not mistake the interpretations put on the results of modern research for the results themselves" (Talk about new books, 1901, p. 817).

differentiating between the science and the philosophy of (for example) intellectual life. Brennan presented more scientific studies than did Maher and, in fact, broadened his definition of scientific psychology between 1937 and 1941. *General psychology* (1937) still emphasized introspection as the method of study for scientific psychology, but *Thomistic psychology* (1941) defined psychology as "a study of the acts, powers, and habits of man" (p. 50). Donceel (1955) included considerable treatment of scientific psychology in a text intended for philosophy courses, keeping to the Neoscholastic outline of the soul's powers for chapter organization. Brennan and Donceel emphasized the topic of the human person more than Maher. This development represents a shift from the earlier Neoscholastic approach, which had focused on the soul and its faculties, to a more phenomenological trend, which emphasized the person as such.

Gruender, well known for his *Psychology without a soul* and a 1920 textbook, later wrote in *Experimental psychology* (1932) that all too often, psychologists claim to avoid philosophical discourse, but then make philosophical claims dogmatically. Gruender recognized the boundaries of experimental research, but he did "not attempt the impossible" (p. 12) of never engaging in philosophical discussion. He conceded the importance of the observation of behavior, but only as a supplement to controlled introspection. As was typical of the Neoscholastics, Gruender also included ordinary self-observation as an important source of psychological data. Indeed, noted Gruender, experimentation relies on ordinary experience; otherwise language could not be used in experimentation. That being said, half of Gruender's text focused on topics of sensation and on what in the Neoscholastic tradition are called the inner senses: attention, memory, and imagination. After chapters on instinct and thought, he concluded with the will, focusing on researches of Narciss Ach, Albert Michotte and E. Prüm, and others. Much of this final chapter deals with the empirical and philosophical approaches to the question and meaning of the freedom of the will. He criticized John B. Watson and Edward B. Titchener for their theories, which he considered unable to account for the results of studies such as those of Ach and Michotte. Because Gruender differentiated between scientific and philosophical psychology, he had a clear sense of what belonged to each.

Pace's student, Thomas Verner Moore, wrote textbooks that systematically integrated Neoscholastic themes while still emphasizing scientific psychology. Moore made an important contribution to Neoscholastic psychology by defining psychology as "the science of the human personality" (1924, p. 9). He directed considerable attention to psychodynamics, emphasizing the importance of impulses and drives, as well as the ultimate freedom of the human will.[18] Whereas Moore kept the various strands of scientific psychology,

---

[18] Boring (1950) suggested that "dynamic psychology seems to fit more readily than other psychologies into the milieu of the Catholic Church, which, being concerned with human responsibility, is especially interested in the nature of human motives" (p. 693). The work

philosophy, and even theology together in his texts, those of the following generation tended to emphasize either philosophical psychology (Royce, 1961) or scientific psychology. I call the latter works "autonomist" texts, since they stressed scientific psychology, and they did not tend to elaborate the philosophical foundations or implications, as did Maher's or Brennan's. Francis L. Harmon's *Principles of psychology* (1938; 1951) reflected his interests in both applied psychology and Neoscholastic philosophy. Harmon had studied with Albert Poffenberger at Columbia, receiving a Ph.D. in 1933. Teaching at St. Louis University, he took a leave and studied philosophy at Louvain in 1938, around the time that his *Principles* first appeared in Husslein's series. Harmon laid out his Neoscholastic principles at the beginning of his text, after which he devoted an entire section to individual differences, with a long chapter on psychological testing. In Timothy Gannon's (1954) text, *Psychology: The unity of human nature*, we see psychology defined along Moore's lines, although he specified "the science of personality" in these terms: "Psychology is the study of the whole range of human experience and behavior insofar as it manifests the reactions of a single, living person to changes within himself and in his environment" (p. 27). Alexander A. Schneiders' (1951) *Introductory psychology* was subtitled, *The principles of human adjustment*, reflecting his interests in counseling, adolescence, as well as personality development generally. *Introductory psychology* began with methodological issues, then turned to personality and adjustment, followed by chapters on sensation, perception, imagery, thought, learning, and memory. The last sections of the text deal with motivation and emotion, and finally on the applications of psychology. The Neoscholastic stress on intellect and will is evident in all these texts, even when they explicitly stress scientific psychology. The philosophical background made a difference.

Sister Annette Walters, CSJ[19] (1910–78) held a 1941 Ph.D. in psychology from the University of Minnesota. She was a driving force within the ACPA and an Executive Secretary of Sister Formation Conference, an organization devoted to advancing the education of American nuns. With Sister Kevin O'Hara, she wrote *Persons and personality: An introduction to psychology* (1953), and she also edited *Readings in psychology* (Walters, 1964). In *Persons and personality*, three aspects of human beings were singled out as relevant to psychology: the person (the essence of who one is, by virtue of our having souls), personality (deals with the "accidents" in the Aristotelian sense of who we are, and character ("the ethical and social concept" (p. 6)). In keeping with this focus, the text had presented psychology in terms of development and adjustment. Walters later wrote in *Readings in psychology* "that psychology is

of Thomas Verner Moore and Magda Arnold, in my opinion the leading Neoscholastic psychologists, supports Boring's contention.
[19] CSJ, Sisters of St. Joseph, a teaching order.

unique among the theoretical branches of knowledge in that it belongs to two disciplines at the same time, that of science and that of metaphysics" (p. xiii). This is a book of readings for college students, which included Neoscholastic philosophical psychologists as well as Catholic and non-Catholic empirical psychologists and psychoanalysts. These texts illustrated how scientific and philosophical psychologies could co-exist.

The experimental tradition

Misiak and Staudt (1954) surveyed the important early experimental work done by Neoscholastically-oriented psychologists, although for the reasons stated at the beginning of this chapter, they did not identify a distinct school. The investigations of the Louvain psychologists, Thiéry, Michotte (especially his early work), and Joseph Nuttin, all had Neoscholastic foundations, as did those of Pace, Moore, and Moore's students at the Catholic University of America. Like Moore, many early Neoscholastics – including Gruender – were sympathetic to the Würzburg school, because of its distinction between sensing and thinking, and the Würzburgers' studies of willing. That experimental studies were part of the Neoscholastic approach is evident from the inclusion of three such studies in a *Festschrift* for Pace (Hart, 1932). The first, by Moore (1932a), is a study of associative learning, with an effort to determine empirically the best mathematical formula to describe the data. In Thomistic terms memory is a sensory and thinking an intellectual power, distinct from the sensory although related to it. So Moore concluded by contrasting associative learning with the general factor of intelligence, g, as derived by Charles Spearman. The contrast for Moore was evidence of the Neoscholastic distinction between sense and intellect: correlation between his measure of associative learning and g was small, leading Moore to state that "the power of association . . . is not cognitive ability" (p. 221). In a quantitative study of "Character and body build in children," Sister M. Rosa McDonough (1932), a graduate of Moore's doctoral program, correlated anthropomorphic measurements with the results of various psychological tests. "The moral development of children" by Sister Mary, IHM (1932) reported the results of her dissertation, which was based on a study of 4,500 school children. As studies in educational psychology, they showed the range of Neoscholastic thought in empirical directions.

In addition to these specific studies, a generation of doctoral students at centers for Neoscholastic psychology produced their own. Such centers included the Catholic University of America, St. Louis University, Loyola University of Chicago, Fordham University, and the University of Montreal (where Noël Mailloux established a psychology program with a Neoscholastic foundation, and where Brennan taught for a time). These doctoral dissertations may not have all emphasized that foundation, precisely because of the Neoscholastic position granting autonomy to scientific inquiry. To the extent that a subsequent generation of psychologists did not receive an education in philosophical psychology, which was more likely after the decline of Neoscholastic thought in the 1960s, this experimental work eased into the scientific mainstream inconspicuously.

Neoscholastic cognitive psychology

In a series of studies, culminating in our work *Cognitive Psychology*, our laboratory has attempted to throw light on the *intellectual* life of man, the very existence of which is commonly denied in modern experimental psychology.

Moore (1948, p. 43)

To get a clearer view of the scope of Neoscholastic empirical psychology, we turn to the investigations into cognition by Moore and his students in the first decades of the twentieth century. Given the distinction between sense and intellect in the Scholastic tradition, it is not surprising that studies along these lines became central in Neoscholastic empirical psychology. The most important contribution to the study of cognition from the Neoscholastics was Thomas Verner Moore's *Cognitive psychology* (1939), which has received significant attention.

Before beginning, a brief word on the relationship between Moore's cognitive psychology and contemporary studies under that heading. Knapp (1985) describes Moore's work as "strangely contemporary" (p. 1315) in its topics and methods, and although it belongs to an earlier period in psychology's history, he points to its value as "alternate cognitive formulation" (ibid.) of psychology that developed, "though perhaps only in Thomistic circles" during the heyday of behaviorism. Surprenant and Neath (1997) find some of Moore's work still relevant to contemporary cognitive psychology, even if "his dynamic and Thomistic views are not as congenial to most cognitive psychologists as his constructivist position" (p. 347). Those "views" indicate the significant differences from the contemporary objects of psychological investigation, as they enabled Moore to move from empirical investigations to the metaphysics of the soul. Finally, Green (1996) argues that the "cognitive" in contemporary cognitive psychology owes much to early twentieth-century Anglo-American ethics and to logical positivism, in that it is concerned with "aspects of the mental that . . . are susceptible to truth-evaluation." Moore's cognitive psychology is a variety of the older "mentalism" in psychology, from this point of view. Moore (1939) did ground his studies of cognition in that of consciousness as "the prime fact of all experience" (p. 3).

Moore's cognitive psychology

Moore received a Ph.D. at the Catholic University in 1903 under Edward Aloysius Pace, with his dissertation, *A study in reaction time and movement.* Afterward, in 1904, he worked in Wundt's lab, although this research, *The process of abstraction: An experimental study* (Moore, 1910), was completed only in the United States after he recovered from tuberculosis. He began teaching philosophy at the Catholic University in 1909, and in 1910 he obtained an appointment in psychology. He visited Lightner Witmer, who coined the term "clinical psychology," in the winter of 1909–10, because of his interest in establishing a clinic similar to the one at the University of Pennsylvania. Moore decided that he needed to study medicine prior to establishing his own clinic. He first returned to Germany and worked in Külpe's laboratory on imagery and meaning, and in 1915, back in Washington, he completed an M.D. in psychiatry with Adolf Meyer. As founder and head of the Department of Psychology and Psychiatry, he directed much research and he published widely. He remained on the faculty at the Catholic University until 1947 (see Neenan, 2000, for a book-length biography).

In accord with the basic Neoscholastic position that the basic powers or faculties of the soul were intellectual and appetitive, two of Moore's important books were *Dynamic psychology* (1924) and *Cognitive psychology* (1939). In the latter, Moore emphasized differences between sensation and cognition, and he argued for a faculty psychology, stressed by the Thomists and attacked by empiricists. Moore and his students (Barrett, 1941; Loughran, 1919; McDonough, 1919; Monaghan, 1935), and others (Gruender, 1937; Mailloux, 1942) agreed on these basic points. The question that haunted them in American psychological circles was whether their philosophical position predetermined the results of their empirical work. To this question we turn after presenting the scope and results of Neoscholastic cognitive psychology.

The organization of *Cognitive psychology*

Moore defined "cognitive psychology" as "that branch of general psychology which studies the way in which the human mind receives impressions from the external world and interprets the impressions thus received" (p. v). *Cognitive psychology* is a textbook, and it has a comprehensive tone. Moore explicitly included both psychiatric and philosophical aspects of cognition, reflecting his stance on the unity of psychology and psychiatry on the one hand, and psychology and philosophy on the other.

Despite his Neoscholastic basis, one gets the sense from the very first section of *Cognitive psychology* that something else is going on as well. He began neither with the soul and its faculties nor with the distinction between empirical and rational psychology, as Neoscholastic texts often did. Instead, Moore discussed consciousness and the nervous system, focusing on psychological disorders, such as multiple personalities, and the psychological consequences of brain pathology, because these topics also address the nature of consciousness. Then he turned to perception, with a long section on the history of theories of perception, before examining the psychology and pathology of sensation and perception. Building on that, discussions of the intellect and memory follow, weaving together experimental and psychiatric material. The book concludes on a metaphysical note, with an analysis of the mind–body problem, and on psychological faculties and their demonstration by means of factor analysis. As we shall see, this final section, rather than being a philosophical "add-on," reflected instead his understanding of the nature of consciousness and reason.

Moore's experimental studies of cognition

Turning to Moore's own research, we begin with *The process of abstraction*, research begun at Leipzig. Moore narrowed the question of the origin of abstract ideas to one of recognizing a common element in a group of visual figures that the experimental subject saw but briefly. In the experiments, the basic design was as follows: the subjects viewed groups of five nonsense figures for 0.25 seconds with a 0.25 second interval between each of the 25 groups. The subject was to stop the rotation "as soon as he was certain that he had seen some figure repeated" (p. 119). Then, he was "to describe his state of mind during the experiment, and especially to tell what it was that he first noticed" (p. 120). Among his results, several stand out: first, mental images of the common element were unessential to its recognition; for Moore, images functioned like illustrations in a novel. Second, subjects said that they first saw *that* something was familiar but recognition was only complete when a judgment, which need not have been verbalized, took place. For Moore, "the chief factor" in percep- tion, enabling recall and recognition, is the concept to which the things seen are assimilated. These concepts are not images, and Moore concluded that his work supported the notion of imageless thought.

This study was emblematic of others that Moore conducted over the next decade. Perhaps his most influential research was on "The temporal relations of meaning and imagery" (Moore, 1915) and "Image and meaning in memory and perception" (Moore, 1919b), carried out initially in Külpe's Munich lab (with Külpe as one of his subjects), and completed in Washington (where Pace was one of the subjects). Moore combined a quantitative study of reaction time with introspective reports. The experimenter presented objects, pictures, and written and spoken words by various means and instruments, with the subjects releasing a telegraph key when they recognized that the word or drawing represented a real something (nonsense words and drawings were used as a control). Different tasks were put before the subjects, such as to indicate when they had the meaning of the object represented, or to indicate when they had a mental image of the object. The results were shorter reaction times to meanings than to images. According to Moore, a meaning indicated "a definite mental process *sui generis*" (1915, p. 225). He developed a theory of meaning as a mental structure different from sensations, images, and feelings, the product of the mental function of perception, which occurs outside of consciousness (1919b, pp. 184–7).

What is a "meaning," then? According to Moore (1939), a meaning has a general character, in contrast to a particular one; by contrast, sensations refer only to particulars. Meaning has no sensory qualities, and it is often expressed in a definition. Meaning is not localized in space-time. A meaning is considered necessary to the perceptual act, whereas a memory image is experienced as unessential to the act. In short, the meaning is a "thought-content" (Moore, 1919b, p. 221), a concept. In drawing out the philosophical implications of this finding, Moore (1939, pp. 555–9) argued for the Thomistic view of the human soul, according to which the concept is a purely spiritual activity, requiring no bodily organ. Moore argued against the empiricist view, as expressed by Titchener, that images in the context or fringe of another image were the meaning of that image. Titchener referred to kinaesthetic images especially as this context. For Titchener, a meaning was not a mental structure nor did imageless thought take place, as the Würzburgers and Moore maintained.

Experimental studies in response to Moore's experimental work

Such studies in perception and meaning were widely conducted in the first decades of the twentieth century. Moore's finding that meaning is a mental structure distinct from the image provoked further study. Edward Chase Tolman (1917), in his first published study, modified Moore's 1915 study on imagery and meaning. Tolman found that for some subjects, reaction time to imagery was briefer than to meaning, suggesting to Tolman a "compromise position" (between Titchener and Moore) "that 'meaning' depends upon image but is itself distinct from the latter" (p. 138). This statement, vague though it be, did restate the basic Aristotelian view. Moore (1917) in reply found Tolman's results did not disconfirm his own findings, which he contrasted to the Aristotelian theory. It is important to note that Moore corrected, in his own mind, Aristotle and Aquinas on the basis of experimentation. Studies counter to Moore's were carried out along Titchenerian lines by Harry Porter Weld (1877–1958) and also by the future quasi-Gestaltist, Raymond H. Wheeler (1892–1961). Weld (1917) found shorter reaction times for imagery for some subjects, to which Moore (1919, pp. 172–4) replied that that represented experimental conditions and did not refute his view. Wheeler (1923) criticized both Moore's research methods, which were those of Külpe, arguing that "an analytical attitude" during introspection would have resolved Moore's imageless meanings into kinaesthetic sensations and images. Wheeler thereby claimed to have vindicated the sensationalism that Moore had attacked. Wheeler proposed his own theory of meaning as the overt or covert response to stimuli. I have not identified a specific reply by Moore to Wheeler, but Moore (1924; 1939) in various places argued against the kinaesthetic theory of meaning.

Moore (1939) later noted that psychology's interest in thought had waned after this period. Later work on thinking, from the time during Moore's lifetime, however, found room for Moore's studies. George Humphrey (1889–1966), summarizing some fifty years of research on cognition in *Thinking* (1951), concluded that while Moore and the Würzburgers were correct in their critiques of the Titchenerian position, the former underestimated the role of the image. Humphrey concluded, therefore, that "we may think a proposition . . . in such a way that the activity in question falls within none of the sensory modalities" (p. 129). This conclusion did not lead him to a Neoscholastic view of the soul, however. Floyd Allport (1955), in reviewing previous studies of meaning – he mentioned Moore but reversed his results on image and meaning – concluded that meaning was still poorly understood in psychology (p. 575).

Moore's statistical studies

In the 1930s, Moore turned increasingly to statistic studies of the results of objective tests (for example, Moore, 1931, 1932b, 1933; Neenan, 2000, p. 179). When Moore studied in Wundt's lab, he met Charles E. Spearman (1863–1945). Moore took up Spearman's statistical methods of factor analysis in the study of intelligence, personality factors, and symptoms of mental illness. For Moore, Spearman's studies – and further research done by Moore and his students – demonstrated a number of things. First of all, "The work of Spearman and his school tends in general to accentuate a fundamental difference between sentience and the eduction of relations in which Spearman seeks the essential nature of judgment" (Moore, 1939, pp. 359–60).[20] Second, statistical analysis supported the idea that "one thing, whatever its nature, underlies a goodly number of cognitive operations" (Moore, 1929, p. 29). Third, factor analysis favored a faculty theory of mind. Moore found in Louis Leon Thurstone's (1887–1955) development of factor analysis a development of Spearman's work. Thurstone cited Moore's work in his important essay, "The vectors of mind" (1934), agreeing with its basic thrust to use factor analysis to discern basic psychiatric symptoms.

Danziger (1990) writes that many psychologists "claimed that their statistical findings reflected on the nature of fundamental human functions or capacities" (p. 150), believing that their techniques were "theory-neutral" (p. 152). Moore held to this position, and it was one of the weaknesses of his approach, one that would lead the following generation of Neoscholastically-trained psychologists to repeat the divorce of psychology

---

[20] Moore tried to bring Spearman to the Catholic University faculty in the 1930s, and Spearman did come as a visiting professor in 1932 (Neenan, 2000, p. 179).

from philosophy that their non-Scholastic peers had largely made a generation earlier. Yet Moore did not claim that theory was irrelevant in statistics. He argued (1934) that to understand the distribution of values around a mean in psychological testing, one must take into account the workings of formal causality, namely, the intention of the person to do the test. He concluded that "the mental testing movement has advanced far beyond the progress of sound psychological theory. Its further development awaits a much needed advance in the psychology and philosophy of the mind" (1939, p. 603). As important as statistical studies were in Moore's research program, he noted that "though mathematics enables us to demonstrate the existence of mental faculties and to give a descriptive definition of them, philosophy is necessary for a satisfactory study of their essential nature" (1948, pp. 37–8).

Cognitive studies from the Catholic University of America

The Catholic University of America produced a number of doctorates with dissertations in Moore's line of research. One relatively early study done by Agnes McDonough (1919), a student of Moore, looked at "The development of meaning." Using Weld's (1917) design, subjects were presented with unfamiliar words together with illustrations, with subjects asked to indicate when they had either the meaning or an image under different conditions. McDonough found a difference between meaning and image, with the former becoming more important as subjects became familiar with the words, and the image faded in significance. In addition, as subjects got to know the words, "the meaning follows so suddenly on the exposition of the card that subjects confess difficulty in describing what actually took place in consciousness" (p. 463). McDonough concluded noting the significance of memory and experience in the development of meaning, and that meaning is one of the "structures of mind" (p. 475). Edward Aloysius Monaghan (1935) used a variety of mental tests, many of which had been developed at the Catholic University in the previous years, and analyzed factors of cognition, memory, and attention, underlying which was what he called a "super-general factor common to all groups" (p. 36). To explain this finding, he pointed to the formal cause of the individual's efforts in doing the tests. Sister Mary Constance Barrett (1941) studied the imagination, combining a review of philosophical and psychological literature with an empirical investigation, using simple tests of memory and imagination with school children. Factor analysis, according to the author, distinguished the two faculties. While not a sophisticated study in one sense, in another it showed remarkable range, presenting Aquinas on the inner sense, the views of contemporary Neoscholastics, as well as modern psychological literature. These three studies illustrate the direction of empirical research taken along Neoscholastic lines.

Neoscholastic psychology's investigative practices

Moore's Neoscholastic cognitive psychology had a well-defined philosophical and theoretical basis, it used empirical methods widely practiced in the psychologies of the day, it had a home in higher education, it produced publications, and its findings were taken seriously by important contemporaries. Moore helped to train a generation or more of psychologists who went on to found departments, enter applied areas of psychology, and found the American Catholic Psychological Association, which existed between 1947 and 1970. However, it failed in its efforts to turn North American psychology from its primarily empiricist grounding toward an Aristotelian one. It failed to get the soul reinstated to pride of place in psychology. To understand the complex development and legacy of this tradition, Danziger's (1990) approach is helpful, looking at the "investigative practices" of psychology, that is, the actual activities of psychologists within their social contexts. Danziger distinguishes three concentric circles of such social contexts: the experimental situation, the research community, and the professional environment (p. 7). To understand Neoscholastic psychology's investigative practices, this scheme will have to be elaborated. Ignoring for present purposes the narrowest circle, that of the actual experiments, I turn first to the second circle, the research community, and then to the third circle, that of the wider Catholic community. In the second circle, Neoscholastics faced three groups: other Neoscholastic psychologists, Neoscholastic philosophical psychologists and philosophers, and the American psychological community. The first of these three was the smallest, residing primarily at Catholic colleges and universities, and they were primarily priests and nuns. With them, Moore and others shared much, including a sense of minority identity as Catholics in a predominantly Protestant country often hostile to Catholics.

The philosophical psychologists, also academics and primarily clergymen, did not concede that psychology was primarily a natural scientific discipline. As we have seen, they viewed empirical investigation, because it deals with particulars, as inferior to philosophical psychology, which dealt with universals, higher things than particulars. Philosophy was the more fundamental science. As Brennan (1940a) noted, scientific experiences cannot establish or repeal "the basic propositions of philosophical psychology" (p. 163). So in principle, this second group could evaluate the scientific psychologists, but the latter group could not evaluate the former, except when doing so on philosophical grounds. We have seen how Moore disputed this claim, but in the years before the Second Vatican Council (1962–5), the Neoscholastic philosophical psychologists held the trump card, namely, Vatican support for Scholasticism as the Catholic philosophy. The complex relationships between these two groups, the scientific and the philosophical psychologists within the Neoscholastic tradition, took place in different contexts, for example, in often contentious efforts to establish scientific psychology in Catholic colleges and universities.

Was Moore's psychology too Thomistic? Sufficiently Thomistic?

Robert J. Kantor (1940) reviewed *Cognitive Psychology* and found, not unpredictably, that it suffered a serious defect scientifically: "it must be a foregone conclusion that all factual evidences coordinate with the original scholastic premises" (p. 249). Peter Hampton (1941) seconded this verdict in another review. This indeed was the opinion of many, and it was one against which Neoscholastic psychologists fought. When Misiak and Staudt wrote *Catholics in psychology*, it was in part to show that Catholics, which meant at that time mainly Neoscholastically-trained psychologists, could be "real" scientists, just like the rest. But one thing separated the bulk of the Neoscholastic psychologists from many other psychologists, and that was that they did not divorce psychology from philosophy. The philosophical questions lurked always near the surface and they had to address them.

If they did not address them, someone from their other constituency, namely Neoscholastic philosophers, would bring them up. While Barrett's (1941) dissertation concluded by affirming the Thomistic account of memory and imagination, she pointed out that in the twentieth century, discord proceeds apace in the Neoscholastic community "on account of differences in the evaluation and interpretation of experimental evidence unknown to the older Scholastics" (p. 18). On matters of faith, however, there was no discord, at least not among the psychologists. This group did not publicly dispute Vatican pronouncements, even where, as in the modernist crisis of the early twentieth century, psychological topics could have been at issue. Moreover, canon law, codified in 1918, explicitly denounced certain philosophical positions as contrary to the faith – such as materialism. The Neoscholastic psychologists were loyal churchmen in disputing materialistic and empiricistic interpretations of psychological research and in furthering a view that was deemed closest to Church teaching. Moore was a fine example of this approach.

At the same time, there was ample room for intellectual combat. Brennan (1940a) disputed much of the philosophical basis of *Cognitive psychology*. He disapproved of Moore's deviation from Scholastic terminology and argued that Moore got some of Thomas's terms wrong, especially in his treatment of the intellect, although he found Moore's evidence for the distinction between images and concepts convincing. Brennan criticized Moore's suggestion that mental testing will not develop without "advance in the psychology and philosophy of the mind" (Moore, 1939, p. 603). For Brennan, this statement violates a Scholastic principle which claims that philosophy is distinct from science in that the former has its ground in "public experience" (1940a, p. 163) and as helpful as science may be, it is not necessary for philosophy. Scientific psychology, in other words, could never overturn the philosophical anthropology of Aristotle or Aquinas. Moore, as we have seen, did dispute both Aristotle and Aquinas on the role of images in thinking, even as he affirmed the basic

Thomistic position differentiating sensing and thinking. Some of Brennan's criticisms of Moore stick, in particular where Moore gives a rather Cartesian definition of the person or personality as "a living, conscious, thinking substance" (Moore, 1939, p. 42), as opposed to a definition that included the body.

Noël Mailloux, like Brennan a Dominican, was involved in both empirical and applied psychology. Mailloux (1942) criticized Moore for deviating from Thomistic principles. He found Moore's account of perception too intellectualistic, indicting thereby Moore's account of the role of meaning in perception. Mailloux held that only a Scholastic theory fully accounted for the factual evidence, and he criticized Moore (and Agostino Gemelli) as Neoscholastics "who manipulate experimental techniques with perfect dexterity," but "as soon as they venture upon philosophical terrain, show signs of a too hasty and insufficient assimilation of the main Scholastic theses" (p. 272). In particular, Mailloux criticized Moore's theory of perception by contrasting it not with Aquinas's, but with that of Cajetan (1469–1534), the sixteenth-century theologian, commentator on Aquinas, and defender of Catholicism against Martin Luther.[21] For Cajetan and for Mailloux, there is a perceptual "thinking," the "cogitative power," which "attains the singular substance" (p. 280) but not the universal, distinct from a purely intellectual grasp. Hence the charge of "intellectualism" against Moore, whose concept of meaning, the result of the act of perception, did transcend the particular.

Moore replied to both Brennan and Mailloux in *The driving forces of human nature* (1948), saying, "Let us look up from the texts and commentaries at least long enough to have a glance at what is available in the present" (p. 45). He was attempting to "bring ancient truths into contact with the developments of the present" – Leo XIII's agenda for the Thomistic Revival – by doing empirical work rather than commentaries.

But there was more to it than this. It is, finally, a mistake to consider Moore's psychology, which was the template for many empirical Neoscholastically-oriented studies, purely Neoscholastic. It owed much to non-Thomistic psychology, especially Külpe's psychology and American functionalism. Most un-Scholastic of Moore was his emphasis on consciousness, a category arising with the empiricists and not the Scholastics. So Moore did not simply apply Aristotelian conceptions to empirical givens in a predetermined fashion. In

---

[21] "His commentaries on the *Summa Theologica*, the first in that extensive field, begun in 1507 and finished in 1522, are his greatest work and were speedily recognized as a classic in Scholastic literature. The work is primarily a defense of St. Thomas against the attacks of Scotus. In the third part it reviews the aberrations of the Reformers, especially Luther. The important relation between Cajetan and the Angelic Doctor was emphasized by Leo XIII, when by his Pontifical Letters of 15 October, 1879, he ordered the former's commentaries and those of Ferrariensis to be incorporated with the text of the *Summa* in the official Leonine edition of the complete works of St. Thomas, the first volume of which appeared at Rome in 1882" (Volz, 1908, p. 147).

this way, we see the influence of the surrounding psychological world in North America playing an active role in Moore's treatment of the subject. He had, of course, also to take notice of the Catholic theological community. In his attempts to address both the psychological and the philosophical community, insisting upon the validity of both approaches, he did not accommodate either group to its satisfaction.

The wider Catholic community – Applied Neoscholastic psychology

For the third circle, that of the professional environment, the Neoscholastics again faced a complex situation. In addition to whatever academic, governmental, and public groups that all academic psychologists faced, the Neoscholastics faced the Catholic community as well. Many of the Neoscholastic psychologists were members of the clergy, including Moore, Brennan, Mailloux, Barrett, and Gruender. By canon law, all that they published that dealt in any way with matters of faith and morals had to be allowed by their superiors. Thus we find Cognitive psychology had a nihil obstat by the censor of his order, J. Edward Rauth, and an imprimi potest by Moore's abbot, Edmund Kelly, in addition to ecclesiastical approval from the archdiocese of Baltimore (including the nihil obstat by Fulton J. Sheen, of the philosophy department at the Catholic University). Relationships here were complex. For example, Rauth, the Benedictine censor, was a younger member of Moore's Department of Psychology and Psychiatry, and an empirical researcher himself, investigating topics such as eidetic imagery, intelligence testing, and psychophysics.[22] John W. Stafford, CSV, a student of Albert Michotte, and the censor for The driving forces of human nature, had been appointed by Moore to teach psychology at the Catholic University and, at Moore's recommendation, was his successor as head of the department in 1947.[23] Fulton Sheen, well known outside of philosophy as a radio (and later an early television) celebrity with his program on Catholic teachings, was highly critical of psychoanalysis, and was vocally critical, in 1945, of how psychology was taught in Moore's department. Archbishop Michael J. Curley, who gave the imprimatur to Cognitive psychology, "occasionally chided Moore for his theories" (Neenan, 2000, p. 166). Archbishop Curley seemed a benign influence, as I read Neenan's account, but there was no guarantee that this needed to be the case. In any

---

[22] Rauth (1886–1945) had received a Ph.D. from the Catholic University of America in 1926, and was in the psychology department from 1922.

[23] CSV, the Clerics of Saint Viator, or Viatorians. Stafford did not continue Moore's efforts to integrate philosophical and empirical psychology, but moved the department "into the mainstream of American psychology education" (Neenan, 2000, p. 200), although the undergraduate study of psychology included a "coordinating seminar and reading list" that included Plato, Aristotle, the New Testament, Descartes, Wundt, etc. (Stafford, 1950).

event, being a member of the clergy meant for Moore and others that the Church hierarchy commanded respect and obedience.

Beyond this type of relationship, there were other ties. In her dissertation, Sister Miriam Reinhart (1931) acknowledged the support she had received from the "Rev. John J. Murphy, Diocesan Superintendent of Schools, Columbus, Ohio, and to the Sisters and children in the schools where the tests were administered" (p. v). Sister Mary Constance Barrett also had access to school children in her study of memory and imagination with permission of "the Very Reverend Monsignor J. Anthony, pastor of St. Teresa School, Cincinnati, Ohio, and the Sisters of Mercy" (Barrett, 1941, p. i), who taught there. Monaghan (1935) ran his series of tests to 450 ninth graders in six Detroit parochial schools, with the teachers administering them over a period of six weeks. Examples like this could be multiplied, and permission to participate must indicate that the schools and their pastors found the studies useful. Finally, Catholic colleges and universities appointed graduates of Moore's program, such as Timothy J. Gannon, who started the Psychology Department at Loras College in Dubuque, Iowa, in the 1930s.

Neoscholastic psychology had a strong applied component. By the 1930s, Catholic education saw the value of using psychological tests and counseling, although work in this area extended back at least to the 1920s (M'Graw and Mangold, 1929). Support from this third circle of Neoscholastic psychology's investigative practices enabled it to thrive. Sister Rose (1936) of St. Mary's Academy in Navoo, Illinois, argued for "a more scientific organized program of guidance" in Catholic high schools, in light of the rapid increase in the numbers of children attending high school and the demands of the modern economy. She called for intelligence testing as well as vocational testing and guidance. She cited a study of 130 schools, of which 36 used mental tests in vocational guidance. Brother Henry C. Ringkamp (1936) reported results of a guidance project organized by the Education Department of St. Louis University, which involved a battery of intelligence, aptitude, achievement, and personality tests given to high school students, concluding with a recommendation that all the Catholic high schools in St. Louis should adopt such a program.[24]

Moore had started a psychological clinic in 1916 in a Catholic hospital, and in 1937 it moved to the Catholic University as the Child Center (Misiak and Staudt, 1954, p. 195). Fordham University and Loyola University of Chicago opened similar centers before World War II. Still, M. Gertrude Reiman (1942) of the Catholic University's Psychology and Psychiatry Department could complain that Catholic education was slow to adopt mental testing and guidance clinics, in part because of fears of exposing children to "non-Catholic

---

[24] Ringkamp mentioned Walter G. Summers, SJ, chair of Fordham University's psychology department as an authority on vocational guidance.

principles" (p. 434). Moore (1936; 1940) engaged the debate, arguing for psychological services provided by Catholics, if only they received the education in psychology.[25]

In the 1940s, Eugenie A. Leonard (1946), of the Education Department of the Catholic University, reported the results of a survey she conducted on counseling programs in 1,156 Catholic high schools across the United States. Most of the teachers were religious (priests, brothers, nuns) and 86 percent of the schools had some kind of guidance program, with 86.6 percent of the schools using intelligence tests, with smaller percentages using achievement, aptitude, and personality tests, and 21 percent having "specialized counselors" (p. 281). This indicates widespread acceptance of psychology's conception of mental abilities, while at the same time providing a religious context for its use. For example, Leonard noted that 86 percent of the schools provided religious counseling, that is, guidance aimed at finding vocations to the religious life among the students, and that for Catholics, vocational guidance chiefly implied religious life. It would seem that the school administrators and the local clerical hierarchies, representatives of the widest circle in Neoscholastic psychology's investigative practices, to some extent came to trust psychology, and that Catholic higher education promoted it. Much of the work of Moore and his colleagues was directed at this audience, within which there remained mistrust and hostility to psychology.

I shall illustrate only briefly some of the other ways Neoscholastic psychologists contributed to applied areas. It seems clear, though, that a Neoscholastic foundation posed no barriers to applied psychology. As a result of demands for psychological services in Catholic communities, despite internal opposition, there were ample opportunities to make psychology useful.

Alexander A. Schneiders (1909–68) devoted considerable attention to mental health, especially among adolescents, and to mental testing (1963). For some years, Schneiders was a colleague of Charles Doyle, SJ at Loyola University of Chicago, which opened a child guidance clinic in 1941. At the University of Montreal, Mailloux (1953) described how in the context of a "Thomistic ideology, which has constantly played the role of a very actively integrating agent" (p. 1), the *Institut de psychologie* conducted training and research in clinical psychology. In addition, Institute members studied topics such as intelligence testing and public attitudes. Across the Atlantic, André Godin (1915–97) – who had an M.A. in psychology from Fordham – and others addressed psychological aspects of religious education and of moral and religious development. Sister Mary Amatora (1904–80) contributed significantly to educational psychology in the 1950s and 1960s. For example, in addition to her own research in child personality, she edited several special issues of the journal *Education* in the mid-1950s on topics such as Child Guidance (volume 74, no.

---

[25] This topic will be developed further in Chapter 7.

3), Teacher–Pupil Relationships (volume 75, no. 1), and The Exceptional Child in the Regular Classroom (volume 76, no. 2). She taught at St. Francis College in Fort Wayne, Indiana.

Perhaps the most prominent contributor to applied Neoscholastic psychology was Charles A. Curran (1913–78), who did post-graduate work with Carl Rogers (Wauck, 1980, p. 7) and wrote extensively on Rogers' nondirective or client-centered therapy. Curran's early work, *Counseling in Catholic life and education* (1952), had a clear Neoscholastic framework, and he tied together the Thomistic virtue of Counsel with the practice of counseling. He justified Rogers' nondirective approach by differentiating between three activities: (1) education, which deals with the generalities of living well; (2) guidance, which is group-specific education; and (3) counseling, which deals with a particular person facing unique life situations. In the counseling situation, the client's decisions are replies to the specific situation that a unique person faces, not simply application of rules. In Curran's later work (e.g. 1966) he sought a discourse other than the Neoscholastic, although one can see the conceptual continuities with his earlier efforts.

Psychiatrists made even further contributions in the applied field: Rudolf Allers (1941), James H. VanderVeldt and Robert P. Odenwald (1952), John R. Cavanagh and James B. McGoldrick (1953), Francis James Braceland (1963), and Conrad Baars (1970) are names worthy of note.[26]

Later experimental studies

Later experimental researches along Neoscholastic lines include Henryk Misiak's (1967) experimental studies of critical flicker-fusion and its clinical applications, and Magda Arnold's (1962) development of a system for measuring motivation using the Thematic Apperception Test. Arnold criticized the psychoanalytic assumptions of drives and wishes in the analysis of projective tests, stressing instead the whole personality and the person's cognitive grasp of his or her situation. In particular, she drew on the Thomistic categories of the "inner senses" without using the term, seeing imagination (and not the unconscious – which she characterized as the imagination acting without the individual's guiding it) as formative of the stories that reveal motivation and values. *Story Sequence Analysis* presented some of the dissertation research done under her direction at Loyola of Chicago, including that of Leo McCandlish (1958),[27]

---

[26] We shall return to some of these contributions in Chapter 7, when we look at the Guild of Catholic Psychiatrists.

[27] Leo McCandlish went on to have a career in clinical and forensic psychology and serving on the Diocese of Dallas marriage tribunal, after having taught psychology at the Catholic University in Puerto Rico.

who studied academic achievement and Thomas Leo Quinn (1962),[28] who investigated motivation among members of a religious order. Arnold's welding of Thomistic categories with modern psychological research and theory proved to be robust. While Arnold clearly articulated the Neoscholastic foundation of her empirical research, Misiak did not, stating repeatedly that psychologists insist "on barring any bias of philosophical doctrines from the domain of psychological research" (Misiak, 1961, p. 128). Nevertheless, this claim to be able to bar philosophical presuppositions from intruding into experimental research had its ground in Neoscholastic thought, as we have seen with Lindworsky, whom Misiak and Staudt (1954) cited with approval. Arnold, on the contrary, straightforwardly asserted the theoretical framework and its philosophical foundations, even if in terms more like Moore and less like Brennan.

The decline of Neoscholastic psychology

Within these contexts, religious and secular, natural scientific and philosophical, Moore and others forged psychological objects, such as meaning, cognition, faculties, and the soul. While we have focused on meaning, there were others, such as Moore's version of "personality," that also sought to bridge the scientific and the philosophical, the religious and the secular. While "meaning" and "personality" continue to thrive in psychological discourse, Moore's interpretations of them have not.

What all this meant for Neoscholastic cognitive psychology was that it fell on the rocky ground of mainstream American psychology, which largely ignored it. Even the dim interest in Moore in more recent cognitive psychology shows no interest in the implication that concepts, being immaterial, argue for the spiritual nature of the intellectual power of the soul, as it did for Moore. Moreover, these objects fell on the arid ground of Neoscholastic philosophical psychology, which had no real interest in the theoretical formulations of Moore or his colleagues.

Ironically, the greatest success of Neoscholastic cognitive psychology may have been its insistence on scientific method. For the generation following Moore, this emphasis, coupled with the major shifts in the Church and American psychology, provided a path for American Catholic psychologists to assimilate almost seamlessly into the broader and less problematic mainstream. That the Neoscholastic underpinning could be first downplayed, then ignored, and then discarded, suggests that the methodological commitments were not as theory-neutral as

---

[28] Quinn (Brother Michael Quinn, FSC) was born in 1922 and died in 2009. He taught psychology at Saint Mary's College in Moraga, California, from the 1950s and received his doctorate in psychology in 1963. He also served as president of St. Mary's during the 1960s.

Moore supposed. The earlier work of his group, with their taking up of the Würzburg approach, was compatible with a Neoscholastic framework, because the object of this type of investigative practice was the mind or consciousness itself (see Kusch, 1999). As Sister Miriam Reinhart (1931) explained it: "The Würzburg psychology of Külpe and his followers was a distinct improvement on the ancient psychology in which the psychologist analyzed his own mind and then wrote his psychology. Külpe insisted on the experimenter making use of a number of observers each one of whom was to give a detailed account of what went on in his own mind" (p. 1). Külpe's psychology was more compatible with the Neoscholastic but not completely so, since "consciousness" is not synonymous with "soul." Indeed, consciousness as a category arose after the development of scholasticism, and we saw that Moore did tread on Cartesian ground in his psychology of consciousness. We have seen how Moore was not simply Neoscholastic in his philosophical position, along this line. But there is an even larger gap between a Neoscholastic view and a statistical one, since statistics deal with aggregates, not with individuals, and it was the individual soul, and the soul as such, that was the real object of Neoscholastic psychology. For Moore, however, statistical analysis was impossible without an underlying theory and philosophy, and he argued for recognition of formal causality and the soul's faculties in his statistic studies. Moore's work constructed two bridges. The first was between Neoscholasticism and science, because Spearman's statistical methods seemed to confirm basic tenets of the philosophy. The second bridge, between the Neoscholastic psychologists and their peers in psychology, was the result of Moore's emphasis on statistics. But the increasing emphasis on statistical thinking had the effect of attenuating theoretical discourse. As a result of the division within Neoscholasticism between the empirically-minded and the philosophically-minded, Neoscholastic psychology undermined its own basic thrust.

When Misiak and Staudt published *Catholics in psychology* (1954), they included a frontispiece, a portrait of Cardinal Mercier, the "patron saint" of Catholic psychologists, so to speak. And the book received a "*nihil obstat*" from none other than "Mr. Psychology" himself (Stevens, 1968, p. 589), Edwin G. Boring (1954), who pointed out that Misiak and Staudt "conduct a gentle propaganda, for they believe strongly that there is no conflict at all [between Catholicism and science] and that the way to prove the fact of harmony is to show that Catholic psychologists do not feel the conflict and that their research does not show it" (p. xi). Yet eight years later, Misiak (1962) could still lament that "Catholic contributions ... to American psychology in the last seventy years, that is, since the establishment of experimental psychology at the Catholic University, have been meager and insignificant ... While philosophical psychology has always held a prominent place in the curricula of Catholic schools, scientific psychology was long neglected and rarely taught" (p. 21). The failure was seen, in large part, as one of education.

The limitations of Catholic higher education became a lively topic in the 1950s, and Neoscholastic philosophy as the integrating core of the curriculum came under attack. The theologian Gustave Weigel (1957), in a widely read article, criticized the teaching of philosophy at Catholic colleges as taught by rote and aimed at apologetics, leading to a deadening of student interest in philosophy. This was but one indication of discontent with Neoscholasticism, which Gleason (1995) describes in detail. Neoscholasticism came under fire for stifling the autonomy of academic disciplines, and for presuming the existence of a Thomistic synthesis in philosophy that historical research was showing never really existed. The psychologists' complaints were, then, part of this larger story.

The autonomy of psychology and of the Catholic psychologist

The independence of psychology from philosophical and theological discourse was much discussed. Moore (1948), in *The driving forces of human nature*, defended the use of terminology not derived from scholastic thought: "There is room for publications using a terminology that can be understood by the physicians and psychologists of the present day. Some Neoscholastic writers make their works unintelligible to modern readers by the use of highly specialized terminology" (p. 45, n. 112). He was responding to a critique of his earlier work, *Cognitive psychology* (1939), by Brennan, to which we referred earlier. For Brennan, psychology's autonomy is restricted, the psychologist needing the philosopher more than vice versa. This argument was repeated by Louis J. A. Mercier (1944) in a critique of a paper by John W. Stafford, CSV, Moore's successor at the Catholic University. Mercier stated that experimental psychology could not study the freedom of the will, because scientific psychology has a deterministic framework. He argued that because human nature is the composite of spirit and matter, another conception of psychology is needed: "What we need is evidently a distinctly humane or humanistic psychology recognized to be both physical and metaphysical which will devise a special methodology through which both the physical and metaphysical aspects of man can be studied" (p. 256). The object of psychological statements, from this corner, meant that psychology can never sever its ties with philosophy.

Misiak and Staudt (1954) sought to redefine the relationship between philosophical and scientific psychology, which is why they objected to Roback's assertion of a Neoscholastic *school* in psychology. Philosophical foundations do not unite psychologists; rather, "the methods, the tools, and the language we are going to use" provide the bonding material (p. 14). Catholics who are also psychologists can thus collaborate with their non-Catholic peers, even if the latter are materialists, for as psychologists they can agree on methods and findings, despite the philosophical foundations dividing them. This assertion of psychology's autonomy represented a changed approach on two levels. First, it accentuated the Neoscholastic conception of the proper autonomy of psychology and distanced itself from philosophical psychology with its claim to the foundations of psychology. In the ongoing conflicts within the American Catholic community over psychology,[29] as expressed by Virginia Staudt Sexton (1991a), all too often the hierarchical superiority of philosophical psychology trumped psychology's autonomy. Misiak and Staudt's stance, defining psychology on methodological grounds – a familiar strategy in American psychology – did boundary-work to support psychology's autonomy. At the same time, this shift in terms meant an abandonment of the soul as the fundamental concept for all psychology.

Henry R. Burke (1953), a charter member of the ACPA, in reviewing a revised edition of Brennan's *General psychology*, criticized it for not addressing sufficiently the contributions of scientific psychology:

> Those whose professional training admit them to inclusion among the 9,000 or more members of the American Psychological Association cannot regard the book as a text they would wish to have used by Catholic Students who hope to survey the field of modern psychology or to qualify for professional recognition in it. Because Catholics have and will insist on using texts like this one, they are practically unrepresented and have almost no standing among professional psychologists.

> (p. 5)

Burke raised a practical consideration: if Catholic higher education allots the scarce resource of student time to philosophical psychology, students will not know enough empirical psychology and thus Catholics will continue to be isolated and underrepresented in mainstream psychology. Such a fear, we will recall, prompted Cardinal Mercier and Pace fifty years earlier. The Neoscholastic synthesis was proving cumbersome and unworkable. Moreover, at least some Catholic psychologists perceived a new openness in mainstream psychology to philosophical issues in the decade after 1954. Royce (1986) could write that in 1960, "reductionism then dominated American psychology, with psychologists saying that man is nothing but conditioned reflexes" (p. 321), but he saw the tide turning with the establishment in 1962 of the Division of Philosophical Psychology in the APA.

Misiak and Staudt (1954) further alleged that Pace's earlier assertions of "the harmony between philosophy and modern psychology ... seem superfluous now" (p. 80). Schneiders (1951), a strong advocate for a distinctively Catholic position in psychology (in addition to other things, he edited the *Catholic Psychological Record*), could yet write that "it would be most incorrect ... to regard psychology as a mere adjunct to philosophy" (p. 10). A decade later

---

[29] See below, Chapter 5, for discussion of the furor over Fulton Sheen's criticism of psychoanalysis in the late 1940s and early 1950s.

Royce (1964) suggested ceasing the apologetics: psychology was dropping its "adolescent defensiveness" vis-à-vis philosophy, and Catholics needed no longer apologetically argue that they were not "enslaved by medieval dogmas" (p. 1). By the end of the 1960s, the autonomy of psychology seemed assured in Catholic circles, and Catholic scientific psychologists – with notable exceptions like Magda Arnold (1977) – no longer referred to Neoscholastic concepts.

The situation in psychology demanded another type of accommodation. Scientific psychology had to be mastered on its own ground, and this called for newer approaches, reflected in textbooks such as Gannon's. Misiak (1951) called for a cleaner cut between scientific and philosophical psychology, without forgetting the importance of the latter:

> Students in our colleges become not infrequently baffled or disturbed in studying Boring's History [*History of Experimental Psychology* (1950)] and seeing the gradual disappearance of 'soul,' 'psychic,' 'mental' and even 'conscious' from psychology, and experiencing the anti- or a-philosophical attitude of modern psychology. To cope with this problem, the reviewer suggests the following things: (1) Make sure that the student has sufficient knowledge (from other courses) of the soul, free will, and the difference between man and animal. (2) Make the student realize that Boring's book is neither a textbook of psychology nor philosophy but history. (3) Impress upon him that it is better for modern psychology if it is free, at least at this stage of development, from any philosophy and if the study of man is based on the methods of science. (4) Supplement Boring by giving a survey of Catholic psychologists from Mercier and Fröbes to Michotte and T.V. Moore.
>
> (p. 7)

The statement, "at least for this stage of development," is the key one. It assumed that the meaning of "scientific" in scientific psychology was the natural scientific model developed in the late nineteenth century. At the same time, Gannon (1954) wrote: "Unfortunately, a strong prejudice bars many present-day psychologists from giving serious consideration to the soul" (p. 25). He did not mean the Cartesian concept of a soul, of course, but the Aristotelian one: "The concept of an entelechy, or of some intrinsic unifying principle, is as necessary to organize and unify our understanding of psychological reactions as the actualizing principle itself is to the constitution of the personality" (ibid.). Gannon included a statement about the immateriality and immortality of the human soul as philosophical and not psychological or as theological conclusions, in keeping with Neoscholastic principles. So long as the Neoscholastic synthesis held together, this conjunction of natural scientific psychology with a psychology with a soul could flourish. When the Neoscholastic glue failed, new approaches had to be found to address the questions that the Neoscholastics raised. A basic ingredient of the new glue was Moore's definition of psychology as the science of personality, adopted by Gannon as well as by Arnold and Gasson (1954a) and others.

By the end of the 1960s, Catholic psychologists as a group felt that they had achieved autonomy from philosophy and assimilation into mainstream psychology. A Neoscholastically-trained psychologist, Mother Margaret Gorman (1966), as we have seen in Chapter 2, could address the American Catholic Philosophical Association in 1966 with proposals that would have been unthinkable thirty years earlier: that Neoscholastism's place was historical, that it had provided a paradigm for integrating the new and the old, and that it certainly was not a system simply to be embraced. At the same time, in college education, the discontinuation of texts like Brennan's meant the decline in the teaching of Neoscholastic psychology, and afterward the education of future psychologists was less likely to include course work in philosophical psychology.

One can view this outcome as the success of Neoscholastic psychology, insofar as it produced a psychology that surpassed its early flourishing, and as its failure to produce an integrated philosophical and scientific psychology. Raymond McCall, who did institution-building in psychology at DePaul and Marquette Universities, saw that the hoped-for synthesis of empirical and philosophical psychology was in fact lacking: "I feel strongly here that if psychology in the Catholic university is to be more than a combination of empiricism and pious intentions . . . it must become increasingly sophisticated philosophically without losing its scientific character" (1954a). For McCall, one way that psychology could become "increasingly sophisticated philosophically" would be to broaden its philosophical basis. Neoscholastic psychology failed in that it succeeded in launching psychology programs in Catholic higher education, with this success marking its failure to achieve a viable psychology with a soul.

Decline of Neoscholastic philosophy

Psychologists were asserting independence from a Neoscholastic framework that was collapsing. This coincided, and not accidentally, with an increased interest in academic freedom at Catholic colleges and universities, and in a removal of some of the Vatican restraints on Catholic intellectual life. As a symbol of the change, the *Index of Forbidden Books* (*Index librorum prohibitorum*, 1948), which listed texts deemed dangerous to the faith and had last been issued in 1948, was discontinued in 1966. McMullin (1967) described the rapid collapse of Neoscholasticism as the result of its having been imposed on Catholic higher education. Philosophers were abandoning the Neoscholastic ship and "the blame for this can be squarely placed on the post-*Pascendi* policy of supporting a philosophy by theological imperative instead of a constant and anxious re-thinking" (p. 14). Moreover, theologians and philosophers who had studied the history of Scholastic thought argued for plurality in the interpretation of Aquinas's philosophy and they described a variety of Thomisms. These disputes came to a head with the Second Vatican Council, "which relaxed the requirement, which Leo XIII had laid down in *Aeterni Patris*, that the philosophy and theology of St. Thomas be used, practically to the exclusion of other systems, in the education of future priests. In that sense then Thomism no longer enjoyed its place of honor as the Church's 'official system'" (McCool, 1994, p. 160). Significant aspects of what had been supposed to be Aquinas's thought were the work of sixteenth- and seventeenth-century Scholastic philosophers, which the Neoscholastics had assimilated with that of Aquinas. Ironically, Neoscholasticism proved to be a modernist philosophy, closer to the moderns it criticized than to the medievals it championed.[30] While the details of the philosophical disputes need not detain us, their effects were significant for Catholic psychologists. One effect was especially decisive. If the Neoscholastics had been wrong, and there had been no Thomistic *system*, but rather a variety of scholasticisms in the middle ages – if, in other words, there was no single, integrated architecture containing all truth – then the path was cleared for other philosophical approaches in Catholic higher education. In a 1966 survey, 21.4 percent of the philosophy faculty in Catholic colleges aligned themselves with existential-phenomenology, "strongly in second place" to Thomism (McMullin, 1968, p. 372). Similarly, psychologists who saw the necessity of thinking through the philosophical foundations of their science expanded their horizons. This opening occurred at the same time that "the third force" was beginning to make itself felt in American psychology.

From Neoscholasticism to phenomenology and humanistic psychology

While the majority of psychologists educated in Catholic universities entered the mainstream by the 1960s, some continued the philosophical critiques and questions of the Neoscholastics, even though direct influence became increasingly vague. For this group, the flight from Neoscholasticism became in part a movement to phenomenology and existentialism, because these new European movements "offered more foothold to the Christian philosopher than the empiricist alternatives" to Neoscholasticism (McMullin, 1967, p. 13). McCool (personal communication, September 18, 2003) pointed out that there were in fact two currents in Neoscholastic philosophy: the one as represented above by Maher, Brennan, Moore, and Arnold, and a second that took root at European centers such as Louvain. This second tradition emphasized the activity of

---

[30] This statement is the conclusion of Steel (1992). See also Rosemann (1999, p. 4) for a concise summary of this position. One modernist aspect of Neoscholasticism was its insistence on the separation of philosophy and theology – precisely the separation that enabled Catholic psychologists to see Neoscholasticism as a strong competitor to positivism and materialism in psychology.

subjectivity more than the first and took a lively interest in the developments in phenomenology. Mercier's successor as head of the Institute of Philosophy, Leon Noël, published the first French-language study of Husserl's thought in 1910, "Les frontières de la logique" (Ladrière, 1992, p. 57). The turn to phenomenological thought at Louvain was set with the rescue of Husserl's *Nachlass* by the Franciscan priest Hermann-Leo Van Breda, which drew many, including Maurice Merleau-Ponty, to Louvain. While there, he lectured on perception in Michotte's laboratory.

There was something of a disconnection between the two traditions,[31] especially with the growing autonomy of the psychology departments. Amedeo Giorgi, who has championed the phenomenological approach in psychology since the 1960s, was a graduate student at Fordham in the 1950s. Indeed, while he was studying psychology, phenomenologically-oriented Neoscholastics in the Louvain tradition (including Joseph Donceel) were in the philosophy department. But psychology students at Fordham did not study philosophy (Giorgi, personal communication, September 19, 2003), despite the psychology department's interest in integrating psychology and philosophy, because of the emphasis on experimental research.[32] Taking this account as typical, many younger psychologists with an interest in the philosophical foundations of psychology did not find themselves continuing the tradition emanating from Neoscholastic psychology. While some of the basic questions remained, the generation that came of age after Vatican II raised questions about the scientific nature of psychology that the older tradition had not. The Neoscholastic philosophical overlay of empirical psychology had lost its appeal.

The examination of the meaning of science in the second, more phenomenological variety of Neoscholasticism proved more incisive. Along these lines, Steel (1992) bluntly writes that Mercier's concept of philosophy remained too "scientistic" (p. 215), because it accepted the positivist conception of science without question. Van Breda gave refuge to Stephan Strasser, an Austrian who fled after the Anschluss, in the Husserl Archives at Louvain. Strasser studied in

---

[31] Gillespie (2001) writes, referring to the period between World War II and the Vatican Council (1962–4): "Louvain, however, with its progressive influence was a long way from America, where Catholics were cautious and conservative and still feeling the effects of the Americanism and Modernism controversies" (p. 192).

[32] W. Norris Clarke, SJ, of Fordham's philosophy department wrote that a Jesuit education underlay the interest in synthesis: Jesuits had "3 years of scholastic philosophy and 4 years of theology" before they came to empirical psychological studies (personal communication, December 18, 2003). In Clarke's estimation, "at that time [1950s and 1960s] the empirical field was expanding rapidly and demanding more and more time to become proficient in it. It was inevitable then that as the number of Jesuit professors declined, the number of people equipped or willing to take the time to do this ideal synthesis declined also." This account underscores the dominance of a particular opinion of what "science" means in psychology, of course. (Father Clarke, born in 1915, died in 2008.)

1944 with Alphonse de Waelhens, an author of important works on phenomenological philosophy and psychology. Strasser, who had a foot in both
Neoscholastic (1957) and phenomenological thought (1963), observed that
Mercier's conception of scientific psychology presupposed experimental
research as its empirical ground, that is, experience as defined by the inductive
sciences of nature. Strasser (1951) argued against the position taken by Brennan
and Arnold that scientific facts do not reflect, in greater detail, common
experience. They are carefully chosen data, arising from technical principles
(p. 710). Strasser had close ties to Duquesne University in Pittsburgh, where a
graduate program in phenomenological psychology was established in the early
1960s. According to Alden Fisher (1957), the natural sciences reconstruct the
world on the basis of abstractions which, while derived from common experience, do not simply reflect the lifeworld. With this distinction between ordinary
experience and its scientific reconstruction, the relationship between philosophical and scientific psychology ceased to be that as assumed by Mercier,
Brennan, and the other Neoscholastics. The new distinction opened a critique
of scientific psychology, one that would stress the differences between natural
scientific and human scientific psychologies. Giorgi (1970) argued for a "human
science psychology" on phenomenological grounds that would be neither
philosophical psychology nor natural scientific psychology. Others, such as
McCall[33] (1983), who had already written in Neoscholastic terms, made similar
arguments.

Representative of the new mood in Neoscholastic thought, as inspired by
phenomenology, was William L. Kelly's presentation at the inaugural meeting
of Division 24 of the APA. Kelly (1965) was critical of the "modern neoscholastics of the older tradition" (p. 435), such as Brennan and Klubertanz,
for their conception of the nature of scientific psychology as a natural science:
"Such neo-scholastics feel that there is but one concept of experimentation – the
strictly quantifiable, which is in their opinion diametrically opposed to the
philosophical method and hence unrelated to it. For them the philosophical
method is a dianoetic, intuitive-deductive intellectual grasp of the intelligibility
of man" (p. 439). Scientific psychology really had nothing to offer Neoscholastic
thought, given this conception of empirical science, according to Kelly. The
older Neoscholastics limited their discussion to introspective psychology
and behaviorism. According to Kelly (1965), "the relation ... [between
Neoscholastic philosophy and scientific psychology] should be mutual"
(p. 441), and he charged that it was not. In order to make it mutual, at least
two changes in Neoscholastic thinking were necessary. First, as indicated, the
nature of the empirical basis of psychology and philosophy must be reconsidered. The Neoscholastic division of labor between psychologists who dig up the
details and philosophers, who deduce their meaning, would not suffice. Second,

---

[33] For further information on Fisher and McCall, see Chapter 8.

Neoscholastic thought must turn from its "essentialistic, apersonal philosophy of human nature" (ibid.) to a concept of the person:

> The concept of person will give an apt basis for the synthesis of the intelligibility of man obtained on various levels of abstraction, as well as a continuity of the various disciplines which study man. It also is a concept which does not lose any of the advantages which [James E.] Royce's and Klubertanz' philosophy of human *nature* offer. But the emphasis is more synthetic.
>
> (pp. 440-1)

Compared to the manuals of Mercier and Brennan, Kelly moved in a phenomenological direction, emphasizing the dynamics and contextualized character of the human person. In his distinctions of levels of investigations, he used as examples the work of Jaspers, Marcel, Merleau-Ponty, Igor Caruso, the *Verstehende* psychology of Dilthey and Spranger, and Felix Krueger's *Ganzheit* psychology, all of which countered the reductionism prevalent in American scientific psychology.

When Donceel revised *Philosophical psychology*, he included more phenomenological thought, especially on the topic of the person. Donceel (1961) stated that the traditional Neoscholastic approach viewed the person as an object, that is, "considered from the outside, as an individual belonging to a certain species" (p. 444). The newer, phenomenological approach *added* to this tradition by considering the person as a Self or an "I." The phenomenologists have investigated this aspect of the person, especially as embodied, using the phenomenological method: the effort "to describe what is given, simply as it is given" (p. 445). While Donceel noted the limitations of this new method, namely, that it cannot reveal "realities which we know only through reasoning from their effects" (p. 446), nevertheless phenomenology makes a genuine contribution to Neoscholasticism.

The new contributions did more than that, however; they helped to break up Neoscholasticism. If philosophical inquiry is not limited to an "intuitive-deductive intellectual grasp," but must also be phenomenologically descriptive, and if the empirical ground of psychology is no longer conceived narrowly experimentally, but more broadly phenomenologically empirically, then the division of labor between philosophical and scientific psychology breaks down. Adrian van Kaam's synthesis, reminiscent of Mercier, did not emphasize the soul or human nature. Instead, van Kaam (1967a) characterized existential psychology as the study of "the intentional-functional behavior of persons who exist with others in a meaningful world" (p. 729). Fisher's translation of Merleau-Ponty's *The structure of behavior* helped to introduce a psychology that was philosophically rigorous and systematically empirical. As an indication of the changing ground, Misiak and Sexton (1966) ignored Moore, mentioned Pace only in conjunction with the founding of the laboratory at the Catholic

University, and referred to Mercier only briefly in terms of the roots of
psychology in philosophy. By contrast, they devoted two chapters to phenomenology and existentialism. They found hope in the newly emerging "third
force" in psychology, which puts the emphasis on "man as a person, on his
unique subjective problems, and on the use of any methods capable of advancing our knowledge of man" (p. 454). In this definition, the older Neoscholastic
approach was attenuated: absent the eternal soul. In their subsequent work
(Misiak and Sexton, 1973), they expressed the hope that humanistic and
phenomenological thought would live up to its promise. Earlier they had
prefigured this moment: "Catholic psychologists accept the Neo-Scholastic
philosophy ... because in their opinion it is the best system at present ... If
another philosophical system were to be developed which would harmonize
better with the two other sources of knowledge, science and faith, the same
Catholic scholars might embrace this system" (Misiak and Staudt, 1954, p. 279).
As philosophical systems all became suspect in the following decades, and as the
history of psychology moved from a "grand narrative of progress" in a realization that psychology has varied beginnings and trajectories, the meaning of
philosophy and psychology became increasingly open questions.

In addition to a movement from Neoscholasticism to phenomenology, there
was a movement from Neoscholastic to humanistic psychology. The specifics
will be discussed in Chapter 8, but consider that many Neoscholastically-
trained psychologists picked up Moore's definition of psychology as the science
of personality.[34] Gannon (1954) claimed the centrality of the study of personality for psychology, noting that "the task of psychology is not to set forth the
schematic of an electronic robot" (p. 413), a critique of behaviorism for its
seeking mechanistic explanations (p. 206). Gannon was equally critical of
psychoanalysis. The truncated views of the human person in behaviorism and
psychoanalysis became a recurrent theme in the humanistic movement, and the
Neoscholastics had already voiced such critiques. Arnold and Gasson's *The
Human Person* (1954a) is a good source for showing the leading edge of
Neoscholastically-trained psychologists articulating a humanistic approach:
contributions included discussions of Viktor Frankl (at the time untranslated
into English) and client-centered therapy, as well as Allport, Maslow, and Kurt
Goldstein on personality. James E. Royce (1986) observed that a non-dualistic
conception of the self "was Aristotle's solution, which was perfected by Aquinas
in the Middle Ages. This conception of the self is reflected today in many
holistic and humanistic psychologies" (p. 322).[35] A sign of a transition from
Neoscholasticism to humanistic psychology was Vytausus Bieliaukas's (1974)
entry in the *New Catholic Encyclopedia*, where he states that "humanistic

---

[34] Further implications of the category of "personality" will be addressed in Chapter 9.
[35] The word "perfected" indicates the Neoscholastic view of Royce. Recent scholarship on the
    Middle Ages disputes the claim in that verb.

psychology has already opened the doors to study of all those psychological phenomena which can be called transcendent or transpersonal, data which were closed off in principle by the inherent philosophical limitations of behaviorism and Freudianism" (p. 370). Neoscholastic psychologists had argued for the theoretical importance of human freedom and choice, for the significance of spirituality in human life, and for the autonomy of higher psychological acts. Again, they argued against determinism in psychological theorizing. All these were themes championed by the Third Force, which came to include many who had been Neoscholastic psychologists or trained by them.[36]

The fate of the soul: Psychology and religion again

The Neoscholastic solution to the problem of science and religion lay in granting science its proper autonomy and in situating it within a hierarchy of knowledge. At the summit of knowledge gained by human reason unaided by Divine Revelation lay metaphysics, which studies the ultimate causes of things. This partitioning and hierarchical arrangement gave room for scientific psychology to develop. The nature of the human soul, however, remained both the pole star and a stumbling block for Neoscholastic psychologists. While psychologists did not discuss the soul in psychological contexts except when explicitly dealing with philosophical issues, the concept of the soul did have some significant implications for psychological research and practice. Moore's analysis of human intelligence and Arnold's study of emotions both assumed the distinction between perception and intellect that the Neoscholastic saw as implying the spirituality of the human soul. When Charles A. Curran articulated principles of nondirective psychotherapy, he also assumed the objective existence of moral goods and the reality of God. With the movement away from Neoscholastic formulations, considerations of the soul changed too. If some Catholic psychologists, drawing on Jung and others (Gillespie, 2001, pp. 104–5), still explicitly spoke of the soul, for the most part the discourse changed to the person, the self, the I–Thou relationship, and concepts such as existence and Dasein (Royce, 1986). These concepts, while still keeping psychologists focused on the uniquely human aspects of psychology and thus countering reductionistic tendencies, do not have the theological denotations that soul carries.[37]

---

[36] A partial list would include: Adrian van Kaam and others who taught at Duquesne University in Pittsburgh (Frank Buckley, Amedeo Giorgi, Edward Murray), Charles A. Curran, Raymond McCall, Alden Fisher, Joseph Nuttin (at Louvain), Virginia Staudt Sexton, Henry Misiak, and Francis Severin.

[37] Heidegger (1962) writes: "If 'death' is defined as the 'end' of Dasein . . . this does not imply any ontical decision whether 'after death' still another Being is possible . . . or whether Dasein 'lives on' or even 'outlasts' itself and is 'immortal'" (p. 292). Pickstock (1998) criticizes this reduction of the question of immortality to an ontic question, suggesting that it could be thought ontologically, such that "reality could be approached in an optative

They thus fostered the development of a psychology that deals with religious and spiritual aspects of life without being tied to a specific religious tradition as was Neoscholasticism. While psychology and religion remained knotted together in many ways, the soul as a stumbling block was removed along with Neoscholasticism. Schneiders (1951) conceded that a complete conception of personality requires philosophical considerations, yet "we must accept the fact that psychologists as a group have given up the idea of a complete interpretation and prefer to leave the problems of the soul to philosophy" (p. 10). Together with the withdrawal of the soul from the conversation, the partition and hierarchy of knowledge also faded from view. Humanistic psychologists, for example, did make claims for knowledge of human spiritual life, and for the most part did not defer to ecclesiastic authority. This was especially true as the human potential movement fused with humanistic psychology in the 1960s (Smith, 1990) and with the rise of transpersonal psychology (Taylor, 1999). When this development took place, interestingly enough, then humanistic psychology often came into conflict with religion (Vitz, 1994). The science/religion relationship in psychology took on new form at this point.

Conclusion

From the 1890s until the 1960s, a Neoscholastic tradition existed in psychology. Its tone was set by Cardinal Mercier, who sought to integrate the findings of experimental psychology with the fruits of centuries of philosophical inquiry. The chief strengths of Neoscholastic psychology were its attempt at integration and its resistance to reductionistic conceptions and practices in psychology. Neoscholastic psychology did not sidestep the implications for human beings of psychological research and praxis, and the subsequent generations, represented by Thomas Verner Moore and Magda Arnold and the ACPA, sought to carry out the synthesis, even as they championed the autonomy of a natural scientific psychology. This unique blend of philosophical and empirical psychology occupied a difficult position. It existed between two orthodoxies, that of the Catholic Church defending its tradition against what it saw as an onslaught of modernism, and that of scientific psychology, often militantly anti-philosophical and narrowly empirical. Neoscholastic psychologists felt that they must be natural scientists as psychologists, and as Catholics, they must address philosophical questions and, especially, be wary of modernism. So they

mood of desire, hope, or faith" (p. 113). Neoscholastic formulations kept open, even if at arm's length for empirical psychology, such a question. Moreover, in its position on the special creation of the soul, it asserted that the existence of the individual was a gift to that individual, and not a possession. Scientific psychology assumes that one's life is one's possession, e.g. in its understandings of personal responsibility, choice, and self-determination.

strove to realize an ideal of a psychology, adequate both philosophically and methodologically. This ideal represented one important chapter in the relationships between the science of psychology and religion in the twentieth century. What was at stake for the Neoscholastics was the human soul, and not only as a philosophical concept that underlay psychology. For as Leo XIII had argued in 1879, "false opinions, whose seat is the understanding, influence human actions and pervert them." Quite literally, then, for Neoscholasticism, the fate of the soul was at stake in psychology. Thus, while psychology could have its autonomy, it could never cut its ties with philosophy or with Church teachings. . Insofar as materialism, positivism, and rationalism "subvert the very foundations of religion," as Canon law stated it (*Codex iuris canonici*, 1918), the stakes were too high simply to let psychology go its own way. Psychology was the crucial science in the fight for the soul. Neoscholasticism sought to balance this concern with the freedom proper to any science. At the same time, the Neoscholastic synthesis remained an idealization, for the basic conceptions of its metaphysics could never suffer challenge by anything produced by the psychologists – thus making psychology ultimately pointless from the philosophical perspective, and philosophy a rarefied irrelevancy for psychologists.

While it flourished, however, Neoscholastic psychology produced many contributions in theoretical, experimental, and applied areas of the discipline. So long as the soul was a relevant psychological concept, boundary-work delineating the place of the psychologist, the philosopher, and the ecclesiastic authority was the order of the day. After Neoscholasticism, the soul was quietly dropped from psychological discourse. Moreover, with the collapse of Neoscholasticism in the wake of philosophical and theological critiques of mid-century, many Catholic psychologists turned to phenomenology and existentialism and humanism for their conceptual orientation. Their Neoscholastic predecessors, but not the questions the Neoscholastics had raised, were forgotten.

Psychology as the boundary: Catholicism, spiritualism, and science

We do not deny that there is a spiritual world and we are more emphatic in asserting the personal survival of the soul after its separation from the body than any spiritist can be. We are also prepared to admit that the spirit world, with the consent of God, can manifest itself to mortals and exercise over them, as the case may be, a beneficent or malign influence. If Spiritism said no more, we would have no quarrel with it. But its fantastic and grotesque embroideries on these plain truths and the practical conclusions it deduces from them, we repudiate most energetically.

Charles P. Bruehl (1920a, p. 401)

Whatever their limitations, the Neoscholastics had an expansive vision of human life. Death was not its end, and philosophically – not theologically – they argued that the facts of human life led to the conclusion that we are ensouled, that the soul is immaterial, and that we have an immortal destiny. Their philosophical psychology was, in their own terms, spiritualistic. They rejected materialism and phenomenalism. The spiritual world is real, we have access to it, and it has its powers, promises, and dangers. Mainstream psychology, with some exceptions, such as the all-encompassing William James, held the spiritual world at arm's length, after a brief love affair with the psychic researchers (Coon, 1992). As Coon points out, many of the new psychologists, James included, embraced positivism and naturalism, to the exclusion of the claims of Spiritualism. James did, however, urge the study all the phenomena, including those of interest to the Spiritualist community. James' interests extended beyond narrow efforts to establish a scientific psychology. He hoped "that in order for some new 'popular religion [to be] raised on the ruins of the old Christianity' there would have to be a renewed 'belief in new *physical* facts & possibilities'" (James to Davidson, quoted in Coon, 1992, p. 144). This secular religion would demonstrate the reality of the beyond and our duties in relation to it, without requiring dogma or institutions. The Neoscholastics, affirming the reality of the phenomena of the spirit, disputed this anti-institutional conclusion.

The squeamishness of the experimentalists was not shared by all who had psychological interests, and given that psychology is not defined solely by the academics, we see that psychology in other contexts was very much a spiritual psychology. I refer here to that broad sea of interest in the influence of the mind over the body and, with it, to the expansive view of mind that has characterized much of American popular religion and psychology from colonial times onward. Called the "shadow culture" by Taylor (1999) and "unchurched spirituality" by Fuller (2001), this tradition has taken various forms over the past three hundred years. In most cases, it involves the incorporation of non-Christian, pantheistic or quasi-pantheistic views of the universe into some form of Christianity. In more recent years, under the umbrella name of "New Age" thought, the Christian component may be muted and relativized, Christ included among those enlightened beings who appear from time to time, and who foreshadow the inevitable evolution of human consciousness to a higher state. Early nineteenth-century forms included Transcendentalism, Swedenborgianism, mesmerism, and phrenology – all of which shared the beliefs that we are more than we realize we are, that we have ties to the higher reaches of the cosmos, that we are connected in some fundamental way to the All, and that – and for many, this was the clincher – insofar as we realize this connection, we find healing and happiness. In the late nineteenth century, this therapeutic focus became much more explicit in movements such as New Thought, Mind Cure, Christian Science, and others. Men such as Phineas Parkhurst Quimby used hypnosis to attune themselves to the souls of others and show them the way out of their difficulties. This whole area is immensely important for understanding the rise of psychology and the acceptance and pursuit of psychotherapy in North America. More than that, however, it represented a cultural reply to the dominant intellectual trends that often succumbed to materialism and positivism.

What characterizes this unchurched interest in things spiritual is its "combinative" attitude, an open "mingling of religious beliefs and cultural practices" (Albanese, 2000, p. 20), a term Albanese prefers to the rather pejorative term, "syncretistic," implying a thoughtless and often heady cocktail of ideas. A combinatory approach, by contrast, draws upon "visionaries and practitioners" from a wide variety of cultures and times in search of truth. More specifically, what characterizes this psychologized religious-spiritual interest is a belief in an unconscious or subconscious mind. This unconscious is not that cauldron of drives and desires that Freud spoke of, but a higher self, connected with the All, which unites us with others and opens the paths to the realization of our potentialities. The application of this belief extends from the crass – the tapping of our potential for fortune and success – to the sublime, the realization of *satori* or some other form of "cosmic consciousness" (Bucke, 1901). Over the course of the twentieth century, this combinative trend in North American culture has become progressively more mainstream. Taylor (1999) argues that in transpersonal psychology, that product of the spiritual awakening of the 1960s and 1970s, the visionary culture that lay in the shadow of Anglo-American Protestant religiosity became institutionalized (p. 277). This emergence is perhaps a unique cultural manifestation of a "spiritual but not religious" mentality. These "seekers" (Roof, 1993) constitute today perhaps 20–25 percent of the American population (Saroglou, 2003, p. 478). And among their churched peers are many who combine their Christian dogmas with other beliefs and practices (Pacwa, 1992). This trend has become so widespread that the Vatican issued a statement on the merits and the limitations of "New Age Spirituality" (Pontifical Council for Culture and Pontifical Council for Interreligious Dialogue, 2003).

In this chapter we look at the history of this popular "visionary psychology" (Taylor, 1999) from the end of the nineteenth century, with particular emphasis on Catholic responses to it. For convenience's sake, we will look at three different manifestations of this spiritual psychology. First, we turn to the end of the nineteenth century, when New Thought, Mind Cure, Spiritualism, and the beginnings of psychotherapy were surfacing. We will look for evidence of Catholic participation and reaction to these developments. Second, we turn to events at the shrine at Lourdes, where Catholics defended miraculous cures akin to what the Spiritualists and Christian Scientists were claiming to do. Finally, we turn to the work of James Joseph Walsh, author of *Psychotherapy*, an early twentieth-century work that sought to reconcile scientific medicine, Catholic teachings, miracles at Lourdes, and the psychology of suggestion. In each of these areas, psychology itself was the boundary between science and religion.

Hypnotism, spiritualism, and mind cure: Catholics and the first wave of psychotherapy

The late nineteenth century witnessed an upsurge in forms of healing. In many respects, they represented a modernization of what had always been present in culture: the myriad of ways that people address life's sufferings and uncertainties, including disease, misfortune in love and commerce, distress of all kinds, and death. Many of these forms have traditionally been outside the circles of elite culture, now tolerated, now embraced, now suppressed. Fuller (2001) and Taylor (1999) point out that these techniques and rituals of healing have long been a part of American culture. Before the modern period, such rituals often manifested as types of popular religion that combined the prevailing orthodoxy with local – and often much older – cultural and religious symbols, rituals, and practices. The use of Easter eggs in Christian celebrations of the resurrection of Christ is one contemporary survival of an older form, the original meanings long forgotten and repressed. Fuller (2001) describes how in colonial New England, there was widespread practice of witchcraft, astrology, and magic, and that in addition to European herbal and magical remedies the colonials brought with them, they learned from the native inhabitants as well. A literary example of this combinative knowledge is that of Roger Chillingworth, Hester Prynne's evil husband in Nathanial Hawthorne's *The Scarlet Letter*. Chillingworth combined alchemy and Native American healing techniques, as well as a cruel form of care of the soul, and used them on Arthur Dimmesdale, Hester's conflicted lover. Chillingworth may not be a benevolent example of the kind of popular religion and healing that I mean, but he is an example of how the colonists may have mixed things together without ecclesiastical approval. At the end of the nineteenth century, as the United States migrated toward being an urban and industrial nation, these traditional religious and healing impulses took new form. Between Hester Prynne and Phineas Quimby, the rise of the natural sciences and the Enlightenment critique of religion had occurred, and popular forms of religiosity and healing took new shape that accounted for these developments, which "should have" had the effect of suppressing them altogether.

The powers of the mind: spiritualism and mind cure

Miles Coverdale, the protagonist of Nathaniel Hawthorne's 1852 *The Blithedale Romance*, falls ill the day he arrives at the utopian community that he has joined to usher in a new epoch of fraternity, equality, and liberty. During his somewhat protracted illness, he wasted away which – in line with solid nineteenth-century beliefs – he interpreted as a spiritualizing of his being. On recovery he found, at least on one occasion, that he now had keener intuition into the soul of the most appealing member of Blithedale Farm, the beautiful Zenobia:

> But there is a species of intuition – either a spiritual lie, or the subtle recognition of a fact – which comes to us in a reduced state of the corporeal system. The soul gets the better of the body, after wasting illness, or when a vegetable diet may have mingled too much ether in the blood. Vapors then rise up to the brain, and take shapes that often image falsehoods, but sometimes truth. The spheres of our companions have, at such periods, a vastly greater influence upon our own, than when robust health gives us a repellent and self-defensive energy. Zenobia's sphere, I imagine, impressed itself powerfully on mine, and transformed me, during this period of my weakness, into something like a mesmerical clairvoyant.
>
> (Hawthorne, 1852, p. 57)

Beside discovering for himself a potentially spiritual benefit of fasting, Coverdale expressed here some of the important themes of nineteenth-century spiritual thought, bringing together mesmerism, Spiritualism, and that sensitivity to the inner life of others that proved so important in Mind Cure and New

Thought and, indeed, in the kind of empathy often proposed as essential to the practice of psychotherapy in the twentieth century.

The phenomena discussed here overlapped considerably. In the founding documents for the Society for Psychical Research, we read that the Society came into existence because it was time to investigate "that large group of debatable phenomena designated by such terms as mesmeric, psychical, and Spiritualistic" (Objects of the society, 1883, p. 3). While these things are more distinguishable after more than a century of study, at the time there was considerable doubt. What they all had in common was the trance: that altered state of awareness that was neither pure sleep nor pure waking consciousness. Did it provide access to the world of the spirits? Did it enslave the will to that of the mesmerizer? Did it free up latent abilities that perhaps lie within everyone to communicate with others without language or sense data, and to see what is happening in distant places? These questions and others swarmed around these phenomena.

Two of the important new forms that appeared in the nineteenth century fall under the names of Spiritualism (or Spiritism) and Mind Cure. Spiritualism had various beginnings. Fuller (2001) describes, in addition to the well-known Fox sisters, with whom spirits communicated by table rapping in the 1840s in New York state, the life of Andrew Jackson Davis (1826–1910), whose career captured many of the characteristics of this secularized religion. Davis found Christian teachings, "no matter how liberal its cast" (p. 39), unpalatable, and he craved, apparently, a variety of religious experiences. Fuller recounts how in 1843, Davis participated as a volunteer at a lecture on animal magnetism, also known as mesmerism: "When mesmerized, Davis performed such feats as reading from books while blindfolded, telepathically receiving thoughts from those in the audience, or traveling clairvoyantly to distant locales" (ibid.). Thus he launched his seeking and his career. He became a medium, and his records of communications with the spirit world became published in popular works. Fuller writes:

> One of the first spirits to instruct Davis was none other than Emanuel Swedenborg. Or, at least, so Davis's contact in the spirit world frequently identified himself. From Davis on, spiritualism absorbed and popularized the metaphysical teachings of Swedenborgianism, Transcendentalism, and mesmerism . . . Spiritualists fully accepted Swedenborg's belief in the inner divinity of the person as well as his conception of the basic continuity between the material and the spiritual worlds.
>
> (p. 40)

In addition to the Spiritualists' promise of direct access to a benevolent spirit world, which had the merit of providing evidence for the immortality and immateriality of the human soul, the Spiritualists' social mores were progressive. Fuller observes that:

Spiritualist leaders paved the way for innovations in the way we describe God so as to balance male and female imagery. In fact, the entire religious outlook encompassed what appear in retrospect to have been the most liberal, progressive, and liberating intellectual currents of their generation.

(p. 41)

Sharp (1999) notes a similar trend took place among Spiritualists in France at the same time, the mid-nineteenth century, in a somewhat different cultural and religious climate:

Spiritism, like a variety of cultural movements in the nineteenth century, attempted to integrate Enlightenment ideals of reason, science, and progress into a more traditional, religious understanding of the world. These movements, from Saint-Simonian socialism and Fourierism to the 'universal religion' of deistic freethinkers in the 1860s, offered alternatives to the materialism and positivism of the secularists and to the increasingly ultramontane position of the Catholic Church.

(p. 283)

That is, Spiritualism promised to "reconcile science and religion" (Fuller, 2001, p. 41). In part, it did so by providing experiential evidence for the existence of the spiritual dimension of life, thus making spiritual affirmations a matter of empirical evidence rather than mere belief. In addition, Spiritualism offered a new type of religion, one freed from the dictates of dogma or clergy. In Davis's words, "American Republicanism will be transformed into tyranny unless individual man declareth himself independent of all political and ecclesiastical Institutions" (Davis, 1872, p. 479, cited in ibid., p. 43).

Freedom from the prevailing orthodoxies of the day had in many instances a political edge, as Fuller notes. In fact, Spiritualism provided a medium in which many social innovations could take place. It was an arena in which nineteenth-century women's rights flourished, as Moore (1975) indicates: "The efforts of some feminist leaders after the American Civil War to liberate women from 'the narrow limits of the domestic circle' received strong vocal support at nearly every Spiritualist convention held in the latter part of the century" (pp. 211–12), a point to which we shall return. Mediums could give voice to any number of controversial topics, such as divorce, without being held responsible for what they said, since they were not speaking in their own voice.[1]

---

[1] Spirit possession is a phenomenon known world-wide. Moore (1975) cites an anthropological study that concluded: "possession trance was more common in rigid societies where simple decision making was fraught with danger from internal and external social controls" (p. 208). He concludes that that structure was operative in the nineteenth century: "Mediums who in trance acted out forbidden desires or expressed repressed aspects of their personality were often making the only approach to reality which their society and culture allowed them" (p. 217). This helps explain some of the connection between radical politics, unchurched spirituality, and Spiritualism up to the present day.

The Spiritualist movement was as much a medical as a religious movement. Taylor (1999) describes how Davis was visited not only by the spirit of Swedenborg, but also by the great Greek physician, Galen. According to Taylor, Galen

> gave Davis knowledge of a therapeutic system based on the premise that disease afflicted only the bodies of living beings but not their internal spiritual life. God within was the internal creative spirit, and one's contact with him was the essence of health and healing. To be disconnected from this source was to court disease.
>
> (p. 110)

The growth of what Taylor calls an "occult psychotherapy" (ibid.) must include mention of Phineas Parkhurst Quimby (1802–66) who, like Davis, came from a working-class background. Both men had been influenced by Charles Poyen, a French follower of Mesmer who lectured throughout New England in the 1830s.[2] Quimby learned the techniques of mesmeric trance induction, and at first, when he mesmerized his assistant, Lucius Burkmar, the latter would "diagnose and prescribe treatments for patients selected randomly from the audience" (p. 111) at public lectures. As Quimby's conception of what was taking place progressed, he abandoned intermediaries, and he developed a form of what could be called psychotherapy. Taylor describes it in these words: "He diagnosed by visual imagery, sometimes using mesmeric passes, but mainly he talked with his patients, listening to what they said about their beliefs and working with them to overcome self-defeating attitudes" (p. 112). In these sessions, he entered a trance state, so that he could "suffuse the patient's mind with magnetic healing fluids" (ibid.). The essence of Quimby's teaching was that beliefs are the cause of sickness and of health.

Quimby's ideas and practices were continued by many others, including Mary Baker Eddy, the founder of Christian Science,[3] Warren Felt Evans (1817–89), Julius and Annetta Seabury Dresser, their son Horatio W. Dresser – who studied philosophy under William James and received a doctorate from Harvard in 1907 (Braden, 1963, p. 160) – and others, established what came to be called "Mind Cure" and "New Thought" movements. Evans, like Quimby, used intuitive means to diagnose and cure, and like

---

[2] Braden (1963) writes: "In 1838, a Dr. [Robert H.] Collyer gave a lecture and demonstration of a curious phenomenon, mesmerism, which had been introduced into America some two years before by the Frenchman, Charles Poyan [sic] ... This amazing new force ... had created a great furor in New England ... It at once attracted the inquisitive mind of P. P. Quimby" (p. 48). See Rodgers (2006, pp. 128–9).

[3] See Fuller (2001, p. 47), Taylor (1999, pp. 146, 150–1), Meyer (1980, pp. 37–40), and Janet (1925/1976, vol. 1, pp. 55–64) for discussions of the stormy relationship between Quimby and Eddy.

Quimby, held that disease is a matter of wrong belief. Taylor (1999) summarizes Evans' conception of healing:

> Evans believed that disease resulted from a disturbance in the spiritual body, which affected the physical body through Swedenborg's law of correspondence. Egotism was thought to be antagonistic to one's inward spiritual nature, as when external sensory desires gain control of one's inner self. Material concerns then predominate over our inner Christ nature. "Matter," Evans wrote, "was only spirit made visible to the mind."
>
> (p. 145)

Practitioners of New Thought, which became a term in the 1890s (p. 146) and an organization, the New Thought Alliance (see Meyer, 1980, p. 36) in the early twentieth century, used a variety of techniques, including visualization and overt suggestion.[4] The essence of the Mind Cure was that the mind could cure the body, that healing meant aligning oneself with one's true nature, one's spiritual nature. Needless to say, there have been many permutations of these ideas over the past century, and they are still very much with us.

Catholic responses: Psychology as the boundary between science and religion

Fuller (2001) points out that Spiritualism provided Americans raised in Protestant traditions something that the Catholics already had: an abundance of mediators in the spiritual world: "The Protestant traditions that dominated American religious thought had long repudiated belief in the efficacy of prayer to saints or to the Virgin Mary. American Protestants consequently stood alone before a remote, wrathful God" (p. 41). These spirit mediators, however, could be approached without the assistance of the Church, one of the likely motives for the appeal of Spiritualism in nominally Catholic countries, such as France (Sharp, 1999). Catholic responses to these nineteenth-century innovations were many. On the one hand, the Church and the Spiritualists alike were opposed to the materialism which enlisted many of the prominent thinkers of the day, especially after mid-century, when vitalism was a spent force. On the other hand, the Church tended to view with jaundiced eye many of the claims made by these fellow affirmers of the immaterial world.

What we see in the Catholic treatment of hypnotism, Spiritualism, and mental healing was a complex use of medical and psychological categories to delineate boundaries between the natural and the supernatural, between science and religion. Since hypnosis at the end of the nineteenth century had achieved recognition as an effective medical and psychological procedure, it could not suffer the same fate as animal magnetism of an earlier day, as simply a

---

[4] Horatio W. Dresser (1919, p. 153) wrote that the term 'New Thought' was first used in 1889.

misguided religious movement. Catholic response to hypnosis, then, emphasized it as a natural phenomenon, explainable in medical and psychological terms, even when its dangers were emphasized. Catholic opposition to positivism and materialism led Catholic thinkers to support Spiritualists in some of their claims to have had commerce with disincarnate spirits without, at the same time, supporting Spiritualists' interpretations of whom these spirits were. This approach demanded rejection of what Catholics saw as a reductionistic skepticism on the part of many, who viewed all Spiritualist claims as the product of deception and self-deception. The same argument in favor of supernatural intervention, although in a different setting, such as the miracle cures at Lourdes, was employed against medical and psychological dismissal of those events. Bernadette, who beheld the Virgin Mary at Lourdes, was not a medium in Catholic eyes, and it was important for the Church to ascertain that some of those cured at Lourdes – and they were primarily women – were not hysterics or sufferers of functional diseases, and to certify that they suffered from organic diseases. However, deception and self-deception were urged to explain the claims of Mary Baker Eddy and the Christian Scientists, because they made theological claims that the Church viewed as heretical. Christian Science healing had to be merely the work of suggestion. This complex boundary work served to fight against positivism and materialism by using, selectively, the very categories that had been turned against the claims of the Faith.

The Catholics and hypnosis: A question of the will

Consider the Catholic response to hypnotism, which can be characterized as cautious and nuanced, and which in some ways resembled how the Church responded to psychology and psychoanalysis in particular in the twentieth century. Such similarity of response is quite in order, indeed, since psychoanalysis and dynamic psychology in general can be seen as the outgrowth of mesmerism (Ellenberger, 1970). "Hypnotism" was not the name used to describe mesmerism until James Braid in the 1840s coined the term. Braid also proposed an explanation of it in terms of the workings of the nervous system, an account much different from that of Mesmer. Mesmer had earlier proposed that healers such as himself directed a subtle fluid that pervaded the entire cosmos through the body of the person to be healed. This fluid took the form, in living beings, of "animal magnetism" (p. 63).[5] However, since mesmerism or hypnotism (the two terms

---

[5] Ellenberger (1970) observes that Mesmer, "being a son of the Enlightenment," "was seeking a 'rational' explanation and rejected any kind of mystical theory" (p. 62). Those mystical theories were forthcoming and combined with hypnotic phenomena and techniques. Earlier explanations of such phenomena would have frankly included spiritual beings. Ellenberger notes, moreover, "with his uncanny powers, Mesmer is closer to the ancient magician than to the nineteenth-century psychotherapist" (p. 69).

were sometimes synonymous, sometimes not) combined with Spiritualism in a variety of ways, there were multiple conceptions of what actually took place in hypnotic trances. Nathaniel Hawthorne, a sympathetic and critical observer, has one of his characters in *The Blithedale Romance* (1852), a young, ethereal woman named Priscilla, appear as the "Veiled Lady," mysterious and enigmatic. The description of her in a stage performance shows the blending of the hypnotic trance with the Spiritualist attunement to the beyond: summoned to the stage of a New England village hall, the Veiled Lady does not respond when some of the rubes come on stage and shout in her ear and make all sorts of noises to startle her:

> "These efforts are wholly without avail," observed the Professor, who had been looking on with an aspect of serene indifference. "The roar of a battery of cannon would be inaudible to the Veiled Lady. And yet, were I to will it, sitting in this very hall, she could hear the desert-wind sweeping over the sands, as far off as Arabia ... Nor does there exist the moral inducement, apart from my own behest, that could persuade her to lift the silvery veil, or arise out of that chair."
>
> (pp. 236–7)

We read in this description one of the alleged characteristics that concerned Catholic response to these confusing phenomena: the subjugation of the will.

In a review of then recent books, the author of Hypnotism and theology (1890) posed the question that was crucial from the Catholic perspective:

> Can a Catholic, without violence to his conscience, assume the position of a hypnotizer, or subject himself freely to the strange influence of its manipulations, or, in fine, knowingly and willfully lend his aid to its practice? Not a few theologians of a high order appear to condemn the practice without distinction. They allow no alternative to the explanation of hypnotic phenomena between imposture and preternatural or demoniac agencies.
>
> (p. 258)

While some theologians doubted naturalistic explanations of what were still being called "magnetic phenomena" (Hypnotism and theology, 1890), there was at the same time sufficient interest in them by priests and the laity to necessitate a clearer understanding.[6] Other theologians had a more benign

---

[6] For interest among priests: this 1890 article in the *Catholic World* observed that "for the practical guidance of priests in a matter which is threatening to become more and more of universal application, we propose briefly to show what hypnotism ... is" (p. 259). Eleven years later, a brief editorial in the *American Ecclesiastical Review* (The dangers of hypnotism, 1901), a journal for the clergy, we read: "In view of a systematic propaganda which is being made throughout the country for what is called 'Suggestive Therapeutics,' and the fact that not wholly ineffectual efforts have been made to introduce these methods among the Catholic clergy as a means of furthering their Samaritan work, we again direct attention to the danger involved in all hypnotic experiments" (p. 78). So presumably some

view, and Rene Holaind, SJ (1836–1906), writing in the *American Ecclesiastical Review*, noted that the Abbé Méric studied with both Charcot and Bernheim, as had the Abbé Schneider (Holaind, 1895, p. 120).[7] Hypnosis for Holaind was not intrinsically evil, although it was "unquestionably dangerous" (p. 121). One fact seemed certain: hypnosis had real power, namely, the power of one person to influence and perhaps control the will of another. The *Catholic World* reviewer noted that because of this power, state and national governments were restricting the practice of hypnosis, largely because of pressures from the medical community (Hypnotism and theology, 1890).

Part of the difficulty with hypnosis had to do with its Spiritualist aura, as this review made clear: "we must not ignore the fact that the main body of modern hypnotists define hypnosis as a state distinct from mesmerism and clairvoyance, as well as from so called spiritism" (p. 259). Holaind (1895) also complained about these associations. Admitting an analogy between them, the *Catholic World* review proceeded to spell out what the hypnotic state is, drawing on Charcot's stages of the hypnotic trance. This distinction was important, and it indicates that it took considerable effort to isolate the natural from the supernatural in this area. The explanatory model that the review presented as the most likely dealt with the will: "The condition to which a subject under the influence of the hypnotizer is reduced is practically this: A man resigns his person to the will of another. The conscious energy of the latter enters apparently into the physical organism which has been abandoned by its own native will-power, and governs it at pleasure" (Hypnotism and theology, 1890, p. 264). This condition was clearly dangerous, said Catholic and other commentators at the time.[8] Nevertheless, hypnosis had its merits, and so it could not be dismissed out of hand: "the strangest effect of all, produced by the exercise of a foreign will upon a diseased organism, is the complete or at least

---

priests were trying hypnosis out with members of their congregations. By this time, of course, hypnosis was a respectable technique. Recall that in 1882, Mercier had gone to Paris to study with Charcot, who did much to make hypnosis a part of "normal medicine," as did his contemporaries Hippolyte Bernheim and Ambroise Liébeault. The latter two championed the "suggestion" theory, in contrast to Charcot's neurological explanation for hypnosis. As for lay interest, evidence includes articles in the *Catholic World* and letters to the editor there in November 1889, where the editor supplied some readings by Catholic authors on the topic.

[7] Holaind was a professor of Ethics and Sociology at Woodstock College, the Jesuit seminary, and a lecturer at Georgetown University on natural and canon law at the end of the nineteenth century.

[8] An example of a non-Catholic who shared the concern about the ill-effects of hypnosis on the will, Henry Rutgers Marshall (1908), past president of the American Psychological Association, wrote a letter to the *New York Times* critical of the Emmanuel Movement, then at its peak: "But it is the control by the individual's self, so efficient in the building of character, that is broken down whenever hypnotic or any allied form of suggestion is employed in Therapeutics" (p. 8). For the context for Marshall's letter, see Caplan (1998, pp. 138–9).

partial cure of different physical ailments with such modifications of temperament and disposition as accompany a normal state of health" (ibid.). The review cited evidence that hypnosis cures by means of the nervous system, but then admitted that the causes were still unknown: "Yet, would it be lawful to conclude thence that they are preternatural? Not at all" (p. 266). The treatment came with dangers; however, the most important were it tended to produce a kind of passivity in the recipient and, worst of all, the possibility that an unscrupulous operator will direct the hypnotized person to evil and immoral acts. The review concluded with a caution: "Leave it to the hands of science" (p. 271). In other words, let the amateurs steer clear of it, for it has powers and possibilities that we do not understand.

Note that its effectiveness was not in dispute. In the same year, 1890, in the *Catholic World*, a magazine that had a lay readership, the physician Joseph T. O'Connor (1890) explained hypnotism along the lines of the Nancy school, that is, as the effect of suggestion. He presented findings that showed that hypnosis had substantial healing effects, but there were dangers as well, especially if too frequently employed. For repeated hypnosis rendered the will weak and the person was then susceptible to the will of another. In other words, hypnosis made one mentally (and perhaps morally) passive and suggestible. O'Connor emphasized more than once that hypnosis had nothing to do with spirits or with Mesmer's subtle fluids, and held that it was a legitimate although limited therapeutic agent. Holaind (1895) drew a parallel with anesthesia, which had been subject to the same charge, that it put someone at the mercy of another. Nevertheless, both had their place, and Holaind, like O'Connor, urged ethical guidelines for its use, including informed consent and the constant presence of a witness during hypnotic procedures.

Hypnosis raised a number of significant questions. William James' *Principles of Psychology* (1890a) discussed, in treating of hypnotism and related topics, the possibility of secondary personalities appearing. Roger Smith (1997) writes that the evidence for multiple personalities was used in France to argue an anti-clerical line, given the insistence of Catholic and other conservative authors on the unity of the soul. William Seton (1835–1905), Civil War veteran, author, and grandson of Elizabeth Ann Seton,[9] wrote widely on scientific topics in the *Catholic World*. In "Wonders of the nervous system," Seton (1890) concluded with a discussion of "unconscious cerebration" (p. 461) and of hypnosis or "artificial somnambulism" (p. 462). Post-hypnotic suggestion works, because "in the trance the idea suggested would seem to be transformed into an act with such marvelous rapidity, *by the intensely excited automatic action of the cerebro-spinal system*, that the intellect, the Ego, has not time to rouse itself and exert its authority" (p. 463). This cerebro-spinal system, Seton asserted on Bernheim's

---

[9] Elizabeth Ann Seton (1774–1821) was the first American-born person to be canonized a saint in the Catholic Church.

authority, is "apparently endowed with a consciousness of its own" (ibid.). Seton's distinction here was not between recent and more primitive divisions of the nervous system, a distinction some of his contemporaries made between the brain and the spinal cord. By the cerebro-spinal system, Seton meant the central nervous system as such, and by the Ego he meant, by implication, the soul, which is not material, although it relies on the nervous system. So he speculated that the nervous system could have its own consciousness, somehow independent of the soul. And with hypnosis comes danger, for with the Ego out of play, an unscrupulous hypnotizer could implant criminal or immoral suggestions into this inferior consciousness. But given the benefits of hypnosis, Seton thought that the procedure worthwhile. He concluded with a note of wonder: "let us say that the evidence points to vastly greater potentialities in the automatism of the cerebro-spinal system than we ever imagined" (p. 464), a note in keeping with the intense interest in what other writers called "subliminal consciousness" as containing great potential for the future.[10]

Seton (1899) returned to this topic in an article centered on the question of "secondary consciousness," reviewing the evidence from hypnotic trance, mediumships, automatic writing, and related phenomena. Seton argued that it would be wrong to assume "two distinct, normal personalities in every human being" (p. 656). He acknowledged that the new science of psychology was bringing to light aspects of the mind that the "old-time psychologists – albeit well versed in metaphysics – made no serious attempt to analyze" (ibid.). Especially important was the evidence for unconscious mental activity, associated with "higher and lower levels within the nervous system" (ibid.). When there is a disintegration of the functioning of the nervous system, either by mental illness or by hypnotic suggestion, then something like a secondary consciousness appears. Seton affirmed, that is, a dissociation theory of mental illness and hypnosis: "it is now held by good authorities that at least half the secret of hypnosis lies in this dissociation of the controlling consciousness from the reflex organic consciousness" (p. 657). So there is no autonomous secondary self in a healthy nervous system, but nervous activity underlying mental life is subject to disintegration. Seton thus gave a psychological account of hypnosis, mental illness and, implicitly, of Spiritualistic phenomena.

Seton did praise modern science for secularizing – not his word – mental illness: the study of the nervous system "rescued the subject of mental disorders from the region of mystery and superstition, and for convincing the world that insane persons are neither demoniacs nor witches" (ibid.). This kind of boundary making had been characteristic of the Catholic response to hypnotism for

---

[10] Seton (1890) devoted much attention to the ways that vital and psychological activities become automated with experience, and it was in that context that he introduced the term "unconscious cerebral action" (p. 457). See Edward Reed (1997) on notions of secondary consciousness as they played out in nineteenth-century psychologies.

at least fifty years by the time that Seton wrote that. In 1840, the Vatican had been pressed for a ruling on the use of magnetism. That ruling was as follows:

> Consult the standard authors, and bear this in mind, that, when every false doctrine is rejected, as well as every kind of witchcraft, and any explicit or implicit invocations of the devil is repudiated, *the mere act of using physical means, otherwise lawful, is not morally wrong*; provided that it be not made subservient to an end unlawful or in some way evil. But the use of causes and means purely physical to obtain effects or results truly supernatural, in order to explain these effects physically, is nothing but a deception, both unlawful and heretical.
>
> (cited in Holaind, 1895, p. 122)[11]

Some Catholics persisted in seeing here a condemnation of all uses of magnetism, and to remove ambiguity, in 1856, a further decree on the topic was issued. While affirming the legitimate scientific use of magnetism, this decree condemned what it termed its abuses: "yet the malice of men has gone so far that they neglect the lawful study of science, and rather seek occult things to the ruin of souls and to the detriment of civil society itself; boasting, as they do, that they have found a new way to magic and divination" (cited in ibid., p. 124). Here was boundary work at its finest point. The Holy Office condemned Spiritualism again in 1898 (Pace, 1912).

Georges Surbled's (1910) article on hypnosis for the *Catholic Encyclopedia* concluded that hypnosis "is a dangerous, if not a morally detestable, practice. In the process of suggestion the individual alienates his liberty and his reason, handing himself over to the domination of another" (p. 609), showing that the Catholic position remained divided on the question. Surbled (1855–1913), a physician, also found that the use of hypnosis waning: "psychology has derived but little illumination from hypnotism, and physicians recognize that, from a therapeutic view-point, suggestion is almost void of results. In the hospitals the practice of hypnotic methods is manifestly on the decline" (p. 610). This appears to be a valid observation. Ellenberger (1970) writes that with Charcot and Bernheim, "official medicine" recognized hypnosis, and that for twenty years following 1882, hypnosis flourished, only to suffer "a swift decline" (p. 171). The reasons were many: not everyone who wanted to practice hypnosis was good at it (the story of Freud's limitations here is legendary); hypnotizability was a variable talent and hard to pin down; most important, deliberate and sincere dissimulation on the part of those who were hypnotized cast

---

[11] Pace (1912) specified that it was the Congregation of the Inquisition that issued this decree. In 1908, Pope Pius X changed the name of this organization to the Supreme Sacred Congregation of the Holy Office. In 1965, it became the Sacred Congregation for the Doctrine of the Faith. In 1983, the "Sacred" was dropped and it became the Congregation for the Doctrine of the Faith. The present pope, Benedict XVI, was the head of the Congregation at the time of his election to the papacy in 2005.

aspersions on the whole enterprise. Psychoanalysis and simple suggestion won the day for the next several decades, and hypnosis slipped away, the Veiled Lady fading as mysteriously as she had arrived.

Or did she? An alternate reading is that hypnosis permeated everywhere in western societies through something like social osmosis. In the next decades, as Mary Watkins (1977) shows, psychotherapeutic techniques employing imagery, progressive relaxation, and a host of dynamic psychologies doing dream analysis and the like became standard forms of attempting to cure the souls of modern men and women. All used "suggestion," considered by some as the core phenomenon of hypnosis. Hypnosis pervaded popular culture in story and mass entertainment (the radio drama, *The Shadow*, broadcast from the 1930s to the 1950s, illustrates this). Finally, there was a resurgence of hypnosis, especially after World War II in academic and clinical settings (Hilgard, 1987, p. 298). With increased attention to things like the importance of relaxation (using hypnotic strategies) for dealing with "stress," hypnosis has found a respectable home in modern psychology.

Catholics and spiritualism: New revelations?

If the following section seems to stray far from the usual haunts of contemporary psychology, then it is important to recall that in the nineteenth century and in the early twentieth, the questions raised by Spiritualism were of the essence to those who pursued psychology. Spiritualism is one of the root stocks of psychology, one that may prove all the more important as psychology, no longer centered in North American and Western European interests, grafts new branches to this root. Moreover, the Spiritualist's questions were vital to some of the earliest proponents of what came to be called the New Psychology. Fechner pursued psychophysics in part because he wanted to prove the immortality of the soul. Brentano lamented that psychology no longer focused on what had made it, from antiquity, the "science of the future," namely, the future of the soul after death. James speculated that psychic researchers would make an even greater contribution to a natural scientific psychology than biologically minded researchers. Many of the first generation of psychologists sat with mediums in séances, as did Carl Jung, and even though many were skeptics, they learned much about the workings of the mind from them. Given the endurance of what we now call transpersonal psychology, with intimations of the continued existence of the human personality beyond the grave among some of its advocates, we cannot dismiss nineteenth-century debates over Spiritualism as out of place. All the more so when examining, as we are doing here, the boundaries between religion and psychology – for the Catholic Church had decided opinions about Spiritualist claims, and they about the claims of the Church.

Catholic opinions about Spiritualism varied considerably. The establishment of Christian Spiritualism, accusations of fraud and/or demonic activity, and proposals of psychological explanations, were among them. Christian Spiritualists included Florence Marryat (1837–99), a popular English novelist who "found that her religion failed to reassure her on the fundamental question of life after death" (Oppenheim, 1985, p. 38), Marie Sinclair, Countess of Caithness (1830–96), and others (Thurston, 1933, pp. 57–8). Like many Protestants and Anglicans, these women held that "Christian Spiritualism was a viable response to the anxieties of life in the nineteenth century" (Oppenheim, 1985, p. 76). Fraud was a common charge, and typical of the charges was an article (with photographs) in the *Catholic World* exposing one of the "haunts" of the Spiritualists (Earle, 1899). If the Catholic Spiritualists, especially before Vatican pronouncements made attendance at séances forbidden for all but the most scientific of purposes for Catholics, found solace in the new spirituality, the debunkers dismissed the movement entirely. Other Catholic positions took Spiritualism seriously, but made critical distinctions.

While admitting that deception, self-deception, and hallucination played some role in séances and other manifestations of the spiritual realm, Catholic writers in the nineteenth century affirmed with the Spiritualists that the spiritual realm exists. In "Spiritism and spiritists" (1869), Orestes Brownson,[12] the former Universalist minister and Transcendentalist, complained that "because contemporary science recognizes no invisible existences, and no intelligences above or separate from the human" (p. 290), scientists cannot understand what is going on in Spiritualism. Brownson asserted that after all the smoke is cleared, "there is still a residuum inexplicable without the recognition of a superhuman intelligence and source" (p. 291). The Catholic viewpoint was that it was possible for a superhuman intelligence to communicate with the living during séances. The question was: which intelligent beings? Brownson disputed the claim that Spiritualism proved the immortality of the soul, a claim often at the heart of Spiritualism as an unchurched spirituality. All it proved, according to Brownson, was that spirits exist, and in no way do Spiritualist claims contain "a revelation, supplementary to the Christian revelation" (p. 292). The testimony of the spirits was dubious: "There is nothing to support this assumption [of human immortality] but the testimony of spirits that

---

[12] Brownson (1803–76), along with Isaac Hecker, the founder of the Paulists (the order of priests to which Thomas Verner Moore belonged, before he became a Benedictine), was one of the notable converts of "native Americans" to Catholicism in the nineteenth century. Brownson, after leaving the ministry, worked with Robert Dale Owen and Fanny Wright in their campaign against the inequalities of marriage laws, and he became an advocate of workers' rights. Brownson then became a Unitarian minister, founded a journal, and had wide influence as a writer on equality and against property as based on natural law – Martin Van Buren blamed his defeat on Brownson. In 1844 he converted to Catholicism. He became a fiery apologist, meriting praise from Pope Pius IX. He wrote critiques of many liberal Christian views, and Spiritualism, especially in its alignment with liberal views, was subject to his attacks (Brownson, 1908).

often prove themselves lying spirits, and whose identity with the individual they personate, or pretend to be, we have no means of proving" (p. 293). Brownson concluded that the spirits were demons. His arguments chiefly rested on what the spirits said. They contradicted Church teaching in many areas: they denied the resurrection of the dead (ibid.), they "know or can say nothing of the beatific vision, which proves that they are not blessed angels" (p. 297),[13] and – most damning – they were "unanimous in declaring that there is no devil and no hell. God may not be absolutely denied, but his personality is obscured, and he appears only in the distance, as an infinite abstraction, being only in the sense in which, Hegel might say, being and not-being are identical" (ibid.). (It is shocking, perhaps, to think that demons read Hegel.) The kind of pantheistic theology allegedly propounded by the spirits was in keeping with some of the Romantic sentiments of the day. Brownson's accusation, however, assumed a kind of unanimity in the Spiritualist community that did not exist. Buescher (2002) reports that at the second annual meeting of the Massachusetts Spiritualists Association in 1867, the membership debated language defining their organization. They argued whether "the preamble should contain language that set Spiritualism apart from Christianity" (p. 564). Buescher also notes that the editor of the Chicago newspaper, *The Spiritual Republic*, found objectionable the anti-Christian language in the statement issued by the Massachusetts group (ibid.). Braude (2001) writes that while an American Association of Spiritualists began in 1865, it collapsed a decade later, largely because Spiritualists as a rule distrusted organizations. They tended to be strong advocates of individual rights, and many left the church and other restrictive organizations in pursuit of freedom. This was true especially of women, who suffered more political oppression than did men.

Brownson (1869) offered further evidence for the demonic source of Spiritualist pronouncements: the Spiritualists support radical political causes, many of which Brownson had supported before 1844. These "furious radicals" (p. 297) aspired to nothing less than a new religion:

> The new form of religion will free the world from the old church, from bondage to the Bible, to creeds and dogmas, the old patriarchal systems and governments, and place the religious, social, and political world on a

---

[13] Lynn Sharp (1999) reports: "Colleen McDannell and Bernhard Lang argue that a 'modern' conception of heaven was born with Swedenborg in the late eighteenth century. This heaven, material and sensual, would be popularized by spiritists and Protestants throughout the nineteenth century. In contrast, Catholic heaven remained that of the sixteenth-century reformers, one of contemplation carried out in the sight of God, up until the late twentieth century. Spiritism incorporated a material, Swedenborgian heaven, including reunions with beloved family members and teaching heaven as an active place" (p. 286). This shows that Brownson in his 1869 *Catholic World* article was sensitive to the conflict between Catholic and non-Catholic views of the afterlife, and that he took an *ad hominem* approach to the conflict.

higher plane, and moved by a more energetic spirit of progress. This is the mission of spiritism.

(ibid.)

This radicalism took specific form in the area of morals and marriage. Among the devious suggestions of the spirits were that "only voluntary obedience is meritorious; forced obedience is no virtue" (p. 298). In response, Brownson argued that the Spiritualists make no distinctions in kinds of love, thus laying the ground for "the grossest corruption and the most beastly immorality" (ibid.). He claimed that Spiritualism especially corrupted marriage. Spiritualists "very generally look upon the marriage law as tyrannical and absurd, and assert the doctrine of free love" (ibid.). What "free love" meant was that "the marriage is in the love, and when the love is no more, the marriage is dissolved. None of our sentiments depend on the will; hence, self-denial is unnatural, and immortal" (ibid.). For the Spiritualists, then, a loveless marriage is as unlawful as prostitution. Naturally, "woman's-rightism is only another product of the same shop," and the leaders of the women's rights movement "are spiritists or intimately connected with them" (p. 299). If nothing else, Brownson's article shows how Catholic concern with spiritualism was more than theological, and that the Spiritualists were not simply concerned with the ethereal world.[14]

Braude's (2001) study supports at least part of his argument: "While not all feminists were Spiritualists, all Spiritualists advocated women's rights" (p. 58). Many of those who became seriously interested in Spiritualism came from religious denominations that already stressed individual freedom, such as the Quakers. Others came from liberal Protestant congregations, such as the Universalists. While some Spiritualists rejected key tenets of Christianity, others did not; in this, as in many other things, North and South differed, with Southern Spiritualists seeing more compatibility with Christianity than did Northerners. In New Orleans, as reported in the Spiritualist newspaper, *The Banner of Light*, "among the Creole and Catholic portions of our populations" Spiritualism has been more readily accepted than among Protestants, in part because "the creed of the Catholic Church does not deny the possibility of spirit communication" (quoted in ibid., p. 30). In line with the Spiritualist main appeal – the consolation of hearing from dead loved ones – the Spiritualists did tend in an "Arminian" direction, that is, a rejection of the Calvinist teaching on predestination in favor of a belief that all may be saved, and they rejected the idea of hell (p. 38). Most of the beliefs surrounding the Spiritualists were in line with Protestant liberalism, except that Spiritualism gave people something to hold on to when faced with death. Other Spiritualist beliefs came from

---

[14] To add a psychological note, Brownson's tone also suggests conflicts between his former and current views.

Swedenborgianism and Transcendentalism, but without the need for submission to the teachings of a master. Anyone who so chose, could verify for him- or herself the truth of Spiritualism by attending a séance. The fact that the Catholic view so consistently stressed the demonic dangers lurking in Spiritualism is an indication of the appeal of direct experience of the spiritual world unmediated by clergy or liturgy.

Interpretation of Spiritualism in terms of the demonic were repeated in a series in the *Catholic World* (Spiritualism: Chapter I, 1873; Spiritualism: Chapter II, 1873; Spiritualism: Chapter III, 1874). Like sincere Spiritualists, the Catholic viewpoint held that in séances, one really did have communication with disembodied spirits. They differed solely in deciding who the spirits were. This series of articles, drawing on contemporary research into Spiritualism by the London Dialectical Society (1871) and on the history of magic and witchcraft, dealt with three interpretations of what happens in séances in naturalistic terms: humbug, unconscious cerebration, and psychic force. While admitting that showmanship and deception play their role in Spiritualist circles, the author (Spiritualism: Chapter I, 1873) was unconvinced that fraud explained everything, especially revelations made that neither the medium nor the recipients of the messages from the beyond could possibly have known in advance, messages that subsequent investigations appeared to verify. In the same way, the thesis of unconscious cerebration could account for some but not all the phenomena. The author (ibid.) drew on William Carpenter's (1813–85) notion of "unconscious cerebration."[15] Carpenter opposed the evidence of Spiritualism presented to the Dialectical Society. He had previously addressed somnambulism and mesmerism, concluding that, in the words of the 1873 article, "you may have received unconsciously into your cerebrum the information in question, or have unconsciously elaborated it from premises so received, and may have communicated it to your informant by unconscious muscular action" (p. 147). "Psychic force" was an alternative hypothesis; this was the postulate of a kind of subtle fluid, similar to "animal magnetism," pervading the entire cosmos, and capable of moving and being moved by the human imagination. The author drew on the work of Henry More, the eighteenth-century English

---

[15] Carpenter was a leading English physiologist of the day, rooted in the British empiricist tradition of David Hartley, James Mill, and others. He was also a "devout Unitarian" (Reed, 1997, p. 121). Alexander Bain, John Stuart Mill, and Thomas Huxley all knew and drew on Carpenter's work. His major work was *Principles of human physiology*, which appeared in numerous editions. Carpenter helped develop the notion of "unconscious cerebration." In his eyes, this concept had a theological dimension, as Reed explains: "Just as God designed the universe to act on its own most of the time, so our minds allow our bodies to act automatically in many instances, Carpenter maintained, on the basis of 'unconscious cerebration'" (pp. 78–9). Carpenter saw unconscious cerebration as an explanation of hypnosis, and he introduced the idea of "suggestibility" (Reed, 1997, p. 79), seeing it as a way to account for Spiritualist phenomena.

Platonist, to explain further the idea of psychic force – first and foremost, it can influence matter, especially the nervous system. By being given shape by the imagination, it can affect the body more generally: images, via psychic force, can influence the shape of marks on a fetus when the mother's imagination is stimulated in some strong fashion; produce bruises and sores on the skin (especially when one is "shocked," a good nineteenth-century term); produce what we call placebo effect ("cases of recovery from the gravest illness, some of which involved the arresting active, organic mischief, are recorded as brought about by the vehement impression made upon the imagination by a remedy supposed, but never really applied" (p. 155)); perhaps psychic force can even influence external objects, as frequently recorded in history and in Spiritualist literature. The article (Spiritualism: Chapter I, 1873), in sympathy with the Spiritualist community (p. 156), concluded that the psychic force hypothesis left some things unaccounted for, and that it seemed employed largely because scientists have a prejudice against the hypothesis that spirits were actually involved in Spiritualism. The author contended the following, after this review of the naturalistic hypotheses of unconscious cerebration and psychic force:

> Whilst reiterating my belief that the mind has many mysterious powers capable of being brought into active operation by various influences, and that these are, in all probability, operative in several of the phenomena of spiritualism; granting, moreover, that it is hardly possible to define precisely the extent of the soul's co-operation in the production of these phenomena, I contend, notwithstanding, that the psychic-force hypothesis is the result of a non-natural and inadequate analysis of the phenomena of spiritualism . . . So far as we have any indication of a thaumaturgic element in the mind, it manifests itself in the supreme efforts of the imagination, kindled by emotion, and abstracted and concentrated by expectation; whereas, in the mass of spiritualistic experiences, imagination in those concerned seems distinctly to fall short of its highest stages.
>
> (ibid., p. 165)

The author, drawing on Catholic teachings, concluded that "one of the causes most active in spiritualism . . . is the devil" (p. 337).

Acknowledging that the Spiritualists argue against materialism, this article claimed that Spiritualism belonged to a long tradition, extending back to the Pagan worship of Diana, to the Gnostics of the early Christian centuries, and to witchcraft (Spiritualism: Chapter III, 1874, p. 613). Spiritualist accounts combine "Platonism with something of the color and rhythm of modern science" (p. 620), thereby claiming what later scholars would assert, that Spiritualism accommodated some very traditional beliefs with modern science (Fuller, 2001; Taylor, 1999). The Catholic position, however, was that the Spiritualists encountered things that modern science, in its materialistic form, do not acknowledge. Writing in the *Catholic World* in 1899, A. L. Dutto argued against materialists' claims that "the supernatural is impossible; therefore it does not exist" (p. 80), instead saying that visions do occur: "True supernatural visions carry with them the seal of their own genuineness, producing effects impossible to account for on natural grounds" (p. 83). He cited as examples the Apostles' experience of Pentecost and the visions of St. Teresa, including evidence that she levitated during her trances. The aim of this article was not Spiritualism; rather, it was the truth of visions that Scripture reported and that occurred throughout history, especially in the lives of the mystics. Dutto strove to refute the claim that all these were hallucinations. Thus we see that while the Catholics and the Spiritualists were much in opposition, they still had much in common.

By the end of the nineteenth century, the skeptics had the upper hand. Taylor (1999) summarizes the findings of the American Society for Psychical Research as supporting "the reality of the unconscious" (p. 170) and of "useful techniques for gaining access to unconscious states" (ibid.).[16] Not that Spiritualism ever died out; it continues to this day. But the main trend was actually the modernist direction of immanence. In studying the Society for Psychical Research, Cerullo (1982) observes that leaders of the Society, such as Edmund Gurney and Frederick W. H. Myers, sought "to fashion psychical research into something quite different from orthodox Spiritualism. It was to be not a verification of the spirits without, but an homage to the ineffable within" (p. 54). This direction, in keeping with the mainstream of scientific thought in de-emphasizing the intervention of disincarnate beings and emphasizing the unconscious, the subconscious, or subliminal consciousness, was essentially, to use the official language of the Church in the decades to follow, modernist. Immanence, however, was also the Spiritualist's direction. With close ties to Transcendentalism, but without its elite status, Spiritualism "struck many Americans as concrete proof of the immanence of God and as a literal interpretation of Emerson's advice to seek truth within their own souls" (Braude, 2001, p. 46). Spiritualism participated, one may say, in the modernist trend without, at the same time, denying the literal reality of life after death and of the spiritual world. It did seek a reconciliation of religion and scientific modernity.

Georges Surbled (1898), whose negative assessment of hypnosis we considered above, also addressed Spiritualism. His account shows some of the difficulty in defining the boundaries between spiritualism and Catholicism. While Surbled opposed the use of hypnotism, he had no doubt but that it produced real effects.[17] He thought that neither Charcot's theory that hypnosis follows

---

[16] Ellenberger (1970) had earlier affirmed the importance of Spiritualism for the rise of dynamic psychology, because it "indirectly provided psychologists and psychopathologists with new approaches to the mind" (p. 85).

[17] Surbled held that hypnosis had great power. In 1891, he reported that after witnessing a "public exhibition of hypnotism, an intelligent man, aged fifty-two, of healthy antecedents, was profoundly impressed by what he had seen, and continued to talk of the wonders of

from a weakened nervous system nor Liébeault and Bernheim's theory of suggestion accounted for all hypnotic phenomena. Surbled (1898; 1910) argued that the old theory of animal magnetism, a *fluide magnétique*, would again prove its value in explaining hypnosis. This magnetic fluid is nothing supernatural, Surbled wrote, but will be shown to be "le fluide électrique *vital*" (1898, p. 185), the vital electrical fluid or the "nerve force" of nineteenth-century medicine. Such a fluid would help explain what seemed to Surbled to be the mysterious "nervous sleep." Surbled invoked an ancient lineage of the concept of this vital fluid, tracing it back to Galen, Ficino, Paracelsus, and Mesmer. He argued that this fluid was a physical phenomenon, and he contrasted it to the Spiritualist notion of some kind of intermediary between the soul and the body, called various things, such as the "astral body" or a "fluid," which mediums can emit and direct. The way that the Spiritualists understood this fluid, Surbled argued, had the effect of "materializing" the soul (because the fluid was somehow both corporeal and incorporeal) and rendering Spiritualism, despite its overt claims, a form of positivism and pantheism (pp. 265–6). Surbled made a thin distinction between vital fluid, which is material, and the Spiritualist's fluid, which is semi-spiritual in nature, to account for hypnosis and to discount Spiritualism. Surbled's speculations point to a complexity of the Catholic position vis-à-vis Spiritualism: Catholics affirmed the existence of the spiritual world but objected to the Spiritualists' materialistic conception of that world and to secular commerce with it. Moreover, the Church opposed Spiritualist teachings while at the same time invoking for itself a lineage including Ficino and Paracelsus, who could both be claimed by the Spiritualists as well.[18]

As we shall see, direct communications from the Beyond were not out-of-bounds for Catholics, and some apparitions were warranted. It all depended on who was communicating with whom, on this side and the other side of the great divide between the temporal and eternal worlds.

In light of the modernist controversy, it is interesting to look at Edward Pace's (1912) interpretation of Spiritualism in his article for the *Catholic Encyclopedia*. Pace, after reviewing the history of Spiritualism and of its scientific investigation, noted that philosophical presuppositions affected how investigators interpreted what they found:

> For those who denied the existence of a soul distinct from the organism it was a foregone conclusion that there could be no such communications as

'animal magnetism' for days after the performance. Soon, however, he began to act rather queerly and in about two weeks became acutely maniacal and died shortly after of encaphalitis. During his delirium all his thoughts were of hypnotism and he was continually making passes as if he had subjects before him. Dr. Surbled regarded his death as the direct result of the impressions made upon an excitable brain by the public hypnotic performance" (The evils of public hypnotizations, 1891, p. 99).

[18] Especially Paracelsus, who was held in high esteem by Theosophists: see Waite (1894) as an example.

the Spiritists claimed. This negative view, of course, is still taken by all who accept the fundamental ideas of Materialism. But apart from any such a priori considerations, the opponents of Spiritism justified their position by pointing to innumerable cases of fraud which were brought to light either through closer examination of the methods employed or through the admissions of the mediums themselves.

(p. 222)

For Pace, there were three hypotheses for explaining genuine events, such as information conveyed during a séance that the medium could not have known: (1) telepathy, originating in the action of the "subliminal consciousness" (p. 223), a hypothesis in "accord with the recognized facts of hypnosis and with the results of experimental telepathy" (ibid.); (2) the supposition of a subtle or astral body "which in certain persons (mediums) can escape from the material organism and thus form a 'double'" (ibid.). This supposition, which Surbled had also attacked, was in accord with the teachings of Theosophy. (3) The Spiritualist belief that disincarnate spirits communicate to the living through mediums. If one accepted this third hypothesis, the question then became, to be sure, the identity of the spirits. Since some of the communications from the spirits "antagonize the essential truths of religion, such as the Divinity of Christ, atonement and redemption, judgment and future retribution, while they encourage agnosticism, pantheism, and a belief in reincarnation" (ibid.), these spirits could not be sent by God, and could be demons. While not denying the Spiritualist interpretation, Pace held that "a critical investigator will cling to the idea that phenomena which now seem inexplicable may eventually, like so many other marvels, be accounted for without having recourse to the Spiritistic hypothesis" (ibid.). (The other marvels alluded to were probably those of hypnosis, under its earlier incarnation of mesmerism and magnetism.) Even more crucial for Pace was the danger of Spiritualism as alleged proof of the immortality of the soul:

> Those [e.g. the Neoscholastics] who are convinced, on philosophical grounds, of the soul's immortality may say that communications from the spirit world, if any such there be, go to strengthen their conviction; but to abandon their philosophy and stake all on Spiritism would be more than hazardous; it would, indirectly at least, afford a pretext for a more complete rejection of soul and immortality. In other words, if Spiritism were the sole argument for a future life, Materialism, instead of being crushed, would triumph anew as the only possible theory for science and common sense.
>
> (ibid.)

For Pace, clearly, the philosophical arguments he and other Scholastics provided were a more sure foundation for the soul and its immortality.

Official Church pronouncements on Spiritualism included those already mentioned in relation to magnetism. Those were not the last: In 1898, the Holy Office forbade "Spiritistic practices, even though intercourse with the demon be excluded and communication sought with good spirits only" (p. 224). In 1917, the Holy Office replied in the negative when asked: "Whether it is allowed either through a so-called medium or without one, and with or without hypnotism, to assist in any Spiritualistic communications or manifestations, even such as appear to be blameless or pious, either asking questions of the souls or spirits, or listening to their answers, or merely looking on, even with a tacit or express protestation that one does not want to have anything to do with evil spirits" (cited in Griffin, 1967, p. 577). Griffin added, by way of clarification, that this interdiction did not "preclude legitimate scientific study" (ibid.). If psychological theories of Spiritualist phenomena tended to become dominant in the twentieth century, especially among those who found therein evidence for unconscious mental activity, whether it be the repressed unconscious of psychoanalysis or the subconscious that potentially opened upon "the more," as William James put it, for the Church those interpretations in terms of immanence did not foreclose the possibility that "the more" was something sinister at work, for with the Spiritualist community, the Church affirmed the reality of the immaterial world.

A Spiritualist alternative to the Catholic position appeared in *The debatable land between this world and the next* (1872), by Robert Dale Owen (1801–77), the son of the British social reformer, Robert Owen. Robert Dale Owen had already established himself as an abolitionist, an advocate of women's rights, and as a legislator and diplomat when he came to write this book. He began with an exhortation to Protestant clergy, denouncing the very recent proclamation of papal infallibility at the first Vatican Council, and also the failure of the Reformation to make significant progress over the past three centuries. We lived, he wrote, in an age of indifference to religion, when skepticism and rationalism abound. Was it possible, he asked, that progress be made in every science and endeavor, but not in our knowledge of the soul? He argued that "Spiritual science" (p. 47) could and has advanced through Spiritualism. Countering the rationalism and modernism of a Rénan, whose *Life of Jesus* (1864) sought to demythologize the gospels, Owen (1872) claimed that the same "signs and wonders" (p. 155) that Jesus and the Apostles worked – healing the sick, speaking in tongues, casting out spirits – were still happening, and that, contrary to the "Catholic and orthodox Protestant belief" (p. 157), they were not miracles – that is, they were not exceptions to natural law. They were, on the contrary, done according to the natural laws that hold between the material and the spirit worlds. Why was this position important to Owen? Because with "the progress of science, the belief in the miraculous is melting away, [and] the ultimate result will be disbelief in the alleged miracles of the Gospels; and we shall fall back on Rénan's conclusion that Christ countenanced fraud" (ibid.). Spiritualism provided "direct evidence that immortality *is* brought to light now, among us – that the apostolic gifts *are* reproduced at this day and are not restricted to the Roman Catholic Church" (p. 161).

Contrary to what Catholic writers were claiming, according to Owen the spirits presented views *"in strict accordance with the teachings of Christ"* (p. 170), although these alleged teachings did not include many things central to Catholicism. In any event, for Owen, just as no living man is infallible, neither are the spirits, and regarding "side-issues and non-essentials, it would seem that the same variety and uncertainty of opinion exist in the next world as in our own" (p. 171). With that proviso, he listed fourteen points that "intelligent Spiritualists" (ibid.) agree upon, such as: immortality, continued progress in the moral and spiritual life after death, no eternal damnation, higher and lower lives in the thereafter depending upon the character of the person, and an absence of answers as to burning theological questions, such as the divinity of Christ (p. 176). However, the spirits do denounce a core belief of Calvinism, the "original depravity" of men and women (p. 177).

Brownson's reply to Owen in the *Catholic World* was relentless. In "Owen on Spiritism" (1872), Brownson repeated the charge that Spiritism proved only that demons can hoodwink susceptible mortals, and that Owen's Christianity, such as it is, "has not a trace of Christianity of Christ, and is as little worthy of being called Christianity as the bald Unitarianism of Channing, or the Deism of Rousseau, Tom Paine, or Voltaire, or the Free Religion of Emerson, Higginson, and Julia Ward Howe" (p. 812). Apologetics and rhetorical venom aside, Brownson gave a fair evaluation of the variety of Christianity Owen did support. But it is also true that Owen was more concerned with rationalist than with Catholic reactions to his work, and he addressed two main fears of the living, death and divine wrath: The Spiritualists confirmed that "in strictness there is no death" (Owen, 1872, p. 171), and that "the sleep which goes by the name of death being but a brief transition-slumber from which, for the good, the awakening is immeasurably more glorious" is not "God's wrath" (ibid.).

One further Catholic interpretation of Spiritualism has Herbert Thurston, SJ (1856–1939), as its representative. Thurston was a prolific writer of essays and books on Spiritualism and history. He was a member of the Society for Psychical Research (SPR).[19] He disagreed with the Catholic physician, James Joseph Walsh (1925), who held that Spiritualism was simply trickery, and Thurston cautioned against accepting too readily the belief that it was only a matter of demonic intervention. Since we know so little about the realm of the spirit, it is best to be cautious. Affirming the Church's official teaching as prudent, he did point to some conversions to Catholicism among Spiritualists. Still, his main point was that "if the Church has banned Spiritualism, she has

---

[19] The SPR did not officially affirm any particular explanation for the topics it investigated, as stated in its constitution: "Membership of this Society does not imply the acceptance of any particular explanation of the phenomena investigated, nor any belief as to the operation, in the physical world, of forces other than those recognized by Physical Science" (Objects of the Society, 1883, p. 5).

not banned psychic research, neither has she, despite a widespread impression to the contrary, pronounced all the phenomena of mediumship and the various forms of automatism to be necessarily diabolic in origin" (Thurston, 1933, pp. 83–4). Thurston argued that to dismiss all reports of spirit manifestation as false puts Catholics in an uncomfortable position, because the same kind of first-person testimony is also used as evidence in the canonization process (p. 249). If one dismisses the former, why not the latter? Thurston's questions went in a theological and a psychological direction. On the former, he wrote that much of the testimony of Spiritualists does not contradict Catholic teaching and, indeed, is compatible with it.[20] On the psychological side, Thurston held that telepathy and clairvoyance, which seemed to him plausible, pointed to natural abilities that at least some people have. Just as the Church has "accepted hypnotism as a phenomenon of psychic experience which does not necessarily suppose the intervention of any diabolic or evil influence" (p. 229), so will the Church accept natural telepathy and natural clairvoyance as purely human acts.

On this point of psychical research as a legitimate topic, whatever the fate of other Spiritualistic claims, Thurston had Catholic company. He cited a passage of Mercier's *Manual of Modern Scholastic Philosophy* in support of the possibility of psychic powers: "A similar explanation [i.e. of cerebral action capable of some sort of transmission from the brain of the operator] may possibly account for telepathy, which etymologically means sensation at a distance. Of this phenomenon examples are by no means rare" (Mercier, 1916, vol. 1, p. 290, quoted in Thurston, 1933, p. 246). He also cited the investigations of Alois Gatterer, SJ, who concluded that telekinesis and materializations happen sometimes in séances (Gatterer, 1927), and the work of Lucien Roure, SJ (1917). To these names we can add Étienne De Greeff, who studied apparitions, and Julian Ochorowicz, who studied the medium Eusapia Palladino (Misiak and Staudt, 1954, p. 62 and pp. 175–6).

A Catholic alternative to spiritualism

Under the first [thesis] we are driven to maintain the Roman Catholic and orthodox Protestant belief in the Exceptional and the Miraculous. If, defeated by scientific progress, we fail to sustain this dogma, then the

---

[20] "Obviously there would be no purpose in praying to angels or saints if they did not know that we *were* praying or did not know what it is we ask. Many – I think most – devout Catholics believe that this knowledge is shared by the souls in purgatory; indeed, for all we know, it may be the common and necessary attribute of all disembodied spirits, including the souls of the lost, that they possess a telepathic and clairvoyant knowledge of distant occurrences ... What I am anxious to insist on is that while the belief that disembodied spirits know what passes on earth is perfectly familiar to Catholics, it impresses the non-Catholic public as a new discovery or a rash hypothesis" (Thurston, 1933, p. 301).

wonderful works of Christ and his disciples take their place beside the labors of Hercules, and other tales of heathen mythology.

Robert Dale Owen, *The Debatable Land* (1872, p. 157)

The *American Ecclesiastical Review* published in 1894 a brief review of a book that contained the testimony of a woman, a Mrs. A. E. Whitehead, who had been converted to Catholicism after getting involved in séances and coming to the conclusion that the devil had a hand in them (Review of the book *A convert through spiritualism*, 1894). The book, *A convert through spiritualism*, included a Preface written by Richard Frederick Clarke, S. J. Clarke (1839–1900) wrote extensively on religious and spiritual matters in the second half of the nineteenth century, including *Theosophy: Its teachings, marvels and true character* (1892b). Among his works, moreover, were *Lourdes: Its inhabitants, its pilgrims, and its miracles* (1888) and *Medical testimony to the miracles of Lourdes* (1892a). What is striking here is what we may call the Catholic equivalent of Spiritualism: a young woman, susceptible to trances, had visions of a being from the spirit world, and she acted as a kind of medium for messages from the world of spirits. There were differences, of course: the apparition claimed to be the Immaculate Conception, that is, Mary, the mother of Jesus.

There were many claims made in nineteenth-century France of apparitions of Mary, but Lourdes became the center for pilgrimages, a tradition that continues to this day. At Lourdes, too, the cures became central to the meaning of the pilgrimages, not the claims of others that they too had had visitations of the Immaculate Conception. The parallels and divergences between the miracles at Lourdes and Spiritualism are many, and they are worth noting in order to see how in the nineteenth century, boundaries were drawn between the emerging science of psychology and the Catholic faith.

Bernadette Soubirous (1844–79) was fourteen years old in 1858, when she experienced a series of eighteen apparitions of a girl[21] who called herself, eventually, the Immaculate Conception. Traditions in the region of the Pyrenees, in addition to standard Catholic views, held that souls of the dead might make their presence felt, and so early on, some of the women of Lourdes thought that maybe the visitation was of a recently deceased woman of the area, who had been known for her piety (Harris, 1999, pp. 57–9). Through some of the things that Bernadette said, as well as through her behavior, locals decided that the apparition was neither a devil nor a dead person's soul. Bernadette was tested both by physicians, as ordered by the prefect, and by her neighbors; the former to see if she were insane, the latter to see if she were possessed. Harris

---

[21] Bernadette insisted that the apparition was a "little girl" who, Harris states, bore "little resemblance to orthodox notions of what the Virgin should look like" (1999, p. 57). "Bernadette refused to guess at the presence's identity, calling it merely *Aquéro*, the patois for *cela*, an indefinable being, certainly not human but not necessarily divine" (p. 5).

summarizes the findings: "Bernadette seemed to differ from these pathological or diabolical examples because of her capacity to perform sensible tasks while in her trance … The influence of the apparition was thus utterly benign" (pp. 63–4). The most significant difference between Spiritualist apparitions and Bernadette's, however, was the answer to the question, who are you? The local curé, Abbé Dominique Peyramale, had asked Bernadette to ask the girl her name, after the apparition had told Bernadette that a chapel should be built on the site. On several occasions she asked, and each time she received no answer. Finally, one day, *Aquéro* replied: "The girl in white appeared [to Bernadette at the grotto], and Bernadette pressed her to say who she was. After repeating the question four times, *Aquéro* finally put her hands together, looked heavenwards and spoke: 'Que soy era Immaculada Councepciou': 'I am the Immaculate Conception'" (p. 8).[22] There had been earlier apparitions of the Virgin as Mary Immaculate, but the timing of the Lourdes apparition was important. Pius XI had declared the Immaculate Conception of Mary Church dogma in 1854.[23] As Harris (1999) writes, "The apparition's statement thus brought together the disparate worlds of rural piety and the Vatican, and provided a tremendous comfort to a papacy beleaguered by the hostility of liberal, rational and democratic movements" (p. 14). Thus, in contrast to what many mediums transmitted, Bernadette reported nothing contrary to Church teaching and had, indeed, affirmed the latest teaching of the Church. For Abbé Peyramale, "the words explained the whole purpose of the apparitions" (p. 81). They made, moreover, subsequent miraculous cures at Lourdes significant in the political-scientific controversies of the day: anticlerical forces would have to explain them away, and Catholics would have to prove in modern ways the reality of the miracles.

Local ancient traditions made grottoes and springs places of healing, and so it was perhaps inevitable that healing took place at the site of the manifestation of the Immaculate Conception, although Bernadette did not report that that was the purpose of apparitions. But even early pilgrims sought healing as well as repentance, as was the custom at such shrines. These early sojourners combined Christian and pre-Christian elements in their rituals with the waters at Lourdes. Harris emphasizes how these rural people "seemed not to distinguish between *santé* (physical health) and *salut* (spiritual well-being), and in their rites sought to break down the boundaries between the material and the spiritual" (p. 293). Church officials sought to distinguish the miraculous intervention of God and potentially magical properties of the water at the grotto. Through the 1870s, moreover, there was little concern with medical confirmation or "proof" of the

---

[22] Harris (1999) describes the oddity of this reply: "To use an event to describe a person sounded awkward, even discordant" (p. 8).

[23] The dogma of the Immaculate Conception states that Mary, the mother of Jesus, was born without taint of original sin.

cures, the narratives being primarily moral in tone (p. 300). Significantly, many of the stories describe illness in decidedly pre-modern ways, at odds with the emerging biomedical model of the late nineteenth century. Harris recounts one such: "Such was the case of Léontine Aubain, whose illness began with the inflammation of her fingernails, developed into an abscess in the envelope of her spinal cord and left her with an inert leg and hip. She seemed to view her symptoms as part of an underlying invasion, a view of illness that was central to these women's conception of cure as a release through wholesale and crushing ejection" (p. 308). Such stories call to mind those that Barbara Duden (1991) found in the notebooks of an eighteenth-century German physician, descriptions of illness and the body that are incomprehensible if one assumes, as we tend to do, the experience of our bodies and illnesses in biomedical terms. That the experience of the body and illness has a history is important to note, especially as we try to understand subsequent events at Lourdes. It was not, at Lourdes, simply the case that many of the pilgrims lived a non-biomedical experience of the body, however; they also lived what we can call a liturgical experience of the body. Harris (1999) writes:

> Whether the cure was in the pools or near the Eucharist, sufferers related their experience as radical and instantaneous. This belief, however, was often contradicted by the rest of their statements, which showed how the emerging sense of well-being often extended over several days and many encounters. Despite this, most indicated a certain moment of miraculous transformation, even if full implementation took longer.
>
> (p. 317)

These cures were holistic, moreover, in that there were strong spiritual elements: repentance, worship, prayer, and something often like an exorcism. This pattern captures much of what Pickstock (2000) describes as liturgical which: "fuses the most realistic with the most ideal. It is realistic in the sense that all our deliberate behaviour and reflective thought is grounded in a pre-conceptual *life-world* ... This reality which everything else assumes has also an *ideal aspect*, for these original patterns privilege certain shapes, sounds or whatever, over others. Here lies the origin of some sort formations, certain unquestioned value ... on which all else depends, even if ... this transcendence lies metaphysically in the immanent world" (p. 160). What this means is that everyday events always point beyond themselves to some "ideal value," meaning, in the case of Lourdes, the mysteries of Christianity. Liturgy mediates the public and private, the personal and the eternal, such that personal joys and sorrows, sufferings and delights, always and at the same time have significance in the light of "cosmic patterns" (p. 161). To take the healings at Lourdes as liturgical events means that in the illness and its cure – and the absence of healing, or the prayer that others may be healed instead of the pilgrim (Harris, 1999, p. 311) – both *santé* and *salut* were operative. So the cure can be instantaneous and drawn out, for the temporality of the liturgical has a complex structure. As Pickstock (2000) shows with regard to medieval liturgy, there is a repeated approach, an ascent that is repeatedly renewed. In the same way, moments of "miraculous transformation" can take time.

What appeared to be pre-modern modes of living the body and time met with considerable resistance, even from ecclesiastical officials, who may have desired to retain them. As Clarke (1888) explained the dilemma:

> When we approach the border-land of the miraculous we have to exercise the greatest possible caution. If it seems ungrateful to question Our Lady's wonder-working power by any attempt to explain, on natural grounds, a change of the supernatural character of which there seems to be very little doubt, yet, on the other hand, in this critical and skeptical age it is very injurious to religion if its advocates lay claim to a direct intervention of God's wonder-working power where the ordinary laws of nature may possibly have produced the phenomena under investigation.
>
> (pp. 73–4)

By the time Clarke visited Lourdes in the 1880s, there had already been considerable attention given to drawing the boundary between the natural and the supernatural in the cures that sometimes occurred there.[24] A first medical report of 1860 examined cures from two perspectives, the ecclesiastical, using criteria that the Church had drawn up in the eighteenth century (Harris, 1999, pp. 321–2), and the medical, with the physician Henri Vergez eliminating from the list of miracles those cases where the cure could be interpreted in terms of mental influences, such as powerful passions or the imagination. In 1883, a *Bureau de Consultations*, or Medical Bureau, was established, because "the Church accepted both the need for scientific verification and for many of the epistemological criteria of modern medicine" (p. 307). Under the direction of Baron Dunot de Saint-Maclou, a physician, Thomist, and ultramontanist (pp. 325–6), the medical examination gained increasing prominence in the evaluation of cures, enabling "the penetration of medical epistemology despite the shrine's pervasive miraculous mood" (p. 327). This work continued under Gustave Boissarie, who took over from Saint-Maclou when the latter died in 1891. Boissairie's goal was to use "science to back up religious belief" and "to force physicians to confront the special happenings at the Grotto" (p. 330).

---

[24] Sometimes: Clarke (1888) reported that "The percentage of those who are completely freed from their maladies there is very small indeed. I scarcely like to venture on any sort of conjectural average, but I imagine that, if five per cent of the sick are cured in any given pilgrimage, the average would be regarded as a very large one . . . But one benefit, I do not hesitate to say, attaches to every pilgrimage, that the sick, even if they are not healed, even if no improvement takes place in their condition, invariably go away comforted, and with fresh grace to bear with patient resignation the sicknesses which it has pleased God to inflict upon them" (pp. 76–7).

To deal with the skeptics, then, the Church used psychological criteria to distinguish true from assumed miracles, true miracles being the residue when all natural causes for the healing have been exhausted. As Clarke (1888) put it:

> If the various forms of hysteria and paralysis [taken as a functional disease] were the only diseases healed, we should join hands with the skeptic, or at least to acknowledge that there is no clear and incontestable evidence of the power of God acting directly and immediately on the body. Unless we concede this, we are liable to render our own position indefensible ... A man who should declare the numberless cures of nervous maladies at Lourdes to be all of them due to Our Lady's wonder-working power to heal, may be a pious enthusiast, but is neither a prudent man nor a trustworthy advocate of the cause he is defending.
>
> (p. 96)

That is to say, that the only real miracles, or the only ones that stand up to skeptical doubt, were those of medically certified organic disease. All others were suspect, because they might have been brought about by any number of natural, including psychological, factors. The one most often cited by the end of the century was suggestion.[25]

Suzanne Kaufman (2005) has analyzed the controversies over miracles at Lourdes, showing how both sides used the newly developing mass media to argue their points. Whereas critics of the claims for actual miracles occurring at Lourdes reduced the observed effects to mind cure and suggestion, "Catholic doctors were quick to undermine the very credibility of the suggestion thesis by attacking the expertise of Charcot and others" (p. 177). As the debates over Lourdes continued, not only were doubts cast upon alleged cures, but they were also sown on the medical community's competence by both supporters and detractors of the shrine. Critics accused Catholic doctors of ignorance of the cause and nature of the diseases they diagnosed, and

---

[25] Georges Bertrin (1910) argued against the suggestion-hypothesis in the *Catholic encyclopedia*: "we confine ourselves to organic diseases. Can suggestion be used efficaciously in diseases of this nature? The most learned and daring of the suggestionists of the present day, Bernheim, a Jew, head of the famous school of Nancy, the more advanced rival of the Ecole de la Salpêtrière, answers in the negative" (p. 390). Pierre Janet (1925/1976) objected strenuously to Bertrin's presentation of suggestion: "Bertrin ... seems to have a very hazy notion of suggestion. It is, he writes, 'a well-known force; ... we quite understand what it can do, and we understand even better what it cannot do.' But science is far from making any such claim ... As for Bertrin, some of his opinions concerning suggestion are very remarkable: 'To induce suggestion there must be a clear, categorical, authoritative affirmation. Hope has no influence in psychotherapy [!] ... Suggestion does not occur when the would-be suggester begs instead of ordering.' Doubtless some suggestions have an imperative character, but it is no less certain that well-marked suggestion can be effected without anything like an order; in fact, suggestion by insinuation is often far more potent. It is really surprising that anyone so incompetent as Bertrin should venture to undertake such studies" (Vol. 1, p. 50).

supporters questioned the motives and knowledge of doctors who doubted claims for miracles. "The suggestion thesis soon cast disrepute not only on the doctors at Lourdes but on the entire French medical profession as well" (p. 181).

If, at Lourdes' Medical Bureau, physicians came to exercise great authority – because of battles with the Church's philosophical and political enemies, even if only the bishops could make a final ruling that a given case was miraculous – what we see is a version of what was happening elsewhere, most prominently, in France. Jan Goldstein (1982) writes that in the Third Republic of the 1870s and 1880s there was an "anticlerical crusade, and the psychiatrists of the Salpêtrière school participated in it enthusiastically" (p. 230).[26] In part, Goldstein observes, this was for professional reasons: "The clergy, after all, were the traditional healers of the maladies of the soul and hence significant rivals of the professional new-comers, the psychiatrists" (ibid.).[27] In 1882, the French government established "a chair in the diseases of the nervous system" (p. 233) and Charcot was named to that chair. It was at this time that Charcot's theories of hypnosis and hysteria were on the ascendant, and they played their role in anticlerical attacks. Emile Littré, a physician, "once Comte's chief disciple" (p. 222), and promoter of positivism, along with Comte, Herbert Spencer, and John Stuart Mill (Ellenberger, 1970, p. 225), developed "retrospective medicine," "the reinterpretation of past phenomena, misunderstood in their own time, according to the categories of medical science" (Goldstein, 1982, pp. 234–5).[28] For Littré, demonic possession, miracles such as happened at Lourdes, and mystical experiences were all hysterical in nature.[29] Charcot affirmed Littré's retrospective diagnoses, using his categories

---

[26] Recall that this was the period during which Mercier studied with Charcot.

[27] One of the persistent themes in the boundary work between psychology and religion has to do with competing professions. Hale (1971) writes: "Since the 1870's some had observed that the physician seemed to be taking over the role of the priest. In 1907, probably following [Pierre] Janet, Lewellys F. Barker, son of a Quaker minister and professor of medicine at the Johns Hopkins University, argued that more people were turning to the physician 'when in psychic difficulty or when in need of mental and moral direction and physicians, whether they like it or not, are thus forced into responsibilities of "confessor" and "moral director"'" (p. 139). The British physician, Clifford Allbutt (1910), did not like it and warned against physicians becoming confessors: "Let us beware lest the resentment of the laity against 'spiritual direction,' against the curious inquisition of the priest into the casuistical paths of naughtiness, may be turned against ourselves" (p. 760). See also, below in Chapter 7, remarks of Cardinal O'Connell critical of the Emmanuel Movement which, in his eyes, confused the roles of physician and priest. On medical opposition to the Emmanuel Movement because of its threat to medical expertise, see Caplan (1998).

[28] In recent years, there have been numerous criticisms of this "presentist" type of history. In fact, critical approaches explicitly point to the limitations of this naïvely empiricist type of history (see Munslow, 1997).

[29] A review of a biography of St. Theresa of Avila, in the *Catholic World* (Talk about new books, 1890, p. 550) complained that the author, Mrs. Bradley Gilman, reduced the saint's mystical experiences to those of hysteria: "Mrs. Gilman's conclusion seems to be that what

of the stages of hysteria.[30] The Lourdes' physicians conceded some of this, at least in their determination of miracles at Lourdes, in not counting as miraculous instances where hysteria could be diagnosed.[31]

Writing in the *Proceedings of the Society for Psychical Research*, Arthur Thomas Myers (1851–94), a physician, and his brother, Frederic W. H. Myers, the psychical researcher, reviewed cases of alleged miraculous cures, concluding that what happened at Lourdes happened elsewhere as well, without invocation of the Virgin, and that the evidence thus far produced by Boissarie was insufficient.[32] What Mind Cure and Lourdes both showed, however, was the promise of "psycho-therapeutics," the use of the mind to heal the body. Like Jung after them, the Myers concluded with a melancholic modernist air: "We have discovered that faith will heal; our difficulty is to find something in which to have faith" (1894, p. 207). Catholic doctrine had really nothing to do with the Lourdes' phenomena: what happens there happened in the temples of Aesculapius in ancient times. Did faith healing show, they wrote, that "self-healing must needs be felt to depend ultimately on something behind and above the Self? It may be that the inmost effort must still be a religious one, and to change man deeply it needs a touch upon that mainspring deep in man" (p. 209). The formerly miraculous, according to this view, was the domain of psychology.

A Catholic critique of Christian Science and other forms of new thought

So the boundary between the miraculous and the natural came to be defined in medical terms, with psychological phenomena between science and the natural on the one side, and religion and the supernatural on the other. This same criterion appeared in polemical articles by Adrian Feverel (1912a; 1912b; 1913a; 1913b) and other Catholic writers on Christian Science.[33] Mary Baker Eddy, the

---

is known as Christian Mysticism is one thing in fact and essence with the 'Faith Cure' and the 'Christian Science' of the present day. St. Theresa, to her mind, 'lays herself open to the accusation of being called hysterical, if not insane' " (p. 552). So retrospective medicine was already widely practiced before the end of the nineteenth century.

[30] Charcot's stages of hysteria were within twenty-five years dismissed as the product of suggestion and dissimulation.

[31] Mercier, in *The origins of contemporary psychology* (1918), took Littré's philosophical positions to task as inadequate in its epistemology and its anthropology. Since Mercier had spent some time at La Salpêtrière, we can see that his Neoscholasticism aimed at precisely the kinds of conclusions that Littré and Charcot were making.

[32] Both Myers made significant contributions to psychical research and were leading members of the Society for Psychical Research. Frederic Myers' work included *Human personality and its survival of bodily death* (1908). Arthur Myers worked extensively with his brother, providing medical expertise in their investigations.

[33] Other psychologists, such as Henry Rutgers Marshall (1909), were equally critical of Christian Science for the "absurdity of its modes of explanation of the facts with which it deals" (p. 296). William James (1890b) held that what Christian Scientists were able to do

founder of Christian Science, had been cured by Phineas Parkhurst Quimby in 1862. Eddy took Quimby's mental healing and combined it with an idealistic reading of Christianity in *Science and Health*, which first appeared in 1875.[34] Caplan (1998) calls it the "first major text of the American mental healing movement" (p. 74). Christian Science differed from Spiritualism in many aspects, and Mary Baker Eddy was critical of the "materialism" of the Spiritualists, their insistence in the reality of the spiritual through effects such as mediumship, the moving of objects, and the materialization of the spirits during séances. Like the Spiritualists, however, in Christian Science there was an emphasis on healing the sick through spiritual means and criticisms of "regular" medicine. Whereas the Spiritualist healers worked by various means, such as by touch and by "consultations" with venerable healers from the past, for Christian Science, healing occurred when the ill person realized the unreality of illness.[35] Feverel (1913a) noted that: "It is owing primarily to this doctrine, this belief that sickness can be eradicated without medical or surgical science, that its increase in membership has been so rapid" (p. 466). In this regard, then, Christian Science had an appeal similar to that of Lourdes. There were, of course, significant differences, and Feverel summarized the Christian Science teaching this way: "There is no disease. The seeming reality of it, like the seeming reality of sin, is but an illusion of the 'mortal mind.' Destroy this illusion, this belief, and the disease will vanish into the nothingness from whence it came" (ibid.). Feverel proceeded to argue that "Eddyism" as Christian Science was disparagingly called, could not really cure anything:

> The cures of "science" are seldom, if ever, authenticated, and when they are, we find them of such harmless diseases that they are practically worthless as proofs of the efficacy of Eddyism in curing disease ... The testimonials, too, are a proof of the humorist's witticism, for the bulk of them chronicle relief from nervous troubles, and are mostly indited by women.
>
> (p. 468)

The only good to come of Christian Science was that it has promoted a psychotherapeutic or psychosomatic approach in medicine: "Indirectly, certainly, it has forced the attention of scientists to the really scientific examination of the influence which the mind can exercise over the body. Mental therapeutics

---

was more important than any difficulties with their accounts for how they did it (see also Taylor, 1996).

[34] There was much controversy concerning Quimby's influence on Eddy; see Braden (1963) for one side of the dispute.

[35] Christian Science shared with other spiritual movements in nineteenth-century America a belief in what Warren Felt Evans (1817–89) called "the mental cure" (Taylor, 1999, p. 145): "Disease, Evans wrote, was not so much a physical derangement as it was an abnormal condition that arises from wrong belief."

is now an established branch of scientific study, and through its means nervous diseases are more readily cured and are more agreeably treated than formerly" (p. 470). But against organic diseases, diseases carried by "germs" (p. 471), that is, against biomedically defined diseases, Christian Science is powerless. At best, for Feverel, it was mental therapeutics in religious guise, with dangerous and, from the Catholic perspective, false premises.

Other Catholic criticisms of Christian Science made the same point. An editorial in the *Catholic World* (Editorial notes, 1899) made the argument that one reason for the success of Christian Science was "the materialism of the medical profession." Medicine ignored the soul and "the psychological influences of mind over matter." Christian Science could claim to have worked cures, and how did it do so? By being able to "stimulate the psychological agencies to bring about a cure." Hawley (1899) admitted, begrudgingly I think, that Christian Science succeeded to some extent, but how? It was not its religious doctrines, which are wrong from a Catholic perspective. Rather, "Christian scientists have availed themselves of this power of auto-persuasion as a therapeutic agent – sometimes, it must be confessed, with beneficial results" (p. 516). In this regard, it was like hypnotism, applying "the doctrine of suggestion" (ibid.), but never could it "restore a lost eye or member, or even straighten a club-foot" (ibid.). Again, only functional diseases respond to suggestion. Insofar as there is truth in Christian Science, it is a psychological and not a religious truth.

We have here the same criterion as was used in the arguments for genuine healing at Lourdes, namely, that the only real cures would be those that are biomedically verifiable, and the accusation that the only healing that did occur were of functional – and hence not "real" – ailments. The clinical gaze, to use Foucault's (1973) term, became the arbiter for the intervention of God into human affairs. The presence of a functional or psychological disorder and the effectiveness of what could be termed psychological treatment became proof of the absence of Divine intervention. We have here an example of a broader trend: the alliance of what became an orthodox medicine with the mainstream churches. The Catholic Church in France was not alone in its move in this direction. Starr (1982) describes how in the state of Missouri, at the beginning of the twentieth century, Presbyterians and Methodists supported state licensing and examining of physicians, because they "were alarmed at the growing popularity of Christian Science and Weltmerism, a local mind-cure cult" (p. 105).

Pierre Janet provided a positivist interpretation of the miracle in his comprehensive history, *Psychological healing* (1925/1976). Making an argument similar to Hawley, Janet noted that miracles are lawful phenomena: "The god who works miracles does not cure any chance comer, nor cure in a haphazard fashion. You will find it useless, at one of these sanctuaries, to ask that the god or the wonder-working fluid shall restore an amputated limb or remove the scar of a wound" (vol. 1, p. 48). Following Charcot (1893), Janet asserted: "we must study the science of miracles so that we may be able to reproduce them at will. Day by day ... the domain of the supernatural is being restricted, thanks to the extension of the domain of science. One of the most notable among scientific victories over the mysteries of the universe will be achieved when we have tamed, have domesticated, the therapeutic miracle" (vol. 1, p. 48). The dominant Catholic response at the time faced the dilemma that Janet noted: "Nothing will persuade the adepts of Lourdes that the miracles worked at the shrine of Aesculapius were genuine" (vol. 1, p. 43). We have seen that this was the argument used against Christian Science successes. "Not genuine" meant not biomedically verifiable. "Not genuine" meant psychological in nature. So Boissarie (1891) emphasized that the medical personnel at Lourdes exercised great caution and took their time to decide on instances of miracles. They stood outside the crowd of enthusiasts who in their fervor hail each claim of a cure as a fact (p. 271). The terms in which the miraculous occurred would have to be medical, not the mere testimonies of the faithful.

Moreover, as evident from the quotation above from Feverel, there was a gendered aspect to this debate. As Braude (2001), Moore (1975), and Buescher (2002) demonstrate, the Spiritualist movements drew women in part because they gave them opportunities that they were otherwise denied, even if, at the same time, these movements played off stereotypes of femininity. It was part of Catholic criticism of Christian Science and anything associated with it to disparage them because of the prominence of women in them – and to indicate the dangers to morality. So Ernest Hawley (1899), writing on "The vagaries of Christian Science," denounced it for what he saw as loosening moral bonds:

> We have often thought it a great misfortune that persons, especially women, of superficial understanding and acquirements should be seized with the mania of posing before the world as teachers and philosophers. If they get a little notoriety ... their example breeds dissatisfaction among others to their sex, who forthwith begin to imagine there is nothing more noble than to stalk upon some platform or pulpit expounding to an interested and admiring audience some new-fangled notions on religion or economics.
>
> (pp. 509–10)

Hawley tied Christian Science and Spiritualism to efforts to secure "female rights" (p. 510), denouncing all in terms of pride and the exaltation of self-will.[36] His article is a searing critique of *Lessons in truth* (1894), a book by H. Emilie Cady (1848–1941) that dealt with Christian Science and related

[36] Moore (1975) writes that "female mediums almost always went on the stage as 'trance' mediums. In this respect they differed significantly from their male counterparts ... [T]he female medium who gave public performances stood in defiance of St. Paul's admonition against women preaching in public – an admonition that most American churches still heeded in the nineteenth century. Speaking in trance was good theater. It was also a way to blunt the defiance" (p. 204). These observations, indicating the cultural basis for the bias of

movements.[37] Dismissive as he was of Cady, he also ridiculed the *Woman's Bible*, a commentary on Scripture written by Elizabeth Cady Stanton and others. Controversial in its day, even among advocates of women's rights, it has been republished often over the past century. For Hawley (1899), however, the idea behind Stanton's commentary, namely that the Bible as we have it expresses an "altogether too masculine stand-point" (p. 510) was laughable. In mentioning Stanton's work in conjunction with Cady's, one sees some of the cultural dynamics at work in these Catholic critical evaluations of Christian Science and of other popular spiritual movements of the day. Just as the positivists reduced Catholic claims of miracles and mystical ecstasies to the hysteria of women, so did some Catholics reduce the experiences of the Spiritualists and the Christian Scientists to them.

The problem, shall we call it, for these Catholic writers, with Christian Science was that it was effective and popular. According to Hale (1971), New Thought and Christian Science were in the first decade of the twentieth century, "the most popular mental treatments" (p. 245) available. Moreover, "in 1908 there were 85,000 [Christian Scientists], a solid phalanx of upper-middle-class citizens" (ibid.). Hawley called Christian Science neither Christian nor scientific. So what was it? It "is really no other than a system of mental therapeutics dressed up in a pantheistic garb" (1899, p. 515). Its truth was that it understood how the mind works:

> Now, the element of truth in this system is, that it avails itself of a very remarkable psychological fact, viz.: the extraordinary power of persuasion upon the human mind and body. It is well known to psychological students that a persuasion which has acquired a deep root in the mind will, in many cases (though by no means in all), produce a favorable or unfavorable condition of the body, according to the nature of the persuasion. This fact, we think, can only proceed from the dynamic and substantial,

Hawley and others, make a good starting point for reflection on Jacques Lacan's (1990) psychoanalytic paradox that woman does not exist (p. 40). It seems that for mainstream Protestant and Catholic writers of the late nineteenth century that statement was true. Hawley and the others unwittingly provided an explanation for their position by associating these women who spoke in public and their spiritual claims with hysteria, hypnosis, and psychotherapy. To use a shorthand, what we see here is that "sex" and "sexuality" occupied the borderland between psychology and Christian religion, including Catholicism, then as now.

[37] *Lessons in truth* is a key text for the Unity School of Christianity (Unity Church), which like Christian Science was related to the New Thought movement of the late nineteenth century. Cady was a homeopathic physician whose writings came to the attention of the founders of Unity, Charles and Myrtle Fillmore. *Lessons in truth* was first serialized in Unity's magazine beginning in 1894 (Braden, 1963, pp. 244–5). Meyer (1980) counts her among the leaders of this "applied therapeutic religion" (p. 36). Elizabeth Cady Stanton was an abolitionist and a feminist with interests in Theosophy (Stevenson-Moessner, 1994, p. 684).

yet altogether mysterious, link which subsists between body and soul, permitting them to react reciprocally upon one another.

(pp. 515–16)

Christian Scientists "have availed themselves of this power of auto-persuasion as a therapeutic agent – sometimes, it must be confessed, with beneficial results" (p. 516). It works exactly, then, as does hypnotism, so that Christian Science is "of a purely natural and psychological order" (p. 517). This charge of Hawley was not psychology-as-religion, although many of his arguments would be used later in that argument; it was rather a form of psychotherapy posing unwittingly as religion. But articles such as this conceded something that would prove contentious in the twentieth century: they admitted that psychotherapy existed and could be effective.

If Christian Science was a challenge to the Church by being itself a church, many in the New Thought movement disavowed the churches altogether. Before the term was a lightning rod in Catholic circles, they were modernists. Quimby was no spiritualist and he thought that spiritualist effects "might well be explained on the basis of the effect of mind on mind" (Braden, 1963, p. 54). In some respects, Quimby's views resembled those of Charcot's "faith cure," and there was even a like anticlericalism. He wrote: "The two most dangerous to the happiness of man . . are priests and doctors. These two classes are the foundation of more misery than all other evils, for they have a strong hold on the minds of the people by their deception and cant" (quoted in ibid., pp. 59–60). The "deception and cant" are the false beliefs that create disease. For Quimby and New Thought, the cure of disease lay in the science of right thinking. No institutionalized beliefs were necessary.[38] The Catholic response found itself between a new religion and a new science.

James Joseph Walsh and mental therapeutics

At the turn of the twentieth century, materialism, positivism, and determinism were political and religious fighting terms. They were often used in anticlerical and anti-Catholic writings, and Catholics often used their counterparts to score political and religious points. With medicine's increasing scientific prestige, a physician who was scientific in spirit, and simultaneously a champion the freedom of the will and an opponent of materialism, could make great con-tributions to the Catholic cause.[39] In addition, if this physician could present a

---

[38] "Quimby was very radical in opposing doctrinal conceptions of Christ. He uniformly called Jesus 'a man like ourselves,' that he might win for the Master new recognition as the founder of spiritual science. To him 'the Science of the Christ' was greater than a religion" (Dresser, 1921, p. 10).

[39] Starr (1982) writes that in the second half of the nineteenth century in the United States, there was medical as well as religious sectarianism: "More than a qualified analogy links

theory of healing that would provide an account for the miracles at Lourdes and show the deceptive and/or purely natural, psychological, causes of Spiritualist, New Thought, and Christian Science healing, that would be service indeed. If, to cap it all off, this scientific medicine could be presented in at least vaguely Neoscholastic terms, the edifice would be complete. Such, I believe, were the terms in which James Joseph Walsh (1865–1942) thought.

Walsh, a Pennsylvania native, entered the Jesuit order after graduating from St. John's College (later renamed Fordham University) in 1884, but poor health forced him to withdraw from the order. He received an M.D. from the University of Pennsylvania in 1895. After graduation, he studied in Europe with Virchow and Ramon y Cajal; moreover, he studied neurology at La Salpêtrière with Fulgence Raymond, who succeeded Charcot there (Vandereycken, 1993). He taught medicine and physiological psychology, and he was associated with Fordham University's medical school until it closed in 1921 (ibid.). He was a prolific writer, addressing medical topics, the history of science, and the history of religion. He is most remembered for his 1907 book, *The thirteenth, the greatest of centuries*, which title gives an indication of his Catholic apologetics.[40] Ella Marie Flick (1945) quoted one of Walsh's collaborators, the physician Austin O'Malley, who stated that Walsh held that "I do not think man has ever made a bit of progress; his mind is today just the same as it ever was, excepting that now it is occupied mainly with trifles" (p. 305). This decidedly anti-positivist view was noted by a reviewer of Walsh's (1911a) *Old time makers of medicine*: "This book, like all of Dr. Walsh's, is dedicated to the proposition that in medicine and surgery and the other sciences there is nothing new ... that was not paralleled or in large measure anticipated in medieval times" (Review of the book *Old time makers of medicine*, 1912). That was Walsh's main message, yet he was simultaneously up to date. Nowhere was that more true than in his writings on psychotherapy.

"Psychotherapy" became a topic in *Index Medicus* in 1906 (Hale, 1971, p. 146), a sign of its having arrived as a legitimate medical subject. Hale lists some of the indicators that in the first decade of the twentieth century, psychotherapy had become an increasingly influential type of treatment of illness:

> In 1904 and 1906 Pierre Janet lectured in America, lending European prestige to the native medical psychotherapeutic movements. In 1905 a popular European text, Paul Dubois's *Psychic Treatment of Nervous*

---

religious and medical sects; they often overlap. The Mormons favored Thompsonian medicine and the Millerites hydropathy. The Swedenborgians were inclined toward homeopathic medicine. And the Christian Scientists originated in concerns that were medical as well as religious. In America various religious sects still make active efforts to cure the sick, while the dominant churches are more or less reconciled to the claims of the medical profession and have abandoned healing as part of pastoral care" (p. 95).

[40] There were eleven editions published between 1907 and 1942, the year of Walsh's death.

Disorders, translated by two neurologists who later became psychoanalysts, launched a new interest among general physicians. In 1906 a popular movement for psychotherapy was founded by physicians and by priests of the [Emmanuel] Episcopal Church in Boston and spread across the nation. By 1907 psychotherapy was hotly debated by neurologists, and in 1909 the first American medical congress on psychotherapy was held in New Haven.

(p. 138)

In addition to Hugo Münsterberg's *Psychotherapy*, 1909 also saw, the prominent psychoanalysts – Sigmund Freud, Carl Jung, Ernest Jones, A. A. Brill, and Sandor Ferenczi – as well as Adolf Meyer, come to Clark University in Worcester for the conference organized by G. Stanley Hall, founder of the American Psychological Association. In 1912, more to the point, perhaps, Jung returned to New York and lectured at Fordham University, where he presented his own theory of the unconscious, including the ideas which helped precipitate his break with Freud.[41] When Walsh began writing about psychotherapy, then, it was in the air as something new, and there were clear religious overtones to the practice and the discussion.

Walsh's first books on medicine were general in nature, but he was interested in moral issues, such as the book he and Austin O'Malley wrote, *Pastoral medicine* (1906). A major work was *Psychotherapy* (1912; 1923).[42] In addition, he wrote *Health through will power* (1919) and other popular works on psychotherapy, as well as the article, "Psychotherapy" (1911b) for the *Catholic Encyclopedia*. There, he defined psychotherapy in characteristically early twentieth-century terms:

> Psychotherapy is that branch of therapeutics which uses the mind to influence the body; first, for the prevention of disease by keeping worry from lowering resistive vitality; secondly, for reaction against disease during progress by freeing the mind from solicitude and tapping latent energies; thirdly, after the ailment retrogrades, to help convalescence through the removal of discouragement during weakness by inspiring suggestions.

(p. 549)

In twenty-first-century terms, Walsh was writing about psychosomatic medicine or even, more fashionable recently, health psychology. But in 1911, and

---

[41] Hale (1971) writes that Smith Ely Jelliffe invited Jung to Fordham, and that previously, he had invited Ernest Jones, the English psychoanalyst and biographer of Freud. Jones "declined because he thought a Jesuit University an 'unsuitable' platform for a discussion of psychoanalysis" (p. 358). In the following chapter, we shall see, albeit briefly, why Jones held such an opinion.

[42] The first and revised editions are the same for most of the book. He added several new illustrations, but the primary new material in 1923 was Appendix 3, "Mental Healing in our Day" (pp. 781–815), in which he presented a more sharply critical view of hypnosis.

until psychoanalysis became the dominant form of psychotherapy in the United States, his depiction reflected the general consensus on the nature of psychotherapy (see, e.g. Riggs, 1923).

Psychotherapy was useful, according to Walsh, not only for functional diseases, but also for organic diseases, by addressing the anxiety and depression that can interfere with the patient taking steps to get better. Psychotherapy also has its role in the treatment of "such affections as depend on mental influence" (Walsh, 1911b, p. 551), such as phobias (which Walsh called "dreads"), although "the greatest usefulness of psychotherapy is in alcoholism and in the drug habits" (p. 552). Walsh sought to demystify the influence of the mind on the body and to show that the various forms of mind cure, as well as most cures by means of scientific medicine, were, in effect, faith cures. Hence he explained the success of New Thought and Christian Science – as the result of suggestion (Walsh, 1923, p. 100). From the mass of cures by ordinary, natural means, Walsh distinguished genuine miracles, which he himself had witnessed at Lourdes.

How does the mind influence the body? Walsh offered what in contemporary terms we can call a cognitive model of psychotherapy. The basic means by which psychotherapy acted was through focusing the patient's attention. Walsh's writings typically drew on anecdote and other medical writers to make his points, making them "very readable" as one reviewer noted (Review of the book *Psychotherapy*, 1913). So in discussing attention, he noted its basic mechanism in these terms: "Every one has had experiences of aches, or actual pains, or discomfort quite annoying while one is alone, but that disappear while in pleasant company or occupied in some absorbing occupation" (Walsh, 1923, p. 84). These common examples suggested the means by which attention affected bodily processes in sometimes significant ways. Walsh did not presume to understand how this process worked, although he posed some solutions, drawn from neurological research. He favored Ramon y Cajal's "neuroglia theory," in which the movement of glial cells, allowing or inhibiting contact between neurons, might explain how mental activity could direct or fail to direct neural activity.[43] When neural activity is inhibited, the parts of the body that are innervated by those neurons can malfunction, thereby causing or worsening disease. Walsh (p. 123) also mentioned the synapse theory, championed by Sherrington and McDougal, although he preferred the neuroglial theory. But what did these neurological accounts attempt to explain? They sought to account for how psychotherapy, by redirecting attention, can unleash the "reservoir of reserve energy" that everyone has and that is the basis for the effectiveness of mental action in the treatment of disease. To reach this supply of reserve energy, it is important for a patient not to give up, and Walsh drew on

---

[43] This was essentially a theory of the nervous system's ability to change with experience, a topic that is receiving much attention today.

William James' (1907) account in "The energies of men" to bolster his argument on this point.

Walsh associated disease with fatigue, that seemingly omnipresent category of late nineteenth-century and early twentieth-century thought about the body and work (Rabinbach, 1990). For Walsh (1923), "men and women may die simply because they give up the struggle. Men and women who *will not give up* seem able to overcome severe illness that would take away ordinary people" (pp. 92–3), because they thus draw upon hidden reserves of energy.[44] This basic approach was developed in one way by Walter B. Cannon, the physiologist also influenced by James' "The energies of men" in developing his endocrinological conceptions of homeostasis, and in a vitalistic way by Walsh. But for Walsh, the direction for the future lay in re-asserting the existence of a vital force "which guides and controls and co-ordinates the different portions of the body" (p. 132). This vital force, which he did not call the soul (but that was what he meant), is the real basis of psychotherapy:

> This vital force behind the nervous system contains stores of energy that can be called on for therapeutic purposes. It is the directing, co-ordinating and energizing force which controls the central nervous system, and enables it to accomplish its purposes. It is the disappearance of this force at death which leaves the body without vital activity, though no physical difference between the dead and the living body can be demonstrated ... This vital force supplies the energy that we call the will, and underlies the process called "living on the will" which so often serves to maintain existence when there is every reason to think that a fatal termination is due. The amount of energy thus available is limited, but is much more powerful than has been thought. It is of the greatest possible service in preserving health and eliminating disease.
>
> (pp. 133–4)

Walsh gave this essentially Cartesian account a Neoscholastic gloss by citing Mercier on the unity of mind and body, on how "everything that happens to one part affects the other" (p. 794). What Walsh achieved with his vitalistic

---

[44] Walsh (1923) explained a possible neurology of attention in healing in these terms: "Even more important, perhaps, than any other of the functions attributed to the neuroglia cells, is the rôle they may play in enabling the individual to concentrate attention on a particular subject, or at least to use a particular portion of the brain, by bringing about a more active circulation in that portion than in any other. Ramon y Cajal attributes this power to the perivascular neuroglia cells. Every capillary in the brain has thousands of these little pseuopod prolongations. When the cells in a particular region contract, the blood vessels of the part are pulled wide open and a larger supply of blood flows more freely, stimulating the nerve cells by which it passes and supplying them with nutrition for the expenditure of energy that they may have to make. This is the physical basis that underlies attention" (pp. 124–5).

theory, however, was a means to bridge medical knowledge with practical moral teachings stemming from then-current Catholic teachings on the will.

While Walsh attended to many aspects of patients' lives in order to help them deal with their illnesses, his description of the process of suggestion is perhaps closest to how he actually practiced psychotherapy. In one passage, he discussed how he prepared patients with functional illnesses and addictions for health-giving suggestions:

> The patient should be put into a comfortable position, preferably in a large, easy arm-chair, should be asked to compose himself in such a way as to bring about thorough relaxation of muscles, and then to give his whole attention to the subjects in hand. Occasionally the arms should be lifted and allowed to fall, to see whether relaxation is complete, and the knee jerks may be tested, to show the patient that he is not yet allowing himself fully to relax ... The patient should then be made to feel that the tension in which he has been holding himself, and which makes it so difficult for him to relax, has really been consuming energy that he can use to overcome the tendencies to sensory or motor disturbance, or to supply the lack of will which makes him a victim of a drug or other habit.
>
> (pp. 197–8)

Walsh emphasized that this kind of relaxation technique differed from hypnosis in that the patient was awake, and that this "hypnoidal state," as it was sometimes called, "instead of making a patient dependent on his physician [as hypnosis tended to do], teaches him to depend on his own will" (p. 198). This relaxed state allowed the patient to concentrate on healing suggestions.[45]

This entire process was, of course, completely natural. There was no reason to include, beyond the vitalistic theory of the will, anything supernatural. Thus,

---

[45] This description is strongly reminiscent of how psychotherapy was conducted in the Emmanuel Movement. In *Religion and medicine* (Wooster, McComb, and Coriat, 1908) we read: "While I have absolutely no prejudice against hypnotism in safe hands, and while I know its employment to be almost necessary in certain disorders, I doubt very much whether it is necessary or peculiarly beneficial in the treatment of the ordinary neuroses. The method of suggestion which I have found to be most effective in dealing with the large number of nervous persons who come to us is first to make the patient calm and quiet. I place the patient in a comfortable reclining chair, instruct him how to relax his arms, his legs, his neck, head and body, so that there shall be no nervous tension or muscular effort. Then standing behind him I gently stroke his forehead and temples, which has a soothing and a distracting effect. Without attempting to induce sleep I inform him that his body is resting and that his mind too will rest, that he will not let his thought run on unchecked, but that it will lazily follow my words, and that when I make a useful suggestion to him he will repeat it to himself. I then tell him that all nervousness is passing from him, that everything is still within him, that his heart is beating quietly and regularly and that he is breathing gently and slowly. I suggest to him that he is entering into peace, that his mind is abstracted and his thoughts are becoming vague and indistinct" (pp. 65–6). See Caplan (1998) for the context.

hypnosis, Christian Science, Spiritualism, and the use of any type of device or ritual in psychotherapy served only to persuade the patient to have confidence in the physician or the healer. All medicine relies on faith cure to a large degree: "Whenever men have believed deeply and with conviction that some other being was able to help them, many of their ills, or at least conditions from which they suffered severely, have dropped from them and their complaints, real or imaginary, have disappeared" (pp. 77–8). As Walsh surveyed the history of medicine, he noted that many drugs and treatments appeared, which for a time proved helpful, yet most of which later proved to be ineffective. He believed that there were maybe two dozen drugs that really had any specific effects, and that most – if not all – drugs cured by virtue of their acting as "placebos" (p. 88). Even the use of prayer in healing works primarily by natural means, by "soothing the mind and making it ever so much less amenable to disturbing influences than it may be when left to itself" (Walsh, 1928, pp. 105–6). If that is true of prayer, so is it true of Christian Science and other forms of mind cure. Faith "acts through the definite conviction that there is to be a direct interference with the ordinary course of nature in the patient's behalf" (Walsh, 1923, p. 78), which being a favorable suggestion, can be curative. Indeed, it was not only religious faith that was effective; Walsh pointed out that with new scientific remedies "faith in the scientific discovery had acted through the mind of the patient so as to bring about an amelioration of symptoms, if not a cure of the disease" (Walsh, 1911b, p. 550). The initial successes and the later failures of hypnosis were examples of how patient and practitioner expectations aided and then hindered healing. Walsh was convinced that psychoanalysis was another form of faith healing, and that it would share the fate of hypnosis.[46]

If faith cures are natural, are all such cures natural? Walsh took on the criticism, developed by Charcot, Littré, and others, that all instances of what appeared miraculous had natural causes. At the end of his *Catholic Encyclopedia* article, as well as in *Psychotherapy*, Walsh addressed the question of miraculous cures. "After a visit to Lourdes and careful study of 'La Clinique de Lourdes,' I am convinced that miracles happen there" (Walsh, 1923, p. 79). His argument?

> It is often said that the cures at shrines and during pilgrimages are mainly due to psychotherapy – partly to confident trust in Providence, and partly to the strong expectancy of cure that comes over suggestible persons at

---

[46] While in 1911 Walsh spoke favorably of hypnosis, and pointed out the dangers of repeated use, in 1923, he wrote: "Probably the greatest joke on the medical profession during the nineteenth century was the use of hypnotism as a curative measure and above all as a remedy that was said to work wonders for the severer psychoneuroses" (p. 800). As for psychoanalysis, he stated: "psychoanalysis has done for the twentieth century, so far, what hypnotism did for the last quarter of the nineteenth. We now know that hypnotism was merely induced hysteria, that is a state of intense supersuggestibility brought on by various modes of suggestion" (p. 790).

these times and places. Undoubtedly many of the cures reported at shrines and during pilgrimages are of this character. An analysis of the records of cures carefully kept – as, for instance, at Lourdes – shows, however, that the majority of accepted cures have been in patients suffering not from mental persuasions of disease, nor from neurosis, nor from symptoms exaggerated by anxiety, but from such very concrete affections as tuberculosis, diagnosed by one or more physicians of standing, ulcers of various kinds, broken bones that have long failed to heal, and other readily demonstrable organic affections. When cures are worked in such cases, some force beyond that of nature as we know it must be at work.

(Walsh, 1911b, p. 552)

This conclusion completed the edifice: psychotherapy exists and works, thus explaining the Spiritualistic and other heterodox forms of healing, and miracles occur in cases of organic disease and demonstrable physical defects. Materialism is defeated by vitalism, Spiritualism by the Christian faith.

Psychology on the boundary

Among the many beginnings of psychology, especially of psychotherapy, the movements discussed in this chapter played a significant role. Although most academic psychologists sought distance from the Spiritualists and others who invoked immaterial forces in their healing work, some then as now have cultivated the spiritual side of therapy. Where boundaries were drawn between the natural and the supernatural, where materialism was defended and opposed, one would expect that the Catholic Church would take a decided position. What is striking in this story, however, is how, from the middle of the nineteenth century, the Church found in the emerging biomedicine a bulwark against which to protect its position regarding proper relationships with the supernatural.[47] The Spiritualists may have unwittingly had commerce with demons – but if Spiritualists did heal disease, they had success only with functional or psychological disorders. Christian Science may have been pantheistic and idealistic – and when healings occurred, only the power of suggestion was at work. The Church's position was clear: the dogmas or teachings of such groups, because they were false, could not provide an adequate account for why healing took place. The cures found their explanation in natural causes, and these causes were found in medicine. Significantly, the medical explanations were psychological. Psychological explanations marked the boundary, protecting orthodox religion and what was becoming orthodox medicine from the invasion of Spiritualism and mind cures. The division of labor, that gave the body to medicine (as to the state) and the soul to the Church, and so defined what religion meant in the modern age, was secured.

[47] As mentioned in Chapter 1, this bulwark was methodological naturalism.

When the tables were turned, as happened at Lourdes, we find analogies and similarities discounted. Bernadette was not a medium, *Aquéro* was not a soul of a dead neighbor, and by what she said to Bernadette, she was not a demon either. Then came the cures. The many found them all miraculous, and the skeptics, summarized by Charcot's (1893) paper on faith cures, found them to be the product of suggestion. The Medical Bureau's investigations sought to differentiate those cures that could be called miraculous on biomedical grounds, in order to combat anticlerical forces. Any cure of a psychological or functional disorder was considered, at least for the record, not miraculous. The miraculous was what defied medical and psychological explanations, *because it healed the body as understood biomedically*. Again, psychological explanations marked the boundary between the workings of nature (and of natural science) and the workings of the Divine.

Across the boundary two irreconcilable regions existed: on the far side lay the realm of demons, the Immaculate Conception, and the hand of God, which would stretch out to heal broken bones and restore tubercular lungs. On the near side lay the realm of nature as understood by natural science and bio-medicine. In between lay the borderland of the psychological. For the Church, this border was the limit of the natural. For the Spiritualists and the Christian Scientists, it was our access to the Beyond.[48] Access to this borderland, which we can also call the subconscious or unconscious, or subliminal consciousness, or more skeptically the realm of suggestion, was in itself peculiar, and this only added to its problematic status. This middle place, where functional diseases emerge, where apparent visitations of the dead appear, where the two objectivities on either side become confused, would continue to trouble science, medicine, and the Church for the next century. This borderland between the supernatural and the natural became, over the next century, the place where the soul, driven from natural scientific psychology, found a home. The soul, if it were to be found, would from henceforth not be found by means of Neoscholastic deductions, but in the liminal places designated by the subconscious and the unconscious, by the symbol and the transference. The existence of the subconscious called into question the neat boundary between nature and the supernatural, a theological theme that would only be questioned beginning in the 1940s, after a 300-year run.

But to pursue that route, we need to turn to Freud and the psychoanalysts on the one hand, and to Jung and his Catholic supporters and critics on the other. The plot thickens.

---

[48] James (1903) sounded this note, too, in saying that if God speaks to us, it is primarily through the subconscious mind: "*if there be* higher spiritual agencies that can directly touch us, the psychological condition of their doing *so might be* our possession of a subconscious region which alone should yield access to them" (p. 242, emphasis in original).

Psychoanalysis versus the power of will

The primary Catholic objection to the New Psychology in the early years was its submitting the human mind to the experimental laboratory. Did the very existence of an experimental psychology presuppose a "psychology without a soul" and thus suffer from a fatal flaw at the very moment of its birth? While this question was the topic of much debate in the early years of the twentieth century, the participation of noted Catholic thinkers significantly decided the issue. Mercier, Pace, and Moore, taking up the letter and spirit of Pope Leo XIII's 1879 encyclical, *Aeterni Patris*, sought to demonstrate theoretically and experimentally that a scientific psychology has its proper grounding in Scholastic philosophy and that, indeed, Scholastic philosophy benefits from the precise findings of an experimental psychology. Mercier argued that Scholastic thinking more adequately provides the theoretical and anthropological basis of experimental psychology than did its competitors, Cartesianism, Kantianism, and phenomenalism.

Experimental studies, however, remained remote to the burning issues of the Church. The challenges posed by psychophysics and the minute examination of sensation, perception, and memory had primarily theoretical implications. Not so for those offered by the scientific treatment of troubled mental life. In the middle of Catholic controversies over the meaning of psychotherapy stood Sigmund Freud and psychoanalysis – for here was a theory and therapy of the soul, one that challenged the authority and rationality of religious approaches to the cure of souls.

Early Catholic responses to psychoanalysis

For a variety of reasons, there was immense interest in psychoanalysis in Catholic circles. Psychoanalysis, first of all, captured the imagination of several generations; indeed, it fascinates to the present day.[1] Both philosophically and practically, psychoanalysis challenged Church positions. In place of Neoscholastic

---

[1] Psychoanalysis was popular in the United States after Freud's 1909 visit to Clark University: "by 1918, almost 50 articles about psychoanalysis had appeared in such popular magazines as *McClure's, Ladies Home Journal* and even in *The Nation* and *The New Republic*. Some 170

stress on the rationality of the human soul and freedom of will, psychoanalysis uncovered unconscious motivation of precisely the kind – the sexual – that Catholic moral theology worried about. On the side of praxis, psychoanalysis seemed to threaten Catholic *cura animarum*, the cure of souls, in particular, the sacrament of confession. The analyst appeared as a secular confessor who could not absolve sin, but who seemed to dissolve it into neurotic, irrational symptoms. Such were the fears.

With his writings on religion, Freud threw down the gauntlet. In *Totem and taboo* (1913/1952), *The future of an illusion* (1927/1961) and *Moses and monotheism* (1939), Freud argued for the irrational roots of religious beliefs and practices in the vicissitudes of human desire, and for science and reason to replace religion. This was not "psychology as religion," to cite Paul Vitz (1994), it was psychology instead of religion. Other analysts contributed to an analysis of religion as an irrational enterprise. Ernest Jones, the English analyst, saw in Catholicism's veneration of Mary and the celebacy and vestments of the priesthood failures to resolve the Oedipus complex, and as "the change of the masculine to the feminine attitude" (1922/1964, p. 373).

Given these Freudian views, early Catholic reaction was predictable.[2] Looking at commentaries on psychoanalysis in Catholic periodicals such as *The Commonweal, America, Catholic World*, and in *The Ecclesiastical Review*, a journal for priests and others in the religious life, between the years 1920 and 1950, we find a number of patterns. One was the "flash in the pan" argument, the belief or the wish that Freud would go away. Paul Hanly Furfey (1929) claimed that "psychoanalysis has gradually lost favor" (p. 238), without dismissing its contributions to psychiatry. James J. Walsh (1930), whom we met in the previous chapter as a pioneer in psychotherapy, cited Knight Dunlap, an experimental psychologist, who pronounced psychoanalysis unscientific. Walsh lumped psychoanalysis with phrenology and hypnotism as pseudo-sciences. A *Commonweal* editorial three years later declared that "psychoanalysis has about run its course, as a contribution to both medical and literary thought" (Farewell to Freud?, 1933). William J. McGarry (1939), former president of Boston College and inaugural editor of the journal, *Theological Studies*, declared shortly after the death of Freud in exile in London, that he had few disciples and that his theory was being repudiated.[3] Unscientific though it

---

articles were published about psychoanalysis in the medical school journals of America between 1912 and 1918" (Rieber, 1998, p. 376). A contemporary observer, E. Boyd Barrett, SJ, an enthusiastic supporter of psychotherapy, wrote that psychoanalysis "is certainly now in process of 'vulgarization,' judging by the space given to it in the daily press" (1924a, p. 1).

[2] This dispute was more evident in the English-speaking world according to John C. Burnham (1985), because the "territorial claims between psychology and theology were disputed on a frontier often remote from the center of intellectual and cultural developments in the European heartland" (p. 322).

[3] This genre continues to flourish. See, for example, Frederick Crews (1995), "The unknown Freud."

may have been, psychoanalysis, these writers noted, had been popular, especially among the educated classes – but no longer, they hoped.

Another response, along the lines of Furfey, was to acknowledge the effectiveness of psychoanalysis in the treatment of neurosis (see McGucken, 1922), but to point to theoretical limitations. Many credited psychoanalysis as a treatment for neurosis, as did Boyd Barrett (1924a), who only drew the line at spiritual guidance: There the analyst had no business. Aidan Elrington (1933), an English Dominican at Blackfriars, Oxford, went further, accommodating psychoanalysis within Catholic thought in bold imaginative strokes. He wrote that "Eros (or natural love) with its symbol, the Phallus" was the center of psychoanalysis, and "Caritas (or supernatural love) and its symbol . . . the Cross" (p. 675) the center of Catholicism. Through "substitution" and "sublimation" caritas replaces eros: "Hence the Church's attitude to sex. She preaches the crucifixion of the flesh, i.e., the substitution through grace of the Cross of Christ, for the Phallus of the Ego Eros. This sublimated Ego is identical personally with the unsublimated Ego, but the former is dominated by the 'Id' of Caritas, the latter by the 'Id' of Eros" (pp. 675–6). Elrington (1936) held that psychoanalysis complemented Catholic philosophical anthropology on the basis of its contributions to "the interplay of appetite, desire, and phantasy . . . which cannot be reduced to or synthesized in any metaphysical system, yet are nevertheless individual expressions of that human nature, the *universal* character of which is alone considered in the traditional philosophical psychology" (p. 599).[4]

Elrington's views, which challenged Neoscholastic orthodoxy in suggesting that science (psychoanalysis) could challenge philosophical teachings on the soul, did not express those of the majority of published opinions within Catholic circles of the time. The primary objection to psychoanalysis was that Freud's conception of the human person was contrary to that of Catholic teaching formulated Neoscholastically: "For it drops out of question man's free will, and it seeks the cause and procedure of rational life completely in the irrational; it goes into the cellar to explain what is on the upper floors" (McGarry, 1939, p. 606). In so doing, and in making of religion a product of infantile fantasies, it has "aided the collapse of morals" (p. 607). William J. McGucken, SJ, of St. Louis University, summarized the value of psychoanalysis vis-à-vis Neoscholastic philosophy by saying "what is new is not true and what is true is not new. Much that Freud teaches is as old as Aristotle" (1922, p. 493). The "new [that] is not true" included the elimination of free will and the "absorption in the sexual" (ibid.). Herbert S. Schwartz (1937) described how Freud's teachings had captured the imagination: "For all its distastefulness, we think about ourselves today in the manner of the psychoanalysts. The interesting fact is that we discover our acceptance of a theory before we realize

[4] More on Elrington, who was a colleague of Victor White, below in Chapter 6.

what we have accepted: we have changed our intellectual habits through an appeal to our imagination . . . What we have accepted is essentially this proposition: that what is disagreeable is true" (p. 659). Schwartz pointed out that what makes incest and narcissism disagreeable is the very fact of human rationality, as rooted in human nature as the primitive drives that Freud exposed. For Schwartz, "the theological contrary of psychoanalysis . . . is not Christianity but Christian Science" (p. 661), for the former claims that goodness is an illusion and the latter that evil is. For Schwartz, then, psychoanalysis has an incomplete theology, the complete version of which the Church has, in accounting for both good and evil in human nature.

One common query about psychoanalysis delved into its relationship to the sacrament of penance, because of their common confessional nature. Early attempts to describe psychoanalysis in Catholic writings naturally compared the two. McGucken (1922) conceded that "confession, extra-sacramental as well as sacramental, has its therapeutic value" (p. 495). Sister M. Jeanette, OSB (1931), explained that: "The Catholic Church has applied this method in the confessional for nearly 2,000 years" (p. 131). Now, her intention in this comparison was to demystify psychoanalysis and to indicate its potential usefulness, nothing more, by comparing something new with something familiar. Other writers stressed the dissimilarities between analysis and confession: "even if you strip psychoanalysis of its most nauseous Freudian characteristics it is still essentially different from the Sacrament of Penance" (Religion marries psychiatry, 1949), because the latter can grant absolution of sin and because in confession, one admits to acts committed with conscious intent.

Charles P. Bruehl (1876–1963), a priest who taught philosophy and psychology (Connelly, 1979, p. 195) at St. Charles Seminary in Philadelphia from 1914 until 1952, wrote widely on philosophical and ethical matters over the course of many decades. He had received a doctorate in philosophy at Louvain in 1904. He had been writing on the state of modern philosophy, and on spiritism, in 1920, and he next turned his attention to psychoanalysis (Bruehl, 1921a) and psychology in general (Bruehl, 1921b). In 1923, he published a series of articles on psychotherapy as well as a pamphlet on psychoanalysis. While seeing the value in psychoanalysis – it has increased our understanding of mental life, especially its psychopathology – Bruehl (1923e) criticized it for overemphasizing the unconscious, such that "it eliminates free will as a determining factor and reduces the conscious life to a state of secondary importance" (p. 2). Bruehl was concerned with psychoanalysis's "erotic inquisitiveness" (p. 15), a recurrent criticism of analysis that was picked up in the 1950s by Pope Pius XII's addresses on psychiatry. For Bruehl, the main danger occurred when the analyst "usurps the office of the physician of the soul" (p. 21). The Catholic must protest that the "Catholic practices of asceticism and confession" are good for the soul and guard "against mental disturbances" (ibid.). Moreover, "there can be no permanent recovery from nervous disease except through will-training, a matter which the psychoanalyst sadly neglects" (p. 15). We shall see that will-training was a recurrent theme throughout this period. It prominence indicates that in the Catholic view, the will was trainable and that the good life promoted mental health.

Because of Bruehl's interest in ethics, his series on psychotherapy in 1923 was significant in that he saw merit in its rise, even if psychoanalysis proper was problematic. In fact, Bruehl claimed that psychotherapy "reinstated mental and spiritual forces" (1923a, p. 174) into medicine. He emphasized that having a "life-purpose" is conducive to mental health and that "religion gives a commanding and stimulating life-purpose sufficient to engage all the faculties of man" (p. 175). For Bruehl, psychotherapy that ignores the contributions of religion to mental health was ignoring a powerful ally.

One further writer on this topic is particularly noteworthy: John A. O'Brien (1893–1980). O'Brien was noted for his apologetic work and writing, but it was also the case that he had a doctorate in psychology from the University of Illinois. His research was in educational psychology (O'Brien, 1926) under B. R. Buckingham.[5] After 1939, he taught theology at Notre Dame University. O'Brien (1938) claimed that psychoanalysis "had its origin through the discovery of the therapeutic effects of confessing or revealing the secret causes of inner discords to a sympathetic auditor or father confessor" (p. 223). He had no doubt but that psychoanalysis, by which he meant the cathartic method of dredging up memories that caused symptoms, was successful, comparing the discovery of unconscious memories to the discovery of treatment for cancer (p. 228). But, O'Brien argued, the confessional was better for mental health than psychoanalysis, because the priest in the confessional acts as Christ's "human ambassador" (p. 229), and because in confession there is divine forgiveness. Hence, confession benefits mental health. It is worth noting that O'Brien thought that psychiatry was sometimes necessary.[6]

Neoscholasticism and psychoanalysis

In the Catholic community in the inter-war period, psychoanalysis received enormously differing interpretations. Three figures stand out: Edward Boyd Barrett, Thomas Verner Moore, and Rudolf Allers. Their interpretations of

---

[5] Burdette Ross Buckingham (born 1876) was a prominent educational psychologist, who edited the *Journal for Educational Research* and taught at the University of Illinois.

[6] Rudolf Allers (1938), noting that some said that analysis was replacing the confessional, differentiated the two, insofar as the psychotherapist "is told not of guilt and sin, but of symptoms which trouble the patient and cause suffering" (p. 402). The therapist can never say, he wrote, *Ego te absolvo*, but nevertheless, there exist cases in which it would be good for the priest to know something of mental illness and for the psychiatrist to know something of sin.

Freud emerged in part from a distinctive perspective, the Neoscholasticism of the first half of the twentieth century, although each of them viewed that tradition in very different ways. Boyd Barrett was a lay analyst with academic training in experimental psychology. Moore and Allers were practicing psychiatrists, so they had a perspective that their academic Neoscholastic colleagues did not. Their Neoscholastic orientation was a mixed bag when it came to their analyses of Freud. On the one hand, they were able to recognize philosophical deficits in Freud, as well as the necessity for psychology to have an adequate philosophical foundation. On the other hand, they viewed psychoanalysis as in a mirror, either seeing a systematic character that it did not have – which Neoscholasticism in the ideal did – or criticizing it for not having one. Boyd Barrett's story is more complex, so with him we begin.

E. Boyd Barrett: From Jesuit to psychoanalyst

Edward John Boyd Barrett (1883–1966), Irish-born, entered the Society of Jesus in 1904 in his native land. His scholastic studies included a stint at the University of Louvain (1906–8). After a brief return home, in 1908 he returned to Belgium to study at Mercier's Institute of Higher Studies, where he concentrated on psychology in Albert Michotte's laboratory (Barrett, 1930, p. 113). His research was an introspective study of "the happenings in the mind when a 'choice' is made" (ibid.). *Motive force and motivation tracts* (1911) was reviewed as an important contribution to the study of conation (Dearborn, 1913). Boyd Barrett (1930) wrote – please note the date, as it will be significant in his interpretation of such events – that while "everywhere the precision of the method employed was praised" (p. 114), in the Church, eyebrows were raised: "Among ecclesiastics, however, it awakened considerable misgivings. It was thought to be inimical to the old proofs of the freedom of the will. In particular, American Jesuits were disturbed and they denounced the book at Rome and demanded that it should be re-examined. Re-examination, however, resulted in its complete and official vindication" (ibid.).[7] With Boyd Barrett, there was much antagonism between psychology and Catholicism, although not all was negative. Bruehl (1921a, p. 643) cited his experimental work as a "valuable contribution" to psychology, mentioning his name

---

[7] He continued: "The reaction of Jesuits of my own province to my thesis surprised me . . . Only a few took the trouble to read my book. Two or three were generous with their praise. The rest made it the subject of jokes and sarcasm. My provincial opposed its publication at first on the ground that not a single copy would ever be sold. His fears proved groundless, for the one edition published was sold out. . . . In general, my brethren made light of the effort I had made by repeating *ad nauseum* the story that a certain secular priest, who had a car, wrote to Longmans, Green and Co., for the book on *Motor Traffic* written by the Irish Jesuit called Barrett" (Barrett, 1930, p. 115).

alongside Lindowsky, Michotte, Gruender, and others. Boyd Barrett also published *Strength of will* (1915), a more traditional book with practical implications for will-training, based in part on his Louvain investigations.

Boyd Barrett was ordained in June, 1917, and from 1920 to 1922 he studied biology and psychology with Charles Spearman at the University of London. He recounted that he "saw clearly that the shortcomings of the old scholastic psychology were due to the scholastic ignorance of" biology (Barrett, 1930, p. 189). In addition to his esteem for modern science, Boyd Barrett also publicly proclaimed, during a debate on "British misrule" (p. 194) of Ireland, that he was an "Irish Republican," a supporter of independence. He wrote that this was daring for a Jesuit to say, as he belonged to "the most reactionary Order of the most conservative of Churches!" (ibid.). Neither his psychological interests nor his political sympathies played well with his superiors.

While Boyd Barrett was already familiar with psychoanalysis from readings, living in London he attended lectures at the Tavistock Clinic by Hugh Crichton-Miller (1877–1959), the clinic's founder.[8] Boyd Barrett recounted that "the lectures turned my mind definitely in the direction of my becoming a priest-analyst" (p. 195). He conceived of an ambitious plan for Catholic psychological clinics:

> I saw myself selecting and training in psychology and psycho-therapy a group of intelligent and temperamentally suitable young priests. I saw them, in various places, opening, in connection with Catholic churches and colleges, private clinics where advice and treatment for scruples, delusions, superstitiousness, phobias, sex trouble, and all forms of semi-religious morbidities might be dealt with. I saw them talking and acting as priests who knew and understood well the religious standpoints of their patients, but, on the other hand, utilizing in their counsel and direction the best methods of psycho-therapy ... To my mind there existed a border-land, peopled with strange problems, between religion and psychology and such problems could only be solved by a priest-psychologist.
>
> (pp. 197–8)

He "began to undertake psycho-analytic work and to lecture and write on psycho-therapy" (Barrett, 1927, p. 325). He wrote articles for the English Jesuit publication, *The Month*, and he received inquiries "from Catholics who were suffering from 'nerves' which they thought to be connected up with religion" (pp. 198–9). One woman in particular came to see him and, although he had no opportunity to treat her psychologically, he was convinced that "a non-priest analyst would possibly have misunderstood the religious factor that was driving her on the rocks. A priest unskilled in psychology would possibly

---

[8] For Crichton-Miller's positive, perhaps modernist, evaluation of religion, see Miller (2008).

have diagnosed the case as one of devil-possession" (p. 199). Only a combination, a priest-analyst, would have had the necessary background.[9]

This plan was not to be. In March, 1922, he was informed that his final vows were postponed,[10] a severe reprimand that he later interpreted as meaning he would not be allowed to pursue his dreams for psychology. After return to Ireland, exiled to Mungret College in Limerick, which for him and probably for his superiors was a backwater, where he taught reading and spelling (Barrett, 1927, p. 327), he continued to write about psychology, this time for the *Irish Ecclesiastical Review*. The Irish Jesuit censors approved the first of the series, but then rejected the rest. He became convinced that "nothing I now wrote on psychology would be allowed publication in Ireland" (pp. 223–4). He did give "consultations to priests and Jesuits suffering from nerve troubles" (p. 327), and he worked on *The new psychology*. *America* published a series of nine articles of his on psychology between October 6 and December 1, 1923, no doubt suggesting greener pastures across the western ocean. In 1924, he took his final vows and was sent to New York, there, as he was told, to get "facilities for my work in psychology and psycho-therapy" (p. 329).

Instead, he discovered that he had been appointed to teach sociology at Georgetown University. When he protested that he knew nothing about that field, he was assigned to teach catechism, although he was promised a course in the spring semester, 1925, in psychology, and he was listed as a "Professor of Psychology" for the university. He again wrote essays on psychology, only to have them rejected as "dangerous" by the Jesuit censors in the United States. However, *America*, a Jesuit publication, began to publish his psychological articles, until his provincial, L. Kelly, S. J., ordered him to stop (Barrett, 1930, p. 243).[11] He was also invited to speak at Fordham, and after objections by his provincial, he was allowed to proceed with the following conditions: "No matters touching on sex were to be alluded to. There was to be tremendous emphasis given to the freedom of the will; the immortality of the soul; the spirituality of the soul" (Barrett, 1927, p. 332).

---

[9] In *The Jesuit enigma* (1927), he wondered in retrospect: "Would my Superiors allow me to do this kind of work? Would they maintain the old attitude that the Confessional was the place for psycho-therapy, and that Confession was the sufficient remedy for all 'diseases of the imagination,' as they were called" (p. 326).

[10] Members of religious orders, such as the Jesuits, take a series of temporary vows, before the final vows. Boyd Barrett's were delayed, he wrote, because in the opinion of his superiors he had been disobedient on occasion, and because they thought he had too high an estimate of his own views (1927, p. 203).

[11] This second series began on December 13, 1924, with a promissory note for studies of character types, including Wanderers, Cleptomaniacs, Pyromaniacs, Drug Fiends, Dipsomaniacs, and Gamblers (Barrett, 1924b, p. 198). Five articles in the series appeared, with the last, "Wanderlust" (Barrett, 1925b), being the only one that painted a symptom picture. The previous essays set the foundation for the particular studies that were to follow. He compiled them in a book, *Man: His making and unmaking* (Barrett, 1925c).

At the end of the 1924–5 academic year, he was told he was no longer needed at Georgetown, and that he would be returning to Ireland. His break from the Jesuit order occurred then. By August, 1925, he had been dismissed from the Jesuits. He later said that he "ran" from them.

Just before his departure from the Jesuits, he published *The new psychology* (Barrett, 1925a).[12] At perhaps his bitterest moment, he recalled the delays in its publication:

> As I knew that this work would be rejected by the Irish Jesuits, I sent it to America, hoping that American Jesuits would be more broad-minded and understanding. They, however, held it up for nearly eighteen months and then decided that unless I added fulsome praise of scholastic psychology, and omitted certain perfectly innocuous passages, it could not be published. Having submitted to these humiliating and stupid conditions, I published the work, and within a week the first edition was sold out. It apparently satisfied a need that the Catholic public of America had felt for a frank description of the new methods of mind-healing written in an open-minded tolerant manner.
>
> (Barrett, 1927, pp. 327–8)

The book served him well. He soon was set up in Greenwich Village, where he saw patients for psycho-analysis. (We shall see that this term had a broad meaning at the time.) He lectured and wrote and kept a practice going for some years. He was openly critical of the Church at this time, writing about abuses of power, including *While Peter slept*, that received significant press.[13] In *The Jesuit enigma*, he discussed George Tyrrell's criticisms of the Jesuits sympathetically, and he compared his own situation to that of Tyrrell (pp. 336, 338), as someone who strove to be loyal to the Church and to his Order but who was defeated by an authoritarian structure. He even compared his being turned away from his residence in New York in that fateful time of 1925 to what he called the first shot being fired in the Irish war for independence during the Easter Rising:

> Back in 1916 I had seen the first shot of the war of independence in Ireland. It was an Easter Monday morning. I was walking through the centre of

---

[12] The title may be problematic, given that the phrase, "the new psychology," had been used to describe experimental psychology in its origins. Graham Richards (2010) explains. Between the world wars in Britain, the term had been dusted off and used again, and he says that "it would have been less confusing had it been called 'The New New Psychology,' since it was actually a reaction against 1880–1890's American 'New Psychology' which was typically focused on experimental psychophysics. This 'New Psychology,' by contrast, tackled more obviously relevant issues regarding the roots of human emotions, feelings and behavior" (p. 334). Boyd Barrett appropriately entitled his book then, although if he could have listened to Richards, he would have modified the name slightly.

[13] Just how anti-Catholic his writings were would be a matter of historical research, but they were – and still are, as judged by a search of the internet – used by anti-Catholic extremists.

Dublin along the north side of Stephens Green. I saw the barricades that the Irish Volunteers had erected but thought that they only represented an elaborate game of bluff. Suddenly I heard a sharp order "Halt!" I looked around and saw a young soldier, in green uniform, standing pistol in hand. He had called to a cabby, who was driving his horse and cab along the street, to stop. The cabby looked at him, cursed, and whipped up his horse. The volunteer raised his pistol, there was a sharp report, the first shot of a long war had been fired, and a cabhorse lay dead. It would be hard to conceive of a more inglorious or petty beginning to a life and death struggle between two nations, but a beginning it actually was.

The memory of the old cabhorse lying on the pavement in front of the Shelbourne Hotel, and the small pool of blood under its head, often returned to me at this time.

(1930, pp. 248–9)

In 1930, he saw his "flight" from the Jesuits as an act of independence from a tyrannical system.

After practicing psychotherapy in New York and marrying in 1931, he returned to Ireland in 1932 (Ó Conluain, 1991), settling in Ulster, and he began researching and writing *The Great O'Neill* (1939), a historical novel about the sixteenth-century Irish hero, Shane O'Neill. Afterward, he moved to the Santa Cruz area in California, to the town of Soquel. There he bought a ranch, which he named "Benburb," "after the Great O'Neill's castle in the north of Ireland."[14] In 1948, after many years of soul-searching, he returned to the Church (Ex-priest explains return to church, 1948). When his wife died in 1964, he was permitted to function again as a priest. His health was failing, though, and he died in the Jesuit infirmary at Santa Clara University in 1966 (Hayne, 1966).

One of the articles Boyd Barrett wrote while still in London, "Psycho-analysis and Christian morality" (Barrett, 1924a),[15] is also one of the earliest Catholic expositions of and responses to psychoanalysis in the English language. It is a cautious essay, critical of the excesses of some Freudian interpretations yet intrigued by its successes:

What then should be the attitude of Catholics towards Psycho-Analysis? We believe that Catholics should be thankful and grateful to those who have developed this new therapeutic method, which does, and has done, much good, and which we believe to be *per se* quite lawful. But we think that, however much they may regard analysts as healers of mind and body,

---

[14] This information comes from the Bowens (2009). Croswell Bowen's grandmother, Elizabeth McCarthy, was a friend of the Boyd Barretts, and she had contact with Edward (called "Jack" by friends) when he came to the United States, according to this account.

[15] The publication cited is a reprint from *The Month*, February 1921.

they should refuse to regard them as spiritual guides ... For the Catholic, the priest is appointed by God to guide and direct in spiritual matters.

(p. 16)

As we have seen, it was already at this time that Boyd Barrett was formulating his idea of the priest-analyst, so that this passage, and this essay, reads less like a cautionary tale for Catholics than it does as an argument for psychoanalysis in the Church. Indeed, Boyd Barrett's principle objection to psychoanalysis – with the obligatory criticisms of the popularizers who sensationalize it, especially in emphasizing sex – was that the analyst is forced, by the nature of their treatment, to act as a "spiritual guide" (p. 15) without the necessary training. Boyd Barrett saw no conflict between this "new psychology" and scholastic psychology, because the former is empirical and the latter rational (p. 14). This was Mercier's approach to the new psychology, but of course, Mercier was dealing with experimental and not psychoanalytic psychology.

While emphasizing cautiously the value of psychoanalysis, Boyd Barrett yet saw its real limitation as a form of treatment. In psychoanalysis there is really "nothing very new" (p. 13) that spiritual guides and confessors did not already know in their scrutiny of the human soul, and there is in addition a weakness: "How can analysts face the reconstructive part of their work? ... The weak will of the moral degenerate has to be built up! ... It is a moral and religious problem – calling for will training and religion" (ibid.). This criticism indicates the direction of Boyd Barrett's own version of analysis, a combination of a form of psychoanalysis with his will-training as described in *Strength of will*. The value of psychoanalysis is the discovery of unconscious causes of neurosis. One gets the impression that Boyd Barrett's essay was written with more than the psychoanalytic "censor" in mind. The hermeneutics of reading it demand attention to the audiences that he had to address, above all, his order.

The new psychology (Barrett, 1925a) attempted to carry the Mercier program into psychoanalysis: it had been "captured" (p. 19) by the materialists but it could be put to good use in Catholic hands. Boyd Barrett presented psychoanalysis as a type of "biological psychology" (p. 29) insofar as it deals with "instinct, passion and habit" (p. 25). Thus, psychoanalysis is a scientific form of psychology – an empirical form, in contrast to the rational form of Neoscholastic psychology, which provides a kind of framework within which to interpret psychoanalytic findings.[16] As we have seen, Boyd Barrett claimed afterward to have been chaffing at the bit here, later objecting to having to provide continual reassurances – which he did – that this new psychology was compatible with the scholastic system. Psychoanalysis has proven its value

---

[16] He asserted the compatibility of psychoanalysis and Thomism, in part because the Thomists had an appreciation of unconscious mental activity: the agent intellect acts outside of awareness, the *species* and instincts as well, and finally, the actual act of choice in willing is unconscious (Barrett, 1923a, p. 610).

during World War I in the treatment of hysteria, with its "frankly biological" outlook (p. 20). Unconscious ideas, repressed in the "vast halls of memory" that St. Augustine described, are the causes of neurosis, and the recollection and working through of those experiences is the essence of psychoanalysis.

Boyd Barrett's psychoanalysis was not, strictly speaking, that of Freud's, any more than were many practitioners' methods in that day. The authors that Boyd Barrett referred to included W. H. R. Rivers, Adolf Meyer, and Hugh Crichton-Miller, as well as A. A. Brill. It was, we can say, basically a psychoanalytic approach, but not an orthodox approach, no more than was Rivers' (1922). Boyd Barrett's eclecticism is apparent in his discussion of methods to use in "mind cure":

> We shall now sketch in a general way the new methods of psycho-therapy. The four essential elements of a good method are:
>
> 1. Mental exploration.
> 2. Suggestion and persuasion.
> 3. Psychical reeducation.
> 4. Physical rebuilding.

(Barrett, 1925a, p. 150)

The first step was psychoanalysis, including potentially the abreaction of repressed material. In this step, Boyd Barrett fused the Catholic practice of confession with psychoanalysis. He wrote:

> There is no doubt that this phase of Psycho-therapy, the exploring of the patient's mind, is all-important and must never be omitted. Indeed, there is hardly a detail about a patient's history, character, or mental states that is not worth knowing. Trifling incidents in his life are worth noticing and remembering. The more complete the knowledge gained of the patient, both as regards his virtues and vices, the better hope there is of understanding the source of his malady.

(1923a, p. 55)

This insistence on detail may have stemmed from how the sacrament of confession was understood, particularly in Ireland in the latter half of the nineteenth century. Mary Lowe-Evans (1990), describing the place of confession in the novels of James Joyce, discusses how confessional practices focused on detailed accounts of acts and thoughts, especially those involving sex, which were generally viewed as being particularly grievous sins.[17] Foucault (1978) argued that dissemination of confessional practices in modernity has been the way in which the "truth" of sexuality is disclosed. In Boyd Barrett's version of psychoanalysis, we see one way in which that dissemination actually occurred. Because Boyd Barrett was trained as a priest and thus heard confessions, the

---

[17] Boyd Barrett's comments on sex before his break with the Jesuits were highly critical, while after the break, he was critical of the Church's negative attitudes towards sexuality.

transition to a secular confession with to some extent a common goal of healing, was one he could make. While Boyd Barrett agreed with Rivers in his criticism of Freud – holding that not all unconscious conflict was sexual in nature – he still maintained that such motives could not be entirely ruled out, either.[18]

He did make at least one direct comparison between psychoanalysis and confession, in those cases where a person comes to the sacrament with a psychological disorder. The priest:

> Comes upon many cases of perversion and degeneracy – and upon those border-land mental states where it is exceedingly difficult to determine how far responsibility exists. If responsibility is absent, there is of course no sin. If the abnormality is such as to "darken the reason or incapacitate the will," there is no sin. The priest then must needs be a gifted psychologist if he is to be able to determine the power and control of the obsessions or hysterias of his penitents.
>
> (1925c, p. 143)

That expertise was precisely what Boyd Barrett had hoped to cultivate, to no avail. However, this passage shows the extent to which the confessional was itself a boundary region where the new psychology and the old cure of souls met. The confessional had important similarities to the analyst's couch.

This is not the complete picture, however. In part, Boyd Barrett's emphasis on personal details revealed in analysis may be a reaction against the way that confession was practiced at the time. As we shall see in Chapter 9, a manualist

---

[18] In *The magnificient illusion*, Boyd Barrett (1930) briefly depicted his own attitude toward hearing confessions: "I found such admixture of the purely 'natural' in confession that my mind was disturbed. There was so much ignorant superstition in the way in which sins were confessed. Nervous men, obviously driven by sheer fear of hell, would 'to make sure' go to ridiculous extremes in recounting their sins. Incapable of judging or reasoning, in the presence of fear they would pour forth a torrential stream of self-accusations. On the other hand, many women would draw out their empty confessions obviously for the sole purpose of having a quiet tete-a-tete with a man. Some superstitious souls would relate incredible experiences, others bereft of faith would confess their crimes, solely for the comfort to be gained by exteriorizing their mind wounds. But, on the other hand, there were many who made really edifying confessions, full of faith in the supernatural grace that was won thereby. With honest purpose of amendment they told their sins, and with sincerity they expressed their sorrow for having committed them. Though interested in my work as a confessor, I never felt curious as to who the penitents were who confessed such and such sins, or as to the details of the sins themselves. I was amply satisfied with the very minimum of information needed with a view to absolution, and my sole preoccupation was to put the sinner right with God and send him or her away happy and strengthened" (pp. 161–2). His being satisfied with the very minimum is at odds with his interest in the details when practicing as a therapist. The discussion of the meaning of self-disclosure in the confessional and in analysis is a prime example of what Foucault called "intrinsic contradiction," since what was at stake was the place of self-disclosure in two radically different techniques of the self.

tradition dominated moral theology in the first half of the twentieth century. This tradition emphasized a legalistic approach to sin, so that Catholics would confess what and how often they had violated God's law. This approach did not lend itself to deep personal revelations in the confessional. Indeed, as Boyd Barrett (1928) wrote in "The drama of Catholic confession":

> Relying on his experience, the writer is inclined to dissent from the view that confession, as a general rule, affords a healthy model of self-revelation such as psychologists desiderate. It is too fragmentary, too artificial, and too coercive in character to be a health-giving mode of release ... The "fragmentary" nature of confession results from the custom, encouraged by the church, of confessing isolated sins. A Catholic, when he commits a grievous sin, is supposed to hasten to confess *it* to the priest without connecting it in any way with the complexus of his life.
>
> (p. 198)

Moreover, he observed that "the thing which is of serious consequence to the penitent, and about which dwells the penitent's most profound anguish, is not subject matter, in the theological sense, for confession, and confessors will point out to the penitent that the confessional is not the place for discussing such matters" (p. 199). Confession gave consolation to some, he continued, but its constraints made that end difficult. So that self-revelation in psychoanalysis can achieve what the formalized ritual of confession could not. In this sense, Boyd Barrett defined analysis in relation to confession, arguing in effect that the sacrament, as he saw it practiced, was insufficiently confessional.

It is worth a digression to address an implicit rebuttal to Boyd Barrett's position. Bruehl (1923b) noted that psychotherapy "calls for very delicate disclosures and sometimes for an unbaring of the innermost self" (p. 202), which makes it a practice subject to abuse. It can produce moral decay, because a person starts to dwell upon, for example, "forgotten sexual experiences" (Bruehl, 1923c, p. 221) and be tempted afresh. As Bruehl wrote: "sordid memories of the past should not be stirred up except where it is really necessary. Moral theologians, for that reason, discourage frequent general confessions, since with the memory of past lapses, are not rarely revived old temptations to embarrass the penitent" (ibid.). From this point of view, the formality of confession and the emphasis on law served the purpose of keeping attention focused on contrition and reformation, not the sometimes sordid past. Bruehl's views, however, like Boyd Barrett's, linked the confessional to the analyst's office.

The second part of psychotherapy included the use of hypnosis (which Freud rejected) – here Boyd Barrett referred to Rivers in partial support for its use. Psychical reeducation included will-training and religion, which Boyd Barrett had explored in *Strength of will* (1915). Finally, physical rebuilding referred to a variety of means to build stamina, including the Mitchell rest-cure and other techniques drawn from pre-psychoanalytic treatments for neurasthenia. He cited Crichton-Miller (Barrett, 1925a, pp. 153–4) in support of the inclusion of these methods. The older treatments for neurasthenia and other nervous diseases were still current in the early 1920s. Boyd Barrett also argued for the inclusion of more intuitive powers, including telepathy, which he called "soul-speech" (p. 285 ff.). This inclusion was less dramatic than it may now seem, because of the early history of psychotherapy, where the boundaries between psychical research and therapy were fluid. Boyd Barrett thus combined the Mind Cure of the late nineteenth century with a form of psychoanalysis.[19]

In summary, Boyd Barrett's psychotherapy brought together many of the then current types of mental healing: psychoanalysis (drawing on Catholic confessional practices), hypnosis and suggestion, will training (the distinctively Catholic contribution to the mix), Mind Cure, and the older "Dr. Diet and Dr. Quiet" of the Mitchell cure for neurasthenia. His work is a good compendium of the range of practices available at the time.

When Boyd Barrett left the Jesuits, he first set up his practice on MacDougal Street in Greenwich Village. This address placed Boyd Barrett in the heart of the psychoanalytic world of New York City in the 1920s.[20] The Village was a center for radical ideas and experimental styles of living. Nathan Hale (1995) writes that "the popular stereotypes of the analyst and the analytic process had been established before World War I: the uncanny analyst, who combined the qualities of secular priest, uncondemning listener, and scientific soul surgeon; the magical power of catharsis to dispel neuroses" (p. 95). Much, including what Boyd Barrett did, was included under psychoanalysis, and Boyd Barrett was one among many lay analysts. It was in a way the Wild West of psychoanalysis, and we must not read too much Freudian orthodoxy into what "psychoanalysis" meant in those years. Boyd Barrett (1929a) contributed an essay, "The psychoanalysis of asceticism," to *Sex in civilization*, edited by another lay analyst, Samuel Schmalhausen (Hale, 1995, p. 69), and V. F. Calverton. This book located Boyd Barrett decidedly on the left of the great cultural divide that was opening in American society. Boyd Barrett for a

---

[19] In "Hypnotism and Telepathy" (Barrett, 1923c) he defended telepathy against the charge that it was a form of spiritism, and claimed that telepathy may play a role in psychotherapy. He concluded with the thought that telepathy and clairvoyance might in the future "be reduced to practical arts. Scholastic psychology will not have to recede from any of her great theses, if that day comes, but will rejoice in the new and striking manifestations of the spirituality and vital power of the soul" (p. 131). Thus Boyd Barrett picked up the earlier interest, that we explored in Chapter 4, claiming them as purely natural capabilities that some or all may have. Like William James, he saw the future of psychology as having great promise in elucidating these phenomena.

[20] McGucken (1922) observed with some contempt that "perhaps the most ardent champion of Freud in America are folk of the Greenwich Village type, that strange race ever on the search for new gods" (p. 485).

while stepped into that breach, with his searing criticisms of the Catholic Church, *While Peter sleeps* (1929b).

The heart of the matter dividing the Church and psychoanalysis of whatever variety was, for Boyd Barrett, sex. In *The new psychology* (1925a), he gave it an important but limited role in human life:

> The sex-instinct is only *one of many instincts and it occupies a subordinate position*. It is subordinate to the self-preservation instinct ... Further, beyond question, in those who are normal, and untainted by any hereditary disease or by evil personal habits, the sex-instinct is subject to the control of the will for its exercise. And in those of heroic virtue it can be so crushed and deadened that its presence ceases to be felt.
>
> (pp. 314–15)

In particular, sex has nothing to do with religion: "Sex has to do with the sensible, the material; religion with the super-sensible and immaterial ... *Love* plays a part in religion as in sex, but in religion it is the rational desire and striving after spiritual good, in sex it is the bodily, sensible, cravings for physical pleasure ... *Religion deals with eternity; sex with the present time*" (pp. 315–16). These passages are from the final chapter, "False theories of religion," a chapter that to this reader at least seems unnecessary to the argument of the book. Given what Boyd Barrett said elsewhere, my guess is that this chapter was included to throw a bone to the Jesuit censors, who had already considered his writings on psychology "dangerous." What is striking about Boyd Barrett's statements about sex and religion is that they reflect neither orthodox psychoanalysis, which did not see sexual drives as one among many, nor Neoscholastic orthodoxy, which would not have bifurcated the sensual and the spiritual so radically. Boyd Barrett's views reflected instead the broader type of psychoanalysis represented by Rivers, on the one hand, and a quasi-Cartesian, quasi-Jansenistic theology that permeated much of popular Catholicism at the time and later (Royce, 1964).

Two years later, Boyd Barrett sounded a different note. Writing of the Jesuits, he said: "No doubt the Order saw at an early date in the development of psychoanalysis, that research into the science of sex, and a fuller biological and physiological knowledge of what sex meant, would discredit the Society's attitude and teaching in the matter" (Barrett, 1927, p. 294). He described the conditions that were given to him for lectures on psychoanalysis that he was to give in 1925:

> I was next invited by the authorities of Fordham University to deliver a course of public lectures on the "New Psychology" during Lent, each Sunday afternoon, at the Jesuit Public Hall in West Sixteenth Street. All arrangements were duly made, permissions received, and the Lectures were widely advertised. Already tickets had been sold, when the Provincial issued a ukase to Fordham University forbidding the course of Lectures.

At once there was an uproar and the Fordham authorities protested so strongly that the Provincial had to compromise. The compromise took the form of a series of restrictions on the lecturer. The lectures should be submitted for censorship in advance. No matters touching on sex were to be alluded to. There was to be tremendous emphasis given to the freedom of the will; the immortality of the soul; the spirituality of the soul, etc. Also, as I discovered afterwards, an official syndicus (spy) was appointed by the Provincial to attend the lectures and to report to him on them.

(p. 332)

Rather than take the bait of Boyd Barrett's polemic here, a digression on the role of the will in pre-psychoanalytic Catholic conceptions of the soul is in order. Early on, emphasis on the will was the counter to exploration of the unconscious.

A digression on the will

At all events, it may be laid down as a law that there can be no permanent recovery from nervous disease except through will-training, a matter which the psychoanalyst sadly neglects.

(C. P. Bruehl, 1923e, p. 15)

We have already noted that hypnosis raised the specter of someone surrendering his or her will to another. In Neoscholastic psychology, the will and the intellect were the two purely spiritual powers of the soul – hence, their importance for any psychology, theoretical or practical. Maher (1918/1933) defined the will as "the faculty of inclining toward or striving after some object intellectually apprehended as good" (p. 395). Freedom of the will was a concept tied to that of "moral liberty," the freedom to act ethically. This is not the place to enter into a full discussion of the will, which would require consideration of the doctrine of the Fall, the weakening of the will as a result, and the role of grace in acts of the will. Suffice it to say that the will was central to Catholic teachings about the human condition, and so it was natural that psychotherapy be tied to the will. This was as apparent in Walsh's *Psychotherapy* as it was in Boyd Barrett's *New psychology* and Moore's *Dynamic psychology*. For Walsh, as we have seen, psychotherapy meant the influence of the mind on the body, usually delivered through suggestion from doctor to patient. The thinking behind this for Walsh (and also for Moore, let it be noted) was not, strictly speaking, only scholastic in nature: in addition, there was vitalism, the positing of a "vital force" in the individual, driving the machinery of the body. Vitalism postulated an irreducible "vital principle" that distinguished living from non-living beings. That is, vitalism rejected the notion that physical and chemical explanations could explain living beings without remainder, and the vital principle was that remainder. For Walsh, "this vital force supplies the energy that we call the will" (1923, p. 133). Psychotherapeutics consisted in the mobilization of this vital energy or will for purposes of preserving health and fighting disease, as well as for combating "evil tendencies" (p. 134). By exercising "will power," one can "tap reservoirs of energy" (Walsh, 1919, p. 11), enabling one to endure and prevail in even dire circumstances.

Strengthening will-power had been a common theme in American psychotherapy. For the popularized form of psychoanalysis that was spreading across the land in the years around 1920, however, "trying to fight one's neuroses by will power was a waste of energy" (Hale, 1971, p. 402). Psychoanalysis was seen, then, as denying the will's freedom and power, and that was a source of contention in the Catholic world.

Walsh (1923, p. 790) found psychoanalysis simply another form of "mind cure," and he contrasted it to the more virile will-training. Describing its use in the treatment of psychoneuroses during World War I, Walsh (1919) said that the essence of the treatment was suggestion, re-education, and discipline. An extreme example was *torpillage*, the use of pain caused by electric current applied to the functionally paralyzed organs of hysterical soldiers: "the man who would insist on maintaining a false attitude of mind towards himself, though that attitude of mind was not deliberate, and least of all not malingering, was simply made to give it up" (pp. 264–5). To avoid further pain, the patient would start to relinquish the symptom. It seems paradoxical to strengthen the will by the use of force, but the idea was that the pain of discipline would make the person realize that the source of change lay within his own power.[21]

Boyd Barrett did not recommend this torture as a therapeutic device, to be sure, but he appealed to the same type of steely masculinity as the epitome of the one in whom the will is awake. The man of will is strong, and he becomes something like a hero from an Ayn Rand novel: "Our lives will become more solitary and more independent. In spite of ourselves we shall grow somewhat cold and serious and rigid. Some of the flower and bloom of our natural manner will be lost and we shall be less lovable. Those who admire us from afar will talk vaguely of telepathy, psychic influence and magnetism, and use many meaningless terms" (1915, pp. 54–5). It was precisely this prototype of the man of will that Boyd Barrett (1929a) later condemned after his break from the Jesuits. What he intended in *Strength of will* was a type of will-training that would awaken a person to the fact of the will within and the means to strengthen it, on analogy with athletic training. Boyd Barrett understood that will-training was

---

[21] Lewis Yealland (1918) practiced this type of treatment in World War I. Moore (1924, p. 296) thought electrical treatment of hysterical paralyses useful. The contrast with a psychodynamic approach was depicted in the novel *Regeneration* (Barker, 1991), where Rivers reacts with horror to this torture-cum-treatment. Class differences accounted in large measure for the differences in treatments, with officers more likely to get the talking cure, and enlisted men the electrical prod and "re-education."

not the same as character development and that the latter was of course more important. His exercises consisted of three stages: educative (becoming aware of the will in oneself), curative (correcting defects of will, such as impulsiveness or hesitation), and strengthening. The exercises were essentially meaningless, in that they had no end beyond themselves, just as push-ups are meaningless, beyond strengthening certain muscles. The will exercises consisted of practices such as standing on a chair for ten minutes a day for a week, keeping an introspective record of one's experience. With these exercises, Boyd Barrett claimed that one could achieve self-mastery (p. 174).[22]

Boyd Barrett drew on Catholic traditions of asceticism for this will-training, saying that will-training "without relation to religion and morality, is in the great part meaningless" (p. 35). He referred to Catholic religious practices, such as regular reception of the sacraments, fasting in Lent and Advent, daily prayer, and so on, as means by which the will is trained. He thus alluded to the notion of *cura animarum*, which was held to be the means by which the Church leads souls to their salvation. This approach to well-being was reflected in Bruehl's (1921b) assessment of the relative merits of psychoanalysis: "Mental disturbances are due in most cases to lack of will control, for will is supposed to be the censor of our conscious life and to hold in check all evil tendencies. The ascetically trained will is the best cure for mental troubles that are not produced by organic lesions or functional irregularities" (p. 541). The theologian Fanning (1908) described the rationale behind these ascetical practices:

> if . . . the people be truly desirous for their own salvation, obedient towards their pastor, zealous to obtain and employ the means of sanctification, and mindful of their obligations as members of a parish to enable their pastor to institute and improve the parochial institutions necessary for the proper furtherance of the object of the Church, we shall have the true idea of the cure of souls.
>
> (p. 572)

The cure of souls was largely a matter of practices to aid in the divine work of salvation, building character in the process. This was the context within which the Catholic community would have understood the new psychotherapy, which in its own way claimed to cure souls in their sufferings. How could the person be cured if not with the use of his or her will? How, if not by psychoanalysis?

---

[22] Assagioli (1973) included some of Boyd Barrett's exercises as ways of strengthening the will, but he saw strengthening of the will as but one aspect of a more comprehensive will-training. Studying the links between earlier modes of such exercise, traditions of spiritual development, and more contemporary forms, such as those of van Kaam and Assagioli remains to be done.

In 1947, in the wake of criticisms of psychoanalysis by then Monsignor Fulton Sheen (more on this controversy below), Harry McNeill (1947), recognizing what he called rivalry between Catholicism and analysis, took the occasion to castigate "our so-called will training," the Catholic default alternative to psychotherapy: "in the absence of correlative intellectual self-searching, [will-training] produces hard, cold, inhuman characters who take pride in their rigidity" (p. 352), precisely the character type praised by Boyd Barrett in *Strength of Will* and later condemned by him. Will-training – esteemed because of its recognition of human rationality and moral responsibility – was insufficient, because it neglected affective aspects of human nature. In retrospect, will-training rested more on the overly-rationalistic Cartesian view that self-consciousness adequately provides self-knowledge.[23]

Testing psychoanalysis at the Catholic University of America

When Boyd Barrett was in Washington and not allowed to practice psychoanalysis, he said that he was informed that Thomas Verner Moore had had his clinic closed by Church authorities. "A few days later I found Fr. Moore, and discovered that his clinic was not only not closed but was flourishing" (1927, p. 331). He still was unsuccessful in getting the Jesuits to let him integrate psychotherapy and religion.

As we have noted before, Moore was widely acknowledged as the foremost Catholic psychologist and psychiatrist of his day. He had worked as an army psychiatrist during World War I and he wrote that, "the war neuroses offered a valuable opportunity for studying emotional conditions and enabled me to delineate a group of emotional disorders, the *parataxes* which lie between the normal emotional reactions or *psychotaxes* and the major psychoses" (1948, p. 46).[24] With psychiatric training behind him, he could address the most important contribution to that field in the new century.

Perhaps the earliest Catholic responses to Freud came from Moore's department, in two contributions to *Psychological Studies from the Catholic University of America*, published as part of the *Psychological Monographs* series, which was dedicated to publishing research articles from around the nation. Moore (1919)

[23] We return to this theme in Chapter 8, in a discussion of the meaning of obedience in the religious life.

[24] Harry Stack Sullivan (1964) credits Moore for the term *parataxic*, which was so important to Sullivan's conception of interpersonal relations: Sullivan used the term to "indicate sundry maladjustive or nonadjustive situations, some of which might be called in more conventional language 'neurotic'" (p. 41). Moore's (1924) use is slightly different, more intrapsychic than Sullivan's: a parataxis is "an impulsive drive to react to difficulties in some particular way . . . that becomes abnormal by virtue of its intensity or prolongation, or bizarre character and which may be the preliminary stage of a serious breakdown" (p. 422).

and Paul Hanly Furfey[25] (1919), Moore's student, addressed the role of symbolism in psychological life. Furfey's contribution was his masters thesis under Moore. He examined the relationship between the dreams of individuals and the myths of a culture, and in the course of this presentation, discussed psychoanalysis extensively. Critical of Freud's narrow conception of libido as sexual (even granting the broad meaning of sex in Freud's work), Furfey assimilated libido to "the Thomistic concept of appetition" (p. 360). What this meant was that Furfey stressed the role of the intellect in desire: "a man desires a thing because he thinks it will be good for him" (p. 361). As a result, a dream is not only a wish fulfillment: it reflects conscious life in general, and so deals with "scruples, fears, doubts, anxieties, and so forth, as well as with wishes" (p. 362). Arguing for unconscious mental activity, by drawing on such events as automatic writing, Furfey found that the unconscious is not simply composed of drives but could also manifest intelligence. Turning then to myths, Furfey suggested that they often express "primitive philosophical speculation" (p. 379). The earliest people, then, used the same mental processes that we do, but given their level of intellectual development, myths resulted. Furfey in effect sketched out what we can call a "Thomistic psychoanalysis," in that he acknowledged the place of drives and desires, as did the psychoanalysts, but insisted on the place of the object (as the goal of desire) and on the role of the intellect in desire. Like others from the time, we see with Furfey a conception of psychoanalysis that extends beyond Freud, to include others who were not "orthodox" analysts. Furfey made extensive reference to the work of Jung, as well as the American psychiatrists William Alanson White and Morton Prince. In fact, he cited such writers more than he did Freud.

Moore's (1919a) article was his first statement on psychoanalysis. He affirmed that it did provide cures for mental disorders, but he questioned if psychoanalytic explanations for those cures were adequate. He argued that Freud's theories had to be tested scientifically in order to determine their validity. His study was an interesting use of introspection – which Freud distrusted as a method because, he claimed, it cannot access the unconscious – in order to capture something at the edge of the range of introspection. Moore described experiences of falling asleep and nodding off, in which he found himself thinking in images rather than discursively: hence the title, "hypnotic analogies," moments similar to dreams, but occurring in the twilight of waking consciousness. He found evidence to support Freud's notion of dreams as

---

[25] Furfey (1896–1992) came to the Catholic University of America in 1917 to study psychology, but completed a doctorate in sociology. He was a member of the Catholic University's sociology department, a prolific writer, and researcher. A considerable amount of his research dealt with developmental topics and intelligence testing. Furfey's "engagement with the social sciences was profoundly shaped by Moore …. Moore combined his study of psychology with very practical social reform work" (Rademacher, 2007, p. 32).

drawing on and addressing moments and conflicts of daily life, but he discovered no support for the theory that repression acts as a censor in dream work, making the manifest content of the dream symbolic in order to disguise the wish and avoid censorship. Instead, he concluded:

> Any thought whatsoever may be expressed in symbols, and is likely to be so expressed if it is the last thought in mind just before going to sleep. Symbols are the language of sleep, logical concepts the inner language of our everyday life. Dreams, therefore, are symbolic not that we may not understand them, but simply because they must be expressed in the language we are capable of using when we are asleep.
>
> (p. 396)

Theoretically, Moore compared hypnagogic imagery to sensations in their relation to thought. That is, for Moore, dream imagery are phantasms in the Thomistic sense of the term. Except for this last point, Moore's attitude towards Freud's theoretical formulations reflected a wider appropriation of Freud by such psychologists as W. H. R. Rivers who, while using psychoanalytic techniques in therapy, and affirming the role of unconscious conflict, extended the range of types of thoughts and conflicts that are psychologically significant in understanding dreams – and symptoms.

Thomistic dynamic psychology

Moore's *Dynamic psychology* (1924) "gave perhaps the most extensive place to Freud's ideas of all the textbooks of the period" (Shakow and Rapaport, 1964, p. 158). In this book and elsewhere, he elaborated a dynamic psychology. Moore's position was that Freud had contributed to the understanding of the etiology of mental disorders and to their treatment, but that his theoretical conception was largely unscientific. Freud did not, Moore said, engage in the experimental or statistical studies that would test his major hypotheses. He credited Freud with the development of the understanding that mental disorders have a source in the patient's life history: "We perhaps owe to Freud, more than we realize, the development of our present class of psychogenic mental diseases. For before his day, the tendency was certainly to look upon everything as some kind of physical disease of the central nervous system" (Moore, 1924, p. 259). While he did not find psychoanalysis to have universal relevance, he did affirm that: "In my experience, psychoanalysis is of particular value in the parataxes of anxiety in civil life. Wherever there has been established in the past a pathological association between emotional incident and abnormal behavior, psychoanalysis is of distinct help" (p. 261).

Theoretically, Moore found many psychoanalytic concepts wanting. In discussing Freud's typology of id, ego and superego, Moore tended to assimilate

Freud's categories into his own, without a reckoning of striking theoretical differences. For example, he wrote:

> We all recognize that everything in a human being is not conscious, though we may not be familiar with the term id as the designation of the nonconscious aspect of the organism. We are all familiar with the conscious mind, which keeps us in contact with external reality, and see no reason why we should not speak of it as the ego. And each of us has lived with his own moral conscience and known its approval and felt its disapproval. But we have not termed it a superego. Nor have we all regarded conscience merely as a portion of our own minds with which it behooves us to be at peace. Some of us at least conceive the possibility of a "true light that enlighteneth everyone who cometh into the world," and know that God has ways of speaking to the mind of man through the channel of natural reason as well as by supernatural grace.
>
> (Moore, 1951, pp. 37–8)

Moore found the core of psychoanalytic theory – the relation of neurosis to sexuality and the origin of neurotic conflict in infancy – as lacking empirical evidence (pp. 43–4). His assessment was that Freud's psychopathology "has its roots not in empirical findings but in the lively imagination of its author. Freud was an interesting writer with a happy gift of inventing a captivating terminology" (p. 55).

Moore emphasized the contributions of Freud the therapist: "His fundamental technique of mental analysis was an important contribution to psychotherapy" (ibid.). Psychoanalysis did influence Moore's practice significantly. Like Adolf Meyer, with whom he studied, Moore saw the etiology of much mental disease in "maladjustment" to the difficulties of life. "Chronic emotional strain" and "acute emotional experience" contribute to the formation of parataxes and more severe disorders, though he did not posit one type of etiology for all disorders. His therapeutic style centered on having the patient begin with his life history and then proceeding to an analysis of free associations to elements of the life history. The analysis of dreams often aided in the therapy, although Moore did not hold, as did Freud, that dreams only and always refer to repressed infantile wishes, although he thought that some could. With Alfred Adler, he held that some dreams are attempts to work out a solution to the difficulty facing the patient. But in his use of the technique of free association, Moore employed the essential element of psychoanalysis.

Moore could be directive or nondirective in therapy, as the situation demanded. Drawing on Alphonse Maeder, an associate of Jung who stressed the prospective function of dreams (Ellenberger, 1970, p. 815), Moore wrote that "I here took [Moore is recounting a case history] the role that Maeder ascribes to the psychoanalyst, that of a friend who helps the patient to know himself better and to rule himself" (Moore, 1951, p. 122), and he gave the patient direct advice, to remain faithful to his wife. Moore noted that Freud urged against such advice giving, saying that the analyst should be "physician and educator" and not mentor. But Moore observed that Freud also criticized conventional sexual morality in analysis, claiming that it had its basis neither in "veracity nor wisdom" (p. 123). Moore concluded that "when Freud says that he cannot spare his patients the task of listening to his criticism of moral principles, it shows that he himself has assumed the role of mentor, but as guide to evil and not to good" (ibid.). Nevertheless, the "methods of psychoanalysis are good and useful" (ibid.).

If the essence of neurosis is maladjustment, then healing entails new adjustments to life demands. Such a change can come only when the patient has sufficient insight so that he can, in freedom, make a decision. For example, Moore recounted: "Toward the end of his interview I said to the patient, 'Now you understand your condition. What are you going to do about it?' I explained that a psychiatrist can only help the patient to see himself in a true light, but the patient must work out a solution" (p. 126). Moore cited, in this context, the notion of a "will to health" formulated by Otto Rank, and that the patient had to fight "for freedom from anxiety" (p. 127) as a life task of the moment.

Moore's eclecticism reflected his practical interests in psychotherapy as well as his Neoscholastic philosophical orientation. If there is some truth in psychoanalysis, then recognize it and apply it, if it be helpful. Moore's psychology was eclectic in part because it was a functional psychology, although he meant by "function" the activity of our mental faculties, and not only our adaptation to reality: hence his emphasis on adjustment. However, lest Moore be seen as just another promoter of social conformity, I need to mention two items. First, his Neoscholastic background showed in his emphasis on "volitional adjustment" (Moore, 1948, p. 388): "For volitional action . . . is rooted in intellectual understanding." Therapy cannot ignore the spiritual reality of the human soul, with its faculties of intellect and will: "We are trying to get the mother [of a child with behavior problems] to understand herself, to become focally aware of a faulty attitude towards the child, and to lay that attitude aside and adopt a new attitude. But to lay aside an old attitude and adopt a new one . . . is a volitional act, and sometimes it demands a great deal of personal effort" (pp. 388–9). Moore used a variety of direct and indirect means to facilitate this change, including direct teaching and indirect appeals to the imagination. So Moore, like his contemporary Boyd Barrett and those in the Church who sought to train the will, and like Otto Rank earlier and Roberto Assagioli later, appealed to the will of his patients out of respect for the dignity of the human person. However, Moore did not think that will training was the way to go, for it neglected the insight necessary for the patient to will willingly. Second, adjustment included "adjustment of man to God in the supreme social order." The development of the spiritual life is part and parcel of adjustment:

But the end of man is to know his Creator, the Supreme Intelligence, and work silently and humbly with Him fulfilling the little duties of the moment in the harmonious development of God's supreme social order. To recognize God's absolute supremacy and attempt to do all in one's power to carry out the will of God is to love God. And whoever sets about doing this to the best of his ability enters upon the way that leads to the mystical union of the soul with God.

(p. 413)

Drawing on St. Augustine, St. John of the Cross, and St. Thérèse of Lisieux, Moore described the path of contemplation. This spiritual adjustment – the word employed here analogically – was not, strictly speaking, within the competence of the psychotherapist. Moore assumes, rather, the necessity of a religious life and spiritual guidance. However, such adjustment is important, given the nature of the human person.

Furfey (1929), at this time the member of the Sociology Department at the Catholic University of America, also linked psychoanalysis and ascetical theology. For him, Freud's teaching on unconscious desires beneath our conscious decisions and actions was something known in ascetical theology, which has long analyzed the human capacity for self-deception. Furfey saw Freud's contribution as extending this knowledge to the workings of unconscious self-deception as a partial explanation for neurosis. Like Moore denying the sexual etiology of all neurosis, Furfey held that Freud's techniques enable an analysis of our "subterfuges" (p. 241). Psychoanalysis "has furnished a technique which has made possible the treatment of many mental diseases before which psychiatrists stood quite helpless" (ibid.). At the same time, Furfey dismissed the extravagant claims of Freud's theory and their extension into "a religion" (p. 242) by some psychoanalysts.

In the period between the 1920s and the 1950s, then, a Neoscholastic framework provided a way to draw on psychoanalytic concepts and practices, without either dismissing them or embracing them uncritically. The examples of Boyd Barrett and Moore, however, show that the reception of psychoanalysis was tied to many things besides philosophical considerations. For Boyd Barrett, psychoanalysis was part of an individual struggle with his order. For Moore, ever the institution-builder, psychoanalysis was but one tool in the toolbox.

Conflicts and accommodations

The 1940s saw a new wave of conflict between the Church and psychoanalysis. Rudolf Allers' critique of psychoanalysis first stirred the waters, although it was his colleague at the Catholic University, the then Monsignor Fulton J. Sheen, who created the storm. Ranged on the other side were Catholic psychologists and psychiatrists who, in the manner of Moore, took what was useful in psychoanalysis and did not subscribe to a rigid psychoanalytic orthodoxy. In the 1950s calm returned, in part because Pope Pius XII nodded favorably in the direction of psychiatry, and in part because of the influence of French writers on psychoanalysis, including Roland Dalbiez (1893-1976) and Jacques Maritain (1882-1973), more sympathetic to Freud than many American Catholic philosophers. Many such writers appeared in new publications, especially *Cross Currents*, a quarterly journal begun in 1950, that brought an international perspective to American Catholics.

Rudolf Allers' philosophical refutation of Freudian theory and practice

In contrast to Moore's eclectic accommodations with psychoanalysis stands the Neoscholastic refutation of Freud by Rudolf Allers (1883-1963), for some years Moore's colleague at the Catholic University. Allers attended medical school at the University of Vienna, where he studied briefly under Freud. After receiving a medical degree in 1908, he was an instructor in psychiatry at the University of Munich. During World War I, he was a surgeon in the Austrian army. For twenty years after the end of that war, Allers taught and did laboratory work in the medical school at the University of Vienna; he also had a private psychiatric practice. In 1934, he received a degree in philosophy from the University of Milan, where he studied at the instigation of Agostino Gemelli (1878-1969), the Italian psychologist and Neoscholastic philosopher. In 1938, he became a professor of psychology at the Catholic University of America; ten years later, he left for Georgetown University, where he was a professor of philosophy. His major psychological works include *The Psychology of character* (1931), *The new psychologies* (1933), *The successful error* (1941), and *Existentialism and psychiatry* (1961).

Allers' psychotherapeutic approach was essentially Adlerian.[26] James E. Royce, SJ, the psychologist and philosopher, who had had the happy fortune of having attended courses given by both Moore and by Allers, summarized Adler's and Allers' theory of neurosis in straightforward textbook terms:

> Alfred Adler's theory centers around ego: pride and selfishness ... The child is always weaker and inferior to his surroundings, but basic ego-assertiveness soon goes about making up for that, in ways which can easily lead to maladjustment. In spite of fear that he would be misunderstood, Adler used to say he could simplify his theory down to four words, "all neurosis is vanity." Rudolf Allers follows him with a similar truism demanding some explanation. He calls the neurotic an 'ambitious

---

[26] In an obituary notice in the *Journal of Individual Psychology* (Rudolf Allers, 1883-1963, 1965), we read that Allers "'belonged for a time to the inner circle of Adler's collaborators,' as he himself stated it ... He separated himself from Individual Psychology in 1927."

coward' – the combination of ambitious pride and cowardly indecision leads to oscillation between excessive pretense and feelings of guilt over failure to achieve.

(Royce, 1955, pp. 252–3)

Allers stressed character development in both adults and children. With Adler, he emphasized the future more than the past in psychotherapy. With Adler, he claimed that every neurotic has a "wrong 'life plan'" (Jugnet, 1950/1975, p. 77). His use of associations and dreams in therapy strike me as resembling that of Moore. For Allers, as for Moore, there was no single way to practice psychotherapy, because each patient is "an absolutely unique person" (p. 78). The therapist's "task is primarily that of understanding, of discovering the hidden forces which make an individual behave in a manner that throws him into conflicts, causes suffering, or incapacitates him for a normal and efficient life" (Allers, 1948, p. 474).

Allers' *The successful error* was a Neoscholastic critique of psychoanalysis by a man with both philosophical and clinical credentials. Unlike some of his contemporaries in American Catholic circles, he did not seek accommodation with Freudian thought. Nor did he dismiss Freud as a mere flash in the pan. Allers claimed that Freud had specific achievements: the attempt to understand and treat neurosis, the theoretical importance of early childhood in the development of personality and, "in an age of unduly exaggerated intellectualism, [psychoanalysis] has made visible the influence of non-intellectual factors within the human personality" (Allers, 1941, p. 259). Freud's greatest achievement, however, was unintentional:

> The discovery that mental treatment is capable of healing certain bodily troubles, that it may result in a total change of attitudes, has delivered mankind from the bondage of biologism. Not every thing is due to heredity, to bodily constitution, to an immutable set-up of personality, decreed by blind fate. The dominion of mind is reestablished.
>
> (p. 260)

Not only unintentional, but ironic, since Freud sought to denigrate the human person through his materialist and hedonistic philosophy.

Allers' position was that psychoanalysis was a heresy (p. 202). Heresy, Allers explained, following Hilaire Belloc, "consists, in taking out one part of a system and replacing it either by some other things or by leaving its place unfilled" (p. 241). Freud's heresy occurred when the conception of "the unity of human nature" (p. 242), which psychoanalysis reaffirms after centuries of being lost because of "the spirit of Cartesian philosophy" (ibid.), was perverted by Freud's "philosophy of materialistic monism" (ibid.). Allers pointed out that "the idea of person is an offspring of Christianity" (p. 243). Psychoanalysis developed a distorted conception of the human person, and that is its heresy.

Allers argued that the philosophical basis of psychoanalysis could not be separated from psychoanalytic method, and here he departed from Moore. He claimed to hold to a stricter understanding of what psychoanalytic technique actually was:

> The essential elements of psychoanalysis as a method are said to be free association and interpretation. This statement is, however, not quite true, or at least, not quite complete . . . Psychoanalysis falls to the ground if we refuse to believe in the existence of the Oedipus-situation or in the existence of libidinous bonds between parents and children or in the process of sublimation or in the effects of repression.
>
> (p. 162)

Allers' point was that psychoanalysis did not consist simply in a technique, for example, free association, but that it also entailed the interpretation of the associations and a decision to break off associations that, as experience shows, can be endless. So psychoanalytic method was inseparable from psychoanalytic hermeneutics. The mere use of associations in psychotherapy did not make the therapy psychoanalytic:

> It becomes necessary for the psychoanalyst, therefore, to have some method on hand for determining when to break off the chain of associations. He alone can know whether a point sufficiently removed from the actual mental event has been attained . . . We can never know whether some matter coming to the surface after resistance has been broken has any importance unless we have previously the knowledge of, e.g., the Oedipus-situation. This is one point in which the necessary and indissoluble connection between theory and method becomes visible.
>
> (pp. 163–4)

If psychoanalytic method was inseparable from interpretation, then we must know the basis of Freudian hermeneutics. Here is where Allers thought psychoanalysis a failure. For the analyst, the relationships among the freely associated ideas were causal in nature: "Causal relations of this kind can be stated only if the peculiar idea of dynamism and of mental energy as it has been developed by Freud is recognized to be true. If this conception is rejected we are allowed only to state a relation of association . . . but not causation" (p. 165). Free associations may be used by the psychiatrist without Freudian canons of interpretation, but psychoanalysis as such ties together the method of free association with a strict determinism of mental contents on the basis of instinct theory.

For Allers, "there is no psychology without a philosophy" (p. 168). Freud's implicit philosophy was defective, and much of *The successful error* was an exposition of it. In summary, Allers described Freud's philosophical foundation in these terms: "A philosophy which denies free will, ignores the spirituality of the soul, and with shallow materialism . . . knows of no other end than pleasure, is given to a confused but nevertheless obstinate subjectivism, is blind to the true nature of the human person – such a philosophy cannot have even one point in common with Christian thought" (pp. 199–200). Freud's was a materialistic philosophy, because he reduced meaning between mental events to those of physical cause–effect relationships. Freud's materialism was hedonistic, since the ultimate effect of the causes operating unconsciously in the mind is pleasure, i.e., the satisfaction of an instinctual drive. Because of this defective philosophical basis and its implication for therapy, "One has to conclude that a Catholic ought to beware of getting too close a contact with Freudian ideas" (p. 210).

Fulton Sheen's denunciation of psychoanalysis

In a Lenten sermon at St. Patrick's Cathedral in New York City, on March 9, 1947, Monsignor Fulton J. Sheen initiated a new round of debate over Freud. Sheen claimed, according to the *New York Times*, that Freudianism was an "escapism," when what really is needed to make men whole is the sacrament of confession, and that it was based on "materialism, hedonism, infantilism and eroticism" (Sheen denounces psychoanalysis, 1947). At this time, psychoanalysis was flourishing in New York and the United States, in part because of the flight of German psychoanalysts to the United States during the Nazi regime, in part because of the contributions of analysts to the war effort, and in part because of the boom in clinical psychology and psychiatry after the war. Gillespie (2001, p. 53) suggests that Allers influenced Sheen. Both men taught at the Catholic University during the same period. In addition, Neoscholastic psychologists, such as Robert Edward Brennan (1940) and Hugh J. Bihler, SJ (1940),[27] had had favorable responses to Allers' work.[28]

Sheen, a philosophy professor, was well known for his radio program, "The Catholic Hour," of which he had been the host since 1930, with a wide and ecumenical audience.[29] His sermon thus fell on fertile ground, because his "golden voice"[30] spoke with the authority of the Church in the ears of many. The sequent furor was confused, with charges and counter-charges, mainly based on the report in the *Times*, amplified by a general lack of distinction among "psychiatry," "psychoanalysis," and "Freudianism" in the Catholic

[27] Bihler contributed many reviews to *America* from the 1930s to the 1950s. He taught at the Jesuit seminary, Woodstock College in Maryland. He had studied psychology with Karl and Charlotte Bühler, and with Johannes Lindworsky.

[28] The controversy over Sheen's sermon has been discussed by Massa (1999), Reeves (2001), Nussbaum (2007), Heinze (2004), Lally (1975), and Gillespie (2001).

[29] His television program, "Life is Worth Living," which began in 1952, would bring him even greater fame. He was a pioneer in the new medium and understood it well.

[30] "Golden-voiced Msgr. Fulton J. Sheen, U. S. Catholicism's famed proselyter, pulls 3,000 to 6,000 letters a Sunday, but is on the air only four months a year" (Radio Religion, 1946).

community, and lack of clarity regarding which one Sheen condemned. The fact that an orthodox Freudian orientation dominated New York psychiatry (see Hale, 1995, p. 277) at the time made the distinctions even less visible. The sermon was one in a series that Sheen delivered that Lent, their common theme being the necessity of finding our true purpose in life, which is "to know, love, and serve God," Sheen here quoting the *Baltimore Catechism* with these words. (All Sheen's Lenten sermons for that year were summarized in the *Times*, by the way.)[31]

Protests from leading Catholic psychiatrists and psychoanalysts such as A. A. Brill at first received no reply from Sheen. In July, the controversy flared again, when four leading Catholic psychiatrists denounced Sheen's charge "that the practice of psychiatry is irreligious" (Msgr. Sheen's attack hit by psychiatrists, 1947). The four were Edward A. Strecker (1886–1959), Leo Bartemeier (1895–1982), Frank J. Curran (1904–89), and Francis J. Gerty (1892–1994). The initial *Times* article did not say that Sheen said that, "psychiatry was irreligious." His remarks implied that, at least according to Curran, who resigned in protest from his position as head of the Psychiatry Department at St. Vincent's Hospital, a Catholic hospital in New York City, and from his archdiocesan duties as psychiatric expert to the matrimonial court and as a psychiatric consultant (Psychiatrist quits in Catholic clash, 1947). He protested the fact that neither Sheen nor the archdiocese had clarified or corrected what to Curran were intemperate remarks. Curran wrote to St. Vincent's: "as a result of the newspaper publicity given to Msgr. Sheen's speech, private patients of mine as well as hospital patients of St. Vincent's stated that they could no longer come for psychiatric treatment or even consult a psychiatrist because they would be committing a sin if they did" (ibid.). So even if Sheen had not equated psychoanalysis or even Freudianism with psychiatry, that was how it was taken by eminent psychiatrists and by ordinary Catholics. The archdiocese stood by Sheen. He delivered another series of Lenten sermons from St. Patrick's Cathedral the following year.

The day after Curran's resignation was reported in the press, Sheen tempered his position to some extent, stating that he had been misquoted. He distinguished between psychiatry as a science and psychoanalysis as an ideology (Msgr. Sheen lays errors to press, 1947; Sheen, 1949). Lawrence Kubie, a noted psychiatrist and a leading member of the New York Psychoanalytic Institute, questioned Sheen's honesty (Sheen criticized by psychoanalyst, 1947), and two years later, Bartemeier, as president-elect of the American

---

[31] Sheen was not the only one to call psychoanalysis an *ersatz* religion. Among others, Betty Friedan, in the *Feminine mystique* (1963), made the same accusation. Like Sheen, she accused Freud of promoting pleasure over responsibility, and of making "private vice sinless" (Hale, 1995, p. 346). So the distortion, "Freudianism," was not Sheen's alone, and it touched a nerve in American life.

Psychiatric Association continued to accuse Sheen of misunderstanding psychoanalysis and psychiatry (Freeman, 1950). Part of the reason for the continued criticism of Sheen was that he continued to attack what he called Freudianism, which he paired with Marxism as two tempting forms of materialism (Mount St. Vincent marks centenary, 1947). Sheen continued his attack on his television show, "Life is Worth Living," in the 1950s, and in his bestseller, *Peace of soul.*[32]

The controversy crossed the Hudson River and into the rest of the nation. Harry McNeill indirectly criticized Sheen in the July 25, 1947 issue of *Commonweal,* a leading Catholic magazine, when he objected to Catholics taking "pot shots" at Freud. McNeill sought an even-tempered position, stating that of course there were tensions between psychoanalysis and Catholicism, because they both plowed the same field, character formation. Freudians, he said, had a lot to learn from Catholics, and then, speaking as an analyst, said that Catholics had things to learn from Freud. He proposed, among other things, that Catholics could learn about the developmental approach, because "our traditional psychology is largely philosophical and based upon an analysis of traits common to adults" (McNeill, 1947, p. 352). McNeill, along with other psychologists (Burke, 1953), expressed dissatisfaction with the overly rationalistic approach of Neoscholastic philosophical anthropology. McNeill's article was summarized in *Time* magazine on August 4, giving the conflict national coverage, largely, no doubt, because of Sheen's celebrity. McNeill was taken, implicitly, as the synthesis of the divergent views of Sheen on the one hand, and the psychiatrists, such as Curran, on the other.

It is important to note that Sheen did single out one psychiatrist for praise. In his letter to the *Times* defending his remarks, Sheen stated that he had referred people to the one "I believe to be the outstanding psychiatrist in New York City, Dr. Bernard L. Pacella" (Msgr. Sheen lays errors to press, 1947). Pacella had been quoted in the *Times* in the story reporting Curran's resignation from St. Vincent's as saying: "I'm uncertain whether Monsignor Sheen's views necessarily represent the official views of the Catholic Church. My opinion is that Monsignor Sheen was expressing his own views on the matter. I think the whole matter should be dropped. The controversy has been needlessly enlarged" (Psychiatrist quits in Catholic clash, 1947). It was not dropped, at least not right away, but this does raise the question: who was Bernard L. Pacella?

---

[32] In reviewing *Peace of soul,* Braceland (1949) found it "distressing" that Sheen continued his "widely publicized quarrel with psychiatry" because "the quarrel only added to the worries of the already harassed Catholic psychiatrist and made him even more suspect in the eyes of the public and his colleagues" (p. 192). Nussbaum (2007) describes how in 1959 Sheen seemed "converted" to the views of the Catholic psychiatrists. But by then, Pope Pius XII had already praised psychiatry and offered conditional support for psychoanalysis. We return to this topic in Chapter 7, in discussing the Guild of Catholic Psychiatrists.

196 PSYCHOLOGY AND CATHOLICISM: CONTESTED BOUNDARIES

Pacella (1912–2007) was a New York psychiatrist and psychoanalyst. At the time of the Sheen controversy, he was in the Department of Psychiatry at the College of Physicians and Surgeons, Columbia University, and a member of the Department of Experimental Psychiatry at the New York State Psychiatric Institute and Hospital. In 1947, the year of Sheen's controversial Lenten sermons, Pacella had published a study of the effects of electric convulsive therapy on the personalities of psychiatric patients (Pacella, Piotrowski, and Lewis, 1947), a topic to which he devoted much research. He was no enemy of psychoanalysis, and in fact, during his career, he was "President of the Margaret S. Mahler Psychiatric Research Foundation, a member of the Board of Directors of the Sigmund Freud Archives, the Freud London Museum, and the New York Psychoanalytic Society and Institute, and President of the American Psychoanalytic Association" (Pacella, 2007). Pacella was interested in the relationship between religion and psychiatry, and he contributed to the early development of pastoral psychology in Catholic circles the decades following 1947.[33]

Sheen's high regard for Pacella makes the situation less than clear-cut; however, it indicates that Sheen did not intend to condemn psychiatry plain and simple. In that respect, he was more in harmony with the Pope's later statements, even if he was intemperate in his 1947 sermon.

The controversy simmered until the mid-1950s, when a series of statements by Pope Pius XII clarified the place of psychiatry and even psychoanalysis, so long as they respected the human person. The Pope's pronouncements were prompted in part by the Sheen controversy. Ernest Jones, who had been a close colleague and apologist of Freud's, asked Bartemeier in 1949 to succeed him as president of the International Psychoanalytic Association.[34] But before accepting, Bartemeier consulted with the Pope, asking him his views on psychoanalysis. He found Pius well informed, and with praise for Freud's discoveries about the mind urged Bartemeier to take on the role if elected (Bartemeier, 1972).

After the Sheen controversy

Throughout the next decade, defenses of psychoanalysis and more nuanced critiques of it appeared in Catholic circles. Contributors to it included Gregory Zilboorg (1949), a convert to Catholicism and friend of Thomas Verner Moore, and William C. Bier, SJ (1957), the driving force behind the American Catholic Psychological Association. The Pope's private support for Bartemeier had not been sufficient. An article by Monsignor Pericle Felici in *The Bulletin of the Catholic Clergy of Rome* (April 1952), asserted that Catholics

---

[33] See below, Chapter 9.

[34] See above, this chapter, for mention of Jones' reductionistic interpretation of Christian teachings.

who practice psychoanalysis or enter into analysis are committing a mortal sin, because of Freud's pansexualism (the incident is discussed in Gillespie, 2001, pp. 18–19). In two addresses, Pius affirmed the benefits of psychiatry, while admitting the dangers of erroneous views of the human person. In *The moral limits of medical research and treatment* (1952) he warned against" the pansexual method of a certain school of psychoanalysis" that seeks to awaken "every appetite of a sexual order which is being excited or has been excited in his being, appetites whose impure waves flood his unconscious or subconscious mind" (p. 7) for therapeutic purposes. In a subsequent clarification, *L'Osservatore Romano* (With reference to psychoanalysis, 1952) noted that "there are other psychoanalytic methods which are not infected with the vice of pansexualism; that furthermore, all the systems of psychoanalysis have in common certain principles, methods and psychic experiments which are in no way contrary to natural ethics and Christian morality" (p. 17). The following year, at the invitation of Bartemeier (Gillespie, 2001, p. 19), the Pope addressed the topic, *On psychotherapy and religion* (Pope Pius XII, 1953), and while affirming the competence of psychotherapists in their work, he also declared that the Christian psychologist and psychotherapist must affirm a fundamental attitude: "Psychotherapy and clinical psychology must always consider man (1) as a psychic unit and totality; (2) as a structured unit in itself; (3) as a social unit, and (4) as a transcendent unit, that is to say, in man's tending towards God" (p. 4). Within that attitude, the autonomy of psychology as science and therapeutics was granted. All in all, this document shows an appreciation of the contributions of psychoanalysis, even as it mistrusts certain forms of it. The mistrust promoted some continuing criticism, essentially repeating Sheen's 1947 charges (for example, McAllister, 1956).

Psychologized spirituality in post-war America

Sheen's animus against Freud had another source, in addition to his legitimate criticism of some of the philosophical bases of analysis. As with any such controversy, however, Sheen and his opponents had much in common. Here, it was that Sheen's approach to peace of soul was psychologized. Sheen made the move to a psychologized apologetics deliberately, because he held that "modern man" would only listen to such a means of persuasion.

When Brill objected to Sheen's depiction of analysis in 1947 before an audience of rabbis, he observed that "this 'unreasonable attack on Freud had something to do with the successful run of Dr. Joshua Loth Liebman's book, "Peace of Mind"'" (Dr. Brill replies to Msgr. Sheen, 1947). Liebman, like Sheen, was a successful radio religious personality, with appeal to Christians as well as Jews (Heinze, 2004, p. 205). While Liebman "befriended Christianity" (p. 223), his bestseller, *Peace of mind*, aimed its criticism against "irrational guilt – and Christianity's alleged encouragement of it" (p. 222). His gentle version of psychoanalysis proposed a "theology of *self-acceptance*" (p. 223) in place of self-condemnation. Liebman did not shrink from taking aim at the confessional, and he argued for the superiority of the analytic couch over the confessional booth: rather than encouraging guilt and the seeking of atonement, psychological help "does not require that you feel sorry for your sins as long as you *outgrow* them" (Liebman, 1946, p. 30). Sheen's Lenten remarks, just months after Liebman's book appeared, seem a direct response to the theology of self-acceptance advocated by Liebman: "There is no morbidity in confession. You don't look so much on your sins as you look upon your Saviour, who restores you to relationship with the Heavenly Father" (Sheen denounces psychoanalysis, 1947). It was a battle of media titans; both Liebman and Sheen were charismatic orators with large ecumenical audiences. Sheen expanded upon his contrast between psychoanalysis and confession, clarifying them to some extent in *Peace of soul*, the title an allusion to Liebman's book. There he expressed no opposition to psychiatry, but instead he stressed the positive value of guilt, confession, and atonement. Finally, playing with the word, "psychoanalysis," Sheen (1949) wrote that "the world needs psychosynthesis; some psychiatrists have recognized this – Jung, in his idea of 'rebirth,' and some followers of Freud, who have called their theory 'active psychoanalysis'" (pp. 145–6), the latter term referring to the approach of Sandor Ferenczi, Freud's Hungarian colleague, who engaged analysands more directly and personally. Sheen also quoted Victor White, the Dominican scholar who was at that point Jung's friend and collaborator. He referred approvingly to Alfred Adler's willingness to intervene in therapy to educate his patients (p. 147), and to Carl Rogers' nondirective approach. While keeping the attention on the reader's relationship with God, Sheen was mindful of the plight of modern individuals, and he concluded the chapter on "Psychoanalysis and confession" with this consideration: "Regular confession prevents our sins, our worries, our fears, our anxieties from seeping into the unconscious and degenerating into melancholy, psychoses, and neuroses" (p. 146). The equation of sin with worries, fears, and anxieties is a category mistake, for the latter three are not moral ones. Nevertheless, the equation fit the emerging psychologized spirituality of the post-war period, exemplified by Liebman, who anticipated major themes of humanistic psychology and psychospirituality, and by Sheen, who did not.

Resolution and dissolution

Dalbiez' *Psychoanalytic method and the doctrine of Freud* (1936/1941), much like Moore's earlier work, differentiated between Freud's method and his theory. Dalbiez argued that the method successfully treated many mental disorders, and he criticized what he saw as excesses of Freud's theory. Dalbiez saw Freud's contributions, too, in his exploration of the lower reaches of human nature.[35] Even though Allers (1939) criticized Dalbiez for this separation of method and theory, a separation Allers thought impossible, his approach became the default position, as it provided a way for Catholic psychiatrists to employ what was seen as a valid mode of treatment. Several years later, Zilboorg (1949) mentioned the work of other European Catholic thinkers who took a more positive view of psychoanalysis, including Jacques Maritain, the prominent Thomistic philosopher. Maritain made a clear demarcation between the sacrament of confession and psychoanalysis, arguing that confession does not cure neurosis and psychosis, a statement at odds with the implications of Sheen's depiction of the effects of the sacrament. In Maritain's clean break between the two, Zilboorg saw the promise of theologians and psychiatrists working together. Beginning in the 1950s, the journal *Cross Currents* introduced Americans to the debates over psychoanalysis and religion in European circles, including publishing in 1956 the Maritain essay Zilboorg cited. In the preface to a collection of articles by Catholic thinkers on psychology, *Cross currents of psychiatry and Catholic morality*, Francis J. Braceland (1964), the Catholic psychiatrist who did much to reconcile psychiatry and the Church, observed that *Cross Currents* "helped to ease the then inflammable relationship between religion, psychiatry, and psychoanalysis" (p. v). In particular, he referred to the very Maritain article Zilboorg had summarized the year before *Cross Currents* began publication, saying that "it was Maritain's paper originally which gave the coup de grace to the shibboleth that confused psychoanalysis and confession" (p. ix). A further indication of the influence of the journal in Catholic circles, Bier (1957) quoted with approval an essay by Maryse Choisy,[36] which had appeared in *Cross Currents* in 1951, and which was included in the 1964 collection.

In addition to the authors in that volume, *Cross Currents* published Carl Rogers, C. G. Jung, Max Scheler, Maurice Merleau-Ponty, and representatives of the so-called "New Theology." Such writers represented the new ways of thinking that began to influence Catholic circles in the years leading up to the Second Vatican Council.

By the mid-1950s, Catholic consideration of Freud and psychoanalysis turned from a narrowly conceived opposition between Neoscholastic and Freudian thought. Two trends occurred at roughly the same time. Psychoanalysis began to lose its standing in American psychiatry, and the Neoscholastic movement in philosophy began to wane. We have already

---

[35] Paul Ricoeur (1977) wrote that Dalbiez was his first philosophy teacher, and that he placed his own work in the company of Dalbiez. However, Ricoeur did not agree that Freud's genius lay in the exploration of the lower reaches of our nature; he held that Freud offered a theory of culture.

[36] Choisy (1903–79) was a writer who founded the journal, *Psyché*, a review of psychoanalysis and the human sciences that ran from 1946 to 1963.

considered the second, so we turn our attention to the first. When Sheen delivered his controversial sermon, psychoanalysis dominated American psychiatry, to the extent that the two were considered synonymous in the minds of many. While psychoanalysis dominated psychiatry in the immediate post-war years, by the 1960s, its influence declined. Fewer psychiatrists entered psychoanalytic training (Hale, 1995, p. 302). Psychoanalysis' scientific credibility, which earlier was taken for granted by its Catholic critics, suffered when serious doubts were raised over its effectiveness. From the 1960s, the medical model of mental illness resurfaced with a vengeance, as new drugs appeared and behavioral approaches made strong inroads into clinical psychology. The length and the cost of classical psychoanalysis did not contribute to any "successes" measurable in functionalist terms. Psychoanalysis fell from grace, not to disappear, but to wield power in psychiatry no longer.

In addition, post-war psychoanalysis, especially the ego psychology that flourished in America, began to be seen as one variant among many. As in the 1920s, when "psychoanalysis" meant many things to writers like Boyd Barrett, in the 1960s, a medicalized ego psychoanalysis no longer defined the term. Object-relations psychoanalysis and the more sociological forms of analysis such as that of Fromm and of Horney, took root. I would here draw a parallel with Neoscholasticism. Just as the latter did not disappear, but lost much of its intimate connection with ecclesiastical power, so too psychoanalysis remained, but lost its hold on medical (or at least psychiatric) power, at around the same time, the 1960s. So the conflict that surfaced at first in the 1920s, and then again in the 1940s, represented a collision of two ways of thinking, tied to sources of power – or to two forms of power/knowledge. Today, there is no conflict between analysis and confession, in large part because not many people trouble themselves about either. Centers of power released them, and they withered.

Beyond Neoscholasticism, beyond psychoanalysis

A new approach was gathering strength, one that moved away from both a narrow interpretation of Freud and an overly rationalistic philosophical approach, characteristic of the Neoscholasticism of the first half of the twentieth century. This new look drew on phenomenological and existential philosophies. Already in the early years of the century, psychiatrists such as Ludwig Binswanger, Eugene Minkowski, and Karl Jaspers, sought to synthesize psychoanalytic thought and the philosophies of Husserl, Heidegger, Bergson, among others. In the 1940s, Jean-Paul Sartre and Maurice Merleau-Ponty, whose philosophical work took the contributions of empirical and clinical psychology seriously, were having an effect on psychiatric thinking (May, Angel, and Ellenberger, 1958). But the pieces of evidence I shall concentrate on came from Walker Percy and Rudolf Allers.

Walker Percy (1916–90) was a physician and – more famously – a brilliant novelist. In 1957, he wrote a two-part essay for *America*, entitled "The coming crisis of psychiatry" (1957a; 1957b). There he pointed to signs that psychiatry was at the point of surpassing its biological orientation, citing the work of Erich Fromm, *The sane society*. What Percy addressed – as he did in his novels – were people who are perfectly "normal" and yet alienated from themselves, "lost in the cosmos," suffering anxiety that did not need to be cured but recognized as "a summons to authentic existence" (Percy, 1957b, p. 416). Percy drew on Fromm (with telling criticisms of his Marxist interpretation of alienation) and the existentialists (Marcel, Sartre, Ortega y Gasset, and others) as approaching the "scholastic view" (p. 415) that transcendence is, "an inveterate trait of human existence" (p. 417). Unless psychiatry recognizes the centrality of the human desire for transcendence, it will only worsen the alienation that moderns suffer. Percy saw hopeful signs that the "medical ministry" of psychiatrists and the "religious ministry" could work together: "The lines [between them] are fluid indeed at present, but it is a hopeful sign that men on both sides now appear to recognize that there *are* lines to be drawn and legitimate areas of cooperation marked out" (p. 416). Percy's essays pointed to innovations in psychiatry and psychology on the horizon at the time in existential and humanistic psychology.

Rudolf Allers (1961) gave a series of lectures at the Institute of Living in March, 1959, at the invitation of Francis J. Braceland, its Director, whom we met above in praise of Jacques Maritain. In these lectures, Allers explored the coincidence of the simultaneous rise of psychoanalysis and existential thought in the twentieth century. Stating explicitly he was not delivering a critique of Freud, Allers declared that Freud prepared psychiatry for existentialism (p. 27), by developing a historical viewpoint on the patient's symptom picture. That is, what was new with Freud was the biographical approach he took in the treatment of mental disorders (p. 23). In this regard, psychoanalysis was implicitly aiming in the same direction as Dilthey's human sciences: "We explain nature, but we understand the mind" (Dilthey quoted, p. 27). According to Allers:

> Freud's psychology was a compromise. He stands at a point where two intellectual ages were ready to pass over the one into the other. What he overemphasized belongs largely to an age that was passing away, though, of course, much of what his age had discovered and thought retains its value. What he implied and did not realize, that is, the biographical side, belongs to the age that began around 1900 and whose traits grew into full visibility after the First World War.
>
> (p. 28)

For Allers, the "biographical" is the equivalent of the "existential" (ibid.).

Allers' examination of existential thought takes us beyond this chapter. Suffice it to say, that for Allers, "existential analysis is ... analysis of the world as it is experienced by the individual" (p. 49). A major contribution of existential and phenomenological thought was precisely this concentration on the uniqueness of the individual. This valuation of the human person, for Allers, was a genuine contribution to philosophical and psychological thought. It seemed to Allers, as to many American Catholic psychologists, that the humanistic approach exemplified in this existentialism was the antidote to the reductionism and materialism of so much American psychology. What we see in these lectures is a concern that extends beyond the particular frameworks – even the Neoscholastic – that occupied the boundaries of Catholicism and psychology: as Allers stated it simply, the issue was "the patient's person or being" (p. 81). If there is one golden thread that runs through this historical maze we are exploring, that is it: the "person" as a category. We will find it again and again and, in the end, we will come to grips with it.

6

From out of the depths: Carl Jung's challenges and Catholic replies

We could reappraise Jung's life-long effort to reinterpret, not so much science, philosophy, society, or even psychiatry, but theology.

James Hillman (1975, p. 228)

Forty years ago, one could speak confidently about ours being a secularizing age: the more science and technology progressed, the more religion receded (Cox, 1965). Carl G. Jung could write about "modern man in search of a soul" (1933) because secularization meant that religious symbols, rituals, and beliefs lost their meaning for an ever increasing number. There were for the first time in history entire nations, especially the Soviet Union, dedicated to atheism. The Positivist dream was being fulfilled.

But it has not happened that secularization simply progressed. The public sphere became increasingly areligious, but this remains highly contested ground. If much of Western Europe seems contentedly secular, in the United States, as in many nations in the east and the south, intense religious ferment explodes on the cultural and political stages. Religious and spiritual issues, once on the fringe of mainstream psychology, as represented by the American Psychological Association, have come front and center. Even biomedicine, that bulwark of secularized views of the body and illness, acknowledges more readily the spiritual and religious dimensions of medicine and their usefulness in preserving health and fighting illness. One cannot speak of desecularization, however, for secularization proceeds apace. The situation is more complex and fragmented, and within the dominant secularized and tolerant culture, there are pockets of resacralization and large areas where religious views, often hostile to the natural sciences, hold sway. Most telling of all is the increasing presence among us of those who are "spiritual but not religious" (Fuller, 2001; Saroglou, 2003), those simultaneously secularized and engaged with the sacred.

If we turn to the question of spirituality in psychology, in relation to the Catholic Church, the work of Carl Jung (1875–1961) is most prominent. One of the most important psychologists of the twentieth century, his work rarely finds a place in academic psychology, although it has influenced literary, religious, and cultural studies in the universities. Jungian psychology verges on "pop" psychology, despite Jung's enormous erudition, and despite the lack of the easy optimism and the positive thinking that characterizes popular spiritualized psychology. Jungian psychology thrives at independent institutes and through the practice of analytical psychology. It has shown its vitality, moreover, with those, such as James Hillman, who continue to invigorate it. Catholic takes on Jung and the Jungians are various as well, and this chapter addresses Catholic (mis)appropriations of Jung.

For the most part, Catholics in psychology who took Jung seriously were not those who sought to develop a natural scientific psychology. For the latter group, Jung was out-of-bounds, since he did not follow the canons of positivistic psychology; and because Jung was a physician and part of the Freud–Adler–Jung trinity, he was not of immediate concern to the experimentalists. But since Jung took seriously the questions of soul, symbol, and ritual, of the significance of religious and spiritual life in relationship to psychological well-being, there were others who were drawn to Jung. At the same time, Jung's views of Christianity were not orthodox, especially if by orthodox one means Neoscholastic. Indeed, he could be called a modernist.

Looking for the soul in the wasteland

In the 1936 movie, *The Petrified Forest*, Alan Squier (played by Leslie Howard) is traveling west across the United States to drown himself in the Pacific Ocean. He has gotten as far as the Petrified Forest of Arizona and in this dry and lifeless country, he comes across an aspiring and beautiful poet, Gabrielle "Gabby" Maple (Bette Davis), who reads to him a poem by François Villon. He tells her that the only book he has in his knapsack is "*Modern Man in Search of a Soul* by Doctor Ju . . .". He never makes the ocean, for in the climactic confrontation with the archetypal outlaw of the American west, Duke Mantee (Humphrey Bogart), he sacrifices his life in love and despair. He was one of countless moderns, the "hollow men"[1] who could no longer believe and live the cultural and religious traditions that had once held life together. Such people were Jung's patients.

Just what the relationships are between Jungian psychology and religion is a matter of debate,[2] but one thing is certain, Jung took religion seriously, and for

---

[1] Squier tells Gabby about the hollow men, cut off from nature, cut off from the past, and not suited, as was she, to the new world that was being born.

[2] This debate, still ongoing, includes many (Angers, 1959–60; Arraj, 1988; Dourley, 1995; Frei, 1953; Heisig, 1973; Noll, 1994; Pacwa, 1992; Shamdasani, 1998; Stein, 1985). This list is but a sample.

that reason, many Catholics have taken Jung seriously. Foremost among them was the Dominican theologian Victor White. He found in Jung a psychologist who addressed the question of the growing irrelevance of religious faith. White affirmed Jung's observation that: "Among all my patients in the second half of life ... there has not been one whose problem in the last resort was not that of finding a religious outlook on life. It is safe to say that every one of them fell ill because he had lost that which the living religions of every age have given to their followers, and none of them has been really healed who did not regain this religious outlook" (Jung, 1933, p. 264; as cited in White, 1953, p. 47). Some (Angers, 1959–60) seemed to have heard only this sentiment of Jung's, and praised his compatibility with Christianity. However, White more than once quoted Jung as having said that analytical psychology is "religion *in statu nascendi*"[3] because "in the vast confusion that reigns at the root of life there is no line of division between philosophy and religion" (White, 1960, p. 37, quoting Jung, 1954). For White, this was not a limitation of psychology, but rather, it pointed to its limits and to the courage of the Jungians to face the real issues arising in therapy. Other Catholics (Gemelli, 1955; Von Gebsattel, 1947) have heard only Jung's intimation that psychology intrudes into religious territory, and condemned Jung as making his psychology a substitute for religion.

Whatever the further evaluations of Jung's psychology, here at least was a psychology that did not dismiss religion as obsolete in a scientific age. Recall that this was a time, the first half of the twentieth century, of the development of "a psychology without a soul" and of the active hostility to religion by some of the major psychologists, such as Freud and Watson. Psychology and psychotherapy were to "drive the last nails in the coffin of Divinity" (White, 1953, p. 3) as the sciences replaced religion as the way to truth and life.

There was ambiguity in Jung's diagnosis of the modern condition, an uncertainty that has shadowed him in Catholic circles. According to White (p. 69), "contemporary religious skepticism is due less to a widespread belief that the Gospels and creeds are positively untrue, than to the widespread feeling that they are irrelevant" (see also White, 1960, p. 69). Jung's experience showed him that when this happened, anomie, meaninglessness, and mental illness could result. Neurosis and psychotherapy both dwell in the hunger for "the more" that alone can satisfy human life, and Jung's psychology reckoned with those experiences, inner and outer, wherein something numinous, something "more" intruded into ordinary life. The symbols and images of those experiences provided the material for therapy and understanding of the human psyche in its sufferings and joys. Religious dogma was irrelevant for many in coming to terms with such experiences, precisely because it did not connect with individual experience. Dogma could be, Jung observed, a defense against religious experience, rather than, as in the Catholic position, a distillation of authentic

[3] i.e. "in a nascent state."

religious experience – God's revelation to humanity. Jung's psychology can be read as an *Aufhebung*[4] of Christianity (Homans, 1995) and as fostering a secular spirituality. Jung's philosophical affinities with modernism and his critical assessment of modernity made for complex relationships with Catholic thinkers.

One point of contact between Jung and Catholic thinkers in the first half of the twentieth century was anxiety over the implications of modernity. For Jung as for the Catholics, modernity meant loss of the nurturing ground of religion with its beliefs and traditions, and consequently, it meant existence adrift. Because we were adrift, the whole fabric of contemporary society was at risk, there being no greater and unknown destructive force than the human psyche. From it must come whatever hope we could have for the future. For Jung, the modern individual "has come to the very edge of the world, leaving behind him all that has been discarded and outgrown, and acknowledging that he stands before a void out of which all things may grow" (Jung, 1933, p. 197). For the Church, this condition was that of modernism, a triumph of agnosticism, positivism, and atheism. For both Jung and the Neoscholastics, the consequences were catastrophic: loss of a religious foundation, collapse into a "mass age," a collapse being realized in fascism and communism. This concern with the shadow of modernity and with modernism forms the backdrop for the points of common interest between Jung and Catholic thinkers before the Vatican Council.

So Jung's psychology addressed the very concerns that the modernists, such as George Tyrrell and Ernesto Buonaiuti, insisted upon as vital for the future of the Church. Like Tyrrell, for Jung dogmatic statements were provisional. There is something "Jungian" in the observation Tyrrell (1910) made after his excommunication:

> Whether in the history of nations, or in the world of organic life, he [the modernist] recognizes that such revolutions often belong to the normal course of development; that the larval life runs its course evenly, up to a certain point, only to prepare the way for a perfectly normal reconstitution. He is convinced that Catholic Christianity cannot live much longer on the old lines ... The time has come, he thinks, for a criticism of categories ... He believes that the current expression of these ideas is only provisional, and is inadequate to their true values.
>
> (p. xx)

In *Psychology and religion* (1938), Jung spoke of religions "replacing immediate experience by a choice of suitable symbols invested in a solidly organized

---

[4] *Aufhebung* is a term from Hegel, meaning to negate something and to preserve it by seeing a more profound and interiorized meaning in it; a movement from the particular to the universal.

dogma and ritual" (p. 52, cited in White, 1960, p. 71). For both Tyrrell and Jung, there was a disconnection between authoritative propositions and the life of the soul; for both, the inner experience of what transcended our conscious egos was of utmost importance. How much more there was between Jungian psychology and modernism, viewed in the light of *Pascendi*, remains to be seen.

Analytical psychology as an empirical science

Before 1960, Catholic theologians, such as White and Raymond Hostie (1957), granted Jung his contention that he was an empiricist, a natural scientist. Indeed, Jung did make that claim throughout his career (see, e.g. Jung, 1938, pp. 2–3), and as long as he was a natural scientist, his work could be taken seriously by theologians, and his forays into philosophy and theology dismissed as amateur. Few "really" empirical psychologists would have agreed with Jung's self-assessment in his day, and the scant attention given Jung in natural scientific psychological circles reinforces this judgment (e.g. Misiak and Staudt, 1954). So with Jung, even more than with Freud, the questions of this book become more complex. As this is a study of the relationship between psychology and Catholicism, understood in terms of that between science and religion, what to do with someone like Jung, who (as Homans, 1995, argues) walks the line between science and religion? His psychology dwells on the boundary not from any failure in conceptualization, but because Jung sought in an uncompromising way, as Hostie (1957, p. 213) stated it, *homo psychicus*. For Jung, whatever else symbols, rituals, dogmas, scientific theories, works of arts, social structures, and ways of life may signify, they also signify the psyche: hence Jung's readings of mythologies, alchemy, the dreams and expressions of his patients, and Catholic dogmas, such as of the Trinity. Because he absented himself from what he called the "metaphysical," that is, the theological claims of symbols and dogma, focusing instead on their archetypal significance and their relationship to the individuation process, Jung's work can be called scientific. To the extent that his analysis sought to revitalize dogmas and make them relevant in the modern age, whatever their new vitality and relevance may mean for the traditional understanding of the dogma, Jung's work can be called religious.

If Thomistic thinkers were to engage Jung's thought, they had to step across the clear and distinct boundaries of their psychology. This was not always recognized – theologians such as Gebhard Frei, an early lecturer at the C. G. Jung Institute, assumed that Jung was doing empirical psychology and did not cross into philosophical territory. Other Thomistic theologians, including Victor White and Raymond Hostie, were inclined to the same opinion as Frei. This standard Thomistic marker facilitated dialogue with Jung:

> We should confront and accept the wealth of empirical data which Jung
> offers us and recognize its profound significance. At the same time we shall

pursue our own traditional procedure in the paths of "rational psychology." This clashes not at all with the findings of empirical psychology, and
has its own weighty themes of the soul's spirituality and immortality.
Neither empirical nor rational psychology clashes with our faith.

(Frei, 1953, p. 237)

Jung affirmed the limits of his inquiry, as in his opening remarks in *Psychology
and religion* (1938):

I approach psychological matters from a scientific and not from a philosophical standpoint. In as much as religion has a very important psychological aspect, I am dealing with it from a purely empirical point of view,
that is, I restrict myself to the observation of phenomena and I refrain from
any application of metaphysical or philosophical considerations ... This
point of view is the same as that of natural science. Psychology deals with
ideas and other mental contents as zoology for instance deals with different
species of animals.

(pp. 2–3)

Coupled with this disclaimer was his insistence that his inquiries had a practical
goal, the care of his patient, "the psychically sick and suffering human being"
(Jung, 1953, p. xiv), and that "therapy along purely biological lines does not
suffice, but requires a spiritual completion" (p. xvi). Because of this therapeutic
intent, Jung's interests were not merely observational; he had to assist the
patient's return to living, and this return included a spiritual aspect:

[The physician] cannot prescribe for his patient just any *Weltanschauung*
assumed to be a living system; but, by dint of careful and persevering investigation, he must endeavour to discover where the sick person feels a healing,
living quality, which can make him "whole." He cannot be concerned at first
as to whether this so-called truth bears the official stamp of validity.

(p. xv)

A particular religious belief or practice may or may not have, for a given patient,
a "healing, living quality" and attention to this was vital to Jung's psychotherapy. And many of Jung's patients were "moderns," for whom their religious
traditions no longer had this "healing, living quality." Jung addressed himself
especially to these moderns (Homans, 1995, p. 154). So despite the claim to be a
natural scientist, a claim that need not be discredited on the basis of a narrowly
conceived "science," insofar as he was also a physician, he could not have been
only a natural scientist. This was the point that some of the Thomists did not
appreciate. Given the therapeutic implications of analytical psychology, Jung
could not conceive of his psychology in terms compatible with those of
Neoscholastic psychology, with its neat division of labor.

Jung's empirical approach was not that of the British tradition, stemming
from Locke. For Jung, "empirical" meant anything experienced (Christou,

1963), including, and especially including, dreams and fantasies, which main-stream scientific psychology studied as objects, but did not consider scientific modes of being present to objects.[5] Nor, as scientific "objectivity" solidified in the twentieth century, were they considered scientific facts, for they were not observable to anyone but the dreamer. At the same time, Jung at times employed the discourse of positivistic science to account for his psychology and his patients. Even in the "Foreword" to White's *God and the unconscious*, Jung (1953) gave his oft-presented view on the evolution of the psyche:

> I try to impress on my pupils not to treat their patients as if they were all alike: the population consists of different historical layers. There are people who, psychologically, might just as well have lived in the year 5000 B.C., i.e., who can still successfully solve their conflicts as people did 7000 years ago. There are countless barbarians and men of antiquity in Europe and in all civilized countries and a great number of medieval Christians. On the other hand, there are relatively few who have reached the degree of consciousness which is possible in our time.
>
> (p. xxiii)

In this last group, with the most evolved consciousness, belong the moderns: "The values and strivings of those past worlds no longer interest him save from the historical standpoint . . . Indeed, he is completely modern only when he has come to the very edge of the world, leaving behind him all that has been discarded and outgrown, and acknowledging that he stands before a void out of which all things may grow" (Jung, 1933, p. 197). These moderns, whom traditions no longer bind, have "built up . . . a psychology" (Jung, 1953, p. xxiv) to deal with the loss and re-creation of meaning. This interpretation agrees with that of Homans (1995), for whom analytical psychology, like psychoanalysis, is "culture-making," that is, not only an interpretation of culture, but also a (re-) creation of culture from the shards of what fell apart beginning with World War I. Murray Stein (1985), acknowledging this interpretation of Jung vis-à-vis Christianity, points to its limitation in understanding what he deliberately calls Jung's "treatment" of Christianity: to view Jung as a quintessential modern, cut off from a tradition yet finding life unbearable without it, is to "focus too sharply in the direction of his personal existential dilemmas and psychological pathology" (p. 16). Most important, this view fails to answer a key question: "Why did Jung want Christianity to evolve?" (p. 17). Stein's point is well taken, but there is reason to tarry with analytical psychology as modernist for a while, for the simple reason that for Catholic thinkers in the first half of the twentieth century, that would have been a major question, a stumbling block that could

---

[5] This is an important area that cannot be addressed here. For a general orientation, see Devereux (1967), for whom events "at the observer" are also data, the most important data in psychology and other social sciences.

not be avoided. So, granting that Jung's relation to modernity is an insufficient access to the question of psychology's relationship to Catholicism, it is a necessary one. We will have recourse to other angles of approach after considering the question of modernity.

All psychology – not just analytical psychology – is "culture-making," a point stressed by recent historical studies (e.g. Smith, 1997). Jung's psychology is not, therefore, unusual in this regard. What does distinguish it is the deliberate way Jung's work sought to provide therapy (Stein, 1985) to the culture on a collective level. What also distinguishes it from some other schools, including to some extent psychoanalysis, is that Jung's psychology was not taken up by and large by academic psychologists. In North America, for example, Jung's work on psychological types and his early word-association investigations had an impact, but as Ernest Hilgard (1987) observed, "as Jung's theory of personality developed, it became more difficult to comprehend and – by contrast with the reception given Jung's views by a broad spectrum of readers outside of academic psychology – most psychologists came to pay little attention to it" (pp. 496–7). Smith (1997), noting that Jung's biological speculations "lay outside the new science of biological genetics," claims that Jung's thought "acquired authority because of the insight and order he brought to clinical material, to comparative mythology and to seekers of an integrated and fulfilled subjective life, not for a contribution to natural science" (p. 743). However, most of the Catholics who took up Jung, especially in the middle half of the twentieth century, assumed, with Jung's statements to support them, that he was a natural scientist.

Jung and the Catholics

In 1944, Jung received a manuscript from one H. Irminger, who urged that Jung recognize that Catholic teachings complete his psychology. Jung replied with a long letter, and with an unsent letter as well, subsequently published posthumously as "Why I am not a Catholic" (Jung, 1976). In the letter of September 22, 1944, he said that he would not accept any credo because his "pursuit is science" (to Irminger, in Jung, 1973, p. 346), although he considered himself a Christian. He linked dogmatic assertions with totalitarianism. The "schism" between Catholics and Protestants he found within himself, which caused him conflict. Worse than this schism, however, was the "Antichristianity" ruling the Soviet Union and Germany. The spiritual response will fail if dogma is asserted; rather, the Church must come to terms with "the scientific spirit" (p. 347). Finally, he asked Irminger: "Have you ever noticed that I do not write for ecclesiastical circles but for those who are *extra ecclesiam*? I join their company, deliberately and of my own free will outside the Church" (p. 350), because he was a scientist and responding to his patients, for many of whom the salt of the Church had lost its savor.

Running throughout the relationships between Jung's thought and the Catholics, as it did throughout other areas of psychology, was the polarity of *science* and *dogma*. It is difficult to hear that last word without a negative overtone. It would be another few decades before this legacy of positivism would begin to be seriously questioned in psychology. In the period to which we turn, the period that ended with Jung's death and "the sixties," science was non-dogmatic and religion was non-scientific. That theme plays through much of the following. What we will examine is not so much Jung's work, but the Catholic response to it. We consider distinct groups of Catholic thinkers who appropriated Jung's analytical psychology:

(1) Neoscholastically-oriented psychologists, such as Thomas Verner Moore (1924), Agostino Gemelli (1955), and Magda Arnold (1954), who criticized Jung's epistemology and praised his innovations vis-à-vis Freud.
(2) Theologians and historians of religion who presented at the Eranos conferences, which Jung helped organize, beginning in 1933. The list of Catholic participants included Louis Beirnaert, S. J. (1964), Ernesto Buonaiuti (1935/1968b; 1937/1954; 1941/1968c), one of the leaders of Italian Catholic modernism, Jean Daniélou (1954), Martin Cyril D'Arcy (1953), Jean de Menasce (1945/1968), Henri-Charles Puech (1936/1968), and Hugo Rahner (1945/1968; 1957/1963). These men shared Jung's research interests in myth, symbolism, and the history of religions.
(3) Theologians concerned with pastoral counseling and with the experiential or subjective aspects of religion: examples include Raymond Hostie (1957; 1966) and Josef Goldbrunner (1955; 1956).
(4) Victor White (1943b; 1953; 1960) who, because of his close collaboration and conflict with Jung, belongs in a category all to himself.
(5) A brief look at some of White's contemporaries, who were Catholics and Jungians, will lead to the end of the chapter.

The Neoscholastic psychologists on Jung's psychology

There was limited interest in Jung among those closely associated with the Neoscholastic movement. The psychiatrist Karl Stern (1906–75), a Jewish convert to Catholicism, asked in 1948 why, aside from Victor White, "Jung has received so little attention by Catholic psychologists" (Stern, 1948, p. 33). Stern raised the question because Jung "was the first one to follow the roots of the neuroses to where they transcend the biological layer" (ibid.), and because Jung in his psychotherapeutic work arrived at observations "some of which bear a startling resemblance to 'observations' of the mystics" (ibid.). Stern commented only briefly on this question, suggesting that Jung was less systematic than Freud, and that he tended toward Gnosticism and "some sort of non-committal mysticism" (ibid.). Despite the seeming compatibility, Jung's emphasis on the unconscious and his "metaphysical" speculations did not play well with Neoscholastically-oriented natural scientific Catholic psychologists.

Thomas Verner Moore gave an early assessment of Jung in *Dynamic psychology* (1924). He viewed Jung mainly in light of and as an improvement upon the psychoanalysis of Freud. For Moore, Jung improved on Freud in his psychotherapeutic practice by emphasizing the active participation of the therapist in the transference relationship and in leading the patient to a new psychological synthesis "in accordance with the individuality of his patient" (p. 273). He cited Freud's criticism that Jung reduced "psychotherapy to the level of pastoral advice" (ibid.), but Moore often found a more directive approach therapeutically necessary: "It is only when they find a satisfactory solution to the problems that confront them and an outlet for the driving forces of human nature, that is fully satisfactory, that the baneful efforts of their mental malady commence to dwindle" (p. 274).[6] Moore's primary criticism of Jung was his use of the "ontogeny recapitulates phylogeny" theory; that is, the view that individual psychological development repeats the psychological evolution of the species. That Jung did hold to a version of this theory was evident in his first "Jungian" writing, *Symbols of transformation* (Jung, 1967a, p. 25), originally published in 1912. As a result, Moore also disputed the claim in this theory that "primitive" people used symbolic thought and not logical thought: "Both types of thought are as old as the race" (1924, p. 277). Moore thus disputed a prevalent view, that so-called primitives were incapable of rational thought. Thomistic anthropology, in which the human soul did not evolve, even if the human body did, provided the basis for Moore's counter-claim. This difference in opinion carried considerable force, since it implied that religious thought was not "primitive" as Jung at the time, along with many others, asserted. But there was no extended debate here, probably because Jung did not begin in earnest to address Catholic dogmas psychologically until the 1930s.[7]

Agostino Gemelli (1878–1959), a Neoscholastic psychologist whose influence spread far beyond Italy, had a negative view of Jung's theories, especially where they touched on religion. While Gemelli (1955) credited Jung with affirming a "psychology with a soul" (p. 82), he criticized the "vagueness and imprecision" (p. 85) of Jung's writings. Certainly, if one took Neoscholastic manuals as a reference point, Jung's writings would have looked unsystematic, for the Neoscholastics strove to present a rational system of concepts that they deduced from first principles, and Jung's insistence that he was not engaged in metaphysics, as well as his stresses on the limits of rationality and the importance of symbolic thought would have seemed to them confused. At the same time, Jung's writings were tantalizingly attractive for Catholics, and Gemelli

---

[6] That Freud's criticism was off base did not seem to occur to Moore.
[7] Moore (1948) made only brief mention of Jung and did not comment on the latter's work on Catholic dogma or symbols.

wrote to warn Catholics not to give in to Jung's seduction. While Jung did accord value to religion, his writings show "that he does not really understand the dogmas and the rites of Christianity about which he speaks," because "he lives in complete isolation in his own ideological world" (pp. 58–9). For Jung, Catholic dogma is "a useful and sometimes indispensable surrogate for those who are not in a condition to face the direct experience of the numinous" (p. 107), and by implication, only a surrogate. Proceeding from "the empirical methods of psychology" (p. 108), even Jung's form of empirical methodology (see pp. 62–3), is an inadequate way "to demonstrate the existence of God, to convince oneself of the truth of dogmas" (p. 108). For that, one needs philosophical and theological contributions. Gemelli condemned "the unpardonable error" (ibid.) of Catholics trying to use Jungian psychology to further religion, because "revealed truth ... does not proceed from man and 'even less from the psyche' (my [Gemelli's] emphasis)"[8] (ibid.), as an error against both religion and against scientific method. Jung's psychology failed to bring together the truths of psychotherapy and the truths of Christian faith. In reply, one could say that Jung never intended to bring these truths together; however, to some Catholics, he seemed to do so, and hence the appeal of his psychology.

In commenting on an address by Pope Pius XII to the Fifth International Congress of Psychotherapy and Clinical Psychology in 1953 – where Gemelli was honorary president (Colombo, 2003, p. 344) – Gemelli (1955) asserted that although it did not mention Jung by name, Pius's speech "suffices to demolish the fundamental basis of Jung's thought" (p. 142). How? By opposing Jung's view that the "dynamism" of the human soul toward the infinite, toward God, which Pius claimed that "scientific research" had established as the "most fundamental and the most elementary [dynamism] of the soul" (quoted in ibid.), is *the* basis of religion. On the contrary, claimed Gemelli, echoing *Pascendi*, "clear and certain knowledge of God by means of his natural and positive revelation" (ibid.) is the basis of religion. Gemelli opposed the proposition that religion has its ground in merely irrational and affective impulses. For Gemelli, Jung's crediting religious dogmas and symbols as psychically real did not suffice to break the subjectivistic circle within which Jung's concepts circulated, because revealed truth is objective truth. Gemelli's position was that psychology as an empirical science has its limits (with which Jung would have agreed), and because of those limits, it must defer to other sciences, in the broadest sense of that term, such as theology, in order to grasp other and more central truths (with which Jung would not have agreed). Beyond science, moreover, is faith, a gift through which God reveals Himself as transcendent to any possible religious experience. For Gemelli, Jung's vagueness muddied the

---

[8] Quoting Raymond Hostie. On the "unpardonable error" and Gemelli's criticisms of Victor White, see below in the discussion of White.

waters between psychology and religion and was thus counterproductive to mutual understanding.

Magda Arnold (1954) shared Gemelli's position to some extent, dismissing Jung for "ignoring the conclusion that religious experience without objective foundation can only be a delusion" (p. 11). This criticism went to the heart of the Neoscholastic criticism of Jung. What it indicated was a refutation of Jung's conception of religion. For the Neoscholastics, religious experience, no matter how intense or numinous, did not necessarily signify anything unless and until it was evaluated against the objective content of Revelation, as preserved within the dogmas of the Church. Yet there was more to Jung than this, for Arnold. She adopted a position similar to that taken by Catholic thinkers, such as Roland Dalbiez (1936/1941), who separated Freudian techniques from Freudian theory. Arnold embraced Jung's innovative psychotherapeutic technique of "active imagination," but without Jung's archetypal theory. Arnold called her approach in psychotherapy "intregral analysis," and she developed it on the basis of active imagination and dream interpretation (Arnold and Gasson, 1954a, p. 508). Both techniques she saw as ways of "exploring personality organization and the self-ideal" (pp. 508–9). Both dream and fantasy story exhibit the work of the "creative imagination," which is useful in therapy under the following condition:

> Only where the necessity for action in the real world is excluded, as in storytelling, doll play, and other forms of imaginative expression which have been utilized for projective tests, will imagination be able to work without interference. When it works freely, it always illustrates problems with which the person is preoccupied, and illustrates them accurately.
>
> (p. 417)

What next? These images were not archetypal manifestations, the gods within, for Arnold. They were stories, and "our awareness of the significance of imaginative productions gives us an opportunity for reorganizing our life, actively reshaping it toward the self-ideal as imagination has portrayed it" (p. 512). Here again was a similarity to Jung, in that for him, the goal of the individuation process would be relationship with the Self. But for Arnold, the self-ideal is not Jung's archetype of the Self. As John Augustine Gasson, SJ (1904–88), Arnold's collaborator, depicted it, it was more communal and traditional than Jung's Self (for Jung, Arnold, and Gasson's "ideal-self" would be a truncated and rationalistic version of the Self):

> The human person must determine his goal and direction for himself progressively, not only in the over-all pattern of his life, but also in many smaller segments of his behavior. This direction or goal is the ideal of the perfect person as the individual conceives him. Needless to say, this self-ideal is not an idealized version of one's self, but it is human nature at its best incarnated in a concrete person. We strive not toward something but toward someone whose perfection we gradually make our own. In all

human history there is only one man so perfect that even his enemies have
to acknowledge him as such: Jesus Christ.

(Gasson, 1954a, p. 193)

Now the ideal-self in question here is not the self I want to be, but the self I
ought to be (p. 194), and the ideal-self is not a psychological construct but a
"transcendent, objective, absolute standard" (ibid., n. 6), derived from knowledge of human nature. This Thomistic form of psychotherapy shared, then,
with Jung, an emphasis on the imagination and the dream, on the future, and on
a self as the goal of all our strivings, even to the point of identifying the ideal of
self with Christ; unlike Jung, Arnold and Gasson delimited psychology,
acknowledging philosophical and theological knowledge-claims that transcend
those of psychology. In so doing, they bound the individual in therapy, implicitly at least, to the community to which he or she belonged.

   This last observation finds support in Gasson's look at Jung's interpretation
of the Spiritual Exercises of St. Ignatius Loyola. As a Jesuit, Gasson would have
been very familiar with the Exercises. He (Gasson, 1954b) viewed Jung's reading
of the Spiritual Exercises as flawed because, he said, "the ideal of personality, for
Jung, is the freedom of absolute independence, where the individual is subject to
no law but his own will" (p. 554). Gasson misconceived Jung in a serious way
here. Indeed, for Jung, the individual, meaning the ego, is as subject to the
constraints of the "objective psyche" as to those of the physical world. The ego is
not the Self, which is an archetype and never completely conscious. A task of the
ego in individuation is to cultivate a relation to the Self, often, especially in the
Christian West, symbolized by Christ. Still, Gasson had a point, because he saw
that Jung's conception of individuation pulled one away from traditional
communities, quite the opposite of the goal of the Exercises.

   This sample of critical appreciations of Jung's psychology by Neoscholastic
psychologists shows a limited and in some cases ill-informed reading of Jung.
To summarize the assessments of the Neoscholastic psychologists: (1) Jung's
psychology suffered from a lack of conceptual clarity and it ignored the canons
of an empirical science by treading into theological ground; (2) Jung's refusal to
go beyond the limits of experience indicated a subjectivistic bias, in that he did
not acknowledge the transcendent truth of Christian doctrine and Divine
revelation; (3) Nevertheless, Jung broke the bounds of the worst features of
modern psychology in his emphasis on the future, on the imagination, and on
the necessity for a religious orientation to living.

Modernity and the spirit: Catholic thinkers
at the Eranos conferences

The Eranos conferences, founded by Olga Fröbe-Kapteyn (1881–1962), began
in 1933 in Ascona, Switzerland. The historian of religion, Rudolf Otto,

suggested the name, Eranos (Greek for "banquet") to Fröbe in 1932, for meetings at "a place that would lend itself to spiritual encounters among seekers, scientists and lay people" (Jaffé, 1977, p. 208). Fröbe had met Jung two years earlier at Graf Keyserling's School of Wisdom (ibid.). Fröbe, with Jung's advice, invited leading scholars in the history of religions east and west, in mythology, and in related areas.[9] The scope of the meetings was anything but purely academic.[10] As Ernesto Buonaiuti (1937/1954), one of the regular participants in the early years, stated: "We are here to receive the tradition of a life that is not extinct. We are here to carry on a tradition which, even though it does embrace the distant past, also looks towards the future with confidence and eager expectation" (p. 240). Eranos, then, confronted analytical psychology with the riches of humanity's spiritual traditions.

A number of Catholic thinkers participated in the Eranos conferences in the years before Jung died. They were historians and theologians; none was a psychologist, and they had various levels of interest in Jung's psychological interpretations of myth and religion. It would be safe to say, however, that they shared the sense of the spiritual crisis of the modern epoch.[11]

Ernesto Buonaiuti and the Ecclesia Spiritualis

In 1904 Buonaiuti (1881–1946) was a priest teaching "Church History at the Pontifical University of the Apollinare in Rome" (La Piana, 1969, p. 8). His 1905 article, "Dogma and history" compared Tradition, one of the two sources of revelation according to Church teaching, to something like the unconscious in the individual: "in this obscure world of collective spiritual experience ... Christianity lives its most intensive life. This may seem a paradox, but it is

---

[9] "Initially, Frau Froebe had conceived of Eranos as a gathering of modern Platonists; but she, and Rudolf Otto whom she had consulted about the founding of the gathering, determined that a voice was missing – that of C. G. Jung. Jung, in his fifties, well established in his profession, was convinced that expressions of the human psyche find resonance and reflection at different times and in other places because of the universality of the human mind with its base in the archetypes of the unconscious" (Scott and Scott, 1982, p. 228).

[10] Wasserstrom (1999) observes: "The turn East, the turn inward, and the turn to myth were each vectors on this one immense trajectory from the urban century to primordial immediacy. Now, at the origins of things as such, authentic relations with the gods would be rectified" (p. 103). While these words do not apply completely literally to the participants I will discuss, they do suggest the tenor of the meetings.

[11] Here are the dates of the *Eranos-Jahrbücher* publications of the Catholic participants: Beirnaert (1949); Buonaiuti (1933–9, 1941); Daniélou (1953, 1954, 1962); D'Arcy (1952); de Menasce (1944–5); Pettazzoni (1950); Puech (1936, 1951); Rahner (1943–5, 1947–8); and White (1947). Note the dates; except for Puech in 1936, none of the others spoke during the years Buonaiuti did. Hakl (2001) writes that Frau Fröbe wrote to Jung on April 18, 1939 that a number of "Vatican professors [including Raffaele Pettazzoni, who later spoke at Eranos] would be interested in Eranos but that they would not come, because they had suspected Bounaiuti's attendance" (p. 110, n. 34).

true nevertheless that tradition, so understood, prepares the future while remaining faithful to the past" (p. 10). This decidedly non-Neoscholastic view of tradition and of dogma – which for the Neoscholastics has not evolved since Christ instituted the Church – was denounced, and Buonaiuti lost his position at the pontifical university. When Pope Pius X's encyclical condemning modernism appeared in 1907, Buonaiuti – partly in self-defense – published an anonymous refutation, *The program of modernism*. In 1915, Buonaiuti obtained a chair in the History of Christianity at the secular University of Rome (p. 12). Continuing to research and publish, his works regularly received official condemnation and placed on the Index of Forbidden Books. In the mid-1920s, he was excommunicated (pp. 13–14). In their negotiations with the Mussolini government, leading to the Lateran agreements in 1929, Church officials pressed for Buonaiuti's removal from his post, and they succeeded in having him removed from teaching duties. In 1931, he lost his university position altogether for refusing to sign a loyalty oath to the fascist government.

Buonaiuti was among the speakers at the first Eranos conference. Otto knew him, and Buonaiuti had translated *Das Heilige* into Italian in 1926 (Otto, 1984).[12] Every year between 1933 and 1941, Buonaiuti spoke at Eranos, except for 1940, when only two spoke and one of them, Jung, had done so more or less at the last minute. These were difficult years, to be sure, with fascism in Italy and the Nazis in Germany, and then the war in 1939. When Jung in 1942 had requested financial support for Eranos from a Swiss foundation, he stated: "I therefore consider this enterprise to be in the greatest sense important for the spiritual national defense. It fulfills one of the most vital cultural tasks of the present moment" (in Jaffé, 1977, p. 206).[13]

The existential situation of Buonaiuti, then, was dire. At odds with both Church and State, he nevertheless saw the renewal of the Church as his duty.[14] In no way could he be called a Jungian, but the major themes in his Eranos papers were compatible with Jung's interests, although he did not, to my knowledge, offer an opinion on the specifics of Jung's theories. Like Jung, he distrusted rational systems for accounting for religion, and he held that in part the spiritual crisis of the west was a result of the rigid and abstract thought of both the Catholic and Protestant churches in recent centuries. In 1934, he sounded a theme similar to that of Jung at the same time, namely the loss of a spiritual depth that characterizes the modern world:

[12] Buonaiuti was also a friend of another inaugural speaker at Eranos, the historian of religion, Friedrich Heiler (Dedola, 2006).

[13] The philosopher of religion, Alfons Rosenberg, exiled in Switzerland, stated that "gewollt oder nicht gewollt war Eranos eine Antwort auf das Verderben des Geistes" (Dedola, 2006). ("Intentionally or not intentionally was Eranos an answer to the corruption of the spirit.")

[14] Buonaiuti knew Angelo Giuseppe Roncalli (1881–1963) on personal and friendly terms. Roncalli was the future Pope John XXIII, who did instigate a process of renewal in the Church with his convening of the Second Vatican Council in 1962.

This schism [the Reformation] robbed modern man of the *symbols* by which to make himself known to his fellows, and deprived him of the vision of what lies beyond experience and beyond political exigencies. Since then our journey through the world has become an atomized and planless wandering of fugitives, without aim, without friends to receive us. Now that we have lost all receptivity to the solemn, intangible norms of the transcendent, we have arrived at the belief that the only possible life discipline is the discipline which is maintained by the rod and ordained by human priesthoods.

(Buonaiuti, 1934/1968a, pp. 176–7)

Like Rudolf Otto, Buonaiuti claimed that "the ascending stages of religious life are characterized by an increasing conviction that to win the favor of the numen, under whose imperious rule our existence moves, . . . what is necessary is that we subordinate our social life to another sphere – that of mutual service and universal love – which rests upon the conviction that there is a redemption capable of raising us from the sensory world into the transcendent world of the spirit" (Buonaiuti, 1937/1954, p. 242). While Buonaiuti, as did Otto, claimed the numinous to be transcendent, he also found the spirit within the human soul: in place of "an external, servile discipline" that marks contemporary Christianity, he could "only recommend a transformation of the spirit, an appeal, above all, to the forces of the unconscious, to the hypersensitive forces of our transcendental calling" (Buonaiuti, 1935/1968b, p. 199).

Buonaiuti basically agreed with Jung's diagnosis of the "spiritual problem of modern man": western consciousness became captivated by the external trappings of spiritual life when it developed in a one-sidedly rational direction. At the same time, social life has devolved into that of the masses that had little inward sense.[15] Again, like Jung, the development of the individual and of the religious life can occur in seemingly unconventional ways, although with Buonaiuti there was not only the emphasis on the individual per se and his or her inwardness but on the new forms of community. So much they had in common, in the Eranos spirit. The big difference between them, and this is important, was that Buonaiuti did not locate the numinous, the *mysterium tremendum*, in the unconscious. It seems clear from his writings that the Holy was, indeed, "wholly other," to use Otto's (1923) term for what surpasses human understanding and the world of the senses. In the end, Buonaiuti was no psychologist, but his writings supported Jung's diagnosis of the one-sidedness of modernity and, hence, the need for something like analytical

---

[15] "The *Exercitia* [the Spiritual Exercises of Ignatius Loyola] offer a practical guidance, suited for those shapeless, average masses who let themselves be governed by elementary, tangible conceptions, who submit readily to a military organization in which obedience and mechanical adaptation to a bureaucratic discipline are looked upon as the principal virtues" (Buonaiuti, 1935/1968, p. 193).

psychology, although for Buonaiuti the direction to go would be toward an *ecclesia spiritualis*, a church of the spirit.

The term, *ecclesia spiritualis*, seems to have originated with Joachim of Floris (1132–1202) in the twelfth century, although the idea is older, much older in Buonaiuti's opinion, for whom it is the direction of the evolution of human spirituality.[16] Buonaiuti was a leading scholar on Joachim, including a book published the same year he refused to sign the loyalty oath (Buonaiuti, 1984). Ernst Benz, his student in the early 1930s and later Eranos speaker, wrote extensively on Joachim.[17] According to Joachim, there are three stages in the development of Christianity: the Age of the Father (the Old Testament), the Age of the Son (with Christ), and then the Age of the Holy Spirit, "which would signify full revelation and the establishment of eternal peace among men" (Buonaiuti, 1937/1954, p. 239). Buonaiuti's interpretation was stark:

> Joachim of Floris was a great optimist. The church of St. Peter scorned and condemned the new visitation of the spirit, proclaimed by the Calabrian seer. The *ecclesia spiritualis* was mercilessly driven from the enclosure of the visible church, and we may well say that from then on, from the beginning of the thirteenth century, the Christian message ceased to be an effective instrument of universal salvation in Europe.
>
> (ibid.)

Thomistic rationalism and Church disciplinary measures were two indications that the spirit had fled the institution, for Buonaiuti. In many respects, Jung's views affirmed Buonaiuti, although Jung, if anything, was more cautious, not wanting to dismantle institutional Christianity, because of the havoc that would ensue. But for Jung, the evolution of human spirituality in the west was essentially what Buonaiuti described.[18] Writing to Victor White in 1953, Jung (1975) observed:

> ... the more you begin to look forward beyond the Christian aeon to the *Oneness of the Holy Spirit* ... The state of the Holy Spirit means a restitution of the original oneness of the unconscious on the level of consciousness ... The later development from the Christian aeon to the one of the S. spiritus has been called the *evangelium aeternum* by

---

[16] In the Christian tradition, the idea is found in St. Paul. Later: "Gnosticism, Marcionism, Montanism – the three great 'heretical' movements of the second century – are all attempts to defend the *ecclesia spiritualis* against the forces of profanation which menaced its innermost being" (Buonaiuti, 1937/1954, p. 232). To be sure, Buonaiuti did not see these three *as* the spiritual church, but he did see them as saying something that pointed to the danger of the church becoming carnalized.

[17] Benz spoke at Eranos 16 times between 1953 and 1978, including an address on Joachim of Flora in 1956 (Benz, 1957).

[18] I have not found any direct reference to Buonaiuti in Jung's writings.

Gioacchino da Fiori [Joachim of Floris] in a time when the great tearing
apart had just begun.

(p. 136)

This tearing apart included "the rise of alchemy, Protestantism, the
Enlightenment, and natural science" Jung wrote in *Aion* (1968, p. 150), and
he associated this tearing apart with Joachim's having been seized "by the
archetype of the spirit" (p. 85).

Buonaiuti (1937/1954) gave the future progress of the Church a decidedly
introverted cast: "When man receives and partakes of these values, he is enabled
to escape from the blind servitude of sensory experience and to achieve the
absolute freedom that lies in the inner, intuitive vision of God. The fundament
and touchstone of the spiritual church is a 'gnosis,' a subtle interwovenness with
the realities of the spiritual world" (p. 243). This gnosis is not knowledge in the
ordinary sense of the term, Buonaiuti wrote, for knowledge as we speak of it is
grounded in sense perception (p. 244). Gnosis "is the power to recognize
absolute values through inspiration, through a spiritual grasp, a psychic sensibility, without the intermediary of sense perception ... gnosis and mysticism
are fully synonymous and equivalent" (ibid.). On this basis, the development of
the spiritual church is founded:

> Today the *ecclesia spiritualis* needs for its foundation no geographically
> limited units, no official groups organized in accordance with ecclesiastical
> articles and rules. The *ecclesia spiritualis* comes into being when here and
> there, of their own free will but no less firmly and effectively, all those band
> together who have become aware that future salvation does not depend on
> the mechanical development of our industry and technology, or on any
> fixed regulation of our economic and social life, but solely on the revival of
> a world of mysterious values, which evade all empirical judgment, and
> reveal themselves only to faith and love.

(p. 245)

He distinguished two forms of mysticism, the first solitary and the second
communal (ibid.). The first he identified with the Neoplatonists, and this one
has close ties to the Jungian way of individuation (see Hillman, 1973). For
Buonaiuti, however, the second mystical way places ethical relations between
human beings as its highest expression. Buonaiuti (1941/1968c) saw the
Protestant Reformers as over-reacting to the externality of the Roman
Church and thus leading to modern individualism: they "made the mystical
Christ into a chaos of atoms scattered in the world" (p. 163). In making Christ
into "a pledge of redemption," the reformers created a view of Christ who is "in
no way distinguished from the mythological figures of the old mystery religions
of initiation" (ibid.). In stressing simultaneously the mystical and the ethical,
Buonaiuti sought an *ecclesia* that was neither caught in externals nor a

repetition of a mythologem. In these ways, his vision differed from Jung's and from some others at Eranos.[19]

The psychological significance of Manichaeism and Gnosticism

Henri-Charles Puech (1902–86) was Professor of the History of Religions at the Collège de France between 1952 and 1972. An authority on Manichaeism and Gnosticism, he worked with primary sources newly discovered in the twentieth century, including the Nag Hammadi Codices, a major discovery of Gnostic scriptures made in 1945. An American purchased part of this collection, containing the Gnostic Gospel of Truth, for the C. G. Jung Institute in 1953, when this part became known as the Jung Codex (Grant, 1960, p. 19); Puech, along with Gilles Quispel (1916–2006), C. A. Meier (1905–95) of the Jung Institute, and others actively sought the purchase. Puech, Quispel, and Michel Malinine edited and published the texts (see Robinson, 1977 for a detailed account). Interest in these documents appears to have been the main connection between Puech and Jung.

Puech's first Eranos lecture, "The concept of redemption in Manichaeism" (1936/1968) is of interest because of Jung's profound disagreement with the idea, identified with Augustine and championed against Jung by Victor White (see Jung, 1975, pp. 58–61), that evil is a *privatio boni*, a privation of the good and not a something in itself. For Jung, evil is the opposite of good, psychologically speaking, and thus it has as much reality as does good. Puech presented the Manichaean doctrine that good and evil were cosmic opposites. In this salvation history, good would triumph over evil but only by containing evil and after having lost some of "the light" to evil's darkness. Puech, then, presented a myth that echoed Jung's archetypal theory of evil. Puech even attempted a psychological reading of the Manichaean myth:

> This myth may well correspond to a psychological experience which would lend it profound meaning. The essence of matter is ... *concupiscentia*, and

---

[19] These others were those Wasserstrom discusses in *Religion after religion*. Jung also found Protestantism "onesided" and plunged into "countless subjectivisms" (Jung, 1973, To Pastor H. Wegmann, December 6, 1945, p. 396). Jung and Buonaiuti shared the conviction that Christianity was evolving into something other than its traditional forms. For Jung, "the individuation process is a development on the native soil of Christianity" (p. 397). But whereas Buonaiuti distrusted Germanic thinking, in particular Hegel, Jung embraced it in his reading of the history of Christianity, as expressed by Peter Homans: "for Jung, the traditional beliefs in God, Christ, the Trinity, and the church were all necessary background for the modern individual if he was to understand himself in a new way. Traditional Christianity was the indispensable context for individuation. Paradoxically, it was there in order to be put aside. In Jung's mind, analytical psychology evolved out of the Christian tradition, in a historical sense, and the end result was just as religious – but not theological – as the context out of which it emerged" (1995, p. 185).

the essence of evil is lust for pleasure ... comparable if not identical with
the sexual urge, the libido. This violent, devastating urge strives darkly for
satisfaction. It develops freely in the unconscious or semiconscious, which
for the Manicheans is matter, but is inhibited by consciousness, which is
the good and the light ... I am very much inclined to interpret his myth –
the assault of darkness on the realm of light – as a projection of the
Manichaean experience of sin.

(Puech, 1936/1968, p. 270)

The only path of salvation, and that is available only for the elect, is gnosis, or
the secret knowledge that gives power.

Puech developed a psychological interpretation of Gnosticism as well,
including a 1951 Eranos presentation on "Gnosis and time" (Puech, 1952).
He wrote that Gnosis constitutes "an ego in search of a divine and eternal self"
(Puech, cited in Rigolot, 2000). Quispel observed that Puech "pointed out that
the center of every Gnostic myth is man, not God. These confused and
confusing images of monstrous and terrifying beings should be explained
according to Puech in terms of the predicament of man in search of himself.
The discovery of the Self is the core of both Gnosticism and Manicheism"
(Quispel, 1980, p. 22). It is fair to say that Puech, along with Quispel, Jung, and
others, helped to bring Gnosticism to the attention of the modern world. At
the same time, Puech's interpretation of Gnosticism protects it from Catholic
theological criticism. Jung's own approach did not make the same differentiation between Gnostic and Catholic symbolism, since all God-talk is
about archetypal forms.[20] For Jung, Gnostic spiritual writings in the early
part of the Christian epoch too easily led to psychological inflation, or the
identification of the ego with the Self. Christian insistence on the historical
reality of the Christ myth protected believers against such inflation. Today,
however, with a more differentiated consciousness and a livelier appreciation
of the shadow of modern rationality, Jung thought that "disparagement and
vilification of Gnosticism are an anachronism. Its obvious psychological symbolism could serve many people today as a bridge to a more living appreciation
of Christian tradition" (Jung, 1969b, p. 292). Future ages might link scholars
such as Puech and psychologists such as Jung to the beginnings of a Gnostic
revival. There are sufficient indications in Jung that he thought such a revival
was in the stars.

---

[20] Quispel (1980) pushed the link between Gnosticism and archetypal psychology further, in
his account Jung's notion of synchronicity, or an acausal connection between events. The
Catholic thinkers of the generation under consideration did not address synchronicity,
which does seem to break the Kantian constraints of the earlier Jung. For Quispel, the
Gnostics understood the concept of projection, except that for them, it was not we humans
who project a God and world (or even God-images and worldviews) but "the world and
man are a projection of God" (p. 31).

Returning to the sources

It is no longer possible to disassociate, as was done too much in times past, theology and spirituality. The first was placed upon a speculative and timeless plane; the second too often consisted only of practical counsels separated from the vision of man which justified it.

Daniélou (cited in D'Ambrosio, 1991, p. 535)

In the middle decades of the twentieth century, a movement called *ressourcement* appeared in Catholic theological circles. It signified a return to the ancient and medieval sources of Christianity in order to renew the Church in the modern world. It also was a reaction to the heavy hand of Neoscholasticism, which was, as we have seen, ahistorical and exceeding rationalistic in its philosophizing and theologizing.[21] Several of the Catholic speakers at Eranos addressed this *ressourcement*, and one, Jean Daniélou, SJ (1905–74), was one of the leaders in this movement. Daniélou had written a "manifesto" for the *ressourcement* movement in 1946 that Réginald Garrigou-Lagrange, OP, a Roman Neoscholastic theologian who had the ear of Vatican officials, saw as "a return to Modernism" (Nichols, 2000, p. 9) for its alleged historicism, anti-intellectualism, and dismissal of Thomistic theology. For Daniélou, what others called the "new theology" was an attempt to move from a theology that has lost connection with spirituality: "[Scholastic theology] gives no place to history. And moreover locating reality as it does more in essences than in subjects it ignores the dramatic world of persons, of universal concretes transcending all essence and only distinguished by their existences" (Daniélou, cited in ibid., p. 5). While there is more to the story than this, and the Neoscholastics need not be whipping boys of theological progress, my point is that Daniélou's position was compatible with Eranos sensibilities, his objections to the Thomists sounding similar in tone if not in spirit to remarks Jung made to the Thomist Victor White and others.

These were Catholic scholars looking back in order to go forward. What Daniélou, Jean de Menasce, Louis Beirnaert, and Martin D'Arcy all shared was a view of ancient symbols as invigorating the life of faith in the contemporary world, a view rooted in a realization that for many moderns, the roots of faith had withered in a mechanized and rationalized age. This renewal brought them face to face with myth, and to the relationship between Christianity and myth. From a Jungian perspective, this was the main point.

Jean de Menasce (1902–73), born in Alexandria, Egypt, and a convert to Catholicism from Judaism, studied ancient Iranian religions and Islam. After

---

[21] This movement has been successful in terms of the early Christian texts made available. The *Sources Chrétiennes* is a series of bilingual texts from the Patristic and medieval eras. It began in 1941 with Daniélou, Henri de Lubac, SJ, and C. Mondésert, SJ, and now has more than 530 volumes. We shall consider *ressourcement* in more detail in Chapter 10.

1936, he taught at the University of Freiboug in Switzerland. His 1945 Eranos lecture, "The experience of the spirit in Christian mysticism" (Menasce, 1945/ 1968) brought a theological perspective to what he saw as a largely psychological audience. In an un-Jungian approach, he argued that the symbolic expression of mystical experience "can be explained only by a postulate of an extrapsychological nature" (p. 326), especially if we are to distinguish illusion and truth in such experience. Mystical experience is conditioned by the individual having the experience, "not only with sensory images, usually charged with affectivity, but also with more or less impure judgments and ideas" (ibid.). To comprehend what is going on in such experiences, the experiential form of the experience needs to be brought into contact "with the very first and undeniable reality, which is that of faith" (p. 328). If we do not do so, we cannot understand Christian mysticism, and de Menasce criticized psychologized readings of spiritual experiences:

> The psychologist who denies the reality of God can only do so [i.e. explicate the symbolism of mystical experience] by applying methods valid in psychology in the strict sense to the realm of the superconsciousness. He, too, must pass beyond the experience itself and, in order to explain it, must have recourse to the reality which it seeks behind the symbols. But seeking it everywhere else than in a sphere which absolutely transcends the human psyche, he must need find it either in pure biological instinct, or in a social instinct regarded as the quasi-historical dictate of the collective unconscious.

(pp. 326–7)

At the same time, de Menasce wrote, biological and collective unconscious factors do condition our experience, and they need to be taken into account. Indeed, to understand the mystical experience, psychological factors operating in the life of the mystic must be understood, but they alone are insufficient. What is also needed is recognition that an Other, the Spirit, is at work here, drawing the soul onward in love. As to discernment of truth and falsity in such experience, for de Menasce that is where spiritual guidance comes in, since the experience is not only personal but also collective, in the sense of belonging to the Church as a community. Thus, while not denying the importance of psychological understanding, de Menasce asserted the higher claim of the Church in assessing the claims of spiritual experience.

Jean Daniélou and Louis Beirnaert addressed mythic symbolism in early Christian writings and rituals. Daniélou, in 1954, spoke of "The Dove and the Darkness in Ancient Byzantine Mysticism," focusing on the writings of Gregory of Nyssa, the fourth-century Patristic writer who founded Byzantine mysticism (Daniélou, 1964, p. 270). Three themes of Daniélou's essay stand out for psychology: (1) Gregory has described the spiritual life in terms that psychology today needs to know. Especially significant is Gregory's concept of *epektasis*, constant transformation, for the spiritual life: "the 'reality' of man is not to *be* spiritual, but continuously to *become* so" (p. 280). This concept marked a reversal of the ideal of life for the ancient world, which saw change primarily as decline and immobility as good (because perfect). Gregory acknowledged the movement of desire, a circular movement reflected in natural rhythms, a kind of "repetition compulsion," although Daniélou did not use this term. Such movement is, for the Platonist, illusory. Gregory helped institute a revolution in ancient thought, in that, in his words, "this indeed is perfection: never to stop increasing in the good, and to set no limit to perfection" (Gregory, quoted in ibid., p. 283), or in other words, "every perfection . . . is the beginning . . . of a greater good" (p. 293). (2) Gregory took up symbolic and mythic speech current in his time, including that of the Gnostics, and employed it in a new way. Thus the image of the "wings of the soul," employed by Plato in his *Phaedrus*, was also used by the Gnostic Basilides, as well as earlier Christian writers, such as Clement of Alexandria. Similarly, the "darkness of God" that Gregory developed occurred earlier in Philo, from whom Gregory borrowed it (p. 285), had its most significant earlier explication in the Gnostic Valentinus in the second century. (3) We cannot interpret Daniélou's return to this source as an indictment of modern psychology. If we follow his line of thinking, to overvalue the past and disparage the future would be in the spirit of Plato, not Gregory. As Daniélou put it, "For Gregory on the contrary the future is better than the past" (p. 290), this meant, obviously, in a non-Positivist sense.

At the same time, Daniélou criticized Jung's interpretation of the relationship of myth to the spiritual life: "Christian biblical revelation owes nothing to myths. It deals with unique divine acts, unprecedented and unfounded in human life . . . The Cross of Christ is not a cosmic symbol of the four dimensions, but the wretched gibbet on which the Savior of the world was hanged" (Daniélou, 1957, pp. 31–2). Yet the originality of Christian symbolism did not mean a merely iconoclastic view of myth. Daniélou, as did Louis Beirnaert[22] (1906–85) and Hugo Rahner, showed how attention to the myths enriched Christian understanding. Daniélou quoted Gregory on this point: "For if God transcends knowledge, what is grasped by the spirit is not He . . . For never to achieve satiety in this desire is really to see God" (Daniélou, 1964, p. 287). Beirnaert (1964) developed a similar idea in discussing the significance of water in baptism in his 1949 Eranos talk. The archaic meanings of water in terms of death and renewal receive heightened significance in the sacrament. By implication, mythic and other symbolic images of water do nothing but enhance the experience. Thus, while revelation may owe nothing to the myths, our experience of spiritual and religious realities does owe something to them, indicating a role for the psychologist in the life of the spirit. Moreover, as Beirnaert noted,

---

[22] Beirnaert made significant contributions to the relationships between psychoanalysis, including Lacanian psychoanalysis, and religion.

acknowledging with Jung the universality of archetypal images, the novelty of Christian symbolism relative to the myths does not gainsay "the permanence of the old meaning" (p. 28). The Church to its peril would ignore the mythic aspects of the religious life:

> To the extent that a sacramentalism (or, more generally, any religious representation) neglects to make use of archetypal figures and reduces its ritual to a schematic unfolding, it loses its efficacy over the pagan man which slumbers in each of us – it fails to evangelize the depths. That is when the archetypes which slumber in the depth of the psyche create themselves idols and cause paganism to rise again.
>
> (p. 29)

The paganism Beirnaert no doubt had in mind – he was writing these lines in 1949 – spurred mass movements, such as Nazism, in the twentieth century. Jung frequently stated that Christianity had failed to evangelize the depths, and that it was a veneer because of a lack of psychological understanding.

Martin Cyril D'Arcy (1888–1976) addressed "The power of Caritas and the Holy Spirit" (1953) in the 1952 Eranos conference. He distinguished two loves, both important, "the one which works to the good of the self and the other which is self-oblivious" (p. 324). To describe these loves, D'Arcy turned many ways, drawing on myth and Jung's psychology, among other sources. He spoke of "two archaic or primordial loves [that] ... can be described in terms of animus and anima or of masculine and feminine and both are active, though with unequal strength in every individual" (p. 292). He wove these images together with specifically theological considerations of the Holy Spirit, leading to conclusions such as the following:

> Love is no episode, it imposes itself like a divinity, regulating, inspiring, and offering the promise of an undreamt – of perfection. It is like a ruse of nature, and those who keep its rules know this and are grateful for what it has revealed. At the end the animus and the anima have thrown off their swaddling-clothes and attained their majority; the one in its freedom and self-possession, a peer of the spirits and clothed in knowledge; the other prepared for the ordeal of self-sacrifice and committed to an ideal which does not count the cost.
>
> (pp. 300–1)

In this way did D'Arcy, as did the other Catholic thinkers discussed in this section, draw upon Jungian themes to deepen their theologies, without losing their bearings in the psychological seas.[23] For them, the myths count, even if

---

[23] Privately, at least, Jung panned D'Arcy's Eranos talk, as he wrote to Victor White: "we had occasion to hear Father D'Arcy. It was a flop! The good man was completely at sea and had no idea what kind of audience he was confronted with. He gave a beautiful sermon that was

Christianity witnesses the introduction of something new, a historical dimension that transforms myth.

Hugo Rahner and the recovery of the Patristic tradition

Hugo Rahner, SJ (1900–68), elder brother of the theologian Karl Rahner, was Professor of Church History and Patrology at the University of Innsbruck from 1937; the Nazi regime and the war forced Rahner and the theology faculty to Switzerland until 1945. Rahner spoke at Eranos in five different years between 1943 and 1948. *Greek myths and Christian mystery* (1957/1963) collects many of his Eranos contributions. Rahner sought to define a new "Christian humanism" in these essays, in which he described an "ancient Christian psychagogy. Behind the concealing images of Greek mythology I seek to trace a way of ascent to the heights of Christian illumination" (p. xviii). In this, and like Daniélou, he followed the lead of Patristic writers, such as Clement of Alexandria who, as Christian Greeks, saw their myths reflecting truths that Christ later revealed. This made Greek myth, then, relevant for understanding Christian mysteries, especially those dealing with the destiny of the human soul. Like Daniélou and the others just discussed, Rahner turned back to the sources in order to move forward. He differed from them in his emphasis on myth.

Although Jung found Rahner "too careful" in his interpretation of the imagery used by Patristic writers (To Victor White, October 5, 1945, in Jung, 1973, p. 386), still he found Rahner's work valuable: "Your researches help to bridge that difficult gap which separates the modern consciousness from the living myths of antiquity" (To Hugo Rahner, November 20, 1944, in ibid.). Indeed, Rahner's investigations of the history of mythic symbolism, particularly as taken up by Christian writers in late antiquity and beyond, argues for the continuing – even up to the present – relevance of myth. That moderns do not live with this iconic tradition supports Jung's point about contemporary ignorance of this profoundly symbolic language. Rahner even argued that the ability of Christian writers, such as Clement of Alexandria, easily to "baptize" such stories as that of Odysseus lashed to the mast as his ship passed the Sirens, and of Hermes giving Odysseus the herb called moly, so that Circe does not enchant him and turn him into a pig, pointed to archetypal elements in myth. Now by archetype, Rahner (1957/1963) meant something different from Jung's conception:

> Catholic theology would here speak of our common human nature which is directed towards God. It would declare that it is this "religiosity" – which

so good in style that I could not help making the remark afterwards that he must have gotten the wrong calendar, namely the one of 1852" (Lammers and Cunningham, 2007, p. 207). In his witticism about the calendar, Jung spoke a criticism that he often did about theologians (including Victor White) that they were out of date, "medieval" in mindset.

always expresses itself in the same basic forms – that renders this human nature accessible to a possible revelation by the speaking God . . . Though, therefore, the evidence for their existence is in many cases debatable, the attempted identification of these archetypes and their use in other religions besides the Christian, does not imply that nature and revelation are thereby being reduced to a common level.

(pp. 14–15)

To be sure, Jung disagreed with Rahner's formulation of the archetypes, because it was not "scientific." Jung did not find Thomistic terminology "appropriate for contemporary man if one wants to give him any understanding of the human psyche" (To Hugo Rahner, August 4, 1945, in Jung, 1973). It is debatable how "scientific" Jung's conception of the archetypes is, but that is not the main point here. While Rahner was sympathetic to Jung's exploration of psychic depths, his emphasis was elsewhere.

Rahner was interested in pointing us moderns back to the psychological riches of antiquity, a legacy that has been overlooked in the modern epoch. In his 1945 Eranos lecture, "Earth Spirit and Divine Spirit in Patristic Theology," Rahner (1945/1968) repeatedly stressed that the Patristic writers "knew more than we do of the depths of the human soul; they had not yet forgotten that in the lowest 'abyss' of this inferno, there dwells a *daimon* fallen headlong from heaven, and they also knew that down in these ultimate depths, the conversion and the triumph begins, because there is another spirit, the divine spirit, that penetrates even deeper into the caverns of the soul" (p. 136). The language he used in this passage, foreign to the ears of natural scientific psychologists, was that of these early Christian writers who spoke to their contemporaries, the mythological-philosophical-religious discourse of the Mediterranean basin of the first Christian centuries. Rahner drew more on Clement of Alexandria than on Jung, and when he spoke of the "patristic doctrine of the 'discerning of spirits'" and called it a "dogmatically sound yet subtly observant psychotherapy" (p. 143), he meant that these forces do indeed transcend the psyche, and they not only personified, immanent, and unconscious forces. By reading the Patristics, "we might learn (and what a gain that would be for our present-day therapy) that one can speak only stammeringly and imperfectly of the psyche and its mysterious forces, if one has forgotten about heaven and the demon, about the vision of God to which the divine spirit empowers us, and the blindness of Satan into which we can fall" (p. 143). But in meaning it in this way, Jung could reply, as we have seen, that Rahner wrote as a medieval, and that he did not address moderns in search of a soul. Jung wrote repeatedly that psychology, as science, could not make transcendent claims.

This lack of a common ground between Rahner and Jung and, as we shall see, between Victor White and Jung, continues to haunt relations between the Jungian tradition and Catholic thought to this day. While there is general agreement that there is a spiritual and religious crisis in the west, its causes and remedies are variously understood. Jung did say that the "Catholic ... has to squander his best energies in papering over the crumbling Church walls" (To Pastor H. Wegmann, December 6, 1945 in Jung, 1973, p. 398), and the Protestants "are equally to blame ... that the evolutionary process within the Church has not proceeded more rapidly" (p. 397), the evolutionary process of individuation. Rahner's assessment differed dramatically, as he pointed to the loss of relatedness to the transcendent as the major issue. Relations between Jungian thought and Catholicism still hang from the horns of this dilemma. As evidence to the ongoing nature of this contested boundary, I point to an interim report presented by the Vatican's Working Group on New Religious Movements. The report deals with New Age religions, and Jung is among the inspirations for this new religiosity, a psychologized spirituality. The report, however, if taken to represent Jungian thought, presents only a caricature, because for Jung, identification with a god is tantamount to psychosis:

> From Jung's time onwards there has been a stream of people professing belief in the god within. Our problem, in a *New Age* perspective, is our inability to recognise our own divinity, an inability which can be overcome with the help of guidance and the use of a whole variety of techniques for unlocking our hidden (divine) potential. The fundamental idea is that "God" is deep within ourselves. We are gods, and we discover the unlimited power within us by peeling off layers of inauthenticity. The more this potential is recognised, the more it is realised, and in this sense the *New Age* has its own idea of *theosis*, becoming divine or, more precisely, recognising and accepting that we are divine. We are said by some to be living in an age in which our understanding of God has to be interiorised: from the Almighty God out there to God the dynamic, creative power within the very centre of all being.
>
> (Pontifical Council for Culture and Pontifical Council for
> Interreligious Dialogue, 2003, Section 3.5)

And one of the key New Age locations is, indeed, Monte Verità, the site of the Eranos conferences: "The *Eranos* conferences have been held there every year since 1933, gathering some of the great luminaries of the *New Age*. The yearbooks make clear the intention to create an integrated world religion. It is fascinating to see the list of those who have gathered over the years at Monte Verità" (Section 7.3). It is, indeed, although from this report one would not suspect that that list included prominent Catholic thinkers, especially during the years that Jung was in attendance.

Care of the soul: Theologians and analytical psychology

From the 1940s, Catholic theologians and spiritual directors criticized and adapted Jung's psychology. Raymond Hostie (1920–99), a Belgian Jesuit with a doctorate in theology from the University of Louvain, had studied at the Jung Institute in Zürich. He made significant contributions in the area of pastoral counseling and spiritual direction, including *Pastoral Counseling* (1966).[24] An early work was his *Religion and the Psychology of Jung* (1957), a theological and philosophical critique of analytical psychology, ending with a consideration of the relationship between psychotherapy and spiritual direction. Hostie reviewed the changes in Jung's approach to religion, from his early views as an "agnostic positivist" (p. 140), to his later view, from about 1940, that religion is not a stage to be outgrown, but "a genuine experience of the numinous ... the culmination" of human development (p. 148). For Hostie, Jung was an "empirical investigator" (p. 160) who unfortunately suffered from "ignorance of metaphysics and ... incompetence in the religious field" (ibid.), which led him to "take up matters which in theology and philosophy had long been settled" (p. 161). He credited Jung with realizing the importance of religion for life and for trying "to bring religion and psychology together" (ibid.).

Hostie addressed the charge that Jung sought to replace religion with analytical psychology, which Hostie (1957) disputed: "Jung wants to give all these people [who have lost religious faith] – and they form the majority of his patients – a real chance to recover their religious attitude – which is quite a different thing from instituting a new creed or cult" (pp. 170–1). In this light, Hostie tried to spell out the relationship between spiritual direction and psychotherapy, acknowledging the limits of each – for the former, in treating neuroses, and for the latter, in dealing with religious difficulties. Here, Hostie took Jung to task: "His psychological revaluation of religion is not generally speaking a first step on the road to faith but an obstacle to any deeper understanding of the real meaning of faith" (p. 180). While crediting Jung with aiding "indirectly toward a better appreciation of anything non-genuine in religious attitudes and of the repercussions that psychic dispositions can have in symbolic representations of revealed truths" (p. 209), Hostie claimed that Jung overstepped the boundaries of psychology and made misguided forays into theology:

> Whether he is discussing the significance of mandala centres, or examining the problem of evil, or deciphering the meaning of quaternary and ternary symbols, he sets up his facts and psychological explanations against dogmatic truths, though at the same time extolling the exceptional efficacy of the latter from the psychological point of view. By proceeding in this way he undoubtedly goes beyond the field of psychology. And therefore I feel obliged to refuse to his views, thoroughly tried and tested as they have been above, any real value in connection with the study of actual dogma.
>
> (p. 210)

[24] He also addressed problems of the spiritual life from a sociological direction in *The life and death of religious orders* (Hostie, 1983), where he proposed that religious orders have a lifespan.

Jung crossed that boundary not in his theoretical stance, but in his practical one, for as a doctor, Jung sought to help his patients. Jung crossed over from psychology to "practical religion" (p. 218) especially in *Answer to Job* (Jung, 1958) where, despite his claims to the contrary, he criticized dogmatic statements because of the psychological damage they caused his patients – specifically in locating no evil in God, but only in us humans. For Hostie, then, Jung succeeded in depicting the "religious function" as rooted in the psyche, but failed by not coming to terms with revealed truths, which "have their source in God" (p. 222). When Jung violated that boundary, he no longer dealt with *homo psychicus*, the object of psychology, but with revelation, which for Hostie as for all the Catholic thinkers we encounter here, has its source beyond us, even if such events take shape only in human experience and language.

Jung caustically replied, after having read the book sent to him by Hostie. He chided Hostie for not keeping in mind "that I am an empiricist whose concepts have – as such – no content, since they are mere *nomina* that can be changed as convention requires" (Jung, 1975, pp. 244–5). He made the familiar defense that "I have no doctrine and no philosophical system" (p. 245). On the contrary, Hostie had detected a philosophical system, and found it "regrettable that Jung has not seen fit to reconsider the shaky philosophical assumptions on which his fundamental position rests" (Hostie, 1957, p. 108). Jung closed by charging that since Hostie was a Jesuit, "there is no personal opponent with whom one could come to an understanding" (Jung, 1975, p. 245), i.e. that membership in the order militated against individuation.

Victor White was critical of Hostie's book in two reviews.[25] In "Two theologians on Jung's psychology" (1955), he addressed the boundaries of theology, philosophy, and psychology. White took Hostie to task for letting "his own philosophical interests predominate" (p. 383), and Jung to task for being "not always too well informed about what constitutes Christian orthodoxy" (p. 385). Finding Hostie engaged too much in apologetics, White held that the theologian should be addressing, as did Jung, "the raw material and crying need of perplexed human souls. Only so can theology appear in its true role as primarily concerned with the *Verbum salutis* and the *salus animarum*" (p. 388). In the later review, White (1958) criticized Hostie for "reading ontology or epistemology into purely psychological description" (p. 61), White taking Jung's position that it was possible to isolate empirical description from philosophical conceptions. At the same time, White affirmed Hostie's critique of Jung's confusing usage of "God-complex" and "God," observing that an analyst would not similarly confuse a "mother-complex" with a patient's "mother." Again, White stressed that Jung's position as "a practical psychologist

---

[25] The first review is of the original French edition of Hostie's work, *Du Mythe à Religion: La psychologie analytique de C. G. Jung.* The second covers the English translation (Hostie, 1957).

concerned with human conflicts" (p. 60) made the boundaries between analytical psychology and theology justifiably vague.

A very different reply to Hostie came from Robert F. Hobson (1920–99), a practicing analyst but no apologist for Jung. His review was, he wrote, of a personal nature because:

> I write as a personal witness to the falsity of Hostie's statement that Jung's work cannot bring anyone nearer to a more meaningful experience of dogma, although he, himself, might say that this essay only goes to prove his assertion. To a Christian, analytical psychology has many defects. It lacks a coherent psychology of group relationships and a satisfying theory of love ... But I am thankful for Jung's researches and ideas which have helped me towards a more vital life in the Holy Catholic Church by underlining Blake's conception of "the great task".
>
> (Hobson, 1958, p. 69)

Hobson found the methodologies of both Hostie and Jung defined by anxiety. In Hostie's "anxiety to protect the dogma from irresponsible psychologists, he writes as if there were a great gulf fixed between psychology and theology or even religion" (pp. 64–5). And Jung, though welcoming "the co-operation of theologians ... often seems over-anxious to write only 'as a psychologist'. Fortunately, he fails to do so" (p. 69).

Josef Goldbrunner (1910–2003), a German priest with a doctorate in philosophy from Munich and in theology from Freiburg, wrote extensively on spiritual direction and religious education. As early as 1940, he "showed enthusiasm for the possible uses of depth psychology in problems of pastoral care ... [but he] accused Jung of 'psychologizing' religious dogmas away" (Heisig, 1973, p. 208). Later, Goldbrunner refined his views, and he was anything but dismissive of Jung's work. In taking up the challenge of Jung, Goldbrunner contributed to a new orientation in Catholic spirituality, as Bohr (1999) writes:

> Between 1900 and 1950 the manuals of ascetical and spiritual theology, such as Adolfe Tanquerey's The Spiritual Life and Reginald Garrigou-Lagrange's The Three Ages of the Interior Life, were based, for the most part, on neo-scholastic presuppositions and were highly individualistic in their approach ... A new focus on the historical understanding of human existence began to shape Catholic theology and spirituality in the 1950s – in the works by such authors as Pierre Teilhard de Chardin, Hubert van Zeller, Thomas Merton, and Josef Goldbrunner.
>
> (p. 75)

In his Individuation (1956), Goldbrunner did not so much present Jung's ideas as apply them to pastoral care and spiritual direction. This distinction is important because it can help to avoid the seemingly endless debate, as Heisig

(1973) ably presents it, whether these religious thinkers did or did not get Jung "right." For example, Stein's (1957) review of *Individuation* accurately claimed that "the first half of the book fails to fulfill its purpose in so far as a number of Jungian concepts are – perhaps inevitably – distorted" (p. 112). But the distortions were applications of Jung's concepts in a different context. Goldbrunner, like other post-Neoscholastic Catholic thinkers in mid-century, drew on personalist and phenomenological as well as Thomistic sources, and the personalist approach stands out in Goldbrunner. With this in mind, his appropriations of analytical psychology made a contribution to spirituality, pastoral care, and religious education. Certainly, Goldbrunner (1956) was critical of Jung's professed refusal to engage in metaphysics as "a positivistic, agnostic renunciation of all metaphysics" (p. 161).[26] But Jung, he continued, was no mere positivist, since "it must be added at once that he has penetrated and extended brutal positivism and fought for the 'reality of the psyche.' He has acquired a new province for empirical knowledge" (p. 162). Goldbrunner took Jung to task for his history of consciousness schema, in which Protestantism and the Enlightenment represented an advance on medieval Catholic thinking. At the same time, Goldbrunner saw that Jung did address the "spiritual problems of the present age" insofar as:

> the religious problem of many people is that they would like to believe, but cannot conceive faith as a reality. They feel that their attitude toward religion is inauthentic, provisional, that it has not evolved from the core of their personality. No pastoral effort that is based merely on theological doctrine can help them overcome their difficulty since such people lack the capacity to respond to a purely theological approach: their spiritual life is undeveloped.
>
> (p. 203)

Analytical psychology, that is, offered supplementary knowledge of the human soul that could be taken up by the Church.

Goldbrunner expressed concern that Jung's conception of individuation would lead to "private religions" – forms of a secular spirituality that we have repeatedly encountered – because of Jung's skeptical attitude toward the truth claims of religion and philosophy. But for Goldbrunner, truth-claims influenced the psyche and made a difference for how we live our lives:

> That attitude of the highest part of the soul, the intellect, the "eye of the soul" (Augustine) has an influence on the life and experience of the psyche.

---

[26] Goldbrunner sent Jung a copy of *Individuation*, and Jung (1973) replied with a letter on May 14, 1950, with thanks and an apologetic for his renunciation of metaphysics: "Psychology is, strictly speaking, the science of conscious contents. Its object therefore is not metaphysical, otherwise it would be metaphysics . . . Everything that man conceives as God is a psychic image, and it is no less an image even if he asseverates a thousand times that it is not an image" (p. 556).

Different metaphysical views are bound to have a different effect on the organism of the soul and be reflected in the experience of the soul. Metaphysics opens a man's eyes to realms above and the self-experience of his psyche will be differently constituted in such a man than in one whose skepticism has closed the "eye of the soul" with a bandage and which forces it to look exclusively within.

(pp. 173–4)

The latter direction was the one that Goldbrunner saw Jung looking, producing a kind of "hot-house" psyche enclosed upon itself. So Goldbrunner re-interpreted individuation in an Augustinian fashion – as a process leading not only to the unconscious depths of the psyche and its core, the Self, but through the Self to others and to the Other. Indeed, his most creative distortion of Jung's thought occurred when he suggested that the Self, the "God within," the unknowable center of the psyche for Jung, could be called "conscience" (p. 183), because "the Self is the organ with which the Truth can be received and with which man comes to see the demands it makes on him, the demand that it should be followed and performed" (ibid.).[27] Drawing on Romano Guardini and Viktor Frankl, Goldbrunner's articulation of "conscience" argued that individuation, if it is to have spiritual meaning must include an orientation beyond the individual and the splendors of the psyche. Indeed, for Goldbrunner, the individuation process leads from confrontation with the Self to the I–Thou relationship, the I–We relationship, and then to the encounter with Christ or, in other words, from projection to "personal encounter" as projections are withdrawn (p. 196). Jung's psychology was to be, for Goldbrunner, the handmaid of spirituality, just as philosophy was, in the Thomistic tradition, the *ancilla theologiae*.

More pointed in its appropriation of analytical psychology was Goldbrunner's *Heiligkeit und Gesundheit*, translated as *Holiness is wholeness* (1955), although it might be better understood as *Holiness and health*, words that reflect the thesis more sharply. According to Chester Michael (1999, p. 125), for Goldbrunner, "a natural, psychologically whole person will also be a holy person."[28] Goldbrunner acknowledged that "the striving after holiness produces a crisis in the body and makes for ill-health" (p. 13), and he differentiated "legitimate imperillings of bodily health" from the illegitimate ones "caused by false attitudes, by false ways of life" which are "mutilations" but which "have become so identified with the very notion of holiness that one

[27] The call of conscience described this way as the totality of the personality resembles roughly how Heidegger (1962) described the call of conscience as from Dasein to Dasein.
[28] Michael writes that according to Jung, "Jesus commands us to be whole just as God is whole" (p. 125). No mention is made here of the question of integrating evil, which was one of the sources of disagreement between Jung and White. For Jung, God's wholeness would include the darkness of evil, whereas the Christian view is that "in Him there is no darkness at all."

almost has to smile when calling a man a saint, as if to apologize for his manifest oddity" (p. 14). To distinguish the two types of illnesses, Goldbrunner asserted that "modern psychotherapy" could be of great value. Goldbrunner diagnosed modern spirituality as having a faulty duality of body and soul. Now was the time to understand anew both of them. For the body, he wrote: "What we need are spurs to force us into life, not a bridle to curb an exuberant *joie de vivre*" (p. 20). Modern asceticism depreciated the body and its forces in an unhealthy way, in a way that did not promote sanctity but illness and distorted human beings.[29] Similarly, Western Christian spirituality's over-emphasis on the intellect has resulted in "the increase in the spiritual diseases known as neuroses" (p. 23). In a passage that shows the influence of Jung on his conception of spirituality, Goldbrunner (1955) wrote:

> The morbid reaction of the soul against the urge to perfection indicates that it cannot live under such conditions, that the ideal of holiness pinches and impedes it, like a garment that is too skimpy and badly cut. Such a human being does not live his own life but another, one artificially forced upon him. He does not live his own truth but a lie. It is now possible to define spiritual disease: a man becomes spiritually ill when he lives against *his* truth. A man is spiritually healthy if he is living *his* truth. It follows that there is no universal way to perfection, but each must find his individual way.
>
> (pp. 26–7)

What Goldbrunner found in Jung was a corrective to a distorted vision of the human person that existed in the Church: "The defection from the Church in the West is not merely a rejection of Christian faith; it is partly due to a feeling that the Church does not accept the whole of human nature, that inside the Church the deeper levels of the personality cannot breathe and live" (pp. 30–1). In this assertion, Goldbrunner implicitly rejected the Neoscholastic conception that the empirical sciences do not challenge the conclusions of philosophical psychology. Instead, Goldbrunner saw that Jung's psychology had something to teach the Church.

The integration of Thomism and analytical psychology

Victor White, like Hostie and Goldbrunner, was interested in the theological and practical implications of analytical psychology for a Christian anthropology. The irreconcilable disputes between White and Jung on the nature of evil and the status of Christ vis-à-vis the Self overshadowed other potential contributions to a philosophical anthropology. White's relationship to Jung has

---

[29] Recall here McNeill's criticism of will-training discussed in Chapter 5.

been the subject of much scrutiny (Arraj, 1988; Charet, 1990; Lammers, 1994; Lammers and Cunningham, 2007; Weldon, 2007). What led White to analytical psychology? To some extent, this question begs for an answer in terms of White's biography, but in another way, the question asks about White's conceptions of philosophy and theology that led him to the same type of phenomena that Jung investigated. Finally, what were the social and historical contexts in which this dialogue occurred? This last is important, because White did something that many of his Catholic contemporaries did not do: recognize the inadequacy of the Neoscholastic division of labor between empirical and rational psychology and, moreover, recognize the legitimacy of a "merely" empirical psychologist, such as Jung, to cross over and deal with theological questions.

The English Dominicans and Jung

White was not the only English Dominican interested in psychology and Jung. Others included Aidan Elrington (1870–1942),[30] Norbert

---

[30] Elrington, the eldest, had studied science at Louvain, and then taught biology at the Angelicum in Rome, but in 1920 he was returned to England because "his lectures were 'not scholastic enough'" (Tugwell and Bellenger, 1989, p. 228). After serving as superior at Oxford from 1921 to 1929, he left for other assignments, including running a home "for mentally defective children" (p. 228). He was one of the founders of Blackfriars, Cambridge, where he served until his death. During the 1930s, Elrington wrote a series of articles on psychology for *Blackfriars*, which explored in general terms the relationships between psychology, both experimental and therapeutic, and Catholicism in general and Thomistic thought in particular. Elrington (1936) acknowledged the limitation of the traditional Scholastic psychology: "the great difficulty with which one is confronted in the attempt to turn this science of the soul to practical account in dealing with modern psychology lies in the archaic language in which it is formulated, and not even in the English versions is the difficulty quite overcome. Any attempt to revise or adapt the language of the Schoolmen is liable to falsify the meaning of the original" (p. 594). The last of these rather introductory essays reported on the International Congress for Psychotherapy, which met at Oxford (and for the first time in England) in the summer of 1938. One of the main speakers was the president of the Congress, C. G. Jung. The political machinations of this meeting were either unknown or simply not reported by Elrington (1938). This meeting of the International General Medical Society for Psychotherapy was highly controversial, as was the Society itself. The Nazis sought to control it, and Jung's involvement in the Society during the 1930s has been debated as to whether it indicated that Jung did or did not have Nazi sympathies. Holding the conference in England in 1938 had a twofold intention: to ensure that the Society was indeed international and not Nazi-dominated, and to legitimate German participation. The meeting at Oxford coincided with Freud's escape from Vienna to London (see Bair, 2003, pp. 445–58). Freud arrived in London on June 6, 1938. Elringon's article is important because it verifies that Jung was on the Blackfriars radar in 1938, just around the time that White was chaffing at the restraints of the Thomistic atmosphere at Oxford. Jung received an honorary degree at Oxford on this occasion. Elrington (1938)

Drewitt[31] (see Cunningham, 2007, p. 313), Thomas Kehoe (1905–81),[32] and Gerald Vann (1906–63). Of the four, Vann's work is more important for our consideration. Vann's spiritual writings emphasized human creativity as an expression of the Trinitarian nature of human beings, made in the image of the Creator (Nichols, 1997), and in this light, he drew on myth to connect Christian life with the unconscious sources of our vitality. Like Hugo Rahner, Vann held that "the Church must learn to re-actualize the potential for *symbolic* thinking" (cited in ibid., p. 136). Mythic forms and stories in Christian teachings do not reduce Christianity to myth. Nor do they, as Jung interpreted them, point to a dichotomy of the historical Jesus and the cosmic Christ: the former, the man who lived long ago, the latter the life of that man "vanished behind the emotions and projections that swarmed about him" (Jung, 1969a, p. 154). For Vann (1959), the situation is the reverse: "Whereas all the myths, profoundly true as they are psychologically, are quite obviously in the realm of fantasy, not of history, the story of Christ is inescapably real and matter of fact ... The pattern is there, indeed, but at long last made flesh" (p. 19, cited in Nichols, 1997, p. 137). So Vann's writings drew on Rahner, Jung, Beirnaert, White, Eliade, Joseph Campbell, and others, in his effort to fire the imagination. Again, like Jung, but with that important difference of assuming the objective truth of Christian doctrine, Vann called for the necessity of accentuating the "feminine" in the spiritual life. "We live in an age which is marked, psychologically" he wrote, "by an appalling hypertrophy of the masculine over the feminine aspects of living: of action over contemplation, of scientific, commercial, go-getting activities over poetry and prayer and the pursuit of wisdom" (p. 12). This conventional way of stating a polarity had profound implications for Vann, who saw the necessity of psychological androgyny in the spiritual life (p. 97). Like Jung, he saw the danger of doctrine without its vivification by the imagination; unlike Jung, he took doctrine as more than a product of the psyche.

briefly recounted Jung's opening speech, which emphasized both his debt to Freud and the diversity of psychotherapeutic viewpoints in existence. After mentioning a number of other talks, Elrington in conclusion drew attention to two items: first a talk, "Psychological Problems of the Mature Personality," by William Brown, who "laid stress on the necessity for a more spiritual outlook in psychotherapy" (p. 681). Second, Elrington observed that, "psycho-analytic theories were on the whole at a discount, the major emphasis being rather in the direction of Jungian psychology" (ibid.). I have not read any account of White's attendance at this conference.

[31] For Drewitt: correspondence with Jung in 1937 (see Jung, 1973, p. 237) and *Blackfriars* articles: (Drewitt 1937a; 1937b; 1938).

[32] Kehoe was a friend of White's, and he wrote a review (Kehoe, 1952) of the German edition of *Answer to Job*, some three years before White published his own review (of the English version). Kehoe's review was somewhat more favorable (see Lammers, 1994, p. 320).

238 PSYCHOLOGY AND CATHOLICISM: CONTESTED BOUNDARIES

White Before Jung

White was born in 1902 in England, the son of an Anglican clergyman. He converted to Catholicism around the age of nineteen, entered the Dominican Order, and was ordained a priest in 1928. He resided at Blackfriars, the Dominican college at Oxford founded in 1921, teaching, writing, and working at the Dominican journal, *Blackfriars*, for much of the rest of his life (see Lammers, 1994, pp. 45–7; Weldon, 2007 for further details). The theological and philosophical atmosphere at Blackfriars was Neoscholastic, but not White: his understanding "of Aquinas ... differed from the 'official' Thomism that predominated among his colleagues" (Lammers, 1994, p. 48), although he was in good company in the Catholic philosophical world generally, with the leading Thomists of the day, Jacques Maritain and Étienne Gilson, also being non-Neoscholastics. Much but not all of White's writings before 1942 dealt with matters Scholastic. After that date, much of his writings addressed analytical psychology.

In 1940, White went through a personal crisis:[33] "Suddenly, or perhaps, not so suddenly, theology ceased to have any meaning for me at all: I could not get my mind into it, or anything to do with it, except with horror, boredom and loathing" (White, in Cunningham, 1992, p. 48).[34] Hayman adds that, "Given 'compulsory leave of absence' from Blackfriars, he was not allowed to go within six miles of Oxford" (1999, p. 385). In September of that year, Donald MacKinnon, a Protestant theologian teaching at Oxford, introduced White to John Layard (Cunningham, 1992, p. 48). Fergus Kerr, OP (2004b) recounts the story that MacKinnon:

> was among the first Oxford dons to have good relations with the Dominicans, quite recently returned to Oxford. He saw a good deal of Victor White, then thinking his way out of a certain Thomism into a more "apophatic" interpretation for which he is remembered ("of the nature of God we can say nothing") as well as beginning to come to terms with the work of Carl Gustav Jung. (Victor White was introduced to John and Doris Layard by Donald MacKinnon.)
>
> (p. 266)

---

[33] For greater detail, see Weldon (2007).

[34] Aidan Nichols, OP (1997) adds that White's "anguish of soul in 1940 did not, it may be surmised, turn entirely on inner-psychological factors. He was much shaken by two events: one was on a vast scale: "the approach of war and the challenge it brought to those Catholics who, having sought a Thomistic renascence of social morality, and a Distributist recasting of the social substance, now saw these hopes frustrated with the coming of quite different agenda" (p. 56). The war forced White to give up "the hope which, as a convinced student of Maritain's *Humanisme intégral*, animated him the 1930s for a 'new Christendom,' analogically related to the old" (p. 58). The other event of 1940 entailed severe disappointments in his efforts to foster ecumenism with the Orthodox church (pp. 58–60).

John Layard (1891–1974) was at the time "President of the Oxford University Anthropology Society and was at one time running three Jungian discussion groups" (Cunningham, 1992, p. 49).[35] By this time, he had already established a reputation as an anthropologist and psychologist. Earlier, as a student at Cambridge, he had traveled with W. H. R. Rivers to the New Hebrides, where he conducted anthropological research, later publishing *The stone men of Malekula* (1942), based on this research. Layard, prior to his Jungian days, had been in psychotherapy with "Homer Lane because of a hysterical paralysis, and he was fond of telling how in a few interviews he was cured ... and the influence of Lane persisted throughout Layard's life" (Fordham, 1975, p. 216). Michael Fordham recounted how Layard struggled with the writing of *The stone men* and so entered Jungian analysis with Helton Godwin Baynes, a friend and translator of Jung (Bair, 2003, pp. 306–7). He also spent time in analysis with Jung.

Layard was in some respects an unusual choice of psychotherapist for White. The influence of Homer Lane meant a radical interpretation of the relationship between the individual and society, teachings that Layard in the 1920s conveyed to W. H. Auden and Christopher Isherwood in Berlin: "According to Layard, '"God" really means our physical desires, the inner law of our own nature' and the Devil is then 'the conscious control of those desires – something we should avoid at all costs.' Sin is disobedience to the god of our desires" (Lucas, 1999, p. 120). All illness, including cancer and hysteria, arises from such disobedience. Such teachings did not reflect Jung, to be sure, but Layard formed his own synthesis of Jung and Lane, and Layard's lack of orthodoxy was reflected in Fordham's obituary notice, which described Layard as "a healer rather than an analyst" (Cunningham, 1992, p. 48; Fordham, 1975, p. 217). Layard's path did not end at Homer Lane, and Nichols (1997, p. 54) records that Layard and his wife, Doris – who wrote occasionally for *Blackfriars* – converted to Catholicism.

White's Thomism

The character of White's writings before 1942, when he began to address analytical psychology, shows that his interests could not be contained in a narrowly conceived Neoscholasticism. For White, the personal and the experiential were also matters of importance for theology and philosophy. He did, however, retain the Thomistic conviction that truth cannot contradict truth, since God is the creator of all. An early essay was his *Scholasticism* (1934), which traced the history of this mode of doing philosophy. For White,

[35] Cunningham lists as members of some of these groups MacKinnon, White's fellow Dominican, Richard Kehoe, an Anglican priest/psychologist, L. W. Grensted, and others. Layard and several other Jungians, including Vera von der Heydt, had left London in 1940 to escape the bombing (Cunningham, 2007, p. 313).

scholasticism was a way of philosophizing, and not a closed system. He was especially critical of the "conservative theologians" of the twelfth century, who had "lost contact with the dynamic ideas which swayed the world in which they lived and, in effect, repudiated the claim of their theology to provide the pivot for a synthesis of all human knowledge" (p. 18).[36] Thomas's approach, by contrast, emphasized the autonomy of reason, and that science was one of the ways to know God. Moreover, perhaps in response to the charge that Thomism was overly intellectual, White asserted that for Thomas, science was but one way to come to know the world and its Creator: "There were other, mystical and affective ways, whereby the profoundest wisdom is attainable" (p. 25). The limits of human knowledge were essential to Thomistic teaching in other ways, too, and White credited Aquinas with a historical sense: "the Fathers of the Church, for all the reverence due to them, were not inerrant, that modes of speech differ in different times and places, and that patristic pronouncements sometimes demanded considerable re-statement and even to be explained away. He showed a live historical sense of doctrinal evolution" (p. 22).[37] Finally, he noted that Aquinas "tells us that the human mind is situated between two realms which are in great measure impenetrable to it: the *Mysterium tremendum* of the Divinity above which blinds us by its very brightness, and the dark enigma of matter beneath" (p. 26).[38] For all this, White held that Thomas had an encompassing vision, including heaven and earth, and that the modern mind had lost it. White's Thomism would seek that breadth and engage the new and the challenging.[39]

White's (1939) review of Kierkegaard's journals provides another indication of the temper of White's thoughts before he seriously engaged Jung. White found Kierkegaard important "especially for the Catholic reader" (p. 807). What struck White?

> In isolating himself from the common run of men whose elemental instincts are unconsciously repressed, or consciously suppressed and sublimated, Kierkegaard establishes in effect a new community with what is

[36] I do assume that in making this comment, White was probably also indirectly alluding to some of his contemporaries, and that he did so indirectly because of rigorously antimodernist atmosphere of theology at this time.

[37] Nichols (1997) stresses the role that White assigned to Anselm of Canterbury in initiating scholasticism and as providing the agenda for White's own Thomism: "that agenda is neither (with theological Modernism) deconstructionist nor (with the most unimaginative of contemporary neo-scholasticism) merely repetitive, but 'constructionist' in both preserving tradition (a *sine qua non*) and building upon it" (p. 62).

[38] Compare this with a remark Jung (1933) made around the same time: "In my picture of the world there is a vast outer realm and an equally vast inner realm; between these two stands man, facing now one and now the other" (p. 120). Both realms are realms of our unknowing. The difference is as important as the similarity: for Jung, that other realm is "inner," whereas for White and Aquinas it is transcendent.

[39] See Lammers (1994, pp. 49–53) for a reading of *Scholasticism* emphasizing the Thomistic view that truth cannot contradict truth.

common to, though hidden from, in all men. In becoming an "exception" he establishes a new affinity with "the common man," and perhaps what scandalises us most in reading him is the scandal caused by self-recognition. In psychological terms he reveals the Unconscious. In theological terms, he opens new vistas of the havoc caused by original sin.

(p. 802)

Here, already, White was synthesizing Thomism and depth psychology. It was a path that took him to the boundary of theology with a psychology of the unconscious. In an important essay, "Thomism and 'affective knowledge,'" White (1943b) argued that "an intellectualist philosophy which is content to ignore or make light of affective experience ... must forfeit the claim to be either truly intellectualist or truly philosophical" (p. 9).[40] Especially when it comes to knowledge of God, affective knowledge is most important, because "the Object of Divinity is *lovable*" (p. 12). Drawing on the traditional association between *Sapientia* (wisdom) and *Sapor* (taste), White cited Aquinas, who said that contemplation "consists rather in *taste (sapore)* than in knowing *(sapere)*" (p. 13).[41] In developing this notion of affective knowledge, White drew on the classical and medieval understanding that in coming to know something, human beings come to "transcend in various ways and degrees the limitations of their own identity and in a certain sense *become another*" (White, 1944b, p. 321). That is, the capacity for knowledge implies "the insufficiency of each creature in its own limited particularity" (p. 324). This insufficiency encompasses more than a potential for knowledge in human beings, for it points to our incompleteness and fundamental lack of self-sufficiency. In general, "in our own human experience, this inclination [to change] is expressed in what we call *desire, appetite, affect, love*" (p. 325). The longing is for our "particular good or end" (ibid.). This brings Thomistic thinking to "purely psychological phenomena," White wrote (ibid.). The validity and importance of affective knowing makes understandable, intellectually, White's interest in the psychology of the unconscious. The related notion of "insufficiency" makes understandable, too, some of the boundary disputes between White the Thomist and Jung the modern thinker, because the radical incompleteness of the soul, no matter how splendid and powerful be the manifestations of the unconscious, points to the need for otherness.

---

[40] See Lammers (1994, pp. 56–65, and Nichols, 1997, pp. 62–3) for further discussion of this series of essays.

[41] This citation comes from Aquinas's *Commentary on canticles*, chap. i. Solomon's *Song of Songs* was a favorite text for medieval spirituality, as it accentuated the affective and amorous relationship between the soul and God. See Illich (1993), *Vineyard of the text* for further discussion on tasting and knowing. The relationship was a commonplace in the medieval period.

"Tasks for Thomists" (1944a) shows again the range of White's Thomism. Among the tasks was "a fuller appreciation of individual personality" (p. 101). White found such an appreciation in the work of Jacques Maritain, among others. And here, in the exploration of the nature of the person, White saw common ground between Thomism and Jung's thought. Thomas's analysis of the human person could help us past:

> the most deplorable outcome of Descartes' cogitations ... the almost inextricable confusion in subsequent thought between "the man *who* exists" (the Person or Self), "*what* he *is*" (the essence or nature) and "*what* he *has*" (the rest). The tendency of man in practice to identify his Ego with his acts, habits, moods, temperaments, even in rarer moments with the generic "essence" of "humanity" is notorious. But nothing but disaster can ensue when this confusion is elevated to a theory, or the confusion rendered so inextricable that every way of escape from its ravages becomes blocked. What a man *has* and should *use* inevitably becomes identified both with *what* he is, and both with the Self or Person *that* is and *has*. Applied to ethics this leads to the inevitable substitution of means for ends, and the consequent elevation of racial, group, class or individual peculiarities to the position of ultimate values.
>
> (p. 103)

Here White justified his turn to analytical psychology and to other non-Thomistic modes of thought. They aid in overcoming this "inextricable confusion" that has reigned in Western thought in the modern age:

> The immense vogue of Indian philosophy and yoga, as well as that of Jung's psychology, seems to be largely due to the fact that they offer both a theory and a technique of escape from this illusion and this oppression. The latter, with its clear differentiation of the Ego and the Self, the former with its processes of "discrimination" of Jiva from Atman and of both from the "gunas" and their manifestations, undoubtedly represent a salutary recall to the *philosophia perennis*.
>
> (ibid.)

This recall did not begin, wrote White, until Kierkegaard, and it has continued with Buber and with Maritain. I have quoted extensively from this essay because it contains the philosophical nucleus for White's encounter with Jung and analytical psychology. White sought to renew Thomistic thought by encounter with these others, because all thought, like all beings, are characterized by a radical insufficiency.

Central to White's concerns was the mystery of the person – which he associated with Jung's idea of the Self. White returned to Aquinas, where he found an insight that would further make a turn to Jung philosophically appropriate. In considering the person, Aquinas held that while we can come to know qualities and characteristics, what I am as a subject is outside such conceptual knowledge:

> perception of the self or "I" is and can be only "non-quidditative," exper-
> imental and existential ... *That* I am is a certain "experience" given in
> knowledge (and, love) of the other and more fully in perception and love of
> the Self; *what* that "I" in its singularity is, is beyond the range of intellectual
> apprehension, for "I" am subject and not object.

(p. 105)

Beyond our ordinary self-perception, in moments when "the Subject-Object distinction is wholly transcended" (ibid.) would there be an adequate way to think the Knower. This way leads to what is called "mystical experience," wherein "the 'Self' perceived (still purely existentially, and indeed in the last analysis negatively) is God Himself" (ibid.). Such a rehabilitation of Thomistic thought would enable philosophy to meet the challenge of the East – and although White did not say it, the challenge of Jung.

Archetypes, "The elusive frontiers of theology and psychology"[42]

The White–Jung relationship provided the most intense boundary-work between psychology and Catholicism in the twentieth century. Much has been written on it, focusing on their disputes over the nature of evil and the relationship between Christ and the archetype of the Self. First, we turn to White's forays into this uncertain domain, and at his interpretations of Jung's ideas. Then, we situate the White–Jung dialogue within the context of a pressing theological question of the day.

Lammers (1994) and Weldon (2007) provide much of the needed background of White's brand of Thomism and how it facilitated a dialogue with Jung. In addition, we must add White's emphasis on the pastoral and teaching aspects of theology. The importance of psychology for theology here cannot be under-estimated, and White would have known the line from Aquinas that stated: "Knowledge is according to the mode of the one who knows; for the thing known is in the knower according to the mode of the knower" (Aquinas, 1948, prima pars, q. 14, art. 1, reply to objection 3, p. 73).[43] This last point alone would have

---

[42] This phrase comes from White's (1943a) review of a book on psychology and religion.

[43] Moreover: "It is impossible for any created intellect to see the essence of God by its own natural power. For knowledge is regulated according as the thing known is in the knower. But the thing known is in the knower according to the mode of the knower. Hence the knowledge of every knower is ruled according to its own nature. If therefore the mode of anything's being exceeds the mode of the knower, it must result that the knowledge of the object is above the nature of the knower." (Aquinas, 1948, prima pars, qu. 12, art. 4, reply to sed contra, pp. 51–2). This position incorporates a stress on both the transcendence and the immanence of God, which White insisted upon in his *theological* disputes with Jung.

justified White's interest, in that for Jung, "the mode of the knower" includes consciousness and its types, introverted and extraverted, the personal unconscious, and the collective or objective unconscious. Most important for Jung, the mode of the knower has instinctual and archetypal structuring elements, which are our fundamental ways of being present to the world and ourselves.

At Layard's suggestion, White sent Jung three of his papers in 1945: "The frontiers of theology and psychology," "St. Thomas and Jung's psychology," and "Psychotherapy and ethics." A year later, White visited Jung at Bollingen, and in 1947, he presented two talks at the Eranos conference. High hopes for an integration of the two sciences began to founder, and "by May 1950 White felt that their discussion of *privatio boni* had reached deadlock" (Cunningham, 1981, p. 322). Cunningham writes that this disagreement was part of a larger one, namely, on the one hand White's attempts "to spell out a thomistic basis for Jungian psychology" (p. 326), and on the other hand, Jung's belief in the impossibility of metaphysics. Charet (1990) adds the important observation that Jung and White may have been working at cross-purposes, that "the significance of Jungian psychology lay less in what is said about the Christian doctrine of God than in what it said about Christians as persons" (p. 434). There is truth in this remark, although just what a "person" is leads to the Christian doctrine of God, since the concept of "person" was worked out originally in that context of the nature of the Trinity.

White saw in Jung's psychology an extension of the Thomistic conception of the soul. This was the challenge Jung presented on a theoretical level – the notion of the collective unconscious in particular carried theological implications. "Jung has in fact," he wrote, "and even in spite of himself, given a point to Tertullian's *anima naturaliter christiana* such as has never been exhibited with such clearness before" (White, 1953, p. 57). White was struck, in his most optimistic moment, with a similarity between Jung's individuation process, or what White called the "integrating or redemptive process," and the "redemptive functioning of faith and grace as known to Christian experience" (pp. 57–8). Since the concept of archetype is so problematic in psychology, it is worthwhile to dwell on White's assessment of its value for the dialogue between psychology and theology. It is in "this sphere of the archetypes that the contacts and collisions between religion and psychology most manifestly occur" (White, 1960, pp. 47–8). Why? Because archetypes refer to non-personal elements in the psyche that are best described in terms of symbols, and that have mythological, religious, and spiritual form. In order to relate to them constructively, what Jung called a "religious" attitude is necessary on the part of the person. In relation to the ego, the conscious identity of the person, the archetypes present themselves as transcendent. At the same time, the archetypes can act with force on the conscious personality, derailing its explicit projects and inspiring transformative changes. The cause of a lack of psychological well-being is, ultimately, lack of relatedness to the stirrings of archetypal powers. Jung's conception promoted the "symbolic life," as it is called, in regard to what lies within as well as with what lies without. White asserted that the archetypes are "the raw material of religion, the endopsychic, 'built-in' determinants and patterns of religious behaviour" (p. 205). Jung's conception of the psyche was, for White, the "nature" of the soul that grace perfects. Jung's views made the transition from nature to grace thinkable. And practicable.

Not that White took Jung's characterization of the archetypes uncritically. In *Soul and psyche* (1960), recognizing the "mercurial" character of Jung's mind and writings,[44] making them difficult to pin down (p. 53), White concluded that "we leave open the question of [the] 'existence'" of the archetypes (p. 229). He proceeded to disentangle some of what he found to be confusions in Jung's thought about archetypal images in their relationship to that which transcended the psyche.

To appreciate White's criticisms, it helps to see how he saw "The theologian's task" (White, 1956): "Theology is the attempt to understand, to make intelligible, what we accept by faith" (p. 4). The theologian need not – as the Neoscholastics tended to do – restrict inquiry to "methodological investigation of the content of revelation by rational methods" (p. 9), although such were not excluded. Following Thomas Aquinas, White (1943b) also saw value in "affective knowledge," or "an affective, mystical approach" (1956, p. 10) as a way of theologizing, and from this point of view, a theologian could learn much from Jung's explorations of the psyche. Coupled with this emphasis on affective knowledge White, again faithful to Aquinas but going against the Neoscholastic grain with its – ironically – modernist emphasis on systematic conceptual knowledge, insisted that "we do not know the Divine Nature at all, and that it is utterly (*omnino*) unknown to us." Why is God utterly unknown? Because:

> For St Thomas knowledge of anything whatever is impossible without some sort of mental image, form or *species* of what is known, however vague, incomplete, and such images or forms must be something definite and finite. There can therefore be no such image or form of the Infinite, and any such image or form which is taken to represent the divine essence will positively misrepresent it ... God must be outside all classes and categories, as well as outside the possibility of being imaged or conceived.
>
> (p. 17)

---

[44] This characterization of Jung's writings is more than a way of speaking. James Hillman (1975) depicted Jung in these very terms: "Jung's style of writing psychology takes various forms ... Like Hermes whose winged feet touch down as well in Hades as on Olympus and who carries messages from every one of the Gods, Jung's hermeneutics knew no barriers of time or space – Chinese yoga, Mexican rites, contemporary historical events, hospital patients, modern physics ... So Jung's way of writing seems to have been under the tutelage of Hermes who is most active in borderline conditions of the psyche, where fields touch on each other" (p. 156). This mercurial and often hermetic style has its limitations, to be sure; but it is also a unique opening on the real.

246 PSYCHOLOGY AND CATHOLICISM: CONTESTED BOUNDARIES

This does not mean, to be sure, that there are no images of God or rational assertions about the divine nature. It does mean, however, that images and assertions must be understood within this overarching *via negativa*.[45] The main point is that although we do not and cannot know *what* God is, we can know *that* he is" (p. 18), and this "knowing that" is a matter of faith.[46]

Any psychology that claims to have found images of God and of gods in the life experience of patients must thus get the theologian's attention. But in addition to this stance of White's was his position that there is much of the Platonic in Aquinas, that Aquinas was not simply an Aristotelian. This now generally acknowledged aspect of Thomas's work is important, because what White (1956) emphasized of the Platonic tradition was its "exemplarism," that is, "this world as an imitation, a participation, a shadow, and thus as a symbol, a sign, a sacrament, of a transcendental world" (p. 63). A symbolic view of the world, theologically speaking, corresponds in important ways with Jung's emphasis on the symbolic life as in keeping with our psychological constitution.[47]

Back to the archetypes. White's theological orientation gave him a different approach to the archetypes than did Jung's psychotherapeutic one. Thus the criticisms that White directed at Jungian interpretation of archetypal experiences, which White did not doubt occurred, and occur with great significance for the individual concerned. First, White made the objections that numinous experiences do not always have religious significance and that religious phenomena are not always numinous. Non-numinous religious experiences indicate the *rational* character of religion, in distinction to Jung's (and hence, Rudolf Otto's) emphasis on the irrational or suprarational character of religious experience. Second, White argued for the transcendence of God in any human experience, a transcendence even of the archetypal forces of the objective psyche. Essential to psychotherapy, he wrote, is the aim:

---

[45] To clarify this point: "All human words originally signify some creature or effect of God, and therefore, at best, some reflection or refraction of the boundless Light of God – which remains darkness to us. They can therefore only be *applied* to God, and as applied to him have a meaning which we cannot grasp, though this meaning has some relationship (*analogy*, based on causality) to the meanings with which we are familiar from our experience of creatures. Even the name 'God' or 'Deus' itself can be derived only, St Thomas insists, from some created *effect* or *work* of God" (White, 1956, p. 21).

[46] Fergus Kerr, OP (2004a), addressing White's "apophatic Thomism," concludes that White and others "insist so strongly on the famous statements by Thomas Aquinas according to which we know what God is *not*, but not what God *is*, that they play down his equally plain statements that we can know something about God by reflecting on the world which is God's doing" (p. 120). To insist strongly on the latter claim, however, probably would have foreclosed any meaningful dialogue with Jung, given his often-claimed non-metaphysical position.

[47] It is worthwhile noting that while Jung's philosophical orientation has often been seen as Neokantian, Hillman (1973) argued that Jung is better seen in the Neoplatonist tradition.

to help their patients precisely to distinguish their *imago* or complex from reality: to enable them to become conscious that, for instance, their father-imago or mother-complex is precisely *not* their "real" father and mother, and so to withdraw the projection and dissolve the identification. Why then, we must ask, do Jung and his followers so consistently confuse God and the God-imago or "archetype of Deity" right from the beginning?

(pp. 52–3)

Following the *via negativa*, White asserted that all our images, no matter how powerfully felt or life-changing they prove to be, are not God, even if these experiences call us to a religious approach to living.

On the other hand, Jungian research has shown that archetypal images are "the raw material of religion, the endopsychic, 'built-in' determinants and patterns of religious behaviour" (p. 205). Even though the Christian symbols cannot be fully accounted for by means of archetypal analysis, they do correspond to archetypal patterns (p. 206) and, here citing Hugo Rahner, White claimed that Christianity "took over the archetypal forms already familiar" (p. 207) in the Mediterranean world. White's interests here were also pastoral, and he questioned the nature of the images of God and of the soul given to children in their religious education. "How do [these images] correspond with their actual psychological needs and with the archetypal processes which ... take place in them" (ibid.)? The insufficiency of religious education in this regard is "a frequent cause" (ibid.) of adults abandoning the faith and often of their neuroses. White cited Tertullian's claim that the "soul is naturally Christian" (see White, 1960, p. 206), arguing for a deep basis of agreement between theology and psychology. But at this juncture it is important to address a significant divide within Catholic theology at the time that White was writing, a divide that relates directly to White's interest in the archetypes.

Archetypes and the division between the natural and the supernatural

Aidan Nichols, OP (2005) indicates that White's Thomism, with its emphasis on affective knowledge of God, coincided with great turmoil in Catholic theology over the so-called "nouvelle théologie" or "new theology," which before the Vatican Council of the 1960s met with significant opposition from some powerful theologians for its critical stance on Neoscholasticism. In 1950, the encyclical *Humani Generis* "reiterated the importance of scholasticism" (Wood, 1992, p. 394), with de Lubac and other proponents of this so-called "new theology" put on notice. White alluded to the "new theology" in *Soul and psyche* (White, 1960): "Hebrew and Christian religion, it is true, convey a message which can never be derived from the archetypes alone, but that message was never independent of them, let alone alien to them" (p. 206).[48] The central issue here was whether God is the ultimate goal of human longing, a topic addressed by de Lubac and by *Humani Generis*. According to David Schindler, Henri de Lubac's book, *Le surnaturel* (1946), which created the stir over the nature of human ends, asserted:

> Neither the Fathers nor the great scholastics had ever envisioned the possibility of a purely natural end for human persons attainable by their own intrinsic powers of cognition and volition, some natural beatitude of an order inferior to the intuitive vision of God. For these earlier thinkers, there was only one concrete order of history, that in which God had made humanity for himself, and in which human nature had thus been created only for a single destiny, which was supernatural.
>
> (Schindler, 1998, p. xvii)

A "purely natural end" would be, for our discussion, the archetype of the Self without an opening to the God whom it symbolizes but who transcends it. This position, stressing immanence to the exclusion of transcendence, was Jung's. One result of this stress was an all too sharp division between nature and the supernatural. Jung's position, close to what *Pascendi* condemned, was the mirror image of what the anti-modernists emphasized, the transcendence of God and the minimizing of religious experience. If all the gods are within, then there need be nothing beyond nature, however wonderful and filled with synchronicities it might be. If God's transcendence is emphasized in order to counter modernist claims for religious experience, then human relations with God are purely external, and we cannot know Him from within – as speaking through the subconscious, as James (1903) stated. White sought to embrace both poles of this opposition, this paradox of the relationship between God and humanity. In this instance, the one-sidedness belonged to both some of the theologians and to Jung.

For de Lubac (1965/1998), the human paradox can be summarized in the following terms: "human nature 'has not been created to remain within the state of nature,' but is in fact destined 'for a state far above its powers'" (p. 137). De Lubac cited White on two occasions, where White defended de Lubac's thesis against his critics. Nichols (1997, p. 117, n. 28) notes White's "*guarded* welcome" to de Lubac's thesis, which is indeed evident in White's (1949a) review of de Lubac's book.

A sharp division between nature and the supernatural dates back to the sixteenth century in theological disputations about the meaning of God's freedom and, more specifically, to the question: does God have to give His grace to mere mortals? If God must grace us, then grace is not a gift. (The arguments are long and deep, and they are beyond the scope of this book.) Scholastic

---

[48] Moreover: "In the archetypes, the theologian, the pastor and the religious teacher may find that point-of-contact . . . between the Word of God and the 'natural man' which has been the subject of much theological discussion in recent decades" (p. 206).

theologians, such as Cajetan and later Suarez, proposed the hypothetical possibility of this pure nature. The significance of the arguments is, however,
relevant for our story. If there is the possibility of a "pure nature," and "purely"
natural ends for human life, independent of God as the goal of human living,
then the supernatural is in some sense irrelevant to our lives:

> The theory of "pure nature" ... encouraged a progressive alienation of
> spiritual experience from engagement in history and, in parallel to this, a
> growing secularization which was conceived as an alternative to the vision
> of man founded on Transcendence. "Wanting to protect the supernatural
> from all contamination," they had de facto exiled it from the living spirit
> and from social life, and the field lay open to the invasion of secularism.
>
> (Forte, 1996, p. 731, quoting de Lubac, *Mystère du Surnaturel*)

De Lubac did not collapse nature and the supernatural into one order, but he
also did not affirm a dualism between them either:

> For de Lubac, the pair nature-supernatural must be thought of as "a
> relationship of opposition, of spiritual otherness and of infinite distance;
> that if man so wills it, it resolves itself finally into an association of intimate
> union". However, even in the closest union, there is distinction ...
> Therefore the alternative to extrinsicism is not immanentism,[49] but trans-
> formation, incorporation, adoption, where the supernatural remains
> totally other, not identified with nature, but where nature becomes a
> "new creation," qualitatively different.
>
> (Wood, 1992, p. 398, quoting de Lubac, *A Brief Catechesis on
> Nature and Grace*)

White was involved in this effort to re-think the relationship between the
natural order and the supernatural in light of the theory of the archetypes.

What was significant about this theological dispute is that de Lubac's thesis
meant that neat divisions between psychology and theology were possible only
in very abstract terms, and that they fail utterly if one is concerned, as both
White and Jung were, with actual suffering human beings. As White (1949a)
put it, "preoccupation with an alleged quasi-autonomous 'pure nature,' 'natural order' and 'natural end' may all too easily foster ... results that must
be disastrous for the spiritual life" (p. 72). As we live in a "science-ruled and
science-threatened age" the questions of "the *relevance* of Christ's grace and
salvation to nature" (p. 73) are our questions. False partitioning of nature and the

---

[49] Extrinsicism is the position that nature and the supernatural are completely distinct, the
position that results in the concept, "pure nature." Immanentism is the converse, holding
that "grace would do nothing more than make explicit and complete what is already
potentially present in nature" (Forte, 1996, p. 726). The former position was aligned with
the Neoscholastics, the latter with a Jungian position. White, with thinkers like de Lubac,
was holding the poles together.

supernatural, upon which the modern peace between the natural sciences and theology rests, no longer suffice. At the same time – and this is the tension that White sought to maintain – the partitioning cannot be overcome by asserting either the absolute autonomy of science (Jung's position) nor the submission of science to theology (the fideist position). Neither Jung nor White avoided the agony of the modern opposition between science and religion.

What was the significance of this theological dispute in the context of White's dialogue with Jung? It made for a theological reading of the theory of the archetypes. It did so by disputing the sufficiency of Jung's claim to be empirical and non-metaphysical. Jung did not want to make theological claims, but he asserted that the unconscious is full of gods. It is this fullness, as White pointed out, that Jung had – despite his claims – a metaphysics. In contrast to the position that all the gods are within the psyche, was the position upheld by White and by de Lubac (1965/1998):

> For Christians created nature is no kind of divine seed. The "depths" of the spiritual soul, that "mirror" where the image of God is reflected secretly, is indeed, as Tauler says, the "birthplace" of our supernatural being: but it is not its seed or embryo. It is indeed our "capacity" for it – to take a word used by Origen, St. Bernard, St. Thomas, and many others – but that does not make it a participation in it, even initially or distantly, "which needs but to be developed and enriched." It is not even the promise of it, so long at least as the objective promise has not been heard there. The longing that surges from this "depth" of the soul is a longing "born of a lack," and not arising from "the beginning of possession."
>
> (p. 84)

De Lubac distinguished this position from those of "natural mysticism" such as the Buddhist and the Gnostics, for whom the soul contains or is the seed of the divine. Jung's position was closer to the latter than to de Lubac's position. For White (1949a), in his review of Surnaturel, the issue was that "an excessive dualism of grace and nature all too easily obscures man's desperate need of grace, even in order to be natural" (p. 72). White stayed within the tension, seeking to overcome this dualism, this dichotomy of the natural and the supernatural without collapsing it, challenging the one-sidedness of both the Neoscholastics and of Jung.

Job, Jung, and White

Hence the ultimate dispute between Jung and White after publication of Answer to Job (Jung, 1958). Lammers (2007) has the clearest insight into what led to the break between Jung and White. Although White's review of Answer to Job, which coincided with Jung's wife, Emma, being diagnosed with a terminal cancer, was the moment of the break, Lammers sees their friendship going into decline after 1948, specifically, after White's (1949b) review of Jung's Eranos contribution, "Über das Selbst" (On the Self). White criticized Jung's "quasi-manichaean dualism" (p. 399) in his syncretism of various mythic and religious symbols in depicting the Self. Jung replied to this scolding in kind (Lammers, 2007, p. 263; see Lammers and Cunningham, 2007, pp. 140–3). The break between the two men had many roots, personal and theoretical. For present purposes, however, the latter take precedence, and we can see their paths diverging on the issue of God's transcendence. For Jung, as for the Jungian John Dourley, who has championed Jung's position, *the* source of religion was the psyche (see Dourley, 2007). That is, unlike White – and George Tyrrell – Jung decried extra-psychic intrusion of the divine into human life. For Jung, the psyche was full; for White, it was an unfillable lack. This was so even as White also affirmed the rootedness of religion in the archetypes, and that moderns were isolated from the inner, emotional, instinctual, hence archetypal roots of religion – thus the emptiness of much contemporary religiosity.[50]

The sad ending of the White–Jung friendship in the context of White's review of *Answer to Job* is a complex story. Jung's book on Job is one of the most remarkable psychological studies of the twentieth century, a tour-de-force that is ambiguously an account of the development of the psyche as revealed by a history of symbols from Scripture and Church history, a study of the archetype of the Self, and an apocalyptic account of modern consciousness, armed with the dark god of the atom bomb at the end of the Christian era, the Age of Pisces.[51] It would take considerable time to sort out the issues evoked, so instead I turn to White's own bombshell, his review of *Answer to Job*. The review contains *ad hominem* arguments against Jung, at one point saying that the book reflects "the clear-sightedness and blindness of the typical paranoid system which rationalizes and conceals an even more unbearable grief and resentment" (p. 59). But we would do well not to personalize the conflict over *Job*, even if the personal was intrinsically involved. Much of *Answer to Job* and of White's review sound like – to use a Jungian word – "Shadow" boxing over the nature of evil. Jung's position, that God or the God-image must contain evil as well as

---

[50] In a letter in reply to an article by Charles Burns, an English Catholic psychologist with an interest in Jung, White wrote: "Jung has proved up to the hilt that his collective archetypes are precisely (as he claims) the psychological counterparts of biological instincts, that religion, in some form or another (conscious or unconscious) is the regular psychological instrument for the assimilation and organization of instinctive, emotional and other experience, and that it can be as little neglected in the treatment of psychoneurosis as can the digestive and excretory organs in the treatment of dyspepsia" (White, 1950, p. 290).

[51] Dourley's (2007) account places Jung's narrative on Job into a Hegelian mold: "Hegel had described divinity as an absolute, creating history as the theatre in which divinity overcame its split with humanity in the unification of its opposites in human history, a position close to Jung's in his *Answer to Job*" (p. 278).

good runs counter to the Christian view of God, and would be an inadequate God-image. White (1960), writing after the storm of *Job* seems to have passed,[52] made two relevant points. First, God as the unknown is "beyond the *opposites* of good and evil" (p. 151) because anything we say of him is analogical at best. Second, acknowledging the complexities of evil in human life, with natural disasters as evils, for example, and with our calling some things "evil" when the fault really lies in our one-sided assessment of them, still there remains *malum culpae* or sin, which in the theological sense must be avoided and not integrated into the total personality, and certainly cannot be attributed to God. While there is much more to say on this issue, it suffices to say that on this point, the reality and nature of evil and of God, there proved to be much room for significant discussion between a theologian and a psychologist both entering, with fear and trembling, into the contested ground between psychology and religion.

With the publication of the letters between Jung and White (Lammers and Cunningham, 2007), we see how complex that contested ground was for them – and for us. On November 8, 1953, White wrote to Jung about his doubts, about his lack of faith: "If Christ is no longer an adequate and valid symbol of the Self, and in fact very inadequate, one-sided, unintegrated and harmful, then must not one choose – at whatever the cost?" (p. 216). This confidential letter must not be cited as White's final position, but as an indication of the turmoil he suffered. He wrote to Jung that "I must get out" (ibid.). He did not leave the Order or the Church. To that end, Jung played a significant role, replying to his letter on November 24. Jung wrote, in the course of (in effect) summarizing the argument in *Answer to Job*, that White's suffering was in fact "the imitatio Christi" that "leads you into your own very real and *christlike conflict* with darkness" (p. 220). Jung reproved White, saying, "It would be a lack of responsibility and a rather autoerotic attitude if we were to deprive our fellow beings of a vitally necessary symbol before they had a reasonable chance to understand it thoroughly ... Anybody going ahead is alone or thinks he is lonely at times, no matter whether he is in the Church or in the world" (p. 221). White (Lammers and Cunningham, 2007) replied that Jung's words "ring the bell" (Letter to Jung, November 29, 1953, p. 223). Given the consolation White got from this letter, which put him in the *Job* narrative, White's scathing review of the book when it appeared in English is all the more puzzling, suggesting deeper layers of suffering.

---

[52] Earlier, in the middle of an existential crisis over his vocation and his relationship with the Church – a crisis aggravated by the anti-modernist oath he was obliged to sign – White wrote to Jung: "To me it is now obvious that Christ had a shadow AND that he projected it; possibly on the devil, certainly on the Pharisees" (Lammers and Cunningham, 2007, letter to Jung, March 4, 1954, p. 228).

The medium and the message: Spiritualism, Jung, and White

One complicating factor in any neat classification of Jung as another Kantian – denying access to the real beyond the psyche – has to be his concept of synchronicity. Defined as an acausal connection between events, such as a dream and a simultaneous event (the so-called prophetic dreams), synchronicity harkens back to the spiritualism of the late nineteenth and early twentieth centuries, a stream of thought so important to Jung's psychology, as Charet has shown. In 1947, White (in Lammers and Cunningham, 2007, p. 87) described to Jung some dreams by and "spooky" events associated with an English woman, Barbara Robb, a devout Catholic, whom White was helping. Jung replied with a touch of skepticism about an incident of some extraordinary roses, but found the dreams suggestive of synchronicity, since they dealt with him, whom Robb had not yet met. Synchronistic events surrounding Robb suggests she was something like a medium for White, and then for Jung, who met her in 1951. Jung referred to her as White's "soror mystica" (referring to a companion of an alchemist), as an anima figure ("If ever there was an anima, it is she, and there is no doubt about it," Jung (in ibid., p. 169) wrote to White after the 1951 meeting), and White labeled her an "introverted intuitive," i.e. something of a visionary – that White did not know quite how to deal with (p. 170).

   In addition to the exchange of dreams as part of their correspondence and relationship, White and Jung at times described consulting the *I Ching* in the course of psychological reflection. For Jung, the *I Ching* was a kind of divination that worked by synchronicity, that is, by means of an acausal connection between an external and internal event. Jung sent White a copy of the English translation of *I Ching or The book of changes* (Wilhelm, 1967), to which Jung had written a Foreword, in 1950. Jung's Foreword described how he interpreted the book and the accompanying form of divination – throwing coins or sticks, reading the pattern, and comparing them to the corresponding part of the text – in terms of synchronicity. In part, he wrote:

> The *I Ching* insists upon self-knowledge throughout. The method by which this is to be achieved is open to every kind of misuse, and is therefore not for the frivolous-minded and immature; nor is it for intellectualists and rationalists. It is appropriate only for thoughtful and reflective people who like to think about what they do and what happens to them – a predilection not to be confused with the morbid brooding of the hypochondriac ... I have no answer to the multitude of problems that arise when we seek to harmonize the oracle of the *I Ching* with our accepted scientific canons. But needless to say, nothing "occult" is to be inferred ... The irrational fullness of life has taught me never to discard anything, even when it goes against all our theories (so short-lived at best) or otherwise admits of no immediate explanation.

> (Jung, 1967b, pp. xxxiii–xxxiv)

Given this view, in the exploration of the psyche in its archetypal depths, with an eye towards one's existential situation, reading the *I Ching* was as likely a technique as reading a dream or a slip of the tongue. But Jung's willingness to consider it seriously as being based on an understanding of the psyche does show that he was not simply a Kantian. The soul manifests itself in many ways, including those "in the world."

In the letter of 1953 described above, in which White's crisis is laid out, he began the letter by saying that he had "just asked the I Ching if I should write and report to you on my present miseries!" (p. 216). Again, when facing going to Rome to take the anti-modernism oath, he said he had received "considerable help from your letter, urgings from superiors and colleagues, and a big kick from the *I Ching*" (in Lammers and Cunningham, 2007, p. 247). The *I Ching*, like the dream, pointed to the roots of psychological life in the image and the symbol.

Assessing White

Lest it be seen that this contested ground simply posed one side, the theologians, against the other, the psychologists, it needs noting that someone like White, who became identified by many with Jungian psychology, received considerable criticism from the Catholic side. Gemelli, whom we have seen was hostile toward Jung, reviewed *God and the unconscious* "with an attack on White's orthodoxy" (Heisig, 1973, p. 206).[53] Within the Dominicans, White faced difficulties as he became identified with Jungian psychology. White's interest in Jung cost him an appointment as Regent of Studies at Blackfriars, Oxford, in 1954 (Lammers, 1994, p. 99; Nichols, 1997, p. 54).

In 1959, after the storm over *Answer to Job*, the Master of White's Dominican Order wanted White to withdraw *God and the unconscious* from publication, although the English Provincial, who had earlier blocked White's promotion, defended White as a loyal Thomist.[54] Nichols (2005) holds that in one sense White's project failed, in that the distance between the "orthodox Catholicism of a Thomistic stamp and Jung's thought as a whole" is unbridgeable.

---

[53] White wrote to Jung (Lammers and Cunningham, 2007, August 25, 1956, p. 274): "I wonder if you saw the vicious attack on you and me by Padre Gemelli ... All this notwithstanding an Italian translation of my book [*God and the unconscious*] is to appear next month: the authorities of the diocese of Milano have not only given the imprimatur but have (I am told) insisted it be published. But I am told that there is likely to be fierce opposition. Maybe I'll even get on the Index!"

[54] Nichols (1997) writes: "the Master of the Order, Fr Michael Browne, asked for the book to be withdrawn (in fact it was already out of print), at least the English Provincial, Fr Hilary Carpenter, took the opportunity to make amends for his scuppering of Fr Victor's regency by paying tribute to his qualities as a religious as well as his passionate adherence to the *sana doctina* of St Thomas" (p. 109).

Nevertheless, he sees its worth in "ending this unnatural divorce" (Nichols, 1997, p. 116) between "spirit" and "matter" in the contemporary world. This is a loss, one might say, of the sacramental view of the world. Indeed, Nichols signals the "crucial role played in the practical exercise of Catholicism by the *image*" (p. 113) in many ways, to which both White and Jung have contributed an understanding.

Weldon's (2007) theological study of White adds to this picture. She directs attention to the role of the image in White's appropriation of Jung. Like Jung, for White the image can express what we cannot grasp either perceptually or rationally. In other words, the image is a mode of apprehension of the real. White's view of the image was, moreover, sacramental: the image (the symbol) is both universal – its archetypal aspect – and particular – Christ was *this* person who lived at *this* time and place, and who there revealed God. That is to say, the image, here meaning especially the Christian image, is both immanent in the psyche and transcendent of it – revelation of what exceeds it. God is immanent and transcendent. White's efforts to articulate this, in the face of modernist emphasis on the former and anti-modernist emphasis on the latter, were a significant accomplishment. Finally, she indicates that White, in what she calls his "post-Jung years" (that is, after 1955), as a Christian theologian concluded that "Catholicism *answers* the very needs which empirical psychology has disclosed" (p. 194). Her claim is that Catholic symbols in the fullness of their expression most clearly direct the soul to what it desires.

What about Catholic psychologists? What did they think of White's efforts? As many were attempting to separate and link natural scientific psychology and Catholicism, they had little tolerance for Jung. William C. Bier, SJ (1953d), reviewing *God and the unconscious* expressed distrust of Jung's psychology, noting that "many Catholics, reacting against Freud, have embraced Jung more for what he *said* than what he *meant*" (p. 4). For Bier, what Jung said about God was incongruous with Catholicism, and confusion results. Raymond Henri Shevenell, OMI (1908–2003) of the University of Ottawa[55] was no doubt typical of many in dismissing any attempts to build bridges between Thomism and Jungian psychology (Shevenell, 1960). Raymond McCall (1954b) also had little patience for the project: "Jung regards himself as an empiricist, but is far from the opinion of his scientific colleagues who, almost without exception, think of him as an incurable 'mystic,' however inaccurately they may employ that term" (p. 241). The review that came closest to the deepest difficulty was written by Gregory Stevens, OSB (1953), from Thomas Verner Moore's former Priory of St. Anselm's. Stevens wrote that his attempt to understand White's writing was like "trying to grasp a handful of mercury" (p. 501). Taken

---

[55] He was a professor of philosophy and psychology between 1935 and 1955, and founded the School of Psychology and Education at Ottawa. He was involved in counseling and psychological assessment.

as an image, he was right. And that may set the agenda for further efforts to explore this most contested of boundaries.

In White's circle

In 1954, White was among the "Catholic analysts group" (Lammers and Cunningham, 2007, p. 227) to start a clinic in London. Called the More Clinic, its aim "was to meet the needs of patients in a Catholic atmosphere by modern psychological methods" (Weldon, 2007, p. 63).[56] The clinic closed in 1959 as its members aged or died (p. 258). In addition to this circle, there were other prominent Catholic Jungians, including Eve Lewis and Vera von der Heydt. Lewis (1962) addressed the very theme central to White in studying children, as Michael Fordham noted in his review: "Her thesis is that children inevitably develop a natural religion of their own caused by the activity of archetypes. Religious instruction needs to be adapted to these developing systems while giving place for the home influence and the child's individual characteristics" (Fordham, 1963).

The most prominent of this group – and in no way am I surveying all potential Catholic Jungians – was von der Heydt (1899–1996). Her Jewish father had become Protestant; her mother, of German and Irish descent, was a Lutheran. An émigré from Hitler's Germany, she moved to England in 1933, and she converted to Catholicism in 1937. She later wrote:

> On Sundays, however, I used to go and sit for a while in some church. More and more I was drawn to the Brompton Oratory where I used to look at a lovely statue of Jesus pointing to His Sacred Heart. In my mind I spoke to this figure, and in my mind I heard Him speak to me. After quite some time I knew what I had to do and I became a Roman Catholic. Actually I did not "become" a Catholic, for I realised that I had been one all my life. I had no difficulties with dogma; for me dogmatic statements were then, as they are now, expressions of inner truths experienced through the ages by different people in different ways and understood and verbalised from different levels.
>
> (von der Heydt, 1976, p. xii)

---

[56] Staff included Victor White, Fr. Francis O'Malley, F. B. Elkisch, a Jungian analyst and author (see Elkisch, 1946,) and Dr. Ruth Sandemann (Weldon, 2007, p. 258). Dom Oswald Sumner, OSB, Toni Sussmann, Anges Selo, and Eve Lewis were part of the Catholic Analysts Group (Lammers and Cunningham, 2007, p. 227, n. 4). I have not been able to ascertain if these two groups were identical, but they certainly overlapped. The clinic name may simply have been a more formal appellation. Sumner and Elkisch co-authored "Psychologie moderne et introspection" (1949), dealing with Jung. Sumner presented twice to the Guild of Pastoral Psychology: *St John of the Cross and modern psychology* (Sumner, 1948) and *St. John Climacus – The psychology of the desert fathers* (Sumner, 1950). Sumner was a psychotherapist as well as a priest; he "studied under Jung and lectured at the Jung Institute, Zurich" (Lammers and Cunningham, 2007, p. 155, no. 36).

During the bombing of London, she went to Oxford, where she entered analysis with John Layard. She was in Layard's Jungian discussion group at Oxford with Victor White and others, including Toni Sussmann (Cunningham, 1992, p. 49; Lammers, 2007, p. 255). After the war, she went to Zürich for analysis with Jung and Jolande Jacobi. She subsequently returned to London (Costello, 1997). She addressed the fact that some of her colleagues viewed her being a Jungian Catholic as a contradiction. She wrote (von der Heydt, 1976) that "I have quite often been asked how I can be a Jungian analyst and at the same time a member of the Roman Catholic Church" (p. 107). Acknowledging that some theologians and some analysts point out intellectual difficulties in combining the two, von der Heydt answered: "Jung's approach and attitude to man in the universe has enriched my faith and kept any doubts I may have healthily in consciousness. Conversely my faith has illuminated many of Jung's ideas and helped me to understand what he was trying to do." In an obituary, Costello (1997) points to how the climate has changed for someone like von der Heydt: "It was [in the early 1950s] also much more difficult to be seen in London as a Jungian analyst and a believer in a religious faith. All that has changed in the period of forty years" (pp. 331–2). In part, no doubt, because of von der Heydt.

In dealing with the intersection of psychology and religion, she seconded Jung's contention that for many modern people, Christian dogma means nothing. With Jung, she held that "the neglect of the religious impulse underlies the neurosis of our times" (von der Heydt, 1977, p. 179). Moreover, she affirmed Jung's contention that westerners, whether or not they are Christian, need "to understand the essential dogmas of the Christian Church as representing psychic truths" (p. 181). That is, whether or not they "believe" in Christianity, Christian symbols and teachings are effective in their psyches. Acknowledging that Jung "did not fully understand Catholic doctrine" (p. 178), von der Heydt saw analytical psychology as being important for Catholics, because of the possibility of connecting the often arid realm of dogma with personal experience of the numinous: "A creed is a positive framework when the symbols of the Church are alive and meaningful; when dogma is a personal experience, belief is transformed into *pistis*, trust, and the opposites religion and creed, the courage to experience, and insight in the reality of symbolic formulations are united in a dynamic process" (p. 177). Since it has been the psychologists who have explored the depth dimension of experience, the clergy and others in the Church dealing with "the psychically sick and suffering human being" (ibid.) can learn something that they did not know.

During the course of those forty years, von der Heydt made significant contributions to analytical psychology. In "The Treatment of Catholic Patients" (von der Heydt, 1970) she dealt with specific conflicts that arose with her Catholic patients, and in one particular, she objected to Jung's contention that dogma becomes a defense against religious experience. Her rebuttal was that confession and communion, being sacraments, were not only symbols (i.e. representations). As sacraments, "they are experienced as a reality" (p. 74), the reality of the presence of God. As such, unless a person celebrates the sacraments "from superstitious fear, from habit, moralistically and legalistically" (ibid.), which no doubt happens often enough, the *numen* is there. Von der Heydt discussed one patient for whom this was clearly the case. She understood what was happening as an archetypal event, but also by means of a passage from St. John of the Cross as explicated by Michael Fordham (1905–95), the prominent English Jungian analyst. The passage is: "when they are powerless to prevent it, impure acts and motions arise in the sensual part of the soul; this happens even when the spirit is deep in prayer, or taking part in the Sacrament of Penance or in the Eucharist" (quoted in ibid., p. 77). The patient, an unmarried Catholic woman sent to her by a priest, started analysis because she had an orgasm when the Host touched her tongue when she received communion. This symptom distressed the young woman as "utterly blasphemous, wicked and terrifying" (von der Heydt, 2002, p. 4). Von der Heydt did not simply see this symptom as contrary to the young woman's conscious spiritual intentions. The woman felt the physical sensation as blasphemous "because she regarded her body and its needs as wicked and terrifying" (ibid.). The patient came to recognize "that she had to link this experience to her total attitude of 'hate' for her body, and that from the centre of her being 'something' was pushing her to recognize the reality of her bodily needs as well as those of her spiritual side" (ibid.). The symptom was not something to be eliminated but a meaningful symbol, emerging from the Self, the image of God within her. Though von der Heydt did not make the connection in that article, elsewhere, in discussing the psychological significance of the dogma of the Assumption – which Jung had seen as of enormous importance for the modern age – von der Heydt (1976) expressed a similar thought: "The Incarnation is the descent of the spirit-man, thereby spiritualizing matter, earth, woman. The Assumption is the ascent of woman, earth, matter, thereby materializing heaven" (p. 76). This woman, then, experienced the numinous character of the sacrament. The symptom was symbolic and sacramental.

Von der Heydt made contributions in other areas where psychology and Catholicism meet, in essays on prayer (as "a turning inward and conscious directing of libido towards the divine image" (p. 90) and on guilt and loneliness. Her work exemplified the complementarity of Jung's work and Catholic spirituality, particularly where the religious concern was with the hollowing out of ritual and faith, leading either too rigid conformity or to indifference.

Dissolving boundaries

With Jung's work, perhaps more than with any other psychological theory or system that we consider in this book, the boundary-work between psychology and religion was at its most intense. There are a number of reasons for this, but first and foremost is that, as Victor White affirmed, Jung (whatever the limitations of his metapsychology) did address the psychological and spiritual sufferings of his contemporaries. At the level of human pain and suffering, a boundary or liminal existential position, the intellectual and institutional divides between psychology and religion dissolve. It remained easy, however, to dismiss Jung. For the Neoscholastics, Jung's lack of clearly defined boundaries between the empirical and the philosophical, his complicated theoretical framework, which he often denied having, and the still-present modernist crisis, precluded serious treatment of analytical psychology. Jung's rejection of metaphysics made it possible to repeat the familiar arguments against such positivistic-subjectivistic-phenomenalistic-Kantian positions. If analytical psychology had been simply a variant of empirical psychology, then for Catholic thinkers of the first half of the twentieth century, the boundaries would have been clear. But Jung's work did not fit into that mold, for a variety of reasons: he expanded the empirical approach to include what people experience in dreams and fantasy; he developed techniques such as amplification and active imagination for exploring what emerges often unbidden in our inner experiences and to understand what happened in analysis; he had, as critics charged, a confused philosophical foundation; he was ill-informed about some basics of Catholic theology; he was not only a detached observer of the human condition, but he was also a physician concerned with the well-being of his patients. But Jung's psychology did not fit the mold of "scientific psychology" for a deeper reason, and it was Hobson who grasped this: the issue was anxiety over the boundaries between psychology and religion.

Anxiety is not only an emotion; it is, in Heidegger's terms, a disposition or an attunement to fundamental structures of human existence. In being anxious, one confronts one's finitude, death – the possibility of one's own impossibility. In addressing the phenomena that it did, analytical psychology locates us in the boundary situations where Jung found his patients. The experience of the God-image, the experience of not being master of one's own house, i.e. the eruption of the archetypal or numinous in dreams, symptoms, and daily life, the emphasis on death, on the soul or psyche (however understood), the suffering of illness and madness, all locate us anxiously in the world. We find things and ourselves otherwise; existence has actualities and possibilities beyond what we had unanxiously considered. Coupled with this is the modernist context for the boundary-work between psychology and religion, with the persistent questioning of certainties and even dogmatic formulations, making anxiety not only a potential personal attunement to analytical psychology, but one, I would say, that is inherent in our historical moment, insofar as both psychology and the Christian religion matter.

For this reason, Goldbrunner's (mis)appropriation of Jung was close to the mark. His work faced the endemic uncertainty and flux of the century and saw in Jung's psychology elements that offer the possibility of a new synthesis of psychology and religion. White hit the mark as well, understanding that with the hypothesis of the archetypes, Jung posed a serious and important contribution to a conception of the human person. And more: a contribution to survival of civilization, threatened as it was and continues to be. Here the emphasis of the Eranos speakers, from Buonaiuti to Daniélou, so divergent in other ways, on the necessity of a return to the sources in the early Church, in myth, and in the wind of the spirit, not to repeat or restore what had been lost, but to break through the husk of dried up Western culture, on the individual and the collective level, sounds a theme in common with Jung. What was at stake was the soul.

7

Institutionalizing the relationship

There would have been no contested boundaries between Catholicism and psychology if there had not had been places – physical locations and social institutions alike – where the lines could be drawn, divisions of labor proposed, social groups formed, and authorities created. In this chapter, we turn to some of these places. Primary institutions were psychology departments at Catholic colleges and universities, because they educated the cadre of psychologists who later created other institutions and staffed the – eventually – growing number of psychology departments, child guidance clinics, and other centers of applied psychology in the Catholic community. So we look briefly at the founding of psychology departments at Catholic universities in the early years of the twentieth century. Then, we turn to three organizations of Catholics in psychology: the Chicago Society of Catholic Psychologists, the American Catholic Psychological Association (ACPA), and the Guild of Catholic Psychiatrists (not psychologists, strictly speaking, but in the psychological field nonetheless). The focus will be primarily on the ACPA, as that was the group that made the biggest impact on the Catholic community during the years of its existence, 1948–70.

These institutional responses to psychology presupposed an attunement to the new discipline's usefulness in addressing difficulties, especially in education. In the early years of the twentieth century, there was not only a push from Catholic psychologists to incorporate the discipline into the community; there was a pull from others in the community to bring it in.

The promises and perils of applied psychology

In 1908, Henry Herbert Goddard, the American psychologist working at the New Jersey School for Feebleminded Boys and Girls published an English translation of Alfred Binet's intelligence test. Goddard saw its potential to assess mental abilities, especially academic ones (Benjamin and Baker, 2004, pp. 43–4). In an early Catholic response, James J. Walsh (1914) warned that this Binet-Simon test must be used with caution, because it can blind educators to the individuality of the student: "a great deal of modern education and social science seems to have a definite tendency to treat all men alike and to make identical criteria for them, above all, attempts to develop in the same way" (p. 109). This criticism sprang from a belief that education and the social sciences neglect what is most important, the soul. It would be a warning repeated over the years, even when testing was deemed worthwhile.

Mental testing indicated psychology's promise – and danger. Following World War I, intelligence testing, having been perceived as successful in army selection procedures, was widely popular. With some ambivalence, the Catholic press began discussing it. The ambivalence showed in "Colleges and Psychological Tests" (de St. Denis, 1921) with the author stating that the tests, despite "the prevalent popular opinion" cannot determine what kind of work a person is suited for, and "I do not know of any reputable psychologist" (p. 6) that would claim that they do. Then, in conclusion, he wrote that most psychologists "cater ... to popular demands than to facts" (ibid.) regarding the tests.

This ambivalence, suggesting that many saw psychologists as both scientists and charlatans, echoed over the succeeding years. Charles P. Bruehl (1920b) saw in "the attempt to substitute psychological tests for the old-time examinations ... another indication of the drift toward materialism" (p. 588). John A. O'Brien (1921), however, writing in the same journal as Bruehl, the *Ecclesiastical Review*, saw great merit in the use of "mental tests as an auxiliary device for the proper classification of pupils" (p. 137), among other things.[1] Joseph Husslein (1922a; 1922b) also saw promise and peril in applied psychology. The promise stemmed from its potential to increase not only industrial efficiency but also worker satisfaction. The peril arose from three considerations: (1) psychological tests may promise more than they can deliver; (2) they may, as did "scientific management" (or Taylorism)[2] serve "capitalistic purposes rather than human needs" (Husslein, 1922a, p. 383); because (3) this new psychology neglects the reality that "labor has a human soul, divine in its destiny, immortal and precious far beyond the dross of wealth and profits" (ibid.). The new psychology could safely concentrate on applied topics in industry and education, so long as in the background, the larger context was secure.

The ambivalence was shared outside the Catholic community, moreover. Michael Sokal (1984) points out that in the wake of the psychologists' army work during World War I, zealous psychologists made "vastly overstated claims for the tests, despite the fact that ... the testers knew that there were important aspects of what they were measuring about which they knew little" (p. 283). By the mid-1920s, some of the enthusiasm died and with more limited claims, testing continued to be used. So Catholic interest and caution mirrored the general society on tests.

---

[1] Recall O'Brien's criticisms of psychoanalysis, discussed in Chapter 5.

[2] See Benjamin and Baker (2004, pp. 127–30) for a discussion of Taylor, scientific management, and its contentious role in industrial relations. Husslein's opinion that scientific management was anti-labor was one that he shared with labor unions.

Despite the ambivalence, some Catholic educators argued for the inclusion of mental testing in Catholic education, so long as teachers understood the limits as well as the potentials of testing. Austin G. Schmidt, SJ addressed the potential and limits of intelligence testing from the point of view of a teacher. Schmidt (1883–1960) was involved with Catholic education throughout his career. In 1912, when still a scholastic,[3] he was co-founder with William Lyons, SJ, of Loyola University Press, for the express purpose of publishing textbooks for Catholic schools. He remained with the press, later as director, for decades. He later earned a Ph.D. in education at the University of Michigan, with a dissertation entitled *The effect of objective presentation on the learning and retention of a Latin vocabulary* (1923c). In the same year, at the height of the public controversy over testing, Schmidt published a series of six articles in *America*, the Jesuit periodical, promoting the judicious use of intelligence tests in Catholic schools. He (Schmidt, 1923b) described his own experience with testing, stating that it had shown teachers the academic potential of some students who were not doing well in school. He carefully specified what the tests[4] can do, namely, assess the ability of children to succeed academically – not whether they will, since that is based on many other factors as well, and not students' suitability for a particular career. Intelligence tests, he wrote, could only do what teachers already do when they claim a student is "bright" or not, but the tests have the advantage of being quick to administer. They do not measure the soul, only "native intelligence . . . in so far as it has been developed by environment and accelerated or retarded by physical causes" (Schmidt, 1923a, p. 141). Tests prove useful in ascertaining the academic abilities of students, but cannot be used without other means, especially the observations of teachers.

This call for the judicious use of tests was repeated a couple of years later by Sister Josefita Maria (Manderfield y Salazar), SSJ (born 1880), who had a Ph.D. in education from the University of Pennsylvania.[5] She advocated the use of intelligence testing to deal with students who repeatedly fail, and who are often kept back in school until they are "promoted," or dismissed from school when they get too old to continue (Maria, 1925). She advocated the Winnetka Plan, which was developed in Winnetka, Illinois in 1919, using ideas drawn from John Dewey's progressive education. It provided such students with ungraded classes, wherein they could progress at their own rate, picking up each year where they left off in the spring, in order to avoid repeating a grade

---

[3] The Jesuit term for someone on the path to priesthood within the order after an initial period of being a novice.

[4] He referred specifically to the Stanford-Binet and the Otis tests.

[5] Her graduate research was published: *A comparative study of three social groups in the parochial schools of Philadelphia* (University of Pennsylvania education thesis, 1922) and *The status of religious instruction for children under sixteen years of age, with special reference to Pennsylvania* (Ph.D. thesis in Education, University of Pennsylvania, 1925). SSJ stands for Sisters of St. Joseph, a Philadelphia-based order.

entirely. In subsequent articles, she urged the diagnostic use of intelligence tests (Maria, 1927) and their use in vocational guidance (Maria, 1931). In the latter article, she wrote: "If the choice of an occupation, of a life work, is to be done scientifically then without doubt we must use psychological tests. Psychology is a science, and the aim of all science is certainty" (p. 137).

What this review suggests is that while there was much opposition to psychology in the Catholic world of the early twentieth century, among those who labored in the field of education, there was much interest in it. They did not seem to fear that psychology would be soulless, because it would be incorporated into the larger governing setting of Catholic education. They saw the potential, as did others in the field of education, for its usefulness. At the same time, such use of testing succeeded in bringing into the Catholic community psychology's discursive objects, such as "intelligence." However, it is important not to overstate the extent to which the efforts of educators such as Schmidt and Josefita Maria were successful. There continued to be resistance and disinterest in psychology's applied potential for education (and for child guidance) for decades to come. What was also necessary was the establishment of psychological institutions within the Catholic world.

Before leaving this topic, however, a final note on the driving force behind this interest in testing, especially among the writers in *America*. This periodical, founded by the Jesuits in 1909, advocated Catholic positions in social justice issues, inspired in part by Leo XIII's encyclical, *Rerum Novarum*, of 1891.[6] Seeking a "middle course" between laissez-faire capitalism and socialism, these Catholic thinkers fought for workers' rights and sought governmental regulation of minimum wage and child labor, among other things. These positions constituted Catholic participation in the progressive movement of the early twentieth century. So it is no accident that Joseph Husslein, Thomas Verner Moore, Paul Furfey, John A. Ryan, and others, including Paul L. Blakely, SJ (who supported Moore's call for greater attention to the "problem child in the parish school" at the National Catholic Education Association (NCEA) meeting in 1930, for instance) saw the potential of scientific psychology. As Rademacher (2007) said of Moore – the statement could be extended to many whom this chapter considers – he combined psychology and practical social reform in his efforts, because he promoted the Church's social teachings.

Psychology in Catholic higher education

In one sense, the story of the establishment of psychology departments at Catholic universities was no different than their founding in most American colleges and universities. Enormous changes took place in the waning years of

---

[6] See Pope Leo XIII, *The great encyclical letters of Pope Leo XIII* (1903, pp. 208–48). The Latin title came from the first words of the Latin text: "Of new things."

the nineteenth and the early years of the twentieth centuries in higher education. There was increasing specialization of subjects taught and the administrative creation of departments. At the university level, an increased dedication to the faculty as producers of new knowledge, especially scientific knowledge, came to the fore during the Progressive Age. The broader picture has been covered elsewhere (Gleason, 1995; McGovern, 1992). In general, Catholic institutions were slower to form scientific psychology programs than their secular peers, but there were notable exceptions. What follows is not meant to be a complete account of these departments, but rather of how several helped to institutionalize psychology within the Catholic community in the United States. To this end, I focus on graduate training, because that led to the spread of psychology, and to the application of psychology in Catholic settings. Misiak and Staudt (1954) listed four "noteworthy departments of psychology" (p. 256), and it is this group that are of interest here.

St. Louis University

Psychology as a branch of philosophy first was taught at St. Louis University in 1883 (Overby, 1990, p. 3). Primarily a philosophical course on the soul, this subject was taught not only in the School of Philosophy and Science, but also in the schools of "Commerce and Finance and Education" (pp. 3–4). Over the next two decades, a number of scholars, including Thomas Aloysius Hughes (1849–1939), noted for his history of the Jesuit order and author of *Principles of anthropology and biology* (1890) taught a variety of philosophical psychology courses.[7] Hughes' course in 1885 included topics such as "reflex action and intellect" (Overby, 1990, p. 4). Only with the arrival of Hubert Gruender (1870–1940), SJ, did the situation change.

Gruender came to St. Louis University in 1907 to teach philosophy. After studying experimental psychology with Külpe in Berlin in 1912–13, he returned to St. Louis. Gruender investigated and taught topics such as sensation, including color blindness, but he always kept an eye on the philosophical foundations of the science. His textbook and laboratory manual, *An introductory course in experimental psychology* (Gruender, 1920), probably indicates the character of his courses. Gruender's Neoscholastic psychology sought a synthesis of philosophical and empirical psychology, as we have seen above (in Chapter 3). Gruender was named professor of psychology in 1917, almost a decade before the university formed a psychology department. When it began in 1926, Gruender was the chairman, and he was joined by Raphael C. McCarthy, SJ, William J. Ryan, SJ, and William D. Commins.[8]

---

[7] See Chapter 3, for a dispute Hughes had with Pace over modern psychology and education.

[8] Overby (1990) claims that St. Louis University had "the oldest psychology department at a Jesuit university" (p. 12).

But for a department really to institutionalize relationships between psychology and the Church, it needed a graduate program. A masters program began in 1927, in a department that drew on Jesuit faculty from several departments (1929–31), including sociology (taught by Joseph Husslein, SJ, whom we have met earlier in this chapter), moral theology and religious history (Overby, 1990, p. 21). As a result, "the philosophical stance of the department . . . persevered in bucking the trend toward behaviorism . . . The central tenets of the behaviorist school, particularly the denial of free will, were anathema to the Thomistic perspective of a Jesuit university" (ibid.).

Raphael McCarthy left St. Louis in 1936. In the mid-1930s, Francis L. Harmon became part of the department, and in 1940 Francis T. Severin, SJ joined it. With World War II, the graduate program was suspended (Severin, 1953). With the arrival of Walter L. Wilkins in 1949, the masters program returned (Overby, 1990, p. 33). Wilkins, with a Ph.D. in 1933, had trained as a clinician during the war, and in St. Louis he forged links between the department and the Veterans Administration Hospital as well as the Archdiocesan Guidance Center (pp. 33–4).[9] Wilkins left St. Louis in 1959 for a post at the Navy Medical Neuropsychiatric Research Unit (Davenport, 1990, p. 41) in San Diego,[10] and Harmon in 1961 for a position in personnel at the Department of Agriculture (p. 26). A doctoral program began around this time, with the first doctorate awarded in 1964:

> At the start of the 1967–68 academic year the clinical and general-experimental graduate programs were well established. . . . By this time we had graduated 37 Ph.D.s (22 clinical, 15 experimental). Of these 18 became academics, 2 entered non-academic research, and 15 went to clinical settings.
>
> (Davenport, 1990, p. 49)[11]

Even before the doctoral program began, the department had had a strong interest in topics and services relevant to relationships between psychology and the Church. Commins, who taught there between 1926 and 1931, wrote on educational issues (Commins, 1937) and "was involved in the administration of the intelligence tests given to all freshmen" (Overby, 1990, p. 13). McCarthy's work in the area of "mental hygiene" (p. 17), especially in childhood and adolescence, had wide influence in Catholic circles, and he was "on the lecture circuit" (p. 16) during those years. Courses in "tests and measurements" were taught from the late 1920s, and there was much work in educational

---

[9] Overby (1990, p. 34) credits Wilkins with the founding of the ACPA, along with Doyle and Bier.

[10] Davenport (1990, p. 41) states that one reason Wilkins left was "his frustration with the lack of progress towards establishing a Ph.D. program."

[11] Three of the first dissertations were by Nancy Y. Brown, John F. Cross, and Gerard Egan. Brown and Cross subsequently taught at St. Louis University.

psychology – and with the Education Department (pp. 18–19). Various courses in applied psychology populated the curriculum over the decades, as well as the more philosophical courses (p. 36).

What emerges from this look at the psychology department at St. Louis University is that, during the years preceding 1965, psychology took shape there that had philosophical, experimental, and applied foci. Especially in the first and third of these interests were the connections with the Catholic community established. Further investigations into the involvement of the department in education would show, no doubt, the extent to which psychology made an impact in the lives of children, adolescents, and their families.

Doyle and Loyola University of Chicago

One of McCarthy's students at St. Louis was Charles Ignatius Doyle, SJ (1889–1973). After entering the Jesuits and completing theological studies, Doyle worked for *America*, the Jesuit magazine, from 1927 to 1931. While there, he wrote the occasional article on psychological topics. It was in 1931 that he began graduate work in psychology at St. Louis under McCarthy. While a number of masters degrees were conferred in these early years at St. Louis, only one doctorate was awarded in psychology, and that was to Doyle in 1933. Doyle's dissertation, *An Experimental Investigation of the Process of Inductive Discovery with Groups of Closely Similar Problems of Variable Complexity*, was a study of learning based on Binet (Overby, 1990, p. 24). He then went to Loyola University in Chicago to teach psychology. The psychology department was established there in 1934, when the "Department of Philosophy and Psychology," created in 1931, was divided.[12] Alexander Schneiders and Marcella Twomey (1901–89) joined him in the department in the mid-1930s. Twomey worked as a psychologist for the Bureau of Child Study in Chicago, which was under the Board of Education. She "taught the first practice course in individual psychological testing in 1934" and two years later, she proposed a new course, "Clinical Psychology of Childhood" (Wauck, 1980, p. 4).[13] Schneiders' strengths were in applied areas, and he "immediately set about establishing a student counseling and testing service which also assumed responsibility for all entering Freshman testing as part of admissions" (Wauck, 1980, p. 4). When Vincent Herr, SJ (1901–70) joined the department in 1939, Doyle began to put his energies into the establishment of a psychological clinic for children.

---

[12] Wauck (1980) writes that at Loyola, a departmental system was set up in 1926, and that George Mahowald, SJ, the head of the philosophy department, "began to equip a psychological laboratory" (p. 1) in 1927.

[13] Twomey (1936) wrote "The question of intelligence tests."

Herr, an American with a masters degree in psychology from St. Louis University, had studied with Charlotte and Karl Bühler before receiving a doctorate from the University of Bonn, where the Würzburg approach was still practiced, in 1939.[14] Herr became chair of the department in 1945. After the war, the doctoral program began (in 1946), the clinical psychology program developed, and among the new faculty members were Frank J. Kobler in 1946, Magda Arnold in 1952, Charles A. Curran in 1955, Leroy Wauck in 1963, and Eugene Kennedy in 1969.[15] At least into the 1950s, philosophical psychology was still taught at Loyola, but Wauck claimed in 1970 that there was at the time little difference between Catholic and secular programs.

With Herr in the department, Doyle turned to forming the Loyola Center for Child Guidance and Psychological Services (later called the Charles I. Doyle, SJ, Center), which opened in 1941. By 1945, the demands of the clinic were such that Doyle stepped down as chair, and Herr took over that position. Doyle ran the clinic until 1963. In the 1950s, the staff at the clinic included Arnold, Kobler, Twomey, and William Joseph Devlin, SJ, as a consulting psychiatrist. Graduate students received training there in "interviewing, testing, counseling, remedial reading, and play therapy" (Snider, 1953, p. 2). Like St. Louis University, Loyola developed a program that included a number of specialties, and also like its fellow Jesuit university in Missouri, established itself in the community at the local, diocesan, and state level.[16] One significant project resulted from a 1956 National Institute of Mental Health grant. Gillespie (2001) describes the scope of the work, which included the study of psychological characteristics of seminarians and priests, as well as the establishment of pastoral counseling classes for seminarians (pp. 60-1). *Psychodynamics of personality development* (1964), by the psychiatrist, Devlin, was based on his lectures for the Loyola Mental Health Project. The book, intended for priests and seminarians, was published after Devlin's untimely death, with Herr, Kobler, Doyle, and others (including William Guppy, who later taught at

[14] At Bonn, Herr studied under the Catholic psychologist, Siegfried Behn (1884–1970), who in 1931 continued the work of Oswald Külpe's school. Behn wrote on pedagogy, aesthetics, and ethics, among other topics (see Misiak and Staudt, 1954, pp. 222–3). He edited Külpe's papers on aesthetics: *Grundlagen der ästhetik: aus dem nachlass* (1921).

[15] Wauck (1980) lists some of the graduates of Loyola's program who went on to found or build psychology departments at other Catholic colleges, including: Marquette (LeRoy Wauck, George Zimny, and Eugene Welsand), Villanova (Eugene Welsand and Eugene Albrecht), St. Mary's in California (Frederick Whalen), and Seattle University (James Royce, SJ).

[16] For example, Wauck (1980, p. 11) details how he and Tom Kennedy, another Loyola alum and fellow faculty member, were active in the Illinois Psychological Association (IPA). They worked to get legislation registering psychologists in Illinois. Wauck was nominated three times to be president of the IPA. He also served on the archdiocesan marriage tribunal in Chicago for many years (at least 20, he informed me in 1999). Wauck served on the Board of Psychological Examiners, as did other Loyola faculty (Frank Kobler and Rod Pugh).

Seattle University) aiding in the publication.[17] Gillespie also describes psychological studies of a group of priests and bishops carried out by Loyola psychologists, the latter studies funded by the National Conference of Catholic Bishops. These accomplishments indicate great institutionalization of modern psychology in Catholic circles by 1970.

Fordham University

Fordham has probably the most interesting pre-history of the four, since Carl Jung spoke there in 1912, when he and the neurologist, Henry Head, famous for his studies of pain and the nervous system, received honorary degrees. However, the invitation came from Fordham's medical school, where James Walsh was dean at the time.[18] Fordham discontinued its medical school in 1921. Also before the psychology department began, there was a Mental Hygiene Department in the School of Social Services in the 1920s, with Walsh back on the faculty, teaching physiological psychology (Behnke, n. d.). Psychology was also being offered in the School of Psychology, Measurement and Elementary School Supervision in the late 1920s. So even before the psychology department officially began, Fordham had a longtime involvement in the greater New York area in applied fields of psychology. As at other Catholic colleges, philosophical psychology was taught in the philosophy department, and it was from the philosophy department that the psychology department was formed by Walter G. Summers, SJ (1889–1938) in 1933 (William C. Bier, 1953c). Among the first faculty was Dorothea McCarthy (1906–74), who had joined the Education Department in 1932. From the start, work at the masters and doctoral levels was part of the curriculum, while the undergraduate program began somewhat later, in 1939. While Summers was an experimentalist, with research in lie detection, he established guidance courses and Fordham's Child Guidance Clinic, first at St. Vincent's Hospital, and then on campus in 1937 (William C. Bier, 1953c). Fordham developed a number of connections with area hospitals and agencies over the years, contributing in areas of mental health and law enforcement, to name two. For present purposes, what stands out in Fordham's history is the role of William C. Bier, SJ. The founder of the ACPA – to which we shall turn

[17] Devlin (1905–61) had a doctorate in psychology from the Catholic University in 1943 with a dissertation entitled *The effect of certain pharmacological preparations on the emotions of normal and psychotic individuals* (Devlin, 1942). He then went on to an M.D. from the Loyola University medical school. Gillespie (2001, p. 58) states that Thomas Verner Moore had hoped that Devlin would replace him as chair of the Department of Psychology and Psychiatry in Washington.
[18] Walsh was dean when Head and Jung spoke in September; he resigned under pressure in November of the same year in what appears to have been a power struggle with the president of the university.

anon – Bier was instrumental in a number of areas that helped to establish psychology in Catholic circles. Foremost among them was a series of conferences on pastoral psychology, held between 1955 and 1977, to which we will turn in Chapter 9.

The Catholic University of America

Catholic University had the oldest of the four psychology programs. Edward Aloysius Pace began teaching psychology in 1891, after returning with a doctorate in psychology from Wundt's institute in Leipzig. Psychology courses were taught first under theology and then under philosophy, until a department was established in the school of philosophy in 1905. Right from the beginning, Pace disseminated scientific psychology widely in the Catholic world. In the summer of 1896, for example, Pace lectured on psychology at Catholic Summer Schools in Plattsburg, New York, and Madison, Wisconsin, as well as on pedagogy at St. Mary's Convent, Notre Dame, Indiana. Records show similar activity throughout the last decade of the nineteenth century and the first of the twentieth.[19] While Pace set the pace, so to speak, his colleague, Thomas Edward Shields (1862–1921) was the psychologist who, from 1902, sought to advance Catholic education by drawing out the implications of empirical psychology (Shields, 1917).[20] This activity shows concretely how Pace and his colleagues were bringing psychology to the Catholic community in the early days of the new empirical psychology. Shields focused on religious education as the core of all education, and he combined empirical findings with Aristotelian principles, arguing against rote memorization in the young, countering that since mental development begins in sensation, feelings, and imagination, stories and music should play critical roles in early education. This activity also suggests receptivity on the part of Catholic teachers to the value of scientific psychology.

The early program was largely in experimental psychology until Thomas Verner Moore taught the first clinical psychology course, "A clinic for the examination of defective children" (Stafford, 1953) in 1916. Graduate education in psychology preceded the undergraduate program, which began in the

[19] For example, in 1900, he lectured "about two hundred teachers in the parochial and public schools of Chicago ... The subjects were treated with a practical view on the bearing of psychology on the work of teachers" on the following topics in psychology: sensation, imagination, association, thought, emotion, will, mental development, and the soul (University chronicle, 1900). In 1901, he gave lectures to the Sisters of St. Joseph in the diocese of Springfield, Massachusetts.

[20] Shields (1916) wrote: "It would, indeed, be difficult to overstate the benefits which education has derived in recent years from the biological sciences both directly and indirectly through modern psychology" (p. 233). Shields became head of the newly created Department of Education at the Catholic University in 1909. Shields and Pace founded the Catholic Educational Review in 1911.

1940s (Stafford, 1950). Graduate studies leading to the doctorate began in 1921, and it is significant that in addition to a dissertation using "empirical methods," students had to "acquaint themselves in a practical manner with the problems which a psychologist may be called upon to handle in a school, clinic, and the vocational bureau" (quoted in Stafford, 1953). A generation of scholars emerged, some of whom established psychology programs elsewhere: in addition to Sommers beginning the department at Fordham, James Moynihan, SJ, set one up at Boston College (Gillespie, 2001, p. 45), as did Timothy Gannon at Loras College.

Always with an eye to the Church's teachings on social justice, Moore sought to open a child guidance clinic, and to that end obtained a medical degree from Johns Hopkins in 1915. His clinic for children opened in 1916 at Providence Hospital – "the first psychiatric outpatient department in Washington" (Gillespie, 2001, p. 38) – and in 1937, the clinic moved to campus (Moore, 1948, p. 46). From the beginning, the clinic had the cooperation of social services in the District of Columbia and of Catholic Charities (Neenan, 2000, p. 104). In 1926, he helped establish St. Gertrude's School of Arts and Crafts for developmentally challenged girls near the university campus (Peixotto, 1969, p. 847).

In 1939, Moore obtained a grant from the Rockefeller Foundation to develop the Child Center further to provide training in psychiatry and, according to what Neenan (2000, p. 195) reports, it was the first such training program in a Catholic setting.

In 1936, Moore published results of a study on the incidence of mental illness among members of the religious life (1936b; 1936c). While he had found that the overall rate of mental illness among priests and other religious was lower than the general population, if mental illness as a result of syphilis is excluded from the data, the rate is higher. Moore suggested that such a life is attractive to some "pre-psychotic" personalities. In follow-ups to this study, a series of dissertations were completed under Moore's supervision – Thomas J. McCarthy (1942), H. R. Burke, SS (1947), B. G. Lhota, OFM (1948), and most significantly, William C. Bier, SJ (1948a). By the end of the 1940s, the psychological assessment of applicants to seminaries and religious communities was gaining momentum, but I delay discussion of this topic for the moment, and will return to it when looking at Bier's initiatives with the ACPA.

Chicago Society of Catholic Psychologists

In 1936, Doyle, together with "a student from De Paul University, one from Mundelein, another from a teachers' college representing the Chicago Public Educational field" (Sister Mary Roberta Roberts, 1947, p. 3) organized the Chicago Society of Catholic Psychologists. From the start, it was conceived as a regional association. Membership was open to "all in Chicago and vicinity who are interested in psychology" (Announcing the first meeting of the Chicago Society of Catholic Psychologists, 1936), including students, philosophers, sociologists, and others. Doyle was the first secretary-treasurer. The first general meeting was held on May 16, 1936 at Loyola University, at which time a constitution was adopted. The purpose of the Society was:

> An organization to create a sense of solidarity, to stimulate study and research, to acquaint workers in various parts of the field, philosophical, experimental, and applied (the last-named including especially psychiatry, education, child guidance, and social work), with the principles, viewpoints, and methods of those working in other branches of psychology, and finally, through the group consciousness thus aroused, to lead to a closer integration of theoretical and applied psychology with the principles of Scholastic philosophy and of the Catholic Church.

> (ibid.)

To illustrate how these intentions were actualized, here is a list of the speakers from the first general meeting:

> Comerford O'Malley, C. M., De Paul University, "The Rational Approach to Psychological Investigation';
> Marie A. Halliman, Chicago Normal College, "Education of the Child for the Future";
> John W. Stafford, C. S. V. (St. Viator College), "Catholic Participation in the Mental Hygiene Movement";
> Eligius Weir, O. F. M. (St. Francis College), "The Psychological Effect of Penal Servitude."

> (ibid.)

Other topics over the next few years included psychoanalysis, intelligence testing, and personality theory. Doyle (in Sister Mary Roberta Roberts, 1947) later recounted that the presentations were of the nature of a "practical discussion" (p. 3).[21]

Membership in the early years grew rapidly. Doyle (1937a) reported 110 individual members, with Barat College, De Paul University, Immaculata College, Loyola University, and Mundelein College as institutional members. Rosary College (now Dominican University) joined them that year. By the end of that year, Doyle (1937b) reported 129 individual and 12 institutional members.

Early members included Sister M. Thomas Aquinas, OP, of Rosary College, Sister M. Dolores, OSB, a Professor of Education and Philosophy at De Paul

---

[21] I have been unable to locate any publications of the Society, and perhaps they do not exist. Doyle (1937a) wrote that, "members have been asking about the publication of our proceedings. They want the papers and discussions issued in permanent form. Plans are still indefinite, for lack of adequate funds."

University, Alexander A. Schneiders, Vincent Herr, SJ of Loyola University, and Miriam Loughran Rooney. Rooney (1897–1988) had been educated at Trinity College (the women's college associated with the Catholic University), with a masters degree in psychology. Her thesis with Moore (Loughran, 1919) was published in the *Psychological Monograph* series. Her doctoral dissertation, *The historical development of child-labor legislation in the United States* (Loughran, 1921) was done at the Catholic University, with Ryan and Moore as her readers. She did statistical research for the U.S. Army during World War I, legal research for the Children's Bureau, as well as work with the National Catholic Welfare Conference in the early 1920s. She was a Professor of Psychology at Loyola University from 1923 and at Mundelein College from 1931. In the 1940s, she was vice-president of the Chicago Society. This brief overview of Rooney's career samples the kinds of people and interests drawn to the Society.[22]

A later member of the Chicago Society was LeRoy Wauck (1920–2009). Wauck obtained a bachelor's degree in psychology in 1941 and after serving in the Navy during the war, he returned to Loyola, where he earned a doctorate in psychology in 1956. He established a psychology department at Marquette University in the 1950s, then taught at De Paul University from 1958 to 1963, at which time he returned to Loyola, where he taught until retirement in 1983 (Graydon, 2009). In addition, he was a clinician and heavily involved in Catholic education in the Chicago area. He held offices in the Chicago Society, stating with some humor: "Many of us took turns serving as President after being 'elected' by one of Charlie's [Doyle] 'nominating' committees" (Wauck, 1980, p. 6). He also wrote that the Society was "strong and vital through the fifties" (p. 6). During this period, as Doyle reported (in Sister Mary Roberta Roberts, 1947), the Society could claim influence: "one of the by-products of the organization was a quickening of interests in the field of psychology among the members in the region of Chicago, Ohio, and Missouri. And through the Middle West we can trace from that, the establishment of two or three different branches of psychology and a number of laboratories in colleges that formerly did not have them" (p. 3). Probably because the Society was not limited to psychologists, it could have had this kind of widespread effect.

Before turning to the national organization prefigured in important ways by the Society, it is worth noting that the history of the Chicago Society illustrates the confluence of three aspects of American social life in the interwar years: increasing extension of psychology into applied areas, especially education; Catholic culture, with its own institutions that were at their peak of flourishing,

---

[22] She presented a paper at the 1939 spring meeting of the Chicago Society on "Personality in sociology." Information on Rooney: Vita in Loughran, 1921, p. 113; *American Catholic Who's Who*, vol. 7 1946–7, p. 381. For Sister M. Dolores, see ibid., p. 396.

and larger American interest in using science to improve life. We see the interrelations between psychology, the Church, and the larger society even more strongly in the next two organizations we consider.

The American Catholic Psychological Association

During and after World War II, there was great foment in American psychology. Psychologists participated actively in the war effort, supplying a variety of psychological services and conducting research. In 1944, the American Psychological Association (APA) re-organized and incorporated the American Association of Applied Psychology, signaling expansion of the field and a turn in the field generally toward an applied emphasis.

This turn was not only psychology's to make. Mental health had become a political issue at the federal level. Herman (1995) calls this "job of maintaining mass emotional control" (p. 241) an impetus behind significant legislation. The problem of the "adjustment" of returning veterans was one big concern. The 1944 "Servicemen's Readjustment Act" (called the G. I. Bill), originally proposed to avoid mass unemployment (Edmondson, 2002, p. 824), authorized veterans to receive educational benefits, swelling the number of college students in the subsequent years. Between 1944 and 1951, over 2,300,000 veterans attended colleges and universities. They could attend Catholic institutions under the Bill, as it did not discriminate against religiously sponsored schools, and enrollment at Catholic colleges grew from 569,136 in 1945 to 1,261,565 in 1947 (Gleason, 1995, p. 210).[23] The National Institute for Mental Health was established in 1946, which funded training and research in psychotherapy (Baker and Benjamin, 2005). In 1947 the Veterans Administration (VA) began funding training programs in clinical psychology at universities across the country, including two Catholic universities: Catholic University and Fordham (Baker and Pickren, 2007, pp. 21–2; Capshew, 1999). The effect of these government programs was to provide growth opportunities to Catholic higher education.

The moment was right both politically and economically for Catholics to move out of their "ghetto" into the mainstream of American society (Massa, 1999, p. 34). The period in which "discrimination against Catholics to keep them out of posts of leadership, regardless of their merits" (Ellis, 1956, p. 148) was ending. In the late 1940s, there was little Catholic participation in psychology, a situation that had changed by the time the American Catholic Psychological Association (ACPA) voted to re-organize into a non-sectarian

[23] "The insularity of Catholics broke down dramatically with the G. I. Bill ... 'The G. I. Bill may have had more of an impact on the Catholic Church than the Second Vatican Council,' observes David C. Leege, director of Notre Dame's ongoing study of Catholic parish life" (Berger, 1987, p. 64).

group in 1969. The time during which the ACPA existed, 1948–70, marked a distinct historical moment for the United States, for psychology, and for American Catholics. At the beginning of the period, American Catholics touted a distinct culture and self-conscious sense of inferiority; by the end, the general sense was that Catholics had assimilated into U.S. society. The history of the ACPA is part of that narrative. It is not a story of significant strides in theory or research. It is one of building institutions within the Catholic community, through an emphasis on higher education and applied work in psychology (see Staudt, 1955). And a story of how, some twenty years after its founding, the organization transformed itself into an ecumenical association.

A Catholic ghetto?

Although the first half of the twentieth century witnessed a flowering of a distinctive Catholic culture, by mid-century, a widespread and contentious opinion circulated that American Catholic intellectual life was seriously deficient. The causes of a perceived lackluster performance in the arts and sciences were manifold: the Church had long been preoccupied with assimilating immigrants, who had more pressing needs than higher education; the aftermath of the Americanist and modernist crises of the early twentieth century had had the effect of concentrating much intellectual activity within a tight circumference, centering on apologetics; and economic constraints in Catholic higher education left little time for faculty research and publication. For the eminent historian, John Tracy Ellis (1955), the primary reason why Catholic intellectual life was wanting was a "self-imposed ghetto mentality" (p. 386), which "prevents them from mingling as they should with their non-Catholic colleagues, and in their lack of industry and the habits of work" (ibid.).[24] Now "mingling as they should" was complicated, because in the period between the world wars, there was suspicion among non-Catholics about Catholic commitments to democracy and the American way of life. Vatican support for Franco was a major issue, and "political Catholicism" was feared as inherently fascist (Gleason, 1995, p. 262). This is not the complete picture, yet such criticisms did result in Catholic defensiveness

---

[24] The first use of the term may have been by Paul Reinhart, SJ, president of St. Louis University, who in 1950, "warned his fellow Catholic educators to avoid succumbing to a 'ghetto mentality'" (cited in Gleason, 1995, p. 219). Ellis borrowed the term, "ghetto" from Heinrich Rommen (1897–1967) of Georgetown University, who warned against a "flight into a Catholic ghetto" (1955). James E. Royce, SJ (1956) said of Viktor Frankl's *The Doctor and the Soul* that this book "may well signal the end of the ghetto mentality for Catholics in the field" of psychology, not because Frankl was Catholic – which he was not – but because in this book "a really leading European psychiatrist speaks out openly and forcibly for spiritual values" (p. 4).

and self-protection. Moreover, in the 1950s, "anti-intellectualism was closely associated with McCarthyism. Since Catholics were widely assumed to be overwhelmingly pro-McCarthy, Catholic liberals, who abominated the junior senator from Wisconsin, had special reason to be concerned about anti-intellectualism" (p. 288). To speak of a Catholic ghetto was to participate in an internal debate within the American Church. That this analysis resonated within the ACPA was evident by comments made at the 1947 organizing meeting, and in an article by Sister Mary Amatora (Tschechtelin) (1954a), who reviewed studies of leadership in American psychology and science, and found very few Catholics, if any, included.

Yet there was an air of hyperbole in the talk of Catholic ghettos, as the theologian, Martin E. Marty (1982) later noted. He observed that much of Catholic life did not constitute a separate enclave, and American society was in no way monolithic – there being other "ghettos," as many religious and ethnic groups in the United States lived in segregation or isolated themselves from the broader community. Indeed, Catholics were not the most notable of the "ghettoized" cultures, in many respects. Nevertheless, in the 1940s and 1950s, there was a clearly marked Catholic community in the United States, and its members by and large felt, even as they were strongly patriotic, that they belonged to a group apart.

Formation of the ACPA, 1947–50

William C. Bier, SJ (1911–80), was the driving force behind the organization. At the 1946 APA meeting, Bier initiated movement toward an association by speaking with other Catholic psychologists about the idea.[25] On that basis, Bier (1947a) urged psychologists whom he identified as Catholic to attend the 1947 APA meeting and join him in a discussion of a possible organization. His initial appeal was to topics of interest among Catholics: "many Catholic students and teachers of scientific psychology have become aware of the fact that modern psychology poses many problems and occupies areas of study which have no interest for the non-Catholic psychologist, and hence are not subjects treated in the APA meetings." The suggested organization would remedy this exclusion. This may have sounded a "separatist" note to some, for it did not become the

---

[25] Bier's effort took place at the same time that the Catholic Commission on Intellectual and Cultural Affairs began: "The aims of the CCICA as it took shape in 1946 were to mobilize the energies of American Catholic intellectuals ... and facilitate their participation in UNESCO and other bodies working for cultural unity in a broken world. It intended, according to an *America* item doubtless written by [John Courtney] Murray, to be 'Catholic indeed, but not "separatist"'" (Gleason, 1995, p. 225). Murray, a leading theologian, was like Bier a Jesuit. Ellis's 1955 critique of American Catholic intellectual life was given at a CCICA meeting (p. 288).

major focus during the organizational meetings that led to the ACPA.[26] Concerns about a "ghetto mentality" were to be behind the founding.

Doyle's organization in Chicago was the precursor of the ACPA. "In a way, the ACPA was an 'outgrowth' of the Chicago Society, which was in effect absorbed by the ACPA" (Personal communication, LeRoy Wauck, October, 1999). This recollection is supported by what Bier stated at the organizational meeting of the ACPA (in Sister Mary Roberta Roberts, 1947, p. 2). Bier also mentioned the existence of the American Catholic Philosophical Association and related groups in education, sociology, and economics. The type of organization already existed.

At the 1947 APA Convention in Detroit, some 110 people met with Bier (1947b) at Mercy College. The meeting opened with words from Rev. Arthur Reckinger of the college: "We are cognizant of the importance of this field of learning, and are fully aware of the fact that many non-Catholics have brought suspicion upon it. Those of us who have heard confessions know the wrong concepts that teaching of this kind can bring, and any step to counteract such instruction is praiseworthy" (Sister Mary Roberta Roberts, 1947, p. 1). This note of suspicion toward psychology was a familiar one, but it did not dominate the conversation. MIT researcher, Edward Aloysius Monaghan, a former student of Thomas Verner Moore, gave a counter-argument during the meeting:

> I think that all Catholics should accept the fact that psychology is a science, and that it should be developed in Catholic institutions; moreover, Catholic men and women should be encouraged to study the field of psychology. If Catholics participating in the field of psychology would get together and exchange views, it would be better. I believe that we should promote our philosophical ideas. In the advancement of ideas of psychology, I feel there are dangers also, especially if we do not restrict ourselves to the development of science among sciences. We should not take over the functions of the department of Rome.
>
> (p. 6)

The ACPA formed between these two views, representing the primary groups that defined the limits of the possible for the association: it had to appeal to Catholic clerics and educators, many of whom were suspicious of psychology, and it had to appeal to mainstream American psychologists. Not that the APA leadership seemed to have had any objections to the formation of the group. Some in attendance at the 1947 meeting wondered if the APA would support such a move. Raymond McCall, then at St. John's University, suggested that "we should get a sample of non-Catholic opinion" (p. 5) about the formation of a Catholic group. No such study was undertaken, but Reckinger and McCall gave

---

[26] Earlier studies chronicle the history of the ACPA and its two transformations: Gillespie (2001), Kugelmann (2000), Reuder (1999).

voice to the objections that in part lay behind the formation of the association.[27] The Rev. Edwin C. Garvey of Assumption College, Windsor, Ontario, warned "if it [the proposed association] should lead to any isolation, then surely we do not want it" (p. 9). Richard Zegers, SJ, noted that professional societies of Catholics in philosophy, sociology, and history already existed.[28] Sister Annette Walters CSJ, (1910–78) of the College of St. Catherine, observed that an organization of Catholic psychologists might alleviate the mistrust of religious superiors toward psychology and pave the way for it to be "respectable for a religious to be a psychologist" (p. 12).[29]

Over the next year and one half the ACPA took shape, with a constitution approved by the membership in January 1949. The statement of purpose underwent a series of modifications. The original constitution (Constitution of the American Catholic Psychological Association, 1949) stated that the purpose "shall be to promote, as Catholics, the development and integration of theoretical, experimental, and applied psychology" (p. 1). Any ambiguity in this formulation was clarified when an announcement appeared in the *American Psychologist* of the founding of the ACPA: it "aims at furthering the development of psychology in Catholic circles" (Psychological news and notes, 1949, p. 366). A year later, a second aim appeared in the *American Psychologist*: "to further the integration of scientific psychology with a Catholic viewpoint" (Psychological news and notes, 1950, p. 644). Even though Catholics constituted a small percentage of APA membership, the ranks of the ACPA began with a healthy number and increased steadily until the mid-1960s.

Statements of aims were not the only means by which the ACPA defined itself. The group's identity was achieved by restricting membership to those who were (and initially could become) members of the APA. As Bier (1967a) explained it later, "in establishing the Association care was taken to mitigate the tendency that might be created . . . to draw Catholics away from the main body of psychologists" (p. 399). That the ACPA aimed primarily at getting Catholics to participate more actively in scientific psychology was one of Bier's, and the organization's, overriding concerns. To further this end, ACPA meetings were held in conjunction with the annual APA convention. At the 1949 meeting, Bier observed that among the 600 psychologists presenting papers, etc., at the

---

[27] Misiak and Staudt (1954) write that "several prominent non-Catholic psychologists were consulted in order to appraise their attitudes toward the proposed association. Since they were sympathetic and, in fact, lent their encouragement, added confidence was felt by the planners" (p. 262).

[28] Zegers (1909–80) was Bier's colleague at Fordham. Zegers had a doctorate in psychology from Columbia University and did research in visual psychophysics (Rev. Richard Zegers, 70, a professor at Fordham, 1980).

[29] Sister Annette Walters was later active in efforts to improve the education and professional possibilities of women religious. CSJ refers to the Sisters of St. Joseph of Carondelet. See Gillespie (2001) for further biographical information.

convention that year, there were only ten Catholics. In 1949 as well, the ACPA Board of Directors agreed, "that the term 'psychological' refers to modern or empirical psychology, not to philosophical psychology." This restriction broke with an earlier "separate but equal" status between empirical and philosophical (i.e. Neoscholastic) psychology in Catholic higher education, and it was explicitly designed to exclude those who taught only philosophy from membership (Minutes of the April 15th 1950 meeting of the Board of Directors of the American Catholic Psychological Association, 1950, p. 1).[30] The ACPA intended to lead Catholics out of a Neoscholastic ghetto and into the larger domain of natural scientific psychology. Gleason (1989), in looking at a number of groups similar to the ACPA and originating at around the same time, writes: "Metaphorically, the founders were the first Catholic 'immigrants' to these professional worlds" (p. 67), and that a major purpose of these associations was assimilation into the mainstream.[31]

The ACPA functioned as a professional association. Such groups, including the APA, sought to define the boundaries between expertise needed to make scientific knowledge claims and other types of knowledge (or pseudo-knowledge). In other words, as a professional group, the ACPA engaged in "boundary work" (Gieryn, 1983), especially vis-à-vis philosophical psychology. The ACPA resembled other groups seeking to secure professional status by controlling entry into the field by defining "psychology" as an empirical science. It was not primarily attempting to secure the expertise of psychologists per se, although as licensing boards were established during the 1950s, some ACPA members were charter members. Its efforts were to establish psychological expertise within the Catholic community, where it did not yet have a secure foundation, because philosophical psychologists claimed to have theoretical knowledge of the human soul, and the Church had long practiced forms of the *cura animarum*, the cure of souls, and pastoral care.

Being a small group within psychology, and psychology viewed with some suspicion within the American Catholic Church, how did the ACPA exert influence and seek change? Individual action on the part of members was a primary vehicle, aided by annual meetings, which encouraged Catholic psychologists to attend the APA convention, and by the Newsletter, which was

---

[30] At the 1948 meeting, a proposed amendment to the constitution to have "a representative or representatives of the Hierarchy under the caption of Patrons or Honorary Members" was not approved (Sister Mary (McGrath)), 1948 No. 1532, p. 5).

[31] The ACPA was neither the first nor the last of such professional organizations of Catholic of this period. There were templates for such groups: the National Catholic Educational Association began in 1904; the American Catholic Philosophical Association was founded in 1926; the Catholic Round Table of Science (founded 1928); the American Catholic Sociological Society (founded 1938); the Albertus Magnus Guild (for the natural sciences, founded 1953); and the Guild of Catholic Psychiatrists (founded 1952). See Binzley (2007) and Gleason (1989, pp. 66–7) for further background on some of these groups.

distributed widely to Catholic colleges. Another vehicle for influencing the larger community was through the participation of ACPA members at meetings of the NCEA. In the ACPA's initiatives in undergraduate education and in assessment, the NCEA was one important group where the value of empirical psychology was argued and proposals presented.

The ACPA's mission to American Catholics, 1948–67

During its two decades of existence, the ACPA focused on the promotion of psychology among Catholics. There were three major initiatives: promotion of the teaching of scientific psychology at the college and university levels; placement services for Catholic psychologists; and psychological testing for applicants to the religious life.

Scientific psychology and Catholic higher education

The first project of the ACPA was promotion of scientific psychology in Catholic higher education. At the 1947 organizational meeting, Zegers stressed that "one of the first objectives" of the group should be "more psychology in undergraduate education" (Sister Mary Roberta Roberts, 1947) in part to improve the readiness of Catholic undergrads for graduate work in psychology. A related concern was the paucity of good textbooks by Catholics or for use in Catholic colleges. In 1949, the first program of the ACPA included the results of a preliminary survey of Catholic higher education: undergraduate programs in women's colleges (presented by Sister Maurice of Seton Hill College), men's colleges (Alexander A. Schneiders of the University of Detroit), doctoral programs (Frank J. Kobler of Loyola University), and a general overview (Zegers) (American Catholic Psychological Association: Third annual meeting, 1949). Bier (1949) summarized the papers, which showed that three universities (Fordham, Catholic University, and Loyola of Chicago) had doctoral programs, and five had masters programs. Schneiders[32] had sent out the questionnaire in the summer of 1949, and results indicated that 26 percent of women's colleges offered a psychology major, and 24 percent of men's and co-ed colleges.[33] Gender differences were more pronounced than these statistics indicate.

---

[32] Alexander A. Schneiders had a doctorate in psychology from Georgetown (Schneiders, 1934) and taught in a number of Jesuit universities. He published widely, especially in the area of adolescent psychology, and he was a counselor. Bier (1968a) called him a "*Catholic Psychologist*" (p. 65), and this was reflected in Schneiders' interests in distinctively Catholic themes, such as values, guilt, and marriage counseling. That is, Schneiders championed the second of the two aims of the ACPA. His editorship of the *Catholic Psychological Record* reflected his priorities.

[33] The number was higher if majors sponsored by philosophy or education departments were included.

Schneiders included comments made by department heads: One wrote that, "our aim in women's colleges is totally different from that of the men . . . major purpose is to train for family life" (Survey of psychological training in Catholic women's colleges, 1949). At the general meeting in 1949, the membership recommended that the Board of Directors work to promote scientific psychology in Catholic colleges and conduct further research in this area.

At the 1950 ACPA meeting, Schneiders (1950) presented the core program for undergraduate psychology departments, a result of work done by a Committee on Undergraduate Training. While stressing scientific psychology, the Committee did not neglect the importance of "the whole man" in psychology: "The answer to the question of a core curriculum hinges on the nature of psychology itself. Is it the study of personality or behavior; of development; of mind? Is psychology a science? If the answer to these questions is 'Yes' in every case, then such courses as Experimental Psychology, Statistics, Personality, and Development Psychology would be most necessary" (p. 6). In this answer, Schneiders shows how the ACPA sought to reconcile the earlier Catholic emphasis on philosophical psychology with the newer one on scientific psychology: conceding the philosophical aspects implicitly to philosophy and enforcing a mix of methodological and content courses in the psychology curriculum.

Timothy J. Gannon,[34] another former student of Moore and founder of the psychology department at Loras College in 1956, addressed the 1953 ACPA meeting on the place of psychology in the curriculum. He regretted that some Catholic reactions to the philosophical inadequacies of scientific psychology were "violent and untempered," such as when "Catholic colleges . . . have ceased to require a course in general or experimental psychology and have substituted a course in the philosophy of man as a requisite for the liberal arts degree" (Gannon, 1953, p. 597).[35] He sounded the "ghetto" theme by calling such a reaction "like retiring within the walled citadel of philosophy and drawing up the bridge" (ibid.). Not that Gannon rejected the role of philosophy in the development of a psychology of the "human person" (p. 601). The dilemma was this: "How can scientific psychology recover this concept of the basic unity of man without relinquishing its experimental methods and taking flight into that metaphysics of man that has just been rejected as too extreme?" (p. 598). That balance proved hard to maintain.

---

[34] Timothy J. Gannon (1904–91) was an archdiocesan priest in Dubuque, Iowa. He received a doctorate in theology in 1929 and began teaching at Loras College in 1930. After an M.A. in psychology from the Catholic University of America in 1934, he began teaching experimental psychology at Loras. His 1939 dissertation from the Catholic University was entitled *A statistical analysis of some psychiatric diagnostic traits among young men*.

[35] The concerns would have been with materialialistic and other reductionistic tendencies in scientific psychology.

The culmination of this early effort was Bier's report to the 1953 meeting of the NCEA. Sounding themes similar to Gannon, Bier (1953b) stressed the fact that psychology was becoming increasingly an applied field. The political context, including increased governmental funding of clinical psychology, was directly relevant to Bier's argument. His own statistics, based on a list of psychologists working for the VA, for example, was that only 1–2 percent of VA psychologists were Catholic, but about a third of VA patients were Catholic. Bier's argument was that psychology had become a profession and that Catholic patients needed competent professionals who shared their faith. An undergraduate psychology program as part of a liberal arts education was the ideal portal into the profession, according to Bier: "Psychology is a training in how to live – not in the deep spiritual or philosophical sense – but in the practical sense of individual adjustment and social contacts" (p. 197). Bier assumed that Catholic colleges would continue to provide the philosophical and theological context, within which scientific psychology could be presented on its own terms. For the moment, at least, his assumption was correct.

In December of 1953, Bier reported to the membership that, "at least one Catholic college is known to have introduced psychology into its curriculum as a result of this address" (William C. Bier, 1953a). A month later, Charles A. Curran[36] (1954b), ACPA president, sent a copy of Bier's address to the presidents of Catholic colleges throughout the country, together with a questionnaire on the status of their psychology programs. Bier (1955) reported the results of 190 of the 195 questionnaires sent, a 97 percent return, which indicates substantial interest in the question. The survey found that 31 percent of colleges had psychology majors, a higher percentage than the ACPA found in 1949. At the same time, almost 78 percent of all Catholic colleges offered courses in "general experimental" psychology. As a kind of summation of this effort and an indication of the future, the 1960 ACPA symposium was "Problems in the Teaching of Scientific Psychology in the Denominational College," and it included presentations from instructors from a Jewish and a Protestant college as well as from a Catholic college (Symposium – Problems in the teaching of scientific psychology in the denominational college, 1962).

Harry V. McNeill (1950), an early member of the ACPA, addressed the American Catholic Philosophical Association on developments in clinical psychology. McNeill held to a complementary relationship between Neoscholastic philosophy and psychoanalytical approaches to human life, stressing how World War II had changed things for psychology. Psychiatric problems with recruitment, with medical discharges, and with VA disability pensions required an increased use of psychologists for diagnostic and

---

[36] Charles Arthur Curran (1913–78) was a priest and Professor of Psychology at Loyola University of Chicago. He wrote extensively on Rogerian psychotherapy (Curran, 1952; 1958; 1969).

treatment purposes. McNeill referred to the fact that Fordham and Catholic University were two of the 45 universities receiving funds for clinical training. McNeill primarily informed the philosophers what clinical psychology was and how the philosophers and psychologists could work together in higher education. But the message was clear: there was pressing need for more training in clinical psychology. McNeill, who had taught at Fordham, was in 1950 working for the U.S. Public Health Service.[37] In 1957, when he was editor of the New York Society of Clinical Psychologists newsletter, he was one of the seven psychologists appointed to the New York state Board of Examiners of Psychologists (News briefs, 1957, p. 3).

In 1952, the ACPA membership voted to direct the leadership to "write to the President or Chairman of the psychology department in each of the Catholic Universities offering graduate work in psychology, directing their attention to the need for developing clinical training facilities . . . at a level of meeting APA standards for training in clinical work" (Sixth Annual Meeting, 1952, p. 1). To promote graduate education, the ACPA began running, as supplements to its *Newsletter*, brief histories of psychology departments at the leading Catholic universities: Catholic University of America (Stafford, 1953),[38] Loyola University (Snider, 1953), St. Louis University (Severin, 1953), Fordham University (William C. Bier, 1953c), the University of Montreal (Mailloux, 1953), and the University of Ottawa (Shevenell, 1953). The trajectory of the narratives was similar: breaks with philosophy, the establishment of experimental programs, and the turn toward applied topics, especially clinical.

As an indication that the membership took clinical training seriously, some members served on the first licensing boards for psychologists, as states passed certification laws in the 1950s: in addition to McNeill, Sister Annette Walters was on the first board in Minnesota (News briefs, 1951, p. 3), James McGoldrick, SJ (1895–1983), of Seattle University, was similarly named to Washington state's board in 1955 (News briefs, 1956b), and John J. Evoy, SJ, of Gonzaga University, was named to the same board in 1957 (News briefs, 1958a). In addition, as noted regularly in the *Newsletter*, various members were active in state psychological associations.

Placement services

At the 1949 meeting, the ACPA decided to offer a placement service as a way to increase Catholic participation in psychology. The *Newsletter* began in November, 1950, and the first placement announcements appeared in May, 1951, one for the director of the counseling center at the Catholic University,

[37] Like the VA, the Public Health Service began programs in the post-war period for research and training in clinical psychology (Capshew, 1999, p. 171).
[38] Stafford (1950) had published a more extensive history of the department.

and another for an instructor in statistics, experimental, and industrial psychology at the University of Detroit. Such announcements appeared regularly over the years. Between May, 1951 and January, 1959, there were 52 announcements in *the Newsletter*, 21 of which were for teaching, the rest for clinical and counseling positions. I was unable to determine how successful this service was, but since the *Newsletter* included announcements of new appointments of members, I found 12 of the positions listed as having been filled by members. Since all placement announcements were self-reports, there is no way of knowing if this 23 percent figure accurately reflected the success of the placement service. In 1959, its structure was changed, with Paul Centi of Fordham coordinating employment openings and applicants. Centi screened applicants and sought to match them with employers. Such a program continued throughout the duration of the ACPA's existence. If nothing else, the service indicated the seriousness of the organization's intention of getting Catholics involved in psychology. A 1961 survey of ACPA members revealed that salaries in Catholic institutions typically ranged about 25 percent lower than at non-Catholic institutions (Centi, 1961).

Psychological testing of candidates for religious life

The final major initiative of the ACPA was its promotion of psychological assessment of candidates for religious life. The idea did not originate with the ACPA. Moore (1936a; 1936b), as mentioned earlier, first addressed the question of mental illness among the clergy. There was but limited attention to the question of mental health screening of applicants to the religious life until a major impetus after World War II. While there had been some ecclesiastical opposition to the idea, by the early 1950s, there was widespread support for the effort, with Pius XII's directives for seminary training encouraging it (Coville, 1957, p. 396). Tageson (1964) claimed that the movement "really began gathering momentum" when Bier published two articles (Bier, 1953e; 1954a) in the *Review for Religious*, a prominent Jesuit journal. His were not the first for that periodical, with reports going back to 1949. However, Bier seems to have presented the argument persuasively to the religious community, as an editorial preceding his first article in the journal stated:

> When we last published an article on the psychological testing of candidates, a religious superior wrote an indignant letter cancelling his subscription and asserting that such testing interferes with the work of the Holy Ghost. That this is a misconception should be evident to all who read Father Bier's article in the present number.

> (in Bier, 1953e, p. 281)

Bier (1954b) even warned the NCEA against excessive enthusiasm about the merits of psychological assessment. Arguing for the relevance of psychological assessment, Bier (1953e) used a traditional distinction between an "internal vocation," or the call to the person from God, which was clearly not "of a purely natural and profane order," and the "external vocation," which is the discernment and acceptance by others of a person claiming to have a calling to the religious life. Psychological testing could contribute something positive to superiors in religious orders and diocesan seminaries, who had to make difficult decisions regarding applicants.

Bier's involvement was early, and his dissertation (Bier, 1948a) on the use and modification of the Minnesota Multiphasic Personality Inventory (MMPI)[39] with seminarians led to his testing candidates for the New York Jesuit province (Gillespie, 2001). The 1950s saw an increase in activity nationwide. There was, for example, a discussion of "The use of psychological tests in the selection of candidates" for the religious life at Fordham in 1953, with Bier, Sister Mary Martina, CSSF,[40] and George F. Cassidy, a clinician at St. Vincent's Hospital in New York City, as participants (News briefs, 1953). The 1957 ACPA meeting held a symposium on assessment of seminarians and other aspirants to the religious life.[41]

ACPA members were active elsewhere on the topic. In 1956, the National Academy of Religion and Mental Health, which had Bier and Curran on its advisory board, received an NIMH grant to study mental health curricula for theology students, and Loyola University in Chicago was designated as the Catholic university to participate (News briefs, 1956a).[42] Thomas McCarthy addressed the NCEA in 1958 on psychological testing in religious vocations (News briefs, 1958b).

An informal discussion of assessment of religious applicants at the 1960 ACPA meeting drew over 100 participants. At the same meeting, the ACPA became officially involved when its Board of Directors appointed a special committee to study "current practices in the psychological assessment of

---

[39] The MMPI was published in 1942. Bier sought to determine if MMPI scores for seminarians differed significantly from other groups of aspiring professionals. He found some differences, consistent with the specific demands and interests of seminary life.

[40] CSSF, the Congregation of the Sisters of St. Felix Cantalice, the Felician sisters.

[41] Participants (Psychological assessment in religious vocation, 1960) included Bier, LeRoy Wauck, Sister Digna Birmingham, OSB (Order of St. Benedict), and Richard Vaughan, SJ. The same year, Vaughan (1957b) wrote to Bier informing him that he had begun a screening program in San Francisco for the Jesuits there. Vaughan (1957a) advocated testing in a journal for religious. Born in 1919, Vaughan received a doctorate in psychology from Fordham University, and he taught for many years at San Francisco University. He later devoted his time to pastoral and psychological counseling. He served as provincial of the California Jesuit Province from 1971 to 1976.

[42] The Loyola study, the results of which were published in 1962, included reports of research by Magda Arnold and others. Much of the research was done in the form of doctoral dissertations done at Loyola (including LeRoy Wauck's) and also at the Catholic University.

religious vocations" (Fourteenth annual meeting, 1960). The committee, including Bier, McCarthy, Paul D'Arcy, and chairman Walter J. Coville, sent members a questionnaire to determine the extent of existing involvement in such assessment.[43] At the following year's meeting, 257 attended a session on the subject (Symposium – Basic issues in assessment of candidates to the religious life, 1962). Coville (1962a; 1962b) reported on a further survey of members on the nature of assessment work already being done. With a sample of 58 respondents, Coville found that 34 administered "rather complete assessment programs ... [to] 28 communities of male religious, 44 communities of female religious and 2 diocesan seminaries" (1962b, p. 1). Instruments included intelligence, personality, and interest tests.

After a decade of workshops, symposia at the annual meetings, and a 1966 workshop was *Assessment of Candidates for the Religious Life* (Coville, 1968a). This work marked the high point of ACPA efforts to bring psychology to Catholics.[44] Coville, D'Arcy, McCarthy, and John Rooney presented the basic issues and they recommended procedures to use when assessing religious candidates. The volume's appendices included an extensive bibliography of psychological research, a review of instruments used, and sample reports and programs. In keeping with the ACPA's philosophy, Rooney's contribution discussed the parameters for research in this area. Favorably reviewed in both psychological and religious journals, one noteworthy comment was made by the reviewer in the *Review for Religious*: "Whether or not they are actually using psychological testing for screening candidates to religious life, all religious institutions will find this volume of great help and interest" (Review of the book *Assessment of candidates for the religious life*, 1969, p. 535). This remark indicated that the ACPA's effort to bring psychology to the Catholic community had been successful. McCarthy (1965), in his 1964 ACPA presidential address, claimed that this work on assessment was one of two areas where the ACPA spoke "with authority" to the larger Catholic community (p. 2).

In focusing narrowly on the validity and means of administration of psychological tests, ACPA psychologists followed a pattern typical of psychologists at the time. What is less apparent in the ACPA literature on assessment is the

---

[43] Coville (1914–73) had graduated from Fordham with a doctorate in psychology in 1942. He was commissioned as a psychologist for the Navy during World War II. He published in the area of assessment for the Merchant Marines and others before turning to assessment of seminarians. He founded the psychology department at St. Vincent's Hospital in New York, providing practicum training for clinical psychologists. Before his untimely death, he had "succeeded in unifying the psychological testing programs for seminarians for three dioceses in the New York area" (Bier, 1973, p. 6).

[44] Coville (1967) declared that "we are confident today of its validity and effectiveness" (p. 305), referring to psychological assessment for religious life. A further example of the acceptance of assessment at the time is Niemann (1967), who was assistant to the Provincial of the Jesuit Wisconsin Province.

extent to which it was controversial in American society, where the broader political context of testing lay. Only in several remarks do we get a sense of dissent, from "some [clerics] of the older generation" (Sweeney, 1964, p. 372) and from those being tested. Robert Howard Sweeney, CSC,[45] a pastoral psychologist, told the NCEA that much of the opposition to testing among religious superiors of religious orders and of seminaries did concern "infringement of privacy and lack of freedom in the assessment programs" (p. 370), echoing the political battle waged over workplace testing and privacy, with the MMPI in particular, in 1964 (Buchanan, 2002, p. 287). Bier (1971b), referring to his early work from the 1940s, admitted that "certain of the items in the test proved to be objectionable to some of the seminary respondents . . . and this was a number of years before the more general objection was raised to certain MMPI items as an invasion of privacy" (p. 123). Bier's response was to develop a modified MMPI that removed the objectionable items as part of his effort to make it more suitable "for use with religious personnel" (ibid.).[46] The seminarians' objections reflected a widespread sense that the tests were an imposition. Buchanan (2002) discusses how battles over testing in the courts and in the U.S. Congress in the mid-1960s had the ironic outcome of strengthening psychology's grasp of expertise in the testing area. In line with the broader success of American psychologists in this grasp, the ACPA psychologists stressed the necessity of trained psychologists to conduct the testing, to ensure that it was handled professionally. The quiet emphasis on the technicalities of testing in Bier, Vaughan, Coville, and others, was a part of the professionalization of psychology at mid-century.

In another context, however, there was more discussion of privacy issues in assessment. At the 1961 ACPA meeting, Francis F. Reh (1962), of St. Joseph's Seminary, and Bernard J. Ristuccia, CM, of Mary Immaculate Seminary, both addressed privacy in relation to canon law. Sweeney (1964) alerted the NCEA to theological concepts to differentiate what a psychological test could and could not do:

> The person has a strict right to privacy about this *formal element* of moral failure or success, that is, evil choice or virtuous choice, because this fact is known only to himself, to God, and to those in whom he confides. A psychological test does not reveal the formal element of success or failure; it reveals only the presence of certain patterns of impulse, and something of the strength of these impulses.
>
> (p. 375)

---

[45] CSC, *Congregatio a S. Cruce*, the Congregation of the Holy Cross, an order of priests. I have not been able to ascertain that Sweeney was a member of the ACPA.

[46] Bier (1971) obtained permission from the authors of the MMPI and the Psychological Corporation to use his modified version for research purposes. Since face validity was not a concern with the MMPI, Bier's modification was uncontroversial.

Such differentiations were crucial in making room for psychological assessment in the vocational setting. Canon law forbade "religious superiors ... to induce in any manner persons subject to them to make a manifestation of conscience to them" (Ristuccia, 1962, p. 77). Were applicants to seminaries subject to this restriction? Do psychological tests manifest conscience? These two questions were part of the discussion of psychological assessment in Catholic circles at the time. By careful distinctions of the psychological and the spiritual, and by the institution of restrictions on the use of tests and the distribution of results, assessment found a place in the discernment of vocations. McCarthy (1970) summarized the prevailing attitude by stating that, "the principle generally invoked to justify testing priest-candidates is that the motive for doing so is proportionate to any danger [of invasion of privacy] involved for the person being tested" (p. 67). Psychological expertise found a place in the process.[47]

Given subsequent events beyond the time of the ACPA, a word must be said about psychological assessment of candidates for the priesthood in light of the clergy sexual abuse scandal in recent years. If the programs to which the ACPA contributed were as good as claimed, should not they have been more effective in this area? Plante and Boccaccini (1998) write, however, that there were few psychological studies of assessment programs for candidates for the priesthood from the early 1970s to the late 1990s. In addition, "each religious order, diocese, seminary, or vocations director makes their own arrangements for what the evaluation should include and who should conduct it" (p. 364). Despite research done during the 1950s and 1960s, it appears that the changes that swept the Church since then worked against the continuation of that trend. Perhaps the decline in the number of applicants and the defection of many others drew ecclesiastical attention elsewhere, until the abuse scandal made assessment again a vital issue.

Integrating psychology and the faith

The desire for integration proved difficult to define. Coville (1968b) recalled that originally the second goal of the ACPA was "to provide a forum for the discussion of psychological questions of special interest to Catholics," but that this statement of purpose was altered in 1953 to read "to work toward the integration of psychology with Catholic thought and practice" (p. 70). The restatement defined the position of the ACPA as desiring to bridge not only Catholics into psychology but also Catholic thought into psychology.

[47] As an indication of the ecumenical turn following the Second Vatican Council, and of the logic of the transformation of the ACPA into PIRI, Bier, Magda Arnold, David W. Carroll, SJ (a student of Bier), Coville, D'Arcy, Austin Dondero, FSC, McCarthy, and Charles A. Weisberger, SJ, took part in a 1966 symposium organized by the Academy of Religion and Mental Health on the topic of *Psychological Testing for Ministerial Selection* (Bier, 1970), along with Protestant and Jewish clergy.

The goal of integration of psychology with Catholic thought and life pre-supposed the goal of assimilation of Catholics into psychology, because assimilation implied the autonomy of psychology as a science and a profession. Moreover, in part, lingering suspicions about psychology in the Catholic world lay behind efforts at the integration of Catholic thought into psychology. As Gannon (1960) reminded the ACPA in 1958: "However unwarranted, the pursuit of scientific psychology very early became associated with defections from the Faith."[48] Apart from affirming their positions as both Catholics and psychologists, and pointing to the evidence of "the work of Mercier, Pace, Froebes, Michotte, Lindworsky and Moore ... [to] give the lie to the fiction that scientific psychology and Catholicism are incompatible" (p. 62), the ACPA attempted such integration in a number of specific areas. Studies of the ethics of lie detection, of marriage, of non-directive therapy, and of guilt and conscience were some of the topics treated, the authors taking moral bearings from Church teaching. Addressing a central theological issue head-on, Joseph G. Keegan, SJ (1955, March), discussed "Psychotherapy and the Action of Grace." He argued that the psychotherapist must know more than his own discipline in order to treat successfully a psychologically suffering person. There were hopes that as clinical psychology expanded, Catholics would make increasingly significant contributions because of their background in moral theology.

Another important area of integration concerned the relationship between Neoscholastic philosophical anthropology and scientific psychology. Catholic psychologists in the 1940s and 1950s argued that the autonomy of psychology as a science was a benefit for both it and philosophy. Their position was that scientific psychology did not have its own philosophical basis and thus was open to align it with Thomistic thought. Thus, scientific psychology as such could be integrated with Neoscholastic thought, at the theoretical and the practical levels, as we have seen in Chapter 3.

Integration was not a one-way concern in the 1950s. In response to Pope Pius XII's (1958) address on moral aspects of psychological practice, Gannon (1960) deferred to papal authority on matters where psychology bordered on philosophical and theological grounds. He noted in particular that the Pope's definition of personality – "the psychosomatic unity of man in so far as it is determined and governed by the soul" – meant a restoration "to scientific psychology [of] a workable concept of the soul, something that it has sorely needed all these years" (p. 63). Albert F. Grau, SJ (1960, p. 73), viewed this same address as providing "clarifying directives" and not restrictions on psychological practice, especially about respect for the person in counseling and his or her transcendent destiny. In general, the Catholic psychologists took the papal pronouncements as efforts in the work of integration.

---

[48] "In the early years ... the names of Stumpf, Messer, and Marbe were added to the more celebrated apostasy of Brentano" (Gannon, 1960, p. 62).

Voluntary dissolution and reformulation

The magnitude of the changes sweeping society and the Church in the late 1960s helps explain why a successful and stable association decided to alter its identity significantly. The accomplishments of the organization were outpaced by social, religious, and political changes. Catholic colleges had established psychology programs, but the liberal arts foundation that Bier had assumed crumbled as the colleges abandoned Neoscholastic training in philosophy and theology. Bier's earlier assumption that Catholics would teach and work in Catholic institutions and non-Catholics in non-Catholic institutions no longer held. The psychology departments of Catholic colleges increasingly resembled their secular peers (Wauck, 1962). Psychological assessment of candidates for the religious life must have looked different in the late 1960s, as the number of new candidates shrunk and many religious left their orders.[49]

The ACPA might have died a slow death as membership aged and numbers declined. What happened instead is that this voluntary association redefined itself in light of changing conditions. On September 2, 1966, the Board of Directors:

> Gave extensive time to a discussion of the current aim and function of the ACPA. It was observed that, although the Association had enjoyed a steady yearly growth from the time of its founding, this growth seemed now to be leveling off, and for the last year or two the Association was doing little more than holding its own in terms of members. In the present climate of the Church and of ecumenism an increasing number of Catholics are reluctant to identify themselves with any organization that is specifically Catholic. Things have changed greatly in the twenty years since the founding of the Association. There would seem to be good agreement that the ACPA had performed a useful function in encouraging the acceptance of psychology in Catholic schools, and bringing Catholics into membership and participation in the APA, but there seems to be growing obscurity as to what the current function of the ACPA is or should be.

> (Twentieth Annual Meeting, 1966, p. 2)

True to form, the Board appointed a committee to study the question. McCall, Walters, and Wauck were to study the question of "the continuation, modification, or possible dissolution of the Association *prior* to the 1967 meeting" (ibid.).

At the 1967 meeting, the Committee presented responses to the questionnaire sent to the membership, which had a "disappointing" 30 percent return

[49] Coville (1962b) reported that in 1960, there were 42,629 seminarians in the United States. Finke (2000) reports 48,046 seminarians in 1965, the year the Second Vatican Council ended. By 1970, the number had fallen to 28,819, a 40 percent drop in 5 years. In 1990, there were 5,083 (p. 125).

(Twenty-first Annual Meeting, 1967, p. 2).[50] No mandate was found in the results. The Board was directed to do more study and make recommendations. The following year saw a new survey and at the annual meeting, Coville, the ACPA president, addressed the "Changing Directions of the ACPA." Coville (1968b), as did others, pointed out that the ACPA membership was aging, and that this was a major weakness (p. 76). This survey had a better return (55 percent), but the results were ambiguous.[51] The Board of Directors decided to appoint a committee to present a re-structuring plan based on D'Arcy's 1967 presidential address, for an organization with a new name and new ends. D'Arcy (1967) sounded familiar themes – the Church has not benefited from scientific psychology, he claimed, because of the struggles of psychologists to separate themselves from the philosophers and the theologians, and because Church leaders have been biased against psychology. The time was ripe, however, for Catholic psychologists not to isolate themselves in "a professional ghetto" (p. 94), but to be a "group of secure professionals at home among their colleagues" (ibid.). "Autonomy," meant, according to D'Arcy, "'getting out from under the Church' while remaining true to it" (ibid.). This position was to prevail in the ACPA: it seemed, to many (e.g. O'Connell and Onuska, 1967) in the late 1960s, as another form of the Catholic ghetto, even as twenty years earlier, it seemed to be the doorway out.

The argument on the basis of membership numbers seems weak. What is striking is how, despite claims of success in both academia and in assessment, the leadership still felt a lack of recognition by the Church and the philosophical psychologists of the professional status of psychologists. Professionalism, as well as the ecumenical arguments, sound the right note.

The name that was finally chosen was Psychologists Interested in Religious Issues (PIRI).[52] Other events encroached on the deliberations of the committee: Alexander A. Schneiders, the editor of the *Catholic Psychological Record*, died suddenly in the fall of 1968, resulting in suspension and later cancellation of the journal; at the 1968 meeting, a group of ACPA members (Statement on Encyclical *Humanae Vitae*, 1969) raised questions challenging the encyclical of Pope Paul VI against artificial birth control, *Humanae Vitae*. This kind of questioning would have been unthinkable at the time the ACPA was founded,

---

[50] The committee also sent 60 questionnaires to representatives of American psychology – "principally Presidents of APA divisions and Chairmen of major Departments of Psychology" (Twenty-first annual meeting, 1967, p. 2), and reported that 91 percent "were only slightly acquainted or completely unacquainted with the ACPA," a result that I think helped to make the case for the irrelevancy of the ACPA as then constituted.

[51] Results: 22 percent favored continuation of the ACPA; 31 percent a restructuring of the ACPA; 32 percent an APA division on religion; and 15 percent an interfaith and interdisciplinary group (Twenty-second Annual Meeting, 1968, p. 2).

[52] The initial suggestion for a name was the Society of Psychologists Interested in Religious Issues and Trends, or SPIRIT (Restructuring of ACPA, 1969).

and it indicates the tensions within the Church and with the Catholic character of the ACPA.

I would not, however, overstate the discontinuity motif, for there was ample continuity as well, not only among the membership but also in terms of attitudes. PIRI sought and became APA Division 36, a goal consistent with the earliest efforts of the ACPA. PIRI also sought to promote the scientific study of religious phenomena and to have the religious dimension taken into account in personality theories and counseling practice, two goals also consistent with the ACPA.[53] Given the increasing influence of clinical and counseling psychologists in the ACPA in its later years – Coville noted in 1968 that about 49 percent of the membership was in that field, a dramatic change from 10 percent in 1951 – the applied emphasis of PIRI was certainly in line with trends within the ACPA. The conservatism of the organization, even within dramatic change, was evident primarily in the continued desire to be fully involved with the mainstream of psychology, as represented by the APA, rather than be outside that structure.

A digression on the psychology of religion

It is worth emphasizing that the shift from the ACPA to PIRI was a shift to a greater emphasis on the psychology of religion. Misiak and Staudt (1954) called for Catholic psychologists to undertake "a systematic study of religion," noting that "there is still a dearth of solid scientific works" (p. 288). While the years of the ACPA saw some work in this area, years later, Virginia Staudt Sexton (1991b) could look back and say that "the psychology of religion as science does not seem to have progressed as well as the profession" (p. 41). This assessment is supported by the *New Catholic Encyclopedia* entry on "the psychology of religion" (Keefe, 1979), where the main topics included marriage, vocational assessment, pastoral counseling, religious education, moral development, and moral issues such as guilt. All areas could be topics of psychological inquiry, but the weight seemed to fall on the application of psychological expertise in these areas.

There were a number of ACPA member contributions to the psychology of religion, nevertheless. Hendrika Vande Kemp (1984) cites Vincent Herr's *Religious Psychology* (1965) as part of a German tradition "continued by the *Eranos* group in Switzerland, the *Lumen Vitae* group in Brussels, and by the Dominican Fathers Noel Mailloux and Salmon" (pp. 103–4). The publication of *Annotated Bibliography in Religion and Psychology* by W. W. Meissner, SJ (1961) was an important contribution to developing a renewed psychology of

---

[53] In fact, Misiak and Staudt (1954) suggested (p. 287) that in the future, Catholic psychologists would most likely make significant contributions in the areas of "psychology of religion, pastoral psychology, and psychotherapy."

religion, and Meissner himself has played a leading role in that field (Gillespie, 2001). The psychological study of religion was indeed taking off during the years of the ACPA. As a further indication, there were notices in the *Sister Formation Bulletin* for courses such as that on "Psychology and Asceticism" given by Noel Mailloux, OP, as part of a graduate program in Ascetical Theology at Immaculate Heart College in Los Angeles (New graduate program in ascetical theology opened to sisters, 1959). Examples of this type abound, as did psychologists brought on as consultants to address psychological issues in religious communities. Van Kaam's (1964) *Religion and personality* may be seen as the fruit of such collaboration.

The real fruit of these efforts was, to a great extent, the transformation of the ACPA into Division 36 of the APA – for now was the psychology of religion institutionalized within the psychological community. The initial hope of the founders of the ACPA was to some extent realized, at least as a promise of research and application, with that transformation. The fruits of that event lie outside the scope of this chapter and this book.

Re-forming the ACPA

If there was both continuity and discontinuity regarding the purpose of assimilation, what about that regarding integration? The picture is more complex, but one series of events stands out that marked the increased professional autonomy of the membership. In July of 1968, Pope Paul VI released *Humanae Vitae*, an encyclical upholding the Church's absolute opposition to artificial birth control. The letter obviously dealt with matters of interest to the ACPA. The response to the encyclical, however, (Catholic psychologists question Pope's Encyclical, 1968) differed dramatically from the submissive attentiveness that characterized the ACPA's response to the letters of Pius XII on psychology. Sixty members of the ACPA, in a public announcement at the 1968 meeting, "strongly suggested ... that Pope Paul VI's condemnation of birth control rested on a false psychology of man."[54] The statement (Statement on Encyclical *Humanae Vitae*, 1969) included fifteen questions addressed to the encyclical, beginning with: "What is the theory of human nature which is implicit in the encyclical? Does it reflect adequately contemporary psychological thinking and research?" The final question was: "Is there sensitivity to the dilemma which such a document presents to Catholic men of science insofar as it does not integrate the latest scientific findings about man?" While ACPA membership was not alone in protesting *Humanae Vitae*, what is significant was the reversal of the theme of integration. Speaking as scientific psychologists,

---

[54] The same article reported a symposium on celibacy, at which Eugene Kennedy stated that clerical celibacy, "ordered to the service of an institution rather than people, is collapsing in our day."

this group asked if Rome integrated the findings of psychology into its think-ing. This alone would establish the conclusion I draw about the reformulation of the ACPA: it represented a shift in the stance or subject-position of the Catholic psychologist at the end of the 1960s. The psychologist now spoke from the ground of scientific psychology, which has an autonomous position vis-à-vis Catholic thought and teaching.

Announcing the questions on *Humanae Vitae* in 1968 were Sherman McCabe, Louis Gaffney, SJ, Vytautas Bieliauskas and Sister Margaret Gorman.[55] In 1969, the ACPA held a symposium on conjugal love and birth control (organized by Bieliauskas) and another, a psychodrama, on authority and dissent in the Church (organized by Gorman).[56] Gaffney (1971) reviewed historical attitudes hostile to the body and sex in western history and their influence on Church teaching, and he cited first-person experiences of married couples. He found that modern biology and married couples contradicted "much of what has been taught about marriage" (p. 19) by the Church. Bieliauskas (1971) argued that scientific research gainsaid the encyclical's views of female and male sexuality: "since the Pope found it necessary to deal in the encyclical with human nature and to use knowledge from the fields of medicine, biology, and psychology, it is reasonable to assume that he wanted to include the newest available knowledge provided by the these disciplines" (p. 47). That such questioning expressed the views of many members is suggested by the facts that Bieliauskas and Gaffney were nominated for pres-ident of the ACPA in the spring of 1970 (Bieliauskas won), and the following year, Gaffney and Gorman were nominated for president of PIRI (Gaffney won). This dissent represented a position different from that of the early years of the ACPA. For it was not left here for philosophical and theological light to shine upon the brute data of scientific research in order to reveal its truth. Now scientific psychology in its autonomy faced philosophy and theology on an equal footing: the latter had to contend with the scientific findings that should inform their conception of the human person. The old separation of psychology from philosophy, which protected psychology when it lacked status or position in Catholic education from unwanted restrictions by philosophers and theolo-gians, now took on a new significance. Scientific psychology's autonomy meant that it had something to say about the meaning of its data for philosophical anthropology and the moral implications drawn therefrom.[57] Catholic psychol-ogists, assimilated more fully into American psychology, and confident of the

---

[55] See above, Chapter 3, for a discussion of Gorman's paper on the decline of Neoscholasticism.

[56] *American Catholic Psychological Association Newsletter 19*, No. 3 (Summer, 1969), 2.

[57] It was in 1969 that George Miller (1969) in his APA presidential address spoke of a positive image of man drawn from scientific psychology that differed from the cultural image that emphasized external controls. Miller also claimed that psychology was revolutionary in its potential to transform society based on this allegedly new image.

autonomy of their science, asserted a new role in relation to Catholic thought and teaching: Having gained a place, they insisted on being heard.

At the 1969 meeting, a new name and bylaws were discussed. The reconstituted organization would not have the word "Catholic" in it, because "when the ACPA was founded in 1948, there was need to win acceptance for psychology in Catholic circles.[58] This was the first goal of the Association and it has been attained. Now, in the post-Vatican and ecumenical Church, the need is for Catholic psychologists to work with their professional colleagues" (Twenty-third Annual Meeting, 1969, p. 2). There was hope that the new association would lead to an APA division, which it did. On September 4, 1970, the Board approved the change in name and bylaws. The following year, the *PIRI Newsletter* appeared. Five years later, PIRI became Division 36 of the APA. Many of the early officers of the latter had been active in the ACPA. In fact, Eugene Kennedy, president of PIRI in 1975, claimed victory for the ACPA vision, when he stated that: "Becoming a division of the A.P.A. is an accomplishment that reflects the American Catholic presence in many professions. We no longer need to be isolated or defend the authentic professionalism of our scientific commitment" (1975, p. 40).

PIRI's *raison d'être* was the fact that professional psychology had now been accepted in Catholic circles. The goal of the ACPA had been to modernize psychology in Catholic circles: the organization sought to separate psychology from philosophically dominated conceptions of the field in both theory and practice. Despite Kennedy's claim, the formation of PIRI was not only a result of that change, but a further way to accomplish it. Differentiation of modern from Neoscholastic psychology on the theoretical level had been taking place for decades, but the more radical change was the ACPA's promotion of assessment of seminarians, because this established psychological expertise within spiritual and religious settings with long traditions. To be sure, the psychologists could not have established themselves in the process had there not been acceptance of psychological means by Church officials – some of whom were themselves psychologists. But as ACPA president D'Arcy (1967) observed: the "practical psychology of Christian perfection ... has grown up within the

---

[58] Other Catholic professional organizations underwent a similar mutation or ceased to exist: the American Catholic Philosophical Association continues to exist, but has broadened its scope. Its journal, *New Scholasticism*, was renamed the *American Catholic Philosophical Quarterly* in 1990. The Albertus Magnus Guild dissolved in 1969. The American Catholic Sociological Society's trajectory most closely paralleled the ACPA's, changing its name to The Association for the Sociology of Religion in 1971. It still exists. In 1963, its journal changed from *American Catholic Sociological Review* to *Sociological Analysis*, and in 1993, it became *Sociology of Religion*. Like the ACPA, the emphasis shifted to religion proper, studied from a disciplinary perspective. Gleason (1989) summarizes the changes: "Catholics in the 1960s were orienting themselves to new reference groups and taking their values from new sources" (p. 71).

Church through the centuries. Its link with tradition has made it holy, but in the light of modern knowledge, it is inadequate for today's Christian" (p. 94). This observation illustrates that in establishing the autonomy of psychology within the Catholic community, more than professionalism and autonomy was at stake: the ground for knowledge had shifted. There was a shift from a knowledge based on traditions of vocational discernment, especially within religious communities, to one based on natural scientific grounds. "Shift" may overstate the case. There was, rather, an incorporation of natural scientific categories and practices into these traditions – a feat accomplished by insiders such as Bier, Vaughan, Kennedy, D'Arcy, Coville, and others, who brought twentieth-century psychological objects and practices to bear on the religious life.

In 1967, a year after the ACPA workshop on testing of applicants for the religious life, the Catholic bishops of the United States authorized a psychological study of American priests (Kennedy and Heckler, 1972). Kennedy was the chief investigator.[59] He was critical of the assessment model that the ACPA championed, preferring a developmental model (based on Erik Erikson) and a clinical approach, using in-depth interviews. He and the project director, Victor J. Heckler, thought a model based on "health" rather than "sickness" was more appropriate. They even dropped the MMPI, using instead the Personal Orientation Inventory (POI), which drew heavily on humanistic psychological concepts. Many of the consultants of the program were ACPA members. While Kennedy's group claimed scientific expertise on the same grounds as had Bier and Coville, his group moved the terms of assessment in the direction of humanistic psychology. That turn came to demarcate another chapter in the relations between psychology and the Church – a chapter beyond the ACPA.

The incorporation of scientific objects into Catholic discourse and praxis was a significant accomplishment. It was a move from Neoscholastic psychology, which provided the theory for earlier Catholic understanding of the soul, and from ascetical theology, that had provided the ways to describe the praxis of spiritual life, to scientific psychological terms, including "intelligence," "motivation," "personality," and even "personal growth." By 1970, these "psychological objects" (Danziger, 1997) had been incorporated into Catholic education and into the formation of future priests and religious. Intelligence and personality tests had legitimate authority in the selection process. These scientific objects prompted changing patterns of seminary training, in the direction of "development of the total human personality" and "personal

---

[59] Kennedy (born 1928), ordained a Maryknoll priest in 1955, was laicized (officially released from priestly duties) in 1977. He received a doctorate in psychology from the Catholic University of America with a dissertation entitled *The relationship of self-perception to expressed motivation for occupational choice* (1962). He is a prolific author and has been in the psychology department of Loyola University in Chicago since 1962. As of writing, he is professor emeritus.

autonomy" (Rooney, 1972, p. 202). The taking up of scientific psychological terms reflected the political changes that had occurred in the Church and in American society since the beginnings of the ACPA.

What do we make of the voluntary re-organization of the ACPA? The leadership declared success and new aims. The sudden move to an ecumenical group and the bland name of the successor organization suggest that the changes were pushed by greater social pressures, especially within the Church following the Vatican council. The re-organization and the subsequent successful attempt to become a division of the APA, which non-Catholic psychologists joined, indicate that what had been only one aspect of the ACPA's identity, namely its professional character, now came to dominate. While it was no longer relevant to be identified as a sectarian group, it was still valuable to be a group of professional scientists.

Guild of Catholic Psychiatrists

The Guild of Catholic Psychiatrists was the other major psychological group that formed during this period. The use of the term "guild" in its title reveals something of how the group understood itself. In the early twentieth century, an American Guild of St. Luke formed in New York. Catholic physicians, including Charles Edward Nammack, a New York physician and contributor of the article on alcoholism to the *Catholic Encyclopedia* and Joseph J. Walsh, were members. Its goal was to "study the ethical and moral data connected with the practice of medicine" (Tells of a compact to end Grant's pain, 1910). Around the same time, 1910, Cardinal William O'Connell (1859–1944) of Boston brought together a group of physicians, urging them to form a Guild of St. Luke there.[60] What makes this story interesting for our narrative is that O'Connell was specifically interested in combating three trends he saw as dangerous for the practice of medicine from a Catholic viewpoint: Christian Science, materialism, and the Emmanuel Movement. We have already seen how the first two played a part in the early history of the relationships between Catholicism and psychology. O'Connell described Christian Science as an idealist reaction to materialism, both of which misunderstood human nature:

> When I came to my sick room a man who has in his hands a dangerous power and in his brain a dangerous knowledge, I insist upon knowing what is the moral position of that man and what are the principles upon which he acts. Pseudo-science runs perpetually to extremes. One school proclaims an absolute materialism which says there is no soul; that man is nothing more than a brute. The very horror of this view has driven some

---

[60] Anglican Guilds of St. Luke had formed in England in the 1860s and in the United States in the 1880s.

people to the other extreme and simple idealism of which Mrs. Eddy is the high priestess.

(Warns Catholics of Christian Science, 1910)

Then Cardinal O'Connell criticized the Emmanuel Movement, which had begun in 1906 in Boston, a joint effort of two Episcopal ministers and a physician, although by 1910, it had been under attack from both the medical and the ministerial side. The Emmanuel Movement was one of the foundations of psychotherapy in the United States. O'Connell criticized it in these terms:

> Then there is a third school which has a mixture of both and says that as there are both soul and body in man, we must make the priest a physician and the physician a priest. This is Emmanuelism. The Church says all this is wrong. To the Emmanuel Movement she answers that the priest is the minister of the soul and the physician is the minister to the body. She settles the question in this lucid way.

(ibid.)[61]

Two years later, Cardinal O'Connell did organize a Guild of St. Luke in Boston, appointing three physicians as officers and a chaplain (The Guild of St. Luke, 2009).

O'Connell's objections to Christian Science and materialism do not come as a surprise, but why his opposition to the Emmanuel Movement? His statement indicates its grounds. Since the time of the Fourth Lateran Council in 1215, it had been the rule in the Church that priests cannot be physicians (Fanning, 1913) for a variety of reasons, the chief being – as O'Connell stated – that the priest is a minister of the soul. So the Emmanuel Movement was, in Catholic eyes at the time, blurring a long-established boundary.

Catholic physician guilds began forming in earnest in the 1920s, the first appearing in Brooklyn in 1925.[62] When the Federation of Catholic Physicians' Guilds organized in 1931, it joined together loosely (hence, "federation") the several individual guilds. The Federation began a journal, the *Linacre Quarterly*. These guilds focused on the integration of the faith and medicine in its members and on their promotion of Catholic moral viewpoints in medicine and society at large.[63]

---

[61] See above, Chapter 4, for earlier arguments on the roles of physicians and priests in nineteenth-century France.

[62] Or in 1927, according to Valerie DeMarinis (1982, p. 207), who found two different accounts of the Brooklyn Guild.

[63] Guilds had positive connotations in the Catholic world. In Pope Leo XIII's 1891 encyclical on labor, *Rerum novarum*, we find: "History attests what excellent results were brought about by the artificers' guilds of olden times. They were the means of affording not only many advantages to the workmen, but in no small degree of promoting the advancement of art, as numerous monuments remain to bear witness" (Pope Leo XIII, *The great encyclical letters of Pope Leo XIII* (1903, p. 238). Another template for these guilds was

In the first issue of the *Linacre Quarterly*, the editor, Anthony Bassler, clearly distinguished the purposes of guilds from those of professional organizations:

> There is an idea prevalent that these Guilds are medical societies, the members whereof are Catholics. Nothing is more erroneous than this. There are too many medical societies in existence now, and Catholics do not need any to be organized for them, they being welcome as members in all medical organizations. It therefore is clear that the Guilds must be something quite different from professional societies, something that these societies cannot offer, something essentially Catholic and attuned to Catholic ideas and doctrines.
>
> A Guild, then, is an organization the avowed objects of which are the fulfillment of Catholic aims and ideals as they apply to medical men. It therefore has a spiritual basis which, while supplying us with a fundamental principle of action, will give us something to strive for and which must become part and parcel of our whole lives as Catholic physicians ... The spiritual must be the foundation of our every effort, for without it the Guilds will fail as a Catholic activity and achieve no more than a professional debating or clinical society.
>
> (Bassler, 1932)

This template[64] for the psychiatrists' guild gave it a sense of purpose different from the ACPA, for several reasons. First, this 1932 statement expressed no anxiety about the professional standing of Catholic physicians. Later on, Catholic psychiatrists were similarly successful in organizations like the American Psychiatric Association. Physicians did not have the same concerns about professionalism that the founders of the ACPA had. Second, guilds had chaplains and Church officials consistently held prominent positions within them. The ACPA had no chaplain and it did not address directly the spiritual well-being of its membership. However, like the guilds, the ACPA did have an interest in making its members and others knowledgeable about Catholic positions on the discipline-relevant moral issues of the day. This difference stemmed in large part from the fact that in the medical guilds, normally the physicians (and psychiatrists) were members of the laity, because of the differentiation of the roles of priest and physician, whereas this was not the case in psychology.

So for the psychiatrists to form a Catholic organization, formal participation of the Church was necessary, and in the position of the chaplain, it was secured.

the Catholic Club of New York, which was formed in 1871 for the purposes of the spiritual well-being and education of its members and to advance Catholic positions in society (Rooney, 1913). The Federation was formed in 1931, at a meeting of the Catholic Club (Catholic physicians form a federation, 1931).

[64] In 1920, a group of dentists organized the Guild of St. Apollonia in Boston (St. Apollonia is the patron saint of dentists), with the blessing and approval of Cardinal O'Connell. One of its activities was a free clinic for poor children (Keyes, 1924).

The psychologists in 1947 were not primarily therapists, and many of them were priests and nuns themselves. There was no formal distinction between being a religious and being a scientist, unlike the case with physicians.[65] Finally, differentiating the physicians' guilds from that of the psychiatrists and the ACPA, the physicians did not have to convince Catholics that medicine was a good thing. Here the position of the psychiatrists was similar to the psychologists', but the psychiatrists' way of handling it differed. The psychiatric Guild did not directly promote the education of Catholics into psychiatry or set up a placement service. Rather, by aligning itself with the Catholic hierarchy, the Guild made the point that there was no essential conflict between psychiatry and the Church.

Psychiatry had a presence in the pages of the *Linacre Quarterly*. James J. Walsh wrote often for the journal until his death in 1942, although primarily on medical history. Others addressed psychiatry directly, however. In 1947, six months after Sheen's sermon on Freudianism, Raphael McCarthy (1947) wrote on "Common grounds for psychiatrists and priests," and earlier, Joseph Keegan (1943), from Fordham's psychology department, published "The therapist as a person." There were other such articles, and this shows that the physicians' guilds provided a place for Catholic psychiatrists.

Like the ACPA, the Guild began in the shadow of Sheen's sermon denouncing Freudianism, only here some of the psychiatrists who objected to Sheen's over-reaching condemnation were instrumental in getting the Guild started. The Guild began in 1952, and it endured until 1988, although its heyday lasted until 1968, when John R. Cavanagh resigned as editor of the Guild's *Bulletin* and as treasurer of the organization. There are parallels between the fate of the ACPA and the Guild: from inception until 1968, both had some successes, especially in increasing the acceptability of psychology and psychiatry in Catholic life; just as the ACPA promoted psychological assessment of seminarians, the Guild championed such assessment as well as mental health treatment for clergy and religious; in the mid-1960s, stagnant membership numbers were a source of distress in both groups; both had scant name-recognition in their respective fields; and 1968 marked the departure of a strong editor – Schneiders' untimely death, Cavanagh's resignation. The parallels end here. There was no Guild equivalent of PIRI or Division 36 of the APA. The Guild added "National" to its title and soldiered on with diminishing numbers until 1987, when Thomas Kane, a priest who had been on the Guild's Board of Directors for twenty years, and who had founded the House of Affirmation for

---

[65] The 1917 Code of Canon Law forbade the practice of medicine and surgery by clerics, unless they receive an indult (formal permission). A *monitum* (warning) from the Sacred Congregation of the Holy Office in July, 1961, extended (or clarified) this rule to include the practice of psychoanalysis, unless an indult is obtained, so it implied (Monitum from the Holy Office, 1961).

mentally ill members of the clergy, "was fired for embezzlement. Two years later, the House of Affirmation closed and Kane fled to Mexico trailing rumors of financial and sexual impropriety" (Nussbaum, 2007, p. 864). The *Bulletin* ceased publication in 1988, although by then, it had shrunk in size and distribution.

Abraham Nussbaum has written an important history of the Guild, and my account draws upon his. Like the ACPA, the Guild closely held to the prevailing notions of its parent discipline, as Nussbaum notes: "members of the Guild did not significantly challenge the ontology of mid-century psychiatry, but instead showed how to apply psychiatry to the specific needs of the Catholics" (p. 850). The Guild – as might have been expected of psychiatrists, who were of course physicians – respected both medical and ecclesiastical hierarchies. As we saw, the ACPA rejected a proposal to have members of the hierarchy as patrons or honorary members. The Guild, by contrast, had as "associate members" Catholics who were not psychiatrists, most of whom were priests and religious (p. 852). In addition, the Guild had a chaplain, who published regularly in the Guild's *Bulletin*. Still, only Catholic psychiatrists – the membership form asked for the name of the applicant's parish and pastor as well as for medical credentials (again in contrast to the ACPA, where applicants did not have to claim explicitly that they were Catholic) – could be "regular members" and hold office (p. 851). The Guild thus engaged in the same kind of boundary-work as the ACPA, but it allied itself more directly with the Church hierarchy. Both the Guild and the ACPA were Catholic professional associations, with the Guild stressing "Catholic" and the ACPA stressing "professional." This difference reflected the relative status of medicine and psychology in society and the Church in the mid-twentieth century.

Nussbaum draws on the sociological research of John Jerome Lally in the mid-1960s, who had studied the status of Catholic psychiatrists within the profession. Nussbaum interprets Lally's sociological research to say that "the Guild was small both because Catholics were underrepresented within American psychiatry and because non-practicing Catholic psychiatrists rarely joined the Guild" (p. 853). A further survey (Lally, 1975) found Catholics were a small percentage of New York psychiatrists and psychoanalysts because of "self-selection of Catholics away from psychiatry and even more so from psychoanalysis, for reasons including their lack of exposure to positive images of these professions and their perception of serious differences between Freudianism and Catholicism. But we have also suggested the involvement of some institutional selection, of secondary effects, and of feedback" (p. 163). These small numbers are somewhat surprising, given that some of the leaders of American psychiatry during this period were also in the forefront of the intersection of psychiatry and Catholicism: Nussbaum lists six Catholics who were president of the American Psychiatric Association during this period: "Karl M. Bowman, Leo H. Bartemeier, Francis J. Braceland, Francis J. Gerty,

Harvey J. Tompkins, and Lawrence C. Kolb" (2007, p. 859, n. 36). Bartemeier, moreover, served as president of the American Psychoanalytical Association and the International Psychoanalytic Association (p. 859). In addition, Gregory Zilboorg was an active Guild member and one of the most prominent analysts of the time. So in terms of making a presence, the Catholic psychiatrists out-shone their co-religionists in psychology, none of whom held positions in psychology of the same status, with the exception of Noël Mailloux, who was president of the Canadian Psychological Association in 1956.[66] And it was Bartemeier, who "responded to Sheen's provocation in 1949 by inveighing upon Pope Pius XII to embrace psychiatry as licit" (p. 846), which he did in 1953 (Pope Pius XII, 1953).[67] In 1958, Sheen addressed the Guild, stressing the same points that Pope Pius had done in his series of talks on psychiatry. Sheen here was supportive – with the condition that psychiatry keep in mind the true nature and destiny of human beings – of psychiatry. He was optimistic about psychiatry's future (see Gillespie, 2001, p. xii; Guild meeting, 1958, with a photo of Sheen with F. T. Harrington and Clarence J. Kurth, officers of the Guild, included in this issue; see Nussbaum, 2007, p. 865, for further interpretation of the talk).

The constitution of the Guild differed dramatically from that of the ACPA. The Guild's purposes were:

> (1) to acknowledge the existence of God, and to recognize His primary place above all His creatures; (2) to promote the proposition that sound psychiatry has no conflict with Christian moral law; (3) to uphold the principles of the Catholic faith and morality with particular references to the science and practice of medicine and to the specialty of psychiatry; (4) to assist ecclesiastical authorities in the diffusion of knowledge of Catholic medical and psychiatric ethics; (5) to uphold Catholic hospitals in their enforcement of Catholic moral principles in medical and psychiatric practice.
>
> (Cavanagh, 1967)

The Guild thus took a more strongly defined apologetic stance than did the ACPA, which was more concerned with establishing Catholics as credible scientists. The differences represent the fact that the Guild was for psychiatrists, who were engaged largely in providing treatment, and so more concerned with practice, where questions of the relationship between human acts and Catholic morality would have come to the forefront. This encyclopedia article, however,

---

[66] Mailloux "was elected President of the Quebec Psychological Association (1945–46), of the Canadian Society for the Study of Depth Psychology (1952–54), of the Canadian Psychological Association (1954–55), of the Quebec Corrections Association (1962–65), and of the Canadian Corrections Association (1962–65)" (Bélanger and Sabourin, 1997).
[67] See Chapter 5 for greater detail on this incident.

was published a year before Cavanagh resigned as editor from the Guild's *Bulletin*, lamenting the lack of young members and enthusiasm in the organization (cited in Nussbaum, 2007, p. 855). Despite the Guild's stated purposes, however, Nussbaum claims that the Guild failed to develop a Catholic alternative to mainstream psychiatry and that its primary success was in making psychiatry more acceptable in Catholic circles (p. 850). That is, it succeeded in precisely the same way that the ACPA did.

The Guild did not establish the kind of committee structure that the ACPA did. Its major initiatives were sessions held at its annual meetings. Compared to those of the ACPA, the Guild's meetings included a wider variety of participants, with members of the Church hierarchy making regular appearances, and a number of non-psychiatrists, especially theologians, participating. However, the themes presented were similar to those of the ACPA, although there was of course much more on issues relating directly to moral issues that can arise in psychiatric practice. In the first several years, the annual meetings consisted largely of a few major addresses; the membership desired some more practical sessions, however, and by the end of the 1950s, a series of seminars was included in the annual meetings. In 1954, there was a call for the Guild to do something to encourage more Catholic medical students to take up psychiatry (Hayes, 1954), a project similar to that developed by the ACPA. However, Hayes thought that the recruitment could be done without formal action or organization. It appears that no formal action was ever undertaken.

Two years later, John G. Novak (1956), the Guild president, citing dissatisfaction among members about the Guild's annual meetings, wrote "that the Guild should serve the Catholic Psychiatrist; that it should serve as a forum where Catholic psychiatrists could discuss his problems with other Catholic psychiatrists; that the Guild should serve as a source of information to interested Catholics (lay as well as religious) for data relative to psychiatry" (p. 3). These purposes suggest that the Guild was largely made up of practitioners who were, for the most part, not in university settings, since the first aim here was directed toward serving the membership, rather than the membership acting itself as a professional unit toward others. At the same time, the second stated aim was to influence the wider Catholic community, and the Guild attempted it by having influential members, such as Bishop Sheen and Cardinal Richard Cushing, Archbishop of Boston, speak at the annual meetings.[68]

---

[68] Cushing's talk was "A member of the hierarchy looks at psychiatry" (Griffin, 1959). Indicative of the higher status of psychiatry compared to psychology was in the continuation of the account: "The talk [by Cardinal Cushing] was preceded by an academic procession of Guild members, the faculty of the Catholic University, members of Congress and of the Diplomatic Corps, and representatives of the Church, the Government, and the Military" (p. 23).

In 1985, toward the end of the *Bulletin*'s existence, a list of members showed that there were 52 regular and 44 associate members.[69] Before it faded into obscurity, however, it had an impact on the introduction of "psychiatric services into the lives of Catholic clergy and members of religious orders and congregations" (Nussbaum, 2007, p. 860). The Guild's meetings in the 1960s discussed psychological assessment of candidates to the religious life, the mental health training of seminarians, as well as reports on psychiatric out-patient clinics under Catholic auspices. So like the ACPA and the NCEA, the Guild helped to legitimate these topics in Catholic circles. Francis T. Harrington, a Guild member from Dallas, wrote that the Federation of Catholic Physicians Guild had established a committee to prepare a medical examination form "to be used as a permanent health record for members of the Clergy and Religious life" (Harrington, 1960). Harrington was a liaison member of this committee for the psychiatrists' Guild, because the committee "wanted help in arriving at a minimal psychiatric screening examination particularly for the pre-entrance examination of candidates for the Clergy and Religious Life."

On the issue of the psychological assessment for candidates for the religious life, Sister Mary Aloyse, IHM (1961),[70] addressed the Guild, describing the five-year study that she led for her order in California.[71] Sister M. Aloyse (1964) also replied to Carroll F. Tageson's (1964) presentation on "Re-evaluation of psychological testing of candidates for religious life." The specific remarks are less important here than the fact of their presentation, since one Guild purpose was to inform its membership. In a similar vein, Alan A. Zielinski (1964), a priest from Buffalo, New York, described the diocesan outpatient psychiatric clinic. Herr's (1966) presentation of the Loyola NIMH project was also infor-mational for the Guild membership. In these and related ways, the Guild legitimated and spread psychological expertise and conceptual objects through-out the Catholic world.

What institutionalization meant

In these various ways, psychology made a place for itself within American Catholic culture. The biggest impact was the acceptance of modern

---

[69] In 1953, there were 83 members (Gerty, 1953); in 1959, 219 regular and 128 associate members; in 1968, 217 regular and 186 associate members (Nussbaum, 2007, p. 852).

[70] Sister M. Aloyse had a doctorate in psychology from the University of Southern California (Turk, 1971, p. 150), and she was head of the psychology department at Immaculate Heart College in the 1960s. She also published in the *Sisters Formation Bulletin*, a publication of the Sisters Formation Movement, whose executive secretary for several years after 1960 was Annette Walters. This Movement was another vehicle for the legitimation of psychological objects into Catholic life.

[71] Richard Vaughan (1961) published on the same topic in the same year in the *Bulletin*.

psychological objects into the ways that Catholics think about themselves and act upon these thoughts. A distinctive "Catholic psychology" did not develop, and neither did a distinctive Catholic psychiatry. But those were not failures, because they were not the intention of any of these endeavors. During this period, which effectively ended in 1968, boundary lines between empirical and philosophical psychology and between the psychiatrist and the priest helped to legitimate these new disciplines in the Catholic world. The fact that their major proponents were themselves either in the religious life or lay people active in the Church gave the work credibility. But a significant change had been wrought, for now psychological categories were infused into the ways that Catholics understood themselves. However, this change was just the beginning, as we shall see in the next chapter.

8

Humanistic psychology and Catholicism: dialogue and confrontation

We have seen that Neoscholastic psychology kept the philosophical questions of psychology alive. The philosophers and theologians and Church officials looking over the psychologist's shoulders contested the boundaries of psychology. But after World War II, a new social, political, economic, and ecclesiastical landscape began to take shape. The Second Vatican Council (1962–65) and the changes it wrought had an effect on psychology. The American Catholic Psychological Association (ACPA) responded to the changes by redefining itself and its objectives. In discussing that re-organization, and at the end of the chapter on psychoanalysis, I alluded to emerging interest in phenomenology and humanistic psychology. In this chapter, we turn to these two movements and how they provided a new opening for Catholic psychologists.

I will consider those psychologists who were at the intersection of what we can call the "Catholic questions" and humanistic psychology, beginning in the 1950s. I identify these psychologists primarily by their membership in the ACPA. By the "Catholic questions" I mean, on the one hand, those relating primarily to the nature of the human person, and on the other, those relating to how to treat persons, especially in psychotherapy. Those are the Catholic questions, because they were the ones that lay prominently on the boundary between the field of psychology and the domain of the Church.

A list of Catholic psychologists who contributed to humanistic psychology includes a number of members of the ACPA: Charles A. Curran (1945; 1952; 1954a and 1954b; 1969), Magda Arnold (1954a), Adrian van Kaam (1964), Raymond McCall (1975), Alden Fisher (1969), Frank T. Severin (1965; 1973), Henryk Misiak and Virginia Staudt Sexton (1973), Vytautas Bieliauskas (1974), James E. Royce (1964), André Godin (1952), Annette Walters (1954), Eugene Kennedy (1975), and others. They found common cause with leading humanistic psychologists in their dissatisfaction with the philosophical limitations of behaviorism and psychoanalysis, and with the general psychological neglect of study of the deeper aspects of psychological life. There was common ground between these psychologists and other humanistic psychologists in efforts to articulate an adequate understanding of the human person.

Humanistic psychology, as a critical voice within psychology, responded to the anxieties that throughout the twentieth century pointed to threats to human individuality and freedom, especially in light of totalitarianism. Echoing both Enlightenment and Romantic themes, the humanists expressed a strong anti-authoritarian position, one that resonated clearly in Catholic circles in the United States, where controversies over modernism had waxed and waned over the same time.

After the 1960s, Catholic discourse and identity in psychology changed. Terms that bridged Thomistic and humanistic thought, such as *person*, altered contexts after the Vatican Council, and the often radical changes in the discourse of these psychologists seemed to flow seamlessly across the discontinuity of the 1960s. In this context, a new sense of identity formed for the psychologist, one wary of both scientific and ecclesiastic strictures. But we turn first to two items that providè some backdrop for what seemed like dramatic changes.

From Neoscholastic psychology to Humanistic psychology

Theologians break the crust of Neoscholasticism

The Neoscholastic movement in philosophy and theology suffered a serious decline following the Vatican Council, which broke the "monopoly of scholasticism over Catholic theology" (Cuneno, 1997, p. 11). Discontents analogous to those Catholic psychologists had with a mandated Neoscholastic foundation for empirical psychology, especially with the Neoscholastics disregard of twentieth-century innovations in psychology, existed in theological circles. The Neoscholastic attempts at a system of philosophy meant that it took an ahistorical approach (Gleason, 1989, p. 27), so that it held its truths to be timeless, and that the Scholastic "synthesis" could be tweaked but not overturned. French theologians Henri de Lubac (1896–1991) and Jean Daniélou (1905–74) initiated a *ressourcement* in the 1940s, that is, a return to patristic and medieval writings in a renewal of theological thought in the face of the dominant Thomism. Along with other theologians, including Hans Urs von Balthasar, Marie-Dominique Chenu, Yves Congar, and Pierre Teilhard de Chardin, they developed fresh approaches in theology. De Lubac objected to the "rigid scholasticism" (Grumett, 2007, p. 3) of the early twentieth century, criticizing "a kind of so-called 'Thomistic' dictatorship, which was more a matter of government than intellectuality, [which] strove to stifle any effort toward freer thought" (1993, p. 47, quoted in Grumett, p. 4). Subject to restrictions in what he could write during the 1950s, he and other innovative theologians came into their own with the Vatican Council. These events directly involved some of the psychologists under discussion; Curran, for example, served as *peritus* (expert) at the Counsel on the education of seminarians and priests. More generally, the open window encouraged exploration beyond the then current formulations.

The larger social context

The changes observed were not only theoretical. Catholic values and opinions were changing as well. Edward H. Nowlan, SJ (1956) of Boston College reported to the ACPA in 1955 on the results of a number of surveys of Catholic attitudes, among college students in particular: "Take the matters of mercy killing, birth control, divorce, sterilization, and abortion. Church teaching is clear on these points and Catholics in general react accordingly" (p. 1). There were areas where Catholic disagreed with one another, to be sure: "keeping company with non-Catholics, the possible evils of uncontrolled reproduction, censorship of movies, mixed marriages, and borderline moral problems like 'petting' when vaguely defined" (ibid.). Catholics favored gambling, drinking, card playing, and sports on Sunday, Nowlan noted. Fifteen years later, the waters were muddied. In a book review in the ACPA *Newsletter*, M. Irene Wightwick[1] (1970) summarized the major changes in recent decades: "Catholics have gained socially and economically in this confused, unstable America but they are in turmoil regarding spiritual growth and relationships with the Church and its structure" (p. 5). Other data from the time showed that Catholics were not conforming to Church teachings as much as they had in the past.

Summarizing the changes in Catholic attitudes and values that occurred after the Vatican Council, the sociologist Andrew Greeley argues that what changed was the way ordinary Catholics viewed a rule-bound conception of the Church. Nowlan captured the older view, in saying that "Catholics in general react accordingly." Why? For Greeley (2004), it was because "the rules *were* the Church" (p. 33). On almost every measure between 1963 and 1974, American Catholics decreasingly followed Church teachings, especially in the area of morals. For example, in 1963, 56 percent of Catholics thought that contraception was always wrong, but in 1974, that number dropped to 16 percent. Greeley writes that by 2000, that percentage had dropped to 12 percent. This, despite Pope Paul VI's 1968 encyclical, *Humanae Vitae*, that reaffirmed the Church's opposition to artificial contraception, and despite Pope John Paul II's vigorous support for this encyclical. The reasons for this growing independence – or indifference – to Church teaching are manifold and hotly debated. What is significant is that they occurred, and that psychology played its own part, both as camp follower to the changes and as provider of rationales and rationalizations for them. In particular, humanistic psychology played a role, because of its anti-authoritarian stance in some of its varieties.

---

[1] Wightwick taught at the College of New Rochelle. She was the author of *Vocational interest patterns: A developmental study of a group of college women* (1945).

Not only did the Vatican Council sanction philosophical pluralism, but according to some observers, it also sanctioned the "'therapeutic culture' of the contemporary West" (Cuneno, 1997, p. 36). What did this mean? It meant that in addition to looking at personal defects purely and simply as moral matters, as matters of sin and repentance, the door was opened to considering also the psychological and sociological contexts of human failings and sufferings. It meant that psychology and psychiatry had something to offer care of souls. A key document from the Vatican Council, *Gaudium et spes*, stated: "In pastoral care, sufficient use must be made not only of theological principles, but also of the findings of the secular sciences, especially of psychology and sociology, so that the faithful may be brought to a more adequate and mature life of faith" (*Gaudium et spes*, 1965, section 62). We have already seen steps in this direction with Pope Pius XII's affirmations of psychiatry during the 1950s. The Vatican Council continued the move in this direction. The "Catholic Revolution" of the 1960s began in the 1950s at the very latest. The Council played a decisive role, to be sure, but there were already sweeping changes underway.

Neoscholastic psychologists move toward Humanistic psychology

In the 1950s, members of the ACPA looked beyond the confines of Neoscholasticism to trends in American psychology seen as compatible with the basic tenets of Thomistic thought. The work of Gordon Allport, Carl Rogers, Rollo May, and others – the "founders" of the humanistic movement – looked promising. At the same time, there was an influx from Europe of phenomenological thought that bridged Neoscholasticism and the philosophies of Husserl and Heidegger, imports often carried by ACPA members (Allers, 1961; Hoy, 1964; Van Kaam, 1961). Moreover, Catholic journals, such as *Cross Currents*, *Lumen Vitae*, and *Thought*, published articles by and about leading phenomenological thinkers, as well as Rogers (1953), for example. In the *Catholic Psychological Record* and in the ACPA *Newsletter* were many forays into humanistic psychology. Articles by Giorgi (1962) and Fisher (1964) expanded the horizons of the discussion of psychology in Catholic circles. Later in this chapter, we will look at Neoscholastic psychologists who helped import phenomenological thought into American psychology.

Had psychology been only a scientific study of the psyche, it would not have raised the furor it often did and still does within religious circles. Psychology, however, entails theories and practices of treatment, thus crossing into turf occupied by the pastoral activities of the Church.[2] Coupled with the theoretical issues were those of authority and power. Questions of authority involved the

---

[2] Heated and spirited debate on this point is not confined to the Church of Rome, of course. Nor is the confluence of psychotherapy and pastoral care a new phenomenon, as documented by Vande Kemp (1994).

subject position of psychological discourse: who can speak for and about the psyche? Power surfaced in many forms: the position of psychology and psychiatry in the pastoral activities of the Church; psychotherapy as providing an alternative to spiritual direction; and perhaps most important, the psychotherapeutic reappraisals of the ascetical theology of the first half of the twentieth century.

Enter nondirective therapy

The first and perhaps most decisive change in orientation among Catholic psychologists came with their generally favorable response to the innovations wrought by Carl Rogers (1902–87), which he first termed nondirective and, later, client-centered therapy. Rogers was president of the APA in 1947, the year that Bier organized the ACPA. At the meeting in 1947 that led to the establishment of the ACPA, one specific concern that emerged was a desire to integrate philosophical and scientific psychologies. Richard Zegers, SJ,[3] later Bier's colleague at Fordham, further suggested that if the group did form, one "objective would be the placement of more emphasis on the humanistic and spiritual aspects of clinical psychology" (Sister Mary Roberta Roberts, 1947). This meant more of an emphasis on the properly human, as opposed to the reductionist trend of focusing on the lower aspects of human nature, a trend deemed prevalent in much of contemporary psychotherapy, especially psychoanalysis. Recall that 1947 was the year of Fulton Sheen's denunciation of Freudianism, just months before the ACPA organizing meeting. Sheen taught at the Catholic University of America, from which Bier had just graduated, and he and Zegers were both in New York that year.

As the ACPA organized, Zegers' suggestion bore fruit. At the first meeting of the Board of Directors of the ACPA in September, 1949, in planning for the following year, it rejected a proposal brought by Joseph F. Kubis[4] (1911–82) of Fordham University, for a symposium on psychoanalysis, because it was "a controversial topic even for us, and . . . we wanted an opportunity to think this question through ourselves before holding a discussion on it before outsiders" (Minutes of First Meeting of the Board of Directors, of ACPA, 1949). The problem for the Board was that the discussion would not have been closed to non-members of the ACPA, because of the necessity to get space for the meeting from the APA. A committee was formed, with Harry V. McNeill and Bier as members, to consider planning a symposium on psychoanalysis at a subsequent meeting.[5] The ACPA Board of Directors discussed this possible

---

[3] For Zegers' role in the starting of the ACPA, see Chapter 7.

[4] Kubis was a researcher in the area of lie detection and surveillance.

[5] While the title of this section of the Report is "Committee on Psycho-analysis," in the subsequent paragraph one reads: "This is a Committee to Study Problems Presented by ~~Psychoanalysis~~ to Catholic Psychologists" with the stricken word replaced with a

symposium over the next year and a half. In September 1950, the topic changed from psychoanalysis to psychotherapy, and in March 1951, the topic was further narrowed to client-centered therapy, to be presented at the time of the 1951 APA meeting in Chicago. Charles A. Curran, Louis B. Snider, Barry Fagin, and William C. Cottle were proposed as discussants.[6] Some on the Board had wanted to wait yet another year, when the APA was to meet in Washington, D. C., because then Rudolf Allers could have been invited to participate, and he was well known in Catholic circles as a psychiatrist and a philosopher with strong views on Freud. However, this proposal was discarded, because Allers had "shifted out of the field of therapy." The sensitivity of the ACPA Board to psychoanalysis showed also in a report made at the September 1954 business meeting of the ACPA, when Timothy Gannon (Minutes of the Eighth Annual Meeting of the American Catholic Psychological Association, 1954) reported on his attendance at the May 1954 meeting of the Guild of Catholic Psychiatrists. Gregory Zilboorg, a psychoanalyst and Jewish convert to Catholicism who defended Freud against Catholic criticism (Zilboorg, 1949), spoke on the "Borderlands of Psychiatry and Religion." Gannon noted that the Guild "attempted a more elaborate and ambitious program than our Association. He intended this observation as no criticism of either organization" (p. 1), but the differences do indicate the caution of the leadership of the ACPA. Client-centered therapy seemed benign, relatively speaking.

When the Board decided to have the 1951 presentation, Charles A. Curran was selected as one who would make a "positive, favorable presentation" of Rogers (ACPA Board meeting, Catholic U., 1951). Curran had already contributed to the counseling field (Curran, 1945) and was writing another important work, *Counseling in Catholic life and education* (Curran, 1952). When that book did appear, Albert Grau, SJ,[7] of the Catholic University, reviewed it favorably in the ACPA *Newsletter*. Grau (1952) noted that Curran "draws heavily from Thomistic philosophy and theology to justify and explain the counseling process" and that "the nondirective approach is discussed from a thoroughly Catholic viewpoint" (p. 3). This gave Curran great currency within Catholic circles, since he could connect Rogers' understanding of counseling with the Thomistic tradition.[8]

handwritten "*Psychotherapy.*" I conjecture that the change is in Bier's handwriting. There is no indication when the change was made.

[6] Louis B. Snider taught at Loyola University in Chicago, and worked at the university guidance center; Barry Fagin was educational psychologist; William C. Cottle contributed to the field of tests and measurements, counseling, and related areas.

[7] Grau (born 1914) completed a doctoral thesis from the University of Ottawa in 1960 entitled *The maturity concept of student groups of middle-class American culture.* He taught at Georgetown University and Wheeling College in West Virginia.

[8] Curran received the doctorate in 1944 from Ohio State University, working under Carl Rogers. Curran taught at St. Charles College Seminary (1944–53), was a visiting professor at Louvain (1953–4), and from 1955 until 1978, he taught at Loyola University, Chicago

Rogers' views were not unproblematic from a Catholic point of view. The psychiatrist, Frank Ayd (1952), noted in his review of *Psychiatry and Catholicism* (VanderVeldt and Odenwald, 1952) that "the authors' revelation that Carl Rogers has expressed doubts about the ability of Catholic psychologists to do more than superficial therapy without having conflicts between their beliefs and the tenets of nondirective therapy, should be carefully noted, particularly by some members of the clergy who have been inclined to favor this therapeutic method" (p. 467).[9] The chapter on counseling in Vander Veldt and Odenwald's book[10] was written by Grau, and it did raise objections to Rogers' nondirective approach. First, Grau took issue with Rogers' assumption that human nature is simply good: from the Catholic perspective we are also "inclined toward evil and that man, left to himself, is only too prone to follow his evil tendencies because his intellect is darkened and his will is weakened" (p. 100). Second – and in light of the development of humanistic psychology and Rogers' place in it, this might be considered the primary objection – the Rogerian approach "is an anti-authoritarian system, i.e. it is based on the assumption that the source of valuing things lies exclusively in man himself. Man does not admit any authority outside himself, as he is the shaper of his own destiny" (pp. 100–1). Client-centered therapy assumes no "objective norm of morality" (p. 101), and Curran's attempted harmonization of Rogers and St. Thomas (ibid., n. 6) seemed doubtful to VanderVeldt, Odenwald, and Grau.

Despite such reservations, the promise of client-centered therapy as an alternative to psychoanalysis was great. Curran saw Rogers' view of the person as consonant with the Thomistic view (1945; 1952). For Walter Smet, SJ (1954) a reconsideration of the nature of psychotherapy was tied to a critical examination of the objectivist foundations of psychology (p. 81). Taking an existentialist approach, he argued that the "I–Thou" relationship be foundational for psychology (p. 82). To establish Christian principles at the basis of psychology, action was needed immediately, Smet wrote: "Others around us are already taking the lead in a new direction – especially the nondirective group with Rogers, and the proponents of phenomenological (and existential) psychology in Europe" (p. 87). Smet saw in nondirective therapy a preparation for spiritual direction, in that the acceptance the client experiences prepares the way for a mature relationship with God: "Under the influence of the warmth

[9] Frank Ayd (1920–2008), a psychiatrist who pioneered the use of chlorpromazine and other drugs in the treatment of psychosis, helped establish psychopharmacology (Obituary: Frank J. Ayd Jr., 1920–2008, 2008). Ayd advised Pope Pius in 1958, checking his speech on psychiatry for its accuracy.

[10] Robert p. Odenwald (1899–1965) was a psychiatrist. He ran Catholic University's Child Center from 1948 to 1953. He wrote widely on developmental issues, marriage, and psychiatric disorders among children. James H. VanderVeldt (born 1893) wrote on psychiatric and religious themes. He completed a thesis, *L'apprentissage du mouvement et l'automatisme; étude expérimentale*, in 1928.

and *communion* of understanding, of mutual trust and faith, the client comes to experience the unique quality of human relationships that are based upon respect for human freedom – something he has perhaps never experienced before ... He discovers the positive side of himself, and feels a desire to expand it. Accepting himself, the client can then accept others as they are" (p. 543). The new emphasis on the person, on the I–Thou encounter, and the expressed desire to bring such a perspective both to scientific psychology and psychotherapy were powerful incentives in the 1950s.

Rogers' scientific credentials were respectable. He is credited with bringing scientific objectivity to the study of psychotherapy (Gendlin, 1988), and that counted as much as his philosophical anthropology for Catholic psychologists. Curran (1954b), addressing the ACPA as president, spoke for many when he wrote that "Catholic psychologists ... are the object of what the social psychologists might call a 'two-fold stereotype': The one from those Catholics who sometimes tend to suspect everything psychological, the other from those scientists who may tend to suspect that Catholics cannot be true scientists" (p. 1). As Curran and others worked against these stereotypes, Rogerian approaches took root in their thinking.

When *Cross Currents* published Rogers' essay, "Persons or Science: A Philosophical Question" (1953), it planted it in receptive ground. In the article, Rogers mentioned Walter Smet as one of his correspondents with whom he had thought through the topic of the paper (p. 300, footnote; see Capshew, 1999, pp. 227–8 for a discussion of the paper). This article, which later appeared in the *American Psychologist* (Rogers, 1955) contrasted subjective and experiential with objective and scientific approaches to psychotherapy, and it moved toward a position that while not conclusively, at least tentatively, reconciled the two on experiential grounds: "Science, as well as therapy, as well as all other aspects of living, is rooted in and based upon the immediate, subjective experience of a person. It springs from the inner, organismic experiencing which is only partially and imperfectly communicable" (p. 305). This personalistic, phenomenological (in the broad sense) conception of therapy and science contained at the same time the view that would make of humanistic psychology an aid to those psychologists who came to challenge "the rule-bound" Church. For Rogers, in discussing therapy experientially, stated, very theoretically, that as therapy progresses, the client "finds that he is daring to become himself" (p. 291). What did this mean? It meant

> less fear of the organismic, non-reflective reactions which one has, a gradual growth of trust in and even affection for the complex, varied, rich assortment of feelings and tendencies which exist in one at the organic or organismic level. Consciousness, instead of being the watchman over a dangerous and unpredictable lot of impulses, of which few can be

permitted to see the light of day, becomes the comfortable inhabitant of a richly varied society of impulses and feelings and thoughts, which prove to be very satisfactorily self-governing when not fearfully or authoritatively guarded.

(ibid.)

Rogers cast the basis of this acceptance in terms of Buber's I–Thou relationship between persons.

The contrast with Neoscholasticism must have been felt profoundly by many: here was the absence of the rationalistic and often rigid formality of that way of thinking, and absent too was the mistrustful approach to lower psychological functions, such as feelings, and to all things modern. At the same time, if we read Smet's (1954) chapter, "Existentialism and Scientific Systematization" in light of Rogers' article, we detect a difference between them. Smet extolled the subjective (existential) approach: for Rogers, Smet wrote, "reality must be experienced in its immediacy to be known fully, and not explained or defined. He judges reality more by connaturality than by reason. The objectivist's theoretical arguments seem meaningless to him, and he is, therefore, defenseless" (p. 83). So far, this statement affirms the Rogerian approach. Smet agreed with Rogers that the objectivist or essentialist approach to reality expresses personal inclination. But in contrast to Rogers' "idealism" – Rogers (1953) wrote that "science exists only in people" (p. 300) – Smet argued for complementarity: Only when the existentialist and the essentialist approaches "are isolated from each other and one or the other is taken to be the *only* expression of reality that they run the danger of becoming false and worthless" (1954, p. 83). Since both have merit, the essentialist approach of "norms, essences, principles" (p. 82) has validity independently of the existentialist approach. This "balance" Rogers did not propose, as it would have given authority to something other than the "organismic," which was for him, in a sense, infallible. Now the objectivism that Smet wanted to balance with existentialism was natural scientific psychology and not Neoscholastic philosophical psychology. Nevertheless, he did consider the Thomistic "conceptual framework" as a way to compensate for the deficiencies of psychology's "exclusively secularistic orientation" (p. 81). But he rejected that solution, and instead proposed, "the 'I-Thou' relationship be made the basis of psychology" (p. 82). From there, he discussed the complementarity of essentialist and existentialist approaches in psychology as a means of supplying a coherent foundation for a Christian orientation in psychology.

Even granting the differences between Rogers and Smet on the grounds of knowledge in psychology, Smet offered an approach radically different from that of the Neoscholastics. For them, there was no complementarity between the two approaches, even if we call them philosophical and empirical psychology, for nothing empirical (never mind experiential), could shake the secure conceptual foundations of psychology, which were deemed timeless. At best, empirical psychology could add nuance and detail to the elaborate philosophical architecture. What Smet proposed[11] would be proposed, more or less independently, by others. In particular, we will see how Alden Fisher made an analogous distinction. But that difference was not the most important one.

Anthony Barton[12] (1974) provided a later assessment of Rogerian therapy, drawing on both Rogers and Curran. The basis of Rogerian therapy is "the *really natural self*, the organismic-self, ... a fluid-like ground for a firmly realistic valuing process based on a naturally given life of feeling-valuing" (p. 182, emphasis in original). This feeling self often suffers suppression in the course of development, because in order to win and maintain love or positive self-regard, aspects of the self are found, by the child and others, as "bad." For the Rogerian therapist, "the basic problem with the neurotic client ... is that he has departed from his own values by taking on the values of others" (p. 177). The underlying individualism and emphasis on feelings detached from other considerations contained the source of some of the friction between the humanistic movement and Catholic thought. Barton acknowledged Curran's "alternative vision" of client-centered therapy, observing that the self stressed in Curran is not so much the "feeling self" as it was the "prudent, reasoning, judging, perceiving self" (p. 199), indicating thereby how Curran fused a Thomistic with a Rogerian view of the self. Nevertheless, Curran accentuated the subjective experience of the person and also focused on the individual's uniqueness.

Rogers', Smet's, and Curran's trust in the existential – or subjective – indicated a radical shift in attitude, which was characteristic of the humanistic movement in psychology. Smet put it in these terms: "the other person will act in the way we expect him to act. If a psychologist expects his client to behave as if he were the playball of impersonal forces, buffeted by id-impulses, and acts toward him as if he were, then his client will respond according to expectations" (p. 85). This statement, obliquely to be sure, takes aim not only at psychoanalysis, but also at the mainstay of Catholic spiritual direction for the first half of the twentieth century and its articulation in ascetical theology. But before dealing with the older spiritual psychology, the movement away from Neoscholasticism among American Catholic psychologists needs to be addressed.

---

[11] Admittedly, the distinction essentialist/existentialist is not the same as the philosophical/ empirical, although in both the first term is systematic and deductive (in this formulation), and the second term sense-based and inductive.

[12] Barton (born 1934) received a Ph.D. in psychology from the University of Chicago in 1964. Earlier he worked at the University of Chicago's Counseling Center (1957–9), where he met van Kaam. He also was a therapist at Chicago's Catholic Charities Counseling Center, where he met Charles Maes. In 1960, he came to Duquesne University (Maes joined him there in 1961). For some years, he took part "in the workshops sponsored by the Institute of Religion and Personality [van Kaam's institute in the early 1960s] and took part in renewal programs for religious communities throughout the country" (Smith, 2002, p. 146).

From Neoscholasticism to Humanism

Many were the connections between ACPA members and humanistic psychology. Some of the evidence for the interest in Catholic psychologists in the "third force" includes reviews in the ACPA *Newsletter* and collaboration between ACPA members, such as Bier, Annette Walters, and Adrian van Kaam, with leading lights in humanistic psychology (including Rogers, Maslow, and Allport). John W. Stafford, CSV, who succeeded Thomas Verner Moore at the Catholic University and who had contributed to philosophy and to the quantitative study of clinical psychology, was described in 1962 as "an avowed client-centered therapist" (Cavanagh, 1962, p. 51). The publication of *Humanistic viewpoints in psychology* (Severin, 1965) was a key moment, for it brought together various strands of Catholic and humanistic thinking. Severin's book included chapters by ACPA members (Frank J. Kobler and van Kaam), as well as by the Belgian psychologist, Joseph Nuttin, who synthesized humanistic and psychoanalytic approaches, and by the philosopher, Pierre Teilhard de Chardin, SJ. Finally, Misiak and Staudt Sexton, who had earlier collaborated on *Catholics in psychology* (1954), wrote a new synthesis, entitled *Phenomenological, existential and humanistic psychologies* (1973).

It is always challenging to define intellectual and institutional movements – even more so when everyone answers to a different drummer. Humanistic psychology did not have a Freud to define orthodoxy. Humanism meant the inclusion of all things human, especially its highest potential as central topics for psychological study, and this inclusion entailed expanding the limits of psychological research methods. This is humanistic psychology, broadly defined, meant as science, a human science (Giorgi, 1970). To others, humanistic psychology meant a focus on the autonomy and the personally defined potentialities of the individual. For example, Charlotte Buhler (1974) defined humanistic psychology in terms of the "person ... *determining himself*, instead of being directed from the outside," in effect seconding the observation made earlier by VanderVeldt, Odenwald, and Cavanagh. It would be anti-humanistic in this sense to define a person in a priori terms; the mainstreams of psychology, behaviorism and psychoanalysis, assumed that human nature "needed strong outside forces to keep the individual in line and give him direction" (p. 3). While this anti-authoritarian attitude initially was that of the therapist, it soon extended beyond therapy to be an ideal for human relationships generally. According to Anthony Giddens (1991), a mix of self-definition, anti-authoritarianism, and self-actualization characterizes a society of high modernity, so that despite humanistic psychology's marginal position vis-à-vis academic psychology, it reflected and contributed to widely shared views of self-identity in the west. Humanistic psychology in this second sense blended in easily with the political and lifestyle agendas of the New Left of the 1960s and beyond.

Movement among Catholic psychologists from a Thomistic foundation for psychology to humanistic psychology is, of course, a complex topic. Any philosophical and applied trend that contained both a more adequate conception of the person and a non-reductionist approach to science was welcome as an alternative to Neoscholasticism. In addition to connections with American humanistic psychologists, as noted above, there was much interest in phenomenological and existential thought. As the writings of European phenomenologists, existentialists, and personalists became available, they were well received by many Catholic psychologists. A primary example is that of the work of Viktor Frankl: logotherapy represented, in his own terms, an alternative to both Freud and Adler, whom Frankl criticized as not having a complete conception of human life. James E. Royce, SJ (1956) praised *The doctor and the soul* (Frankl, 1955), the first of the Viennese psychiatrist's books to appear in English, for its emphasis on meaning, but also noted that "it is striking that one so insistent on the spiritual should state flatly that all clinical neurosis has an underlying constitutional (biological) cause. This accords, however, with this reviewer's ... growing suspicion that some Catholics may have leaned too heavily on psychogenesis for apologetic reasons" (p. 5). Even before the translation of this book, moreover, there were favorable critical presentations of Frankl by Arnold and Gasson (1954b).

Adrian van Kaam's work represented a philosophical approach that spanned Thomistic and existential–phenomenological thought. Such integrative work was pursued by other Catholic thinkers from the Netherlands and Belgium, including many who also had ties to Duquesne University, where van Kaam came in 1954: Henry Koren, Stephen Strasser, William Luijpen, Hans Linschoten, Remy Kwant (see Smith, 2002). Van Kaam (1961; 1963) helped to bring phenomenological psychological thought to the United States, and his *Existential foundations of psychology* (1966b) constituted a synthesis in the spirit of earlier Thomistic works, such as Mercier's, but one attuned to the positive contributions of psychoanalysis, behaviorism, and other "differential psychologies," as van Kaam called them. Moreover, even before coming to the United States, he "had taught Thomistic philosophical anthropology in the spirit and letter of the original Thomas Aquinas and not that of the later versions of neo-Thomism or neo-scholasticism" (Personal communication, November 16, 1999). Van Kaam, while presenting a philosophical anthropology grounded in Catholic philosophical thought, kept this book in a "pre-theological" context, as he also did subsequently in his work on what he called formative spirituality. After his arrival in the United States, van Kaam studied psychotherapy with Carl Rogers, and he collaborated extensively with Abraham Maslow. Van Kaam's association with Rogers, and his editorial work on such journals as the *Review of Existential Psychology and Psychiatry*, did much to set the framework for the humanistic phenomenological research and writing on psychotherapy that came from the Duquesne school.[13]

---

[13] Van Kaam was the editor of the *Review of Existential Psychology and Psychiatry* in its early years (until the mid-1960s – see Giorgi (1998)). His colleagues at Duquesne, Anthony Barton and Henry Elkin, were associate editors, along with Rollo May. The Editorial Board

In place of experimental settings, characteristic of earlier attempts in phenomenological psychology (e.g. Stumpf and Külpe), the Duquesne school emphasized first-hand descriptions of lived events, attempting to understand them from the point of view of the person experiencing them, not imposing a priori psychological categories on the experiences. The methods, developed most significantly by Amedeo Giorgi (a member of the ACPA in the early 1960s, after his graduation from Fordham), owe much to the humanistic impetus in Allport and Rogers, as well as to existential phenomenological thought.

Like van Kaam, Severin (1909–95), a charter member of the ACPA and longtime faculty member at St. Louis University, sought to enlarge the scope and methods of psychology, in order to make it more meaningfully related to human life as it is lived. His *Humanistic viewpoints in psychology* (1965), called *Discovering man in psychology* (Severin, 1973) in revision, drew together readings primarily from psychologists, although he gave the last word to Teilhard de Chardin.[14] He also explored the implications of Teilhard's interpretation of the evolution of the cosmos and of humanity in essays (Severin, 1967a, 1967b). For Severin, Teilhard had defined the decisive issues facing psychology:

> Modern man feels like a newborn infant opening his eyes to the world for the first time: Everything seems strange and terrifying. For centuries he had grown accustomed to the comfort of a narrow intellectual outlook that neatly arranged small segments of knowledge in isolated categories. Now he must rearrange his whole inner world, finding a new equilibrium for all its contents. A single mental index no longer suffices, for everything is related to everything else and must be appropriately cross-referenced. But more upsetting still is the growing awareness of his own responsibility for the continued progress of evolution.
>
> (1967a, p. 158)

Teilhard (1881–1955) was a fitting thinker for this humanistic psychology – holistic, future-oriented, challenging the reigning paradigms in the natural sciences, engaging in research himself. He was a problematic thinker from the Vatican's point of view. He had been silenced, i.e. not allowed to teach, from the mid-1920s, and in 1962, the Vatican issued a *monitum*, a warning, about his writings because his "works abound in such ambiguities and indeed even serious errors, as to offend Catholic doctrine." Because of this, the Vatican wanted "to protect the minds, particularly of the youth, against the dangers presented by the works of Fr. Teilhard de Chardin and of his followers" (Holy Office, 1962). In 1963, Severin wrote and received permission from his provincial, Linus J. Thro, SJ, to include Teilhard in *Humanistic viewpoints in*

---

in the early 1960s included Gordon Allport, Viktor Frankl, Abraham Maslow, Carl Rogers, Erwin Straus, Paul Tillich, and others.

[14] Theilard was a good friend of Henri de Lubac, who defended Theilard against critics after his death in 1955.

psychology. Severin argued to Charles F. McDermott, SJ, the Vice Provincial, that the readings from Teilhard were necessary, because "De Chardin is one of the few authors who at the present time can say such a thing [as science progresses it will concentrate more on man and find itself increasingly coming face to face with ·religion] to Positivists without being rejected out of hand" (Severin, 1963). Moreover, Severin saw that the time was ripe for the kind of book he had in mind, as he wrote in this letter:

> It is only once in a lifetime that a person can see a new field opening up in which a book has not been written as is now the case in humanistic psychology (as I define it) ... I want to do my best to see that humanistic psychology develops to be a synonym for Christian psychology rather than man-centered psychology with no place for God as some leaders are trying to make it.

Severin, like van Kaam and others, offered a humanistic psychology that was compatible with Catholic understandings of the person, without the defensive tone of much previous Catholic writings on the subject. But this humanistic psychology in the broad sense was but one strand of this complex weave.

Importing phenomenology into North American psychology: Three phenomenological Thomists

> We shall do a service not only to the science of psychology but to confused, harassed, unhappy modern man, who dares not believe in common sense unless it has the stamp of scientific approval.
>
> (Arnold, 1954, p. 36)

In the middle decades of the twentieth century, phenomenological thought arrived in North America and asserted influence in psychology and psychotherapy. At the time, van Kaam (1961) realized that it was not simply a transfer of ideas, but a translation into a different cultural milieu, one not immediately devastated by two world wars. Earlier studies of the beginnings of phenomenological psychology (Churchill, 2000; Cloonan, 1995; Halling and Nill, 1995; Misiak and Sexton, 1973; Spiegelberg, 1972) have used history to promote phenomenology within North American psychology. However, we are interested in how phenomenological thought fell into the opening created by the decline of Neoscholastic thought, and in how such inquiry took up the concerns of the Neoscholastics while putting them into new contexts. This was not as difficult as it may sound, since there was already much interplay in philosophical circles between phenomenological and Thomistic thought.

Awareness of the chasm separating scientific achievement and its ethical use was a constant theme in the post-World War II period, in psychology as elsewhere. Although psychology's technological contributions have been modest, they could contribute to our self-destruction because they directly affect our self-understanding. In an address to the newly founded Division of Philosophical Psychology of the APA in 1963, William L. Kelly (1965) stated that, given the problems facing humanity, it was essential that "an integral conception of man must guide the scientific efforts on man's behalf." Why? Because, he said, "error here could mean genocide" (p. 429). Many psychologists who responded to the threats posed by scientific psychology (regardless of its actual results or power) – engaged in teaching, research, and therapy, many of these psychologists found in phenomenological and existential thought a new way of thinking and speaking about the psychological that promised an effective reply to the "robot" that dominated mainstream psychological images of the human.

According to Spiegelberg (1972), the publication of *Existence* (1958), edited by Rollo May, Ernest Angel, and Henri Ellenberger, was the key event in establishing an awareness of phenomenology in American psychology. Here, we will focus on the "importers" of phenomenology, rather than the "exporters," European émigrés such as van Kaam, Erwin Straus, and Aaron Gurwitsch.[15] Instead, representative philosophical psychologists, members of the ACPA, will occupy my attention: Arnold, McCall, and Fisher. These psychologists, before promoting a phenomenological approach in psychology, had espoused a Thomistic grounding for psychology.

There was much interest in phenomenological thought within Thomistic circles, as contributions to journals such as *Modern Schoolman* and the *Thomist* from the 1940s onwards show, so that Arnold, McCall, and Fisher did not bridge Thomistic and scientific psychologies by way of phenomenology in a vacuum. I will focus on their psychology as a scientific enterprise, and on how they understood philosophy and psychology as separate but related undertakings. Each translated phenomenology onto the American psychological scene in some way: each furthered phenomenological thought through their teaching and writing, and through participation in organizations, such as Division 24, Theoretical and Philosophical Psychology, of the APA.[16] All three were as concerned with psychotherapy as with scientific psychology, and therapeutic praxis contributed to the autonomy of psychology vis-à-vis philosophy: Arnold researched projective testing; McCall conducted research using the MMPI, practiced clinical psychology, and helped found the Wisconsin School of Professional Psychology; and Fisher taught psychiatry in the Medical School of St. Louis University. This pattern fits that of many of the psychologists who promoted phenomenological thought in North America:

[15] I am not dealing with household names in clinical psychology, such as May and Rogers, nor on researchers like Giorgi. Likewise ignored here are those, such as Donald Snyggs (1904–67) and Arthur W. Combs (1912–99), who began to speak about phenomenology before the European influx.

[16] Magda Arnold was president of Division 24 in 1973–4, Raymond McCall from 1980–2 (in addition to other positions in this division), and Alden Fisher was a Member-at-Large of the Executive Committee 1967–70.

academics who also had a strong interest in or practice of psychotherapy. Psychotherapy was the main avenue through which phenomenological thought entered this hemisphere, precisely because in this area, the limitations of a method-bound academic psychology were most strongly felt; in addition, questions of meaning and purpose, which often lead people to therapy, were most directly addressed in phenomenological and existential writers.

Magda Arnold (1903–2002)

Magda Barta Arnold, an Austrian-born immigrant to Canada in 1928, studied psychology at the University of Toronto (Ph.D., 1942, in experimental psychology), and taught there until 1947, when she moved to the United States, teaching at several universities: Bryn Mawr College, Loyola University in Chicago, and Spring Hill College in Mobile, Alabama, from which she retired in 1975. She is the most traditional of the three under consideration, in two ways: she stayed closer to Neoscholastic psychology than did McCall and Fisher, and she emphasized the explanatory, especially the physiological, aspects of psychology as a necessary complement to the phenomenological or descriptive aspects.

Arnold and her frequent collaborator, John A. Gasson, SJ (1904–88), edited papers from a 1951 "Workshop on Personality" into a book for courses in personality theory (Arnold and Gasson, 1954a). They attempted "to formulate an integrated theory of personality based on a Christian understanding of human nature" (p. iii), and its first contribution was "Basic Assumptions in Psychology" by Arnold and Gasson. Here they presented a Thomistic conception of the relations between philosophy and psychology, namely that every psychology has philosophical presuppositions, acknowledged or not, that constitute the basis of psychological research and not its conclusions. Psychology, according to a narrative standard at the time and still current, excludes philosophical discourse because psychology "still suffers from its early struggles to become a science and has not yet outgrown the aggressive and belligerent spirit it developed in its attempt to free itself from its philosophical heritage" (p. 4). Psychology could ignore questions of the nature of human nature only as long as its attention was on elementary mental activities, such as those of psychophysics – again, Arnold and Gasson affirmed a standard narrative of the history of psychology. But "when psychologists begin to study man in his daily living" (p. 6), then the question of human nature becomes figural. Since science intends the "prediction and control of the subject matter" (p. 7), psychologists must ask: "In whose favor are we going to exercise that control? ... Where is man's true benefit" (ibid.)? Psychologists hide behind a fact/value distinction, but they are "being called in by government agencies to help them *decide on action*" (ibid.). Even the question of the existence of God cannot be excluded from psychology, because it concerns the origins and destiny of human life. If one turns to what could be the basic assumption about human nature, four alternatives exist: physical naturalism, critical idealism, psychophysical parallelism, and personalism. The personalist view, to which they subscribed because it best accounts for scientific and ordinary experience, defines human nature as a "compound unit, made up of the principle of organization and the material organized" (p. 14), i.e. in Aristotelian terms, soul and body. They avoided the term "soul" here, because of its lack of currency in American psychology, though in a more philosophical context, Arnold (1977) did speak directly of the human soul. Arnold and Gasson argued that the results of scientific psychological research, especially concerning human choice, development, and psychotherapy, point to the personalistic alternative, and thus necessitate a rehabilitation of final causes in psychology. They concluded that the personalist conception, with its stated understanding that we have an "eternal destiny," is actually more scientific than the mechanistic view.

Arnold, then, disputed the autonomy of psychology vis-à-vis philosophy. Although she found that phenomenological approaches better approximated Aristotelian conceptions of the person than did mechanistic ones, her Thomistic stance prevailed in her work, even when she helped bring phenomenological thought into American psychology. For instance, in *The Human Person*, Arnold and Gasson (1954b) introduced the work of Viktor Frankl to North American psychology. *Ärzliche Seelsorge*, which they summarized, had not yet appeared in English; that would come a year later, with an imprimatur by Gordon Allport (Frankl, 1955). After summarizing Frankl's existential analysis, Arnold and Gasson evaluated it. They found it preferable to Freud or Adler, because it was not reductionistic, and they concluded that Frankl made an important contribution to personality theory and to psychotherapy. Yet they saw limitations in Frankl's theory, in that from their point of view, he did not "follow through the implications of the primary data of existential analysis, *consciousness* (or self-awareness) and *responsibility*" (p. 491). Frankl spoke of values, life tasks, listening for the meaning of one's life, yet he did not ask about the object (the subject) to whom one owes responsibility or who assigns the tasks. Because of this, Frankl was "defenseless against any objectivist assault because he is completely open only to subjectivist understanding" (p. 488), and then "therapy can easily substitute for religion" (p. 491). The personalist philosophy completed Frankl's system, they held.

Arnold's most important contribution to phenomenological psychology was her *Emotion and Personality* (1960). While she did not formally present Thomistic presuppositions, they clearly dominated in the approach. Since a human being is organized matter, an examination of the physiological processes that mediate but do not determine human experience and behavior is necessary and not reductionistic. Prior to the study of the brain functions, however, comes the psychological analysis, since it is the person who feels emotion, not the brain. Basic to this psychological analysis is a phenomenological inquiry, in the course of which she discusses the work of Sartre, Scheler,

May, and others. But her phenomenological analysis "of the whole sequence from perception to emotion and action" (p. 170) assumed that "perception," "appraisal," and "emotion" exist as such, and it does not perform anything like a Husserlian *époche* of these categories of common sense. Phenomenology means, in this context, descriptive presentation and interpretation of the psychological realities of common sense.

From Arnold's perspective, however, this is not a failing to be sufficiently radical in a break with traditional categories, it is a tacit recognition of what has more recently (Bruner, 1990) been called the folk psychological basis of all psychologies, and a hermeneutical conception of the *Lebenswelt*. Not that Arnold said either of these things, but she did affirm the truth of common sense because it springs from everyday awareness and self-awareness on the part of rational beings, namely, ordinary human beings, even though they have not adopted the scientific method. Common sense is "the mother of science," as she put it (Arnold, 1960, p. 6), and scientific abstractions arise from and inform us about specific aspects of it. In psychology, the rejection of ordinary terms, such as *thinking* and *will* often arise from a desire by psychologists to emulate the natural sciences, and they so substitute terms such as *problem-solving* and *tension-reduction*. The substitute terms derive all too often from mechanistic interpretations of the psychological, and Arnold proposed to "return to the common human experience of emotion that is as accessible to the psychologist as it is to the layman and is described by both in the same terms in their daily life" (p. 11). Written before current interest in the cultural shaping of affective life, Arnold's main concern here was the reflexivity of everyday human experience. Her approach undercut the presumptive authority of the expert, not on the basis that the psychologist does not have expert knowledge but rather because anyone is capable potentially of testing this knowledge through personal experience. This undercutting stemmed from her conception of the human person. Thus her phenomenological approach produced a descriptive account of psychological states grounded in everyday experience and expressed in common terms: "Our phenomenological analysis is not meant to give an accurate description of one person's experience which will be used as the literal equivalent of everyone else's experience. Rather, we take the differences in analogous experience for granted and discuss the conditions under which every human being will have a similar but not identical emotional experience" (p. 13). Then and only then can the physiological aspects, as material part of the human person, be analyzed.

Arnold translated phenomenology into American psychology because it was useful in correcting the mechanistic biases of the mainstream. She did not, however, champion any particular version of phenomenology, and she was certainly not a phenomenological purist. Like other Thomistic thinkers, phenomenology as she understood it was a means of staying close to common human experience, recognizing the centrality of reflexivity, and a welcome alternative to idealism and naturalism.

Raymond J. McCall (1913–90)

Raymond J. McCall was a Thomistic philosopher/psychologist who later took up a phenomenological approach. His training and contributions were both philosophical (McCall, 1983) and psychological (McCall, 1975). His understanding of the relationships between them had much to do with his reading of the history of psychology. McCall, like Arnold, appropriated the dominant narrative that psychology emerged and separated from philosophy at the end of the nineteenth century with the rise of the New Psychology. Not only did he appropriate it, he enacted it. He established masters degree programs in experimental and clinical psychology at Marquette University between 1956 and 1961. He even humorously described a rapprochement between psychology and philosophy in terms of psychology abreacting the "cathexis of its birth trauma, and is now quite ready to join forces with its mother, philosophy" (McCall, 1952, p. 83). This theoretical separation from philosophy he felt was fading, and there was appearing among psychologists a willingness to treat philosophical questions as such. Psychology, now in its "adolescence," was reaching out to philosophy; unfortunately, it extended its grasp to logical positivism. Philosophy is more developed than psychology, and in his "stages of scientific development" (p. 86), he declared that psychology is in the first "preinductive" stage, comparable to biology in the eighteenth century. Physics, by contrast, is in the second stage of "inductive and hypothetico-deductive" thinking. In the preinductive stage, there are no general laws established which would state the conditions for the prediction and control of human psychological activity. He stated his mission to psychology in these terms:

> If we have the tact to commend the psychologist for his growing tendency to adhere to the reality of man as experienced, and the forbearance to criticize gently his philosophical naiveté, while pointing unemotionally to the immediate philosophical implications of the experience he is endeavoring to understand, we should find our efforts to communicate not altogether vain.

> (p. 88)

He sought to follow through with this mission in a number of ways.

In a 1942 article, "Truth and propaganda,"[17] he wrote that, "a philosophy that does not constantly renew itself by meditation on and reference to new

---

[17] He delivered this paper after having received an M.A. in philosophy from the Catholic University of America and a Ph.D. in philosophy from Fordham University in 1941. He had begun graduate work in psychology in 1942, and after military service as a Naval officer in World War II, he completed a Ph.D. in "experimental abnormal psychology" in 1951. Between 1936 and 1951, he taught in the Department of Philosophy and Psychology at St. John's University. He subsequently taught philosophy and psychology at De Paul University (1951–6) and psychology at Marquette University (1956–84).

situations and problems as history poses them is a philosophy doomed ultimately to sterile academism, its eternal verities reduced to verbalisms" (McCall,
1942). This urge to renewal was consonant with the impetus of Neoscholasticism
since the nineteenth century. At the same time, it echoed what many scientific
psychologists saw as the limitation of Thomistic psychology, its lack of real
engagement with natural scientific investigation. For McCall, any philosophy
that lacks "constant apposition to and renewal in terms of the order of concrete
action" will wither from lack of interest, even among "its own partisans" (p. 49).
He called for a level of inquiry like that of jurisprudence, one that ties thought to
action. This 1942 essay sounded themes that echoed throughout McCall's writing. In his 1960 presidential address to the ACPA (McCall, 1962), he discussed
psychological theories of motivation in the context of an Aristotelian understanding of human nature.[18] In his 1952 and 1962 articles, he used the term
"phenomenological" without strict definition to mean a description of phenomena preliminary to scientific explanation for them (p. 23). Phenomenology
means, in this context, the gathering of experiences, a step necessarily prior to
the elaboration of lawful relationships between them. This Baconian interpretation of phenomenology was McCall's understanding even after he studied
Heidegger with Medard Boss in 1977.

McCall's turn to phenomenology had two sources, at least. First was his
interest in clinical psychology. Second was his understanding of the logical
development of the sciences, presented in the 1952 article, elaborated in *A
preface to scientific psychology* (1959), and discussed again in *Phenomenological
psychology* (McCall, 1983). The beginnings of his formal writing in phenomenology dealt with a reassessment of psychological defense mechanisms, moving from a psychoanalytic to a functional interpretation (McCall, 1963).

After 1970, his involvement with phenomenological thought deepens. In 1971,
he met Medard Boss at a workshop Boss conducted for the APA. Convinced
that the English translations of Boss were "irredeemably bad" and of Heidegger's
Sein und Zeit "totally incomprehensible to the psychiatrists and psychologists
to whom I showed it" (McCall, 1983, pp. 3–4), McCall spent six months with
Boss in 1977 working out English translations of "fifty to sixty terms which are
key words in Heidegger's system, especially those aspects of his system which
Boss sees as most relevant to psychological questions" (p. 4). What is intriguing
about McCall's approach to phenomenology is that he never concluded that it led
to a human science as opposed to a natural science psychology in the Diltheyian
mode, as did Giorgi and others. For McCall, the decisive issue was not what
methods to use in psychology, but what conception of human nature lies behind

---

[18] McCall's (1962) approach is quite intriguing and has been neglected. It resembles that of
Joseph Nuttin, and it has the advantage over Maslow's theory of motivation in that for
McCall, self-actualization "is not a special kind of motive but an overarching principle
applicable to human motivation generally" (p. 24).

one's interpretations of empirical findings. He acknowledged Boss's mistrust of "scientific method as applied to any aspect of the human condition" because of the almost inevitably "physicalistic and mechanistic" interpretations to which it leads, but McCall distinguished science and scientism. Science is "an admirable enterprise which has opened to man the understanding and control of nature to a degree undreamed of before the seventeenth century, when the systematic application of the scientific method began" (p. 7), whereas scientism is the aping of an outmoded physics by psychology. With Boss as his foil, McCall argued for the importance of scientific method, both for its ability to reach the truth and for its rhetorical value:

> Neither the validity of Boss's highly plausible theories of motivation, diagnosis, and dream interpretation nor the effectiveness of the various psychotherapeutic procedures he advocates will find full acceptance without supportive empirical evidence such as might be provided by frequency counts, incidence figures for various diagnostic categories, reliability measures, outcome statistics, and the like.

(p. 8)

Yet for McCall psychology is still a pre-science, and he criticized behaviorism, psychoanalysis, Rogerian humanism, and neuropsychology for various forms of reductionism. In one way or another, these presumptive scientific psychologies miss the psychological, "knowing (*cognition*), motivation and emotion (*appetition*), or both" (p. 9), categories based in Aristotle and the Thomistic tradition. Behaviorists may use a scientific method, but their explanations of what they discover are not themselves empirical. Propaedeutic to a scientific psychology is phenomenological psychology "as a pre-science whose emergence heralds the possibility of a fundamental change in psychology as an empirical discipline" (p. 131). In a way analogous to how Husserl saw phenomenological psychology as necessarily prior to a positive psychology, for McCall, phenomenological psychology as a pre-science would enable the "the application of the scientific (i.e. empirical) method to psychological phenomena as such, which is to say as they are in themselves and not as construed according to a model or paradigm derived from other sciences such as physics or biology" (p. 97).[19]

[19] McCall's claim that that phenomenology is a preamble to scientific psychology has been subject to criticism within the Thomistic–phenomenological tradition by William L. Kelly (1965) and Stephen Strasser (1951), who point to the limitations of integrating philosophical thought with a natural science psychology. If philosophical thought rises above the sciences and, at the same time, depends on them, then one version of integration is to take the methodological grounds of the sciences on their own terms. For Kelly (1965), that would "inhibit further effort on the part of scientific psychology to broaden the experiential basis of the science and is likely to support the position which would limit that basis to strictly objective, quantifiable, observable facts" (p. 434). Kelly argued for "the inclusion of prescientific data into the meaningful manifold of human

McCall used phenomenology to rectify the foundations of psychology as a science, specifically to form an adequate description and categorization of psychological phenomena. The phenomenological thought of Husserl, Heidegger, and Boss supplied both, although it seems clear that a Thomistic conception of the psychological remained McCall's lodestar. With all this McCall, like Arnold, located his work within psychological discourse, with its emphasis on method and its historical narrative of separation from philosophy, and with its destiny of applicability.

Alden L. Fisher (1928–70)

Alden Fisher, remembered chiefly for his translation of Maurice Merleau-Ponty's *The structure of behavior* (1963), like Arnold and McCall imported phenomenology into North America. Fisher received his philosophical education at St. Louis University (M.A. in 1953), then still a center for Thomistic thought in the United States; his Ph.D. in psychology was from the University of Louvain in 1956, where he studied under Alphonse de Waelhens and where he met Merleau-Ponty. He taught philosophy at St. Louis University beginning in 1956, and in 1960 he also began teaching psychology in the Psychiatry Department at the Medical School at the same university.

In "Psychology or Psychologies – A Study in Methodology" (Fisher, 1957), he addressed types of psychological approaches – philosophical, scientific, and one that had no name, which derives from a phenomenological approach. The first two categories correspond to the division of intellectual labor current in Thomistic circles: there are two psychologies, philosophical and empirical, a division continuing an older tradition of rational and empirical psychologies. In mainstream American psychology, the division was meaningless, since empirical psychology did not recognize philosophical psychology as psychology. In American Thomistic circles, however, it was recognized, and outside North America, the two psychologies were not as sharply separated. Fisher's studies at Louvain put him into contact with thinkers, such as de Waelhens, Merleau-Ponty, and Antoine Vergote, whose work was as psychological as it was philosophical. Fisher recognized the legitimacy of the two psychologies, but in introducing the third, a phenomenological psychology, he articulated a new

experience as potentially useful to the scientific investigator" (p. 422). Kelly, moreover, urged that the term of integration be "the human person" rather than "human nature," and that integration be effected with those trends in psychology that "offer a genuine basis of rapport" (p. 435), such as the *Ganzheitpsychologie* and personalistic psychology. The upshot of Kelly's proposal is the establishment of a new psychological object, the human person, and a breakdown of methodological purity on the part of both philosophy (a move from the "dianotic, intuitive-deductive intellectual grasp of the intelligibility of man" (p. 439)), and psychology (the equation of empirical with natural scientific experimentation).

configuration that did not conform to Thomistic understandings of the two psychologies. For the older Thomists, such as Mercier and Brennan, philosophical psychology provides the ultimate conceptualizations for psychology, with scientific psychology contributing the empirical details to be examined. In contrast to the Thomistic hierarchical model of the sciences was the separation model of the New Psychology, based on a positivistic conception of the history of knowledge. Fisher supplied a third model, in which "the relations of philosophical anthropology and the sciences of man" are based upon "'neither subordination nor simple coexistence' [citing de Waelhens]" (Fisher, 1961, p. 56).[20] This new type of psychology, in which "I am confronted with a different kind of knowledge which is neither [natural] science (as we defined it), philosophy, nor humanistic knowledge, but which is in all events, and whatever you call it, properly a new kind of psychology which opens up a whole new area of possibilities for the study and understanding of man" (Fisher, 1957, p. 157). He later referred to this new psychology under the heading "the sciences of man," and pointed to psychoanalysis as potentially such a psychology (Fisher, 1961). Fisher suggested that the "empirical counterpart" of phenomenology, "be it phenomenological or existential psychology ... remains unsettled in spite of the fact that outstanding individual contributions continue to be made" (Fisher, 1964, p. 140). Fisher's conception of these psychologies differs in a fundamental way from that of Arnold and McCall's, and to it I turn.

For Fisher, philosophical, natural scientific, and this other third psychology all ground themselves in everyday experience, the *Lebenswelt*.[21] The philosophical attitude proceeds by means of "intellectual intuition," staying with the givens of experience (not to be understood in an empiricist fashion), and leading to the "real, necessary, ontological structure of reality" (Fisher, 1957, p. 148). In another place, he described the philosophical project in terms borrowed from Merleau-Ponty and de Waelhens: "to render explicit and thematic that which was only implicit and lived" (Fisher, 1961, p. 72). The scientific attitude, by contrast, begins with an abstractive moment of objectification, followed by one of reconstruction. Reconstructed things replace the *Lebenswelt*; thus, for example, the lived experience of color becomes reconstructed as a secondary quality and

---

[20] In perhaps his final publication, the editing of *Philosophy and science as modes of knowing*, Fisher and his co-editor George B. Murray (1969) stressed this non-hierarchical conception, which contrasts with Neoscholastic views: "Epistemology is viewed as based not on the notion of a 'hierarchy' of types of knowledge – science seen as dealing with proximate causes and philosophy with ultimate causes – but on the idea that the different ways of knowing are complementary, that they are in a sense horizontal and not necessarily to be subordinated one to the other" (p. vii).

[21] Scientific psychology too, a main point for William Kelly, in his critique of how some Thomists, including Klubertanz, see the foundation of scientific psychology in experimentation. See also Strasser (1951).

not as a property of things. Fisher acknowledged his debt to both Thomistic as well as to phenomenological thinkers in this analysis. Scientific psychology, in these terms, has yet to jell, wrote Fisher, because it has not determined its proper object: the abstraction from which science begins (not a reductionism, since one may take a part for a whole and not confuse the part for the whole) has not been settled in scientific psychology. Like McCall, Fisher saw this scientific psychology as developing by means of the hypothetico-deductive method. Given the different orienting attitudes of philosophical and scientific psychologies, "no single proposition from one can be *directly* compared with a proposition from the other, for they are, radically speaking, two different demonstrative knowledges" (Fisher, 1957, p. 153). The third psychology was not, as it was for McCall, preliminary to scientific psychology, or to explanation, as it was for Arnold. Fisher's 1957 article, which up until its last section grounded itself in Thomistic thought, turned explicitly to Merleau-Ponty's phenomenology. He posed the possibility for this psychology to study "a third dimension which we might call the dimension of concrete liberty" (p. 154), that is, neither a study of universals, as in philosophical psychology, nor an objectified study as in scientific psychology. He took as his example the case that J. H. van den Berg used in the beginning of *The phenomenological approach to psychiatry*, which had just been published in English in 1955. Fisher stated that this third psychology, which would seek to understand the individual, begins with attempts to "enter into his world, to see it through his eyes" (p. 155). The second step is a *"reconstruction* of the past in an attempt to understand *why* the actual situation is the way it is" (ibid.). The interpretative problem, and he indicated that Freud saw it too, is that different present situations could be meaningfully connected to the same past: that is – and this is the revelation of concrete freedom – the past did not blindly determine the present. Fisher compared this psychology with philosophical psychology (PP) and with scientific psychology (SP):

> My knowledge in this case is like that obtained in PP in that I find a real, seen, intelligible relationship between a real cause and a real effect. It is quite unlike it in that I am not dealing with objects which cannot be other than they are. This knowledge is like PP and SP in that it involves a systematic investigation and culminates in an organized body of knowledge. It is quite unlike SP in that it starts from and keeps as its real object the reality of the natural attitude, that of spontaneous experience. It does not objectify or make its object into a thing.
>
> (p. 156)

It is not humanistic knowledge either, for it seeks general principles in a systematic effort. It would be a psychology that deals with "man as a free being" (p. 157), that is, "a being who is determined by his past to the extent that I can understand his present in terms of the past and to some extent predict his future; but also a being whose past offers a limited number of possibilities for future lines of action – but always more than one" (p. 156).[22] In delineating these three psychologies, Fisher indicated a move into phenomenological thought that remained grounded in "perennial philosophy."[23]

In these writings he developed a conception of science and psychology that owed a great deal to Merleau-Ponty. Fisher's translation of *The structure of behavior* (Merleau-Ponty, 1963), did much to connect phenomenology with American psychology, as Merleau-Ponty interrogated scientific psychology in a way that acknowledged the contributions of scientific inquiry, that affected his philosophical thinking in a dialectical manner (and not in the top-down manner of the older Thomists), and that argued for the behavioral approach to psychology.

From the citadel to the person

In the pre-Vatican II writings of Catholic psychologists and psychiatrists, the sense of belonging to a group apart is overwhelming. Throughout this period, many Catholics perceived themselves and to some extent were perceived by other Americans as inferior intellectually and academically. At the 1947 Organizational Meeting for the ACPA, Sister Agnes Lucille, SCN of Nazareth College in Louisville, stated that an organization of Catholic psychologists could help "assure us of the confidence of non-Catholics in our ability to teach psychology on an equally high standard ... We are not considered by our students to be on an intellectual par with non-Catholic professors" (Sister Mary Roberta Roberts, 1947, p. 12). Such concerns echoed throughout the next decade, especially with the publication of the work of John Tracy Ellis on the "causes of Catholic weakness" in American intellectual movements (Ellis, 1955). At the same time, there was a strong sense of Catholic identity. In many of the book reviews in the ACPA *Newsletter* in the 1950s were concerns about the suitability of some books for students with an insufficient theological and philosophical education or, even for psychologists, warnings about Canon Law prohibiting Catholics reading books by non-Catholics about religion. Typically, however, this identity expressed itself in interests in increasing the participation of Catholics in the APA and in the writing of textbooks for college courses that would reflect a Catholic orientation while providing a solid presentation of scientific psychology.

---

[22] In "Freud and the image of Man," Fisher (1961) developed further his conception of causality in the human order, showing the convergences among psychoanalytic, phenomenological, and Thomistic thought in this regard.

[23] He was, of course, not alone in doing so, if one considers philosophical thought in the twentieth century. However, among American psychologists, even those with philosophical leanings, Fisher's position was hardly the norm.

The Vatican Council was instrumental in changing much of this sense of being a group apart. It gave sanction to a move to "'open-air Catholicism' in place of 'hothouse Catholicism'" (Pater, 1953, p. 588). To this event and all its complexities, I can give only brief notice. Suffice it to say that one of the outcomes of the Council was a crisis over Catholic identity with changes in what many had seen as immutable, with an abrupt exodus of many priests and nuns from their vows. These changes produced unanticipated outcomes. One notable event, as we have seen, was the critical response of many of the leaders of the ACPA, some of whom also contributed to humanistic psychology, to the issuing of the papal encyclical, *Humanae Vitae*, which condemned chemical and mechanical forms of birth control, in 1968 (Catholic psychologists question Encyclical, 1968). Equally significant were debates within the ACPA over its future (O'Connell and Onuska, 1967; Schneiders, 1967) and, as we have seen, the subsequent re-organization of the ACPA along non-denominational lines.

Charles A. Curran (1969) described the differences between the attitudes of 1950 and 1965. The Church, he wrote, had described itself as a City or a Citadel, "a walled city – impregnable, perhaps, but remote," an image that once made sense but no longer. The new image was that of the Person, "in humble counsel with himself" (p. 290). Curran elaborated the analogy of a person undergoing client centered counseling to describe the process of change that the Church was under-going. Gone apparently was the Thomistic framework, no longer a fixed ground from which to evaluate the contributions of psychology. In place of an emphasis on virtue, as in Curran (1952), the new look emphasized value (Gillespie, 2001, p. 122), a term emphasizing individual choice and variability, unlike the term virtue. *Virtue*, indicating a supra-individual order and carrying hierarchical connotations about human living, did not exist in humanistic discourse.

While there was much continuity before and after Vatican II, there were differences that have proven decisive. The more humanistic orientation (in contrast, to some extent, to a phenomenological orientation) emphasized the uniqueness, the autonomy and the privacy of the individual, some of the characteristics of American humanistic psychology (Sass, 1988). The changes meant a loss of "objectivity," of the certainties of both the Church and the laboratory. Humanistic psychology's anti-authoritarian stance resulted in a shift in the meaning of "person" within this psychological–theological dis-course. In the Thomistic framework, the person had the obligation to develop "right reason," reason in accord with natural and eternal law.[24] Catholic

[24] The changed meaning of *person* did not go unnoticed: "The word 'person' does not bear the same meaning for the modern psychologist or psychiatrist as it does for the Thomist. That holds true for logotherapists including Frankl. For Boethius and St. Thomas person is an 'individual substance of a rational nature,' who continues to be a person so long as he continues to be individual substance in existence, even though he might not be able to operate as such. For psychologists, man is a person only when he seems to be able to operate as a person. A schizophrenic is not fully a person, in this sense. A child deprived of

psychologists such as Curran and Kennedy, employed psychological discourse to describe the spiritual and the religious dimension of human life, a shift found elsewhere (for example, see Stern and Marino, 1970). But an underlying change had occurred in psychological discourse and authority: if prior to 1965, the stress had been on a professional identity as a *Catholic* psychologist, now it was an emphasis on being a Catholic *psychologist*. What this meant was that the psychologists saw themselves as being able to speak on their own terms within the Church. On matters relevant to the Church, within their professional competence, the psychologists were able to make an independent contribution.

The humanistic turn inward was not an abandonment of the communitarian ethos that Thomism marked within the Catholic community. Rather it was a sense that this community was undergoing a creative breakdown. Kennedy took issue with James Hitchcock, a leading Catholic intellectual and critic of liberal interpretations of Vatican II, over the loss of community among American Catholics in the wake of the Council. For Kennedy (1971), "the splintering sense of community" was not, as Hitchcock would have it, "'partly murder and partly suicide'" (p. 131). The loss of "the symbols of our most recent American Catholic cultural experience" was part of the experience of death and resurrection: "The great crisis of the Church centers on whether it can let certain transitional forms of Catholic community die without making the mistake of thinking that this means the end of Catholicism" (p. 133). Kennedy drew on Allport and Skinner (*Walden Two* as a negative image of the Church) and Piaget, as well as on the Gospels, to describe the process of transformation that was occurring. For Kennedy (1975), the president of PIRI as it became Division 36 of the APA, the change was positive: "We no longer need to be isolated in our research interests and we no longer need to explain or defend the authentic professionalism of our scientific commitment" (p. 1).

Humanistic psychology as spiritual psychology

Because humanistic psychology dealt with the higher possibilities of human psychological development, unlike natural scientific psychology, which primarily focused on adjustment, it inevitably addressed spiritual growth and potential. In this way, whether it wanted to or not, humanistic psychology was a spiritual psychology. As in other areas, so too here, it found itself on land already occupied by long traditions within the Church. We now turn to how Catholic spiritual psychology came to incorporate humanistic psychological categories. First of all, however, what the humanists met when moving in this direction must be considered.

love, fails to become a person" (Guinan, 1961, p. 137). We shall return to this pivotal category, person, in the following two chapters.

The older spiritual psychology

Ignoti nulla cupido[25]

The shift in ground from the older ascetical theology or spiritual psychology to humanistic psychology, was most noticeable in how the two dealt with the self and the love of self. In the older spirituality, emphasis was on "mortification" of the self. Self-love was seen as natural, basically good but – with a capital "B" – excessive and extremely difficult to moderate. Because human nature has been distorted by the Fall, we seek our own way, rather than the Way of God and God's ways as defined by the Church. By contrast, the humanists stressed, as we saw with Rogers, acceptance of self, warts and all. Where the older spiritual psychology saw pride (wrong conception of self and distorted love of self) as the chief ill impeding a full human life, the humanists saw excessive self-deprecation as the besetting fault of modern humanity. They saw, essentially, people demoralized by mass society and technology run rampant. Psychotherapy got people in touch with themselves, with their true selves, perhaps for the first time.

Humanistic psychology turned away from a type of spirituality that characterized Catholic practices in the early part of the century. But the humanists did not invent their form of spiritual practice, which could be called the way of acceptance, in contrast to the older way of mortification. That the way of acceptance existed earlier is evident from the descriptions William James (1903) gave of it in his *Varieties of religious experience*, in particular in his chapter of "The Religion of Healthy-Mindedness." Much of the psychological and spiritual attitude of the humanistic psychologists of the mid-twentieth century can be traced to the first flourishing of psychotherapy in the United States in New Thought and Mind Cure that James depicts and defends in this chapter. These forms of spirituality did not take the position that suffering was "something sent from God for our good, either as chastisement, as warning, or as opportunity for exercising virtue, and, in the Catholic Church, of earning 'merit'" (p. 103). By contrast, Mind Cure rejected the notion that we needed such chastisement. Rather, its approach was "anti-moralistic": "Passivity, not activity; relaxation, not intentness, should be now the rule. Give up the feeling of responsibility, let go your hold, resigning the care of your destiny to higher powers" (p. 101). While this is not humanistic psychology pure and simple, it is close to the notion expressed by Rogers of learning to trust the still, small voice that comes from within, and to listen to the "organism" as a sure guide in life. Humanistic psychology was healthy-minded.

By the older spiritual psychology, I mean what was contained in scholastic manuals of spirituality that immediately preceded and accompanied the rise of

[25] "No one desires what he does not know" (Tanquerey 1930, p. 21).

psychology in the late nineteenth and early twentieth centuries. Even limiting consideration to the Catholic tradition, there has not been one way to cultivate spiritual life. The strain I am focusing on is that of spirituality as the science of the perfection of Christian life, as developed in scholastic terms. For present purposes, in part because of his teaching and influence in the United States, I concentrate on the work of Adolphe Tanquerey, SS (1854–1932),[26] who taught at St. Mary's seminary in Baltimore from 1887 to 1902, and whose work, translated into English, was widely influential in American Catholic spirituality. I will also consider briefly another treatment of this spirituality by Thomas Verner Moore, who also wrote in the period preceding humanistic psychology.

Tanquerey was a theologian, but in writing on spirituality, he was dealing with a topic that, because it was practical, designed to guide daily living, was also psychological. *The spiritual life* (Tanquerey, 1930) aimed not simply at the development of one area of living, but "the perfection of the Christian life" (p. 1) as such. This book sought to depict a path to a completely fulfilled human life. Tanquerey was rooted in scholastic philosophy and theology, as well as in many of the Catholic spiritual traditions.[27] To achieve perfection – not fully possible in this life, as he indicated – progressively, a certain training was necessary, and so "ascetical theology" was a synonym for "spiritual science," the word *ascetical* coming from the Greek *askesis*, meaning effort or training, as in athletics.[28] Perfection was not necessary for salvation, Tanquerey observed (p. 23), although something of it was, insofar as the Christian life requires rectification of our fallen nature. But progressive seeking of perfection is important, insofar as a human life is directed toward its final cause, God. The essence of a perfect human life, Tanquerey maintained, is not to be found in the external trappings of the Christian life, for example, in devotions, fastings, etc. Rather, it is found in charity, love. But love demands sacrifice: "in our present state of fallen nature, it is *impossible* for us to love God truly and effectively without sacrificing ourselves for Him" (pp. 163–4).

To say that the goal of human life is love sounds a note that any humanistic psychologist could have endorsed. So there is a certain affinity between *The spiritual life* and the humanists: but the differences in attitude were significant. To them we turn.

Tanquerey's psychology was essentially Neoscholastic. At the same time, he drew on the empirical psychology of his place and time, especially on French

---

[26] SS, the Society of St. Sulpice, an association of Catholic priests dedicated to seminary teaching.

[27] He acknowledged "a certain preference for the spirituality of the French School of the seventeenth century" (pp. vii–viii). He lists the major contributors to this school (pp. xliii–xlvi), and it included J. J. Olier (1608–57), the founder of Tanquerey's order, the Sulpicians.

[28] And it was a "science" in that it was an ordered body of knowledge. This use of the term was common in Latin. In English these days, we tend to equate "science" with "natural science."

character psychology of the turn of the century (see Roback, 1927 for an overview). He listed Paulin Malapert (1862–1937) as his main source for the psychology of character, probably because Malapert was also a priest.[29] Following him, he understood character to consist of psychological dispositions "based on temperament as modified by education and will-power" (p. 8*). The types need not detain us; the main point was that physiological factors while influential are not decisive, because education and individual will take the raw material of character and make something of it.

While the perfection of ourselves is love (of God, of neighbor, of self), Tanquerey reckoned with the fallen state of our nature, the result of original sin. That is, we are inclined to self-seeking rather than God-seeking. As a result, the pursuit of perfection, that is, to pursuit of that path that would make us be what we truly are, involves self-sacrifice, insofar as our nature has been distorted: "our nature inclines us to self-seeking, [so that] we must, in order to react against this tendency, remember that *of ourselves* we are but nothingness and sin" (p. 108). Therefore, some mortification is necessary in the pursuit of perfection. Mortification is self-renunciation, a fight against "the inordinate tendencies of our nature" (p. 364). While warning against superficiality and excess in mortification, Tanquerey stressed that it "is the enemy of pleasure . . . as an end in itself without any relation to duty" (p. 371). Indeed, in his presentation of the path of perfection, Tanquerey drew on metaphors of passionate love (for example, in surrender ourselves to God, in sacrifice of self), of combat (against our sinful tendencies, against the flesh, the world, and the devil), and training (for combat, for athletics). It was, in short, a discourse of the will. Surrender and combat were the two sides of this emphasis on the will. For Tanquerey, there is no love without "the stern discipline of daily self-denial" (p. 168), while sacrifice is "easier if done for the love of God: '*Where there is love, there is no labor*'" (p. 169).[30] The will is the seat of this paradox, since the will as it should be is love, whereas the will as it is, is concupiscence, our distorted desires.

As in Boyd Barrett's book on the will, in Tanquerey, too, there is emphasis on building the muscles of the will. Consider the following:

> In order to obtain a complete victory, it does not suffice to renounce *evil* pleasures . . ., but we must, in order to be on the safe side, sacrifice all

---

[29] He cited Paulin Malapert (1897), *Les élements du carctère et leurs lois de combinaison.* Tanquerey also referred to Alfred Fouillée (1838–1912), philosopher and psychologist, who wrote *Tempérament et caractère, selon les individus, les sexes et les races* (1901); Pierre Jean Corneille Debreyne (1786–1867) and Ange Ernest Amédée Ferrand (1835–99), authors of *La théologie morale et les sciences médicales* (1884), a contribution to pastoral theology; and Frédéric Paulhan (1856–1931), who studied character and other psychological topics, author of *Les caractères* (1902).

[30] Tanquerey quoted Augustine, *De bono viduitatis*, section 26. Augustine was the first important philosopher/theologian of the will. From Augustine, too, comes the idea of the perfection of the will as love, but in our fallen state, it is concupiscence.

dangerous ones, for these almost invariably lead us to sin . . . Besides, we must deprive ourselves of some lawful pleasures in order to strengthen our wills against the lure of forbidden ones.

(p. 104)

Tanquerey endorsed a muscular spirituality that spurned all softness of character. While not promoting it for its own sake, he stressed the place of pain and suffering in the spiritual life, as curative of our faults, chastisement for our sins, and strength needed for the battle that inheres in the spiritual life. The will "should *reign supreme* over the other faculties, but it cannot do so unless we use great tact and make great efforts"(p. 224). This supremacy corresponds with Tanquerey's emphasis on love as the end of human life.

Hence, knowledge of self is impossible without some "distrust of self" (p. 168). Part of the path Tanquerey outlined dealt with developing knowledge of oneself, in order, to be sure, to come to know and love God. But in dealing with self-knowledge, he came most surely to ground that the psychologists would also occupy.[31] The study of psychology and, in particular, psychotherapy, involves the development of self-knowledge. The method that Tanquerey outlined for development of self-knowledge fell under the heading of "examination of conscience" (p. 225), in which one went "from *outward* actions . . . to the hidden causes from which they spring, our interior dispositions" (p. 226). This examination emphasized the goodness or badness of what we found and our responsibilities. In place of a psychotherapist was "a wise spiritual director" to whom we can turn to arrive at improved self-knowledge. Tanquerey gave explicit instructions on how to carry out this examination, drawing on the spiritual exercises of St. Ignatius. He stated that, if carried out to the letter (which Tanquerey admitted was not possible for everyone), it would entail careful scrutiny of all of our actions, day by day. Together with this general examination was the "particular examination," by which one focused on a particular personal defect, seeking always "the *hidden cause of our fault*" and the cultivation of "the *opposite virtue*" (p. 228). The terms of this quest were Thomistic: sensitive appetites, the mind, the will, character, and habits. In other words, Tanquerey did not use the epistemic objects – such as intelligence and personality – that twentieth-century psychology developed (Danziger, 1997; 2003). Tanquerey described, in effect, a highly developed and systematic "technique of the self," to use Foucault's term, except that here, the goal was not simply self-knowledge and self-transformation, but as a result of these acts, the love of God. For the ultimate goal was, as Tanquerey quoted more than once, the following passionate cry: "May I know Thee, O Lord, that I may love thee; may I know myself, that I may despise myself" (pp. 204, 232).

---

[31] Among the authors Tanquerey cites at this point is Basil William Maturin (1847–1915), *Self-Knowledge and Self-Discipline* (1905). Maturin (a convert to Catholicism from the Anglican Church; he died on the Lusitania when it was sunk in World War I), was a writer on the spiritual life, whose work also includes *Laws of the Spiritual Life* (1916).

Moore's *Heroic sanctity and insanity: An introduction to the spiritual life and mental hygiene* (1959) was as rooted in Neoscholastic thought as Tanquerey's, although by the time Moore wrote this book, he had been engaged with modern empirical psychology for more than fifty years. The "heroic sanctity" of the title refers to the criteria that the Catholic Church uses in the course of evaluating someone for canonization as a saint. The thrust of the book was that the pursuit of perfection, in the terms that Tanquerey outlined, is good for one's mental health. Moore did not equate poor mental health with an absence of sanctity, to be sure, but he did argue that "a devout life has a tendency to prevent many psychogenic mental disorders" (p. 236), and that the "preservation and strengthening of virtue, both moral and theological, is a powerful factor in the preservation and establishment of sound mental health" (p. 50). Moore in this book was in effect extending the guidelines that Tanquerey described to include the practice of psychotherapy. At the same time, he wrote, "priests must be given a general introduction to psychiatry" (p. 51). The psychological sciences have a contribution to offer to the pursuit of a fully human life, in other words, but a complete conception of that life must include religious considerations. The individual is not only a self, but a member of a larger community as well. Not that Moore advised imposing religious considerations on the non-religious patient in therapy (p. 50), but with "devout patients," the therapist "should become familiar with the ideals of the virtues" (ibid.). So while Moore was certainly innovative in seeing the value of psychiatry for members of the Church, he in no way abandoned the external framework for living the good life that earlier writers such as Tanquerey stressed.

Self-love, then, in this spiritual psychology, while a good thing, is at the same time distorted and in need of rectification. Love of self was to be subordinated to love of God, and the pole star of one's life is not to be found within, except insofar as the within leads to what transcends the self. To this end, Moore stressed the will. No one can develop a spiritual life except that they take it up consciously and actively. For neither Tanquerey nor Moore would this emphasis on will gainsay Divine grace as necessary. How this tradition was taken up and transformed by Catholic humanistic psychologists will be the next topic.

Humanistic psychology, the will, and obedience

How Catholic humanistic psychologists took up and changed this older tradition requires a further look at the will. Like Tanquerey and others, the humanists continued to talk about the will. Part of what distinguished humanistic psychology from the mainstream was the stance that the individual was an active agent, not a plaything of either environmental contingencies or unconscious forces. Again, this stress on the person as agent was part of the appeal of humanism to Catholic psychologists in the 1950s and 1960s.

Curran's Humanistic spiritual psychology

As mentioned earlier, Charles A. Curran contributed significantly to Catholic appropriations of humanistic psychology. An example of his approach is "What can Man believe in?" (Curran, 1972): here he put the traditional spiritual psychology into a Rogerian key, shifting emphasis in a discussion of faith and belief from the Neoscholastic stress on assent to rational propositions to "an abandonment of the self and a commitment of the self." This understanding of faith he expressed in Rogerian terms as "an unconditional, positive regard both of the ego toward the self and of the ego-self toward others" (p. 8). To believe in others, and ultimately in God, I must first of all believe in myself. What does this mean? Here he drew on his earlier work (such as Curran 1952), in that belief in self "would be a process of taking counsel with the self" (p. 12). "Counsel" for Curran evoked both the counseling process in a Rogerian fashion and the virtue of counsel, one aspect of prudence. This term is a prime example of how Curran put traditional spirituality into a new key. Included in this taking counsel was "a penetrating into the significance and meaning behind the segmented urges of the emotions, instincts, and soma and a recognizing of the particular segmented purpose of each of these actions" (p. 12). This sounds like Rogers' trust in the organism, and indeed it is. However, Curran's counsel taught him some lessons that might otherwise have been missed. While Curran encouraged positive regard to these urges and feelings, in sharp contrast to Tanquerey, who rather promoted vigilance, Curran sidestepped a rosy view of them. First of all, "the soma, instincts, and emotions" had to be integrated "with the awareness of ego in the conscious intellectual and voluntaristic aspects of the self" (p. 14). Second, with allusion to the teaching on original sin, he addressed the tendency of these bodily urges and feelings to be "narrow and restricted to the immediate somatic, instinctive, or emotional need" (p. 17). That is, they deal with the here and now. Why? Because life begins with anxiety, a condition of fear for survival and fear of death. Original sin (he did not use the term in this article) is in a profound sense original anxiety: a "primitive defense" (p. 21), a primitive will to power that is a vital basis for well-being, but one that must be "integrated" into a larger, more complete, sense of self. The fact remains that we do need such integration, meaning that we are initially disintegrated (p. 17).

This initial condition is our primal "will to power," a concept Curran said he borrowed from Adler (p. 29). Even though it is a "narcissistic inversion," it is primary to an adequate sense of self: one must experience oneself as a center of action. Only a person who has this sense can later be in relation with others: "One sacrifices this self-power in giving oneself openly to the other" (p. 32). One must be invited to enter into loving relations: The one who loves "must openly foreswear his need for self-assertion" (p. 33). In love, we enter into a new form of relationship, and "this kind of bind has to be willed. It is free because the opposite is always possible" (p. 34). In such a way, one can love God, too.

Curran wove together the old spiritual psychology with the new. Unconditional positive regard for the self was of the new – at least as compared to Tanquerey, not as compared to all forms of spirituality (see Sommerfeldt, 1991) – yet in a fundamental way, Curran kept counsel with the old. The category of the will was the pivot on which the move from the Neoscholastic to the humanistic spirituality turned.

Van Kaam on obedience: Continuity with the older spiritual psychology

The will played a similar role in the work of the leading Catholic humanistic psychologist of the period, Adrian van Kaam (1920–2007). In *The art of existential counseling* (1966a), van Kaam presented a view of counseling that was at the same time a preliminary for spiritual direction, i.e. preliminary to the type of activity described by Tanquerey and Moore. The therapeutic relationship is an encounter between an I and a Thou, and it has the purpose of "wanting his [the client's] *freedom*" (p. 57), that is, creatively assisting the client in becoming his or her true self:

> My counselee is basically a free person, and not a thing, even when his freedom is stifled or crushed under the weight of his neurotic anxiety and guilt feelings, his destructive habits, his overdependency, his compulsions, depression, and paranoid attitudes. He is never a stone or any other thing, but always basically free. It is precisely the radical nature of this freedom which makes psychotherapy possible.
>
> (pp. 51–2)

We may be basically free, but not actually. In the course of growing up, people experience certain meanings and to an extent, the client's "one-sided world of meaning is not freely and consciously decided upon by him. He may not even be aware that he lives in such a gloomy world" (p. 63). Counseling, then, is "an event of liberation" (p. 62): a liberation to meaning, by discovering the possibilities for life by encountering reality in a less defensive fashion. For van Kaam, drawing on phenomenological thought, this growth in freedom is a move from "impersonal" living to personal living: "Making the impersonal become personal, rooting the unrooted, assimilating the unassimilated, ratifying the unratified, therefore, is as much an essential part of the process of discovering freedom as the transcendence of perceptions and behavior which are incompatible with the totality of one's personality" (pp. 66–7). Stated in other terms, the client becomes increasingly capable of willing.

According to van Kaam, the will is "the core of freedom" (p. 70), but it is often misunderstood. Here van Kaam criticized a widespread notion of the will, enshrined in the term "will-power," which originated in the nineteenth century.[32]

[32] The *Oxford English Dictionary* gives 1874 as the earliest usage of "will-power."

But van Kaam's critique applies to Neoscholastic psychology as well, where the will was described as one of two rational faculties of the soul. Tanquerey, as we have seen, isolated the will as a faculty that could be strengthened. For van Kaam, on the contrary, it was a misconception to consider the will as "an absolute and autonomous power which is isolated from the whole of my personality" (p. 71). To be sure, a Thomist would agree and say that the will is not autonomous and isolated. Such a view distorts the Thomistic conception of the soul. Nevertheless, as we have seen in writers as diverse as Boyd Barrett, Moore, and Tanquerey, the way that the will was said to be trainable made of it something like an autonomous and isolated force within the individual, like a muscle that could be developed. For van Kaam, "I do not have a will, but I *am* a will, or even better, I am a willing person" (ibid.). What earlier Catholic psychologists called will, tends to be what van Kaam called "willfulness," the attempt by the individual to impose a certain meaning on life regardless of other considerations. The earlier metaphors of spiritual warfare and military training (*askesis*) lend themselves to this willfulness. In that older tradition, with its mistrust of the self and its tendencies, to go against the grain, to encourage self-denial, to urge sacrifice, could become a parody of spirituality and become willfulness. For van Kaam, the key questions were: is the self I am denying my authentic self? Or is it a distorted image that I have acquired prereflectively in the course of growing up? Such considerations constitute the way that Catholic humanistic psychologists "encountered" the tradition of spiritual psychology.

For van Kaam, will centers around the human person's "fundamental openness for reality" (p. 72), an interpretation of the phenomenological concept of intentionality. To be open, in the first instance, requires "listening," so that "readiness to listen is already a primary way of willing" (p. 73). But willing includes response to what one hears, as well, and for van Kaam, willfulness is a distortion of this response, and deficiencies of will would be deficiencies of response to the calls of the real. In describing the will in these terms, van Kaam maintained the basic principles of the older spiritual psychology, while correcting what he saw as one of its blind spots, namely, a failure to recognize psychological aspects of the self and self-development. Like Tanquerey, van Kaam spoke of the "perfection" of human life. He, like Tanquerey, stressed the provisional nature of perfection in this life: "To be man is never to be perfect but to strive in willing openness toward a limited perfection which one is allowed to reach in one's life" (p. 77).

A false striving for perfection van Kaam addressed in terms of religious counseling:

> Many people who come for religious counseling have lived their religion in an inauthentic way. Having heard or read about religious perfection, they started to imitate the perfect religious attitudes in their external religious behavior. Soon there came a split between their real personal inner life and the proliferation of perfect manners, customs, and devotions which they

had assumed to the great delight of their excited educators. The latter, animated by the best intentions, did not realize that they were producing a number of neurotics instead of saints.

(p. 69)

The spiritual life requires authenticity: it must be a genuine personal response to the call of God in one's life. While the earlier spiritual psychology would have affirmed that statement as the meaning of vocation, the humanist stress on the "true self" proved to be a two-edged sword. To develop this theme, we turn to van Kaam's insight that the basic meaning of "will" is "listen." And another term for "listen," derived from the Latin, one with a strong spiritual tradition, is "obey."

In the mid-1960s, van Kaam extended these thoughts explicitly to the religious life in *Religion and personality* (1964), *Personality fulfillment in the spiritual life* (1967b), and *Personality fulfillment in the religious life* (1967a). In the second of these books, van Kaam developed the theme of "religious presence" as presence to the "Holy," in the face of which one becomes one's true self: "As my true identity emerges from the Holy, I feel increasingly that I am the responsible creative center of my feelings, attitudes, perceptions, and actions. Contrast this with inauthentic identity which is not centered in the transcendent Holy but in the appreciations, moralistic estimates, approval, and applause of others" (p. 67). This book, as did the others that van Kaam wrote during this period, wove together Thomistic, phenomenological, and humanistic themes and categories in an effort to address spiritual life in the light of the current situation of alienation from the Holy, from nature, and from authentic identity. The theme of obedience, broached in *The art of existential counseling* received more attention in this book – written, as it seems, primarily for Catholics living in religious communities as priests, brothers, and nuns. A key difference between van Kaam's approach and that of some other humanistic psychology of the period was his positive evaluation of tradition and of a communal sense of self. We do not find in van Kaam the same emphasis on listening to the organism that we found in Rogers, for example. Instead of emphasizing a break from the shackles of the past, for van Kaam, "tradition belongs to my very being" (p. 94), although it is necessary to "dialogue" with tradition, in order to take it up authentically.

In so weaving together the tradition of Catholic spirituality with the new phenomenological and humanistic psychology, van Kaam returned to themes of sacrifice (p. 100), discipline (pp. 120–1), and asceticism (p. 155). He defined the last of these in terms of "an asceticism that aims at the uncovering of the religious presence that I am by distancing and detaching myself from the surface appearances of people, things, and situations and becoming aware of their most inner transcendent value emerging from the ground of the Holy" (pp. 156–7). He then turns to the "threefold path" that accomplishes this asceticism: poverty, chastity, and obedience, the three vows that many Catholic religious take. He emphasized in this context "free and spirited obedience" (p. 160), a listening to the call of the Holy as it would announce itself in traditions, communities, and the Church. Van Kaam, in his synthetic mode of thinking, so characteristic of him as of Mercier, did not reject the older spiritual psychology. In fact, in a later, comprehensive work, he (Van Kaam, 1983) asserted that like Tanquerey, he sought not to articulate a particular type of spirituality, but to provide "comprehensive insight" (p. 28).

Van Kaam did not embrace the rosy optimism of Rogers' view of human nature either. While most of *Personality fulfillment in the spiritual life* has an ecumenical stress, characteristic of van Kaam's work in general, in the final chapter, he addressed specifically Catholic themes directly, looking at the place of the sacraments in the Christian life, starting with Baptism, and there he included the teaching on original sin in psychological terms:

> The transmission of original sin leads to a fundamental egocentrism or narcissism which I can never totally overcome. There is a narcissistic bent in me which always threatens my pure selfless presence to reality as it is; my fundamental narcissism stands as a screen between me and my life situation, between me and reality.

> (p. 173)

As a result, existence is never fully actualized, never fully transformed by the spirit in this life (p. 178). In this way, van Kaam's spiritual psychology, as did Curran's, took up the themes of self-sacrifice and self-limitation that characterized the pre-Vatican II spiritual writers such as Tanquerey.

Authentic obedience

Obedience was a central topic in the relationship between the humanistic psychologists and the Church, especially for those in religious orders. Tanquerey (1930), addressing such individuals, defined obedience as "a supernatural, moral virtue which inclines us to submit our will to that of our lawful superiors, in so far as they are the representatives of God" (p. 497). While there are limits to obedience, the thrust of Tanquerey's thought is that obedience requires that we submit "that which we cling to most tenaciously, our own will" (p. 185). When souls are perfect, "they submit their *judgment* to that of their superior, without even considering the reasons for his command" (p. 500). As we have seen, van Kaam would have no objection in principle to these formulations, but he brought a new sensibility to this discourse, namely, an emphasis on personality development and the necessity for an obedience freely given.

If Tanquerey stressed self-submission, and van Kaam, with caveats, agreed, Rogers championed self-assertion. In a book review published in the mid-1960s, Rogers (1967) wrote how in the Catholic Church "the individual has no right to think or search" (p. 13). The book under review was James Kavanaugh's (1967a) *A modern priest looks at his outmoded Church*, a blistering critique of the Church by a disaffected priest. Rogers wrote that the Church is "legalistic, inhuman, with no place for love or for persons, only a place for laws and rules and orders" (p. 13). Rogers here simply affirmed the self-expression of an individual, namely, Kavanaugh, without critique although with judgment. Rogers' emphasis was on the individual and the validation of the experience of the individual. Institutions would have to change to accommodate them.

By contrast, van Kaam and the Duquesne psychologists had an irenic conception of tradition and obedience. There is no real individuality without tradition, for Van Kaam. Indeed, true obedience in the religious life requires a mature personality, for this reason: it requires surrender of one's own judgment, which means it requires surrender of one's self (Van Kaam, 1964). Such an act is a gift of oneself and only a mature person can do so freely, without undue anxiety. An immature or fragile self cannot offer the self as a gift, consciously and with serenity. Van Kaam, like Rogers, assumed that alienation from self is a common feature of modern society, so that much in the way of personality development and therapy is a prerequisite for maturity in the religious life. Along these lines, Charles Maes (1984), van Kaam's colleague at Duquesne, included in the truly obedient mode of existence that "we must listen reverentially and appreciatively to the messages of our bodies, of our emotions" (p. 215), as part of listening to how God speaks to us in daily life. Van Kaam and Maes stressed self-understanding and self-love as integral to the possibility of authentic obedience, whereas for Tanquerey the accent fell on the dangers of self-love.

Margaret-Rose Welch had been a superior in a religious order, the Sisters of the Immaculate Heart of Mary, most of the members of which broke with the Church in 1970. She was then a leader in the spiritual community that formed outside the structure of the Church. She had begun a psychology dissertation at Duquesne University during the time of turmoil before that break, although it was completed later. It addressed obedience among women religious, by means of a phenomenological study based on accounts drawn from members of her order in the 1960s, the years it was in turmoil.[33] She summarized her findings in these words:

> Obedience is a co-constituted relationship, linking the individual and the community, the individual and religious meaning. The absence of direct

---

[33] See Kugelmann (2005a) for a more complete account of the IHM order and its conflict with Church authorities. Among many accomplishments of the IHMs after 1970, Welch and other members of her community founded Casa Esperanza, a community resource center, in a troubled California neighborhood of Panarama City (Cabrera, 1999).

> dialogue between authority and the individual about the meaning of
> obedience is a major cause of felt discrepancies between the ideals taught
> and the actual experience. Obedience practiced in a manner that destroys
> its nature results in experiences of alienation, meaninglessness, and sub-
> jugation. Authentic obedience will provide experiences where personal
> autonomy is linked to a sense of community.

(Welch, 1983, p. xi)

Welch shared with Van Kaam his diagnosis of alienation from self and the
crisis of authority in technological societies, where "the uniqueness of persons, spontaneity, and growth have been suppressed by concern for the
values of the common, the routine, the standardized" (p. 8). Among the
difficulties Welch found was that often there was "an absence of dialogue"
between the superior giving commands and the religious who was to obey,
thus undermining authentic obedience as a co-constituted reality (p. 113),
leaving the religious to experience herself as "unfree, incapable of self-
transcendence" (p. 115). Welch concluded by stating that while the older
conception of obedience proved in the contemporary world detrimental to
the spiritual life, the present danger (in the 1980s) was an over-emphasis on
"isolating individualism" (p. 127). Given the dialogical nature of obedience,
she stated:

> The style and practices of authority prior to the 1970's often communi-
> cated an implicit denial of the individual's dignity and freedom. A present-
> day condition in which some individuals place their own needs above
> those of the community and justify this attitude in the name of their
> own freedom and dignity continues to be a distortion ... The goals of
> autonomy within community should not be confused with individualism
> and domination.

(pp. 126–7)

That is, the humanistic psychological critique of institutions and traditions as
alienating individuals from their own vitality was an important contribution.
But given the historicity of human existence, it is insufficient, and hence the re-
assertion of the place of community and tradition in human life. Welch's
position, like Van Kaam's, attempted a dialectical synthesis of Tanquerey's
thesis of self-submission and Rogers' antithesis of self-expression. In a similar
vein, another Catholic psychologist, William Coulson (1982), who had worked
with Rogers and published widely on humanistic themes in relation to the
religious life, wrote: "No one suggests turning the clock back to the pre-modern
era. But try as we might, we cannot deny the necessity of living within a
framework of tradition" (p. 5). This psychological discourse on individuality
and tradition has had widely different applications, serving both to legitimate
and criticize changes in the modern Church.

Questioning authority in Humanistic discourse

Humanistic psychology was particularly hostile to "Cartesian dualism," and in James Kavanaugh's terms, the Church has been "steeped in a distorted anthropology that was more Cartesian than Christian" (1967a, p. 18).[34] In this hostility, the humanists shared a point with their Thomistic predecessors. Mercier (1902), for example, aimed some of his heaviest salvos at the Cartesians. Both Thomists and humanists strove to articulate a psychosomatic unity as the core of the person, but the former preserved a hierarchical conception of the terms of this unity: the soul is superior to the body as the form of that body. Humanists specifically disavowed such hierarchical conceptions. Rogers, for example, held that the organism was the seedbed of our deepest, truest feelings and orientation to life, which our cognitions and judgments often distort.[35] In the emphasis on attunement to feelings, humanistic psychology did counter the Thomistic stress on the ordering of emotional life in accordance with right reason. What was at stake in these differences, however, was not only a different philosophical anthropology, but also different orientations to authority. While van Kaam and Maes promoted dialogue between the older spirituality and the new, for others, such as Kavanaugh and Rogers, Catholic conceptions of authority hindered individual self-actualization. Rogers' assessment of Kavanaugh's personal journey as narrated in his book was that "a Roman Catholic Priest who has evidently been a thoroughly orthodox and self-righteous priest for many years … finally … becomes a *man*" (p. 13). Institutions and their hierarchical structures were the problem.

When humanistic psychology arrived on the scene, shades of modernism still hovered about, especially where psychology was concerned. Indeed, one could say that in some variants, the humanists had a modernist spirit. For example, Vermeersch (1911), described part of the modernist agenda:

> A spirit of complete emancipation, tending to weaken ecclesiastical authority; the emancipation of science, which must traverse every field of

---

[34] James Royce (1964) had surveyed his Catholic students several years earlier and found that their implicit anthropology was more Cartesian than Thomistic.

[35] *Organism*, as depicted by Rogers (1951), is not the same thing as the *body* of the Thomists. For Rogers, "the organism has one basic tendency and striving – to actualize, maintain, and enhance the experiencing organism … It moves in the direction of greater independence or self-responsibility. Its movement … is in the direction … away from heteronymous control, or control by external forces" (p. 489). For the Thomists, *body* is the matter, giving singularity to existence, and it is the *soul* that gives form and directedness toward species-specific and personal goals. Rogers' "organism" resembles more the irrational parts of the soul as the vital principle of organic life. While Rogers' views resemble those of the *lived body* of the phenomenologists (a resemblance developed by Gendlin (1981)), the phenomenologists emphasize participation more than Rogers' autonomy.

investigation without fear of conflict with the Church; ... the emancipation of private conscience whose inspirations must not be overridden by papal definitions or anathemas.

(p. 416)

Modernism, a spirit of reform by means of the application of the natural sciences, expressed itself psychologically in making one's own experience the arbiter of what is true and good (Mercier, 1910). Psychotherapy especially could fall under suspicion, since it is allegedly the application of science for the care of the soul.

In the pre-Vatican II writings of the ACPA, one finds loyalty and deference when it came to papal pronouncements and Canon Law. In texts such as Cavanagh's (1962), papal writings give the last word in the dispute over values in client-centered therapy. Pius XII's positive statements about psychiatry and psychoanalysis were welcomed as approval. Before Vatican II, the authority of the pope and the higher status of theological knowledge of the soul prevailed over anything the psychologists could have provided. Conformity with Church teachings could be a source of pride in the Catholic community. As Nowlan wrote in the ACPA *Newsletter*: "Non-Catholics are astonished at our conformity; Catholics are amazed that it is not one hundred per cent" (1956, p. 1). At other times, there was concern: "'the central purpose of power and authority seems to be the enforcement of conformity through the suppression of initiative,'" wrote Theodore V. Purcell, SJ (quoting Fichter, 1961, p. 266; in Purcell, 1962, p. 4), in a review of a book about the lives of American priests and nuns.

Humanistic anti-authoritarian discourse took root among the Catholic psychologists. Many chafed against mandated Thomistic "syntheses" of psychology and philosophy that affected higher education. There were anxieties that Catholic education produced authoritarian personalities. The ACPA in 1965 held a symposium led by Annette Walters and Sheridan B. McCabe on "Attitudes, values, and motivational systems of the American college student." Rita Y. D'Angelo (1966) summarized the results, some of which indicated that Catholic students, whether at denominational colleges or not, "showed a significantly higher degree of variables consistent with the authoritarian personality than did Protestant and non-believers" (p. 46). D'Angelo asked "If features of training have served to constrict both intellect and personality, might we, as Sister Annette suggests, expect change on the attitudinal systems of Catholics as a result of the encouragement of breadth of vision, and the understanding and acceptance of others brought about by the Vatican Council" (p. 47)? A year earlier, McCarthy (1965) had raised a similar concern: "the core of all criticisms leveled against Catholic education ... is the fundamental concern over failure to develop individuality" (p. 3). Indeed, McCarthy charged his peers: "Perhaps you can think of one or two other exceptions, but I believe that there has been little conscious effort to speak as *authorities* to our fellow Catholics on those problems

of contemporary import about which we would have expert opinion to offer"
(p. 2). This evidence points to a readiness among Catholic psychologists to adopt
a more independent stance and less of a willingness to defer without question to
ecclesiastical (as to scientific) authority.

With Vatican II, fears of modernism receded. As I mentioned already, many
aspects of humanistic psychology were modernist: its valorization of individual
experience; its anti-authoritarianism; its skepticism toward moral codes. There
were a number of versions of humanistic psychology's anti-authoritarian
stance. As May (1961) described it, the kind of authority characteristic of
modernity was most troubling, for it had led to totalitarian societies: "The
whole existential movement arose in a violent protest against the onmoving
lava of conformism, collectivism, and the robot man" (p. 38, note). Similar
charges against ecclesiastic authority were common, and the events surrounding
Vatican II brought these conflicts into the open in Catholic circles. McCarthy
(1965), in his presidential address to the ACPA in 1964, warned about contemporary "culture that pays excessively high compliment to conformity" (p. 7). In
the new atmosphere, the earlier period in the Church was at times described as
repressive. Kennedy (2001) depicts the pre-Vatican II period as "totalitarian,"
and in other writings applauded the decline of monarchical conceptions of
leadership in the Church. E. Mark Stern (1968) claimed that, "the age we live
in demands more than doctrine" and deplored "the use of force to strangle men's
vision, whether arising from Moscow, the Vatican, or the streets of Chicago." The
alternative was cast in humanistic terms: "People must stand up for what their
experience dictates" (p. 1). So humanistic protests against the hegemony of
various kinds of authorities, in science as in religion, found a place in Catholic
circles. Bieliauskas (1974) summarized the new relations between psychology
and religion in humanistic terms, terms that altered both the objectivistic conception of psychology and the subservient role of psychology vis-à-vis religion.
Quoting Maslow, he presented humanistic psychology as being able to recognize
and study religious and spiritual phenomena because it does not have the
philosophical blinders of psychoanalysis and behaviorism. He called for "cooperation" with religion and theology and observed a "careful, but serious rapprochement between religion and the profession and science of psychology"
(p. 371). The inclusion of this contribution in the *New Catholic Encyclopedia*
suggests his was a consensus position.

Therapy as metaphor for change

Granting that the Church after Vatican II was in a period of change, what was
the nature of this change? In this context, the psychologists formulated what
was happening with a metaphor derived from their own profession: change is
therapy. That is, for meaningful change in the Church to take place, the Church
must undergo therapy. Describing it as therapy ordered the process,

conceptually at least, and gave meaning to the inevitable resistance to change by some elements in the Church. The metaphor was, of course, charged: resistance is "natural," but when overcome, personality growth follows. Openness to change is a sign of psychological maturity, according to this metaphor. Curran (1965; 1966) employed this metaphor in the immediate post-Council period. He turned the metaphor on the conceptual and verbal resemblance between the virtue of counsel as Aquinas had described it, the process of counseling, and the meaning of the Vatican "Council." The analogy indicates both the end and the means to the end, as in the following:

> So, in organizations and particularly in the Church, there must be a certain tolerance for the same kind of negative confusions and conflicts. If they are quickly stifled for fear of their consequences, they may in fact, as in an individual, simply become repressed again and show themselves in disguised but disrupting or impeding forms. Handled confidently and openly, they will perhaps more readily disperse themselves and reveal, upon analysis, the more basic and more valuable impulses that are hidden behind their confusion and negation.
>
> (Curran, 1966, p. 98)

Kennedy (1967) developed the same metaphor – "the Church, if you will, is like a person in therapy, trying to shed its defenses, to open itself to the truth, to become whole and holy again in the sight of men" – emphasizing intimate connections between "holy," "healthy," and "whole." "This conjunction of the three ideas of health, wholeness or unity, and exclusive orientation to one goal is no mere accident of language but a key to what it means to be a person – something you must be before you can be a religious person" (p. 54). This interpretation of the metaphor carries it into contentious territory, the problematic relationship between psychology and spirituality. Other psychologists, writing on the connection between health and holiness, have disputed any necessary connection between the two (O'Connell, 1961). The merits of the issue aside, what does stand out is a reversal of an earlier relationship between psychology and the Church. In the period before the 1950s, Catholic psychologists argued for the autonomy of psychology; here, the claim is made that psychological expertise carries authority in spiritual and ecclesiastical areas. Psychologists are authorities on therapeutic change.

A third use of the metaphor, change is therapy, appeared in Kavanaugh (1967a; 1967b). Writing in a confessional mode, Kavanaugh,[36] at the time a priest, wrote that, "the Church claims to have entered the realm of therapy with Vatican II. It points out the behavioral changes that have occurred. I see them

---

[36] At the time, Kavanaugh (1967b, p. 6) was Director of Educational Services and a counselor at the Human Resources Institute, La Jolla, CA. The cover of this issue of *Psychology Today* shows Kavanaugh, in his clerical garb, standing in front of a broken and dead tree.

and I am not impressed" (1967b, p. 18). He claimed that the Church still "needs therapy. It needs the experience of a group environment where man is offered the freedom to be himself" (p. 19). He described how his own ministry had enslaved people to "dogmas ... [that] are only the empty conceptualizations of an unscientific age" (ibid.), especially those relating to sexuality. He did not hear the anguish of these people in the confessional, but in group therapy, where there was "more genuine concern in this little flock of struggling people than in any Christian community" (p. 18). In Rogers' (1967) review of Kavanaugh's book, he found a powerful indictment of the Church, wondering if Kavanaugh would be excommunicated – he would have been burnt at the stake in an earlier day, stated Rogers. The point of the book was that Kavanaugh is looking "for a community of love and a meaning in life and an end to childish rule-bound living" (p. 13). This implicit reference to the Enlightenment indicates one way that the metaphor, therapy is change, functioned in humanistic circles: as a corrective to outmoded ways of living and understanding the person.

Uncharted territory

The humanistic emphasis on the individual and on authentic relationships made community considerations secondary. These considerations returned in subsequent years when psychologists such as Paul Vitz (1994) accused the humanistic psychologists, in their stress upon the individual, of encouraging self-worship. Carl Rogers' former colleague, William Coulson (1995) depicted excessive emphasis on the individual in some of the extensions of Rogerian therapy, to the detriment of communities and traditions. The humanistic thrust of the 1950s and 1960s already appears an expression of western individualism, as an example of what Richard Sennett referred to as the "death of public man." Yet, as we have seen, other strains of humanistic psychology, represented by van Kaam, emphasized community as well as individuality.

Another topic came to a head in this period. As we saw in Chapter 2, Tyrrell was critical of the Church for its neglect of the importance of affect and the body in its understanding of spiritual life. We saw something of the same in Harry McNeill's suggestion that Catholics have something to learn from the psycho-analysts. Victor White also stressed affective knowledge as well as the imagination in the life of the soul. Now add the psychological analyses that stress embodiment: the ACPA members' criticisms of the encyclical on birth control, critique of "will power" by van Kaam, and the valorization of what we can call the pre-rational by Catholic humanistic psychologists. Embodiment has been a major contested boundary between psychology and Catholicism.

But here the story comes to an end. After the end of the Second Vatican Council, and after the cultural revolution of the 1960s, when the intellectual and cultural trends of the preceding decades burst into the open, the possible relationships between psychology and the Catholic Church multiplied.

Neoscholastic psychology faded into obscurity, even if many of its impulses and questions survived in the work of the humanists and phenomenologists. Those taught by the Neoscholastics, having established psychology departments and clinics, moved on more confident of their place in American society, working with or not working with their local Church communities. After the period covered in this book, in other words, the narrative changed dramatically. It became a new story, one beyond my scope here. For some, it was, with some exaggeration, the promised land of free inquiry and dialogue among equals; for others, with hyperbole, it was the desert where psychology drifted into a secular morass without the guidance of the Church. That is where we are today.

Before we finish, however, there is a further topic to cover. This book has emphasized the contesting of the boundaries. But more than contests take place at boundaries: there is also commerce. And it is to commerce that we now turn.

Trading zones between psychology and Catholicism

Let us turn, now, to areas within the contested boundaries where there has been commerce between psychology and the Church. Drawing on Peter Galison's notion of a "trading zone," we will see how hybrids of psychology and Catholic thought have developed in select areas.

What has happened at boundaries between psychology and Roman Catholicism from the late nineteenth century to the middle of the twentieth? That is what this entire book has been about. One of the things that occurred – as we saw above in examining the institutionalizing of psychology within the Church communities – was the establishment of new institutions within Catholic settings. Many of the psychologists who were active in setting them up were themselves clerics, so it was not as outsiders that they crossed the boundaries. In the course of forming these institutions, interesting things happened. There was the contesting of boundaries, to be sure; however, there was also commerce on the frontier as different cultures got to know each other. Fruitful exchanges across the boundaries had been desired since the beginnings of modern psychology. Charles Bruehl (1923d), who was one of the earliest Catholic commentators on Freud, as we saw in Chapter 5, made a plea for ties between "the psychopathic clinic" and "spiritual guidance." Using the metaphor of the "boundary" that has been the mainstay of this book, Bruehl wrote that the "young science" of psychiatry "is tempted to trespass on foreign territory" (p. 245) in treating the religious difficulties of patients. While he acknowledged the differences between psychotherapy and spiritual direction, Bruehl asserted "there is also, however, a borderland where their jurisdictions overlap and with regard to which there ought to be mutual cooperation" (p. 246).[1] For Bruehl, boundary maintenance was of utmost importance in this cooperation, and if the "psychopathologist ... unwisely and unjustly ventures into the different field of education, vocational guidance and spiritual direction, we deny his competence and denounce his arrogance" (ibid.). The subsequent history of this cooperation in the period before 1965 shows that in the Catholic world, good fences made good neighbors.

---

[1] By way of example, he referred to the "pastoral use of hypnotism" as advocated by Boyd Barrett in a 1923 article in the British Jesuit periodical, *The Month*.

In extending these notions of trading zones and boundary-work to the relationships between psychology and Catholicism, the chapter will examine: (1) the nature of the collaboration in each situation; (2) the status of the collaborators and their claims for expertise and authority; (3) the resulting discursive objects that both groups could agree upon – which we will discuss in terms of the development of a common discourse, such as a pidgin or a creole – and which made collaboration possible.

Trading zones

What happens at boundaries? Two related concepts prove useful in understanding the interactions there. The first is Peter Galison's (1999) metaphor of "trading zones" between different cultures as applied to different sciences working together on a common project, such as the development of radar or of nanotechnology, despite differences in terminology and conceptual frameworks. The coordination of activities on all sides of the boundary do not require homogenization of conceptual frameworks and discourses (Kellogg, Orlikowski, and Yates, 2006, p. 39), and do not need the groups involved to eliminate pre-existing disciplinary boundaries (Galison, 1999, p. 152). Working arrangements may suffice, and they may be temporary and provisional. As Collins and Evans (2002) indicate, the nature of the relationship between collaborators can vary, for the partners need not be equals. In the collaboration, the language of the first group will not be the same as that of the second group, so hybrid languages may develop in the process. As Galison (1999) explains it: "we need some guidance in thinking about the local configurations that are produced when two complex sociological and symbolic systems confront one another. Anthropologists are familiar with such exchanges, and one of the most interesting domains of such investigations has been in the field of anthropological linguistics surrounding the problems of *pidginization* and *creolization*. Both refer to languages at the boundary between groups" (p. 153). A pidgin is a simplified form of communication that is not a full-fledged language, whereas a creole is a language. (Modern English, for example, began as a creole between Norman French and Anglo-Saxon.) Galison provides an example of a 1960s-era textbook in quantum mechanics that, he says, "attempts to create a stable pidgin language" (p. 155) "for an audience outside the subculture of theorists" (p. 154), that is, for the subculture of experimentalists in physics.

The trading zone notion has proven useful in analyzing the developments in cognitive science (Maasen, 2007; Thagard, 2005), and the relationship of gender and science (Keller, 1995), and here the metaphor will be extended further. Thagard (2005), for example, details how those beginning cognitive science came from a variety of backgrounds: artificial intelligence, linguistics, neuroscience, philosophy, and psychology. The places where the exchanges occurred were journals, university departments and professional organizations; however, conferences "are probably the closest analog to intercultural trading zones, as people from various disciplines and countries gather to exchange ideas" (p. 327). Finally, Thagard claims that the "point of intellectual trading zones is the exchange of ideas" (ibid.).

Galison (1999) draws on anthropology to understand the character of a science like physics. Tied to the metaphor of trading zones (an anthropological term) is his contention that physics is not a unified science, but rather it is composed of subcultures that are "intercalated." That is, in physics, "many traditions coordinate with one another without homogenization" (p. 137). The subcultures of physics include theoretical physics, experimental physics, and instrument makers. Even their ontologies can differ, so that there is no one "paradigm" (Thomas Kuhn's term) to rule them all. There is no one "observational language" that grounds them all (contrary to what the logical positivists held). Instead, like subcultures, each sub-discipline "has its own rhythms of change, each has its own standards of demonstration, and each is embedded differently in the wider culture of institutions, practices, inventions, and ideas" (p. 143). Hence, the term "intercalation," chosen to reflect the fact that "the many traditions coordinate with one another without homogenization" (p. 137), seems to apply *a fortiori* to psychology.[2] However, I do not know which set of subcultures to declare definitive in psychology, and this is where the analogy may limp. Theoretical psychology is not as vigorous a growth as theoretical physics, but the rough and ready distinctions between academic, applied, and popular psychologies provide a beginning. Even this division breaks down, when one considers the many theoretical and philosophical approaches in psychology, the more or less independent research and therapeutic traditions, and the failure of anyone to proclaim successfully that psychology has at long last found its paradigm. Some claim that psychology is pre-paradigmatic, but that begs the question of the existence of such a thing. Let us stay with psychology's current reality as intercalated.

This condition has made it possible for some subcultures in psychology to engage in exchange with religious communities and traditions. Some subcultures, in particular the more narrowly defined experimental ones, have no interest in these exchanges, nor do the religious groups seem interested in their wares. But as we have seen, in both theoretical and applied areas of psychology there has been lively interest in the boundaries, and much interest in what the other side has. In these trading zones, there are many crossings and exchanges.

---

[2] Once again, a psychologist is modeling psychology on physics! Only loosely, however, because I do not think that a tripartite model works very well for psychology. What I want to stress is the disunity of psychology (as a strength) and its history of collaboration with other sciences.

Before we can see what has happened in the region between psychology and the Church, we need to recall that at the boundaries warfare also breaks out from time to time. Gieryn's (1983) concept of "boundary work" (already introduced in Chapter 1) proves useful here. He developed it to study how scientific groups establish, maintain, and defend knowledge claims. The boundaries under consideration here are those between psychology and the Church, where assertions of expertise on the same subject matter were made on both sides, the knowledge having arisen, however, from different traditions, discourses, and conceptual and professional criteria. The boundary work most at issue here is that wherein the goal of the psychologists was "*expansion* of authority or expertise into domains claimed by other professions or occupations" (p. 791). Complicating this boundary work is the fact that on the psychological side of the boundary, there were individuals who claimed membership on the other side of the boundary. The psychologists treading on ground cultivated by the Church were themselves primarily priests, nuns, and Catholic lay people. Because these psychologists belonged to the Church, their staking of ground for psychology had a hearing that it might not otherwise have had.

We shall look at a number of areas where the notion of trading zone proves useful to see anew what was going on. The first of these is education. To make inroads into Catholic higher education, the psychologists had to reckon with the existence of a philosophical psychology, as we have seen. Yet the "new psychology" of the early twentieth century had rejected, for the most part, any notion of the soul, a concept central to Neoscholastic philosophical psychology. How the psychologists made a place for their psychology in this context, made this area a prime one for the development of a language that would address both "subcultures," that of the philosophical psychologists on the one hand, and the empirical psychologists on the other. So what exchanges took place? In the work of Thomas Verner Moore (1924; 1939) we see how the psychological term "personality" became central in enabling collaboration, and in Magda Arnold (1954; 1960; see also Cornelius, 2006), Thomistic concepts were adapted for scientific psychology, furthering collaboration across the boundaries of psychology and the Catholic Church.

In the field of counseling, Charles A. Curran (1952) and Raymond Hostie (1966) bridged the gaps between developments in psychotherapy, on the one side of the border, and the traditional *cura animarum* on the other, by a series of translations, in order to further the work of counseling in Catholic institutions. Church officials recognized a need for mental health care but, at the same time, they were suspicious of psychology for its often materialistic conceptual foundations. The psychological object "counseling" thus received special attention in these works.

A significant area is that of pastoral psychology, where the Church had long developed a system of knowledge and of practice for dealing with the trials and tribulations of human life. Again, the psychologists, supplied with their own theories and practices derived from psychoanalysis and nondirective counseling, helped to forge a veritable creole that made collaboration possible between psychology and the pastoral functions of the clergy.

There are other areas that could be pursued, but these will suffice to show the kinds of hybrid structures that emerged over the course of the time between the early-to-mid twentieth century.

Trading zones in education: personality as the key category

One relatively early place where psychology and the Catholic traditions met was in higher education. While we have already looked at the establishment of some psychology departments in Catholic universities, here we turn to some of the ways that the language of the Church and of psychology came together to form a new discourse, one that had currency on both sides of the border – at least in the limited area where the two interacted. Textbooks were one important source of this hybrid language, as they were designed for the students who would become native speakers in this new language (see Thagard, 2005, for a similar discussion of this in cognitive science). While we considered earlier, in the chapters on Neoscholastic and humanistic psychology, the category of "person" and "personality," here we look at it in terms of how it functioned as a kind of pidgin between the Neoscholastics and the empirical psychologists.[3]

Before reviewing some of the work that sought to bridge Catholic thought and modern psychology, it would be helpful to consider a perceived failure to do so. In 1953, John R. Cavanagh, a psychiatrist, and James B. McGoldrick, a Jesuit educational psychologist,[4] published *Fundamental psychiatry* (1953). Leo S. Loomie, a psychiatrist and member of the New York Psychoanalytic Institute, reviewed the book for the *Homiletic and Pastoral Review*, a magazine for the clergy. He criticized the book for its "abandonment of the modern psychiatric point of view and its replacement in the clinic by the scholastic philosophical concept of man. To the authors, the *psyche* in psychiatry is the soul of St. Thomas Aquinas" (1954, p. 656). Loomie thought the book would mislead the Catholic student: "to train Catholic medical students, nurses, or social workers by using this text would be a real hazard ... If their 'psychiatric' frame of reference is that suggested by this book, they will be pretty well cut off from any meaningful communication with their fellows" (p. 658).[5] My intention here is not to endorse Loomie's point of view; rather, it is to indicate the difficulty of

---

[3] Burnham (1985) points out that personality served as a kind of substitute for discarded notions of soul in mid-twentieth-century psychology, but that "personality was read in terms of reductionistic elements from both psychoanalysis and experimental psychology" (p. 332). This points to the labor involved in bringing "personality" into the trading zone under discussion.

[4] A long-time faculty member at Seattle University, see Chapter 7 for further information.

[5] Sister Mary Amatora (1954b) gave the book a positive review.

finding a language common to the Catholic world and the world of the clinic. Cavanagh and McGoldrick intended to bridge those worlds. Loomie did not think that they had succeeded, insofar as they relied too heavily on the Neoscholastic frame of reference – even though that frame of reference was, as we know, essential if bridges were to be built.[6] To find a common language, then, was difficult, and those who resided in the borderland between what were then two worlds were acutely aware of the problem.

Thomas Verner Moore (1924) wrote *Dynamic psychology* with the express purpose of reaching disparate groups. In addition to students, he addressed the book to "spiritual advisors, professional psychologists, social workers, and physicians in their daily work" (p. vi). Thus, he intended it to cross boundaries and appeal to all these groups. He needed a way of articulating his subjects that would make sense to all. It was an effort worthy of a trading zone.

Moore began with a brief overview of "the concept of psychology," starting with Aristotle's discussions of the *psyche*. He observed that Aristotle's works on psychology could really be called works in biology, although he called the Stagirite "the first great psychologist" (p. 4), praising him for his "physiological psychology" (p. 5). After a quick run through the middle ages, Christian Wolff, Fechner and others, we come to the behaviorists, who rejected any study of inner experience. Moore then noted that "there has been a return to the older concept of psychology as the study of the soul" (p. 9), notably in Mary Calkins' self-psychology. Moore interpreted Calkins to mean that psychology is "the science of the individual being" (ibid.), which for him had advantages over psychology as the "science of conscious processes" (ibid.), a definition he traced to Brentano, who proposed dismissing the category of the soul from the science. For Moore, the goal of psychology was not the study of conscious processes as such or "the mental mechanisms of behavior" but "the particular behavior of some individual whom we are trying to influence" (ibid.). This idiographic – to use the term Allport appropriated later – grounding of psychology Moore summarized by saying that human psychology is "*the science of the human personality*" (ibid.).

In choosing "personality"– and "person" – Moore bridged the scientific and theological domains. "Personality," a Gestalt of traits in psychological terms, also referred, in Thomistic terms, to "an individual substance of a rational nature," a definition from Boethius in the sixth century.[7] To the point of a trading zone, Moore did not have to reconcile the differences between these two conceptions, differences that were considerable. Moreover, in using "personality" to span the

---

[6] We have already seen how Brennan criticized Moore for his deviation from a Thomistic discursive framework, and Moore defended his decision to do so in order to reach beyond the Neoscholastic philosophical community.

[7] Moore's concept of personality, as we saw in Chapter 3, bridged the Thomistic view of the person with the psychologists' emphasis on consciousness.

gulf between the psychological and the theological, Moore did something that Allport did as well. It is no accident that, over the next several decades, there was much collaboration between Allport and the Catholic psychologists.

And here Moore made a bridge between the language of Catholic higher education and teachings and the empirical psychologists:

> It is not necessary in a definition of this kind to assume any theory of human personality but only that there are personalities, individual human beings who may be studied from the point of view of their mental life and the mechanisms of their behavior. To say that psychology is the science of the soul assumes at the outset a metaphysical theory. It is better to start on common ground. ... Psychology is merely the science of human beings developed by an analysis of their mental life by experiments, by observations, by everything that will enable us to obtain insight into the minds of men – how they know, how they think, how they reason, how they feel, how they react in the difficulties of life.
>
> (pp. 9–10)

This "common ground" is what I am considering a trading zone.

If he had stopped here, conceding a point important to many of his contemporaries in empirical psychology, his work would not have had much traction in Catholic circles, because the Thomistic "metaphysical theory" of the soul was highly regarded and guarded. Especially with anxieties about modernism, materialistic tendencies in psychology made the science suspect. So Moore steered his psychology back into metaphysical waters in the very next section. On the one hand, "one who would become a psychologist cannot get along without a good knowledge of the principles of physiology" (p. 12). Nevertheless, on the other hand, "psychology . . . is not in the strict sense of the word a natural science" (p. 11), because human behavior cannot be "completely explained or understood by an appeal to principles which are strictly those of natural science" (ibid.). Those principles only go so far, and understanding requires study also of the unconscious and conscious intentions and motives of individuals.

This kind of back-and-forth between the empirical and the philosophical distinguished Moore's efforts to bridge his diverse constituencies and establish a scientific psychology within a Catholic context. For example, he addressed conscious behavior as the distinctive feature of the human personality. Then: "What, we may ask, is the ultimate nature of consciousness?" (p. 15). This question could have been avoided in a secular psychology text, but not in one addressed to the Catholic community. His reply: "Properly speaking, it is no task of psychology, and one may go on and study a great deal about the facts of consciousness without ever knowing anything at all about their ultimate nature" (ibid.). Here, he looked to the subculture of scientific psychologists. So next he turned his head toward the Catholics: "Nevertheless, it may be pardonable to raise the question and suggest a philosophical answer" (ibid.). He did so by bringing into his zone the Aristotelian categories of substance and accident, which were part of the discourse of Catholic higher education. Consciousness is not a substance, he wrote, but a characteristic (an "accident" in Aristotle's term) of a type of substance, and this characteristic cannot be explained by only chemical principles. Rather than jump immediately to the scholastics for a solution, Moore brought up the biologist, Hans Driesch, his contemporary and champion of vitalism in biology.[8] This appeal to Driesch, to whom he returned in the concluding chapters, was to one who had credibility as a scientist and who was not reductionistic. In the language of trading zones, vitalism had currency for Moore.

Unlike the type of theorizing that became prominent somewhat later – Gordon Allport in 1939 noted the decline in big systems in favor of narrowly construed theories – Moore in 1924 proposed a classification of all mental activity. Toward the conclusion of the book, in dealing with volition, Moore included a chapter on freedom of the will. As we have seen above, in the Catholic response to psychoanalysis, and in particular in the work of Boyd Barrett (to whom Moore refers, as we have seen in Chapter 5), the free will was a non-negotiable category for the Catholics. Moore was no exception, but including it in his text risked losing his secular audience. Drawing on psychologists such as Ach and Calkins, on Thomas Aquinas, and on the philosophical reflections of chemists, Moore defended the freedom of the will. Then, in concluding, Moore returned to the topic of the soul. Noting how the idea "is in ill repute" in psychology (p. 402), he proceeded to argue the case for it, explaining how philosophical and scientific presuppositions led to the current situation. Then, drawing on Driesch's vitalism and scholastic thought, he argued for the soul, concluding that its immortality is philosophically justified.

What this last chapter represented was Moore's attempt to get the soul into the trading zone and give it currency there. He had reason to believe that psychology was not totally opposed to the idea, given the work of such notables as Calkins and the psychologists of the Würzburg school. However, it did not turn out that way – the soul did not enter into the exchange between the empirical psychologists and Catholic thought. Moore, however, kept trying. In revising *Dynamic psychology* some twenty four years later in *The driving forces of human nature*, he dropped the last chapter on the soul, but not the ideas behind the chapter. He presented instead arguments on formal causality, a topic he had earlier addressed in the context of factor analysis (Moore, 1934). In "Formal causality and the philosophy of nature," he drew on embryonic studies to say that we cannot understand what happens in foetal development unless we posit a "formative force" (p. 442) that directs the growth and differentiation of the cells. He drew on biologists such as Driesch and Hans

---

[8] We have already seen that Walsh drew on Driesch in his *Psychotherapy*.

Spemann,[9] on Aristotle and Aquinas, and on a critique of Descartes' dismissal of formal causality. His conclusion stated:

> Nature is not a mere swarm of moving particles, but a matrix of *materia prima* [prime matter] in which by laws, known as yet but dimly, formative forces arise, *rationes seminales* [germinal principles], which are akin to concepts, which coordinate development and disappear as ideas flash into consciousness and then cease to be.
>
> (p. 444)

These formative principles, *rationes seminales*, "guide and direct change in nature, like concept in the mind of an artist" (p. 443). In raising this issue, Moore attempted to bring into play a term that had a long history, originating in the ancient world, developed by Augustine, and elaborated later by the scholastics. It was tied to the idea of goal-directedness, since a formative principle directs growth and living toward defined ends. Certainly, Moore was not alone in attempting to return formal (and final) causality to psychology (see Rychlak, 1976), but again, these philosophical terms had at best marginal currency in psychology in the twentieth century. But if we focus on the fact that Moore was establishing what we are calling a trading zone, then his terms did have currency. He demonstrated that being "scientific" was not an obstacle to being "philosophical," and indeed, that the science sub-culture had something that Catholics might find valuable. We shall turn presently to what the Catholic sub-culture did want from psychology.

But first, let us see how some subsequent Catholic psychologists dealt with the conceptions of psychology that Moore elaborated. Some Catholic psychologists who sought to cultivate this trading zone followed Moore directly on this point. One such was Timothy Gannon's (1954) *Behavior: The unity of human psychology*, which we discussed in the chapter on Neoscholastic psychology. Gannon's textbook addressed students in Catholic colleges and universities. Like Moore, he prefaced his introduction of the soul into psychology with a criticism of Cartesianism's division between a mechanistic understanding of the body and a purely spiritual conception of the soul. Like Moore, he thought it good that psychology had rejected that conception of the soul. He made a spirited defense of a broader notion of the soul, saying that the psychologist "is not at liberty to ignore the question and then proceed with his analysis of human experience and behavior as if the answer made no difference" (p. 17). Gannon then presented the Aristotelian alternative, arguing in part that, "in Aristotle's sense the soul by definition is no more supernatural than the foot" (p. 25). Such a concept is as necessary for psychology as "the actualizing principle itself is to the constitution of the personality" (ibid.). Thus Gannon

---

[9] Hans Spemann (1869–1941) received the Nobel prize in physiology in 1935 for his work in embryology. In referring to Spemann, then, Moore referred to someone whose scientific credentials were impeccable.

defended the place of the soul in psychology. Finally, turning attention to the psychological side, he stated that psychology is "the study of the whole range of human experience and behavior insofar as it manifests the reactions of a single, living person to changes within himself and in his environment" (p. 27). Like his teacher, Moore, Gannon stressed psychology as interested in "the single personality meeting the impact of concrete situations" (p. 28).

Gannon's presentation of the category of personality shows most clearly the nature of the text as a trading zone between psychology and Catholic thought. First, he hearkened back to Boethius as having given the earliest definition of personality (person) in the sixth century. Implied in this definition are, "the power of self-directed effort or voluntary control" and "rational insight into one's own mental states" leading to "self-estimate or self-ideal" (p. 414). Gannon argued that Boethius' definition (taken up and refined by Aquinas) "has provided a sound foundation upon which empirical definitions [of personality] could well afford to build" (p. 415). Drawing on personality theorists Gordon Allport and Raymond B. Cattell, he offered his own definition of personality, one that he claimed would be true to both the philosophical and empirical perspectives: "Personality is the unique pattern of mental and physical traits bound together within a living organism which seeks expression in the self-directed pursuit of values and which makes the organism capable of entering into the complex relationships of human society as an active and responsible member" (pp. 416–17). Personality thus appeared the prime object useful for trade between the psychologists and the Catholic world. It carried implications of moral responsibility, important to Catholic thinkers, and it was available to the psychologists as an object of study and for commerce with their colleagues in the empirical psychological world.

Sisters Annette Walters and Kevin O'Hara, who taught at the College of St. Catherine in St. Paul, published *Persons and personality: An introduction to psychology* (1953), as discussed above in Chapter 3. Like the textbooks of Moore and Gannon, this one was addressed to the Catholic college student. This meant addressing the specific issues that such a student would want to encounter, such as attempts "to reconcile the amoral point of view adopted by psychologists with the moral view inculcated by his religion" (p. vii), while simultaneously providing a solid introduction to the field. The title suggested the general framework, and Walters and O'Hara organized the text around a lifespan developmental approach. They differentiated "person" from "personality" in terms of the Aristotelian differentiation of substance and accidents: person referred to "what is unchangeable" (p. 6) and "can be known only by the intellect" (p. 7). Personality, on the other hand concerns our actualized potentials.

> In contemporary psychology, the terms used in discussing personality are frequently the same as those used in philosophy, but the denotative and connotative meanings often differ. The term *person*, for instance, is typically

used as a synonym for *individual* and has no deeper philosophical significance than that; it does not necessarily connote a rational creature. The term
personality is also used in a philosophically naïve sense. Its meaning differs
for psychologists. The definition we are adopting is as follows: "Personality is
the dynamic organization within the individual of those psychophysical
systems that determine his unique adjustments to his environment."

(quoting Allport, 1937, p. 48 on pp. 507–8)

By keeping the focus on "the personality as a whole" (p. 508), Walters and O'Hara
sought to bridge the disparate discourses of Neoscholastic philosophy and
empirical psychology, a strategy facilitated by drawing on Allport, whose interest
in personality was similarly influenced by his religious concerns (Nicholson
(2003, pp. 205–6). That this strategy conforms to Galison's notion of a trading
zone is evident in that the denotative and connotative differences were allowed to
stand, once pointed out, as was the naïve use of the term "personality." In order to
work in the middle ground and prepare Catholic students for psychology, which
was their explicit intention (see p. 641), a truncated notion of "person" and
"personality" was left standing. There was no attempt to be more precise, as such
precision would have cut the text off from one or the other group. The accommodations were primarily to the psychologists, to be sure, but not entirely, as the
discussion of the determinants of behavior made evident.

One term not negotiable in the Catholic world was "free will." *Persons and
Personality* did not omit that topic and related moral ones, but when Walters
and O'Hara did discuss them, the presentation was frankly philosophical and at
times theological, drawing on Aquinas and Neoscholastic writers of Catholic
spirituality such as Reginald Garrigou-Lagrange (1877–1964). That is, not all
the content of this text, as of the others we are considering, belonged in the
trading zone. Writing for Catholic students and teachers, Walters and O'Hara
addressed their sensibilities and concerns, beyond what would have been
necessary for an exclusively psychological audience.

Another contribution to this commerce was *Readings in Psychology*, edited by
Sister Annette Walters (1954). The book was intended for Catholic students just
beginning their studies of psychology, and it contained an impressive selection of
authors in psychology and out, both Catholic and non-Catholic, including
Walters' good friend, B.F. Skinner. With 121 readings (the list is too extensive to
include here), suffice it to say that members of the ACPA were well represented
(Magda Arnold, Alexander Schneiders, James E. Royce, Timothy Gannon, Noël
Mailloux), as were the luminaries of mid-twentieth-century psychology (Allport,
McClelland, Maslow, Gibson, Freud, etc.). The book was part of the College
Reading Series,[10] with Thomas P. Neill as editor of the social sciences part of the

---

[10] Other volumes published by Newman Press included: Thomas Patrick Neill (1959)
Readings in the history of western civilization; Richard Mulcahy (1959), *Readings in
economics*; James Collins (1960), *Readings in ancient and medieval philosophy*; Gordon

series. Neill, a historian, wrote a great deal about Catholicism, and so his name on this volume gave it added credibility in Catholic circles, and he praised Walters for her grounding in both philosophy and scientific psychology. Walters, for her part, did not downplay the assumptions made by many of the psychological authors that diverged from Catholic teaching. She wrote that the book "is replete with valuable scientific information, some of which is almost inextricably mixed with philosophical assumptions unacceptable to the Catholic. In calling your [the student's] attention to these assumptions we do not condemn the scientific validity of the work. We merely try to present these selections to you in such a way that you will be able to view modern psychological literature in the clear light of your Catholic faith" (p. xix). Thus, the book brought into play a complex set of ideas and issues, and it placed them on a common ground. Rather than proposing a solution to the conflicts between the philosophical presuppositions of some psychologists and those of the Church (Neoscholastic philosophy, to be sure), Walters envisioned this as a task – that perhaps some of the readers of the book would accomplish. The book constitutes yet another attempt to establish or perhaps to enlarge the zone of interaction between the Catholics and the psychologists.

In 1951, a group of Catholic psychologists, led by Magda Arnold and John A. Gasson, SJ, met "to formulate an integrated theory of personality based on a Christian conception of human nature" (Arnold and Gasson, 1954a, p. iii). The group included leading Catholic psychologists.[11] The contributions spelled out many of the points of convergence that we have already seen: the distinction between philosophical presuppositions and empirical research, the necessity for consideration of formal and final causality, the unitive nature of the human person. The group thus affirmed Moore's position that psychology is the study of the personality. The collection, *The human person*, was intended to be a "primary text for course in personality" (ibid.). It is in the last chapter, "Religion and Personality Integration" (Gasson, 1954b), that we see how the category of "personality" operated as a term common to the psychologists and the wider Catholic community, how "personality" passed from its empirical psychological to religious meanings. In the trading zone that had been developing, we see that "personality" had become, by the 1950s, jargon.

Gasson discussed the influence of religious ideals and practices on "personality integration," presenting an overview of the Spiritual Exercises[12] of

---

C. Zahn (1958), *Readings in sociology*; Henry J. Koren (1958), *Readings in the philosophy of nature*; and Jean R. Rosenberg (1964), *Readings in metaphysics*.

[11] Charles A. Curran, Vincent V. Herr, SJ, Frank J. Kobler, Noël Mailloux, OP, Alexander A. Schneiders, Walter Smet, SJ, Louis B. Snider, SJ, and Annette Walters, CSJ. At the time, Arnold, Snider, Herr, and Kobler were on the Loyola University of Chicago faculty. See Chapter 8 for further discussion of this book.

[12] The Spiritual Exercises (written 1522–4) provide a systematic structure for prayer and meditation on the life of Christ and on the relation of the individual to Christ. In Chapter 6, I discussed Gasson's critique of Jung's reading of the Exercises.

St. Ignatius of Loyola, the founder of the Jesuits. Gasson presented his credentials, which show how he was as grounded on the religious side as on the
psychological side:

> More than thirty years of experience of making retreats[13] ... and almost
> twenty years' experience of directing men and women ... in the making of
> them ... together with a systematic study of the ascetical and psychological
> dynamics involved in the Spiritual Exercises ... have made the present
> writer sufficiently acquainted with this area of religious living to write
> about it from the inside ... I have observed with a psychologist's eye the
> effectiveness of the Exercises in contributing to the cure of souls sick
> spiritually, some of them psychologically as well.
>
> (p. 549)

Gasson followed one of the basic rules of this trading zone, negotiating psychological meanings with the spiritual: "Since we are making a psychological
analysis of the Exercises, our primary concern will be with the basic driving
forces of human nature [an allusion to Moore's book, perhaps?] on the *psychological* level. Let us remember, nevertheless, that the Exercises are not merely a
psychological device employed by St. Ignatius to achieve a certain psychological
state in those who go through them ... He was concerned with the salvation of a
man's soul" (p. 555). The bulk of Gasson's analysis concerned the way the
Exercises call into question and set on a Christian course the "self-ideal" of the
individual. He attempted to translate the steps of the Exercises into psychological terms, to show how an individual can undergo psychological development during the retreat. For example:

> The third exercise then extends the content of the self-concept to include
> deviant motivation and the sources whence they flow. A hint is given that
> the ideals which the exercitant [the person following the Exercises] had
> actually set up for attainment – "worldly and vain things" – may be in fact
> disintegrating rather than integrating factors in the total "laying out of
> one's life."
>
> (pp. 561–2)

Gasson named some of the motives that drive our behavior – "basic tendencies
to possession, social recognition, and self-actualization" (p. 567) – as purely
natural motives that can be changed in the direction of spiritual perfection.[14] In
the concluding section, Gasson presented the hoped-for outcome of a retreat:

---

[13] He noted: "A *retreat* is a technical expression from asceticism denoting a period of time of
   varying length ... during which a person in silence, solitude, and recollection of spirit
   ponders the truths of Revelation in a systematic way so as to shape his life in accordance
   with them and make his interior supernatural life more vigorous and effective" (p. 550).
[14] The last mentioned, "self-actualization," is a reference to Maslow's theory of motivation. In
   an earlier chapter in the book, Gasson discussed Maslow (p. 187).

"Thus a complete detachment from self is achieved, and the person is set free to move without hindrance or deviation to the pinnacle of self-actualization which is found in thoroughgoing Christlikeness or, what amounts to the same thing, complete integrity, that is, sanctity" (p. 573). Gasson concluded by urging the reader to test this interpretation by making a retreat – a call to empirical verification!

We have already seen, in Chapter 3, that "person" and "personality" were used to bridge another gap: as the Neoscholastic synthesis fell apart, the term "person" established a link between the Thomistic and the phenomenological traditions. As important as that was, it was a bridge and not a trading zone, because the term had to be articulated clearly in terms both traditions, insofar as they were distinct, could comprehend. The work of Donceel and others did precisely that.

If this trading zone did not establish a new language, it did set the rules of engagement between the psychologists and the Catholics, and produced a pidgin for exchange purposes. First, there were the key terms, "person" and "personality" that had currency already on both sides. In focusing on these terms, the psychologists signaled that they were not succumbing to the reductionism that many in the Catholic world saw in psychology. These terms silently carried connotations of a scholastic, Aristotelian anthropology, in which the soul as formal and final cause still had significance, without the psychologists speaking in terms that became increasingly alien in the psychological world. Other terms, such as "motive" and "self-ideal" also resonated in both the psychological and religious register, and they featured prominently in this trading zone.[15] Second, one of the primary rules of this common discourse was that spiritual meanings "completed" the psychological meanings, as we saw in Gasson's discussion of the Spiritual Exercises. This was in accord with the Thomistic teaching that "grace perfects nature," and the psychologists were of one accord that psychology was a matter of nature, not grace, about which the psychologists, as such, could say nothing. This Thomistic principle, along with another Thomistic conception, namely, that the sciences are autonomous within the limits of their own competency, meant that there was something of a division of labor and of meaning in both terminology and in professional roles. Thus, "personality" had distinct but related meanings, either one of which could be the reference, depending on whether the context was theological or psychological. Similarly, a priest as priest had pastoral and liturgical roles and duties distinct from his roles and duties as a psychologist. He could be fully both and, in principle, his theological orientation was irrelevant in his psychological activities. Not absolutely, of course, for that would institute a kind of schizoid position that would have been intolerable. The

---

[15] Boring (1950, p. 693) noted the emphasis on dynamics among Catholic psychologists because of their concern with human responsibility. Another example of this mixed discourse is a textbook by James E. Royce, SJ (1955), *Personality and mental health.*

boundary work performed by distinguishing between philosophical and empirical psychologies helped much in this effort. Third, in exchange for accepting this common discourse, the psychologists could "sell their wares" to the Catholic community, so to speak, and to that we now turn.

Counseling as a trading zone

Catholic psychologists wanted recognition for their work and profession, but more important, they also saw themselves as having things to offer the Catholic world. The first is the general area of counseling and psychotherapy, the second, and more directly a point of exchange, is pastoral counseling.

As we have already seen, for Pope Pius XII and for Catholic psychologists and psychiatrists such as Gregory Zilboorg, psychologists needed to keep the person in mind when theorizing and practicing. One psychologist who did precisely that was Charles A. Curran, in *Counseling in Catholic life and education* – a good example of applied Neoscholastic psychology, already discussed in Chapter 3. There, we saw how Curran drew on the philosophical meanings of "counsel" to connect a Thomistic approach to character development with nondirective counseling. Here, I will briefly indicate how counseling, on Curran's terms, was received, so that his work provided an example of a trading zone.

Evidence for the acceptance of Curran's work exists in the book itself. Curran taught at St. Charles College-Seminary in Columbus, Ohio. His bishop, Michael J. Ready, wrote the Foreword to the book, and Cardinal Eugene Tisserant, a leader in the Vatican, wrote the Preface. Ready (1893–1957) was one of the leaders in the American Catholic Church. From 1931 to 1936, he was assistant secretary general of the National Catholic Welfare Conference (NCWC), and from 1936 to 1944, he was secretary general. This organization was in many ways the public face of the Catholic Church in the United States, and it was involved in many things, including lobbying in Washington. It was the means whereby the bishops addressed the major social issues of the day.[16] So, already involved in social issues before becoming Bishop of Columbus in 1944 (where he served until his death), he set up a Catholic Welfare Bureau and a Diocesan Child Guidance Center (The Bishops of Columbus, 2008). Ready would have thus been inclined toward the kind of work that Curran was doing. Curran

---

[16] As an indication of Ready's many activities: "He came into office [at the NCWC] during the depression and when the Ku Klux Klan was at its height. In 1941, he gave the benediction at Roosevelt's inauguration. During the war, he worked closely with the USO, the War Relief Services, and the National Refugee Service. During the war the NCWC press department also provided information on Vatican views and activities. During Ready's tenure, the conference built an office building for its Washington staff" (Reese, 1992, p. 80). The NCWC was the predecessor to the National Conference of Catholic Bishops. Ready was also the *censor librorum* for Hagmaier and Gleason's (1959) *Counseling the Catholic* and so affirmed the book with a *nihil obstat*.

dedicated the book to his bishop, indicating that the two probably had close ties. Ready's (1952) preface endorsed Curran's book – no surprise in that – and he made the point that "a counselor has as great a need to understand the human person and to know how to offer sound assistance in anxieties and difficulties as a physician has to understand the human body" (p. xii). Curran had the appropriate philosophical and theological credentials, Ready declared, presumably to that part of the Catholic readership skeptical of psychology and counseling. Implicitly, then, Curran's ability to "understand the human person" meant that he had both the psychological expertise and the theological background. Curran's book presented this type of understanding, giving psychological skill a secure place in the Catholic world. Such was the value of "person."

Cardinal Eugène Tisserant (1884–1972) was a leading member of the Curia, the Vatican bureaucracy, having held by 1952 a number of major posts, including head of the Vatican Library. That such a figure should endorse Curran's book is a bit of a mystery, since Tisserant was not directly involved in psychology. In addition to his other duties at the time, however, he had pastoral concerns, including the well-being of Catholic family life and pastoral care in Rome. The strong influence of the communists, too, was something he wished to check (Lesourd and Ramiz, 1964). These interests probably directed his attention to the book, as he wrote (Tisserant, 1952): "in these times when social and political conditions demand of each Christian the maximum of personal responsibility and prudent action in the midst of events which promote both mass emotion and personal turmoil and conflict" (p. xi), Curran's work was timely. Tisserant repeatedly stressed how Curran's book could "help man conquer and control himself" (p. vii), thereby aligning counseling with more traditional moral discipline. Tisserant was aware that counseling is not spiritual direction and not teaching, but counseling helps "to create an opportunity where a person can develop the virtue of counseling in himself and grow gradually able to control his confusing emotions and instincts" (pp. x–xi). He affirmed, that is to say, Curran's use of "counsel" and "counseling" in this trading zone, along with "person." Psychological science, Tisserant insisted, was necessary, especially "in these perilous social and political times" (p. x). His brief remarks reveal two things: first, what the Church hoped to gain by "trading" with the psychologists; and second, how key psychological terms, freighted with theological and Thomistic connotations, showed how psychological expertise could be used within Catholic settings.

Tisserant's endorsement did help, in that his name was invoked to introduce priests to the similarities and differences between psychotherapy and spiritual direction. John T. Burne (1959), a member of the Department of Religious Instruction and chaplain at the Catholic University, in drawing on Curran's book, explained that counseling deals "with problems emotional and motivational had by *normal* people" (p. 539). He described counseling as complementary to spiritual direction, the key difference being seen in the terminology used to describe the Other in both: in counseling, it is the "normal person" with emotional difficulties; in spiritual direction it is the "soul" or the person showing his soul – his or her relationship with and progress toward God. Spiritual direction, at least in its basics, was part of ordinary seminary education, but not counseling, at this point. Burne cited Tisserant's words in Curran's book, where the Cardinal stressed the value of this new science of psychology.

Guidance counseling

Curran's book did much to forge links between the Catholic community and counseling, in part through his hybrid terminology, wherein counseling in the therapeutic sense contributed to the development of prudence, the moral virtue. This was not purely Rogerian therapy and it was not pure guidance, the accepted standard in Catholic circles. Curran's work led in several directions, one of which was guidance counseling in the schools. (We have already seen how Moore's students contributed to this area by means of their testing studies in the schools, beginning in the 1930s.) Guidance counseling became an accepted part of Catholic education, with journals such as the *Catholic Counselor* (which ran from 1956 to 1964)[17] and other journals, including *Catholic Educator* (which was published from 1931 to 1970) devoting attention to it. However, it is to another trading zone, pastoral counseling, that we now turn.

Pastoral counseling

In pastoral counseling, psychology came into direct contact with the age-old *cura animarum*, the cure of souls. The cure and care of souls included the practices of confession and spiritual direction, both of which had been topics of reflection and practice for centuries, and the early twentieth century was heir to traditions that had been cultivated since the Counter-Reformation of the sixteenth century (McNeill, 1951). Confession involved the examination of conscience, and casuistry, the practice of resolving questions of moral culpability in the light of religious teachings. Casuistry had had a great flourishing, with Jesuits taking the lead in the seventeenth century and thereafter. Spiritual direction, which has to do "with the pursuit of higher spiritual attainment rather than with the sacramental pardon of sins" (p. 293), had flourished since the seventeenth century.[18] Both of these practices involved relationships between two people: in confession, the structure was sacramental, liturgical, private, and under a seal of secrecy. Spiritual direction could involve a much more personal relationship. St. Francis de Sales (1567–1622) addressed the

---

[17] The name was changed to the *National Catholic Guidance Conference Journal*, which continued until 1971.

[18] In Chapter 8, we discussed a twentieth-century work of spiritual direction, Tanquerey's *The spiritual life*.

nature of the relationship with the spiritual director in terms typical of his "spirit aflame with the love of God, and of his spiritual charges" (p. 295): "the guide should always be an angel in your eyes: that is to say, when you have found him, do not look upon him as a mere man, nor trust in him as such, nor in his human knowledge, but in God who will favor you and speak to you by means of this man" (*Introduction to the devout life* (1609), cited in ibid.). While not the only possible formulation of the relationship, this passage suggests an intensely personal and highly formalized relationship, in which matters of the will and the fate of the soul were at stake.[19] All this exposition serves to demonstrate is that when psychotherapy came along in the twentieth century, it was not received in the Catholic world with a *tabula rasa*. When defined more or less along medical lines, psychotherapy posed no challenge to these traditions, but when it was applied to the cultivation of the religious life, then the possibilities for boundary-work and exchange were significant.

The care of souls was not lightly delegated to psychology and psychiatry. Schneiders (1959) observed, after over seven years of work in this area, that "we must remind ourselves that the Church, through its priests and hierarchy, has for centuries regarded itself as the primary if not sole custodian of spiritual growth and health, peace of mind, and measured happiness. Understandably, it regards with some skepticism and even resentment the encroachment of other disciplines into the life of the spirit" (p. 5). Nevertheless, there were reasons to overcome the skepticism and even enter into collaboration, altering a boundary conflict into fruitful exchange.[20]

Pastoral psychology and counseling saw rapid growth after World War II. Misiak and Staudt (1954) did discuss earlier contributions to this field, which they described as "psychology applied to the direction of souls" (p. 222). They noted in particular that the journal, *Études Carmelitaines*, had been in existence since the 1920s, addressing various areas where psychology, religion, and spirituality come together. Nevertheless, in 1954, they wrote (p. 288) that Catholics had no periodical like the Protestant *Pastoral Psychology*, and that a systematic work in it was sorely needed.[21]

---

[19] This passage does suggest that St. Francis de Sales was aware of the phenomenon that psychoanalysts describe as transference. Particular kinds of transference – and counter-transference – were esteemed in the traditions of spiritual direction.

[20] As an indication of the sensitive nature of this enterprise, Schneiders (1959) noted in his introduction to a special issue of *Pastoral Psychology* (a Protestant journal) that the issue, "Catholic Viewpoints in Pastoral Psychology," was "undertaken with approval of the Chancery of the Archdiocese of New York, and of the Rector of Fordham University, the Reverend Laurence J. McGinley, SJ" (p. 6).

[21] Misiak and Staudt also mentioned the British group, the Guild of Pastoral Psychology, founded as a Catholic group. It was devoted to Jung's psychology. Prominent among its speakers was Victor White and Vera von der Heydt. Relevant publications of this group include: Adeline M. Matland (1942), *Pastoral psychology* and Vera von der Heydt (1954),

It was around this time that a trading zone came into being, helping to establish pastoral psychology as a discipline. As with other trading zones, we can identify the disciplines that came together to exchange and work on a common project: psychology, psychiatry, pastoral and moral theologies, philosophy, sociology, social work, and education. The psychology in question was that compatible with theology and philosophy, to be sure, the psychology of "person" and "personality." In mid-century, psychiatry meant psychoanalysis, so much of the terminology in early pastoral psychology was psychoanalytic. Competing with it in the 1950s was nondirective or client-centered psychotherapy, which we have already seen was establishing itself as viable in Catholic settings, with some misgivings. Pastoral and moral theologies are two of the more "applied" areas of theology, so to speak, because they dealt with human action in the concrete. The theological and philosophical partners in this venture were, to be sure, largely Neoscholastic. If the early 1950s were the *terminus a quo* for this trading zone, then the late 1960s were the *terminus ad quem*, in that by that point pastoral psychology had become established, and was producing its own "native speakers." From that point forward, it constituted a discipline unto itself. We shall concentrate on the formative period from 1953 to 1967.

In addition to these "sub-cultures," to prolong the metaphor, there had to be a problem that the collaboration was seeking to address. It was largely that of priests dealing with difficult pastoral situations, especially one-to-one relationships with parishioners seeking advice, with individuals in confession, and with people seeking spiritual direction. The situations were many and various, and there was recognition on the part of those collaborating in this trading zone that seminary training did not adequately address the kind of interpersonal relationships that priests were facing. This also meant that many of those who worked in this trading zone were members of the clergy. In addition, many others were nuns, as well as lay men and women. But even in the early years of pastoral psychology, there was some participation by non-Catholics. In fact, pastoral psychology in Protestant circles was already well underway, with pastoral counseling centers beginning to proliferate, and with seminaries often including this kind of pastoral education.

Creating the language of pastoral psychology

One of the earliest books to deal with this area systematically was *Counselling the Catholic* by George Hagmaier, CSP,[22] and Robert Gleason, SJ. During the 1950s, Hagmaier was involved in pastoral counseling, particularly in the areas of sexuality and marriage, and he had taught pastoral psychology at the Paulist

Psychology and the care of souls. I found little influence of this group in the United States during the 1950s and 1960s.

[22] CSP, Congregation of St. Paul, i.e. the Paulists (recall that Thomas Verner Moore belonged to this order until he became a Benedictine).

House of Graduate Studies in Boston. In 1959, he was at the Paulist Institute for Religious Research in New York City. Gleason was chair of the theology department at Fordham. Hagmaier and Gleason sought to carve out an area distinct from traditional cure of souls and from psychotherapy, drawing upon both but in fact establishing a new discipline. They stated that their aim was practical, not theoretical – addressed to priests who often found themselves called upon to venture beyond the skills and knowledge obtained in seminary training. Hagmaier's part of the book came from "an introductory counselling course, taught by a trained instructor to seminarians or young priests who have had little or no formal training in these areas" (Hagmaier and Gleason, 1959, p. xiii). The book showed that its authors were well aware of both boundary-work and a trading zone in formation.

They attempted both tasks, boundary-work and exchange, by defining their topic such that it supplemented – but did not replace – traditional examination of conscience and spiritual direction:

> Unlike many Catholic counselling books, this volume will have very little to say about theology, philosophy, will power and grace in the development of desirable human behavior. Rather than duplicate the many excellent contributions already made in these areas, the authors hope in these pages to highlight the roles which feelings and emotions play in the development of sound or weak human personalities.

(pp. 5–6)

While not questioning at all the singular importance of intellect and will in directing our actions, they did nonetheless stress the "prior influence" of feelings and emotions on them. People cannot benefit from instruction and guidance if they are not emotionally available to receive them, and Hagmaier and Gleason stated: "the emotional life of most of us is in some way stunted, perverted, or otherwise undeveloped so that grace is not always able to work as fruitfully and perfectly as it might" (p. 6). They expanded upon this theme of the wounded character of human emotional life with a developmental perspective, illustrating how the young child's limited cognitive perspective combined with parental misconceptions and often limited ability to love their child could produce emotionally distorted adolescents and adults. These themes of personality distortion as a result of faulty upbringing were of course a staple of mid-twentieth-century psychology, especially as influenced by psychoanalysis. What is of interest here is how this prototype of personality development served to establish a zone where priests could see the value of learning a thing or two from the psychologists. In other words, priests would see something of value to "buy" in this trading zone of pastoral psychology.

Hagmaier and Gleason proposed what in effect was a simplified language so that priests and psychologists could communicate. The stress was on the former learning some of the language of the latter, in order to explicate the guiding thesis of the book: *"experiences* and *attitudes* of *early life determine* to a significant degree the kind of *personality*, the type of *character*, and to some extent the degree of *free choice* which the adult will possess" (p. 18). I have italicized key terms of this mixed psychological–spiritual discourse, *character* and *free choice* representing contributions from the religious side.[23] The text then presented the relevant constituents of personality, drawing explicitly on a psychoanalytic framework. They simplified technical terms, including *id*, *superego*, and *ego*, along with a number of defense mechanisms for use in the pastoral setting. A key contribution of Galison's notion of trading zone is that such translations are not "dumbed down" versions of psychological epistemic objects, but a kind of pidgin language that enables two disparate groups to interact. In this instance, Hagmaier, a member of both "tribes," proposed the terms to his priest-students and to psychologist- and psychiatrist-readers, so that they could discuss together specifically pastoral problems in a common discourse.

Without repeating the complete translation of these terms into the proposed new pastoral language, let me present some of what they said about the id, the superego, and the ego. First, the id:

> At the core man's personality there is a *primal surge of living energy or force* which is without consciousness, beyond rationality and will, outside of place or time ... These forces are healthily expressed when they are channeled into manifestations of love, conjugal sexual interchange, healthy aggression and ambition, creativity and zeal for worthwhile causes. The same substrate of primal energy can be less desirably channeled into expressions of hate, hostility, libidinal excesses, sadistic and masochistic behavior.
>
> (p. 19)

Strictly speaking, this depiction bears only glancing resemblance to the Freudian id. Hagmaier drew upon other discourses as well to make his point in his depiction of the id. He incorporated the broader notion of psychic "energy" and – most important – in indicating the "healthy" expressions of this living energy, Thomistic philosophical anthropology.

Second, the superego:

> Offsetting, as it were, the chaotic and unfettered quality of the primitive urges is that part of man which we might call the *'unconscious conscience.'* The unconscious conscience in each man develops long before his use of reason. Very early in life the young child subtly discovers that there are both acceptable and unacceptable things associated with human

---

[23] Character could be said to come from the psychological side, since Rudolf Allers' study of character was still current in Catholic circles, but by mid-century, the term, with its ethical baggage, had ceased more or less to be a psychological epistemic object.

behavior ... The child seems to absorb, without a great deal of conscious reference, the kinds of attitudes to certain modes of thinking, feeling, and behaving that his parents transmit to him.

(ibid.)

This unconscious conscience is not the "*conscious* conscience" (p. 20), which is "that faculty by which we make a judgment about a kind of behavior over which we have definite control" (ibid.). It is with this conscious faculty that we ought to reflect when we make an examination of conscience in preparation for confession. This was traditional pastoral terminology, with conscience being a faculty whereby we determine the goodness and badness of our actions and thoughts. The "unconscious conscience" is not rational and it really has no place in the examination of conscience. That being said, in the pastoral setting, the two types of conscience were often confused. The terminology of the two types of conscience bound them together for pastoral purposes and simultaneously differentiated them.

Finally, there is the *self*, which is the Freudian ego: "This is the conscious, rational, free component of the human being which makes decisions, is in touch with reality within and without the human organism" (ibid.). Again, this is not precisely the Freudian ego: it is the Freudian ego tempered with Thomistic categories of the rational faculties of intellect and will. The simplification, again, allowed for the two groups to work together, understanding each other well enough for the exchange, without either one having to "buy" the philosophical and theoretical commitments of the other side.

One who was interested in developing this field was Raymond Hostie (1966), whose work we have previously met in the chapter on Jungian thought. While pastoral counseling was under way by the early 1960s, Hostie did not think it yet systematically developed among Catholics. As such, his work provides evidence for how this field came to be in the intersection of psychology and moral theology. Hostie said that: "Pastoral psychology usually purports to be a discipline that puts within the reach of the priest the latest findings and especially the practical applications of counseling, depth psychology and even psychiatry. It has rarely been attempted to integrate it with dogmatic and moral theology" (p. 240). Hostie's book was aimed at priests who found themselves being called upon to provide such counseling and in need of instruction. The book sought to establish – although of course he did not use the term – a trading zone where priests could benefit from psychology. Hostie wrote:

A non-technical vocabulary, therefore, will be used, but the words will gradually give indication of the specialized meaning we have in mind. This decision was not inspired solely by the desire to make the ideas accessible to the reader unacquainted with psychological studies; it seemed highly recommendable to respect the specific nature of the function of the

spiritual counselor, which is only distantly related to that of the psychotherapist or to that of the 'counselor' in the ordinary sense of the term.

(p. ix).

The way that Hostie said he would grapple with this situation was to avoid a
specialized language and use one descriptive of practical and concrete situations.

In fact, he drew heavily on a client-centered discourse, which lent itself to a
non-technical presentation (unlike, for example, a Freudian terminology of
"cathexis" and "counter-transference"). Hostie was no doubt also conversant
with existential literature, since "encounter" was one term he repeatedly used.
An example of what we may call his pastoral creole is this passage, with key
terms emphasized (emphasis added):

> It goes without saying that the *person* who comes to the priest is not in
> control of all his capabilities. He desires to speak about his powerlessness
> and his confusion, but is not able to give an exact description. If the
> spiritual *counselor* first of all does not *accept* the fact that this powerlessness
> will express itself just as it is *being lived* by the *client* – that is, in the form of
> timidity, stubbornness, self-conceit, laziness, obstinacy, discouragement,
> indifference, frivolity, and so forth – then he paralyzes the *client*. For these
> various forms influence not only the contents of the *dialogue*, but also the
> manner of speaking. The *client* must be *permitted to express* his real
> powerlessness just as he is *experiencing it*, otherwise he will never be able
> to see clearly in himself.

(pp. 49–50)

A psychological reader would see in this something like Rogerian unconditional
acceptance, and the passage is written in a clear style, with just enough
psychological terminology to make sense to Hostie's typical reader. The attitude
that Hostie advised the priest to take in this type of situation (which he clearly
differentiated from other forms of interaction with people) also communicated
a therapeutic attitude with clarity:

> The priest, therefore, should have one concern: to forget about his other
> occupations and duties. The client must become the center of his sympa-
> thetic attention so that he may be given the opportunity of working
> everything out himself. By talking to the priest, the client exposes his
> confused state and himself undertakes the treatment.

(p. 50)

Why must the client "undertake the treatment"? Why is it not the priest who
provides the treatment? Because the person must find his center within himself, and
another person, the priest as counselor, cannot do this for the client. Because, as
Hostie stated, combining seamlessly client-centered and Christian sensibilities:
"The counselor owes it to himself to be detached and disinterested. In the conviction
that God has confided a distinctly personal life to his client, he does not arrogate the

right to take away from him the orientation of his own destiny" (p. 54). Again, Hostie described pastoral counseling in these terms: "The spiritual counselor allows the counselee freedom to express himself fully, so that he may become conscious of what he is experiencing and thus be enabled to take an authentic stand" (p. 57). So rather than give advice or lead (that is, be a pastor in the etymological sense of a shepherd), the priest as counselor facilitates the person's self-discovery.

Hostie thus imparted a basic psychotherapeutic approach and a basic vocabulary into this new kind of pastoral setting. Francis L. Filas, SJ (1916–85), who taught theology at Loyola University in Chicago, thought that Hostie had succeeded. Filas (1966), who wrote widely on religious topics, including family life, agreed with Hostie that a non-technical language was fitting for the book, wondering however, if its straightforward approach might strain the patience of a typical clerical reader, because of the discussion of dialogue belabored the obvious. The strongest point of the book, according to Filas, was the "importance of counseling in the life of the priest" (p. 885). This is a significant remark, since it got to the heart of much psychological advice in the area of counseling: the importance of the counselor having been counseled.

Boundary-work in pastoral counseling

Emphasizing as I have the exchanges between psychology and theology, it might be easy to miss the boundary-work that went on simultaneously. Clearly defined boundaries were essential for collaboration at this time. John R. Cavanagh (1962), a psychiatrist who lectured in the School of Sacred Theology at the Catholic University, and whose attempted synthesis of Thomism and psychiatry has been discussed already, cited Bier (1959) and Braceland (1959) in arguing for clear distinctions between pastoral work and counseling: "He [the clergyman] may wear two hats, he may be a professional (secular) counselor, and he may be a pastor. He cannot be both simultaneously" (p. 21). In part, Cavanagh's dictum was based on appropriate training necessary for counseling, and pastors would usually not have it, so that they would not be equipped for it. The other boundary issue, however, was a potential conflict between the nondirective character of much counseling and the primary pastoral concerns of the clergy: "The secular counselor must usually avoid value judgments unless the counselee makes a direct request for information. Under certain circumstances the pastoral counselor may no longer be permissive but must be directive. These statements should not be interpreted as criticism of the secular counselor. Secular and pastoral counseling are two different processes" (p. 25).[24] For these reasons, Cavanagh urged pastoral counseling be limited to conscious conflicts, not unconscious ones.

---

[24] By permissiveness, Cavanagh meant "acceptance" in the Rogerian sense: the counselor abstains from value-judgments (either positive or negative). Cavanagh was emphasizing

Bier had made a similar point, to be sure, and he did so in terms of the developing *lingua franca* of pastoral psychology. In a special issue of *Pastoral psychology*, Bier (1959) made distinctions, spelled out in large part by Curran (1952), between guidance and counseling, adding one between counseling and psychotherapy (which he saw as the purview primarily of the psychiatrist). The priest who would engage in pastoral counseling should limit "himself to helping solve conscious religious problems" (Bier, 1959, p. 12), leaving "deep emotional conflict" (p. 11) which, by implication, is unconsciously motivated, to secular counselors and psychotherapists. While this position differed in tone from Hagmaier and Gleason's, it did use the same terminology. Bier's concern was with clergymen who in their enthusiasm for counseling have attempted a type of counseling that they did not have the training to do, and that was not in keeping with their clerical responsibilities to others.

Specific trading zones

Gillespie (2001, pp. 90–3) describes the creation of the St. John's Summer Institute in Minnesota in 1953 as one important event in the developing collaboration between mental health professionals and Church officials. Kilian O'Donnell, OSB (1957), described the structure of the St. John's Summer Institutes as part of a trend in "workshops on pastoral care and psychotherapy being held under the auspices of religiously affiliated universities, state hospitals, and psychiatric foundations" (p. 253). The faculty was not exclusively Catholic, although the members of the clergy were. O'Donnell recounted that the faculty and clergy met "in their common concern for the human person" (p. 255), a common concern being a *sine qua non* for a trading zone. What is interesting in this description is how the workshops not only provided information but a lived experience of the counseling process, by focusing on group dynamics, attitudes, and feelings of the participants: "During the process of group maturation the participants become emotionally at home with the subject matter, vocalize their anxieties, become individually related to each other and to the seminar leader. Now the period of real growth begins" (ibid.). The subject matter of this trading zone, the emotions and motivations of persons, the differences between conscious and unconscious processes, etc., were mimetically presented. The participants were not simply presented with psychiatric facts, they were invited to be present to themselves in new ways, so that they could fuse together their theological background with the psychological approaches they encountered. Most important, the members of the clergy learned and experienced "the technique of listening" (p. 258). This was the key new element of pastoral psychology, since the clergy were taught in

the role of the priest in the care of souls, which he stressed, put a limit on acceptance by the priest as pastor.

their theological education to be teachers and spiritual leaders. Here, "they heard and saw demonstrated the necessity of talking little and listening much. They were assured that the counselee would not only expose his problem but, if permitted, would also answer it" (ibid.). In this emerging discipline, the participants saw that they had to balance the "juridic and moralistic attitudes towards human behavior" with the "subjective conditions of the individual conscience and the historic act" (ibid.). We have already seen that Hagmaier and Gleason proposed the same type of attitude, one that entailed not abandoning moral theology but blending it with psychological listening.

Fordham's Institutes of Pastoral Psychology

Gillespie (2001, pp. 65–6) recounts Bier's symposia on topics of pastoral psychology that Fordham began to hold in 1955, and which continued until the end of the 1970s. It is to these symposia we now turn, in order to see how a pastoral psychological discourse developed in the trading zone established by representatives of various fields. These summer institutes provide prime examples of a trading zone. Bier (1964b) described their history: "In 1955 the Psychology Department at Fordham University inaugurated a series of Pastoral Psychology Institutes intended to acquaint members of the clergy with the findings of psychology, psychiatry, sociology, and allied disciplines in the belief that the insights provided by these relatively new and fast developing behavioral sciences would prove helpful to clergymen in their pastoral work" (p. ix). While Bier expressed the outcome of the seminars in terms of mutual understanding and division of labor, what also was going on was the creation of pastoral psychology, with its own language and concepts.

In the first six institutes, from 1955 to 1969 (there was no institute in 1967), representatives from a number of disciplines came together to discuss topics of pastoral psychology.[25] The disciplines included theology, philosophy, psychology, psychiatry, sociology, social work, and several others. Let us enter the zone.

In the zone: Significant issues in pastoral psychology

What we have done so far sets the stage for formation of this trading zone. To further understand the driving forces in its formation, I turn to some of the topics deemed important, especially in the early years. Drawing on the first two institutes at Fordham and to Hagmaier and Gleason's book (to be sure, they participated in the early years of the institutes), what we see is that certain areas of human behavior, with decidedly problematic moral implications, were center

---

[25] The topics: personality and sexual problems (1955 and 1957, in Bier, 1964a); addiction (1959 in Bier, 1962); adolescence (1961 in Bier, 1963); marriage (1963 in Bier, 1965); women in modern life (1963 in Bier, 1968b); and conscience (1969 in Bier, 1971a).

stage. These areas reflected Catholic concerns. Absent, for example, were topics such as gambling or theft, which would have worked in the abstract. No, the central topics were guilt and sex. If ever there were topics that invited exchange with the psychologists (especially those with a psychodynamic orientation), these two, often intertwined to be sure, were the ones.

Guilt, psychological and moral

The discussion of guilt brought together representatives from psychiatry (Zilboorg), psychology (Bier and Coville), theology (Gustave Weigel, SJ, and Joseph H. Duhamel, SJ) and a hospital chaplain (Fr. James F. Cox). Zilboorg, a psychoanalyst, disarmed Catholic critics of Freud by conceding that Freud was a "poor philosopher" (in Bier, 1964a, p. 41) but a good clinician. Zilboorg primarily differentiated the work of psychoanalyst and priest on the basis of the difference between unconscious and conscious processes, saying, however, that awareness of unconscious processes would benefit the spiritual director and confessor. At the same time that Zilboorg was seeking common ground with the clergy, he engaged in boundary-work, saying: "one (almost hopelessly) wishes that psychoanalytic studies had learned to avoid passing on things so much beyond their scope as morality, charity and conscience, and that pastoral psychologists and moral theologians would refrain for a while from spending so much time and energy on pointing out the logical and theological errors of the psychoanalysts in matters of morality" (pp. 50–1). For Zilboorg, good fences made for good neighbors: more important than cross-border sniping would be "to appreciate the full value of the two orders of things: the psychological and the spiritual" (p. 51). It is significant that Zilboorg saw the problem in part as one of translation: "the greatest number of present-day psychologists do not know what spiritual is, and deny its existence, and believe that the nonexistence of spiritual experiences can be proved by the translation of these terms into modern psychological terms" (ibid.). What he wanted to avoid was the reduction of problems of conscience and guilt to nothing but those of the superego and unconscious guilt. So Zilboorg, like Hagmaier, differentiated the superego and the conscience, both of which had to be taken into consideration. This result was neither pure psychoanalysis nor pure spiritual direction. Zilboorg, like the others, proposed a new discourse made up of simplified versions of the parent discourses. He concluded, however, by keeping the "child" (pastoral psychology) tied to its parents: "Therefore pastoral psychology must always be the fruit of the joint effort of the psychiatrist and the priest" (p. 53). This solution keeps the boundaries secure, but it does not foresee the growth of the child and its learning to be independent.

Bier in reply to Zilboorg proposed a vocabulary of guilt that took into consideration the distinction between unconscious and conscious psychological activity. Bier suggested names for three types of guilt based on the degree of unconscious activity in their dynamics. "Moral guilt" is the "normal feeling of guilt" which is the "result of sin" (in Bier, 1964a, p. 55) and has its source in conscience. "Neurotic guilt" and the "need for punishment" originate in the superego, and the distinguishing feature of the latter two is that there is nothing objective (or in the case of neurotic guilt, nothing of magnitude) that would make for "normal guilt." Bier's contribution aimed at providing a new language for a new field.

Gustave Weigel[26] translated Zilboorg's and Bier's terms into explicitly Thomistic terms, while at the same time incorporating psychodynamic terms into the scholastic analysis of the soul (psychodynamics were not lacking in the Thomistic view of the soul but Weigel brought in psychoanalytic terms):

> since a man as a totality is dynamized by drives and impulses other than reason, and by drives which are independent of and prior to reason, the same intellect which makes moral judgments in the light of objective and rational motives, simultaneously acts under pressure of unconscious impulses emotionally charged and uncontrolled by reason. When these impulses operate in accord with a projected father-image which is inhibitory and punitive, we have the superego at work. In some sense the superego is more present concretely than is abstractive conscience, but the superego is no more a faculty than conscience is ... Superego and conscience are closely and tightly interwoven when the intellect makes its practical judgment.
>
> (p. 56)

Weigel's point was that "in the concrete moment and in the concrete person the voice of superego and the voice of conscience fuse" (ibid.), so that neither dynamic psychology nor moral theology alone can grasp the situation: both are needed. What Weigel showed was that philosophical and theological discourse could be modified to incorporate psychodynamic discourse in an effort to understand the individual struggling with moral decisions.

Joseph S. Duhamel, SJ, explored what this common ground between moral theology and psychodynamics meant. For Duhamel, psychology contributed new perspectives and treatments that the priest needed to understand, and he suggested that in teaching, priests try to avoid instilling "a neurotic sense of guilt" (p. 58). Coville, the chief clinical psychologist at St. Vincent's Hospital in New York, described a case of excessive guilt and how it arose in the patient's childhood. The thrust of his comments was to distinguish the types of guilt. Duhamel and Coville, from different backgrounds, worked within the new territory demarcated as pastoral psychology, insofar as both accepted the

---

[26] Weigel (1906–64) was one of the most prominent American theologians of the day. He was Professor of Ecclesiology in the Jesuit seminary, Woodstock College, in Maryland.

theological, philosophical, and psychological contributions as making for greater clarity in difficult situations.

Scrupulosity

Scrupulosity is a common complaint in Catholic life. The term refers to an excessive concern with the sinfulness of otherwise innocuous thoughts and deeds. The scrupulous person might confess sins frequently but never receive any subjective relief from anxiety over sins thus forgiven. Someone scrupulous has an exquisitely refined and often childish conscience. Suffice it to say, the scrupulous penitent was a bane of the confessor, who often did not know how to help the person. At the discussion of scrupulosity, Noël Mailloux, OP, with a background in both theology and psychology, reconfigured it in both philosophical and psychological terms: "the spiritual director will feel more inclined to consider scrupulosity as a rather generalized pathological sensitivity of moral conscience, which through the distortion of any one of its functions is bound to upset the pattern of its dynamics as a whole" (in Bier, 1964a, p. 77). In reply, Alexander Schneiders stated that scrupulosity as a moral defect and as a neurosis ought to be distinguished, and Mailloux seconded that idea, saying that scrupulosity is not simply a psychological disorder but a phenomenon *sui generis* (p. 83). These claims by Schneiders and Mailloux are important, as they show that the defining categories of pastoral psychology cannot be reduced to any one of its parent disciplines. These contributors were carving out a new territory.

A digression: Moral theology in the 1950s in the United States

While there were many disciplines that came together to form pastoral psychology, one among them stands out: moral theology. Without the explicit agreement of the moral theologians and the hierarchy of the Church, pastoral psychology could not have been established at the time. So what is moral theology, and what was it then?

Moral theology in the first half of the twentieth century largely dealt with the confessional, and the manuals[27] written by moral theologians were aids for priests in their understanding the morality of human actions. One of the most

---

[27] On the manuals and the manualists: Curran (1999, pp. 2–3) writes that from the time of the Council of Trent following the Protestant Reformation, moral theology developed along juridical lines, with the "priest acting as a judge to determine whether absolution is to be given or denied" (p. 2). The Council of Trent also promoted a "new genre of moral theology, the *Institutiones morales* (generally referred to in English as the 'manuals'), came into existence through the Society of Jesus (Jesuits) ... In 1603 the Jesuit John Azor published his *Institutiones morales* based on the two-year course he taught to Jesuit seminarians ... to prepare future priests to hear confessions" (p. 3). Charles E. Curran discusses the history of the manuals up to the twentieth century, pointing out that for

influential was *A manual of moral theology for English-speaking countries* by Thomas Slater, SJ. Slater (1909) advised the reader in his Preface (as pointed out by Keenan, 2008, p. 142) that works of moral theology are "books of moral pathology," "not intended for edification" (p. 6). In other words, their task was not to teach one how to live a good life but that "of defining what is right and what wrong in all the practical relations of the Christian life" (ibid.). These manuals focused narrowly on actions and carefully analyzed them for their morality. Using Slater as typical of this tradition, we see that he defined the type of actions that were of concern for moral theology:

> The actions over which a man has control are in a special sense called human acts, because they are due to his free choice. That man has the power of free choice, or free will, is clearly taught in Holy Scripture, and is a dogma of faith ... A man must indeed have a motive for action, but that motive does not constrain him to act; if he has the use and control of his reason, he may as long as he is in life perform or abstain from the action proposed to him. Man has the wonderful power, unique in all the visible creation, of directing his mental and bodily activity in this way or that according to his good pleasure; and it is this wonderful power which makes him a moral agent, and which makes it worthwhile to discuss and for-mulate rules of human conduct.

(pp. 18–19)

The major topics of the book, and of manuals like it, were: human acts, conscience, sin, virtue, an analysis of acts in light of the Ten Commandments (or Decalogue), contracts (including all kinds of business relationships), the commandments of the Church, and "the duties of clergy, religious, and 'certain laymen' (physicians and those with different roles in the courts" (Keenan, 2010, p. 12). Keenan writes that the moral theological manuals assumed that human actions could be judged from an ahistorical and universally valid position.

---

various reasons, the manuals were isolated from other areas of theology and as a result, did not become Neoscholastic at the end of the nineteenth century, but "the manuals fully endorsed the spirit of neo-scholasticism, emphasizing the defensiveness of the Church and the failure to dialogue with the modern world" (p. 11). Another critic of the manualist tradition – and a critic of Curran's moral theology, Benedict Ashley, OP – writes that "whereas Thomistic moral theology emphasizes the development of character (virtue) through good action, the moral theology of the manuals reduced virtue to obedience to law, and emphasized casuistry" (Ashley, 1995, p. 76). Ashley briefly treats of the history of the theology of the manuals by noting its roots in Duns Scotus, who "taught that morality is based not on the requirements of human nature as such but on the commands of God or of human authorities in church or state delegated to act in God's name" (p. 77). This manualist moral theology thus became "traditional" moral theology by the twentieth century. The Thomistic revival of the first half of the twentieth century, Ashley continues, raised "serious questions about this 'traditional' moral theology, which, ... was far from purely Thomistic in its structure" (p. 78).

In other words, there was not a sense of the historicity of either human acts or of moral decision-making. However, over the course of the twentieth century, there were decided movements in the direction of taking these histories seriously, leading to major upheavals in moral theology up to the present day.

What is of immediate interest here, however, is how in the manualist tradition, there was increasing consideration of psychological factors. Keenan (2008) shows how this consideration increased from the work of Slater to that of Heribert Jone, a manualist writing somewhat later than Slater. Moral theology by mid-century was already approaching psychology, so that the kind of collaboration between the psychologists and the theologians that we have seen at the Fordham institutes (and elsewhere) did not come out of the blue.

Two examples: in dealing with impediments to voluntary action, Slater followed traditional thinking going back to the ancient world, that ignorance and passion could constrain the voluntary nature of acts and in so doing limit personal responsibility. He referred briefly to insanity. Jone's (1961/1993) manual, while using the same categories as did Slater, expanded on the psychological impediments to moral judgment, and he included discussions of "nervous mental diseases" (pp. 10–13), including neurasthenia, hysteria, compulsion phenomena, hypochondria, melancholia, and psychopathic inferiority.[28] The second example concerns the presentations of conscience in Slater and Jone. Slater (1909) emphasized the rationality of conscience: "conscience signifies a dictate of the practical reason deciding that a particular action is right or wrong. The process by which we arrive at this judgment of the practical reason may be put in the form of a syllogism" (p. 57). This accorded with the Neoscholastic emphasis on reason as the foundation of choice. In dealing with what we can call pathologies of conscience, Slater included three types: strict, lax, and scrupulous. The scrupulous conscience "without sufficient reason apprehends sin where there is none" (p. 58). Jone (1961/1993) repeated the categories, but he gave more attention to the irrational aspects of scrupulosity, saying that "the basic factor in a scrupulous conscience is not so much error as fear" (p. 39). He discussed its symptoms and its causes, including in the latter "manic-depressive impulses or pressure on the brain" (p. 40). Neither he nor Slater discussed referrals to a psychiatrist, as would contributors to the pastoral trading zone.

Keenan (2010) writes that in later manuals, there is a further accentuation of the psychological factors, and "with greater research into human psychology, the manualists' perception of the lay Roman Catholic as a wounded and uncertain penitent became more and more evident [by the eve of the Second Vatican Council]. Though the manualist was always known as a physician of

---

[28] It is interesting that this text of 1961 included neurasthenia which, by then, had become an outmoded diagnosis. Clearly, Jone was drawing on an older psychiatric tradition and had not updated the categories. This suggests only a limited interest in psychology and psychiatry.

souls, now he became the psychiatric care-giver of the inculpable sinner" (p. 30). As an example, consider *Contemporary moral theology* (1958) by John C. Ford, SJ, and Gerald Kelly, SJ. Both men were moral theologians, and Ford in addition contributed to the Fordham Institutes on Pastoral Counseling. They were leaders in this area in the 1950s, squarely in the manualist tradition, although they were aware that other approaches were arising (Curran, 1999, p. 40; McCormick, 1999, p. 47).

Ford and Kelly addressed psychology and psychiatry directly in *Contemporary moral theology*, something of a departure from the manualist tradition. Chief among their concerns was the use of psychoanalytic reasoning to show the constraints on human freedom. In particular, they pointed to the fact that the word "motivation" had different meanings in theology and psychology. In theology, a motive is "a good which is consciously apprehended by reason" (p. 190), and it thus acts as a final cause, drawing a person to it. Psychologically, a motive is an instinctual or emotional urge, and thus an efficient cause, pushing a person to do something. In the theological use of the term, a motive cannot be unconscious, since it is discerned by reason. To overcome this confusion, Ford and Kelly distinguished between someone being influenced and someone being compelled. Catholic moralists must defend, they wrote, the conclusion "that normal men and women *per se* have sufficient freedom in the concrete circumstances of daily life to merit great praise or great blame before God" (p. 200). In other words, the findings of psychology do not undermine the basic truth of freedom of the will, even as they provide a more finely grained analysis of the "impediments" (p. 199) to free choice. Finally, Ford and Kelly concluded their book by speaking of a rapprochement between psychiatry and moral theology. There are many problems that the priest and the psychiatrist face where the services of the other would be beneficial. They cited a number of issues (which should sound familiar): scrupulosity, alcohol and drug addiction, certain forms of masturbation, and homosexuality (pp. 337–8). What this book shows is that by the late 1950s, moral theologians, even in the manualist tradition, were coming to see that psychology had something to offer the priest as confessor. The moral theologians were looking to "purchase" something from the psychologists.

This digression on moral theology also shows something else. The pattern of the moral theological manuals was repeated to a great degree in a work such as Hagmaier and Gleason's *Counselling the Catholic*. Not that it slavishly copied the manuals, and in many respects it was innovative. Nevertheless, many of its chapters addressed topics as did the manuals. "The psychology of human weakness," like Slater and Jone, went through the Decalogue, discussing the morality of various actions. What distinguished Hagmaier and Gleason, however, was greater attention to psychological mitigating factors reducing personal responsibility, and the value of taking into consideration the psychological and life-historical factors that led to a particular action. Like the manuals, the book dealt with masturbation, homosexuality, and alcoholism, although with much greater detail and attention to psychological factors. However, the basic pattern of the book would have impressed priests reading it in the late 1950s as conforming to the basic pattern of the moral theological manual. This similarity, no doubt, aided in the transition to pastoral psychology, especially, as we have seen, the manuals themselves were giving increasing attention to psychology as the century advanced.

Pastoral psychology comes of age

> In our own generation there has developed, within the framework of the general movement in counseling and clinical psychology, something that can be called new in the area of pastoral counseling. The term itself, "pastoral counseling," is new.
>
> John W. Stafford, CSV (1969, p. 4)

In 1957, Bier reported to the larger Catholic community the existence of a number of institutionalized ways that psychology and religion worked together: in the expanding role of Catholic chaplains in mental hospitals (Bier, 1957, pp. 14–15), in invitations to psychiatrists to teach seminarians (including Zilboorg coming to Woodstock College, the Jesuit seminary in New York), and especially in workshops, including those at St. John's University, Collegeville, Minnesota, at Fordham, at Loras College, and at Gonzaga University (pp. 18–19). According to Bier, these efforts were products of mutual respect and collaboration.

By the mid-1960s, the field of pastoral psychology was defined: graduate programs appeared, new journals were founded, and professional organizations developed. In the graduate programs, pastoral counseling and psychology could develop "native speakers" in the new field. At that time, because of the Second Vatican Council's openness to ecumenism, Catholics were joining more frequently with non-Catholics, both Protestant and Jew, in these new enterprises. To the ecumenical groups we turn first, and then to an early master's program in pastoral psychology.

Associations and institutes

There were a number of initiatives in the 1950s and early 1960s wherein pastoral psychological topics and training were studied and discussed. Some of these groups were primarily Catholic, while others had representatives of various religions. Godin (1961) discussed a number of organizations in "religious psychology," including the Academy of Religion and Mental Health, founded in 1955 in New York, and the International Commission of Religious Psychology (Lumen Vitae), begun in 1956 in Belgium, with Godin

384 PSYCHOLOGY AND CATHOLICISM: CONTESTED BOUNDARIES

as secretary (as of 1961). The Academy of Religious and Mental Health included members of the ACPA, Bier and Mailloux, as well as Protestant and Jewish leaders in this field. It was designed to bring the insights of psychiatry, psychology, and religion together for the study of common problems. Here again, a common language had to be formed, in a situation somewhat different from what we have already considered. Earlier, we considered a trading zone language formed within a Catholic context, among theologians and representatives of other sciences, broadly defined. Here, we look at what happened when other religious traditions, which did not use Catholic categories and terminology, were included in the conversation. The two types of interactions occurred simultaneously. At the Academy of Religious and Mental Health's second symposium in 1958, the discussion turned to research in the religious field. Frank Fremont-Smith (1915–74), a physician, an official of the Josiah Macey, Jr. Foundation (which funded the symposium), and the moderator of the discussion in question, noted that the difficulties of religious groups talking together was like that of translation. He suggested that "it would be better to get members of the various religious groups to describe these phenomena in their own words and pull them together for cross reference and for synthesis" (Academy of Religion and Mental Health, 1960, p. 90). This warning about an all-too-quick and ultimately futile common language indicates part of what was going on at the symposium. As an example is this report:

> Dr. Meserve[29] suggested two kinds of research projects. The first arose from Father Bier's statement about man's ontological need for God, which Dr. Meserve accepted with the proviso that it be interpreted to mean the need for some ultimate concern with which the individual is related, of which he is a part, to which he can give himself, and in which he can find peace and strength. This is the fundamental religious experience as Dr. Meserve saw it, though perhaps not stated in terms that would be acceptable to all members of the group.
>
> (p. 89)

Bier's response was not included. What resulted was a desire for research of the "study of the universal character of the fundamental religious experience: man's need for God, or for an ultimate value" (p. 101). In other words, the question of a common language was kept open, in order to accommodate the divergences among the members of the Academy. These proceedings illustrate an effort at a fruitful exchange among various subcultures. Bier seems to have found the exchanges useful, as he continued to participate in them, and in that he also supported the transformation of the ACPA into PIRI and then into Division 36 of the APA. Using him as our guide for understanding this trading zone of pastoral psychology, it would seem that he saw it as beneficial to the Church and

[29] Rev. Harry C. Meserve, DD, represented the Rockefeller Brothers Fund.

to psychology. When the Academy of Religion and Health began the *Journal of Religion and Health* in 1961, Bier, Godin, and J. Franklin Ewing, SJ,[30] were Catholic representatives on the Editorial Advisory Board (Meserve was the editor).

Illustrative of the extent of the trading zone was the contribution to the field from the Conferences of Religious Superiors and Institutes for Catholic Pastoral Counseling at the Catholic University of America (O'Brien and Steimel, 1965). This collection of essays shows the extent to which psychological and spiritual discourses were being brought together.[31] Michael J. O'Brien, CSV (1920–2003) had a doctorate in counseling psychology from the Catholic University (O'Brien, 1957). In 1965, he was the Director of the Viatorian Seminary as well as a counselor at the Catholic University's Counseling Center. His book, *An Introduction to Pastoral Counseling* (O'Brien, 1968) was a relatively early contribution. He later taught at Loyola University in Chicago in the Psychology Department, working with a masters program in counseling that later became part of the Institute of Pastoral Studies by the early 1980s (see O'Brien, 1984). Raymond J. Steimel completed a Ph.D. under William C. Cottle (who was ACPA president 1961–62 at the University of Kansas, and addressed adolescent issues in counseling (Steimel, 1960)). He then taught psychology at the Catholic University and by the late 1960s, he was working in the University's administration. One article in these proceedings illustrates well pastoral psychology as a trading zone. Timothy J. Gannon, whom we have discussed earlier in relation to personality, addressed these institutes. Gannon (1965) found "the common ground" between psychological development and spiritual growth, which he acknowledged as "two different universes of discourse" in "a common subject, man" (p. 3). "Growth" became a key term in Gannon's proposed pidgin (if you will), because it was common to both. He wove together the Thomistic conception of emotions with contributions from psychology, especially those of Magda Arnold. In addition to finding common ground, Gannon – in part because he inhabited both sides of the border – said that it was necessary to "re-think spiritual writings and to re-interpret them in the light of what is now known of the normal functioning of the human personality" (p. 9). In particular, he was critical of how some traditional Catholic spirituality betrayed an "intemperate adulation of intellect or reason" (p. 10), which was contrary to the Christian teaching about the Incarnation. Into this trading zone, then, came terms such as "reason" and "will," reflecting

---

[30] Ewing was an archaeologist who taught at Fordham and a supporter of Teilhard de Chardin, the controversial Catholic theologian.

[31] This was not a unique event, to be sure. The work of many others at the time were involved in similar activities, especially where psychologists, often members of religious orders (such as van Kaam, Godin, Mailloux, Walters) were brought into religious orders as consultants.

the traditions of spirituality, next to "personality," "emotion," and "superego," representing the psychological side. Drawing on Rogers, Maslow, (Charles A.) Curran, Fromm, and others, Gannon spoke of the "indispensable function of positive human affection in the development of personality" as pointing up "some of the deficiencies in the traditional view of spiritual growth ... [which] savors more of the stoic exaltation of reason against non-rational human tendencies" (p. 17). This example shows that in the trading zone wherein pastoral psychology developed, the various sciences and professions met on equal ground, subordinated to be sure to the religious context in which they met.[32]

The American Association of Pastoral Counselors (AAPC) began in 1963. At first it was almost exclusively a Protestant organization, and in 1967, there were only two Catholic priests who were members. However, in 1966, Bernard L. Pacella[33] spoke at the AAPC meeting on the topic of "A Critical Appraisal of Pastoral Counseling." At the time, Pacella was chair of the American Psychiatric Association's Committee on Religion and Psychiatry (Wagner, 1992, p. 38). The creation of the AAPC meant that pastoral psychology moved from a trading zone to a recognized entity. Such a move is part of defining a discipline, with a home turf to cultivate and defend. Catholics were not there at the founding of the organization, but they were invited to join. As we have seen in other areas, as the 1950s progressed, there was increasing ecumenical involvement between Catholic and non-Catholic pastoral counselors. By the end of the following decade, it seems that there was much less emphasis on denominational types of pastoral psychology, the common interests predominating.

Masters Program in Pastoral Counseling

In the 1960s, Catholic pastoral psychology had become sufficiently defined so that master's programs began to appear. A significant one began at Iona College in New Rochelle, New York, in 1963. The summer institutes at St. John's University in Minnesota were one inspiration behind the program as described by Alfred R. Joyce (1966),[34] the first director of Iona's Graduate Division of

---

[32] Gannon (1965) indicated, toward the end of his article, why this critique of tendencies in traditional spirituality were needed, in words that proved prophetic: "And if the high incidence of mental breakdown, and neurotic invalidism, not to mention alcoholism and sexual deviation, continues to baffle and appall us, we would be well advised, not only to pursue the development of more valid screening devices, but we should subject to careful scrutiny spiritual handbooks, books of meditation and traditional ascetical practices for evidences of an image of religious formation that shows little insight into or concern for the psychosomatic unity of man" (p. 19).

[33] Pacella was the psychiatrist named by Fulton Sheen in the 1940s as one he could trust and to whom he could refer people (see Chapter 5).

[34] The program also launched the *Journal of Pastoral Psychology*.

Pastoral Counseling. Celsus Wheeler, OFM, a Franciscan provincial, had attended one of the St. John's summer institutes in the late 1950s and initiated the process that led to the Iona program. Wheeler, Joyce, and George Flanagan, SJ,[35] a psychologist, organized a series of seminars for Franciscans in 1958–9, after which Joyce led the formation of the St. Francis Institute of Pastoral Counseling. Wheeler informed Cardinal Francis Spellman of New York about the Institute and the cardinal encouraged it. In 1962, with the support of the Franciscans, the archdiocese, and Brother Richard Power, president of Iona College, the Institute moved there: "We were still struggling to find ourselves since there was no other program of its type to use as a yardstick of comparison" (Joyce, 1966, p. 7). A year later, a masters program in pastoral counseling began, and true to the dimensions of the trading zone that we have seen developing in this area, the program included course work in psychology, psychiatry, and religion (but no theology, the students being at first all clerics). Moreover, via group and individual counseling of the students, "the faculty has witnessed not only a growth of knowledge in the student, but also a spurt in emotional development" (p. 8). In 1966, the Institute began offering workshops for clergy-men "of all faiths" (p. 9) and for nuns. After 1965, nuns and lay people were admitted into the Institute, but in a separate program. From Iona, the message of pastoral psychology reached other areas of the Catholic community. Joyce wrote:

> For instance, during the past year I, as Director, have lectured at Pope Pius X Seminary, at Dunwoodie Seminary, and at Maryknoll Seminary. I have been the main speaker at the annual meeting of the North Eastern Seminary Association, at the Catholic Alumni Association, at the Fordham University Pastoral Year convention, and at St. Bonaventure University's seminar on marital counseling, Sister Formation Institute, Board of Education, Yonkers, New York. The staff members have acted as consultants to the Family Life Bureau of New York City, helping to set up a counseling service.
>
> (p. 10)

To see the full force of this trading zone, consider this testimonial of an early graduate of the Iona. James E. Sullivan, a Brooklyn priest, who after 16 years of parish work entered the program, wrote:

> Finally, in the technique of counseling, we learned to counsel the *person*, the complete human being, who had not only an intellect and a will but strong emotions and emotional conflicts. While the seminary stressed kindness and thoughtfulness to all persons, it was more a kindness in presenting our teachings and solutions rather than in listening to the problems. People's

---

[35] See Flanagan in "Pastoral dimensions in counseling and psychotherapy," 1970, p. 13.

problems were to be solved by showing them the truth. It was a matter of clear presentation and precise instruction, plus of course the need for God's grace. At Iona we learned that even the clearest presentation of teaching cannot be seen through the *fog* of conflicting emotions, just as persons with the best eyesight cannot see in a mist ... We learned how to listen with warmth and acceptance of the person, with unconditional, positive regard for him – until he was able to accept himself as he was, able to see that he was a person of real worth, just as he was, with all his feelings.

(1966, pp. 30–1)

Anthony Milano (1966) reported that the program had 230 students, with 57 graduates to date, with 33 more anticipated that spring. With this program and others, pastoral psychology had its own ground.

Significant in the pastoral psychology trading zone was that in addition to the course work that would bring together the various disciplines that contributed to it, an emphasis was placed on self-knowledge. That is, pastoral psychology sought not only a certain type of knowledge, a hybrid language of psychology and theology, but also a certain type of person. In contrast to the strong emphasis on intellectual development, as Sullivan described seminary training in the period before pastoral counseling, here was an emphasis on awareness of the feeling self, one possessed of unconscious and often irrational processes. This experiential training, a psychological technique of the self, fostered distinctive self-presence. For the priest, it was a sharp departure from the earlier emphasis on his being a "pastor," that is, a shepherd, of his flock. It meant listening, so that the client could similarly practice these "techniques of the self," to use Foucault's term, which seems appropriate here. More was at stake than the development of a new discipline, pastoral psychology (or pastoral counseling). It was the cultivation of a new (for the clergy) way of being: the Listener to the feelings and emotionally entangled relationships of self and others, who was present to self and other in both conscious and unconscious ways. But this new way of being was not simply the adoption of a form of psychology: it was a blend of the psychological and the theological. Much of the discourse that it developed would not have been heard in non-pastoral settings, and even the assertion, made by Bier, that God was an ontological need of human beings, was not part of the lingua franca of some other religious traditions. The listening required in pastoral psychology was not only psychological; it was also theological, and this made it distinct. It was, to use the term that Victor White took from Aquinas, a gain in affective knowledge.

The theological aspect of this listening helped to distinguish pastoral from secular counseling. The pastoral counselor, especially in the early years, was a priest who also had pastoral obligations to the client, such that the client not only a client, as he or she would have been in secular counseling. The client was, at least potentially, of pastoral concern to the counselor-priest. The balance between the two "hats," as Hagmaier called them, required attentiveness to the particulars of the situation.

Pastoral psychology defined

By the late 1960s, then, pastoral psychology was coming of age. Bier (1967b) wrote an article for it in the *New Catholic Encyclopedia*, a sign that the field had achieved widespread recognition. Bier's definition was narrowly tailored to the Catholic community, even though he had already been involved in ecumenical groups. This limitation reflected, no doubt, the fact that he was writing for a Catholic encyclopedia: "Pastoral psychology is a branch of practical or applied psychology ... In pastoral psychology, the group comprises those who come under the pastoral care of the priest, and the goal is to help them achieve a more adequate and mature spiritual life" (p. 1078). He called it an "ancillary discipline" to pastoral theology by providing priests with skills and knowledge to understand people better who come for counseling, and by providing them with "techniques of helping" (ibid.). However, pastoral psychology was not a science in the strict sense, since it "does not have an independently developed body of scientific data" (ibid.); it draws its data from many other areas of psychology. The core of pastoral psychology is pastoral counseling, defined in ways that we have already seen: in terms of listening and understanding. Pastoral psychology does have a unique goal: "to aid the individual in attaining his eternal salvation" (p. 1080). This is the "ultimate goal" of pastoral psychology, and its "proximate goals" are psychological, helping people to live mature lives making conflict-free decisions. Despite Bier's limits for the field, it did develop its own body of data in the coming years.

Introductions to pastoral counseling were published, providing orientations for priests and other religious who might receive training in it. Eugene J. Weitzel, CSV, edited *Contemporary pastoral counseling* (1969), with contributions by many whom we have already encountered, including Magda Arnold, Alexander Schneiders, and John W. Stafford. Weitzel was a member of the Viatorians, the order to which Stafford also belonged. His doctorate was in theology from the Catholic University in 1966. The book was primarily intended, he wrote, for seminarians and clerics. Richard P. Vaughan, SJ, a long-time member of the ACPA, published *An introduction to religious counseling: A Christian humanistic approach* (1969) addressed the same readership, with an approach that saw religious counseling as differing from "other forms of counseling in that its primary focus is on the religious dimension" (p. 3). The book concentrated primarily, as the title suggests, on a humanistic approach, although Vaughan emphasized that this type of counseling is "undertaken by a person who has a strong commitment to and specialized training in religion" (p. 19). With texts such as these, the field was autonomous.

This matter of an ultimate goal did serve to differentiate pastoral psychology and set the parameters of its hybrid discourse. A few years later, the *Journal of Pastoral Psychology* (Pastoral dimensions in counseling and psychotherapy, 1970) invited contributors to say in their own terms what pastoral counseling was. Richard D. Chesick thought it was the pursuit of childish illusions (i.e. religious convictions) and Sidney Jourard thought that all counseling is pastoral. Between these extremes were those who saw it as a distinct area of counseling. Sullivan, the graduate of the Iona program quoted, above defined pastoral counseling as "God-oriented" (p. 6). Charles A. Curran agreed, saying that pastoral counseling views life *sub specie aeternitatis*, that is, in relation to the ultimate meanings of life.[36] Flanagan, one of the founders of the Iona program, defined it in terms of who practice it, namely clergymen (seconding Bier's encyclopedia article), as did Francis J. Braceland and Leo H. Bartemeier. These were two types of definitions and they led in different directions. That emphasized by Sullivan and the psychiatrists Braceland and Bartemeier focused on *who* does the counseling, namely priests. Curran's delimitation stressed the purpose of the counseling. He continued by saying "that 'pastoral' is something that stands in its own order and is not necessarily arrived at in and through other forms of counseling and psychotherapy" (p. 16). Despite this, Curran too tied the field to "ministers, priests and rabbis" (p. 17) and he hoped it would become an integral part of their work, even if they were not specialists in counseling.

Concluding remarks on pastoral psychology

Subsequent developments altered the field considerably. Over the next few decades, the number of priests and religious declined, and the laity assumed more and more ministerial duties within the Catholic Church. In pastoral care, the same trend happened. There are a number of graduate programs around the country offering graduate degrees in pastoral counseling and psychology, and they are not restricted to priests and nuns. The trend that the Iona program began in the mid-1960s has become the norm. Joyce's (1966) view that non-priests and non-Catholics be admitted to the program foresaw the subsequent development of pastoral psychology. What came to define this area were not so much the professions of the participants, as it did in the years when this trading zone was being formed, but the hybrid discourse and the "ultimate goal" sought. Understood in this way, unique to pastoral psychology was that the relationship of counselor and client was not viewed as a dyadic one, as was secular counseling; rather it was Trinitarian, or in Cavanagh's (1962) words: "It is a three-way relationship of which God is the third member" (p. 20). So starkly stated, this

---

[36] The phrase, *sub specie aeternitatis*, derives from St. Augustine. Jung used it as well, in speaking of life seen in relation to its archetypal structure.

serves to define in part the zone that is pastoral psychology, a psychological field in which relationships are viewed *sub specie aeternitatis*.

Pastoral psychology and homosexuality

To illustrate the dynamic character of pastoral psychology after 1965, it is useful to discuss another topic in addition to guilt and scrupulosity. While these have been, more or less, static categories over the past several decades, topics such as homosexuality have become significantly contentious. Even though, officially, the Church has not altered its stance – homosexual acts, like all non-marital sexual acts, are wrong, and homosexual sex, in addition, is contrary to natural law because it cannot lead to offspring – there has been considerable revision of it in psychiatry, psychology, and among a substantial number of Catholic moral theologians, who find the official position wanting. In this section, we will look at (1) the position of psychology and the Church on homosexuality in the period just preceding and at the time of the rise of pastoral psychology, and (2) the changes that have occurred in the decades following the establishment of pastoral psychology (from 1965 on).

Catholic psychiatrists, psychologists, and moral theologians agreed in the 1950s that homosexuality was objectively sinful.[37] For the former group, it was a psychological disorder as well. There was widespread agreement that homo-erotic activity did not in itself constitute homosexuality; in fact, among adolescents, it was deemed better to assume that it was a developmental stage and not an expression of identity. Paul G. Ecker (1964), a psychoanalyst at the Fordham Institutes, presented homosexuality in Freudian terms as a developmental disorder, although he (and others) raised the question about a genetic basis, without being able to answer it one way or another. Nevertheless: "the probability of homosexuality in the male is increased in direct proportion to the degree of identification with the mother" (p. 162). He concluded that homosexuality was a "perversion ... a symptom, an expression of an unresolved, neurotic conflict" (p. 165). Ford (1964) and Hagmaier (1964) dealt with it from the theological side, both stressing the social stigma that homosexuals face, in addition to often harsh legal sanctions and then, finally, hostility and prejudice from some priests. Their remarks distinguished between the objective sinfulness of homosexual acts and their subjective sinfulness, which may be wanting

---

[37] Not all psychiatrists agreed with this assessment, as is clear from Hagmaier's advice to priests when they seek a psychiatrist or psychologist for a homosexual penitent. The therapist must agree with the statement that, "Almighty God, in His plan of nature, intended that human-kind be heterosexually oriented. The homosexual, regardless of the origin of his tendency, is afflicted with a disorder of nature" (Hagmaier and Gleason, 1959, pp. 182–3). This had to be agreed to because some psychologists and psychiatrists "hold to the rigid determinism of human behavior. If a homosexual is 'born this way,' fate intends that he seek and enjoy perverse sexual gratification" (p. 182).

in a person driven by compulsion. They tended to define homosexuality primarily as a psychiatric problem, as "one of the most difficult psychiatric challenges" (p. 179). Hagmaier urged compassion:

> The true invert[38] ... was either born so, or made so very early in his development. As an adult he faces life as one who is psychologically handicapped. It is a medical error and a moral injustice to call him depraved or perverted. Both these words imply a deliberate *turning away* from a healthy and normal state to a degraded one. The true invert has never had this choice. He has not turned away from anything. Heterosexual affection has never been a reality for him.
>
> (p. 183)

Still, homosexual acts are wrong, and part of the tragedy for the "true invert" is that he "can never entertain the prospect of a legitimate outlet for his drives" (p. 184), since the only legitimate sexual expression is that within marriage (and that without the practice of contraception). The pastoral approach held the line on the objective sinfulness of such sexual acts, but:

> The confessor should avoid speculating about the degree of responsibility involved in the overt homosexual activity of his penitents ... If at all possible, we should avoid discussing the subject with the penitent. Certainly we should not tell him that he is not responsible. On the other hand, we cannot actually determine his guilt either. There are cases, for example, where the penitent must be treated as insane, even though he is completely lucid and in control of his will in all other aspects of his behavior.
>
> (p. 190)

The priest needed to know the limits of his ability to counsel such people, Ford and Hagmaier stressed, and they urged working closely with psychiatry if possible.

Ford and Hagmaier's stance represented a change from the earlier manuals of moral theology. There, homosexuality was dealt with briefly and categorically. Slater (1909) dealt only with sodomy, and that in a chapter (written in Latin, despite the title of his book, no doubt to avoid scandalizing or tempting those who did not need to know about such things), "De peccatis consummatis contra naturam,"[39] which also dealt with *pollutio* (masturbation) and *bestialitas* (bestiality). Jone (1961/1993), in addition to essentially the same chapter, also discussed homosexuality in a chapter, "Sexual Perversity." The main issue was "imputability" or personal responsibility. Jone wrote: "Everyone, even the sexually abnormal and perverted, can and must control himself, since all

---

[38] A synonym for homosexual in much of the literature of the time, seen preferable to the term pervert.
[39] "Consummated sins contrary to nature."

actions are imputable to an individual as long as he has not lost all sense of responsibility and the actions are performed with knowledge and free will" (p. 161). Typical of the manuals was the lack of attention to what Hagmaier stressed, namely, the personal equation. The manuals were "objectivistic," in that they looked only to the action and not at the personal and social context in which the act occurred. Hagmaier and Ford, on the contrary, did, even if they were in agreement with the manuals on the objective immorality of the deeds.

Changes in moral theology and in psychology/psychiatry concerning homosexuality

Moral theology before the 1960s was not really an academic discipline (Curran, 1999, p. 36). Only after the Vatican Council did it become established in that form, moving out of the seminaries and into the universities. At the same time, academic freedom at Catholic universities became an accepted principle, something that it had not been earlier. This has meant a rise in pluralism in Catholic moral theology, especially on the question of the authority of the Magisterium, that is, the teachings of the Church, specifically concerning noninfallible matters (i.e. issues other than teachings about the divinity of Christ, etc.). One of the major topics has been the conflicting positions among moral theologians over the Church's stance against contraception.

This development, which occurred at the same time that in psychology there was a proliferation of approaches other than the natural scientific, which had dominated for the first half of the twentieth century, especially in North America, meant that in both psychology and theology there developed opposition to the assumptions of objectivism. Humanistic psychologists, phenomenologists, and others proposed alternatives to objectivistic behaviorism and psychoanalysis, and some moral theologians, called "revisionists" by Curran (1999), proposed alternatives to what they saw as the "legalism" of earlier moral theology and of official Church teachings in some areas. On both sides, there was greater stress on the experiential, the subjective, and the personalistic. This in turn affected pastoral psychology, which in 1965 was *in statu nascendi*. No sooner born, however, than it began to change, not only because of its internal dynamism, but also because its parent disciplines, especially moral theology and psychology, were focusing more on the person than on human nature, more on the historicity of action than on action objectively understood, more on the authority of individual experience than on institutional authority. As an example, consider the conception of holiness offered in *Holiness and mental health*: "In the pastoral sense, holiness is wholeness, or that which identifies the significance of life with a willingness to transcend the arbitrary boundaries placed on a person because of limited authority. In other words, to become holy may mean to rise above the restrictive conditioning which an unhealthy society may have imposed upon individual aspirations" (Joyce and Stern, 1972, p. vii). Such an approach can be understood partly in terms of the zeitgeist following Vatican Two and the social upheavals of the 1960s.

Beginning in the 1970s, the American Psychiatric Association took steps to de-pathologize homosexuality, with "the last official vestige of a sanctioned medical model" (Minton, 2002,p. 262) disappearing in 1986. Thus, an earlier basis for unanimity among the moral theologians and the psychologists crumbled. But on the theological side, too, there was change, at least since 1970 (Curran, 2008, p. 195). James F. Keenan (2010) observed that historical studies show that the Church has not had a consistent teaching on sexual matters, including sodomy, over the centuries. Historical studies of the changes in moral teachings, however, is insufficient, according to Keenan, because "behind these claims of discontinuity and development, moral theologians have been asserting a third claim: not only does history necessitate develop-ment, but moral theology must also occasion such a development" (p. 46). That is, neither we nor our predecessors know moral truth in its entirety. The interpretation of moral principles in unique historical and personal situations leads to "developments in these principles and eventually in moral doctrines" (ibid.). Moral theology, in this view, must reckon with the historicity of human life. This approach marks a break from the manualists, who did not.

Against this emphasis on history and the personal context, a 1986 letter from the Congregation for the Doctrine of the Church observed:

> An essential dimension of authentic pastoral care is the identification of causes of confusion regarding the Church's teaching. One is a new exegesis of Sacred Scripture which claims variously that Scripture has nothing to say on the subject of homosexuality, or that it somehow tacitly approves of it, or that all of its moral injunctions are so culture-bound that they are no longer applicable to contemporary life. These views are gravely erroneous.
>
> (Ratzinger and Bovone, 1986, section 4)

Similarly, a few psychiatrists and psychologists have attempted to repathologize homosexuality, often for explicitly theological reasons: Vitz (1985) calls homo-sexuality a pathology, "from which one can recover" (p. 10). Such attempts to repathologize homosexuality argue from a Natural Law stance, similar to what one found in the manuals of moral theology.

In contrast, a Catholic theologian, taking a "proportionalist" stance in moral theology, argues against the biological reductionism implicit in the official teachings:

> Currently, official church teaching places homosexual genital acts in the same category as lying, stealing and murder ... Evaluating actions based on the object of the act (that which is done) rather than in a broader context that includes intention, circumstances and consequences has been criticized by some moral theologians as a biologistic and unreliable

rendering of natural law thinking. Biologism can be described as an "oughtness" ascribed to the biological structure of the heterosexual act of intercourse. Here, a moral law is perceived in the way the act is configured, and human sexual acts that do not conform to this structure are said to be immoral.

(Flynn, 2000, p. 16)

Theological critics of proportionalism argue that this approach "justifies acts which are contradictory to the ultimate end of human nature known to us through philosophical and theological analysis" (Ashley, 1995, p. 83). So an act can be morally wrong, not because it violates "biologism" but because it is contrary to an analysis of human nature.

While the issues involved are theological and ethical, they are also psychological, in that they concern intentionality, meaning, and historicity. Much is at stake here, to say the least. What this topic illustrates is the changed context for the exchanges and boundary-work between psychology and theology.

Pastoral psychology has become more contentious and disunified, not only on the psychological side, but also on the theological side. And this brief review has not taken into account the fact that pastoral psychology has become ecumenical over the past few decades.

A final note

The existence of trading zones between psychology and the Church has not diminished the importance of contested boundaries. In fact, to some extent, they have exacerbated them. While the Church may try to rein in the theologians who disagree with official teachings on matters sexual, the psychologists who align themselves with official Church teachings assert that official psychology (the APA) marginalizes their views. In addition, the autonomy of psychology from theology has become an established fact in contemporary society, even in Catholic colleges and universities. So something may be declared contrary to natural law, for example, and be healthy and adaptive in psychological terms. At the same time, some psychologists use theological arguments against allegedly empirically based positions of the APA. Some would call this situation "post-modern." It is certainly post-1965. During the time considered in this book, however, things were relatively straightforward, because the boundaries were clear. All that changed.

10

Crossings

The paths cutting through the borderland between psychology and Catholicism are many. What we have seen has dispelled any notion of a rigid boundary or even of merely opposing forces. The situations have been much more complex, especially where the participants in a particular situation inhabited both sides of the boundary. However, it still makes sense to call the areas explored here a boundary region because psychology in all its variants has constituents other than the Catholics, and because Catholic communities have other interests than those of psychology. Now is the occasion to look back at the schema proposed in Chapter 1 to describe the lines between psychology and the Church. And then to move beyond that schema, not in the direction of erasing the border or of integrating psychology into Catholic thought, but rather, in effect, to make things worse. What I mean by this is to do something similar to what histologists do when they "stain" tissues with substances that make visible structures that would be otherwise undetectable. (Psychology likes to imitate other sciences, as we know.) The substance (if it is a substance, let's not prejudice the issue) that will be applied to this boundary tissue is, of all things, the soul. This stain of mortality and immortality opens up new regions of the frontier between psychology and Catholicism. A curious idea, to re-introduce the idea of the "soul," which psychology discarded at the end of the nineteenth century because of its metaphysical and theological baggage. What I will suggest is that the soul be reconsidered as a psychological object of great import for a number of reasons – not the least of which is reconnecting psychology with the long, fragmented, and complex discourses about the nature and the destiny of human living. To do this, we will need to address once again the questions asked early on: which psychology? Which religion? For it will not be any of the positivistic or Neoscholastic psychologies that skirmished at the borders in days past. It will not be the Church of a century ago, traumatized by the French Revolution and modern science. Yet this journey into the frontier will preserve the essence of idea that started the boundary disputes of the previous century: *vetera novis augere perficere.*

Before 1879, after 1965

Throughout this book, we have concentrated attention on the period between 1879, the symbolic beginning of both the new psychology and the Thomistic revival, and 1965, the year the Second Vatican Council ended. Before that time, Catholic philosophy was not officially Thomistic – at least during the nineteenth century – and after that time, there was an opening to other types of philosophizing, including the phenomenological. Psychology before 1879 was in its early formation on many fronts. Psychology after the mid-1960s underwent considerable upheaval, and the assumption, made by Moore and the founders of the ACPA, that there was one way for psychology to be scientific, came under fire. We can summarize this situation by saying that the period after 1965 was characterized by an explosion of possibilities. In surveying the situation since Vatican II, Gillespie (2007b) concludes that "a series of Catholic individuals and institutions have appropriated psychology to form programs, to frame psychological constructs for religious structures and to face critical moral and legal issues" (p. 130). He sees the story continuing as part of ongoing dialogues of faith and reason.

What that means is that the narrative thread that has tied together the account given here unravels before and after this time. It would require other narratives to recount what came earlier and to continue the history of the relationships between psychology and Catholicism in the following period. This period, beginning in 1965, so it seems to me, is itself coming to an end. A new type of interest in the relations between psychology and the Church is taking shape. I would date this new interest, symbolically, with the issue of the papal document, *Ex corde ecclesiae*, in 1990, which examined the meaning of a Catholic university. What will develop now is not clear, but it will not be a repetition neither of the earlier period, that of Neoscholasticism and the appearance of natural scientific psychology, which has been explored in this book, nor of the period from 1965 to 1990, characterized as it was by the exploration of possibilities and by an enthrallment, if I can put it this way, with the new.

To conclude, then, I would turn to what may lie in store for this relationship as it moves forward. First, a recapitulation of what has come before, and then a turn to what it might mean for the future.

1879–1965

The dominant themes of this history of the contested boundaries between psychology and the Catholic Church are modernism, Neoscholasticism, and natural scientific psychology. The modernist crisis looms over the entire epoch, even that preceding the formal denunciation in the *Pascendi* encyclical of 1907. As it took its various forms in the late nineteenth and early twentieth centuries, psychology sought to be – and was perceived to be – the application of natural science to the life of the mind. This application took many forms, from hypnosis to experimentation in laboratories, from the psychoanalytical couch to unconditional positive regard. The accusation of modernism, or so-called modernism, was that the modernists rejected the past, rejected the fixity of dogma, that they reduced faith to religious experience, and that they saw in the sciences the way to understand and improve life. Psychology – in the broadest sense possible, not in the specific ways rejected by *Pascendi* – was modernist. Older discourses of the soul, of the mind, of habit and virtue, were displaced by the new discourses of consciousness, the unconscious, behavior, and personality, to name a few. Older practices, forged in long spiritual and religious traditions, seemed discarded in favor of the new forms of self-knowledge and self-improvement offered by various types of psychology. Many of the figures that we considered were, essentially, modernists: Tyrrell, Boyd Barrett, Buonaiuti, Kavanaugh. Others, such as Mercier, Moore, Arnold, White, and van Kaam, sought syntheses that surpassed the tired categories of pre-modern/modern.

The questions that surfaced during the period must be understood in the light of the modernist controversy. Even though some of the questions seem outdated today, they retain their significance because of what was at stake. Can one study the soul in the experimental laboratory? For the Cartesians, this simply did not make sense, as the soul is a spiritual entity. But Mercier, Pace, Moore, and the others disagreed, because what psychology studied was not the soul per se, but the person or personality, a composite of soul and body, and psychological acts engaged the latter. One brought a person into the laboratory, not the soul. And what came out of the laboratory was full of promise to address the pressing needs of the day. Child guidance, psychological assessment, mental hygiene, and a host of social problems could be corrected using the insights gained by scientific study. Mercier and Pace knew what was at stake: if Catholics neglected this science, what would become of it in the hands of the materialists and others hostile to the faith? They sought and fought to develop not a Catholic psychology, but a psychology to which Catholics contributed. Misiak and Staudt's *Catholics in Psychology* continued to make the case for this approach until the end of the epoch we have investigated.

This Neoscholastic psychology owed part of its robustness to the fact that it incorporated ideas that were essentially foreign to Neoscholastic philosophy – such as Moore's use of "personality" as the conscious ego. Nor was Moore unwilling to challenge Neoscholastic interpretations of Aristotle and Aquinas when experimental studies showed to him that images were not essential to thinking. Neoscholastic psychology increasingly took on a life of its own. Its trajectory, however, underwent profound modification with the decline, officially and philosophically, of Neoscholasticism in the 1960s. Then, new lines opened up, and this psychology had a destiny that its founders could not have foreseen.

Were the cures at Lourdes the result of miraculous intervention or were they faith cures? How to tell the difference? Psychology in an early form was a knife used to separate the two, if it could be done. Do the spiritualists teach us anything about the soul and the afterlife? At least the spiritualists were not materialists, and they did contribute to the cultivation of psychology in its early years.

But how to interpret their sometimes unorthodox statements? Here, Catholic thought had to weave a narrow path between the materialists and the spiritualists, affirming the soul with the latter for psychology, warning of demonic influences when fraud and self-deception were not at play. The spiritualists and the Christian Scientists pushed the issue of healing in ways that crossed the boundaries between the body and the soul. The neat boundary between those two, and the tidy abstract boundary dividing faith and reason, and science and religion, dissolved in their hands. Psychology proved to be a borderland between science and religion, both on the disciplinary level and on the personal level, as the "subconscious" seemed to be the place where the spiritual world made contact with the material world. The soul, we may say, retreated into this subconscious, banished by natural scientific psychology, despite the philosophical arguments made by the Neoscholastics and others, and despite the long tradition of locating in the soul the human power to reason and gain conceptual knowledge. But then, other ideas intervened, especially psychoanalysis, with a different conception of this shadow land.

What to make of this new enterprise of psychoanalysis? To some, at first, to be a kind of secular confession. But then the questions arose, is analysis necessary for Catholics who have the sacrament of penance? Is it a substitute? Does it deal with things other than sin? It deals with human passions and desires, with longings and actions, with commissions and omissions, just like confession. What is, after all, the relationship between mental disturbance and sin? Do our impulses determine our deeds? What are Catholics to do in the face of mental illness and maladjustment? How are they to provide guidance? Is the will strong or weak? Is will-training enough? Or does it rest on an inadequate conception of psychological life? Can Catholics be psychoanalyzed? Is psychoanalysis like communism, a debased view of human nature? Can the methods and even some of the theories of Freud have a place in Catholic settings? Does Catholicism have something to learn from Freud? What to make of unconscious motivation and desire? These questions were entangled in the social setting of psychoanalysis in the United States, where it was both suspect as science and as dominant in psychiatry in mid-century. The various ways that Catholic psychologists made distinctions, so that Boyd Barrett could develop a distinctively spiritual psychoanalysis, Moore a useful and Neoscholastically orthodox dynamic psychology, and Allers could denounce the entire project and Sheen some of it, show the ways that Freud's thought vexed the Catholic community. Harry McNeill summarized the situation best: each side had something to learn from the other.

Modernism meant that people were cut off from the symbolic roots that nourished meaning and value for ages. What is the place of the symbol in human psychological life? Thinkers and sufferers such as Victor White sought to renew psychological life with a new conception of the tradition, drawing on Jung's archetypes. Here was a psychology with a soul – but what a soul! Was

Jung simply a Gnostic? Was he, as he claimed, a natural scientist studying psychological life by means of analysis? Here was a psychology that took the tradition as having something to say, but what to do with the fact that for many, this tradition did not speak to them? Can we rediscover the myths from within? Is the Christian age passing? What to do with Jung's seemingly – even if he rejected the charge – theological claims? Is Victor White's project of renewing Thomism and the spiritual life of modern men and women possible? If we took nothing else than these questions from our examination of Catholic responses to Jung, that would be enough. But in the Eranos conferences, we see something else that was distinct. Unlike many of his contemporaries Jung, even as he distanced himself from the philosophical roots that underlay his system, did bring together thinkers from many traditions and disciplines. All had something to say about the soul, all had something to teach and learn from a psychiatrist who dealt with the troubles and torments of their contemporaries.

Then came the first waves of the breakdown of the Neoscholastic movement and of natural scientific psychology. Actually, natural scientific psychology did not break down, but it was challenged and psychology became more openly pluralistic. The main point is that as Catholic philosophy and theology sought new routes during the 1950s, humanistic psychology emerged in psychology in North America. Older and seemingly clear dividing lines dissolved. Now, psychologists had something to say about spiritual life. They clearly entered what we can call sacred ground. The most friendly of all psychologies to Catholicism came to be seen by some as the most dangerous – repeating an accusation earlier hurled at hypnosis, psychoanalysis, and then Jung. Can psychologists deal with human spiritual life? Where are the boundaries between what belongs to the Church and what to the psychologists? Is it possible that van Kaam was right, and that in this ever-new psychology lies a re-invigoration of spirituality?

What is significant is that Catholics in psychology for the most part did not simply reject these questions, these thinkers, and what they thought. Simple rejection was an ever-present temptation, and some succumbed to it. But notable and often courageous souls responded to the challenges and findings of modern psychology by becoming themselves psychologists, were scientific in their studies yet without abandoning the Church and letting it fend for itself. Pre-eminent among these thinkers are: Edward A. Pace, Thomas Verner Moore, James Walsh, Victor White, E. Boyd Barrett, Adrian van Kaam, William C. Bier, Annette Walters, Magda Arnold, and others, many others. A litany would be necessary to recount them all.

What they did was to establish institutions within the Catholic citadel in order to forge a psychology that did not succumb to the temptations and reduction-isms of the age. They established trading zones and forged hybrid discourses to make psychology serviceable. They sought to have psychology a faithful hand-maiden of the Church. And at the same time, they sought to be professional scientists. At their best, they were not trying to affirm what they already knew from their philosophy and their theology. Their best service was when they stayed on the border, at home in both lands, and enabling exchange, criticism, and cross-fertilization (to mix a metaphor).

The means whereby these psychologists met the challenges of psychology were, for the most part during this period, Neoscholasticism or some other form of Thomistic thought. "To renew the old by means of the new." Toward the end of the period, as we have seen, phenomenological thought made a difference. It must be said, however, that it did so in large part because it was seen as compatible with Thomism, adding to it a first-person perspective that Thomism largely lacked. The work of van Kaam, Strasser, Donceel, and others in this regard is noteworthy. For all its limitations – its ahistorical stance, its conviction that it represented a system of thought that was unchanged since the Middle Ages, its ties with ecclesiastical power (and in some cases, its ties with political power) – it offered the first several generations of Catholic psychologists in North America a philosophical basis that was conducive to experimental and statistical methods in psychology, with the advantage of avoiding the methodolatry that has plagued American psychology. In the hands of a Thomas Verner Moore and a Magda Arnold, Neoscholasticism gave psychology a foundation that both encouraged empirical research and worked against the implicit and often materialistic philosophical bases that many of their contemporaries held. Both a strength and a weakness of Neoscholasticism was its assumption that "natural science" meant "science" in general, and that the natural sciences are simply rooted in and abstract from common sense. Neoscholasticism also facilitated, as we have seen, the assimilation of Catholics into empirical psychology. Because it seemed to be a *philosophia perennis*, the generation of the 1930s and 1940s could not have foreseen that this philosophical and theological bulwark would later appear as a historical construction like any other. The ahistoricism of Neoscholasticism made its own historical destiny unthinkable.[1]

Questions remain. Does it make sense any longer to think about contesting the boundaries between psychology and Catholicism? Have the institutions, the trading zones, the hybrid discourses made further work in this area meaningless? Is psychology, like medicine, one more scientific authority external to the Church except in significant but isolated contexts? Or has Vatican insistence, often supported by those psychologists who most closely identify themselves as Catholics (in North America, at least), that faithfulness to the Magisterium in all things, including non-infallible statements, is fundamental to Catholic thought, effectively curtailed psychological thought making an independent contribution to Catholic life? Is such loyalty to the Pope's teachings a Catholic fundamentalism (Sommerfeldt, 2009), a search for certainty in a relativistic and nihilistic age?

---

[1] Jean Daniélou, one of the *ressourcement* theologians, criticized Neoscholasticism for its lack of "historical sense. In an existentialist world, it remains resolutely essentialist and objectivist, oblivious to human subjectivity" (D'Ambrosio, 1991, p. 534).

The position proposed here is that psychology is not a fixed entity. It does not have a "paradigm," to use Thomas Kuhn's term, and it is not the kind of science to have one. (Maybe not even the paragon of paradigmatic sciences, physics, has one, if one follows Galison's thought.) Unlike our Neoscholastic predecessors, we do not assume that there is one psychology, and that it is a natural science. Psychology has natural scientific aspects, to be sure. But it has human scientific aspects, it has critical scientific aspects, and – perhaps most important of all for the general public – it has "pop psychological" aspects. Moreover, psychology draws sustenance from and affects the cultural roots from which it springs, and these roots are many. And we can add indigenous psychologies, that is, we can formally recognize that cultural categories are implicit in all psychological theorizing and practices. To pursue these lines of thought would be a significant undertaking, and our task is simpler, although related to these questions about the status of psychology as a discipline.

What remains to be explored is the intersection of psychology as a discipline, broadly defined – with due consideration of its embeddedness in history and culture – with Catholic (and more broadly, Christian) traditions.[2] This means: the intermixing of psychologies with multiple strands of the Catholic intellectual tradition. These strands include philosophies, spiritualities, ascetical and moral theologies, as well as medical, ethical, and political works that were grounded in the Christian west. The list is illustrative, not definitive, as there is much uncharted territory to consider, at least from psychology's point of view.

So we return to the fourfold categorization of the relationships between psychology and the Church introduced in Chapter 1. How have these categories fared in making sense of this history? Their value was heuristic; they were guides only. The first was that of the divorce between psychology and philosophy as foundational for an empirical psychology. What we have seen is that in some contexts, Catholics used that argument to secure a place for psychology within institutions and to secure a place for it alongside a well-entrenched philosophical psychology that seemed out of touch with the contemporary world. Misiak in particular drew on this argument. Primarily, however, the Catholics conceded the place of a philosophical psychology, so that the arguments for the autonomy of scientific psychology were not vicious ones, designed to eliminate the philosophical competition. The "levels of explanation" account of types of sciences and knowledge does characterize much of Catholic participation in psychology over the past century. Superficially, this position was methodological naturalism, but its deep structure was the Thomistic idea of the limited autonomy of the sciences, an autonomy based on the distinction of reason and faith.

---

[2] These considerations could be extended further, to Jewish, Muslim, Hindu, Buddhist, etc., traditions. But an all too easy syncretism could result. For present purposes, the faith tradition of the Catholic Church remains the touchstone.

But even when the independence of psychology was supported, we saw that a host of psychologists, from Moore to Hostie to van Kaam, saw psychology in terms of our second category, bound to philosophy and theology. That lay at the basis of the critiques of Freud, Jung, and Rogers, for example. This position preserved them from methodolatry, because they understood that methods do not interpret themselves. So Moore could bring in notions of formal causality into factor analysis. What they did not do was to inject "biblical facts" into psychology (a variant of the second approach) on an equal footing with empirical facts and theories. This followed from Catholic theology rather than psychology, and it points to a major difference between the Catholic theological influences in psychology in contrast to some Protestant theological influences. Catholic theology rejected liberal Protestant tendencies to "rationalize" scripture (that way lay modernism) and rejected the position – call it fundamentalism – that minimized the ability of human reason to discover truths independently of Divine Revelation. Like many Protestant and Jewish psychologists, the Catholics saw the place of an autonomous contribution of psychology to understanding and changing human behavior and minds. (We will return later to the question of "integration," which belongs to this second approach.)

For the most part, the Catholics did not propose the third approach of a Catholic or Christian psychology, and certainly, none proposed a biblically-based psychology. During the period under study in this book, Catholics were concerned about their intellectual isolation, so that a non-secular and Catholic psychology was not really in contention. At the same time, we can draw something forward from such proposals, namely, the notion that thinkers and texts – including the Bible – from the past have something to contribute to modern psychology. The anti-positivism in this third approach has much to offer psychology, even if psychology cannot become "biblical" without eliminating the very contested boundaries that have been such a fruitful terrain to explore. What are needed would be answers to the questions: whose bible? Whose interpretations?

The fourth approach, psychology instead of religion, has been a path not followed. Or, at least it was not followed during the time covered in this book. It has come somewhat later, sometimes in the form of New Age thinking, stemming from the American tradition of unchurched spirituality. Certainly, a psychologized spirituality has become part of contemporary psychology, but it need not displace religion for psychology. It becomes another stream leading to the vast sea of Christian spirituality, a contribution of our age. What did happen was the incorporation of psychological categories into Catholic discourses about spiritual and religious life, giving it a psychological flavor. Psychology seasoned the stew, so to speak, but did not replace it.

This last approach shows most clearly the "intrinsic contradictions" between psychology and Catholicism, an awareness of which guided the narratives. These contradictions can be easily overlooked in outcomes, in which psychological epistemic objects such as "personality" and "assessment" became assimilated into religious and spiritual practices and ways of understanding. But contradictions they are, especially when we call to mind the question of authority. Who can speak the truth? In what terms can it be done? What is the authority of "science" of whatever form, in Church life? What is the authority of Church teachings and officials in science? What is the meaning of self-disclosure in confession and in psychotherapy? What is obedience? The contradictions stem from the sources of authority on each side: on the one side, that of science, it arises from experience; on the other side, that of the Church, it arises from revelation and tradition. We have seen that sometimes the contradiction is muted, at other times pronounced. It has been especially an intrinsic contradiction because the psychologists we have studied have been Catholics, often in the religious life. And the contradictions are not what they were at the beginning of our story. For the most part, psychological ideas and discourses have been absorbed into the life of the Church, although the life of the Church has been altered as a result. It has become psychologized. One might be tempted to call this a dialectic, except for the fact that any synthesis of psychology and Catholic thought seems to be unstable, always threatening to break down again, especially over the issue of authority and sources of truth. So the story continues.

In what follows, I will sketch out a historical-cultural psychology that explores various formations of human psychological structures and acts, with an eye to invigorating fruitful exchanges among psychologists for whom the Catholic traditions are meaningful. This historical-cultural psychological approach will be, in the words of Hans van Rappard (1998), "historically informed theoretical psychology" (p. 664). The objective is to sketch out a way toward a "fusion of horizons," to use Gadamer's term, of significant works from the past in the Catholic tradition with contemporary psychology, taking into consideration the historical and cultural conditions in which the works were produced.[3] This work will be an interpretative one, not assuming the superiority of either horizon. The goal: a re-invigorated psychology in the Catholic tradition, one wed neither to natural scientific psychology nor to Neoscholasticism. Such a psychology would be both theoretical and applied. For present limited, purposes, we will focus on the theoretical aspects of psychology.

It is not, it must be said, as if psychology is the only discipline in the bunch that has multiple threads and approaches. The same must be said of the others as well. The philosophers and the theologians do not offer psychology (even if

---

[3] As we shall explore in the next section, this attempt to connect with the past to renew the field in the present was central to the *ressourcement* theologians, as D'Ambrosio (1991) explains: "Such a hermeneutical process of application is, in the words of Richard Palmer, 'not a literal bringing of the past into externalities of the present; it is bringing *what is essential* in the past into our personal present'" (p. 553, citing Palmer, 1969, p. 191), with D'Ambrosio's emphasis.

the psychologists desired such security) a pole star by which to steer. Like psychology, or psychologies, these other disciplines exist in the plural, and in the interrogative mode, in a search for truth as we can know it.

A Janus-faced psychology: *Ressourcement* in psychology

The break with philosophy – and theology

Recent histories of psychology, as well as earlier chapters in this book, challenge a narrative, long worn from overuse, which claimed that psychology began as a divorce from philosophy. The new psychology did announce such a break, and it was repeated time and again by such psychologists as Carl Jung, who humbly claimed to be only natural scientists. Yet psychology never had that origin, according to recent histories. That origin is largely an imaginary account that has served a number of purposes, including the establishment of psychology departments and, in the United States, a socially expedient functionalist mentality. Consider what appears to be the most empiricist notion in psychology, namely the operational definition. Where did that come from? The most insider of all insiders, Edwin G. Boring, tells the tale: it owes its esteemed position largely to the influence of a philosophical movement, Logical Positivism, and to a physicist, P. W. Bridgman, whose book, *The logic of modern physics* (1927), helped, philosophically, to steer psychologists away from some significant philosophical issues by defining them as "pseudo-problems" (Boring, 1950, p. 654). So psychology cannot help but raise philosophical questions even when seeking to dismiss them, the answers to which affect psychological research, theorizing, and praxis. I think that this argument has been made successfully in recent years.

That story of origin in a divorce never fit the human science tradition in psychology (see Giorgi, 1970, for an insider history), which never abandoned explicit interest in philosophical questions. This human science tradition, from Dilthey to Bruner, conceptualizes psychological givens as historically constituted. That story of divorce does not fit critical psychology either, especially in social psychology, which is explicitly concerned with ontological and epistemological issues, even in textbooks (see Stainton Rogers, 2003 for an example). That story never fit the Neoscholastic psychologists, of course, who knew that psychological theory and praxis draws from a philosophical anthropology.

These arguments against a break with philosophy should not be taken as evidence against the reality of a break. If one looks at psychology today, it has broken from philosophy. This is evident in many ways, especially in the kind of education deemed necessary for psychologists. Pre-dating the break with philosophy was a break with theological thinking, which extends back to the seventeenth century and its religious wars. Psychology has followed Robert Boyle's teaching that while we cannot agree on matters of religious dogma, we can agree on what is given to the senses. Science after the seventeenth century, we may say, dispensed with theological statements: not that scientists became atheists, but that they renounced theological claims. They abjure trying to address the ultimate causes of things. Perhaps the last generation of natural scientists to make them were in fact the founders of natural science, people like Robert Boyle and Isaac Newton, who engaged in alchemical and magical work – but that is another story! However, it indicates that the theology/science split is not nature- or God-given. It was a historical decision. Looking to earlier periods, we cannot assume its existence.

Stenner (2009) raises the question of the severing of nature from nature's God in the seventeenth century as a theological conclusion. But the creation of a natural realm isolated in principle (metaphysical naturalism) or in a division of labor (methodological naturalism) can be traced back to an earlier distinction. De Lubac saw the "fragmentation" of the cosmos into a purely natural realm and a purely supernatural one as a product of the late Middle Ages, solidified in "the erection of an order of 'pure nature' in the scholasticism of the Counter Reformation" (Dulles, 1991, p. 182) of the sixteenth century. Thus, one way forward in the exploration of the religion/science problematic is the historical examination of what psychology today means by "nature." There are clear strands within the history that this book has considered that point in this direction: the question of psychology (and the subconscious) as the indeterminate boundary between the material and the spiritual in Mind Cure and miracles at Lourdes; the question – raised by Victor White over Jung's version of methodological naturalism – of the nature of the image and the unconscious as our affective access to the Divine; the question of humanistic psychology's spiritual claims as it broke down the barrier between disciplines. Boundary-work, in short, did not leave the boundaries settled.

The implication of the breaks

Nevertheless, the narrative of divorces from theology and philosophy has had important consequences for psychology. It has meant a shrinking of historical perspective, a trend that Gordon Allport (1940) noted in his study of the state of the discipline in 1939: "A decline of another sort is seen in the diminution of historical surveys. After steadily increasing their recognition and acknowledgment of antecedent studies, it looks now as if psychologists have started to declare their independence of the past" (p. 7). The divorce from theology and philosophy meant a divorce from the past: if we do not know about it, we do not have to address it, because it is not real for us, seems to have been the implicit rationalization. Against this declaration of independence, which had a noble motivation in its desire to see things afresh, I oppose Gadamer's (1989) notion of "historically effected consciousness," a ponderous term in English to be sure, but one with great significance for the task at hand. It means that we should learn to understand ourselves better and recognize that in all understanding, whether we are expressly aware of it or not, the efficacy of history is at work. When a naïve faith in scientific method denies the existence of effective history, there can be an actual deformation of knowledge ... But on the whole the power of effective history does not depend on its being recognized.

(p. 301)

What this means for present purposes is this: there is a great project of anamnesis that can be undertaken to understand more fully the contested boundaries between the psychological and the religious. We must even explore the partition between the two, a division that itself has a history. Such an anamnesis would further the development of the discipline of psychology, in that it would challenge the modern discipline with earlier discourses and disciplines about the nature of the soul, human nature, the mind, the person. Beginning with recognition of the historical novelty of modern psychology, it would also provide an occasion to examine its many implicit presuppositions about the nature of the psychological in its relation to the spiritual and the religious. How would such an anamnesis proceed?

Ressourcement

A somewhat analogous situation prevailed in Catholic theology some fifty years ago, when Neoscholasticism provided the dominant discourse.[4] As introduced earlier, in our discussion of Catholic responses to Jung's work, the French theologian Henri de Lubac and others urged a *ressourcement* – a return to patristic and medieval texts and modes of exegesis of Scripture in order to revitalize theological discourse. De Lubac helped to renew theology by a movement to the past, to free theology from a stultified present. He paid dearly for this move in the 1950s, before his ideas took hold at the Second Vatican Council. This return to the sources was not to be a nostalgic rejection of the science of theology as it had developed over 600 years. Von Balthasar (1991), de Lubac's great student, stated the case:

> The outcome of de Lubac's portrayal of history is not at all the wish for a slavish renewal of the old schema – the outward form theology has taken is no longer capable of being forced into such a mold. The result has been rather a rethinking of the synthesis that lived within the schema, of the breadth of the spiritual horizon, the enduring value of the main articulations; theology of the present and of the future will have to emulate all this.

(p. 81)

---

[4] The theologian D'Ambrosio (1991) refers to Gadamer's hermeneutics in order to explain what de Lubac, Daniélou, and others were doing in their re-appropriation of the past.

The terms of de Lubac's *ressourcement* were a renewal of the present by means of a recovery of the past, an approach similar to that of the Neoscholastic movement: *vetera novis augere et perficere*. However, in one way I have under-stated the relationship between de Lubac's accomplishment and what faces psychology. As Gadamer (1989) indicated, the human sciences received a sig-nificant impetus from the scriptural hermeneutics of the eighteenth and nine-teenth centuries, the exegesis of Scripture being a main source of all hermeneutic theory today. An analogy, more strict than I can depict here, holds: scriptural hermeneutics is for systematic theology what human science hermeneutics is for modern psychology. If that be the case, then psychologists could renew psychol-ogy in part by turning to pre-modern ways of interpreting signifiers. Sacred words, first of all, since they have been of primary importance in the western traditions. Following de Lubac, this turn would not be an imitation of the past or a rejection of the modern, but it would be an opening to modes of analysis that seem to me to be begged for in the critiques of the detached viewer and of dreaded Cartesian dualism. Why? Because it requires recovering an engaged way of encountering the word.

The terms of de Lubac's turn to the past are what interest me. He was critical of merely objective methods of textual analysis of Scripture and of certain strains of Neoscholasticism for the same reasons: they thought "that they could contain the mystery within their rational constructs. The kind of theo-logical and exegetical science to which he objects exhibits the same dangerous impulse as that *'curiosa cupiditas'* denounced by Hugh of St. Victor in the twelfth century: 'it wants to explain in order thereby to possess and dominate. It wants to make the infinite Truth its thing'" (D'Ambrosio, 1992, p. 386). In other words, for de Lubac, the reader, the interpreter, is not a detached observer, but someone called into question by what is read. This view of reading fits Gadamer's conception of hermeneutics, in that what we discover by such work of interpretation is not only knowledge of past thought, but self-knowledge.[5] And this self-knowledge can occur on two levels: on the personal level, whereby by means of reflexivity, we come to know ourselves in light of what we know (the theme of such historians of psychology as Richards (2010) and philoso-phers such as Ian Hacking (1999)); and on the disciplinary level, whereby we "remember" what psychology has "forgotten" in becoming merely modern. This latter task is that of anamnesis, a recovery of what has been "unconscious" in modern psychology.

To this end of *ressourcement*, de Lubac and his colleagues initiated a series of translations of patristic and medieval texts, the *Sources chrétiennes*. Viewing the hundreds of volumes of bi-lingual texts in this series makes for a literal experience of a return to the sources. These texts provide what de Lubac saw as

---

[5] Willem van Hoorn (1972) refers also to Habermas on the dialectic of knowledge of the past and knowledge of self in the present.

necessary in his day, a "plunge into history" (*Paradoxes of faith*, p. 154, quoted in D'Ambrosio, 1992, p. 368). In the 1960s, de Lubac's approach to Scripture study and theology played a central role in the Vatican Council's "opening of the windows" of the Church to the modern world. So in cracking the shell of Neoscholasticism at the Vatican Council, *ressourcement* already has affected psychology in the Catholic world, as we have seen. In addition to breathing the air that blew as it listed through those open windows, the time is ripe to engage in a psychological version of *ressourcement*. Many of the texts in the *Sources chrétiennes* address what we can call psychological topics, and would be fitting places to begin.

Ressourcement *in psychology*

Psychology today faces a rigidity of thought similar to what prevailed in theology, with a discredited positivism and its concomitant methodolatry. *Ressourcement* in psychology would begin not with a critique of the scientist tendencies of traditional psychology – named by analogy with the stale Neoscholasticism that de Lubac faced – but with a turn to pre-modern discourses on the mind, soul, and human nature in philosophy, medicine, rhetoric, and theology. The assumption of *ressourcement* in psychology would be that the break with philosophy meant not a denial of the inherent philosophical character of psychological discourse, but a dialectical negation of the dead letter of nineteenth- and twentieth-century empiricism and rationalism, a negation that confirms the status of psychological discourses as philosophical: that is, in the interrogative mode. Such a *ressourcement* is impossible, in this day, without giving attention to those contemporary thinkers who guide a post-colonizing hermeneutics of the past, attuning us to the past as other. These thinkers – Heidegger, Gadamer, Foucault, Lacan, Levinas, de Lubac and others, provide an orientation for a reading in psychology's *ressourcement* (not appropriation) of the past. In conjunction with the contemporary thinkers, we can learn from our predecessors how to read anew.

Ressourcement differs from both presentism and historicism.[6] Both those approaches suffer from a detachment that makes of the past merely the past. *Ressourcement*, following de Lubac, occurs when the reading of texts occurs simultaneously on different levels. Since he was concerned with the reading of Scripture, it was in those terms that he understood hermeneutics: "For Origen and the entire Middle Ages following him, the guarantee for the fundamental distinction – between literal and spiritual (or allegorical) sense – is Paul" (von Balthasar, 1991, p. 77). The letter is fixed, tending to be a dead letter. The letter

---

[6] In case these terms are not clear: presentism views the past as inevitably leading to the glorious present. For the presentist, the past means the present, and the present is superior in knowledge to the past. Historicism relativizes past and present, reducing knowledge to its historical context. With both of these presuppositions, the past does not speak, for it is dead.

is what the presentist and the historicist read. In Scripture, according to de Lubac, "the letter is always being transformed into spirit, promise into fulfillment, in a unique transition, by a mutation that is at the same time conversion and also the condensation of the manifold in the uniquely normative center" (p. 79). Analogously, outside of Scripture, do texts exist for a *ressourcement* in psychology? They, too, have their letter and their spirit. They must be read on at least those two levels. Enough is known about the letter; it is the spirit of the text that interests me in trying to spell out *ressourcement*.

In the history of Biblical interpretation, the level of the spirit of the text has been described in terms of allegory, that is, in terms of moral and mystical senses of Scripture. For example, *The Song of Songs*, that beautiful love poem, is also a story about the history of the Church, also a tale that details how we must follow our true love and not our concupiscence, and a description of the mystical journey to the presence of Christ, the Bridegroom. What characterizes the level of spirit is the fact of the reader of the text not being the subject of the text, but rather, being subjected to it. The reader is not an I, but a You, called into question by the text, by the spirit or word that speaks through the text. At the same time, *ressourcement* did not mean "returning to the past" (D'Ambrosio, 1991, p. 544). As Balthasar stated the case, "no historical situation is ever absolutely similar to any other preceding period; none can therefore furnish its own solutions as so many master keys capable of resolving our contemporary problems" (cited in ibid.; von Balthasar, 1942).

For the *ressourcement* theologians, dipping into the great wells of the past was intended not simply to "recover" what had been forgotten, but it "was expected to serve as a catalyst that would stimulate new ideas" (D'Ambrosio, 1991, p. 545). I think that some of the most gripping examples of *ressourcement* in psychology take up the reading of the past in terms of letter and spirit. After all, *ressourcement* does not begin today. Consider the Oedipus complex and the psychoanalytic project of remembering what we cannot simply remember. Freud's Oedipus continues to haunt the imagination, despite its anthropological and sociological absurdities. Why? It is because Freud captured the spirit of the Oedipus tragedy. There are moral and mystical overtones in the Oedipus story that call us into question in our quests for knowledge, power, and intimacy. Like Oedipus, we strive with good will, only to undermine ourselves by the very actions that turn out to be symptoms, a realization we have only after the fact. After Freud, Oedipus lives again.

The thinkers Jung invited to the Eranos conferences offer a second example of an earlier *ressourcement*, especially given that some of the theologians involved in the movement, such as Jean Daniélou, spoke at the Eranos meetings. We saw how they urged a revitalized interpretation of myth and symbol as necessary for our psychological and spiritual lives. A more recent example is Foucault's reading of John Cassian, a fifth century founder of Western monasticism, on the vice of lust. Foucault was writing a history of sexuality, and

Cassian's hermeneutics of desire was strikingly more intimate and interiorized than what had prevailed among the Greeks and Romans of an earlier day. For Cassian, vice begins in the quietest stirrings of thought and feeling; these must be attended to, if one would achieve the purity of heart necessary for the mystical assent. So much for the letter of Cassian's text on spiritual development: what of its spirit, a spirit unspoken by Foucault? How does it address us? I think that the spirit of Cassian's *Conferences* addresses us in our presumption of non-judgmental acceptance of self-disclosure, both of ourselves and of others. (This is not meant as a defense of psychological moralizing.) We have come to think of acceptance as a kind of democratic virtue because, after all, judgment makes sense only in the context of a relevant community of discourse. This suffocating isolation from what Levinas calls *exteriority* Cassian would no doubt demolish. Self-disclosure, in his terms, searches for the stirrings of vice, not because he was anxious about loss of self-control or because he repressed his sexuality, but because he was seeking the Other, the object of his deepest desire. For him, that could only be done by a death of the "natural" self, so the true self, the spiritual self, could live. So the stirrings of the inner self betray vice or virtue, illness or well-being, insofar as they detract or make possible proximity to this supreme Other. Cassian's spirit calls our lukewarm selves, cooled by a century of psychological self-disclosure, into question. He makes vice live for the reader.

I have not addressed the intricacies of reading for the spirit and the letter. That topic is beyond the scope of this chapter, which only sketches what may now be possible after modernism and Neoscholasticism. I conclude, instead, with a final implication of this *ressourcement* for psychology. It is imperative for psychologists to turn to history as a major source for the renewal and development of our science. Just as the interpretation of Scripture is the basis of Christian theology, so analogously is the interpretation of what our predecessors have said a basis of psychology. After all, we are the result of the long genealogies that produced contemporary psychology with all its rifts and fragments. We turn to the ancients, the medievals, the humanists of the Renaissance, to the poets and the moralists, the theologians and the writers of manuals of casuistry, because they are the sources from whence we spring.

A paradoxical discipline

What to say in conclusion to this convoluted story with many threads? There was no one psychology that we have discussed in the course of this study. Nor were the psychologists we encountered of one mind. Some faced the boundary between psychology and religion with serene assurance, understanding that there was the rock of faith and the truths that the Church affirmed, and knowing that science meant the unprejudiced investigation of nature. Others had less assurance in either ground. The stories are many. Is there anything that holds them together? Even to ask this question invites criticism, as it may express a secret desire for certainty, and may spring from what Edward Aloysius Pace called a passion for unity. But I am not seeking unity. I do seek a way forward. While this has been a historical study, the history of psychology is historically informed philsophical psychology. So I do turn back to all that has been looked at over the course of this book and ask: what was going on?

I would put it in the following terms. Despite the enormous differences in temperament, philosophy, type of psychology, despite the range of assurances of the truths of the faith, from the assertive confidence of some of the Neoscholastics, who could prove the immortality of the soul on philosophical ground, to the excruciating struggles of a thinker like Victor White, and to the agonies of Edward Boyd Barrett, there were a few things that characterize what they were trying to do with psychology. The first and most important of them was that they wanted a psychology that would do justice to a living being that has an eternal destiny. Sometimes this was explicit, as in Neoscholastic psychology where, despite the willingness to contribute to a purely natural scientific psychology, the claims of the metaphysician and the theologian were never forgotten. Even if such considerations did not enter directly into introspective studies or into factor analyses, into clinical judgments or the results of projective tests, even if collaboration with their non-Catholic and even materialist colleagues in psychology was something desired and achieved, there was a remainder. Even though, for the most part, they did not want to make the soul a category of their psychologies, in all truth, it lingered in the background. Like physicians taking the Hippocratic oath, these psychologists seem to say, "Do no harm" to the eternal, transcendent dimension of human life.

Sometimes this was expressed in mundane ways: counselors careful not to abandon the moral rudder of the Church when discussing counseling; Moore's experimental confirmation that the concept was an element of experience distinct from sensation and feeling; Boyd Barrett's incorporation of the parapsychological into his version of psychoanalysis; White's struggles with the relationships between the archetypes and the sacramental; van Kaam's affirmation that counseling has to do with the human being called by the All of reality; above all, the desire to articulate psychologies that would be compatible with revealed truth, even if it could not deal with it directly.

What if we follow Moore in beginning to think through what this observation means? The observation, once again: psychology should do no harm to the intimation of immortality in human living and dying. In Chapter 9, I quoted Moore. Here are some of his words once again: "To say that psychology is the science of the soul assumes at the outset a metaphysical theory. It is better to start on common ground" (1924, pp. 9–10). So in what follows, I will not assume at the outset a metaphysical theory, but stay on common ground. There is a further reason for this abstinence from such an assumption. I think it is important not to retreat from ground claimed by psychology over the past century. I suggest that it is important to avoid two traps, into which psychology regularly falls, because of its social utility. The first trap is to reduce psychology to moral guidance and teaching. Curran (1952) was right. Counseling (the psychological praxis) is not the same as guidance and education. Not that the latter are unimportant, but psychology, especially in its applied areas – everywhere really – because of the uses people make of it, deals with human freedom. Psychology should no more be the handmaiden of moral theology than it should be a handmaiden of politics. I say nothing new here. What I see, however, are calls for closer ties between psychology and the Church, meaning that the Magisterium has a directive role in the counseling session. But the incorporation of the Vatican as a third party in the psychotherapeutic session and in the investigations of human experience and action would make the discipline something other than psychology. It would be some kind of direction and guidance, similar to the training that is cognitive behavioral therapy. Teach them what to do, train them to do it. It would "prove" Church teachings empirically, the way think tanks "prove" the political opinions of their funding sources. If that vision would prevail, then that peculiar historical institution, which flourished in the twentieth century and was called psychology, will be over and done with. Moralizing in psychology is not the worst way to do harm, however. The worst way is to eliminate from the view of people the horizon of their eternal destiny.

The Catholic psychologists have been much more consistent in dealing with the second error than in dealing with the first. But between the moralists and the materialists, there is precious little room for maneuvering, or so it seems. How to address in psychological ways the intimations of immortality?

On not integrating psychology and Christian faith

The French phenomenologist, Maurice Merleau-Ponty, did not develop a philosophy of God or of religion, but in one essay he considered the debate that had occurred between 1927 and 1931 on the question of a Christian philosophy. He referred to the personal effort involved in bridging together two modes of engagement that need not have anything to do with each other. This observation will be my point of departure. For present purposes, I assume that scientific inquiry, including the psychological, is or at least can be philosophical inquiry. All the sciences raise philosophical questions, and this is nowhere more true than in psychology, where we deal with the mystery of the human person.

Merleau-Ponty's observation was that philosophy and faith need not have anything to do with each other. Why? I would claim that this is because philosophical inquiry remains in the interrogative mode. Inquiry, in psychology and in the other disciplines grounded in the lifeworld, is perpetually provisional, reflexively turning on itself to question its categories and means of discovery. It remains a critical activity, grieving at its inability to grasp the gold of truth even in those moments where something glitters, a something turning in the course of time into lead. Faith, by contrast, is not this way of knowing. Faith is a relationship with an Other who said, "I am the Truth" (John 14:6). Faith arises in a call and in a response to a calling. The call does not give us scientific knowledge; indeed, it can even appear as folly in terms of the wisdom of the world. "We see through a glass, darkly" (1 Cor. 13:12), seeking God "the unknown" (White, 1956). These two ways, the philosophical and the religious, thus have radically different points of departure, because in the former, the subject is the knower, while in the latter, the subject is primarily known by that Other who is the Truth.

They may differ, but the ongoing and vexing question of a Christian philosophy, and by extension, a Christian psychology, refuses to go away. That persistence means that in some way the distinction between them is not a division. Rather than try to resolve the question, I think it best to heighten the tension, to proceed into an area that is unknown. There might arise a symbol – a phantasm, Thomistically speaking – that might point the way.

So to proceed into what for the rational mind is a paradox if not a contradiction: what kind of psychology can aspire to something like "integration" with faith?[7] What kind of psychology is up to the task? I draw again on Merleau-Ponty (1964), who provides for me a lead into the darkness: "To say yes to Christianity as a fact of culture and civilization is to say yes to St. Thomas, but also to St. Augustine and Occam and Nicholas of Cusa and Pascal and Malebranche, and this assent does not cost us an ounce of the pains each one of them had to take in order to be himself without default" (p. 142). And so, this integration, if it is even possible, would cost us at least an ounce of pain, because the integration must be grounded in one's living. If there is any integration, it is not in the psychology, it is in the psychologist. This does not mean that only the saintly can do the work, but it does mean that the questions and the quest must be matters of desire for the psychologist.

In considering this topic, we find ourselves like Odysseus on his way home to Penelope – he had to pass between Scylla and Charybdis only once, whereas it seems that we must do so at least three times. So to the first.

---

[7] This was the question raised for a meeting, "Integrated Psychology: True to Science, True to God" (Society of Catholic Social Scientists Regional Conference, April 27–8, 2007, hosted by the Institute for the Psychological Sciences, Arlington, Virginia), in a session entitled: "The Viability of a Truly Catholic Integrated Psychology: Theories in Dialogue." Part of the larger context for this topic is the meaning of reading and study in the modern world. Illich (1993) shows how the relationship between the reader and the text, between the knower and the known, changed with the advent of scholastic reading, which is what we do in psychology, in other sciences, and in philosophy. For the early twelfth century, the question as I have posed it would probably not have made sense. I mention this because it indicates one of the presuppositions, historical as well as cognitive, that underlies this book and that will not be addressed.

Avoiding Positivism of Science and of Religion

The first passage we must make is through the narrow straits of positivism, by which I mean the cult of the fact. Positivism asserts that pure facts exist, undefiled by any mediation. Facts for the positivist simply represent some sense reality. Positivism has dogged psychology since its various beginnings in the nineteenth century. By way of over-compensation, a religious positivism has arisen. By traversing this first passage, we seek to eliminate the illusion of two "positivisms," a positivism of science, which claims to have established for all times a foundation of certain and factual knowledge, and a religious positivism, which claims to grasp factually the truth of God. As Merleau-Ponty (1964) observed: "The innocent co-existence of philosophy and Christianity taken as two positive orders or two truths, still conceal[s] from us the hidden conflict of each within itself and with the other, as well as the tormented relationships which result from it" (p. 143). With this in mind, maybe we can avoid the worst snares and idols of a totalized truth, the goal of positivism.

What is this totalized truth? It is the dream of modern thought and science, the utopia of a system that would contain all knowledge. Totalizing thought has a centripetal movement: it assimilates all things to itself. Totalizing thought seeks theoretical foundations that are secure because they cannot be doubted, and upon that rock it builds its system, fact by fact.

What about religious positivism? It too aspires for an airtight system. It claims a secure factual ground in faith. In psychology, the two can be combined. As an example of this positivism of science and religion, consider again this statement by Bruce Narramore (1973), one of the leaders in theorizing integration between psychology and Christianity: "we are in a position to gather relevant objective data, seek well constructed theoretical views and find improved techniques for applying our biblical and psychological data" (p. 17). Note again the use of the term "data" in this quotation. It serves to legitimate bringing biblical considerations into psychology without abandoning the claim that psychology is a natural science. In what sense except the metaphorical can Scripture provide "data," as that term is employed in scientific discourse? Data are sense data, whereas Scripture claims another authority than that of the senses. Religious positivism apes scientistic positivism, and it distorts the story of St. Thomas the Apostle, he who doubted until he could see the Living Lord: "Because thou hast seen me, Thomas, thou hast believed: blessed are they that have not seen and have believed" (John 20:29). We are those who have not seen. As Victor White (1956), the most psychological of all the Thomists, wrote: "For no man has seen God at any time, and his self-revealing to man in his condition on this earth is adapted to his very limited capabilities, by means of human words, apprehensible deeds and symbols, albeit possessing divine authority and sanction" (p. 6). What to make of these words, deeds, and symbols is a big question, but no religious positivism could be based upon them. From the positivist point of view, words and symbols, words indeed as symbols, are second-best, mere approximations. How can they be the basis of what we know? But they are, in both science and religion.

A more affirmative way of saying that "we see through a glass, darkly," is to say that no experience, scientific, religious, or of any other kind, occurs without mediation by symbolic forms, especially those of language. This consideration shows positivism in science and religion to be an illusion, the illusion of immediate grasp of the thing itself. That experience is mediated symbolically in oh, so many ways, means that we have contact with the real "together with the distance" (Vergote, 1998, p. 142) of otherness, unlikeness, ungraspability.[8]

An implication of the mediated character of experience is that psychology begins *in media res*, in the middle of things, already conditioned by language, culture, and history. Psychology is a work of human culture, one of the contemporary ways we have of coming to know ourselves and of coming to know what to do about ourselves and others. It embodies the strengths and limitations of our current situation, with its paradoxes and penchants.

Avoiding methodolatry and Fideism

If we keep these points in mind, that integration happens only in the person of the psychologist, and that what the psychologist knows is made possible by immersion in a symbolic order, then the following question, and the second passage, arises: are there psychological approaches that foster integration without sacrificing the proper autonomy of the discipline of psychology? To this question, I reply, that it is necessary to avoid the Scylla of methodolatry and the Charybdis of fideism. To steer between these fatal attractions, we stress the personal character of knowledge and of reflexivity.

Methodolatry is the charge that psychology has privileged methods over fidelity to its subject matter. As Chamberlain (2000) points out, it applies as much to qualitative as to quantitative research. While there would be much to say about methodolatry, for present purposes I emphasize that it points to a depersonalized approach in psychology: the psychologist as researcher or thinker should be Anyone, so that one's results can be replicated and verified. Methodolatry thus rests on the conviction that psychological events occur outside of time and history, and outside of the flesh and blood presence of real human beings. To this desire for epistemological purity, I reply to the contrary, that all knowing is personal knowing (Polanyi, 1962). Knowledge implies a knower. Thus, in contrast to the desire for knowledge untouched by

---

[8] Byron Good (1994), the medical anthropologist, drawing on the philosophy of Ernst Cassirer, writes: "Reality is to be found within manifold human experience, and it is through the study of symbolic forms that we have access to distinctive ways of knowing and thus to what is knowable of reality" (p. 89).

human hands, a psychology appropriate to the work of integration needs to be a reflexive discipline.

Reflexivity here means that the psychologist is self-questioning. Who I am makes a difference in practice, research, and theorizing, and reflexivity means attending to these differences. Not necessarily to eliminate them, but to understand how they reveal and conceal self, other, and world. The goal is not bureaucratic impersonality but existential engagement and encounter. If I seek integration between psychology and my faith, this needs to be done reflexively too. What does my faith open up? What does it close off? Reflexivity means, moreover, living with the ambiguity of provisional knowledge, always open to those others who will have other insights.

As we steer away from the Idol of Methodology, let us avoid the Pitfall of Fideism. Fideism is "a philosophical term meaning a system of philosophy or an attitude of mind, which, denying the power of unaided human reason to reach certitude, affirms that the fundamental act of human knowledge consists in an act of faith, and the supreme criterion of certitude is authority" (Sauvage, 1909). Contemporary versions of fideism are biblically-based psychologies, those that in the words of Robert C. Roberts (2000) "try to see how psychology ... looks when brought under the lordship of Jesus Christ" (p. 148), a program which Roberts would extend to biology and to philosophy. Fideism reduces scientific and philosophical thinking to expressions of faith, creating a nice little preserve for groupthink, but forgoing significant reflexive encounters. In distrusting our ability to know, these approaches paradoxically claim to have the secret key to knowledge. Uncertainty in science and philosophy disappears, because our position is guaranteed, not as in positivism by the cult of fact, but now by a cult of authority. Gadamer's conception of the philosophical frame of mind guides us here again toward reflexivity, when he writes: "In philosophy the worst thing is when one cannot take one's own standpoint completely apart and start anew, but rather one believes that once one has settled a certain point, one can simply start out from there" (in Palmer, 2001, p. 62). Scientific thought, as philosophical thought, has its own demands and integrity, and this means, not in a pejorative sense, that faith is one of the prejudices to examine. Reflexively examining one's faith in the context of psychological work is not the same as the self-examination of oneself in the light of faith. It is, rather, the acknowledgment of the relative autonomy of thinking and the limitation of appeals to authority.

Avoiding relativism and foundationalism

The voyage taken thus far may strike some as advocating a kind of relativism. As we steer clear of this vortex, we have to avoid striking the rock of foundationalism. Relativism claims (in the terms developed here) that symbolic structures, especially language, determine and enclose knowledge, and that different symbolic orders give us distinct worlds. Knowledge is socially constructed without remainder. Foundationalism, its mirror image, asserts that there is a system of clear and distinct ideas, expressed unambiguously, that mirrors the real in itself. To relativism, we reply: there are no closed worlds, because worlds collide, trade, intermarry, conquer, assimilate, and learn from each other. The symbolic order is the order of dialogue and of recognition of the otherness of the other. To foundationalism, we reply, in the words of Gadamer (1989), "Even if . . . we are fundamentally aware that all human thought about the world is historically conditioned, and thus are aware that our own thought is conditioned too, we still have not assumed an unconditioned standpoint" (p. 448). In brief, no matter how much we understand our situation, know that it is structured linguistically or symbolically, we remain flesh and blood beings, situated in time and place. We never, in short, attain the status of gods. There is no overarching, context-free, ahistorical, acultural, asocial way of speaking of the world and of ourselves – or of faith, for that matter.

What way steers us between the Empty Space of Relativism and the Rocky Crags of Foundationalism? It is the way of dialogue. Dialogue thrives on differences, recognizes otherness, and has the aim of a conversation. It claims that discourse is the medium of relationship. Each partner in a dialogue engages to some extent in translation, assimilating the other's position to one's own world, and in journeying, becoming a stranger in a strange land. Arguing, fighting, bargaining, complaining, and exchanging are not out of order.

An experiential or empirical psychology

What kind of psychology would be the ship for this journey? This ship needs the instruments of the mediating symbol, reflexivity, and dialogue. It would be a science in the broadest sense of the term, which means that it relies on the givens of experience and not on the gifts of revelation. Yet it should be open to the Word, insofar as the psychologist seeks to be true to science and to faith. But which psychologies achieve the port of fidelity to science and faith? There are many ships.

First, these psychologies must be credible, in principle, to those psychologists who do not seek to integrate their faith and their science, or who do so with other faiths or other high ideals. This condition is a necessary one, for every science has its own proper autonomy, which means that its findings and theories cannot be dictated by external authority, even ecclesiastical authority. The sciences, in this regard, have also the obligation not to overstep their bounds and make claims about things, such as Revelation, that their methods cannot approach.[9] To use Adrian van Kaam's term, psychology must be "pre-theological."

---

[9] Examples of such encroachment abound in psychology, from early materialist interpretations of the human subject and Jung's critique of the doctrine of the Trinity, to

Second, it should be open to the Word of God. Here I will make a controversial claim. The psychology we seek for a *ressourcement* will be a psychology open to the Word, as the Word addresses the person of the psychologist. I mean a psychology that can make it through the narrow straits of positivism. I mean a psychology that renounces the false ideal of the fact/value dichotomy. One does not achieve this renunciation by a wholesale insertion of one's values into one's research, theorizing, or practice, but in part by recognizing the historical, social, cultural, and personal contexts within which one as an individual and as a member of intellectual and other communities operates. Psychology is not an impersonal enterprise; flesh and blood individuals, to whom the world of the psyche is both revealed and concealed, accomplish it. We have presuppositions, biases, and prejudices that we cannot know in their totality – our descendants will see them better than we do – although we can acknowledge that they exist. But these constraints are also our means of encountering the real. The name for this simultaneous constraint and vehicle is language: "Being that can be understood is language," writes Gadamer (1989, p. 474), summing up a century of thought. Thus, these psychologies will acknowledge the mediated character of all experience and all knowing, by means of their reflexive stance. Finally, this openness has a negative criterion: it eliminates from consideration those psychologies that are reductionistic in any sense, because they systematically obscure the possibility of the psychologist achieving any integration. So these psychologies foster dialogue. They are seaworthy ships, to prolong the metaphor yet again!

Such psychologies exist. Each one is a partial answer to the question of integration. Let me name but three, from three different intellectual traditions in psychology. The first is phenomenological or human science psychology. Second, there is critical psychology, which has affected social and health psychologies in particular. Third, there are interesting approaches in the depth psychologies, that is, in those psychologies that start with the notion of the unconscious. This list is not inclusive and, in principle, any psychology, such as cognitive or neurophysiological psychologies, could be the vehicle for the journey. The three discussed here have the advantage of a long tradition of theoretical reflexivity.

There are a variety of phenomenological psychologies, all of which emphasize description and the understanding of meaning as central to psychology. They also reckon with the relationships between psychology and philosophical thought. They include the Utrecht school, which rejected the natural scientific emphasis on method, stressing instead the intellectual and personal formation of the potential phenomenological psychologist. By contrast, American

Seligman's proposal that positive psychology can replace religion. Seligman (2002) would reconceive of God not as a Creator, because that is "hard to swallow for the scientifically minded person" (p. 259), but would see God as the *telos* of evolution and human progress, which positive psychology promotes. Positivism dies hard.

phenomenological psychology, as represented by Amedeo Giorgi, has articulated methodological positions, attempting to be true to phenomenological principles and to bridge the gap with natural scientific psychology. Another variation of phenomenological psychology is that articulated by Adrian van Kaam, whom we have met already. Van Kaam distinguished between pre-theological and theological inquiries into the human condition. In *The existential foundations of psychology* (1966b), he spoke of the pre-theological psychology as an anthropological psychology. He later used other terms and distinguished between psychology and "formation science," but his approach remained the same. He warned against what he called "such false 'hybrids' as theo-psychology and psycho-theology" (Van Kaam and Muto, 1995, p. 143), which arise when we loose sight of differences between disciplines. Psychology is not theology, but he criticized those psychologies that "reject the very notion of transcendence" (p. 141), even though the findings of these "differential theories" can be incorporated into a broader conception of psychology that does recognize the necessity of openness to transcendence. He exemplified this approach in many works, including *The art of existential counseling* (Van Kaam, 1966a).

A more contemporary trend within the phenomenological tradition is that indebted to the thought of Emmanuel Levinas. For these psychologists (see, for example Gantt and Williams, 2002), many of whom are interested in psychotherapy, what Levinas offers is a way of articulating the Other's transcendence of whatever knowledge we may have of him or her. The relationship with the Other is first of all ethical, and ethics, far from being grounded in ontology or philosophical anthropology, grounds them. "Ethics is first philosophy," wrote Levinas (1969), in his account of how language, as exemplifying recognition of the transcendence – or infinity, to use his term – of the Other, is the precondition for knowledge of the Other. There is no concept of the Other, who is not an intentional object, but a face who calls us out of our worlds, conceptual and otherwise. Hospitality, gratitude, guilt, and justice are called forth in our relationship with the Other. Such considerations undermine both foundationalism and relativism in psychological theorizing.

So much for phenomenological psychology, and now to the second type. Critical psychology is a fairly recent trend, arising in part as a result of the so-called crisis in social psychology in the 1970s. The critical character of critical psychology has a number of dimensions: it is critical of the philosophical grounds of natural scientific psychology, arguing, among other things, that psychology is a social institution, which means that it often serves existing economic and political structures in such a way as to naturalize the social, as it is said. Critical psychology, in its reflexive moves to shed light on the implicit commitments of psychological theorizing and praxis, explicitly attempts to promote justice and equality. One way it does this is through qualitative research, one of whose aims is to give a hearing to those whose voices have not been heard in psychology. Critical psychology raises questions about such topics as health, for example, asking whose conception of health does psychology promote (see Murray, 2004)? What, moreover, can critical psychology itself, which largely belongs to the academic and professional spheres of the developed world, learn from the so-called indigenous psychologies from around the world? Critical psychology, with its emphasis on the interplay of the personal and the political, opens up the possibility of questions of integration between psychology and faith, by legitimating such questioning in theorizing and researching.

Finally, there are contemporary depth psychologies. Because therapeutic praxis is their basis for theorizing, questions of the boundaries of the scientific and the religious surface often in urgency. Antoine Vergote (1990), a psychoanalyst and philosopher, has addressed these questions in considerable detail. Critical of reductionistic elements in Freud, Jung, and Lacan, he has studied experiences that both psychoanalysis and religion can illuminate. He holds that "psychoanalysis refers important themes, which also come up in religion, back to the primordial experience of the person, whereas religion lifts them up to a relation with God, which is conditioned but not determined by the psychic depth dimension" (p. 79). He recognizes the boundaries of analytic competence, which "observes only psychic reality – neither the presence nor the absence of God" (p. 92). In this it offers a corrective to often naïve and even presumptuous assertions about what "God wants for me" or for an Other. Here enters the discipline of a psychoanalytic approach, which explores psychic reality with its unconscious character and its play in our lives before and after reflection. Like phenomenological and critical psychologies, Vergote's psychoanalysis stresses the mediation of experience, reflexivity, and dialogue.

Here are three types of psychology that foster the work of integration in the person of the psychologist. They not only remain open to the work of integration, they can contribute to it by the discipline in thought and feeling that they can promote. One thing that all three have in common, to restate the main theme once again, is recognition of the mediated character of experience and knowledge. All that we can grasp is given by means of symbols, myths, discourse, and even instrumentation, symbolic forms giving us access to the real. Blandly put, all knowledge is perspectival. More fully said, all our knowing and doing has contexts, horizons, and direction, which we do not create. They are the gifts and the blinders of our traditions, cultures, and histories. But insofar as these psychologies emphasize as well the personal aspect of knowing, they remain in principle open to the contributions of faith. This openness is important if in our lives we will aspire to some kind of integration between psychology and faith. How can the gifts of faith, coming to psychology from the outside, make a difference?

One thought comes from Jean-Luc Marion (1999), a philosopher who has taken up again the earlier debate over the possibility of a Christian philosophy. After observing that Revelation shows us things that reason and experience cannot know, he suggests that because the revelation that "God is love" transcends reason, "charity opens a field of new phenomena to knowledge, but this field remains invisible to natural reason alone" (p. 255). Charity reveals the other as Other. The psychologist, who seeks integration between faith and science, then, would follow the lead of love. This is but a start, and it would direct attention to what cannot be grasped in our science, and what cannot be contained in our grasp. But it can be intimated even through a glass, darkly. When we practice our psychology with charity, then something of integration takes place.

These psychologies are rooted in the mundane, the sensuous, the material, the bodily, and at the same time, they point beyond this sphere to something universal, transcendent, purposive. What I propose is that these items and, indeed, all psychology, have a paradoxical structure, not integrating psychology and religion.

An indigenous psychology?

These conclusions secure a psychology open to one and all, Catholics and non-Catholics alike. That has been the goal since Mercier, a psychology open to the light of Revelation but not based upon it, grounded in that other light, Reason, that guides all humanity. This analysis seems to rule out an explicitly Catholic psychology, as it rules out an explicitly Jewish or Hindu psychology as well. But there is a presupposition in a call for such a universal psychology, a presumption contested in recent years by advocates of indigenous psychologies. Indigenous psychologies have developed over the past several decades in many countries around the world, and there are varieties of indigenous psychology. The variety that makes most sense in the present context, given the history that we have examined, is one which is not interested primarily importing scientific psychology into a foreign market. Instead, it is that type of indigenous psychology that "is characterized by some form of opposition to, rejection of, or simply distancing from a way of doing psychology that is characterized as Western or American" (Danziger, 2006, p. 270). This type has appeal here because of the character of conflicts between scientific psychology and Catholic thought and life over the past century. While we have seen accommodations and creative syntheses, assimilations and trading zones, for the most part, the underlying commitments of scientific psychology to a type of individualism and to a type of science remained unquestioned, at least until the humanists came along. But the indigenous psychology movement offers an alternative way to frame the whole enterprise of psychology. The indigenous psychologies seek to include local cultural categories into psychology, and not simply import its discursive objects from western scientific psychology, which is seen, rather, as also a psychology rooted in a particular cultural setting. In this area, critical reflection on the nature of psychology meets cultural reflection.

One of the areas addressed by psychologists developing indigenous psychology is the place of religion in such psychologies. As the overview by Allwood and Berry (2006) observes, in some indigenous psychologies, attempts are made to incorporate religious categories: "Philippine IP [indigenous psychology] was described as being influenced by Catholic philosophy and as not separated from religion and philosophy; Indian IP was described as being based on Hindu philosophy; and in Iran, at least some versions of IP are clearly influenced by, or even based on, Islam" (p. 265). Stating this does not solve the problem of what such influence means, but it does raise the question of a Catholic psychology in a new context. However, this proposal goes against the grain of other proposals for a Catholic psychology, one based on natural law moral philosophy (Brugger, 2009). Such a Catholic psychology would not see itself as one culturally-based form of psychologizing, but as having universal application.

But if psychology has its roots in the lifeworld, then psychology has many grounds from which it springs; indeed, there are many lifeworlds (or cultures) from which it has sprung and into which it has been planted – more often as not, as a non-native species. Hence the call for indigenous psychologies, those that draw upon cultural traditions that grasp the psychological, that specify practices of healing and guiding, that map out the course of life and its ends in various ways.

So why not a Catholic indigenous psychology? Why not, indeed! Such a psychology could serve the Catholic culture, just as a Hindu indigenous psychology, a Chinese indigenous psychology, could serve those cultures and draw on their cultural knowledges. As soon as one says this, however, a further complication arises. "Catholic" is not the same kind of category as "Chinese" or "Hindu," since there are Catholic Chinese and Indians. The Catholic psychologies proposed to date are decidedly European and North American in origin, and they have not reckoned with what the theologians are currently reckoning with: namely, the question of the one and the many when it comes to Christianity and world cultures. There is tension between the call for a Catholic indigenous psychology and the call to be a catholic, that is, universal psychology.

This leads to the conclusion that what is called for would be Catholic indigenous psychologies. To some extent, they already exist: pastoral psychology, which formed in a trading zone, as we have seen. But – to further the metaphor – what if we did not stay on the frontier but went into the interior? Might not we find subcultures in psychology that would require a Catholic psychology? Indeed, a Catholic psychology in this sense, would not be *an* indigenous psychology, it would itself be something like a Catholic-indigenous psychology, one that was rooted in a notion of the "people of God" throughout the world. Just as the Church does not, in the ideal, colonize local cultures (an ideal all too often ignored in the past), so such a psychology would address local issues and the global Church.

The soul

However conceived, the center of this paradoxical discipline is the soul. To think anew the possibilities for moving within the boundaries established between psychology and Catholic thought and life, for this *ressourcement*, we shall need some new – and old – categories. The most significant of these is the soul. The soul's dismissal was the foundational condition for the establishment of modern scientific psychology, even though in some quarters – for example, the Jungian and the Neoscholastic – the soul endured. So it is wrong to say that the soul was merely a discarded category in modern psychology. It remained in the "minority reports" of the discipline. That was not the case with the soul in the pre-modern world, where the soul had center stage. Can a meaningful conception of the soul be thought for psychology? There is no question here of conceding the most important category of psychology to the authority of the theologians, since theological formulations of the soul already drew from philosophical and naturalistic (for example, from Aristotle) sources. The soul never was, as affirmed by Victor White, purely a supernatural category. The soul was rejected as methodological (and metaphysical) naturalism prevailed; to consider again the soul is therefore to call naturalism into question, without capitulating to a supernaturalism or to a non-secular psychology. The theologians have something to say, as do the empirical psychologists.

This reflection on the soul should be seen in light of the question of the relationships between science and religion, which have woven their way through this book. Here we can add another narrow strait to sail through: the opposition between naturalism and supernaturalism, first discussed in Chapter 1. I do so by noting that throughout most of history, the category of the soul was only in part concerned with "the spiritual." The soul, in the Aristotelian tradition was the form of a living being, the actuality of an organism (plant, animal, and human), and so belonged to nature. At the same time, the soul has always had in the western tradition a special affinity with death and the beyond. It is a boundary category with a long history as such. So for the purpose of furthering the science/religion dilemma of modern thought, it is, ironically, ideally suited. Automatic rejection of the idea of the soul is as unreflective as passionate insistence on its inclusion. It is the most uncomfortable of categories for psychology, making it grist for our mill.

At the end of Chapter 8, we saw that embodiment was a key location of the challenges made by psychology over the past century to authoritative Church positions. The present analysis on the place of the soul in psychology is also a way to address the issue of embodiment, since the polarity of soul/body haunts it.

So, a commencement. Although it is said that scientific psychology rejected any notion of the soul – so the narrative has gone over the years – in fact, it did not. As we have seen, the Neoscholastics, from Pace and Moore to Arnold and

Gannon, kept soul in psychology. The dynamic psychologists, too, including Victor White and the Catholic psychoanalysts, retained a notion of the psyche. However, despite this, with a few exceptions, they affirmed a dichotomy between empirical psychology, which could presuppose a notion of the soul without addressing it directly, and philosophical psychology, which could formulate it.

Elsewhere in psychology, others did not simply reject a notion of soul as important for psychology. Külpe (1920) for one continued to declare that psychology is the science of the soul. Even Freud, according to Bettelheim (1983), spoke of *Seele*, or soul, as of course did Jung. In other words, what I am claiming is that there is another narrative to be told, one that like many others, has been neglected in how we tell the history of psychology.

It is not that psychology completely dismissed the soul from service, but that psychology has for the most part ignored it. However, if the contested boundaries between psychology and Catholicism (and between psychology and religious traditions in general) are to be explored further in this postmodern and post-colonial world, then the soul must be included in psychology as well. It forms too large a part in many of these religious traditions and discourses to be ignored. Moreover, to actualize a *ressourcement* of psychology, and deal not only with explicitly religious texts, but all those which assume a religious background, or draw upon it, or spring from it, including medical, rhetorical, philosophical, as well as theological texts, psychology must deal with the category of the soul or psyche, for these traditions, which are the sources to draw from, dealt with it.

To begin this task – a somewhat strange thing for an ending – consider several psychological contributions to an understanding and potential significance of the soul. Let me sound again Moore's caution as we begin: "To say that psychology is the science of the soul assumes at the outset a metaphysical theory. It is better to start on common ground." I would modify this statement, however, and state that we will say that psychology is the science of the soul, without assuming a metaphysical theory of what the soul is. It is indeed better to start on common ground. I would, however, make one assumption that is metaphysical. That is, I assume that "soul" and "psyche" and their equivalents in other languages are not empty or meaningless signifiers. I also assume that this category is heavily laden with cultural and historical significance that is difficult, if not impossible, to untangle. Its conceptual ambiguity I take as a good place to start. Soul is, in addition to being a concept in philosophical and psychological systems, also a symbol that points to the depth dimension of human existence. By way of example, consider (for some readers, remember) "soul music," an American, an African-American, cultural phenomenon of the mid-twentieth century. What did "soul" mean in the blues and in "soul music"? According to the ethnomusicologist, Charles Keil (1966) who studied it, using what psychologists would call qualitative research, soul was an ideology in

Geertz's sense.[10] Soul in this context was a symbolic and rhetoric term that addressed identity, community, living, dying, sensing, willing, etc. The question is not to try to define this particular cultural expression as to recognize its existence. Whatever the fate of "soul" has been in academic psychology, it has continued to flourish in common sense and everyday life, in "folk psychology" if you will. As a signifier, a sign, with deep roots in the lifeworld, psychology can include it in its *ressourcement* a drink from this spring as well.

These remarks serve to argue that soul is not an antiquarian object only. Like all thought, as Alden Fisher reminded us, psychology has its roots in the lifeworld. But to further this commencement in departure, we turn to a few contributions for psychology concerning the soul. Consider five sources: first, from Magda Arnold, one of the leading Neoscholastics, and an important empirical psychologist; second, from Victor White, the Thomistic theologian and Jungian analyst; third, from James Hillman, one of the leading "post-Jungians," to use Andrew Samuel's (1985) term; fourth, from Stephan Strasser and Merleau-Ponty, two phenomenological philosophers; and fifth, from John Milbank, leader of the contemporary "radical orthodoxy" movement in theology.

Magda Arnold discussed the soul in many places, to be sure, one of which was "The Concept of Mind in Psychology" (Arnold, 1977). In this brief essay, Arnold presented the Aristotelian concept of the soul as the form of the body (p. 5). She focused on the resulting unity of the organism, of the person, who acts in various ways, and she distinguished sensory and conceptual activity along these lines (as we have seen, Moore studied this distinction experimentally). For Arnold, one implication of this view is that it instructs psychology "to treat each person as an individual, a center of activity and self-determination, and to compare him with others of his kind, thus transcending the 'idiographic versus nomothetic' alternative as well" (p. 7). This now to us familiar emphasis on the person as an organism, that is, an ensouled being, at the same time provides a position whereby psychology can engage in its *ressourcement*, because it has common ground with much of ancient and medieval psychological thought, which now does not appear so antiquated. And it opens up new avenues for the future of psychology. Timothy Gannon, one of Moore's students, whose earlier work (1954) began from the same premises that Arnold sketched, suggested in his final book a way into the future of psychology by drawing on the implication of the organism as an ensouled being: semiotics, the science of signs. For Gannon (1991), a sign is "a relation between the organism and some environmental change that needs to be evaluated in terms of the

---

[10] Keil explained: "A particular ideology can be viewed and analyzed in at least two different ways. It can be interpreted in terms of the socio-psychological conflict, stresses, and strains that give rise to it (this is the usual approach), or in terms of ideological thought, the formulation and interworking of symbols" (p. 165). Keil focused on the latter.

organism's immediate interests and ultimate survival" (p. 238). While not limited to characteristically human signs, such as the linguistic, the study of signs would show its value when this level of signification is addressed. Semiotics emphasizes the unity and interplay between organism and environment. Gannon was not alone in this suggestion. Walker Percy (1975), Julia Kristeva (1989), and Jacques Lacan (1977), to name some of the significant thinkers in this area, also stress the psychological's semiotic character. What Gannon provided, however, was a link between semiotics and the soul, which is not emphasized in the others, with the exception of Percy. Moreover, Gannon's suggestion points in the direction of a link with work in the Jungian tradition, because Jung emphasized the interpretative activity of the psyche vis-à-vis the world. With an emphasis on the sign in Gannon and Percy, however, this line of thinking comes center stage.

Victor White's work has been extensively discussed earlier in this book. At this point, I want to indicate only that for White, psychology deals with signs, and that they are the link to religious life, his chief concern. White was especially troubled, with regard to religious education, with the "impoverishment of images" in the life of the Church, an impoverishment resulting from their one-sidedness and their being uprooted from the archetypal depths of the soul. Like Arnold, Gannon, and Percy, White was Thomistic in his philosophical anthropology, so he emphasized the unity of the person. Unlike them, he stressed the soul's image-making capacity, which to us, in our conscious self-knowledge, is as unknown as the processes of digestion, as an otherness within ourselves, yet ourselves. To grasp this aspect of our psychological lives, White like Jung spoke of image and symbol as the "organs" of the psyche, as objectively real and self-organizing as bodily organs.

Continuing in this line is James Hillman, who has made soul central to his work. In *Re-Visioning Psychology* (1975) Hillman writes: "By *soul* I mean, first of all, a perspective rather than a substance, a viewpoint toward things rather than a thing itself. This perspective is reflective; it mediates events and makes differences between ourselves and everything that happens. Between us and events, between the doer and the deed, there is a reflective moment" (p. x). In an earlier work, he said that in his usage, soul "is really not a concept, but a symbol" (Hillman, 1976), thereby grounding his psychological theorizing in the symbol and the image, rather than in the concept. Hillman's archetypal psychology, and Jung's too, according to Hillman, belongs more to the Platonic tradition in western thought than it does to the Kantian, so often associated with Jung. This way of approaching the place of the soul in psychology differs from the Aristotelian–Thomistic one, to be sure, but what they share is an explicit concern for the soul and its place in psychology. In archetypal psychology, the imagination is primary in psychological life, not perception as it is the Aristotelian tradition. Putting the imagination first makes the questions of death, love, and transcendence of primary importance, not topics to be addressed after the basics of perception and physiology are worked over.

Reconsideration of the soul brings back the topic of the will. We have seen that the will has been a recurrent theme from the beginnings of Neoscholastic psychology to the work of van Kaam. The will played an important role in the praxis of these psychologies, as we saw in will-training and in the emphasis on willing in phenomenological psychology. The will has many aspects to explore, but chief among them is the centrality of the provisional nature of a human person. With acts of will, one becomes what one was not yet. Emphasis on the will would accentuate the fact that psychology deals not with fixed substances, but with subjectivities "on the way."

Stephan Strasser's 1957 book, *The soul in metaphysical and empirical psychology*, presents a development of the Neoscholastic conception of the soul. His study was limited, in that he primarily dealt with introspective studies in treating empirical psychology (although he included an appendix to the English language edition on behavior). The value of Strasser's series of studies is that he approached the question of the soul with a phenomenological method, focusing his investigations on the Thomistic tradition (similar to the work of Donceel, Arnold, and in a different way, van Kaam). After arguing that the empirical and philosophical psychologists do not mean the same thing by "soul," that indeed they do not even speak the same language, Strasser developed the point that whatever soul means, it is not an object and so cannot be known by means of objective knowledge: "That which I am primordially, i.e. in such a way that no exteriority, foreignness, disposability, plurality and real composition breaks its existential immediacy, that is my soul, my spiritual soul" (p. 74), a statement that he quickly qualified by saying that this does not exclude also my being my body. This formulation is but the beginning of Strasser's reflections, and while we cannot present them all, two points need to be made. First, because he dealt with the Aristotelian tradition and saw it prolonged in phenomenological investigations of the lived-body, Strasser related the soul to living, much as Aristotle did. In his concluding study, he writes: "*the psychical being belongs metaphysically to the realm of the besouled body*, the domain of animality, the sphere of sense life" (p. 207). He retained the distinction between empirical and metaphysical psychology, concluding that, "*the empirical psychologist considers the soul through the medium of objectifications and quasi-objectifications.* He grasps the spirit to the extent that it is more or less alien to itself. Thus it becomes clear that he obtains a negative picture of the spirit" (p. 227). It is for the metaphysical psychologist to address the "spiritual being," that is, the being who grasps universals and who transcends limitations of time and place.

Since Strasser recalls the work of Merleau-Ponty, it would be worthwhile to say something about the soul in his work. In *The structure of behavior* Maurice Merleau-Ponty (1963) discussed "The relations of the soul and body and the problem of perceptual consciousness" (p. 185). It was his only prolonged discussion of the soul, perhaps because he found the term, like others, too sedimented with philosophical meaning and thus an impediment rather than a vehicle to understanding.

The category of *form* constituted, for Merleau-Ponty, a way through the conflicting truths of mechanism and vitalism. He saw in psychology's turn to behavior an implicit recognition that neither *ism* adequately comprehends vital and psychological phenomena. "Form" is a perceptual and not an ontological category; there are no forms-in-themselves. A form is a unity, a whole, a meaning or a sense, expressed in the arrangements and activities of a set of particulars, in a situation that embraces the perceiver. Form is not any one of the facts of particulars, and so does not have thing-like character. Neither is form an idea in observing consciousness, i.e. a synthetic judgment that has no empirical existence. Form is a relationship of sense between the perceiver and the perceived, a physiognomic configuration.

For Merleau-Ponty, both vitalism[11] and mechanism err in calling an organism an object, i.e. an assemblage of parts having no reality as a unity. If we attend to the perceptual world, then we are present to an organism as a unity of signification, of meanings expressed in behavior. Such perceived forms are a priori in our experience and not reducible to the elements which subsequent analysis finds in them.

Vitalism, unlike mechanism, at least acknowledges that life differs from inanimate nature, but locates the vital principle as one object among the others. (Moore seemed to succumb to this way of thinking in supporting his Aristotelian conception of the organism with Driesch's vitalism, thereby arguing for a "vital principle" to animate the organism.) The category of form allows us to affirm the distinctiveness of life without presupposing two different substances. Form replaces substance for the understanding of both soul and body. The perspectival character of perception – when acknowledged – enables us to say that all things show themselves through perspective. The "thing" is not a hidden substance producing the perspectives, the phenomena.

This all too brief summary of Merleau-Ponty on "form" prepares the way for a sketch of a phenomenology of the soul, the main points of which are presented in *The structure of behavior*.

First, everyday consciousness experiences a relationship of soul and body, "body" being for such a consciousness not an object, but access to the world. To understand how it happens that an intention produces bodily movement, one cannot begin with body-as-object. I do not intend to move levers and pulleys when I decide to raise my arm. The body I move is, he writes, the living envelope of my actions; it is myself, me as somebody. Insofar as my body

---

[11] Recall that Moore turned to Driesch's vitalism in his defense of formal causality. Merleau-Ponty addresses formal causes without recourse to vitalistic presuppositions, which are, in the final analysis, non-Thomistic and non-phenomenological.

responds to my intentions, soul manifests itself through the new figuration, the gesturing transformation of the body. He states that body is to soul as perspective is to a thing. Body is the manifestation of soul, simultaneously its appearance and concealment. On the level of perceptual awareness, the body (as form) is the appearance of soul. The perceived body in a particular situation is the manifestation/concealment of soul.

Second, further reflection shows that not all acts of behavior can be called "soul." "Soul" and "body" are two kinds of meaning perceivable by self and other. Neither is a substance, for both are relational realities co-constituted by their situations. Using traditional language, Merleau-Ponty says that the soul "acts" on the body when behavior cannot be said to have physical or vital significance, i.e. when behavior is symbolic, establishing the meaning of the situation it inhabits. Soul is a transcendence of the given situation, a creation of meaning.

In interpreting soul as structure or form, Merleau-Ponty confronted physiology. True, the nervous system's integrity is the material cause of soulful structures, for the latter depend upon the former – this is a truth of naturalism. Yet soul is the form of the situated body in symbolic behavior, which form defines the very functioning of the nervous system.

Third, we are warned that soul "as the meaning of the body" and body "as manifestations of soul" evoke external relations. While there is a truth to dualism – timidity and spinal cord injury can keep intentions disembodied – "soul" and "body" are indistinguishable in acts of transcendence. Thus, soul and body are relative terms, whose meanings depend "on whether the 'formation' succeeds or fails and whether the inertia of the subordinated dialectics [biographically and socially predetermined forms of behavior] allows itself to be surmounted or not" (1963, p. 209). He introduced a tension between soul and body: if the former is the transcending of the actual, the latter is the thickness and inertia of the actual. They are the same and different in perceptual experience and "their empirical connection is based on the original operation which establishes a meaning in a fragment of matter and makes it live, appear and be in it. In returning to this structure as the fundamental reality, we are rendering comprehensible both the distinction and union of the soul and body" (ibid.). Ensouling, therefore, is an action requiring effort. Soul has no guarantee; it can be cultivated or it can atrophy in the course of a human life.

To make this point more vivid, I can find no better examples of the soul as observed than those provided by Viktor Frankl (1963) in his account of his imprisonment in the concentration camps. In describing the starvation that the prisoners suffered, he wrote that: "Those who have not gone through a similar experience can hardly conceive of the soul-destroying mental conflict and clashes of will power which a famished man experiences" (p. 48). In particular, loss of face, in all the senses of that word, is synonymous with soul-destruction. And the insight was founded in perception, as we read in this passage:

After many observations we knew the symptoms well, which made the correctness of our prognoses quite certain. "He won't last long," or "This is the next one," we whispered to each other, and when, during our daily search for lice, we saw our own naked bodies in the evening, we thought alike: This body here, my body, is really a corpse already. What has become of me? I am but a small portion of a great mass of human flesh . . . of a mass behind barbed wire, crowded into a few earthen huts; a mass of which daily a certain portion begins to rot because it has become lifeless.

(pp. 48–9)

Hopeless situations, in which a person no longer looks forward to a future; in which terror makes torture and death the price for attempts to transcend an actuality defined by others; in which these others view the person as sub- or non-human: such settings can leave one soulless. Here is an idea of soul as a basis for phenomenological inquiry.

Soul is the form of the situated body in the act of forming. Soul is the appearing, the taking shape, the manifesting face. "Body" is the form already formed; "soul" is the event of its transformation: "The body in general is an ensemble of paths already traced, of powers already constituted; the body is the acquired dialectical soil upon which a higher 'formation' is accomplished, and the soul is the meaning which is then established" (Merleau-Ponty, 1963, p. 210). Merleau-Ponty saw in the upwelling of something novel in the world a phenomenon of the soul. This insight recalls Strasser's thinking through the meaning of the "spiritual" in relation to the soul, namely, that it deals with what goes beyond the here-and-now.

For Merleau-Ponty, soul and body are perceptual givens. The dialectics of human existence operates between the pole of transcendence of the actual and the sedimentation of the new meanings thereby established. To describe this, the momentum of existence, he sometimes spoke of sublimation, and drew on an image from Heraclitus, describing soul in terms of boiling and vaporization. Soul happens as a transcendence of the fixities of sense. These events of sublimating or boiling are the appearance of the phenomenon of soul. Traditional language can be re-appropriated, for we no longer speak here of substances: soul animates, soul transcends, or rather, soul is the animat*ing*, the transcend*ing* of what is.

For Merleau-Ponty: "the connection of the soul and body signifies nothing other than the *eccitas* of knowledge by profiles" (1963, p. 214).[12] The soul is made present in profiles, in actions, in physiognomies, which give the form of the person but also point beyond themselves to other profiles possible and

---

[12] *Eccitas* is ecceity, the "making present," here meaning that what we know we know through profiles or perspectives. We never grasp the whole thing, especially the whole person, in one grasp or manifestation.

impossible. The invisible is given through the visible, the soul through the body. Soul is the invisibility, the hiddenness, given in the presence of the expressive body, in our behavior. And soul is not only hidden from others, it is also hidden from self. We know ourselves, too, only through profiles. What better term than "soul" to express the hiddenness of one's own life? In his discussion of distinctly human behavior, Merleau-Ponty mentioned three: speech, suicide, and revolution. Such acts are soulful because they negate the actual. Such soulful acts are rare, as Merleau-Ponty realized – and his choice of these three reflected his social milieu – because for the most part, behavior is largely determined by social and biological conditions. Such is the ambiguity of our situated freedom. Nevertheless, Merleau-Ponty (1964) sought to articulate a sense of soul in order to prevent the loss of the idea of humanity. In one of his last essays, "Eye and Mind," he wrote that it could happen that people think of themselves of automata – the condition Frankl faced in the concentration camps: "then, since man really becomes the *manipulandum* he takes himself to be, we enter into a cultural regimen where there is neither truth or falsity concerning man and history, into a sleep, or a nightmare, from which there is no awakening" (p. 160).

The psychologist (the empirical psychologist in Strasser's sense) does address the soul directly, despite Strasser's claim to the contrary. What the psychologist studies are ways of becoming, a description of the task of psychology that brings it back to its standard topics: sensing, thinking, remembering, deciding, etc. This brings us to our last contribution to a psychology with soul, to the thought of the theologian John Milbank. Again, only to sketch a possibility, I find that he offers a context for the study of the most mundane psychological topics, such as perception, that extend what we have thus far considered. Milbank (2001a) engages in *ressourcement* himself, arguing that with Descartes, "the soul died, and the subject was born" (p. 335). In pre-modern notions of soul, the self was not enclosed in an interior realm cut off from the outside world. Instead, the soul "opened outwards in the very heart of its interiority to become 'in a manner all things'" (p. 336). Soul was this kind of opening, and Milbank calls the soul "an event or series of events" (p. 337) of this interactive, reciprocal character that characterizes animate life. Most important, he indicates that "what we today tend to think of as objective and subjective were thoroughly confused" (ibid.), which suggests a way of viewing soul that has links to contemporary psychological thought. In particular, Milbank (2001b) draws together insights on perception from Aristotle and Merleau-Ponty. He frames the analysis of what both thinkers mean by "the flesh." By "flesh" Merleau-Ponty referred to something elemental that names the belonging together of the organism and its environment, in that the lived-body both sees and is seen, is both situated and a point of view on situations. This emphasis on the reciprocity of organism and environment enables us to indicate that others in psychology, outside this phenomenological-theological circle, have emphasized the same thing, and in so doing, challenged the primary assumptions of twentieth-century psychology, while still insisting on the scientific status of psychology. Included here would be William James (1912), especially in his *Essays in radical empiricism*, his student Edwin B. Holt, and Holt's students, Charles C. Tolman and James J. Gibson (see Heft, 2001). This tradition of ecological psychology, especially in Gibson's work, dovetails with the ways that Merleau-Ponty and Milbank speak of the soul. So that yet another door is opened for this category in our paradoxical discipline.

Yet Milbank (2001b) the theologian asks: "Yet for Merleau-Ponty, the soul is not immortal. Can one think the soul of reciprocity without God, within immanence?" (p. 502). Milbank refers here to something explicitly theological in a Christian sense, something he finds necessary to think through the question of the lived-body and our being-in-the-world: that the thinking of the flesh, of the lived-body, of the exchanges between lived-body and world cannot be thought without also thinking of the Incarnation, the Trinity, and even the "immortality of the body" (p. 505), which the Greeks never thought. The body, the flesh, despite centuries of ascetical and puritanical suppressions, is a key idea in Christian thought, grounded in the revelations of the Word made flesh and of the Resurrection.

This has not been a complete or systematic review of the various strands wherein psychologists and others over the past century have continued to insist upon the soul as a central category for psychology. Suffice it to say that the soul is still a marginal psychological category, and it cannot be (following Hillman and Strasser) a psychological object. There is, in addition, another psychological category that overlaps that of the soul and which we have seen as its stand-in for the Neoscholastics and others: person or personality. The range of this category differs from soul, in that it has tended to emphasize unity or wholeness and that it is available to empirical research. But these terms, especially "person" point to the same significations as "soul," although from a different angle. In the Thomistic tradition, "person" is an individual rational substance, so that animals and plants are not persons, although they are ensouled beings. This is not the place to develop the relationships between "person" and "soul," only the place to indicate their reference to things in common.[13] "Person" is widely used today in philosophical and theological discourse, especially in personalism, while "soul" remains marginalized.

If the boundaries between psychology and Catholic thought are to be thought through in our time, psychologists need soul. Not as an object of investigation, to be sure, not as a presupposition for research – we do not yet have the category even remotely delimited. To delimit it, *ressourcement* comes first. For the present moment, situated where we are and from where we must take our bearings, the soul is a horizon of our thinking. The soul, that is, frames our work

[13] Vytautas J. Bieliauskas (1958), for one, addressed the relationship in the German psychological tradition.

in non-reductive ways, in league with the philosophers, theologians, humanists of the past and the present, granting them their distinctive tasks and keeping to our own. The soul as horizon keeps us mindful that psychology's work does tread on the ground of others, notably that of the Church and its two millennia of traditions. And mindful that in the direction of that horizon we are bound.

REFERENCES

Academy of Religion and Mental Health. (1960). *Religion in the developing personality: Proceedings of the Second Academy Symposium.* New York University Press.

—(1963). *Research in religion and health.* New York: Fordham University Press.

Albanese, C. (2000). The culture of religious combining: Reflections for the new American millennium. *Cross Currents,* 50(1/2), 16–22.

Allbutt, C. (1910). Neurasthenia. In C. Allbutt, and H. D. Rolleston (eds.), *System of medicine.* (vol. VIII. London: Macmillan. (pp. 727–91.)

Allers, R. (1931). *The psychology of character* (trans. E. B. Strauss). New York: Macmillan.

—(1933). *The new psychologies.* London: Sheed and Ward.

—(1938). Confessor and alienist. *Ecclesiastical Review,* 99, 401–13.

—(1939). Review of the book, *La méthode psychoanalytique et doctrine Freudienne,* by Roland Dalbiez. *The Thomist,* 1, 131–8.

—(1941). *The successful error: A critical study of Freudian psychoanalysis.* London: Sheed & Ward.

—(1948, August 27). The analyst and the confessor (Letter to the editor). *Commonweal,* 48, 474–5.

—(1961). *Existentialism and psychiatry.* Springfield, IL: Charles C. Thomas.

Allport, F. H. (1955). *Theories of perception and the concept of structure.* New York: John Wiley and Sons.

Allport, G. (1937). *Personality.* New York: Holt.

—(1940). The psychologist's frame of reference. *Psychological Bulletin,* 27, 1–28.

Allwood, C. M., and Berry, J. W. (2006). Origins and development of indigenous psychologies: An international analysis. *International Journal of Psychology,* 41, 243–68.

Amatora, M. (1954a). Encouragement of leadership by Catholics in psychology. *Catholic Educational Review,* 52, 587–96.

—(1954b). Review of the book, *Fundamental Psychiatry,* by John R. Cavanagh and James B. McGoldbrick [*sic*]). *Education,* 75(3), 199.

American Catholic Psychological Association: Third annual meeting. (1949). Akron, OH: Archives of the History of American Psychology. Collection: American Psychological Association Division 36, Box 710, Folder 22.

Angers, W. P. (1959–60). Jung's approach to religion. *Downside Review,* 78(250), 36–51.

Announcing the first meeting of the Chicago Society of Catholic Psychologists. (1936). Chicago: Dominican University Archives. Associations, Chicago Society of Catholic Psychologists 1936–1937, Box D, Folder 10.

Appleby, R. S. (1995). The triumph of Americanism: Common ground for U.S. Catholics in the twentieth century. In M. J. Weaver and R. S. Appleby (eds.), *Being right: Conservative Catholics in America*. Bloomington: Indiana University Press. (pp. 37–62.)

Aquinas, T. (1948). *Summa theologica* (vol. I). Westminster, MD: Christian Classics.

Arnold, M. B. (1954). Basic assumptions in psychology. In M. B. Arnold and J. A. Gasson (eds.), *The human person: An approach to an integral theory of personality*. New York: Ronald. (pp. 3–48.)

—(1960). *Emotion and personality* (vol. I). New York: Columbia University Press.

—(1962). *Story sequence analysis: A new method of measuring motivation and predicting achievement*. New York: Columbia University Press.

—(1977, Fall). The concept of mind in psychology. *Philosophical Psychologist*, 11, 4–7.

Arnold, M. B. and Gasson, J. A. (eds.). (1954a). *The human person: An approach to the integral theory of personality*. New York: Ronald Press.

—and—(1954b). Logotherapy and existential analysis. In Arnold and Gasson (eds.), *The human person*. (pp. 462–92.)

Arraj, J. (1988). Jungian spirituality: The question of Victor White. *Spirituality Today*, 40(3), 249–61.

Asad, T. (1993). *Genealogies of power: Discipline and reason in Christianity and Islam*. Baltimore: Johns Hopkins University Press.

Ashley, B. M. (1995). Loss of theological unity: Pluralism, Thomism, and Catholic morality. In Weaver and Appleby (eds.), *Being right: Conservative Catholics in America*. (pp. 63–87.)

Assagioli, R. (1973). *The act of will*. New York: Viking.

Aubert, R. (1981). The modernist crisis. In H. Jedin and J. Dolan (eds.), *History of the Church: The Church in the industrial age* (vol. IX.) New York: Crossroad. (pp. 420–81.)

Ayd, F. J. (1952). Review of the book, *Psychiatry and Catholicism*. *New Scholasticism*, 27, 466–8.

Baars, C. (1970). *Feeling and healing your emotions*. Plainfield, N.J.: Logos International.

Bair, D. (2003). *Jung: A biography*. Boston: Little, Brown and Co.

Baker, D. B., and Benjamin, J. Ludy T. (2005). Creating a profession: The National Institute of Mental Health and the training of psychologists, 1946–1954. In W. E. Pickren and S. F. Schneider (eds.), *Psychology and the National Institute of Mental Health*. Washington, D.C.: American Psychological Association. (pp. 181–207).

Baker, R. R., and Pickren, W. E. (2007). *Psychology and the Department of Veterans Affairs: A historical analysis of training, research, practice, and advocacy*. Washington, D.C.: American Psychological Association.

Barker, P. (1991). *Regeneration.* New York: Viking.

Barrett, E. B. (1911). *Motive force and motivation-tracts.* London: Longmans, Green and Co.

—(1915). *Strength of will.* New York: P. J. Kenedy and Sons.

—(1923a, October 13). What is the sub-conscious? *America,* 29, 609–11.

—(1923b, November 3). Methods of psycho-therapy or mind-healing. *America,* 30, 54–5.

—(1923c, November 24). Hypnotism and telepathy. *America,* 30, 129–31.

—(1924a). *Psycho-analysis and Christian morality.* London: Catholic Truth Society.

—(1924b, December 13). Studies in practical psychology. *America,* 32, 197–9.

—(1925a). *The new psychology.* New York: P. J. Kenedy and Sons.

—(1925b, January 31). Wanderlust. *America,* 32, 365–6.

—(1925c). *Man: His making and unmaking.* New York: Thomas Seltzer.

—(1927). *The Jesuit enigma.* New York: Boni and Liveright.

—(1928). The drama of Catholic confession. *Journal of Religion,* 8(2), 188–203.

—(1929a). The psychoanalysis of asceticism. In V. F. Calverton and S. D. Schmalhausen (eds.), *Sex in civilization.* New York: Macaulay. (pp. 490–503).

—(1929b). *While Peter sleeps.* New York: Washburn.

—(1930). *The magnificent illusion.* New York: Washburn.

—(1939). *The Great O'Neill.* Boston: Hale, Cushman and Flint.

Barrett, M. C. (1941). An experimental study of the Thomistic concept of the faculty of imagination (Monograph). *Studies in Psychology and Psychiatry,* 5(3).

Bartemeier, L. H. (1972). An autobiography of my religion. In P. E. Johnson (ed.), *Healer of the mind.* Nashville: Abingdon. (pp. 59–77).

Barton, A. (1974). *Three worlds of therapy: An existential-phenomenological study of the therapies of Freud, Jung, and Rogers.* Palo Alto: National Press Books.

Bassler, A. (1932). Why the Catholic Physicians Guild? *Linacre Quarterly,* 1(1), 4–5.

Behnke, J. (n.d.). Fordham University department of psychology: Department history. Available:www.fordham.edu/academics/programs_at_fordham_/psychology_departmen/department_history/index.asp.

Beirnaert, L. (1964). The mythic dimension in Christian sacramentalism. In W. Birmingham and J. E. Cunneen (eds.), *Cross currents of psychiatry and Catholic morality.* New York: Pantheon. (pp. 7–30).

Bélanger, D., and Sabourin, M. (1997). In Memoriam: Noël Mailloux, OP, STHL, DPh: 1909–1997. *International Journal of Psychology,* 32, 361–2.

Benjamin, J. Ludy T, and Baker, D. B. (2004). *From séance to science: A history of the profession of psychology in America.* Belmont, CA: Thomson Wadsworth.

Benz, E. (1957). Creator Spiritus. Die Geistlehre des Joachim von Fiore. In O. Fröbe-Kapteyn (ed.), *Eranos-Jahrbuch 25: Der Mensch und das Schöpferische.* Zürich: Rhein-Verlag. (pp. 285–355).

Berger, J. (1987, August 23). Being Catholic in America. *New York Times Sunday Magazine,* pp. 22–7; 64–5.

Bertrin, G. (1910). Notre-Dame de Lourdes. *Catholic Encyclopedia* (vol. IX). New York: Appleton. (pp. 389–91).

Bettelheim, B. (1983). *Freud and man's soul.* New York: Random House.

Bieliauskas, V. J. (1958). Der Seelenbegriff in der Psychologie der Gegenwart. In *Seelenleben und Menschenbild: Festschrift zum 60. Geburtstag von Philipp Lersch.* München: Johann Ambrosius Barth. (pp. 27–41).

—(1971). Masculinity, femininity, and conjugal love. *Journal of Religion and Health,* 10, 37–49.

—(1974). Psychology, religion, and Church. *New Catholic Encyclopedia* (vol. XVI, supplements 1967–74). New York: McGraw-Hill. (pp. 370–1).

Bier, W. C. (1947a). *Letter to Thomas J. Riches, July 1.* Akron, OH: Archives of the History of American Psychology. Collection: American Psychological Association Division 36, Box 707, Folder 5.

—(1947b). *Letter, October 14.* Akron, OH: Archives of the History of American Psychology. Collection: American Psychological Association Division 36, Box 707, Folder 5.

—(1948a). A comparative study of a seminary group and four other groups on the Minnesota multiphasic personality inventory. *Catholic University of America. Studies in psychology and psychiatry,* 7(3).

—(1948b). *Report of the Committee on Organization to the potential membership of the society of American Catholic psychologists.* Akron: Archives of the History of American Psychology. Collection of Div. 36, APA.

—(1949). *Report on the joint Denver meeting of the American Psychological Association and the American Catholic Psychological Association.* Akron, OH: Archives of the History of American Psychology. Collection: American Psychological Association Division 36, Box 709, Folder 9.

—(1953a). *Dear fellow member, December 5.* Akron, OH: Archives of the History of American Psychology. Collection: American Psychological Association Division 36, Box 707, Folder 5.

—(1953b). The place and function of the department of psychology in the liberal arts college. *National Catholic Educational Association Bulletin,* 50, 193–8.

—(1953c, July). Psychology at Fordham University. *American Catholic Psychological Association Newsletter Supplement No. 4,* 1–2.

—(1953d, November). Review of the book, *God and the unconscious,* by Victor White. *American Catholic Psychological Association Newsletter,* 3, 3–4.

—(1953e). Psychological testing of candidates and the theology of vocation. *Review for Religious,* 12(6), 291–304.

—(1954a). Practical requirements of a program for the psychological screening of candidates. *Review for Religious,* 13(1), 13–27.

—(1954b). Psychological tests in the screening of candidates in the minor seminary. *National Catholic Educational Association Bulletin,* 51(1), 128–35.

—(1955, November). ACPA survey on status of psychology in Catholic colleges. *American Catholic Psychological Association Newsletter, Supplement No. 18,* 1–2.

—(1957). *Freud and Catholics.* New York: America Press.

—(1959). Goals in pastoral psychology. *Pastoral Psychology,* 10(91), 7–13.

—(1964b). Preface. In Bier (ed.), *Personality and sexual problems in pastoral psychology* (pp. ix–xiii). New York: Fordham University Press.

—(1967a). American Catholic Psychological Association. *New Catholic Encyclopedia* (vol. I). New York: McGraw-Hill. (pp. 398–9).

—(1967b). Pastoral psychology. *New Catholic Encyclopedia* (vol. X). New York: McGraw-Hill. (pp. 1078–80).

—(1968a). Alexander Aloysius Schneiders 1909–1968: In memory and tribute. *Catholic Psychological Record*, 6(2), 65–9.

—(1971b). A modified form of the Minnesota Multiphasic Personality Inventory for religious personnel. *Theological Education*, 7(2), 121–34.

—(1973, Fall). Walter J. Coville: In memory and tribute 1914–1973. *PIRI Newsletter*, 23, 5–6. Akron, OH: Archives of the History of American Psychology. Collection: American Psychological Association Division 36, Box 706, Folder 1.

—(ed.). (1962). *Problems in addiction: Alcohol and drug addiction*. New York: Fordham University Press.

—(ed.). (1963). *The adolescent: His search for understanding*. New York: Fordham University Press.

—(ed.). (1964a). *Personality and sexual problems in pastoral psychology*. New York: Fordham University Press.

—(ed.). (1965). *Marriage: A psychological and moral approach*. New York: Fordham University Press.

—(ed.). (1968b). *Women in modern life*. New York: Fordham University Press.

—(ed.). (1970). *Psychological testing for ministerial selection*. New York: Fordham University Press.

—(ed.). (1971a). *Conscience: Its freedom and limitations*. New York: Fordham University Press.

Bihler, H. (1940, July 20). Classical interpretation of Freudian philosophy. *America*, 63, 413–14.

Binzley, R. A. (2007). American Catholicism's science crisis and the Albertus Magnus Guild, 1953–1969. *Isis*, 98, 695–723.

Bishops of Columbus, the. (2008). The Roman Catholic Diocese of Columbus. Available: www.colsdioc.org/AboutUs/TheBishopsofColumbus/tabid/276/Default.aspx.

Bishop, R. C. (2009). What is this naturalism stuff all about? *Journal of Theoretical & Philosophical Psychology*, 29, 108–13.

Blackman, L. M. (1994). What is doing history?: The use of history to understand the constitution of contemporary psychological objects. *Theory & Psychology*, 4, 485–504.

Blanshard, P. (1949). *American freedom and Catholic power*. Boston: Beacon Press.

Bohr, D. (1999). *Catholic moral tradition*. Huntington, IN: Our Sunday Visitor Publications.

Boileau, D. A. (1996). *Cardinal Mercier: A memoir*. Belgium: Peeters.

Boissarie, P. G. (1891). *Lourdes: histoire médicale 1858–1891*. Paris: Librairie Victor Lecoffre.

Boring, E. G. (1950). *A history of experimental psychology* (2nd edn.). New York: Appleton-Century-Crofts.

Boring, E. G. (1954). Science and faith: A foreword. In H. Misiak and V. Stoudt, *Catholics in psychology: A historical survey*. New York: McGraw-Hill Book Co. (pp. ix–xi).

Boudens, R. (1970). George Tyrrell and Cardinal Mercier: A contribution to the history of modernism. *Église et Théologie*, 1, 313–51.

Bouscaren, T. L., SJ, and Ellis, A. C., SJ. (1946). *Canon law: A text and commentary.* Milwaukee: Bruce Publishing Co.

Bowen, L., Bowen, B. C., and Ames, M. B. (2009). *About Croswell Bowen (1905–1971).* eOneill.com. Available: www.eoneill.com/library/curse/about.htm.

Braceland, F. J. (1949, May 7). Review of the book, *Peace of soul*, by Fulton J. Sheen. *America*, 81(5), 192–3.

—(1959). A psychiatrist examines the relationship between psychiatry and the Catholic clergy. *Pastoral Psychology*, 10(19), 14–20.

—(1964). Preface. In W. Birmingham and J. E. Cunneen (eds.), *Cross currents of psychiatry and Catholic morality*. New York: Pantheon. (pp. v–x).

—and Stock, M. (1963). *Modern psychiatry: A handbook for believers.* Garden City, NY: Doubleday and Co.

Braden, C. S. (1963). *Spirits in rebellion: The rise and development of New Thought.* Dallas: Southern Methodist University Press.

Braude, A. (2001). *Radical spirits: Spiritualism and women's rights in nineteenth-century America* (2nd edn.). Bloomington: Indiana University Press.

Brennan, R. E. (1937). *General psychology: An interpretation of the science of mind based on Thomas Aquinas.* New York: Macmillan.

—(1940a). Review of the book, *Cognitive psychology. Thomist*, 2, 156–63.

—(1940b). Review of the book, *The successful error. Thomist*, 2, 581–584.

—(1941). *Thomistic psychology.* New York: Macmillan.

—(1945). *History of psychology, from the standpoint of a Thomist.* New York: Macmillan.

Brentano, F. (1973). *Psychology from an empirical standpoint* (trans. A. C. Rancurello, D. B. Terrell, and L. L. McAlister). London: Routledge and Kegan Paul. (First published 1874.)

Bridgman, P. W. (1927). *The logic of modern physics.* New York: Macmillan.

Broman, T. H. (2002). Introduction: Some preliminary considerations on science and civil society. *Osiris*, 17, 1–21.

Brooke, J. (1991). *Science and religion: Some historical perspectives.* Cambridge University Press.

—and Cantor, G. (1998). *Reconstructing nature: The engagement of science and religion.* Edinburgh: T. and T. Clark.

Brother Henry C. Ringkamp. (1936). A vocational guidance project in McBride High School. *Catholic Educational Review*, 34(9), 553–60.

Brownson, H. F. (1908). Orestes A. Brownson. *Catholic Encyclopedia* (vol. III). New York: Appleton. (pp. 1–3).

Brownson, O. A. (1869, June). Spiritism and Spiritists. *Catholic World*, 9, 289–302.

—(1872, March). Owen on Spiritism. *Catholic World*, 14, 803–12.

Bruehl, C. P. (1920a). Spiritism. *Ecclesiastical Review*, 62, 401–12.

—(1920b). A survey of the present condition of philosophy (concluded). *Ecclesiastical Review*, 62, 584–9.

—(1921a). Some new ways in psychology. *Ecclesiastical Review*, 64, 640–4.

—(1921b). The literature of psycho-analysis. *Ecclesiastical Review*, 65, 539–44.

—(1923a, June 9). Religion and neurotic troubles. *America*, 29, 174–6.

—(1923b, June 15). Religion and psychotherapeutics. *America*, 29, 202–3.

—(1923c, June 23). Moral aspects of psychotherapeutics. *America*, 29, 221–2.

—(1923d, June 30). The psychopathic clinic and spiritual guidance. *America*, 29, 245–7.

—(1923e). *Psychoanalysis*. New York: Paulist Press.

Brugger, E. C. (2009). Psychology and Christian anthropology. *Edifications: Journal for the Society of Christian Psychology*, 3(1), 5–19.

Bruner, J. (1990). *Acts of meaning*. Cambridge, MA: Harvard University Press.

Buchanan, R. D. (2002). On *not* "giving psychology away": The MMPI and public controversy over testing in the 1960s. *History of Psychology*, 5, 284–309.

Bucke, R. M. (1901). *Cosmic consciousness: A study in the evolution of the human mind*. New York: Causeway Books.

Buescher, J. B. (2002). More lurid than lucid: The Spiritualist invention of the word *Sexism*. *Journal of the American Academy of Religion*, 70(3), 561–92.

Buhler, C. (1974). The scope of humanistic psychology. *Education*, 95, 3–8.

Buonaiuti, E. (1954). Ecclesia spiritualis. In J. Campbell (ed.), *Spirit and nature: Papers from the Eranos Yearbooks*. New York: Pantheon. (pp. 213–50). (First published 1937.)

—(1968a). Symbols and rites in the religious life of certain monastic orders. In J. Campbell (ed.), *The mystic vision*. Princeton University Press. (pp. 168–187). (First published 1934.)

—(1968b). The *Exercitia* of St. Ignatius Loyola. In Campbell (ed.), *The mystic vision: Papers from the Eranos Yearbooks*. Princeton University Press. (pp. 187–99). (First published 1935.)

—(1968c). Christology and ecclesiology in St. Paul. In J. Campbell (ed.), *The mystic vision: Papers from the Eranos Yearbooks*. Princeton University Press. (pp. 144–67). (First published 1941.)

—(1984). *Gioacchino da Fiore. I tempi – la vita – il messagio*. Cosenza: Giordano.

Burke, H. R. (1947). *Personality traits of successful minor seminarians*. Washington, D.C.: Catholic University of America Press.

—(1953, March). Review of the book, *General Psychology*. *American Catholic Psychological Association Newsletter*, 3, 5–6.

Burke, R. A., CSV (1952). *What is the Index?* Milwaukee: Bruce Publishing Co.

Burne, J. T. (1959). The counselor and the spiritual director. *Homiletic and Pastoral Review*, 59(6), 537–42.

Burnham, J. C. (1985). The encounter of Christian theology with deterministic psychology and psychoanalysis. *Bulletin of the Menninger Clinic*, 49, 321–52.

Byrns, R. K. (1931, May 30). Limitations of the scientific method. *America*, 45, 184–5.

Cabrera, Y. (1999, January 31). Life's work is helping others – Former nun hands over reins at center. *Daily News of Los Angeles*, p. N1.

Cadegan, U. M. (2002). Modernisms literary and theological. *U.S. Catholic Historian*, 20(3), 97–110.

Cady, H. E. (1894). *Lessons in truth*. Lee's Summit, MO: Unity School of Christianity.

Caplan, E. (1998). *Mind games: American culture and the birth of psychotherapy*. Berkeley: University of California Press.

Capshew, J. H. (1999). *Psychologists on the march: Science, practice, and professional identity in America, 1929–1969*. New York: Cambridge University Press.

Carpintero, H. (1984). The impact of the Spanish Civil War on Spanish scientific psychology. *Revista de Historia de la Psicología*, 5, 91–7.

Carter, J. D., and Narramore, B. (1979). *The integration of psychology and theology*. Grand Rapids, MI: Zondervan.

Catholic physicians form a federation. (1931, June 20). *New York Times*, p. 25.

Catholic psychologists question Pope's Encyclical on artificial contraception. (1968, September 3). *New York Times*, p. 15.

Cavanagh, J. H. (1967). Guild of Catholic Psychiatrists. *New Catholic Encyclopedia* (vol. VI). New York: McGraw-Hill. (p. 844).

Cavanagh, J. R. (1962). *Fundamental pastoral counseling: Technic and psychology*. Milwaukee: Bruce.

—and McGoldrick, J. B. (1953). *Fundamental psychiatry*. Milwaukee: Bruce.

Cavanaugh, W. T. (1995). 'A fire strong enough to consume the house:' The wars of religion and the rise of the state. *Modern Theology*, 11, 397–420.

Centi, P. J. (1961, January). Report on survey of ACPA members. *American Catholic Psychological Association Newsletter Supplement No. 49*, 1–2. Akron, OH: Archives of the History of American Psychology. Collection: American Psychological Association Division 36, Box 706.

Cerullo, J. J. (1982). *The secularization of the soul: Psychical research in modern Britain*. Philadelphia: Institute for the Study of Human Issues.

Chamberlain, K. (2000). Methodolatry and qualitative health research. *Journal of Health Psychology*, 5, 285–96.

Charcot, J.-M. (1893). The faith-cure. *New Review*, 8, 18–31.

Charet, F. X. (1990). A dialogue between psychology and theology: The correspondence of C. G. Jung and Victor White. *Journal of Analytical Psychology*, 35, 421–41.

Christou, E. (1963). *The logos of the psyche*. Zürich: Donquin.

Churchill, S. (2000). Phenomenological psychology. In A. E. Kazdin (ed.), *Encyclopedia of psychology* (vol. VI). New York: Oxford University Press. (pp. 162–8).

Clarke, R. F. (1888). *Lourdes: Its inhabitants, its pilgrims, and its miracles*. New York: Benziger Bros.

—(1892a). *Medical testimony to the miracles of Lourdes.* London: Catholic Truth Society.

—(1892b). *Theosophy, its teaching, marvels and true character.* New York: Benziger.

Clarke, W. N. (1968). The future of Thomism. In McInerny (ed.), *New themes in Christian philosophy.* University of Notre Dame Press. (pp. 187–207).

Cloonan, T. F. (1995). The early history of phenomenological psychological research in America. *Journal of Phenomenological Psychology*, 26, 46–126.

Codex iuris canonici. (1918). Rome: Typis Polyglottis Vaticanis.

Coghlan, D. (1909). Dogma. *Catholic Encyclopedia* (vol. V). New York: Robert Appleton. (pp. 89–91).

Collins, H. M., and Evans, R. (2002). The third wave of science studies: Studies of expertise and experience. *Social Studies of Science*, 32(2), 235–96.

Collins, J. D. (ed.). (1960). *Readings in ancient and medieval philosophy.* Westminster, MD: Newman Press.

Colombo, D. (2003). Psychoanalysis and the Catholic Church in Italy: The Role of Father Agostino Gemelli, 1925–1953. *Journal of the History of the Behavioral Sciences*, 39, 333–48.

Commins, W. D. (1937). *Principles of educational psychology.* Oxford: Ronald Press.

Connelly, J. F. (1979). *St. Charles Seminary Philadelphia: A history of the Theological Seminary of Saint Charles Borromeo, Overbrook, Philadelphia, Pennsylvania, 1932–1979.* Philadelphia: St. Charles Seminary.

Constitution of the American Catholic Psychological Association. (1949). Akron, OH: Archives of the History of American Psychology. Collection: American Psychological Association Division 36, Box 707, Folder 5.

Coon, D. J. (1992). Testing the limits of sense and science: American experimental psychologists combat spiritualism, 1880–1920. *American Psychologist*, 47, 143–51.

Cornelius, R. R. (2006). Magda Arnold's Thomistic theory of emotion, the self-ideal, and the moral dimension of appraisal. *Cognition and Emotion*, 20, 976–1000.

Costello, J. J. (1997). Baroness Vera von der Heydt, 1899–1996. *Journal of Analytical Psychology*, 42, 331–3.

Coulson, W. R. (1982). The person in context: Paper presented at the Honors Day Address, College of Notre Dame, Belmont, California.

—(1995). Full hearts and empty heads: The price of certain recent programs in humanistic psychology. In J. M. DuBois (ed.), *The nature and tasks of a person-alist psychology.* Lanham, MD: University Press of America. (pp. 59–86).

Coville, W. J. (1957). The personality assessment of candidates for the priesthood and the religious life. *National Catholic Educational Association Bulletin*, 60 (1), 396–409.

—(1962b, September). Psychologists and the assessment of candidates for religious life: Part I. *American Catholic Psychological Association Newsletter Supplement No. 59*, 1–2. Akron, OH: Archives of the History of American Psychology. Collection: American Psychological Association Division 36, Box 706.

—(1962a, November). Psychologists and the assessment of candidates for religious life, Part II. *American Catholic Psychological Association Newsletter Supplement No. 60*, 1–2. Akron, OH: Archives of the History of American Psychology. Collection: American Psychological Association Division 36, Box 706.

—(1967). Personality assessment program for the religious and sacerdotal life. *Review for Religious*, 26, 305–10.

—(1968a). *Assessment of candidates for the religious life; basic psychological issues and procedures.* Washington, D.C.: Center for Applied Research in the Apostolate.

—(1968b). Changing directions of the ACPA. *Catholic Psychological Record*, 6, 70–90.

Cox, H. (1965). *The secular city: Secularization and urbanization in theological perspective.* New York: Macmillan.

Crews, F. (1995). The unknown Freud. In *The memory wars: Freud's legacy in dispute.* New York Review Books. (pp. 31–73).

Cuneno, M. W. (1997). *The smoke of Satan: Conservative and traditionalist dissent in contemporary American Catholicism.* Baltimore: Johns Hopkins University Press.

Cunningham, A. (1981). Victor White and C. G. Jung: The fateful encounter of the White Raven and the Gnostic. *New Blackfriars*, 62(733/734), 320–34.

—(1992). Victor White, John Layard and C. G. Jung. *Harvest*, 38, 44–57.

—(2007). Victor White, a memoir. In A. C. Lammers and A. Cunningham (eds.), *The Jung–White letters.* New York: Routledge. (pp. 307–34).

Curran, C. A. (1945). *Personality factors in counseling.* New York: Grune & Stratton.

—(1952). *Counseling in Catholic life and education.* New York: Macmillan.

—(1954a, November). The Catholic's role in scientific psychology. *American Catholic Psychological Association Newsletter, Supplement No. 12*, 1–2.

—(1954b). *To the Presidents of our Catholic colleges, January 30.* Akron, OH: Archives of the History of American Psychology. Collection: American Psychological Association Division 36, Box 707, Folder 5.

—(1958). Religious factors and values in counseling. *Catholic Counselor*, 3 (Autumn), 3–5; 24.

—(1965). Psychological aspects of Vatican Council II. *Journal for the Psychological Study of Religion*, 5, 190–4.

—(1966). Vatican II: A new Christian self-concept. *Journal of Religion and Health*, 5, 91–103.

—(1969). *Religious values in counseling and psychotherapy.* New York: Sheed & Ward.

—(1972). What can man believe in? *Journal of Religion and Health*, 11(1), 7–39.

Curran, C. E. (1999). Moral theology in the United States: An analysis of the last twenty five years (1965–1985). In C. E. Curran and R. A. McCormick (eds.), *The historical development of fundamental moral theology in the United States.* New York: Paulist Press. (pp. 22–45).

—(2008). *Catholic moral theology in the United States*. Washington, D.C.: Georgetown University Press.

D'Ambrosio, M. (1991). Ressourcement theology, aggiornamento, and the hermeneutics of tradition. *Communio*, 18, 530–55.

—(1992). Henri de Lubac and the critique of scientific exegesis. *Communio*, 19, 365–88.

D'Angelo, R. Y. (1966). Attitudes, values, and motivational systems of the American college student: Discussion. *Catholic Psychological Record*, 4, 42–8.

D'Arcy, M. C. (1953). The power of caritas and the Holy Spirit. In O. Fröbe-Kapleyn (ed.), *Eranos-Jahrbuch 21: Mensch und Energie*. Zürich: Rhein Verlag. (pp. 285–324).

D'Arcy, P. F. (1967). Psychology and the contemporary Church. *Catholic Psychological Record*, 5, 93–101.

Dalbiez, R. (1941). *Psychoanalytic method and the doctrine of Freud* (trans. T. F. Lindsay). London: Longmans, Green and Co. (First published 1936.)

Daly, G. (1980). *Transcendence and immanence: A study in Catholic modernism and integralism*. Oxford: Clarendon.

Dangers of hypnotism, the. (1901). *American Ecclesiastical Review*, 24, 78–9.

Daniélou, J. (1954). Terre et paradis chez les Pères de l'Église. In Fröbe-Kapleyn (ed.), *Eranos-Jahrbuch 22: Mensch und Erde*. (pp. 433–72).

—(1957). *God and the ways of knowing* (trans. W. Roberts). New York: Meridian.

—(1964). The dove and the darkness in ancient Byzantine mysticism. In Campbell (ed.), *Man and transformation: Papers from the Eranos Yearbooks*. New York: Pantheon. (pp. 270–96).

Danziger, K. (1990). *Constructing the subject: Historical origins of psychological research*. Cambridge University Press.

—(1994). Does the history of psychology have a future? *Theory & Psychology*, 4, 467–84.

—(1997). *Naming the mind: How psychology found its language*. London: Sage.

—(2003). Where history, theory, and philosophy meet: The biography of psychological objects. In D. B. Hill and M. J. Kral (eds.), *About psychology: Essays at the crossroads of history, theory, and philosophy*. Albany: State University of New York Press. (pp. 19–33).

—(2006). Comment. *International Journal of Psychology*, 41, 269–75.

Davenport, D. G. (1990). The birth of the doctoral program and the development of experimental psychology. In J. Korn (ed.), *The history of the Saint Louis University Department of Psychology*. St. Louis: Special Collections, Pius XII Library, St. Louis University. (pp. 41–59).

Davis, A. J. (1872). *The penetralia; being harmonial answers to important questions* (rev. edn.). Boston: Colby and Rich, Banner Publishing House.

de Lubac, H. (1946). *Surnaturel: Études historiques*. Paris: Aubier.

—(1993). *At the service of the Church: Henri de Lubac reflects on the circumstances that occasioned his writings* (trans. A. E. Nash). San Francisco: Ignatius.

—(1998). *The mystery of the supernatural* (trans. R. Sheed). New York: Crossroad Herder. (First published 1965.)

de St. Denis, R. (1921, October 22). Colleges and psychological tests. *America*, 26, 5–6.

de Wulf, M. (1911). Neo-Scholasticism. *Catholic Encyclopedia* (vol. X). New York: Robert Appleton. (pp. 746–9).

Dearborn, G. V. N. (1913). Review of the book, *Motive force and motivation-tracts*, by E. Boyd Barrett. *Journal of Abnormal Psychology*, 7(6), 441–3.

Debreyne, P. J. C., and Ferrand, A. E. A. (1884). *La théologie morale et les sciences medicales* (6th edn.). Paris: Poussielgue frères.

Dedola, R. (2006). *Am Festmahl von Eranos*. Available: www.eranosfoundation.org/ 7A228BD6-3D20-4766-AFDA-6EA38D9E7480.html.

Delaney, H. D., and DiClemente, C. C. (2005). Psychology's roots: A brief history of the influence of Judeo-Christian perspectives. In W. R. Miller and H. D. Delaney (eds.), *Judeo-Christian perspectives on psychology*. Washington, D.C.: American Psychological Association. (pp. 31–54).

DeMarinis, V. (1982). The Catholic Physicians' Guild – origin and direction. *Linacre Quarterly*, 49(3), 205–9.

Devereux, G. (1967). *From anxiety to method in the human sciences*. The Hague: Mouton and Co.

Devlin, W. J. (1942). The effect of certain pharmacological preparations on the emotions of normal and psychotic individuals. *Studies in Psychology and Psychiatry (Catholic University of America)*, 5(6).

—(1964). *Psychodynamics of personality development*. New York: Alba House.

Donceel, J. F. (1955). *Philosophical psychology*. New York: Sheed & Ward.

—(1961). *Philosophical psychology* (2nd edn.). New York: Sheed & Ward.

Dourley, J. P. (1995). The religious implications of Jung's psychology. *Journal of Analytical Psychology*, 40, 177–203.

—(2007). The Jung–White dialogue and why it couldn't work and won't go away. *Journal of Analytical Psychology*, 52, 275–95.

Doyle, C. I. (1937a). *Dear Friends and Fellow-members, February 9*. Chicago: Dominican University Archives. Associations, Chicago Society of Catholic Psychologists 1936–1937, Box D, Folder 10.

—(1937b). *Dear Friends and Fellow-members, November 13*. Chicago: Dominican University Archives. Associations, Chicago Society of Catholic Psychologists 1936–1937, Box D, Folder 10.

Dr. Brill replies to Msgr. Sheen. (1947, July 6). *New York Times*, p. 42.

Dresser, H. W. (1919). *A history of the New Thought movement*. New York: Thomas Y. Crowell.

—(1921). *The Quimby manuscripts: Showing the discovery of spiritual healing and the origin of Christian Science*. New York: Thomas Y. Crowell.

Drewitt, N. (1937a). Catholicism and myth. *Blackfriars*, 18, 103–10.

—(1937b). Faith – love and the supernatural. *Blackfriars*, 18, 514–24.

—(1938). Thomist apocalyptic. *Blackfriars*, 19, 356–63.

Duden, B. (1991). *The woman beneath the skin: A doctor's patients in eighteenth-century Germany*. Cambridge, MA: Harvard University Press.

Dulles, A. (1991). Henri de Lubac: In appreciation. *America*, 165(8), 180–2.

Duminuco, V. J. (ed.). (2000). *The Jesuit ratio studiorum: 400th anniversary perspectives*. New York: Fordham University Press.

Dutto, L. A. (1889, October). Presentiments, visions, and apparitions. *Catholic World*, 50, 80–8.

Earle, E. L. (1899, January). Lily Dale, the haunt of Spiritualists. *Catholic World*, 68, 506–15.

Ecker, P. G. (1964). Genetic and dynamic factors. In Bier (ed.), *Personality and sexual problems*. New York: Fordham University Press. (pp. 152–68).

Editorial notes. (1899, July). *Catholic World*, 69, 572.

Edmondson, E. A. (2002). Without comment or controversy: The G. I. Bill and Catholic colleges. *Church History*, 71, 820–47.

Elkisch, F. B. (1946). Some practical points on Jung's analytical psychology. *Blackfriars*, 27(321), 461–6.

Ellenberger, H. F. (1970). *The discovery of the unconscious: The history and evolution of dynamic psychiatry*. New York: Basic Books.

Ellis, J. T. (1955). American Catholics and the intellectual life. *Thought*, 30, 351–88.

—(1956). *American Catholicism*. University of Chicago Press.

Elrington, A. (1933). Psychoanalysis and Catholicism. *Blackfriars*, 14, 673–8.

—(1936). Is a Catholic psychology possible? *Blackfriars*, 17, 591–9.

—(1938). Psychotherapy at Oxford. *Blackfriars*, 19, 676–81.

Evans, C. S. (1982). *Preserving the person: A look at the human sciences*. Grand Rapids, MI: Baker.

Evils of public hypnotizations, the. (1891). *Medical Record*, 40 (4), 99.

Ex-priest explains return to church. (1948, December 5). *New York Times*, p. 95.

Fanning, W. (1908). Cure of souls. *Catholic Encyclopedia* (vol. IV). New York: Robert Appleton Company. (p. 572).

Fanning, W. H. W. (1913). Medicine and canon law. *Catholic Encyclopedia* (vol. X). New York: Universal Knowledge Foundation. (pp. 142–3).

Farewell to Freud? (1933, February 22). *Commonweal*, 17, 452.

Feverel, A. (1912a). Christian Science I. *Catholic World*, 96(572), 180–90.

—(1912b). Christian Science II. *Catholic World*, 96(573), 360–9.

—(1913a). Christian Science III. *Catholic World*, 96(574), 466–76.

—(1913b). Christian Science IV. *Catholic World*, 96(575), 655–69.

Fichter, J. H. (1961). *Religion as an occupation: A study in the sociology of professions*. South Bend: University of Notre Dame Press.

Filas, F. L. (1966). Mostly as advertised. *Homiletic and Pastoral Review*, 66(10), 884–5.

Finke, R. (2000). Catholic religious vocations: Decline and revival. *Review of Religious Research*, 42, 125–45.

Fisher, A. L. (1957). Psychology or psychologies – A study in methodology. *Proceedings of the American Catholic Philosophical Society*, 31, 144–57.

—(1961). Freud and the image of man. *Proceedings of the American Catholic Philosophical Society*, 35, 45–77.

—(1964). An impressionistic account of the Second Lexington Conference on Phenomenology. *Catholic Psychological Record*, 2, 137–40.

—and Murray, G. B. (1969). Preface. In A. L. Fisher and G. B. Murray (eds.), *Philosophy and science as modes of knowing*. New York: Appleton-Century-Crofts. (pp. vii–viii).

Flick, E. M. (1945). Dr. James Joseph Walsh (1865–1942). In W. Romig (ed.), *The book of Catholic authors*. Grosse Pointe, MI: Walter Romig. (pp. 302–8).

Flynn, E. P. (2000). Responding to the 'gay agenda'. *America*, 183, 15–18.

Ford, J. C. (1964). Homosexuality: pastoral notes. In Bier (ed.), *Personality and sexual problems*. New York: Fordham University Press. (pp. 169–76).

—and Kelly, G. (1958). *Contemporary moral theology, Volume I*. Cork: Mercier Press.

Fordham, M. (1963). Review of the book, *Children and their religion*, by Eve Lewis. *Journal of Analytical Psychology*, 8, 189.

—(1975). John Layard. *Journal of Analytical Psychology*, 20(2), 216–17.

Forte, B. (1996). Nature and grace in Henri de Lubac: from *Surnaturel* to *Le Mystère du surnaturel*. *Communio*, 23, 725–37.

Foucault, M. (1972). *The archaeology of knowledge* (trans. A. M. S. Smith). New York: Harper & Row.

—(1973). *The birth of the clinic: An archaeology of medical perception*. New York: Random House.

—(1978). *The history of sexuality* (trans. R. Hurley) (Vol. I: *An introduction*). New York: Random House.

Fouillée, A. (1901). *Tempérament et caractère, selon les individus, les sexes et les races*. Paris: Alcan.

Fourteenth annual meeting. (1960, September). *American Catholic Psychological Association Newsletter*, 10, 1–2. Akron, OH: Archives of the History of American Psychology. Collection: American Psychological Association Division 36, Box 706.

Frankl, V. (1955). *The doctor and the soul: An introduction to logotherapy*. New York: Knopf.

—(1963). *Man's search for meaning*. Boston: Beacon.

Freeman, L. (1950, May 4). Psychiatry fight by Sheen attacked. *New York Times*, p. 56.

Frei, G. (1953). On analytical psychology: The method and teaching of C. G. Jung. In White, V., *God and the unconscious*. Chicago: Henry Regnery. (pp. 235–62).

Freud, S. (1939). *Moses and monotheism*. New York: Alfred A. Knopf.

—(1952). *Totem and taboo; Some points of agreement between the mental lives of savages and neurotics* (trans. J. Strachey). New York: Norton. (First published 1913.)

—(1961). *The future of an illusion* (trans. W. D. Robson Scott and J. Strachey). Garden City, New York: Doubleday Anchor Books. (First published 1927.)

Friedan, B. (1963). *The feminine mystique.* New York: Norton.

Fuller, R. C. (2001). *Spiritual, but not religious.* New York: Oxford University Press.

Furfey, P. H. (1919). Conscious and unconscious factors in symbolism. *Psychological Monographs,* 27(121), 349–86.

—(1929). Psychoanalysis, behaviorism and the Gestalt. *Thought,* 4(2), 237–53.

Gadamer, H.-G. (1989). *Truth and method* (trans. J. Weinsheimer and D. G. Marshall) (2nd rev. edn.). New York: Continuum.

Gaffney, L. (1971). Psychological reflections on marital love and contraception. *Journal of Religion and Health,* 10, 11–22.

Galison, P. (1999). Trading zone: Coordinating action and belief. In M. Biagioli (ed.), *The science studies reader.* New York: Routledge. (pp. 137–60).

Gannon, M. (1971). Before and after modernism: The intellectual isolation of the American priest. In J. T. Ellis (ed.), *The Catholic priest in the United States: Historical investigations.* Collegeville, MN: St John's University Press.

Gannon, T. J. (1939). A statistical analysis of some psychiatric diagnostic traits among young men. *Studies in Psychology and Psychiatry,* 4(4), 1–44.

—(1953). Function of psychology courses in a Catholic college. *Catholic Educational Review,* 51, 596–603.

—(1954). *Psychology: The unity of human behavior.* Boston: Ginn.

—(1960). The general significance of the Papal Address for the practice of psychology. In W. C. Bier and A. A. Schneiders (eds.), *Selected papers from the ACPA meetings of 1957, 1958, 1959.* New York: American Catholic Psychological Association. (pp. 61–6).

—(1965). Emotional development and spiritual growth. In M. J. O'Brien and R. J. Steimel (eds.), *Psychological aspects of spiritual development.* Washington, D.C.: Catholic University of America Press. (pp. 3–22).

—(1991). *Shaping psychology: How we got where we're going.* Lanham, MD: University Press of America.

Gantt, E. E., and Williams, R. N. (eds.). (2002). *Psychology for the other: Levinas, ethics and the practice of psychology.* Pittsburgh: Duquesne University Press.

Gasson, J. A. (1954a). Personality theory: A formulation of general principles. In M. B. Arnold and J. A. Gasson (eds.), *The human person: An approach to an integral theory of personality.* New York: Ronald. (pp. 165–221).

—(1954b). Religion and personality integration. In Arnold and Gasson (eds.), *The human person: An approach to an integral theory of personality.* (pp. 548–74).

Gatterer, A. (1927). *Der wissenschaftliche Okkultismus und sein Verhältnis zur Philosophie.* Innsbruck: Felizian Rauch.

Gaudium et spes. (1965). Available: www.vatican.va/archive/hist_councils/ii_vatican_council/documents/vat-ii_cons_19651207_gaudium-et-spes_en.html.

Gemelli, A. (1955). *Psychoanalysis today.* Oxford: P. D. Kenedy.

Gendlin, E. (1981). *Focusing.* New York: Bantam.

—(1988). Carl Rogers (1902–1987). *American Psychologist,* 43, 127–8.

Gergen, K. (1997). The place of the psyche in a constructed world. *Theory & Psychology,* 7, 723–46.

Gerty, A. V. (1953). Report of the secretary. *Bulletin of the Guild of Catholic Psychiatrists*, 1(4), 3.

Giddens, A. (1991). *Modernity and self-identity: Self and society in the late modern age.* Stanford University Press.

Gieryn, T. F. (1983). Boundary-work and the demarcation of science from non-science: Strains and interests in professional ideologies of scientists. *American Sociological Review*, 48, 781–95.

—(1999). *Cultural boundaries of science: Credibility on the line.* University of Chicago Press.

Gillespie, C. K. (2001). *Psychology and American Catholicism: From Confession to therapy?* New York: Crossroad.

—(2007a). Patterns of conversation between Catholicism and psychology in the United States. *Catholic Social Science Review*, 12, 173–83.

—(2007b). Psychology and American Catholicism after Vatican II: Currents, cross-currents and confluences. *U. S. Catholic Historian*, 25(4), 117–31.

Giorgi, A. (1962, May). Existential Psychology. *American Catholic Psychological Society Newsletter Supplement No. 57*, 1–2. Akron, OH: Archives of the History of American Psychology. Collection: American Psychological Association Division 36, Box 706.

—(1970). *Psychology as a human science.* New York: Harper & Row.

—(1998). The origins of the *Journal of Phenomenological Psychology* and some difficulties in introducing phenomenology into scientific psychology. *Journal of Phenomenological Psychology*, 29, 161–76.

Gleason, P. (1989). *Keeping the faith: American Catholicism past and present.* University of Notre Dame Press.

—(1995). *Contending with modernity: Catholic higher education in the twentieth century.* New York: Oxford University Press.

Godin, A. (1952). Psychotherapy: A new humanism. *Thought*, 27, 421–34.

—(1961). Trends and groups in religious psychology. *Lumen Vitae*, 16(2), 187–96.

Goldbrunner, J. (1955). *Holiness is wholeness* (trans. S. Goodman). New York: Pantheon.

—(1956). *Individuation: A study of the depth psychology of Carl Gustav Jung* (trans. S. Godman). New York: Pantheon.

Goldstein, J. (1982). The hysteria diagnosis and the politics of anticlericalism in late nineteenth-century France. *Journal of Modern History*, 54, 209–39.

Good, B. J. (1994). *Medicine, rationality, and experience.* Cambridge University Press.

Gorman, M. (1966). Some thoughts on the place of scholasticism in a philosophy of man today. *Proceedings of the American Catholic Philosophical Society*, 40, 17–29.

Grant, R. M. (1960). *The secret sayings of Jesus.* Garden City, NY: Doubleday.

Grau, A. (1952). Review of the book, *Counseling in Catholic Life and Education. American Catholic Psychological Society Newsletter*, 2(6), 2–3.

—(1960). The Pope's remarks and the limits of counseling. In Bier and Schneiders (eds.), *Selected papers from the ACPA meetings of 1957, 1958, 1959.* (pp. 71–7).

Graydon, M. (2009, January 9). Deceased: Dr. LeRoy Wauck: 1920–2009. Psychology professor, clinician. *Chicago Tribune*, p. 39.

Greeley, A. (2004). *The Catholic church*. Berkeley: University of California Press.

Green, C. D. (1996). Where did the word "cognitive" come from anyway? *Canadian Psychology*, 37, 31–9.

Greer, S. (1997). Nietzsche and social construction: Directions for a postmodern historiography. *Theory & Psychology*, 7, 83–100.

Griffin, A. (1959). Tenth Annual Meeting. *Bulletin of the Guild of Catholic Psychiatrists*, 6, 22–3.

Griffin, M. D. (1967). Spiritism. *New Catholic Encyclopedia* (vol. XIII). New York: McGraw-Hill. (pp. 576–7).

Groeschel, B. J. (1983). *Spiritual passages: The psychology of spiritual development 'for those who seek'*. New York: Crossroad.

Gruender, H. (1911). *Psychology without a soul: A criticism*. St. Louis: B. Herder.

—(1920). *An introductory course in experimental psychology*. Chicago: Loyola University Press.

—(1932). *Experimental psychology*. Milwaukee: Bruce.

—(1937). *Problems of psychology*. Milwaukee: Bruce.

Grumett, D. (2007). *De Lubac: A guide for the perplexed*. London: T. & T. Clark.

Guild meeting, 1958. (1958). *Bulletin of the Guild of Catholic Psychiatrists*, 5(3), 35–37.

Guild of St. Luke, the. (2009). Available: www.guildofstluke.org/.

Guinan, M. S. M. (1961). Existential analysis and the human condition. *Proceedings of the American Catholic Philosophical Society*, 35, 125–41.

Hacking, I. (1999). Making up people. In Biagioli (ed.), *The science studies reader*. New York: Routledge. (pp. 161–71).

Hagmaier, G. (1964). Homosexuality: pastoral counseling. In Bier (ed.), *Personality and sexual problems*. (pp. 177–93).

—and Gleason, R. W. (1959). *Counselling the Catholic*. New York: Sheed & Ward.

Hakl, H. T. (2001). *Der verborgene Geist von Eranos: unbekannte Begegnungen von Wissenschaft und Esoterik: eine alternative Geistesgeschichte des 20. Jahrhunderts*. Bretten: Scientia Nova.

Hale, N. G., Jr. (1971). *Freud and the Americans: The beginnings of psychoanalysis in the United States, 1876–1917*. New York: Oxford University Press.

—(1995). *The rise and crisis of psychoanalysis in the United States: Freud and the Americans, 1917–1985*. New York: Oxford University Press.

Halling, S., and Nill, J. D. (1995). A brief history of existential-phenomenological psychiatry and psychology. *Journal of Phenomenological Psychology*, 26, 1–45.

Hampton, P. (1941). Review of the book, *Cognitive Psychology*, by T. V. Moore. *Journal of Abnormal & Social Psychology*, 36(2), 300–2.

Hanegraaff, W. J. (1996). *New Age religion and western culture: Esotericism in the mirror of secular thought*. Leiden: E. J. Brill.

Harmon, F. L. (1938). *Principles of psychology*. Milwaukee: Bruce.

—(1951). *Principles of psychology* (rev. edn.). Milwaukee: Bruce.

Harrington, F. T. (1960). Dear members of the Guild of Catholic Psychiatrists, *September 14. Bulletin of the Guild of Catholic Psychiatrists, 7*, 258.

Harris, R. (1999). *Lourdes: Body and spirit in the secular age.* New York: Viking.

Hart, C. A. (ed.). (1932). *Aspects of the new scholastic philosophy.* New York: Benziger Brothers.

Hawley, E. (1899). The vagaries of Christian Science. *Catholic World, 69*(412), 508–17.

Hawthorne, N. (1852). *The Blithedale romance.* Boston: Ticknor, Reed, and Fields.

Hayes, J. J. (1954). Message from the chaplain. *Bulletin of the Guild of Catholic Psychiatrists, 2*(2), 2–4.

Hayman, R. (1999). *A life of Jung.* New York: Norton.

Hayne, D. (1966, September 3). Edward Boyd Barrett: Shepherd in the mist. *America, 115*, 230.

Heelan, P. A. (1998). The scope of hermeneutics in natural science. *Studies in History and Philosophy of Science, 29A*(2), 273–99.

Heft, H. (2001). *Ecological psychology in context: James Gibson, Roger Barker, and the legacy of William James's radical empiricism.* Mahwah, NJ: Lawrence Erlbaum.

Heidegger, M. (1962). *Being and time* (trans. J. Macquarrie and E. Robinson). New York: Harper & Row.

Heinze, A. R. (2004). *Jews and the American soul.* Princeton University Press.

Heisig, J. W. (1973). Jung and theology: A bibliographical essay. *Spring*, 204–55.

Herman, E. (1995). *The romance of American psychology: Political culture in the age of experts.* Berkeley: University of California Press.

Herr, V. V. (1965). *Religious psychology.* Staten Island, NY: Alba House.

—(1966). Mental health training in seminaries. *Bulletin of the Guild of Catholic Psychiatrists, 13*(1), 17–20.

Hilgard, E. (1987). *Psychology in America: A historical survey.* San Diego: Harcourt Brace Jovanovich.

Hillman, J. (1973). *Plotinus, Ficino and Vico as precursors of archetypal psychology.* Roma: Instituto della Enciclopedia italiana.

—(1975). *Re-visioning psychology.* New York: Harper & Row.

—(1976). *Suicide and the soul.* Zürich: Spring.

Hobson, R. F. (1958). Review of the book, *Religion and the Psychology of Jung*, by Raymond Hostie. *Journal of Analytical Psychology, 3*(1), 64–9.

Holaind, R. J. (1895). The physiological and moral aspects of hypnotism. *American Ecclesiastical Review, 12*, 25–37; 120–34.

Holy Office. (1962). *Warning regarding the writings of Fr. Teilhard de Chardin.* Available: petersnet.net/research/retrieve_full.cfm?RecNum=3490.

Homans, P. (1995). *Jung in context: Modernity and the making of a psychology* (2nd edn.). University of Chicago Press.

Hostie, R. (1957). *Religion and the psychology of Jung* (trans. G. R. Lamb). New York: Sheed & Ward.

—(1966). *Pastoral counseling*. New York: Sheed & Ward.

—(1983). *The life and death of religious orders*. Washington, D.C.: Center for Applied Research in the Apostolate.

Hoy, D. J. (1964). Psychology, theology, and philosophy: Martin Heidegger as intermediary. *Catholic Psychological Record*, 2, 131–6.

Hughes, T. A. (1890). *Principles of anthropology and biology*. New York: Benziger Brothers.

—(1894). Psychology, physiology, and pedagogics. *American Catholic Quarterly Review*, 19, 790–812.

Humphrey, G. (1951). *Thinking: An introduction to its experimental psychology*. New York: John Wiley and Sons.

Husslein, J. (1922a, February 4). The new industrial psychology. *America*, 26, 382–3.

—(1922b, February 18). Industrial psychology in practice. *America*, 26, 430–2.

—(1938). Preface by the general editor. In W. A. Kelly and M. R. Kelly (eds.), *Introductory child psychology*. Milwaukee: Bruce. (pp. ix–xi).

Hypnotism and theology. (1890). *American Ecclesiastical Review*, 3, 257–72.

Ihde, D. (1997). Thingly hermeneutics/Technoconstructions. *Man and World*, 30, 369–81.

Illich, I. (1993). *In the vineyard of the text: A commentary on Hugh's Didascalicon*. University of Chicago Press.

Index librorum prohibitorum. (1948). Rome: Typis Polyglottis Vaticanis.

Jaffé, A. (1977). C. G. Jung and the Eranos conferences. *Spring: An Annual of Archetypal Psychology and Jungian Thought*, 201–12.

James, W. (1890a). *The principles of psychology* (vol. I). New York: Henry Holt.

—(1890b, March). The hidden self. *Scribner's Magazine*, 7, 361–74.

—(1907). The energies of men. *Science, n.s.* 25 (635), 321–32.

—(1912). *Essays in radical empiricism*. New York: Longmans, Green, and Co.

—(1903). *The varieties of religious experience*. New York: Longmans, Green and Co.

Janet, P. (1976). *Psychological healing: A historical and clinical study* (trans. E. Paul and C. Paul). New York: Arno. (First published 1925.)

John Jay College of Criminal Justice. (2004). *The nature and scope of the problem of sexual abuse of minors by Catholic priests and deacons in the United States*. United States Conference of Catholic Bishops. Available: www.usccb.org/nrb/johnjaystudy/index.htm.

Johnson, E. L., and Jones, S. L. (2000a). A history of Christians in psychology. In E. L. Johnson and S. L. Jones (eds.), *Psychology and Christianity*. Downers Grove, IL: InterVarsity Press. (pp. 11–53).

—(eds.). (2000b). *Psychology and Christianity*. Downers Grove, IL: InterVarsity Press.

Joly, H. (1898). *The psychology of the saints*. London: Duckworth.

Jone, H. (1993). *Moral theology* (trans. U. Adelman) (18th edn.). Rockford, IL: Tan Books. (First published 1961.)

Jones, E. (1964). A psycho-analytic study of the Holy Ghost concept. In *Essays in applied psycho-analysis*. New York: International Universities Press. (pp. 358–73). (First published 1922.)

Jordan, M. (1997). *The invention of sodomy in Christian theology*. University of Chicago Press.

Joyce, A. R. (1966). The Iona graduate division of pastoral counseling – A historical view. *Journal of Pastoral Counseling*, 1, 4–11.

—and Stern, E. M. (1972). Foreword. In A. R. Joyce and E. M. Stern (eds.), *Holiness and mental health*. New York: Paulist Press. (pp. vii–viii).

Jugnet, L. (1975). *Rudolf Allers o el Anti-Freud* (trans. C. Gutiérrez). Madrid: Speiro. (First published 1950.)

Jung, C. G. (1933). *Modern man in search of a soul* (trans. W. S. Dell and C. F. Baynes). New York: Harcourt Brace Jovanovich.

—(1938). *Psychology and religion*. New Haven: Yale University Press.

—(1953). Foreword. In White, V., *God and the Unconscious*. Chicago: Henry Regnery. (pp. xv–xxvii).

—(1954). *The practice of psychotherapy* (trans. R. F. C. Hull). Princeton University Press.

—(1958). *Answer to Job* (trans. R. F. C. Hull). Princeton University Press.

—(1967a). *Symbols of transformation* (2nd edn.). Princeton University Press.

—(1967b). Foreword (trans. C. F. Baynes). In Wilhelm, R., *The I Ching or book of changes* (3rd edn.) Princeton University Press. (pp. xxi–xxxix).

—(1968). *Aion: Researches into the phenomenology of the self*. In *Collected works, Vol. IX, ii* (2nd edn.; trans. R. F. C. Hull). Princeton University Press.

—(1969a). A psychological approach to the Trinity. In *Collected works, Vol. XI: Psychology and religion: West and east* (2nd edn.) Princeton University Press. (pp. 107–200).

—(1969b). Transformation symbolism in the Mass. In *Collected works, Vol. XI: Psychology and religion: West and east* (2nd edn.). Princeton University Press. (pp. 201–96).

—(1973). *Letters* (Vol. I: *1906–1950*; trans. R. F. C. Hull). Princeton University Press.

—(1975). *Letters* (Vol. II; trans. R. F. C. Hull). Princeton University Press.

—(1976). Why I am not a Catholic. In *Collected works, Vol. XVIII: The symbolic life*. (trans. R. F. C. Hull). Princeton University Press. (pp. 645–8).

Kantor, J. R. (1940). Review of the book, *Cognitive Psychology*, by T. V. Moore. *Psychological Bulletin*, 37(4), 249–50.

Kaufman, S. K. (2005). *Consuming visions: Mass culture and the Lourdes shrine*. Ithaca: Cornell University Press.

Kavanaugh, J. (1967a). *A modern priest looks at his outmoded church*. New York: Trident.

—(1967b). Religious hang-ups. *Psychology Today*, 1, 16–23.

Keefe, J. (1979). Religion, psychology of. *New Catholic Encyclopedia* (vol. XVII). New York: McGraw-Hill. (pp. 558–9).

Keegan, J. G. (1943). The therapist as a person. *Linacre Quarterly*, 11(4), 73–6.

—(1955, March). Psychotherapy and the action of grace. *American Catholic Psychological Association Newsletter, Supplement No. 14*, 1–2.

Keenan, J. F. (2008). From teaching confessors to guiding lay people: The development of Catholic moral theologians from 1900–1965. *Journal of the Society of Christian Ethics*, 2, 141–57.

—(2010). *A history of Catholic moral theology in the twentieth century: From confessing sins to liberating consciences*. New York: Continuum.

Kehoe, R. (1952). Review of the book, *Antworf auf Hiob*, by C. G. Jung. *Dominican Studies*, 5, 228–31.

Keil, C. (1966). *Urban blues*. University of Chicago Press.

Keller, E. F. (1995). Gender and science: Origins, history, and politics. *Osiris*, 10, 26–38.

Kellogg, K. C., Orlikowski, W. J., and Yates, J. (2006). Life in the trading zone: Structuring coordination across boundaries in postbureaucratic organizations. *Organization Science*, 17, 22–44.

Kelly, W. A., and Kelly, M. R. (1938). *Introductory child psychology*. Milwaukee: Bruce.

Kelly, W. L. (1965). Contemporary psychology and philosophy: Viewpoint of a Neo-scholastic. *New Scholasticism*, 39, 421–50.

Kendler, H. H. (2005). Psychology and phenomenology: A clarification. *American Psychologist*, 60, 318–24.

Kennedy, E. C. (1962). *The relationship of self-perception to expressed motivation for occupational choice*. Unpublished doctoral dissertation, Catholic University of America, Washington, D.C.

—(1967). The twain shall meet. *Journal of Pastoral Counseling*, 2, 52–5.

—(1971). *In the spirit, in the flesh*. Garden City, NY: Doubleday and Co.

—(1975, October). President's message. *PIRI Newsletter*, 25, 40–1. Akron, OH: Archives of the History of American Psychology. Collection: American Psychological Association Division 36, Box 706, Folder 1.

—(2001). Foreword. In C. K. Gillespie (ed.), *Psychology and American Catholicism*. New York: Crossroad.

—and Heckler, V. J. (1972). *The Catholic priest in the United States: Psychological investigations*. Washington, D.C.: United States Catholic Conference.

Kerr, F. (2004a). 'Real knowledge' or 'enlightened ignorance': Eric Mascall on the apophatic Thomism of Victor Preller and Victor White. In J. Stout and R. MacSwain (eds.), *Grammar and grace: Reformulations of Aquinas and Wittgenstein*. London: SCM Press. (pp. 103–23).

—(2004b). Remembering Donald MacKinnon. *New Blackfriars*, 85(997), 265–9.

Keyes, F. A. (ed.). (1924). *The Guild of St. Apollonia: A brief historical sketch*. Boston: The Pilot Publishing Co.

Knapp, T. J. (1985). Contributions to the history of psychology: XXXIX. T. V. Moore and his Cognitive Psychology of 1939. *Psychological Reports*, 57(3, Pt. 2), 1311–16.

Koren, H. J. (ed.). (1958). *Readings in the philosophy of nature*. Westminster, MD: Newman Press.

Kristeva, J. (1989). *Language the unknown: An initiation into linguistics* (trans. A. M. Menke). New York: Columbia University Press.

Kugelmann, R. (2000). The American Catholic Psychological Association: A brief history and analysis. *Catholic Social Science Review*, 5, 233–49.

—(2005a). An encounter between psychology and religion: Humanistic psychology and the Immaculate Heart of Mary nuns. *Journal of the History of the Behavioral Sciences*, 41, 347–65.

—(2005b). Neoscholastic psychology revisited. *History of Psychology*, 8, 131–75.

Kuhn, T. S. (1970). *The structure of scientific revolutions* (2nd edn.). University of Chicago Press.

Külpe, O. (1921). *Grundlagen der ästhetik: aus dem nachlass* Leipzig: Hirzel.

—and Bühler K. (eds.), (1920). *Vorlesungen über Psychologie.* Leipzig: Hirzel.

Kurtz, L. R. (1986). *The politics of heresy: The modernist crisis in Roman Catholicism.* Berkeley: University of California Press.

Kusch, M. (1999). *Psychological knowledge: A social history and philosophy.* London: Routledge.

La Piana, G. (1969). Ernesto Buonaiuti's spiritual vision of life. In C. Nelson and N. Pittenger (eds.), *Pilgrim of Rome: An introduction to the life and work of Ernesto Buonaiuti.* London: James Nisbet and Co. (pp. 5–27).

Lacan, J. (1977). *Écrits: A selection* (trans. A. Sheridan). New York: Norton.

—(1990). *Television* (trans. D. Hollier, R. Krauss, and A. Michelson). New York: Norton.

Ladrière, J. (1992). One hundred years of philosophy at the Institute of Philosophy. In D. A. Boileau and J. A. Dick (eds.), *Tradition and renewal: Philosophical essays commemorating the centennial of Louvain's Institute of Philosophy* (vol. III). Leuven: Leuven University Press. (pp. 41–78).

Lally, J. J. (1975). Selection as an interactive process: The case of Catholic psycho-analysts and psychiatrists. *Social Science and Medicine*, 9, 157–64.

Lammers, A. C. (1994). *In God's shadow: The collaboration of Victor White and C. G. Jung.* New York: Paulist Press.

—(2007). Jung and White and the God of terrible double aspect. *Journal of Analytical Psychology*, 52, 253–74.

—and Cunningham, A. (2007). *The Jung–White letters.* New York: Routledge.

Laveille, A. (1928). *A life of Cardinal Mercier* (trans. A. Livingstone). New York: Century.

Layard, J. (1942). *The stone men of Malekula.* London: Chatto & Windus.

Leonard, E. A. (1946). Counseling in Catholic secondary schools. *Catholic Educational Review*, 44(5), 280–4.

Lesourd, P., and Ramiz, J.-M. (1964). *Eugene Cardinal Tisserant.* University of Notre Dame Press.

Levinas, E. (1969). *Totality and infinity* (trans. A. Lingis). Pittsburgh: Duquesne University Press.

Lewis, E. (1962). *Children and their religion.* New York: Sheed & Ward.

Lhota, B. G. (1948). Vocational interests of priests. *Studies in Psychology and Psychiatry*, 7(1).

Liebman, J. L. (1946). *Peace of mind.* New York: Simon & Schuster.

Lindworsky, J. (1931). *Experimental psychology* (trans. H. R. DeSilva). New York: Macmillan.

London Dialectical Society. (1871). *Report on spiritualism of the committee of the London Dialectical Society*. London: Longmans, Green, Reader and Dyer.

Loomie, L. S. (1954). Fundamental psychiatry. *Homiletic and Pastoral Review*, 54(7), 656–8.

Loughran, M. (1921). *The Historical Development of Child-Labor Legislation in the United States*. Unpublished doctoral dissertation, Catholic University of America, Washington, D.C.

—(1919). Concomitants of amentia. *Psychological Monographs*, 27 (4 [Whole No. 121]), 401–40.

Lowe-Evans, M. (1990). Sex and confession in the Joyce canon: Some historical parallels. *Journal of Modern Literature*, 16(4), 563–76.

Lucas, J. (1999). *The radical twenties: Writing, politics, and culture*. New Brunswick: Rutgers University Press.

M'Graw, S. M. L., and Mangold, S. M. C. (1929). Group intelligence tests in the primary grades. *Catholic University of America Education Research Bulletin*, 4(2).

Maasen, S. (2007). Selves in turmoil: Neurocognitive and societal challenges of the self. *Journal of Consciousness Studies*, 14, 252–70.

MacIntyre, A. (1984). *After virtue: A study in moral theory* (2nd edn.). University of Notre Dame Press.

—(1990). *Three rival versions of moral inquiry: Encyclopedia, genealogy, and tradition*. University of Notre Dame Press.

Maes, C. (1984). Listening, silence and obedience. *Studies in Formative Spirituality*, 5, 211–17.

Maggiolini, A. (1996). Magisterial teaching on experience in the twentieth century: From the Modernist crisis to the Second Vatican Council. *Communio*, 23, 225–43.

Maher, M. (1933). *Psychology: Empirical and rational* (9th edn.). London: Longmans, Green and Co. (First published 1918.)

—and Bolland, J. (1912). Soul. *Catholic Encyclopedia* (vol. XIV). New York: Appleton. (pp. 153–7).

Maier, B. N. (2004). The role of James McCosh in God's exile from psychology. *History of Psychology*, 7, 323–39.

Mailloux, N. (1942). The problem of perception. *Thomist*, 4, 266–85.

—(1953, September). Psychology at the University of Montreal. *American Catholic Psychological Association Newsletter Supplements, No. 5*, 1–2.

Malapert, P. (1897). *Les élements du carctère et leurs lois de combinaison*. Paris: Félix Alcan.

Maria, J. (1925, December 5). What of the repeaters? *America*, 34, 183–4.

—(1927, February 19). Intelligence tests in secondary education. *America*, 36, 452–3.

—(1931, May 16). Intelligence tests in vocational guidance. *America*, 45, 137–8.

Marion, J.-L. (1999). 'Christian philosophy': Hermeneutic or heuristic? In F. J. Ambrosio (ed.), *The question of Christian philosophy today*. New York: Fordham University Press. (pp. 247–64).

Marshall, H. R. (1908, November 24). Psychotherapy. *New York Times*, p. 8

—(1909). Psychotherapeutics and religion. *Hibbert Journal*, 7, 295–313.

Marty, M. E. (1982). The Catholic ghetto and all the other ghettos. *Catholic Historical Review*, 68 (April), 184–205.

Massa, M. (1999). *Catholics and American culture*. New York: Crossroad.

Matland, A. M. (1942). *Pastoral psychology*. London: Guild of Pastoral Psychology.

Maturin, B. W. (1905). *Knowledge and self-discipline*. New York: Longmans, Green.

—(1916). *Laws of the spiritual life*. London: Longmans, Green.

May, R. (1961). Existential psychiatry an evaluation. *Journal of Religion and Health*, 1, 31–40.

—Angel, E., and Ellenberger, H. F. (eds.). (1958). *Existence: A new dimension in psychiatry and psychology*. New York: Simon & Schuster.

McAllister, J. B. (1956). Psychoanalysis and mortality. *New Scholasticism*, 30, 310–29.

McCall, R. J. (1942). Truth and propaganda. *American Catholic Philosophical Association Proceedings*, 44–53.

—(1952). The logic of communication between philosophy and psychology. *American Catholic Philosophical Association Proceedings*, 26, 83–90.

—(1954a, March). Integration of psychology courses with the curricula of other departments. *American Catholic Psychological Association Newsletter Supplements, No. 8*, 1–2.

—(1954b). Review of the book, *God and the Unconscious*, by Victor White. *New Scholasticism*, 28(2), 240–3.

—(1959). *A preface to scientific psychology*. Milwaukee: Bruce Pub. Co.

—(1962). Invested self-expression: Toward a theory of human structural dynamics. In A. A. Schneiders and P. J. Centi (eds.), *selected papers from the ACPA meetings of 1960, 1961*. New York: American Catholic Psychological Association. (pp. 7–26).

—(1963). The defense mechanisms re-examined: A logical and phenomenal analysis. *Catholic Psychological Record*, 1, 45–64.

—(1975). *The varieties of abnormality: a phenomenological analysis*. Springfield, Ill.: Thomas.

—(1983). *Phenomenological psychology: An introduction*. Madison: University of Wisconsin.

McCandlish, L. (1958). *An investigation of a new method of TAT analysis by a prediction of high and low academic achievers*. Unpublished doctoral dissertation, Loyola University, Chicago.

McCarthy, R. (1947). Common grounds for psychiatrists and priests. *Linacre Quarterly*, 14(4), 1–4.

McCarthy, T. J. (1942). Personality traits of seminarians. *Studies in Psychology and Psychiatry*, 5(4).

McCarthy, T. N. (1965). Are they all made out of ticky-tacky? *Catholic Psychological Record*, 3, 1–8.

—(1970). Testing for the Roman Catholic priesthood. In W. C. Bier (ed.), *Psychological testing for ministerial selection*. New York: Fordham University Press. (pp. 47–86).

McCool, G. A. (1989). *From unity to pluralism: The internal evolution of Thomism*. New York: Fordham University Press.

—(1994). *The Neo-Thomists*. Milwaukee: Marquette University Press.

McCormick, R. A. (1999). Moral theology 1940–1989: An overview. In C. E. Curran and R. A. McCormick (eds.), *The historical development of fundamental moral theology in the United States*. New York: Paulist Press. (pp. 46–72).

McDonough, A. R. (1919). The development of meaning. *Psychological Monographs: Psychological Studies from the Catholic University of America*, 27 (6 [Whole No. 122]), 443–515.

McDonough, M. R. (1932). Character and body build in children. In C. A. Hart (ed.), *Aspects of the new scholastic philosophy*. New York: Benziger Brothers. (pp. 226–49).

McGarry, W. J. (1939, October 7). Freud has passed on and Freudianism also dies. *America*, 61, 606–7.

McGovern, T. V. (1992). Evolution of undergraduate curricula in psychology, 1892–1992. In A. E. Puente, J. R. Matthews, and C. L. Brewer (eds.), *Teaching psychology in America: A history*. Washington, D.C.: American Psychological Association. (pp. 11–38).

McGucken, W. J. (1922). The cult of psychoanalysis. *Ecclesiastical Review*, 66, 484–97.

McKeown, E. (2002). After the fall: Roman Catholic modernism at the American Academy of Religion. *U. S. Catholic Historian*, 20(3), 111–31.

McMullin, E. (1967). Presidential address: Who are we? *Proceedings of the American Catholic Philosophical Society*, 41, 1–16.

—(1968). Philosophy in the United States Catholic college. In McInerny (ed.), *New themes in Christian philosophy*. (pp. 370–409).

McNeill, H. (1947, July 25). Freudians and Catholics. *Commonweal*, 47, 350–3.

—(1950). Contemporary developments in clinical psychology. *Proceedings of the American Catholic Philosophical Society*, 24, 81–9.

McNeill, J. T. (1951). *A history of the cure of souls*. New York: Harper & Row.

Meissner, W. W. (1961). *Annotated bibliography in religion and psychology*. New York: Academy of Religion and Mental Health.

Menasce, J. d. (1968). The experience of the spirit in Christian mysticism. In J. Campbell (ed.), *The mystic vision: Papers from the Eranos Yearbooks* (pp. 324–47). Princeton University Press. (First published 1945.)

Mercier, D. (1996a). Opening discourse for the course on St. Thomas' philosophy. In D. A. Boileau (ed.), *Cardinal Mercier: A memoir*. Belgium: Peeters. (pp. 296–313). (First published 1882.)

—(1996b). Report on the higher studies of philosophy. In Boileau (ed.), *Cardinal Mercier: A memoir.* (pp. 344–57). (First published 1891.)

—(1902). *The relation of experimental psychology to philosophy.* New York: Benziger.

—(2002). The encyclical and philosophy. In D. A. Boileau (ed.), *Cardinal Mercier's philosophical essays: A study in Neo-Thomism.* Herent: Peeters. (pp. 543–50). (First published 1907.)

—(1908). The Lenten pastoral. In G. Tyrrell, *Medievalism: A reply to Cardinal Mercier.* London: Longmans, Green, and Co. (pp. 1–21).

—(1910). *Modernism* (trans. M. Lindsay). St. Louis: B. Herder.

—(1916a). Introduction to philosophy. In T. L. Parker and S. A. Parker (eds.), *A manual of modern scholastic philosophy* (8th edn., vol. I). St. Louis: B. Herder Book Co. (pp. 1–41).

—(1916b). Psychology. In Parker and Parker (eds.), *A manual of modern scholastic philosophy.* (8th edn., vol. I). St. Louis: B. Herder Book Co. (pp. 159–339).

—(1918). *Origins of contemporary psychology* (trans. W. H. Mitchell) (2nd edn.). London: R. and T. Washbourne.

Mercier, L. J. A. (1944). Freedom of the will and psychology. *New Scholasticism,* 18, 252–61.

Merleau-Ponty, M. (1963). *The structure of behavior* (trans. A. L. Fisher). Boston: Beacon Press.

—(1964). *Signs* (trans. R. C. McCleary). Evanston: Northwestern University Press.

Meyer, D. B. (1980). *The positive thinkers: religion as pop psychology from Mary Baker Eddy to Oral Roberts.* New York: Pantheon.

Michael, C. P. (1999). *An introduction to spiritual direction: A psychological approach for directors and directees.* New York: Paulist Press.

Milano, A. (1966). Pastoral counseling news. *Journal of Pastoral Counseling,* 1 (2), 79.

Milbank, J. (2001a). The soul of reciprocity, part one: reciprocity refused. *Modern Theology,* 17(3), 335–91.

—(2001b). The soul of reciprocity, part two: reciprocity granted. *Modern Theology,* 17(4), 485–507.

Miller, G. (2008). Scottish psychoanalysis: A rational religion. *Journal of the History of the Behavioral Sciences,* 44, 38–58.

Miller, G. A. (1969). Psychology as a means of improving human welfare. *American Psychologist,* 24, 1063–75.

Miller, W. R. (2005). What is human nature? Reflections from Judeo-Christian perspectives. In Miller and Delaney (eds.), *Judeo-Christian perspectives on psychology.* (pp. 11–29).

Minton, H. L. (2002). *Departing from deviance: A history of homosexual rights and emancipatory science in America.* University of Chicago Press.

Minutes of first meeting of the Board of Directors of the American Catholic Psychological Association, Denver, September 7. (1949). Akron, OH: Archives of the History of American Psychology. Collection: American Psychological Association Division 36, Box 710, Folder 22.

Minutes of the April 15th 1950 meeting of the Board of Directors of the American Catholic Psychological Association. (1950). Akron, OH: Archives of the History of American Psychology. Collection: American Psychological Association Division 36, Box 710, Folder 22.

Minutes of the Eighth Annual Meeting of the American Catholic Psychological Association, September 7. (1954). Akron, OH: Archives of the History of American Psychology. Collection: American Psychological Association Division 36, Box 710, Folder 22.

Minutes of the meeting of the Board of Directors of the American Catholic Psychological Association: Catholic University of America, March 31. (1951). Akron, OH: Archives of the History of American Psychology. Collection: American Psychological Association Division 36, Box 710, Folder 22.

Misiak, H. (1951, January). Review of the book, *A History of Experimental Psychology* (2nd edn). *American Catholic Psychological Association Newsletter*, 1, 6–7. Akron, OH: Archives of the History of American Psychology. Collection: American Psychological Association Division 36, Box 706.

—(1961). *The philosophical roots of scientific psychology*. New York: Fordham University Press.

—(1962). Catholic participation in the history of psychology in America. *Historical Records and Studies*, 49, 15–23.

—(1967). The flicker-fusion test and its applications. *Transactions of the New York Academy of Sciences*, 29(5), 616–22.

—and Sexton, V. S. (1966). *History of psychology: An overview*. New York: Grune & Stratton.

—(1973). *Phenomenological, existential, and humanistic psychologies: A historical survey*. New York: Grune & Stratton.

—and Staudt, V. (1954). *Catholics in psychology: A historical survey*. New York: McGraw-Hill.

Monaghan, E. A. (1935). Major factors in cognition (Monograph). *Studies in Psychology and Psychiatry*, 3 (5).

Monitum from the Holy Office. (1961). *Bulletin of the Guild of Catholic Psychiatrists*, 8, 185–6.

Moore, R. L. (1975). The Spiritualist medium: A study of female professionalism in Victorian America. *American Quarterly*, 27(2), 200–21.

Moore, T. V. (1910). The process of abstraction: An experimental study. *University of California Publications in Psychology*, 1(2), 73–197.

—(1915). The temporal relations of meaning and imagery. *Psychological Review*, 22, 177–225.

—(1917). Meaning and imagery. *Psychological Review*, 24, 318–22.

—(1919a). Hypnotic analogies. *Psychological Monographs*, 27(4), 387–422.

—(1919b). Image and meaning in memory and perception. *Psychological Monographs*, 27 (Whole No. 119), 69–296.

—(1924). *Dynamic psychology*. Philadelphia: Lippincott.

—(1929). The general factor in intelligence. *Proceedings of the American Catholic Philosophical Society*, 5, 26–30.

—(1931). Multiple correlations and the correlation between general factors (Monograph). *Studies in Psychology and Psychiatry*, 3(1).

—(1932a). The analysis of association by its equational constants. In Hart (ed.), *Aspects of the new scholastic philosophy*. (pp. 181–225).

—(1932b). Partial correlation (Monograph). *Studies in Psychology and Psychiatry*, 3(2).

—(1933). The essential psychoses and their fundamental syndromes (Monograph). *Studies in Psychology and Psychiatry*, 3(3).

—(1934). Formal causality and the analysis of mental life. *Journal of Educational Psychology*, 25(6), 401–21.

—(1936a). The clergy and mental hygiene. *Ecclesiastical Review*, 85(6), 598–604.

—(1936b). Insanity in priests and religious: I. The rate of insanity in priests and religious. *American Ecclesiastical Review*, 95, 485–98.

—(1936c). Insanity in priests and religious: II. Detection of prepsychotics applying for admission to priesthood or religious communities. *American Ecclesiastical Review*, 95, 601–13.

—(1939). *Cognitive psychology*. Philadelphia: J. B. Lippincott.

—(1940). The work of a Catholic clinic for problem children. *National Catholic Educational Association Bulletin*, 37, 11–22.

—(1948). *The driving forces of human nature and their adjustment*. New York: Grune & Stratton.

—(1951). *The nature and treatment of mental disorders* (2nd rev. edn). New York: Grune & Stratton.

—(1959). *Heroic sanctity and insanity: An introduction to the spiritual life and mental hygiene*. New York: Grune & Stratton.

Morawski, J. (1996). Principles of selves: The rhetoric of introductory textbooks in American psychology. In C. F. Graumann and K. J. Gergen (eds.), *Historical dimensions of psychological discourse*. New York: Cambridge University Press. (pp. 145–62).

Mount St. Vincent marks centenary. (1947, October 7). *New York Times*, p. 30.

Msgr. Sheen's attack hit by psychiatrists. (1947, July 2). *New York Times*, p. 17.

Msgr. Sheen lays errors to press. (1947, July 21). *New York Times*, p. 8.

Mulcahy, R. E. (ed.). (1959). *Readings in economics*. Westminster, MD: Newman Press.

Munslow, A. (1997). *Deconstructing history*. New York: Routledge.

Münsterberg, H. (1909). *Psychotherapy*. New York: Moffat, Yard and Co.

Murray, M. (ed.). (2004). *Critical health psychology*. New York: Palgrave Macmillan.

Myers, A. T., and Myers, F. W. H. (1894). Mind-cure, faith-cure, and the miracles of Lourdes. *Proceedings of the Society for Psychical Research*, 9, 160–209.

Myers, D. G. (2000). A levels-of-explanation view. In E. L. Johnson and S. L. Jones (eds.), *Psychology and Christianity*. Downers Grove, IL: InterVarsity. (pp. 54–83).

Myers, F. W. H. (1908). *Human personality and its survival of bodily death* (2 vol). London: Longmans, Green, and Co.

Narramore, B. (1973). Perspectives on the integration of psychology and theology. *Journal of Psychology and Theology*, 1(1), 3–18.

Neenan, B. (2000). *Thomas Verner Moore: Psychiatrist, educator and monk.* New York: Paulist.

Neill, T. P. (ed.). (1959). *Readings in the history of western civilization.* Westminster, MD: Newman Press.

New graduate program in ascetical theology opened to sisters. (1959, Summer). *Sister Formation Bulletin*, 5, 14.

News briefs. (1951, November). *American Catholic Psychological Association Newsletter*, 1, 2–3. Akron, OH: Archives of the History of American Psychology. Collection: American Psychological Association Division 36, Box 706.

—(1953, November). *American Catholic Psychological Association Newsletter*, 3, 2–3.

—(1956a, January). *American Catholic Psychological Association Newsletter*, 6, 2–3. Akron, OH: Archives of the History of American Psychology. Collection: American Psychological Association Division 36, Box 706.

—(1956b, May). *American Catholic Psychological Association Newsletter*, 6, 3–4. Akron, OH: Archives of the History of American Psychology. Collection: American Psychological Association Division 36, Box 706.

—(1957, January). *American Catholic Psychological Association Newsletter*, 7, 2–3. Akron, OH: Archives of the History of American Psychology. Collection: American Psychological Association Division 36, Box 706.

—(1958a, May). *American Catholic Psychological Association Newsletter*, 8, 2–4. Akron, OH: Archives of the History of American Psychology. Collection: American Psychological Association Division 36, Box 706.

—(1958b, January). *American Catholic Psychological Association Newsletter*, 8, 2–3. Akron, OH: Archives of the History of American Psychology. Collection: American Psychological Association Division 36, Box 706.

Nichols, A. (1997). *Dominican gallery.* Leominster, Herefordshire: Gracewing.

—(2000). Thomism and the Nouvelle Théologie. *Thomist*, 64, 1–19.

—(2005, September 9). *The rebellious discipleship of Father Victor White: Theology and psychology in a critic of C. G. Jung.* Paper presented at the John Henry Cardinal Newman Lectures: Philosophical psychology, emotions, and freedom, Washington, D.C.

Nicholson, I. A. M. (2003). *Inventing personality: Gordon Allport and the science of selfhood.* Washington, D.C.: American Psychological Association.

Nicolson, M. H. (1960). *The breaking of the circle: studies in the effect of the "New Science" upon seventeenth-century poetry.* New York: Columbia University Press.

Niemann, M. E. (1967). Selecting the seminary applicant. *Review for Religious*, 26, 470–82.

Noll, R. (1994). *The Jung cult: Origins of a charismatic movement.* Princeton University Press.

Novak, J. G. (1956). Message from the president. *Bulletin of the Guild of Catholic Psychiatrists,* 4, 2–3.

Nowlan, E. H., SJ (1956, March). The picture of the Catholic that emerges from attitude tests. *American Catholic Psychological Association Newsletter Supplements,* 20. Akron, OH: Archives of the History of American Psychology. Collection: American Psychological Association Division 36, Box 706.

Nussbaum, A. (2007). Profession and faith: The National Guild of Catholic Psychiatrists, 1950–1968. *Catholic Historical Review,* 93, 845–65.

O'Brien, J. A. (1921). The priest, the school, and modern pedagogy. *Ecclesiastical Review,* 64, 132–42.

—(1926). *Reading; its psychology and pedagogy.* New York: Century.

—(1938). Psychiatry and the confessional. *Ecclesiastical Review,* 98, 223–31.

O'Brien, M. J. (1957). *Differential effects of anxiety on problem solving.* Washington, D.C.: Catholic University of America Press.

—(1968). *An introduction to pastoral counseling.* New York: Alba House.

—(1984). Counselor values – client freedom. *Pastoral Psychology,* 33, 25–34.

—and Steimel, R. J. (eds.). (1965). *Psychological aspects of spiritual development.* Washington, D.C.: Catholic University of America Press.

Objects of the Society. (1883). *Proceedings of the Society for Psychical Research,* 1, 3–6.

O'Connell, D. C. (1961). Is mental illness a result of sin? *Lumen Vitae,* 16, 233–42.

—and Onuska, L. A. (1967). A challenge to Catholic psychology. *Catholic Psychological Record,* 5, 29–34.

O'Connell, M. R. (1994). *Critics on trial: An introduction to the Catholic modernist crisis.* Washington, D.C.: Catholic University Press of America.

O'Connor, J. T. (1890, February). Hypnotism. *Catholic World,* 50, 574–82.

O'Donnell, K. (1957). Psychiatry and pastoral psychology. *Lumen Vitae,* 12 (2), 253–9.

Ó Conluain, P. (1991). Edward Boyd Barrett and "The Great O Neill". *Dúiche Néill: Journal of the O Neill Country Historical Society,* 6, 76–89.

O'Malley, A., and Walsh, J. J. (1906). *Essays in pastoral medicine.* New York: Longmans, Green and Co.

Obituary: Frank J. Ayd Jr., 1920–2008. (2008). American College of Neuropsychopharmacology. Available: www.acnp.org.

Oppenheim, J. (1985). *The other world: Spiritualism and psychical research in England, 1850–1914.* Cambridge University Press.

Otto, R. (1923). *The idea of the holy* (trans. J. W. Harvey). New York: Oxford University Press.

—(1984). *Il sacro. L'irrazionale nell'idea del divino e la sua relazione al razionale* (trans. E. Buonaiuti). Milano: Feltrinelli.

Overby, T. J. (1990). A century of psychology at St. Louis University. In Korn (ed.), *The history of the Saint Louis University Department of Psychology.* (pp. 3–40).

Owen, R. D. (1872). *The debatable land between this world and the next.* New York: G. W. Carleton.

Pace, E. A. (1894). The growth and spirit of modern psychology. *American Catholic Quarterly Review,* 19, 522–44.

—(1895). The relations of experimental psychology. *American Catholic Quarterly Review,* 20, 131–62.

—(1896). St. Thomas and modern thought. *Catholic University Bulletin,* 2, 188–97.

—(1912). Spiritism. *Catholic Encyclopedia* (vol. XIV). New York: Appleton. (pp. 221–4).

Pacella, Bernard L. (2007, February 18). *New York Times,* p. A39.

Pacella, B. L., Piotrowski, Z., and Lewis, N. D. C. (1947). The effects of electric convulsive therapy on certain personality traits in psychiatric patients. *American Journal of Psychiatry,* 104, 83–91.

Pacwa, M. (1992). *Catholics and the New Age: How good people are being drawn into Jungian psychology, the enneagram, and the Age of Aquarius.* Ann Arbor: Servant Publications.

Palmer, R. (1969). *Hermeneutics.* Evanston: Northwestern University Press.

Palmer, R. E. (ed.). (2001). *Gadamer in conversation.* New Haven: Yale University Press.

Pargament, K. I. (1999). The psychology of religion *and* spirituality? Yes and no. *International Journal for the Psychology of Religion,* 9, 3–16.

Pastoral dimensions in counseling and psychotherapy. (1970). *Journal of Pastoral Counseling,* 5(1), 4–27.

Pater, T. (1953). Review of the book, *The Christian dilemma: Catholic Church – Reformation. Thomist,* 16, 585–91.

Paulhan, F. (1902). *Les caractères* (2nd edn.). Paris: Alcan.

Peixotto, H. E. (1969). A history of psychology at Catholic University. *Catholic Education Review,* 66(13), 844–9.

Percy, W. (1957a, January 5). The coming crisis in psychiatry. *America,* 96, 391–3.

—(1957b, January 12). The coming crisis in psychiatry: II. *America,* 96, 415–18.

—(1975). Toward a triadic theory of linguistic signs, thought, and meaning, *The message in the bottle.* New York: Farrar, Straus and Giroux. (pp. 159–88).

Perrier, J. L. (1909). *The revival of scholastic philosophy in the nineteenth century.* New York: Columbia University Press.

Pickren, W. E. (2000). A whisper of salvation: American psychologists and religion in the popular press, 1884–1908. *American Psychologist,* 55, 1022–4.

Pickstock, C. (1998). *After writing: On the liturgical consummation of philosophy.* Oxford: Blackwell.

—(2000). Liturgy, art and politics. *Modern Theology,* 16, 159–80.

Plante, T. G., and Boccaccini, M. T. (1998). A proposed psychological assessment protocol for applicants to religious life in the Roman Catholic Church. *Pastoral Psychology,* 46, 363–72.

Pohle, J. (1912). Theology, Dogmatic. *Catholic Encyclopedia.* (vol. XIV). New York: Appleton. (pp. 580–97).

Polanyi, M. (1962). *Personal knowledge*. University of Chicago Press.

Pontifical Council for Culture and Pontifical Council for Interreligious Dialogue. (2003). Jesus Christ: The bearer of the water of life: A Christian reflection on the "New Age". Available: www.vatican.va/roman_curia/pontifical_councils/ interelg/documents/rc_pc_interelg_doc_20030203_new-age_en.html.

Pope John Paul II. (2000). *On Catholic universities: Ex corde ecclesiae*. Washington, D.C.: United States Catholic Conference. (First published 1990.)

Pope Leo XIII. (1903). *The great encyclical letters of Pope Leo XIII*. New York: Benziger Brothers.

—(1954). On Christian philosophy: Encyclical Letter *Aeterni Patris*, August 4, 1879. In E. Gilson (ed.), *The Church speaks to the modern world: The social teachings of Leo XIII*. Garden City, NY: Image Books. (pp. 31–54). (First published 1879.)

Pope Pius IX. (1999). Syllabus of errors. In A. J. Mioni (ed.), *The popes against modern errors*. Rockford, IL: Tan Books. (pp. 27–39).

Pope Pius X. (1907). On modernism (*Pascendi dominici gregis*). In Mioni (ed.), *The popes against modern errors*. (pp. 180–241).

—(1999a). The oath against modernism. In Mioni (ed.), *The popes against modern errors*. (pp. 270–2).

—(1999b). Syllabus condemning the errors of the modernists (*Lamentabili sane*). In A. J. Mioni (ed.), *The popes against modern errors*. (pp. 171–9).

Pope Pius XII. (1952). *The moral limits of medical research and treatment: An address given September 14, 1952 by His Holiness Pope Pius XII to the First International Congress on the Histopathology of the Nervous System*. Washington, D.C.: National Catholic Welfare Conference.

—(1953). *On psychotherapy and religion: An address of His Holiness Pope Pius XII to the Fifth International Congress on Psychotherapy and Clinical Psychology, April 13, 1953*. Washington, D.C.: National Catholic Welfare Conference.

—(1958, July). Morality and applied psychology: An address to the Congress of the International Association of Applied Psychologists, Rome, April 10, 1958. *Catholic Mind*, 56, 353–68.

Portier, W. L. (2001). Fundamentalism in North America: A modern anti-modernism. *Communio*, 28, 581–98.

Poulat, É. (1969). *Intégrisme et Catholicisme intégral: Un réseau secret international antimoderniste: La "Sapieniére" (1909–1921)*. Tournai: Casterman.

Pratt, J. B. (1920). *Religious consciousness: A psychological study*. New York: Macmillan.

Psychiatrist quits in Catholic clash. (1947, July 20). *New York Times*, p. 5.

Psychological Assessment in religious vocation. (1960). In Bier and Schneiders (eds.), *Selected papers from the ACPA meetings of 1957, 1958, 1959*. (pp. 3–43).

Psychological news and notes. (1949). *American Psychologist*, 4(8), 365–70.

—(1950). *American Psychologist*, 5, 643–8.

Puech, H.-C. (1968). The concept of redemption in Manichaeism. In J. Campbell (ed.), *The mystic vision: Papers from the Eranos Yearbooks.* Princeton University Press. (pp. 247–314). (First published 1936.)

— (1952). La gnose et le temps. In O. Fröbe-Kapleyn (ed.), *Eranos-Jahrbuch 20: Mensch und Zeit.* Zürich: Rhein-Verlag. (pp. 57–113).

Purcell, T. V. (1962, March). Review of the book, *Religion as an occupation: A study in the sociology of professions. American Catholic Psychological Association Newsletter,* 12, 4–5. Akron, OH: Archives of the History of American Psychology. Collection: American Psychological Association Division 36, Box 706.

Quinn, T. L. (1962). *Differences in motivational patterns of college student brothers as revealed in the TAT, the ratings of their peers, and the ratings of their superiors; a validation study.* Unpublished doctoral dissertation, Loyola University, Chicago.

Quispel, G. (1980). Gnosis and psychology. In B. Layton, (ed.), *The rediscovery of Gnosticism.* (vol. I) Leiden: E. J. Brill. (pp. 17–31).

Rabinbach, A. (1990). *The human motor: Energy, fatigue, and the origins of modernity.* Berkeley: University of California Press.

Rademacher, N. (2007). Paul Hanly Furfey and the social sciences: Liberal, radical, and revolutionary. *U. S. Catholic Historian,* 25(4), 23–43.

Radio Religion. (1946, January 21). *Time,* 47, p. 74.

Rahner, H. (1968). Earth spirit and divine spirit in Patristic theology. In J. Campbell (ed.), *Spirit and Nature: Papers from the Eranos Yearbooks.* New York: Pantheon. (pp. 122–48). (First published 1945.)

—(1963). *Greek myths and Christian mysteries* (trans. B. Battershaw). New York: Harper & Row. (First published 1957.)

Ratzinger, J., and Bovone, A. (1986). On the pastoral care of homosexual persons. The Congregation for the Doctrine of the Faith. Available: www.vatican.va/roman_curia/congregations/cfaith/documents/rc_con_cfaith_doc_19861001_homosexual-persons_en.html.

Ready, M. J. (1952). Foreword. In C. A. Curran, *Counseling in Catholic life and education.* New York: Macmillan. (pp. xii–xiii).

Reed, E. (1997). *From soul to mind: The emergence of psychology from Erasmus Darwin to William James.* New Haven: Yale University Press.

Reese, T. J. (1992). *A flock of shepherds: The National Conference of Catholic Bishops.* Kansas City: Sheed & Ward.

Reeves, T. C. (2001). *America's bishop: The life and times of Fulton J. Sheen.* San Francisco: Encounter Books.

Reh, F. F. (1962). Use of the psychologist's report in a diocesan seminary. In A. A. Schneiders and P. J. Centi (eds.), *Selected papers from the ACPA meetings of 1960, 1961.* New York: Fordham University Press. (pp. 71–6).

Reiman, M. G. (1942). Psychiatry and psychology in Catholic education. In R. J. Deferrari (ed.), *Essays on Catholic education in the United States.* Washington, D.C.: Catholic University of America Press. (pp. 427–43).

Religion marries psychiatry. (1949, December). *Catholic World*, 170, 161–5.

Rénan, E. (1864). *The life of Jesus* (trans. C. E. Wilbour). New York: Carleton.

Restructuring of ACPA. (1969, Winter). *American Catholic Psychological Association Newsletter*, 19, 1. Akron, OH: Archives of the History of American Psychology. Collection: American Psychological Association Division 36, Box 706.

Reuder, M. E. (1999). A history of Division 36 (Psychology of Religion). In D. A. Dewsbury (ed.), *Unification through division: Histories of the Divisions of the American Psychological Association*. (vol. IV). Washington, D.C.: American Psychological Association. (pp. 91–108).

Rev. Richard Zegers, 70, a professor at Fordham. (1980, April 10). *New York Times*, p. B19.

Review of the book, *A Convert through Spiritualism*. (1894). *American Ecclesiastical Review*, 11, 155–7.

Review of the book, *Old Time Makers of Medicine*. (1912). *Boston Medical and Surgical Journal*, 167, 772.

Review of the book, *Psychotherapy*. (1913). *Boston Medical and Surgical Journal*, 168 (9), 319.

Review of the book, *Assessment of Candidates for the Religious Life*. (1969). *Review for Religious*, 28, 535.

Richards, G. (2010). *Putting psychology in its place: Critical historical perspectives* (3rd edn.). New York: Routledge.

Ricoeur, P. (1977). *Freud and philosophy: An essay on interpretation* (trans. D. Savage). New Haven: Yale University Press.

Rieber, R. W. (1998). The assimilation of psychoanalysis in America: From popularization to vulgarization. In R. W. Rieber and K. D. Salzinger (eds.), *Psychology: Theoretical-historical perspectives* (2nd edn.) Washington, D.C.: American Psychological Association. (pp. 355–97).

Riggs, A. (1923). Psychotherapy. *Boston Medical and Surgical Journal*, 189(8), 269–73.

Rigolot, I. (2000). La tradition vivante chez les Pères, lecteurs de l'Ecriture. Available: users.skynet.be/am012324/studium/rigolot/TABLE%20DES%20MATIERES.htm.

Ristuccia, B. J. (1962). The psychologist's report and canon law. In Schneiders and Centi (eds.), *Selected papers of the ACPA meetings of 1960, 1961*. (pp. 77–81).

Roback, A. A. (1927). *The psychology of character*. London: Kegan Paul, Trench, Trubner and Co.

—(1952). *History of American psychology*. New York: Library Publishers.

—(1964). *A history of American psychology* (New, rev. edn.). New York: Collier Books.

Roberts, R. C. (2000). A Christian psychology view. In E. L. Johnson and S. L. Jones (eds.), *Psychology and Christianity*. Downers Grove, IL: InterVarsity. (pp. 148–77).

Robinson, J. M. (1977). The Jung Codex: The rise and fall of a monopoly. *Religious Studies Review*, 3(1), 17–30.

Rodgers, A. (2006). Jim Crows, veiled ladies and true womanhood: Mesmerism. In *The house of the seven gables*. In M. Willis and C. Wynne (eds.), *Victorian literary mesmerism*. New York: Rodopi. (pp. 127–44).

Rogers, C. R. (1955). Persons or science? A philosophical question. *American Psychologist*, 10, 267–78.

—(1951). *Client-centered therapy*. Boston: Houghton Mifflin.

—(1953). Persons or science? A philosophical question. *Cross Currents*, 3, 289–306.

—(1967, July). Review of the book, *A Modern Priest Looks at his Outmoded Church*. *Psychology Today*, 1, 13.

Rommen, H. (1955). Catholicism and American democracy. *Catholicism in American culture: Semicentenary lecture series, 1953–54*. College of New Rochelle. (pp. 61–70).

Roof, W. C. (1993). *A generation of seekers*. New York: HarperSanFrancisco.

Rooney, J. J. (1913). Catholic Club of New York. *Catholic Encyclopedia*. (vol. III). New York: Encyclopedia Press. (pp. 452–3).

Rooney, J. J. (1972). Appendix A: Psychological research on the American priesthood: A review of the literature. In Kennedy and Heckler, *The Catholic priest in the United States: Psychological investigations*. Washington, D.C.: United States Catholic Conference. (pp. 183–219).

Rose, N. (1996). Power and subjectivity: Critical history and psychology. In C. F. Grauman and K. Gergen (eds.), *Historical dimensions of psychological discourse*. New York: Cambridge University Press. (pp. 103–24).

Rosemann, P. W. (1999). *Understanding scholastic thought with Foucault*. New York: St. Martin's Press.

Rosenberg, J. R. (Ed.). (1964). *Readings in metaphysics*. Westminster, MD: Newman Press.

Roure, L. (1917). *Le merveilleux Spirite*. Paris: Gabriel Beauchesne.

Royce, J. E. (1955). *Personality and mental health*. Milwaukee: Bruce.

—(1956). Review of the book, *The doctor and the soul. American Catholic Psychological Association Newsletter*, 6 (2), 4–5. Akron, OH: Archives of the History of American Psychology. Collection: American Psychological Association Division 36, Box 706.

—(1961). *Man and his nature: A philosophical psychology*. New York: McGraw-Hill.

—(1964). The image of man and its implications for psychological practice. *Catholic Psychological Record*, 2, 1–8.

—(1986). Philosophical issues and the founding of Division 24, American Psychological Association. *Journal of the History of the Behavioral Sciences*, 22, 321–3.

Rudolf Allers, 1883–1963. (1965). *Journal of Individual Psychology*, 21, 112.

Rychlak, J. F. (1976). Can psychology be objective about free will? *Philosophical Psychologist*, 10(2), 2–9.

Samuel, A. (1985). *Jung and the PostJungians*. London: Routledge and Kegan Paul.

Saroglou, V. (2000). Église(s) et psychologie(s): Bilan et perspectives d'une ouverture prudente. *Revue d'histoire ecclésiastique*, 95(3), 709–53.

—(2003). Spiritualité moderne. *Revue théologique de Louvain*, 34, 473–504.

Sass, L. A. (1988). Humanism, hermeneutics, and the concept of the human subject. In L. A. Sass and R. L. Woolfolk (eds.), *Hermeneutics and psychological theory: Interpretative perspectives on personality, psychotherapy, and psychopathology*. New Brunswick, N.J.: Rutgers University Press. (pp. 222–71).

Sauvage, G. M. (1909). Fideism. *Catholic Encyclopedia*. (vol. VI). New York: Robert Appleton Co. (pp. 68–9).

Schabert, J. A. (1936). General relations between scholastic psychology and modern psychology. *American Catholic Philosophical Association Proceedings*, 12, 103–6.

Scheffczyk, L. (1981). Main lines of development of theology between World War I and Vatican II. In H. Jedin, K. Repgen and J. Dolan (eds.), *History of the Church: The Church in the modern age* (vol. X). New York: Crossroad. (pp. 260–98).

Schindler, D. L. (1998). Introduction to the 1998 edition. *The mystery of the supernatural*. New York: Crossroad Herder. (pp. xi–xxxi).

Schmidt, A. G. (1923a, November 24). Do we measure native ability? *America*, 30, 141–2.

—(1923b, December 15). Classroom uses of tests. *America*, 30, 217–18.

—(1923c). *The effect of objective presentation on the learning and retention of a Latin vocabulary*. Chicago: Loyola University Press.

Schneiders, A. A. (1934). *The anatomy of human personality, a philosophical and psychological investigation into the nature of human individuality, with special reference to its aberrations*. Unpublished thesis (Ph.D.), Georgetown University, Washington, D.C.

—(1950). *The "core" program*. Akron, OH: Archives of the History of American Psychology. Collection: American Psychological Association Division 36, Box 709, Folder 10.

—(1951). *Introductory psychology*. New York: Rinehart.

—(1959). Editorial: The Catholic and psychology. *Pastoral Psychology*, 10(91), 5–6; 64.

—(1963). *The anarchy of feeling: Man's struggle for freedom and maturity*. New York: Sheed and Ward.

—(1967). Catholics and psychology: An editorial reply. *Catholic Psychological Record*, 5, 102–10.

Schultenover, D. G. (1981). *George Tyrrell: In search of Catholicism*. Shepherdstown: Patmos.

Schwartz, H. S. (1937, April 9). Psychoanalysis and the devil. *Commonweal*, 25, 660–1.

Scott, D. J., and Scott, C. E. (1982). Eranos and the *Eranos Jahrbücher*. *Religious Studies Review*, 8(3), 226–39.

Seligman, M. E. P. (2002). *Authentic happiness*. New York: Free Press.

Seton, W. (1890, January). Wonders of the nervous system. *Catholic World*, 50, 452–64.

—(1899, February). The problem of personality. *Catholic World*, 68, 652–8.

Severin, F. T. (1953, May). Psychology at St. Louis University. *American Catholic Psychological Association Newsletter Supplement No. 3*, 1–2.

—(1963). Letter to Rev. Charles F. McDermott, S. J. St. Louis: Midwest Jesuit Archives, Missouri Province Collection, Jesuit Francis T. Severin Personnel File.

—(1965). *Humanistic viewpoints in psychology*. New York: McGraw-Hill.

—(1967a). The humanistic psychology of Teilhard de Chardin. In J. F. T. Bugental (ed.), *Challenges of humanistic psychology*. New York: McGraw-Hill. (pp. 150–8).

—(1967b). Teilhard's methodology for the study of cosmic psychology. *Catholic Psychological Record*, 5, 1–7.

—(1973). *Discovering man in psychology: A humanistic approach*. New York: McGraw-Hill.

Sexton, V. S. (1986). Psychology of religion: Some accomplishments and challenges. *Journal of Psychology and Christianity*, 5, 79–83.

—(1991a). American psychology and philosophy, 1876–1976: Alienation and reconciliation. In H. N. Malony (ed.), *Psychology of religion: Personalities, problems, possibilities*. Grand Rapids, MI: Baker House. (pp. 21–35).

—(1991b). Psychology of religion: Some accomplishments and challenges. In Malony (ed.), *Psychology of religion: Personalities, problems, possibilities*. (pp. 37–43).

Shakow, D., and Rapaport, D. (1964). The influence of Freud on American psychology. *Psychological Issues*, 4 (1, monograph 13).

Shamdasani, S. (1998). *Cult fictions: C. G. Jung and the founding of Analytical Psychology*. London: Routledge.

Sharp, L. L. (1999). Fighting for the afterlife: Spiritists, Catholics, and popular religion in nineteenth-century France. *Journal of Religious History*, 23(3), 282–95.

Sheen criticized by psychoanalyst. (1947, July 22). *New York Times*, p. 16.

Sheen denounces psychoanalysis. (1947, March 10). *New York Times*, p. 18.

Sheen, F. J. (1949). *Peace of soul*. New York: Whittlesey House.

Shevenell, R. H. (1953, November). Psychology at the University of Ottawa. *American Catholic Psychological Association Newsletter Supplement No. 6*, 1–2.

—(1960, November). Review of the book, *Soul and Psyche*, by Victor White. *American Catholic Psychological Association Newsletter*, 10, 6–7. Akron, OH: Archives of the History of American Psychology. Collection: American Psychological Association Division 36, Box 706.

Shields, T. E. (1916). The culture epoch theory. *Catholic Education Review*, 11(3), 233–47.

—(1917). *Philosophy of education*. Washington, D.C.: Catholic Education Press.

Siegfried, F. P. (1891). Catholic psychology. *American Ecclesiastical Review*, 4, 40–54.

—(1897). Review of the book, *Institutiones Psychologicae*, by T. Pesch. *American Ecclesiastical Review*, 16, 98–102. (F.P.S. listed as author.)

Sister M. Aloyse. (1961, October). Evaluation of candidates for religious life. *Guild of Catholic Psychiatrists Bulletin*, 8, 199–204.

—(1964, October). Re-evaluation of psychological testing of candidates for religious life: A discussion of a paper given by Carroll F. Tageson, O.F.M., Ph.D. *Guild of Catholic Psychiatrists Bulletin*, 11, 221–3.

Sister M. Jeanette. (1931). Psychoanalysis. *Catholic School Journal*, 31, 130–2.

Sister Mary. (1932). The moral development of children. In C. A. Hart (ed.), *Aspects of the new scholastic philosophy*. New York: Benziger Brothers. (pp. 250–71).

Sister Mary (McGrath), IHM (1948). *Report of the Secretary on the Business Meeting of the Catholic Group*. Akron, OH: Archives of the History of American Psychology. Collection: American Psychological Association Division 36, Box 710, Folder 22.

Sister Mary Roberta Roberts, RSM (1947, September 11). *Report of the proceedings of the organizational meeting*, Detroit. Akron, OH: Archives of the History of American Psychology. Collection: American Psychological Association Division 36, Box 710, Folder 22.

Sister Miriam Reinhart. (1931). A scale for measuring the g-factors in intelligence. *Studies in Psychology and Psychiatry*, 2(5), 1–42.

Sister Rose. (1936). Redirecting the guidance aspect of our schools. *Catholic Educational Review*, 34(4), 220–32.

Sixth Annual Meeting. (1952, September). *American Catholic Psychological Association Newsletter*, 2, 1–3.

Slater, T. (1909). *A manual of moral theology for English-speaking countries* (3rd edn., vol. I). New York: Benziger Brothers.

Slife, B. D., and Reber, J. S. (2009a). Is there a pervasive implicit bias against theism in psychology? *Journal of Theoretical & Philosophical Psychology*, 29, 63–79.

—and—(2009b). The prejudice against prejudice: A reply to the comments. *Journal of Theoretical & Philosophical Psychology*, 29, 128–36.

Smet, W. (1954). Religious experience in client-centered therapy. In M. B. Arnold and J. A. Gasson (eds.), *The human person: An approach to an integral theory of personality*. New York: Ronald. (pp. 539–47).

Smith, D. L. (2002). *"Fearfully and wonderfully made": The history of Duquesne University's graduate psychology programs (1959–1999)*. Pittsburgh: Simon Silverman Phenomenology Center, Duquesne University.

Smith, M. B. (1990). Humanistic psychology. *Journal of Humanistic Psychology*, 30, 6–21.

Smith, R. (1997). *The Norton history of the human sciences*. New York: Norton.

Snider, L. B. (1953, March). The department of psychology at Loyola University, Chicago. *American Catholic Psychological Association Newsletter Supplement No. 2*, 1–2.

Sokal, M. M. (1984). James McKeen Cattell and American psychology in the 1920s. In J. Brožek (ed.), *Explorations in the history of psychology in the United States*. Lewisburg, PA: Bucknell University Press. (pp. 273–323).

Sommerfeldt, J. R. (1991). *The spiritual teachings of Bernard of Clairvaux: An intellectual history of the early Cistercian Order*. Kalamazoo, MI: Cistercian Publications.

—(2009). *Christianity in culture: A historical quest*. Lanham, MD: University Press of America.

Spiegelberg, H. (1972). *Phenomenology in psychology and psychiatry*. Evanston: Northwestern University Press.

Spiritualism: Chapter I. (1873, November). *Catholic World*, 18, 145–65.

Spiritualism: Chapter II. (1873, December). *Catholic World*, 18, 318–37.

Spiritualism: Chapter III. (1874, February). *Catholic World*, 18, 606–26.

Staeuble, I. (2006). Psychology in the Eurocentric order of the social sciences: Colonial constitution, cultural imperialist expansion, postcolonial critique. In A. C. Brock (ed.), *Internationalizing the history of psychology*. New York University Press. (pp. 183–207).

Stafford, J. W. (1950). Undergraduate psychology at Catholic University. *American Psychologist*, 5, 670–2.

—(1953, January). Psychology at the Catholic University of America. *American Catholic Psychological Association Newsletter Supplement No. 1*, 1–2.

—(1969). Pastoral counseling. In E. J. Weitzel (ed.), *Contemporary pastoral counseling*. New York: Bruce. (pp. 1–18).

Stainton Rogers, W. (2003). *Social psychology: Experimental and critical approaches*. Philadelphia: Open University Press.

Starr, P. (1982). *The social transformation of American medicine*. New York: Basic Books.

Statement on Encyclical *Humanae Vitae*. (1969, Spring). *American Catholic Psychological Association Newsletter*, 19, 3. Akron, OH: Archives of the History of American Psychology. Collection: American Psychological Association Division 36, Box 706.

Staudt, V. (1955, May). Opportunities for Catholic psychologists in research and service. *American Catholic Psychological Association Newsletter, Supplement No. 15*, 1–2. Akron, OH: Archives of the History of American Psychology. Collection: American Psychological Association Division 36, Box 706.

Steel, C. (1992). Aquinas and the renewal of philosophy: Some observations on the Thomism of Désiré Mercier. In D. A. Boileau, and J. A. Dick (eds.), *Tradition and renewal: Philosophical essays commemorating the centennial of Louvain's Institute of Philosophy* (vol. 1). Leuven: Leuven University Press. (pp. 181–215).

Steimel, R. J. (1960). Childhood experiences and masculinity-femininity scores. *Journal of Counseling Psychology*, 7(3), 212–17.

Stein, L. (1957). Review of the book, *Individuation: A Study of the Depth Psychology of Carl Gustav Jung*, by Joseph Goldbrunner. *Journal of Analytical Psychology*, 2(1), 112–13.

Stein, M. (1985). *Jung's treatment of Christianity: The psychotherapy of a religious tradition*. Wilmette, IL: Chiron.

Stenner, P. (2009). Psychology, religion, and world loyalty. *Journal of Theoretical & Philosophical Psychology*, 29, 102–7.

Stern, E. M. (1968). Pastoral counseling and freedom. *Journal of Pastoral Counseling*, 3(2), 1–2.

—and Marino, B. G. (1970). *Psychotheology*. Paramus: Newman.

Stern, K. (1948, October 22). Religion and psychiatry. *Commonweal*, 49, 30–3.

Stevens, G. (1953). Review of the book, *God and the unconscious*, by Victor White. *Theological Studies*, 14(3), 499–505.

Stevens, S. S. (1968). Edwin Garrigues Boring: 1886–1968. *American Journal of Psychology*, 81, 589–606.

Stevenson-Moessner, J. (1994). Elizabeth Cady Stanton, reformer to revolutionary. *Journal of the American Academy of Religion*, 62, 673–89.

Strasser, S. (1951). Désiré Mercier et le problème de la psychologie néothomiste. *Revue Philosophique de Louvain*, 49, 699–713.

—(1957). *The soul in metaphysical and empirical psychology*. Pittsburgh: Duquesne University Press.

—(1963). *Phenomenology and the human sciences: A contribution to a new scientific ideal*. Pittsburgh: Duquesne University Press.

Sullivan, H. S. (1964). *The fusion of psychiatry and social science*. New York: W. W. Norton.

Sullivan, J. E. (1966). The Graduate Division of Pastoral Counseling of Iona College. *Iona Journal of Pastoral Counseling*, 1(1), 28–31.

Sumner, O. (1948). *St John of the Cross and Modern Psychology* London: Guild of Pastoral Psychology.

—(1950). *St. John Climacus – The Psychology of the Desert Fathers*. London: Guild of Pastoral Psychology.

—and Elkisch, F. B. (1949). Psychologie moderne et introspection. *Psyche*, 4, 637–50.

Surbled, G. (1898). *Spiritualisme et spiritisme*. Paris: Ancienne Maison Ch. Douniol.

—(1910). Hypnotism. *Catholic Encyclopedia* (vol. VII). New York: Appleton. (pp. 604–10).

Surprenant, A. M. (1997). T. V. Moore's (1939) Cognitive Psychology. *Psychonomic Bulletin and Review*, 4(3), 342–9.

Survey of psychological training in Catholic women's colleges. (1949). Akron, OH: Archives of the History of American Psychology. Collection: American Psychological Association Division 36, Box 709, Folder 9.

Sweeney, H. (1964). The morality of psychological testing of vocation prospects. *National Catholic Educational Association Bulletin*, 60(1), 370–81.

Symposium – Basic issues in assessment of candidates to the religious life. (1962). In Schneiders and Centi (eds.), *Selected papers from the ACPA meetings of 1960, 1961*. (pp. 65–81).

Symposium – Problems in the teaching of scientific psychology in the denominational college. (1962). In Schneiders and Centi (eds.), *Selected papers from the
ACPA meetings of 1960, 1961*. (pp. 28–62).

Tageson, C. F. (1964). Re-evaluation of psychological testing of candidates for
religious life. *Bulletin of the Guild of Catholic Psychiatrists*, 11, 147–54.

Talk about new books. (1890, January). *Catholic World*, 50, 550–3.

Talk about new books. (1901, March). *Catholic World*, 72, 807–26.

Tanquerey, A. (1930). *The spiritual life: A treatise on ascetical and mystical theology*
(2nd rev. edn., trans. H. Branderis). Tournai: Desclée and Co.

Taylor, E. (1996). *William James on consciousness beyond the margin*. Princeton
University Press.

—(1999). *Shadow culture: Psychology and spirituality in America*. Washington,
D.C.: Counterpoint.

Tells of a compact to end Grant's pain. (1910, April 7). *New York Times*, p. 11.

Teo, T. (2009). Editorial. *Journal of Theoretical & Philosophical Psychology*, 29, 61–2.

Thagard, P. (2005). Being interdisciplinary: Trading zones in cognitive science. In
S. J. Derry, C. D. Schunn and M. A. Gernsbacher (eds.), *Interdisciplinary
collaboration: An emerging cognitive science*. Mahwah, N.J.: Lawrence
Erlbaum. (pp. 317–99).

Thurston, H. (1933). *The Church and Spiritualism*. Milwaukee: Bruce.

Thurstone, L. L. (1934). The vectors of mind. *Psychological Review*, 41, 1–32.

Tisserant, E. (1952). Preface. In C. A. Curran, *Counseling in Catholic life and
education*. New York: Macmillan. (pp. vii–xi).

Tolman, E. C. (1917). More concerning the temporal relations of meaning and
imagery. *Psychological Review*, 24, 114–38.

Tugwell, O P, Simon, and Bellenger, OP, Aidan (eds.). (1989). *Letters of Bede Jarrett:
Letters and other papers from the English Dominican Archives, selected by
Bede Bailey, O.P.* Bath: Downside Abbey.

Turk, M. (1971). *The buried life: A nun's journey*. New York: World Publishing
Company.

Twentieth Annual Meeting. (1966, Autumn). *American Catholic Psychological
Association Newsletter, 16*, 1–2. Akron, OH: Archives of the History of
American Psychology. Collection: American Psychological Association
Division 36, Box 706.

Twenty-first Annual Meeting. (1967, Autumn). *American Catholic Psychological
Association Newsletter, 17*, 1–2. Akron, OH: Archives of the History of
American Psychology. Collection: American Psychological Association
Division 36, Box 706.

Twenty-second Annual Meeting. (1968, Autumn). *American Catholic Psychological
Association Newsletter, 18*, 1–3. Akron, OH: Archives of the History of
American Psychology. Collection: American Psychological Association
Division 36, Box 706.

Twenty-third Annual Meeting. (1969, Autumn). *American Catholic Psychological
Association Newsletter, 19*, 1–2. Akron, OH: Archives of the History of

American Psychology. Collection: American Psychological Association Division 36, Box 706.

Twomey, M. (1936). The question of intelligence tests. *Catholic School Interests*, 14, 66–8.

Tyrrell, G. (1902). *The faith of the millions* (2nd ser., 2nd edn.). New York: Longmans, Green, and Co.

—(1904). *The faith of the millions* (1st ser., 3rd edn.). London: Longmans, Green, and Co.

—(1905). Preface. In F. Thompson, *Health and holiness: A study of the relations between Brother Ass, the body, and his Rider, the soul*. London: J. Masters & Co. (pp. vii–x).

—(1908). *Medievalism: A reply to Cardinal Mercier*. London: Longmans, Green, and Co.

—(1910). *Christianity at the cross-roads*. London: Longmans, Green and Co.

—and Petre, M. D. M. (1912). *Autobiography and life of George Tyrrell*. London: E. Arnold.

University Chronicle. (1900). *Catholic University Bulletin*, 6, 554.

van den Berg, J. H. (1971). What is psychotherapy? *Humanitas*, 7, 321–70.

—(1972). *A different existence: Principles of phenomenological psychopathology*. Pittsburgh: Duquesne University Press.

Van Hoorn, W. (1972). *As images unwind: Ancient and modern theories of visual perception*. University Press Amsterdam.

Van Kaam, A. (1961). The impact of existential phenomenology on the psychological literature of western Europe. *Review of Existential Psychology and Psychiatry*, 1, 63–92.

—(1963). Existential psychology as a comprehensive theory of personality. *Review of Existential Psychology and Psychiatry*, 3, 11–26.

—(1964). *Religion and personality*. Englewood Cliffs, N.J.: Prentice-Hall.

—(1966a). *The art of existential counseling*. Wilkes-Barre, PA: Dimension Books.

—(1966b). *Existential foundations of psychology*. Pittsburgh: Duquesne University Press.

—(1967a). Existential psychology. *New Catholic Encyclopedia*. (vol. V). New York: McGraw-Hill. (pp. 728–9).

—(1967b). *Personality fulfillment in the religious life*. Wilkes-Barre, PA: Dimension Books.

—(1967c). *Personality fulfillment in the spiritual life*. Wilkes-Barre, PA: Dimension Books.

—(1983). *Formative spirituality, volume one: Fundamental formation*. New York: Crossroad.

—and Muto, S. (1995). The theology and pretheology of empirical Christian character and personality formation. In J. M. DuBois (ed.), *The nature and tasks of a personalist psychology*. Lanham, MD: University Press of America. (pp. 141–53).

van Rappard, J. F. H. (1997). History of psychology turned inside(r) out: A comment on Danziger. *Theory & Psychology*, 7, 101–5.

—(1998). Towards household history: A reply to Dehue. *Theory & Psychology*, 8, 663–7.

Vande Kemp, H. (1984). *Psychology and theology in Western thought 1672–1965: A historical and annotated bibliography*. White Plains, NY: Kraus International Publishers.

—(1994). Historical perspective: Religion and clinical psychology in America. In P. J. Verhagen and G. Glas (eds.), *Psyche and faith beyond professionalism*. Zoetermeer: Uitgeverij Boekencentrum. (pp. 3–35).

Vandereycken, W. (1993). James Joseph Walsh (1865–1942), a forgotten psychiatrist. *Biological Psychiatry*, 33, 395–6.

VanderVeldt, J. H., and Odenwald, R. P. (1952). *Psychiatry and Catholicism*. New York: McGraw-Hill.

Vann, G. (1959). *The paradise tree: On living the symbols of the church*. New York: Sheed & Ward.

Vaughan, R. P. (1957a). Moral issues in psychological screening. *Review for Religious*, 16(2), 65–78.

—(1957b). *To William C. Bier, April 29*. Akron, OH: Archives of the History of American Psychology. Collection: American Psychological Association Division 36, Box 710, Folder 7.

—(1961). Psychological examination. *Bulletin of the Guild of Catholic Psychiatrists*, 8(3), 149–55.

—(1969). *An introduction to religious counseling: A Christian humanistic approach*. Englewood Cliffs, N.J.: Prentice-Hall.

Vergote, A. (1990). Confrontation with neutrality in theory and praxis. In J. H. Smith and S. A. Handelman (eds.), *Psychoanalysis and religion*. Baltimore: Johns Hopkins University Press. (pp. 74–93).

—(1998). *Psychoanalysis, phenomenological anthropology and religion* (trans. E. Haasl). Atlanta: Rodopi.

Vermeersch, A. (1911). Modernism. *Catholic Encyclopedia* (vol. X). New York: Appleton. (pp. 415–21).

Vernant, J.-P. (1991). History and psychology. In F. I. Zeitlin (ed.), *Mortals and immortals*. Princeton University Press. (pp. 261–8).

Vitz, P. (1985). Introduction. In G. van den Aardweg (ed.), *Homosexuality and hope*. Ann Arbor: Servant Books. (pp. 7–12).

—(1994). *Psychology as religion: The cult of self-worship* (2nd edn.). Grand Rapids, MI: Eerdmans.

Volz, J. R. (1908). Tommaso de Vio Gaetani Cajetan. *Catholic Encyclopedia* (vol. III). New York: Appleton. (pp. 145–8).

von Balthasar, H. U. (1942). *Présence et pensée: essai sur la philosophie religieuse de Gregoire de Nysse*. Paris: Beauschesne et ses fils.

—(1991). *The theology of Henri de Lubac* (trans. J. Fessio and M. M. Waldstein). San Francisco: Ignatius.

von der Heydt, V. (1954). *Psychology and the care of souls*. London: Guild of Pastoral Psychology.

—(1970). The treatment of Catholic patients. *Journal of Analytical Psychology*, 15, 72–80.

—(1976). *Prospects for the soul: Soundings in Jungian psychology and religion.* London: Darton, Longman and Todd.

—(1977). Jung and religion. *Journal of Analytical Psychology*, 22, 175–83.

—(2002). *Religious aspects in Jung's work.* Guild of Analytical Psychology and Spirituality. Available: www.gaps.co.uk/.

Von Gebsattel, V. E. (1947). *Christentum und Humanismus. Wege des menschlichen Selbstverständnis.* Stuttgart: Ernst Klett.

von Hügel, F. (1909–10). Father Tyrrell: Some memorials of the last twelve years of his life. *Hibbert Journal*, 233–52.

—(1923). *The mystical element of religion as studied in Saint Catherine of Genoa and her friends* (2nd edn. vol. I). London: E. M. Dent.

Wagner, C. A. v. (1992). *The AAPC: A history of the American Association of Pastoral Counselors (1963–1991).* Fairfax, VA: American Association of Pastoral Counselors.

Waite, A. E. (ed. and trans.). (1894). *The hermetic and alchemical writings of Aureolus Philippus Theophrastus Bombast, of Hohenheim, called Paracelsus the Great* (2 vol). London: James Elliott and Co.

Walsh, J. J. (1911a). *Old time makers of medicine.* New York: Fordham University Press.

—(1911b). Psychotherapy. *Catholic Encyclopedia* (vol. XII). New York: Appleton. (pp. 549–53).

—(1912). *Psychotherapy.* New York: Appleton.

—(1914, November 14). Backward children. *America*, 12, 109–10.

—(1919). *Health through will power.* Boston: Little, Brown, and Co.

—(1923). *Psychotherapy* (rev. edn.). New York: Appleton.

—(1925). *Spiritualism a fake.* Boston: Stratford.

—(1928). *The Catholic Church and healing.* New York: Macmillan.

—(1930, December 24). Einstein and Freud. *Commonweal*, 13, 203–4.

Walters, A. (1954). Contemporary personality theory. In Arnold and Gasson (eds.), *The human person.* (pp. 101–26).

—(ed.). (1964). *Readings in psychology.* Westminster, MD: Newman Press.

—and O'Hara, K. (1953). *Persons and personality: An introduction to psychology.* New York: Appleton-Century-Crofts.

Warns Catholics of Christian Science. (1910, May 15). *New York Times*, p. 2.

Wasserstrom, S. M. (1999). *Religion after religion: Gershom Scholem, Mircea Eliade, and Henry Corblin at Eranos.* Princeton University Press.

Watkins, M. (1977). *Waking dreams.* New York: Harper & Row.

Wauck, L. (1962). The status of psychology in Catholic colleges and universities. In Schneiders and Centi (eds.), *Selected papers from the A.C.P.A. meetings of 1960, 1961.* (pp. 49–59).

—(1980). The story of psychology at Loyola 1929–1979. Loyola University Chicago Archives and Special Collections.

Weigel, G. (1957). American Catholic intellectualism: A theologian's reflection. *Review of Politics*, 19, 275–307.

Weir, E. (1936). Summary of discussion in Division B. *American Catholic Philosophical Association Proceedings*, 12, 109–11.

Weisheipl, J. A. (1968). The revival of Thomism as a Christian philosophy. In McInerny (ed.), *New themes in Christian philosophy*. (pp. 164–85).

Weiten, W., and Wight, R. D. (1992). Portrait of a discipline: An examination of introductory psychology textbooks in America. In A. E. Puente, J. R. Matthews and C. L. Brewer (eds.), *Teaching psychology in America: A history*. Washington, D.C.: American Psychological Association. (pp. 453–502).

Weitzel, E. J. (ed.). (1969). *Contemporary pastoral counseling*. New York: Bruce.

Welch, M.-R. (1983). *Religious obedience as a value: An analysis of the experience*. Unpublished doctoral dissertation, Duquesne University, Pittsburgh.

Weld, H. P. (1917). Meaning and process as distinguished by the reaction method, *Studies in psychology contributed by colleagues and former students of Edward Bradford Titchener*. Worcester, MA: Louis N. Wilson. (pp. 181–208).

Weldon, C. (2007). *Fr. Victor White, O. P.: The story of Jung's "White Raven"*. University of Scranton.

Werner, S. A. (2001). Joseph Husslein, S. J., and the American Catholic literary revival: 'A University in Print'. *Catholic Historical Review*, 87 (October), 688–705.

Wheeler, R. H. (1923). Some problems of meaning. *American Journal of Psychology*, 34, 185–203.

White, V. (1934). *Scholasticism*. London: Catholic Truth Society.

—(1939). Kierkegaard's Journals. *Blackfriars*, 20(236), 797–810.

—(1943a). Review of the books, *The Psychology of C. G. Jung*, by Jolan Jacobi, *The Successful Error*, by Rudolf Allers, and *Psychology and Religious Truth*, by Thomas Hywel Hughes. *Blackfriars*, 24(274), 32–4.

—(1943b). Thomism and 'affective knowledge' (I). *Blackfriars*, 24(274), 8–16.

—(1944a). Tasks for Thomists. *Blackfriars*, 25(288), 93–117.

—(1944b). Thomism and 'affective knowledge' (III). *Blackfriars*, 25(294), 321–8.

—(1949a). The supernatural. *Dominican Studies*, 2, 62–73.

—(1949b). Eranos: 1947, 1948. *Dominican Studies*, 2(4), 395–400.

—(1950). Correspondence. *Blackfriars*, 31(363), 289–92.

—(1953). *God and the unconscious*. Chicago: Henry Regnery.

—(1955). Two theologians on Jung's psychology. *Blackfriars*, 36(427), 382–8.

—(1956). *God the unknown*. New York: Harper and Brothers.

—(1958). Review of the book, *Religion and the Psychology of Jung*, by Raymond Hostie. *Journal of Analytical Psychology*, 3(1), 59–64.

—(1960). *Soul and psyche: An enquiry into the relationship of psychotherapy and religion*. London: Collins and Harvill.

Wightwick, M. I. (1945). *Vocational interest patterns: A developmental study of a group of college women*. New York: Teachers College, Columbia University.

—(1970). Review of the book, *Catholics/USA, Perspectives on Social Change*, by William Liu and Nathaniel J. Pallone (eds.). *American Catholic Psychological Association Newsletter, 20*, 4–5. Akron, OH: Archives of the History of American Psychology. Collection: American Psychological Association Division 36, Box 706.

Wilhelm, R. (1967). *I Ching or book of changes*. (3rd edn., trans. C. F. Baynes). Princeton University Press.

Williams, R. N. (1999). A history of Division 24 (Theoretical and Philosophical Psychology). In D. A. Dewsbury (ed.), *Unification through division: Histories of the Divisions of the American Psychological Association* (vol. IV). Washington, D.C.: American Psychological Association. (pp. 65–89).

With reference to psychoanalysis: Translation of an article in *L'Osservatore Romano* of Sept. 21, 1952, interpreting the Address of His Holiness Pope Pius XII. (1952). *The moral limits of medical research and treatment*. Washington, D. C.: National Catholic Welfare Conference. (pp. 15–18).

Wood, S. (1992). The nature-grace problematic within Henri de Lubac's christological paradox. *Communio, 19*, 389–403.

Wooster, E. McComb, S., and Coriat, I. H. (1908). *Religion and medicine: The moral control of nervous disorders*. New York: Moffat, Yard & Co.

Yealland, L. R. (1918). *Hysterical disorders of warfare*. New York: Macmillan.

Zahn, G. C. (ed.). (1958). *Readings in sociology*. Westminster, MD: Newman Press.

Zielinski, A. A. (1964). Focus and philosophy of a diocesan sponsored outpatient psychiatric clinic. *Bulletin of the Guild of Catholic Psychiatrists, 11*(3), 155–60.

Zilboorg, G. (1949). Psychoanalysis and religion. *Atlantic Monthly, 183*, 47–50.

INDEX

Pickstock, Catherine, 147
Pope Leo XIII, 2, 23, 36, 37, 38, 48, 73,
    80, 82, 100, 118, 298
Pope Pius IX, 35, 36, 134
Pope Pius X, 32, 35, 41, 50, 51, 53, 132
Pope Pius XII, 62, 196
    on psychoanalysis and
        psychotherapy, 196–7
positivism
    in psychology, 415–16
Pratt, James Bissett, 47
Protestantism
    evangelical, 13, 14
    liberal, 17, 41, 42
psychoanalysis
    Boyd Barrett and, 174
    Catholic responses to, 25, 127, 166–9
    confession, sacrament of, and, 168, 399
    decline of, 200
    Fulton Sheen and, 193–6
    Furfey on, 185, 189
    Moore on, 189
    Neoscholasticism and, 167
psychological assessment
    in Catholic schools, 102, 261–4
    of candidates for religious life,
        286–8
        Moore and his students and, 271
    of priests, 296
psychological categories
    "motive" in theology and psychology,
        382
    categories of the earlier Catholic
        tradition and, 398
    critical approach and, 403–4
    historically constituted, 405
    in pastoral psychology, 371, 373,
        377, 385
    in Tanquerey's spiritual psychology,
        336
Psychologists Interested in Religious
    Issues, 291, 293–7, See
    American Catholic
    Psychological Association
psychology
    as "culture making", 209–10
    autonomy of, from theology and
        philosophy, 11–14, 19, 74–5,
        294, 296

among Catholic psychologists,
    107–10
Catholic psychologists on, 289
humanistic psychology and,
    346–7
questioned, 107
Catholic, 31, 398, 403, 422, 423
Catholic criticism of, 84, See
    Catholics: opposition to
    psychology among
Christian, 10, 16, 32
history of, as break with theology and
    philosophy, 405–7
human science approach in, 13
humanistic
    as healthy-minded, 333
    compared to traditional spiritual
        psychology of Church, 333
    Neoscholastic psychology and, 29,
        316–19, 345
    van Kaam compared to Rogers,
        341, 342, 343
indigenous, 33, 422–3
Jung's psychology
    as science, 210
    significance of, for boundary-work
        between psychology and
        religion, 258–60
natural scientific, 12
    arguments for separation from
        Neoscholastic philosophy, 84–5
    criticism of, 84
    Misiak and Staudt on methods
        defining psychology's unity, 107
    philosophical foundations of, 86
phenomenological
    Arnold's contributions to, 323
    Fisher on, 327, 329
phenomenology
    McCall and, 327
philosophical foundations of, 321
rational, 76, 88
scientific, 6
the new, 16, 24, 78, 133
transpersonal, 17, 121, 133
used in Catholic critiques of
    Christian Science, 153
with a soul, 424–5
without a soul, 16

Guild of Catholic Psychiatrists and, 302
Liebman, Joshua Loth and, 198
on psychoanalysis, 193–6
criticisms of, 194–5
psychologized spirituality and, 197
psychotherapy and, 198
Shevenell, OMI, Raymond Henri, 255
Shields, Thomas Edward, 80
Siegfried, Francis Patrick, 77
Slife, Brent, 15
Smet, SJ, Walter, 312, 314
Society for Psychical Research, 123
soul, 6
hypnosis and, 130
in Neoscholastic philosophy, 69–70, 76
in Neoscholastic psychology, 116
Jung and White on, 250
soul, category of, 24, 30, 58, 69, 70, 83, 88, 109, 116, 424–34
Arnold on, 322, 426
Gannon on, 359, 426
Hillman on, 427
in Jung's psychology, 399
limitations of, for psychology, 355
Merleau-Ponty on, 428–32
Milbank on, 432–3
Strasser on, 428
White on, 427
Spearman, Charles E., 96, 171
Spencer, Herbert, 60
spiritual direction, 367
Spiritual Exercises of St. Ignatius Loyola, Gasson on, 215, 362–4
spiritualism, 123–6
and psychology, 8–9
Catholic views of, 126–7, 134, 136, 137, 138, 143–4
Christian, 133
Christianity and, 135, 136
criticism of orthodox Christianity, 142–3
Jung and White and, 253–4
modernism and, 139
psychic force, as explanation of, 138
radicalism and, 123–4, 135
reconciling science and religion, 124
skepticism toward, 139
Vatican declarations on, 141–2

spirituality without religion, 17, 27, 121, 203
Stafford, CSV, John W., 101, 316
Stater, SJ, Thomas, 379–81
Staudt Sexton, Virginia, 52, 67, 70
Stein, Murray, 209
Stern, Karl, 211
Stevens OSB, Gregory, 255
Strasser, Stephan, 112, 428
subconscious, 164
criticism of, during modernist crisis, 51
hypnosis and, 131
role in spiritual life, 120
suggestion, 149
supernatural, 406
de Lubac and White on, 247–50
role of biomedicine in determining boundaries with the natural, 163
vs. natural at Lourdes, 148
Surbled, Georges, 132
explanation of spiritualism, 139–40
symbols and images, 186, 207, 214, 215
Beirnaert on, 225
Daniélou on, 224
in Arnold's psychology, 214
Jung's psychology and, 244
Moore on, 185–6
Tyrrell on, 43, 44
von der Heydt on, 257, 258
White on, 246, 247, 254, 255

Tanquerey, SS, Adolphe, 334
Teilhard de Chardin, SJ, Pierre, 318
telepathy, 141, 144, 179
The Blithedale Romance, 122, 128
The Petrified Forest, 204
The Scarlet Letter, 122
theologies, Catholic and Protestant, 403
Thiéry, Arnand, 74
Thurston, SJ, Herbert, 143
Tisserant, Cardinal Eugène, 366
trading zones, 29
Galison's theory of, 352–3
in pastoral psychology hybrid discourse, 388
Twomey, Marcella, 267